THE PRACTICE OF RESEARCH IN SOCIAL WORK

SAGE was founded in 1965 by Sara Miller McCune to support the dissemination of usable knowledge by publishing innovative and high-quality research and teaching content. Today, we publish over 900 journals, including those of more than 400 learned societies, more than 800 new books per year, and a growing range of library products including archives, data, case studies, reports, and video. SAGE remains majority-owned by our founder, and after Sara's lifetime will become owned by a charitable trust that secures our continued independence.

Los Angeles | London | New Delhi | Singapore j Washington DC

THE PRACTICE OF RESEARCH IN SOCIAL WORK

Rafael J. Engel
University of Pittsburgh

Russell K. Schutt
University of Massachusetts Boston

4e

Los Angeles | London | New Delhi
Singapore | Washington DC

Los Angeles | London | New Delhi
Singapore | Washington DC

FOR INFORMATION:

SAGE Publications, Inc.
2455 Teller Road
Thousand Oaks, California 91320
E-mail: order@sagepub.com

SAGE Publications Ltd.
1 Oliver's Yard
55 City Road
London EC1Y 1SP
United Kingdom

SAGE Publications India Pvt. Ltd.
B 1/I 1 Mohan Cooperative Industrial Area
Mathura Road, New Delhi 110 044
India

SAGE Publications Asia-Pacific Pte. Ltd.
3 Church Street
#10-04 Samsung Hub
Singapore 049483

Library of Congress Cataloging-in-Publication Data

Names: Engel, Rafael J., author. | Schutt, Russell K., author.

Title: The practice of research in social work / Rafael J. Engel, Russell K. Schutt.

Description: Fourth edition. | Thousand Oaks, California : SAGE, [2017] | Includes bibliographical references and index.

Identifiers: LCCN 2015038935 | ISBN 978-1-5063-0426-7 (pbk. : alk. paper)

Subjects: LCSH: Social service—Research.

Classification: LCC HV11 .E57 2017 | DDC 361.3072—dc23 LC record available at http://lccn.loc.gov/2015038935

Acquisitions Editor: Jerry Westby
eLearning Editor: Gabrielle Piccininni
Editorial Assistant: Laura Kirkhuff
Production Editor: Libby Larson
Copy Editor: Kristin Bergstad
Typesetter: C&M Digitals (P) Ltd.
Proofreader: Wendy Jo Dymond
Indexer: Joan Shapiro
Cover Designer: Anupama Krishnan
Marketing Manager: Shari Countryman

This book is printed on acid-free paper.

SUSTAINABLE FORESTRY INITIATIVE
Certified Chain of Custody
Promoting Sustainable Forestry
www.sfiprogram.org
SFI-01268
SFI label applies to text stock

18 19 20 10 9 8 7 6 5 4 3

Brief Contents

On the Study Site

Detailed Contents

On the Study Site

Appendix E. Reviewing Inferential Statistics

Preface

There has been tremendous progress by social work professionals and educators in building the profession's research infrastructure. There are now national research centers, federal and foundation research initiatives, institutional support, and dissemination efforts by organizations such as the Council on Social Work Education and the Society for Social Work Research. These accomplishments provide new opportunities for social work graduates and make your research training even more critical.

Whether you are eager to take an introductory course in social work research or you are wondering why you have to take this class as all you want to do is work with people, we hope that by the end of the course, you will understand how important research is—how it can contribute to your understanding of social problems, the human condition, and to micro and macro practice. We use different examples such as domestic violence, homelessness, poverty, child welfare, and aging that cut across the domains of social work practice.

By the end of this book, you should have the skills necessary to critically evaluate the research articles that you read across all your social work courses. You should not just accept findings because they appear in print; rather, you will learn to ask many questions before concluding that research-based conclusions are appropriate. What did the researchers set out to investigate? How were people selected for study? What information was collected, and how was it analyzed? Can the findings be applied to populations not part of the study? To different settings? Communities?

Another goal of this book is to prepare you to actually evaluate social work practice. The various examples demonstrate the methods used by social work researchers to discover the efficacy of interventions, to identify needs, and to test the impact of social policies. Evaluation is a key component of social work practice; it is through evaluation that we determine the efficacy of work with individuals, families, groups, and communities.

Achieving these goals will provide a foundation for evidence-based practice. As part of evidence-based practice it is imperative that you are able to locate research, understand research findings, and critique the quality of the research. You will also need to assess the applicability of the findings for diverse people.

▤ Teaching and Learning Goals: Achieving Social Work Core Competencies

The Council on Social Work Education (2015) has identified competencies essential for social work practice. We have placed a matrix on the back cover noting these core competencies as well as a detailed matrix on the book's website that goes into further detail and specifies where these competencies are achieved in the book. While the text touches on every competency, most of the chapters contribute to achieving five competencies in particular:

Competency 1: Demonstrate Ethical and Professional Behavior (p. 7). A major focus of this book is the ethical conduct of research. You will learn that the ethical conduct of research is comparable to the ethical issues of practice and the ethical conduct of research is an obligation incorporated into the National Association of Social Workers (2008) *Code of Ethics*. For example, both require informed consent. In addition to a separate chapter on research ethics (Chapter 3), 9 other chapters include content on ethics and every chapter has at least one ethics-related exercise.

Competency 2: Engage Diversity and Difference in Practice (p. 7). This book addresses diversity and its implications for social work research through substantive sections and examples. You will come to recognize that there are questions to ask about social diversity in every stage of the research process, from asking a question to reporting and discussing the implications of the research. The book guides you to ask, "Are these findings relevant for the type of clients with whom I work, or are there cultural biases?" Such content is explicitly found in 11 chapters.

Competency 3: Advance Human Rights and Social, Economic, and Environmental Justice (p. **7**). This book addresses methods that support social workers in assessing mechanisms of oppression and discrimination and to have the data to advance social and economic justice. Concomitantly, students will learn how research can also be used as a mechanism of oppression. You will find many examples that deal with poverty and income inequality and efforts to improve economic well-being.

Competency 4: Engage in Practice-Informed Research and Research-Informed Practice (p. **8**). This book prepares you to actually evaluate social work practice—your own and that of others. The various examples demonstrate the methods used by social work researchers to discover the efficacy of interventions, to identify needs, and to test the impact of social policies. You will learn principles of evidence-based practice and how research contributes to enhancing practice. With a foundation provided in Chapter 1, nearly every chapter addresses how the particular subject contributes to evidence-based practice.

Competency 9: Evaluate Practice with Individuals, Families, Groups, Organizations, and Communities (p. **9**). This book emphasizes the importance of monitoring and evaluating interventions through its many examples and offers the knowledge and skills to actually engage in evaluation. To facilitate this competency, there are micro and macro examples. This content is found in every chapter.

A common characteristic of all the competencies is the ability to apply critical thinking to inform and communicate professional ments. This book provides you with the skills to appraise knowledge, whether it derives from research using qualitative, quantitative, or mixed methods or from practice wisdom. You will learn to ask many questions before deciding whether conclusions are appropriate to use in their practice settings. These types of questions are found in every chapter.

Organization of the Book

The way the book is organized reflects our belief in making research methods interesting and relevant by connecting research to social work practice, teaching students how to critique research, and providing the knowledge and methods that students can use to evaluate their own practice. An underlying principle reflected throughout the text is that content on ethics, diverse populations, and evidence-based practice should be infused into the various topics; therefore, almost all chapters have specific sections in each of these content areas.

The first three chapters introduce the why and how of research in general. Chapter 1 shows how research has helped us understand homelessness and its consequences. This chapter introduces students to evidence-based practice and the importance of understanding research in our diverse society. Chapter 2 illustrates the basic stages of research including developing a research question, searching and summarizing the literature, and determining a research approach. Chapter 3 provides the foundation for the ethical conduct of research and scientific guidelines for research.

The next three chapters discuss how researchers design their measures, draw their samples, and justify their statements about causal connections. Chapter 4 demonstrates how broad concepts such as substance abuse, depression, and poverty are translated into measures and how such measures are assessed. Chapter 5 reviews principles of sampling and lessons about sampling quality. Chapter 6 examines issues about causality, using a study of the impact of financial training for low-income participants and a study about the relationship of economic status and depression.

Chapters 7, 8, 9, and 10 present the primary research design strategies: group designs, single-subject designs, surveys, and qualitative methods (including participant observation, intensive interviews, and focus groups). The substantive studies in these chapters show how social work researchers have used these methods to improve our understanding of the effectiveness of different treatment modalities, such as cognitive-behavioral therapy with different population subgroups, as well as our understanding of social work issues with different age groups, including youth and the elderly. Chapter 11 reviews major analysis techniques that researchers use to identify and understand data collected in qualitative research investigations. Reading Chapters 10 and 11 together will provide a firm foundation for further use of qualitative methods.

The next two chapters demonstrate how these research designs can be extended. Chapter 12 describes two methods that build on the previous chapters: secondary data analysis and mixed methods. Evaluation research is the focus of Chapter 13. We illustrate how these primary methods may be used to learn about the effects of social programs. We emphasize the importance of using a logic model to describe a program and to develop evaluation questions.

Chapter 14 provides a basic grounding in preparing data for analysis and using descriptive statistics. While we introduce inferential statistics, we encourage students to read more about inferential statistics on this book's website, **www.sagepub.com/engelprsw4e**. Finally, we finish with Chapter 15, an overview of the process of and techniques for reporting research results and a summary examination of the development of research proposals.

▥ Distinctive Features of the Fourth Edition

To prepare for this new edition, we have incorporated valuable suggestions from faculty reviewers and students who have used the book. The content and modifications also reflect the first author's experiences when using the book to teach foundation-level social work students. It benefits from the increasing research literature on the effectiveness of social work practice. You will find all of this reflected in innovations in approach, coverage, and organization. These enhancements include:

1. *Increased attention to Secondary Data Analysis.* Secondary data analysis now shares a chapter with mixed methods. The content on secondary data analysis has been greatly expanded with attention to how to access secondary data sources and as well as how to assess the utility of a particular data set. Another new addition to this chapter is a focus on the use of Big Data in research. The ethical issues associated with secondary data analysis and Big Data add additional new content.

2. *Reorganization and expansion of mixed methods in social work research.* Chapter 12 describes the uses of mixed-methods designs with social work examples ranging from practice and policy assessment to measurement validity. The philosophical basis for mixed methods is introduced in Chapter 1 and expanded upon in Chapter 12.

3. *Expansion on the implications for evidence-based practice.* In Chapter 1, we describe the steps associated with the evidence-based practice decision model and the challenges of implementing evidence-based practice at the agency level.

4. *Increased content on qualitative methods and analysis.* We have added a new appendix (C) with questions that should be asked when reading a qualitative research article as well as an example of an analysis (Appendix D). There are new sections on community-based participatory research and qualitative methods, conversation analysis, and ethnomethodology. We have expanded content on topics such as focus groups and how to authenticate results.

5. *Emerging research efforts using the Internet and other electronic media.* We begin by addressing ethical issues and Internet research in Chapter 3. In Chapter 9, we expand material about the use of electronic surveys and discuss the implications of cell-phone usage for survey research. Some researchers are now applying qualitative techniques to the Internet, and so we introduce online interviewing and netnography in Chapter 10.

6. *New learning tools.* We have included a vignette about research reported in the popular press that relates to the discussion in that chapter: *Research in the News*. These examples highlight how research informs media stories, and the two questions will help students think about the methodological issues.

In addition to these enhancements, we continue to update and expand diversity content and add new research-related examples. We also provide new and up-to-date studies of homelessness, poverty, domestic violence, aging and other pressing social issues.

We hope that readers of this text will enjoy learning about research and apply the skills and knowledge taught in a research course to their field of practice. Social workers are in a unique position to discover what interventions work, under what circumstances, and with what populations. In so doing, we benefit our clients and broader society.

回 Ancillary Materials

To enhance the use of the book, a number of high-quality, useful ancillaries have been prepared:

Student Study Site

Available free on the web at **www.sagepub.com/engelprsw4e** is a collection of high-quality materials designed to help students master the course content and gain greater insight into social work research. The site contains interactive self-quizzes and eFlashcards, a chapter-length review of inferential statistics, articles from social work journals with guiding questions, web exercises from the ends of chapters with additional online resources, and exercises for SPSS.

Instructor Teaching Site

We provide instructors with a variety of useful instructional materials. For each chapter, this includes overviews and lecture outlines, PowerPoint slides, exhibits in reproducible form, student projects, and a complete set of test questions. There are also lists of suggested film and software resources and links to related websites.

Acknowledgments

O ur thanks to Jerry Westby, publisher, SAGE Publications. Jerry's enthusiasm and support for this project has been crucial, and his patience extraordinary. He is an exceptionally talented publisher and book developer with a clear vision about how best to serve students and enhance their learning. We are also deeply indebted to Laura Kirkhuff, Libby Larson, and Kristin Bergstad, who made this text into something more than just words in a word-processed file. Special thanks are also due to Samantha Levinson (Carnegie Mellon University) for updating the ancillary materials on the instructor teaching site and student study site.

We are indebted to the talented group of social work professors whose suggestions and insights have helped improve every chapter. They are

Kathleen A. Bolland, University of Alabama

April Murphy, Western Kentucky University

Catherine M. L. Pearl, University of Calgary

Mary I. Armstrong, University of South Florida

Elizabeth K. Anthony, Arizona State University

Michel Coconis, University of Toledo

Ericka Kimball, Portland State University

Faith Pratt Hopp, Wayne State University

The increasing focus and attention on interdisciplinary research is reflected in this edition of the *Practice of Research in Social Work*. We are part of a support group of researchers, educators, and authors from other disciplines, including Ronet Bachman (University of Delaware), Daniel Chambliss (Hamilton College), Joe Check (University of Massachusetts, Boston), and Paul Nestor (University of Massachusetts, Boston). Together, we have had open and honest discussions about what works and what does not work in teaching students about the research process.

Reviewers for the third edition were Regina T. P. Aguirre (University of Texas, Arlington), Jude Antonyappan (California State University, Sacramento), Judy Berglund (Saginaw Valley State University), Mary Ann Jones (New York University), Junghee Lee (Portland State University), Kirstin Painter (Texas Woman's University), Janice K. Purk (Mansfield University), and Roosevelt Wright (University of Oklahoma).

Second edition reviewers included Catherine Baratta (Central Connecticut State University), Judy Berglund (Saginaw Valley State University), Michael Fendrich (University of Wisconsin, Milwaukee), Judith G. Gonyea (Boston University), Lisa Hines (San Francisco State University), Michael Kane (Florida Atlantic University), John L. Murphy (University of the District of Columbia), Bassima Schbley (Washburn University), Cathryne L. Schmitz (University of North Carolina at Greensboro), Audrey Shillington (San Diego State University), Abigail Tilton (Texas Woman's University), Carol Williams (Kean University), and Mike Wolf-Branigin (George Mason University).

First edition reviewers included Leslie B. Alexander (Bryn Mawr College), Julie Cooper Altman (Adelphi University), Patrick S. Bordnick (University of Georgia), Fred Brooks (Georgia State University), Jong Choi (California State Bakersfield), Adele Crudden (Mississippi State University), Tim Dyeson (Louisiana State University), Mark Ezell (University of Kansas), James Hanson (University of Northern Iowa), Sanford Schram (Bryn Mawr College), Emily Spence-Diehl (University of Texas at Arlington), Jim Stafford (University of Mississippi), and Gary Widrick (University of Vermont).

We both thank our spouses, Sandy Budd and Elizabeth Schneider, for their love and support (and patience!), and our children, Yael, Meir, and Julia, for the inspiration they provide and the joy they bring to our lives.

Science, Society, and Social Work Research

Burt had worked as a welder when he was younger, but alcoholism and related physical and mental health problems interfered with his career plans. By the time he was 60, Burt had spent many years on the streets. Fortunately, he obtained an apartment in 2008 through a housing program for homeless persons. Although the *Boston Globe* reporter who interviewed him reported that "the lure of booze and friends from the street was [still] strong," Burt had finally made the transition back to a more settled life (Abel, 2008, p. A14).

It is a sad story with an all-too-uncommon happy—although uncertain—ending. Together with one other such story and comments by several service staff, the newspaper article provides a persuasive rationale for the new housing program. Does Burt's story sound familiar? Such newspaper stories proliferate when the holiday season approaches, but what do they really tell us about homelessness? How typical is Burt's story? Why do people live on the streets? What helps them to regain housing?

In the rest of this chapter, you will learn how the methods of social science research go beyond stories in the popular media to help us answer questions like these. By the chapter's end, you should know what is "scientific" in social science and appreciate how the methods of science can help us understand the problems of society.

▣ Reasoning About the Social World

The story of just one homeless person raises many questions. Take a few minutes to read each of the following questions and jot down your answers. Do not ruminate about the questions or worry about your responses. *This is not a test*; there are no "wrong" answers.

- Was Burt typical of the homeless?

- What is it like being homeless?

- Why do people become homeless?

- How do homeless people adapt to a temporary shelter?

- What programs are effective in ending homelessness?

Do a few facts from the newspaper story give you enough information to answer these questions? Do you feel you need to know more about Burt, his friends, and the family he grew up in? Have you observed other homeless persons with whom you would compare Burt? What is the basis for your thoughts about the causes of homelessness? Have you worked in social service programs that provide some insight? How can you tell whether a program is effective? We began with just one person's experiences, and already our investigation is spawning more and more questions.

We cannot avoid asking questions about the social world, which is a complex place, and trying to make sense of our position in it—something of great personal importance. In fact, the more you begin to think like a potential social work researcher, the more questions will come to mind. But why does each question have so many possible answers? Surely, our perspective plays a role. One person may see a homeless individual as a victim of circumstances, another person may see the homeless as the failure of our society to care for its members, and a third person may see the same individual as a shiftless bum. When confronted with a homeless individual, one observer may stop to listen, another may recall a news story on street crime, and another may be reminded of her grandfather. Their different orientations will result in different answers to the questions prompted by the same individual or event.

When the questions concern not just one person, but many people or general social processes, the number of possible questions and the difficulties in answering them multiply. For example, consider the question of why people become homeless. Responses to a 2006 survey of New York City residents, summarized in Exhibit 1.1, illustrate the diverse sentiments that people have (Arumi, Yarrow, Ott, & Rochkind, 2007). Compare these answers with the opinion you recorded earlier. Was your idea about the causes of homelessness one of the more popular ones?

Answers to questions about the social world can vary given the particular details of what we observe or read about a situation. Would your answers be different if the newspaper article was about a family who had lost their home due to

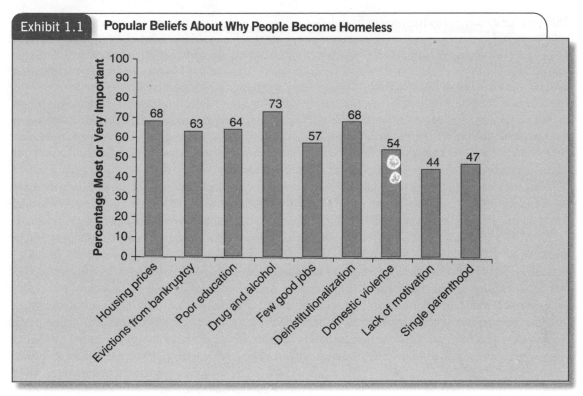

Exhibit 1.1   Popular Beliefs About Why People Become Homeless

Source: Adapted from Arumi, Ana Maria, Andrew L. Yarrow, Amber Ott, and Jonathan Rochkind. 2007. *Compassion, Concern, and Conflicted Feelings: New Yorkers on Homelessness and Housing.* New York: Public Agenda.

foreclosure or a single parent with two children? Responses of large-city mayors to the 2013 Hunger and Homelessness Survey (U.S. Conference of Mayors, 2013), summarized in Exhibit 1.2, demonstrate their differing opinions about what causes families to be homeless in comparison to individuals who are homeless.

Answers to questions about the social world also vary because what people have "seen" varies. The New York City survey (Arumi et al., 2007) reflects this. The elderly were more likely than younger people to see drug and alcohol abuse as a significant cause of homelessness. People of color were more likely than White people to see the absence of good jobs as a key cause. Other studies have found that political perspectives and personal contact make a difference in how people perceive the causes of homelessness (Lee, Farrell, & Link, 2004).

🔲 Everyday Errors in Reasoning

People give different answers to questions about the social world for yet another reason: It is simply too easy to make errors in logic, particularly when we are analyzing the social world in which we are conscious participants. We can call some of these *everyday errors* because they occur so frequently in the nonscientific, unreflective discourse about the social world that we hear on a daily basis.

Our favorite example of everyday errors in reasoning comes from a letter to syndicated newspaper advice columnist Ann Landers. The letter was written by someone who had just moved with her two cats from the city to a house in the country. In the city, she had not let her cats outside and felt guilty about confining them. When they arrived in the country, she threw her back door open. Her two cats cautiously went to the door and looked outside for a while, then returned to the living room and lay down. Her conclusion was that people shouldn't feel guilty about keeping their cats indoors—even when cats have the chance, they don't really want to play outside.

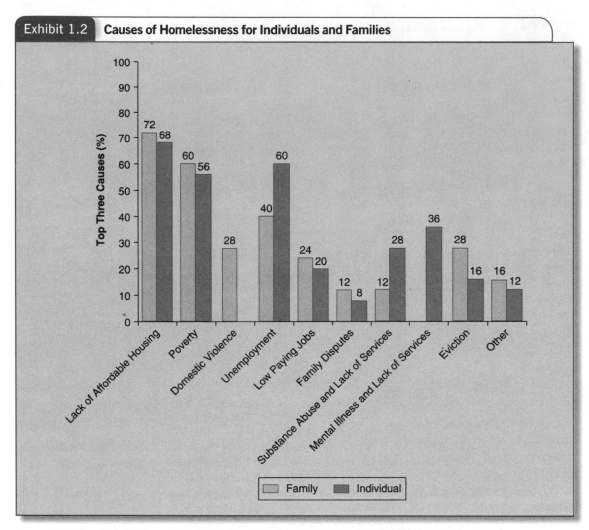

Exhibit 1.2   Causes of Homelessness for Individuals and Families

Source: Adapted from U.S. Conference of Mayors, December 2012. Hunger and homelessness survey: A status report on hunger and homelessness in America's Cities, A 25-City survey.

Do you see this person's errors in reasoning?

- *Selective observation or inaccurate observation.* She observed the cats at the outside door only once.

- *Overgeneralization.* She observed only two cats, both of which previously were confined indoors.

- *Illogical reasoning.* She assumed that others feel guilty about keeping their cats indoors and that cats are motivated by emotions.

- *Resistance to change.* She was quick to conclude that she had no need to change her approach to the cats.

- *Adherence to authority.* She is looking to the "expert" for support for her conclusion.

You do not have to be a scientist or use sophisticated research techniques to avoid these errors in reasoning. If you recognize these errors for what they are and make a conscious effort to avoid them, you can improve your own reasoning. In the process, you will also be implementing the admonishments of your parents (or teacher or other adviser) to avoid stereotyping people, to avoid jumping to conclusions, and to look at the big picture. These are the same errors that the methods of social science research are designed to help us avoid.

Selective or Inaccurate Observation

We have to avoid **selective observation**: choosing to look only at things that are in line with our preferences or beliefs. When we are inclined to criticize individuals or institutions, it is all too easy to notice their every failing. For example, if we are convinced in advance that all homeless persons are substance abusers, we can find many confirming instances. But what about homeless people who left abusive homes or lost jobs? If we acknowledge only the instances that confirm our predispositions, we are victims of our own selective observation. Exhibit 1.3 depicts the difference between overgeneralization and selective observation.

> **Selective observation** Choosing to look only at things that are in line with our preferences or beliefs.
>
> **Inaccurate observation** Observations based on faulty perceptions of empirical reality.

Our observations can be inaccurate. If a woman says she is *hungry* and we think she said she is *hunted*, we have made an **inaccurate observation.** If we think five people are standing on a street corner when actually seven are, we have made an inaccurate observation. Or our observations can be incomplete. If we see Burt sitting alone and drinking from a beer bottle, we would be wrong to conclude that he does not have any friends or that he likes to drink alone.

Such errors often occur in casual conversation and in everyday observation of the world around us. In fact, our perceptions do not provide a direct window onto the world around us because what we think we have sensed is not necessarily what we have seen (or heard, smelled, felt, or tasted). Even when our senses are functioning fully, our minds have to interpret what we have sensed (Humphrey, 1992). The optical illusion in Exhibit 1.4, which can be viewed as either two faces or a vase, should help you realize that perceptions involve interpretations. Different observers may perceive the same situation differently because they interpret it differently.

Overgeneralization

Overgeneralization occurs when we conclude that what we have observed or what we know to be true for some cases is true for all cases. We are always drawing conclusions about people and social processes from our own interactions with them, but we sometimes forget that our experiences are limited. The social (and natural) world is, after all, a complex place. We have the ability (and inclination) to interact with just a small fraction of the individuals who inhabit the social world, especially in a limited span of time.

> **Overgeneralization** Occurs when we unjustifiably conclude that what is true for some cases is true for all cases.

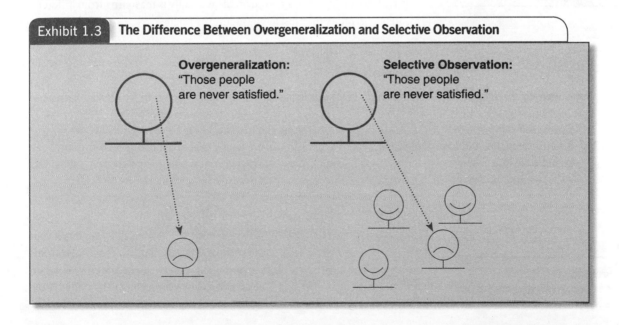

Exhibit 1.3 The Difference Between Overgeneralization and Selective Observation

Overgeneralization:
"Those people are never satisfied."

Selective Observation:
"Those people are never satisfied."

Exhibit 1.4   **An Optical Illusion**

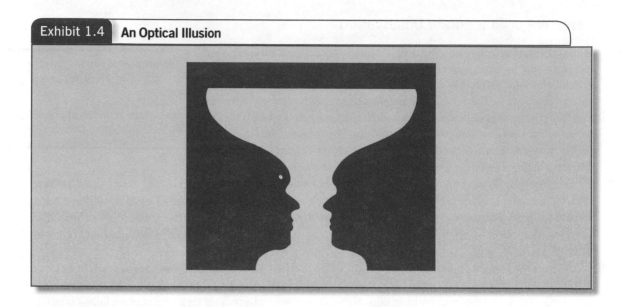

If we had taken facts we learned about Burt, such as his alcohol abuse, and concluded that this problem is typical of homeless persons, we would have committed the error of overgeneralization.

Illogical Reasoning

When we prematurely jump to conclusions or argue on the basis of invalid assumptions, we are using **illogical reasoning.** For example, it is not reasonable to propose that homeless individuals do not want to work if evidence indicates that the reason many are unemployed is a shortage of jobs or the difficulty of finding jobs for those unemployed because of mental or physical disabilities. However, an unquestioned assumption that everyone who *can* work *will* work is also likely to be misplaced. Logic that seems impeccable to one person can seem twisted to another—the problem usually is reasoning from different assumptions, rather than just failing to "think straight."

Illogical reasoning Occurs when we prematurely jump to conclusions or argue on the basis of invalid assumptions.

Resistance to Change

Resistance to change, the reluctance to change our ideas in light of new information, may occur for a couple of reasons:

Ego-based commitments. We all learn to greet with some skepticism the claims by leaders of companies, schools, agencies, and so on that people in their organizations are happy, that revenues are growing, and that services are being delivered in the best possible way. We know how tempting it is to make statements about the social world that conform to our own needs, rather than to the observable facts. It can also be difficult to admit that we were wrong once we have staked out a position on an issue. For instance, we may want our experiences while volunteering in a shelter for homeless people to confirm our political stance on homelessness and therefore resist changing our beliefs in response to new experiences.

Excessive devotion to tradition. Some degree of devotion to tradition is necessary for the predictable functioning of society. Social life can be richer and more meaningful if it is allowed to flow along the paths charted by those who have preceded us. But too much devotion to tradition can stifle

Resistance to change The reluctance to change our ideas in light of new information.

adaptation to changing circumstances. When we distort our observations or alter our reasoning so that we can maintain beliefs that "were good enough for my grandfather, so they're good enough for me," we hinder our ability to accept new findings and develop new knowledge. In many agencies, those who want to reject an idea use those famous words: "But we've never done it that way."

Adherence to Authority

Sometimes it is difficult to change our ideas because someone in a position of authority has told us what is correct. **Adherence to authority** is given because we believe that the authority, the person making the claim, does have the knowledge. If we do not have the courage to evaluate critically the ideas of those in positions of authority, we will have little basis for complaint if they exercise their authority over

> **Adherence to authority** Unquestioning acceptance of statements by authority figures such as parents, teachers, and professionals.

us in ways we do not like. And if we do not allow new discoveries to call our beliefs into question, our understanding of the social world will remain limited. We once had a student in a social welfare history class who came back from Thanksgiving break saying, "You're wrong [about the impact of structural issues on economic well-being]. My parents told me that anyone can get ahead if they want to." In her eyes, her parents were right despite any evidence to the contrary.

Now take just a minute to reexamine the beliefs about homelessness that you recorded earlier. Did you grasp at a simple explanation even though reality is far more complex? Were your beliefs influenced by your own ego and feelings about your similarities to or differences from homeless persons? Are your beliefs perhaps based on stories you have heard about the "hobos" of an earlier era? Did you weigh carefully the opinions of political authorities or just accept or reject those opinions out of hand? Could knowledge of research methods help to improve your own understanding of the social world? Do you see some of the challenges faced by social science?

▣ The Social Scientific Approach

The scientific approach to answering questions about the social world is designed to greatly reduce these potential sources of error in everyday reasoning. **Social science** relies on logical and systematic methods to answer questions, and it does so in a way that allows others to inspect and evaluate its methods. In this way, scientific research develops a body of knowledge that is continually refined as beliefs are rejected or confirmed on the basis of testing empirical evidence.

> **Social science** The use of scientific methods to investigate individuals, groups, communities, organizations, societies, and social processes; the knowledge produced by these investigations.

Social work research relies on these methods to investigate treatment effectiveness, social conditions, organizational behavior, and social welfare policy. While we may do this in our everyday lives, social scientists develop, refine, apply, and report their understanding of the social world more systematically, or "scientifically," than the general public:

- Social science research methods can reduce the likelihood of overgeneralization by using systematic procedures for selecting individuals or groups to study that are representative of the individuals or groups to which we wish to generalize.

- To avoid illogical reasoning, social work researchers use explicit criteria for identifying causes and determining whether these criteria are met in a particular instance.

- Social science methods can reduce the risk of selective, inaccurate, or incomplete observation by requiring that we measure and sample phenomena systematically.

- Because they require that we base our beliefs on evidence that can be examined and critiqued by others, scientific methods lessen the tendency to develop answers about the social world from ego-based commitments, excessive devotion to tradition, and/or unquestioning respect for authority.

▣ Social Work and the Social World

The methods of social science are an invaluable tool for social work researchers and practitioners at any level of practice. The nature of our social world is the starting point for the profession because much of what we do is in response to social, political, and economic conditions. Social work efforts, whether they are aimed at influencing or evaluating policy, working with communities, or engaging in programs to help individuals or groups, emerge in response to conditions in the social world. Our profession works with people from diverse backgrounds and promotes the social and economic participation of groups that lack access to full participation. Through systematic investigation, we begin to uncover the various dimensions of the social condition, the accuracy of our assumptions about what causes the social condition, the characteristics of people with a particular social status or social problem, and the effectiveness of our policies and programs to ameliorate the social problem.

Social policies are often designed based on assumptions about the causes of the problem. If we believe that homelessness is due to individual behavior or pathology—for example, that homeless individuals prefer separation from their friends and family, do not want to take advantage of economic opportunities, suffer from mental illness, or are alcohol and substance abusers—then policies will emerge that focus on treating these pathologies. However, if we believe that homelessness is due to structural problems—for example, the market's inability to provide enough reasonably paying jobs or problems in producing enough low-income housing—then government policies will emerge that might subsidize wages or encourage developers to build lower income housing. If we learn that the causes of homelessness are multidimensional, that there is a bit of reality to both perspectives, different government policies might emerge that both encourage housing alternatives and incorporate support services. Social work research aids us in the task of describing the characteristics of the homeless, their needs, and their prevalence, all of which can guide policy development and the distribution of resources.

The kinds of programs that human service agencies develop are also based on assumptions about the causes of a social problem (L. Martin & Kettner, 2010). If an agency assumes that homeless adults are alienated from society and suffer from emotional or substance abuse problems, then the agency might provide transitional housing with a variety of social services integrated into the program. In contrast, if the agency believes that homeless adults are simply in between jobs or new to a city and just need time to get started, then the agency might offer a short-term shelter. The tools of research allow social workers to examine the extent to which these assumptions are correct and to evaluate the effectiveness of these different programs.

Interventions in human service programs are related not only to assumptions about what causes the problem, but also to different beliefs about what is the appropriate treatment model. Two agencies might have the same set of assumptions about what causes a problem, but might use different practice models to treat the individual or group. The personal problems that Burt faced might have been addressed by using a social systems model of treatment or a cognitive model of treatment. The tools of research allow us to evaluate the effectiveness of different treatment models in different settings, with different problems, and with different subgroups of the population. For example, Russell Schutt's (2011) book *Homelessness, Housing, and Mental Illness* reports the findings of an evaluation of the effectiveness of group or independent housing for homeless persons.

Finally, social work research allows us to challenge perceptions and popular sentiment about those who are in need. Burt reflects common stereotypes about the homeless: They are male; they are substance abusers. Yet we now know, thanks to the work of many researchers, that increasing numbers of homeless people are women with children or people diagnosed with HIV; they have different kinds of needs than Burt, and they require different types of services and interventions in the kinds of housing options offered.

▣ Social Work Research and Evidence-Based Practice

Evidence-based practice (EBP) has emerged in the past several years as a popular model for social work practice. EBP, with its roots in medicine, is described by Eileen Gambrill (2006) as an evolving "philosophy and process

Research In the News

For Further Thought?

WHY DID NEW YORK CITY'S HOMELESS POPULATION INCREASE?

The U.S. Department of Housing and Urban Development's annual count of homeless people reported a 1-year decrease of 4% nationally but this same survey found that the number of homeless people in New York City increased by 13%. Contrary to expectation, New York City's increase occurred at the same time that its economy had recovered. Much of the growth in New York City was attributed to an increase in homeless families who could no longer pay high rents.

1. What would you like to research to better understand why homelessness is increasing in New York City?

2. How might you test the impact of federal budget cuts to support low income housing?

Source: Navarro (2013).

designed to forward effective use of professional judgment in integrating information regarding each client's unique characteristics, circumstances, preferences, and actions and external research findings" (p. 339). EBP's emergence is, in part, a reaction to an overreliance on professional claims about the effectiveness of social work practice. One of the failings of social work professional literature is "that it is rife with claims unaccompanied by evidence" (Gambrill, 2001, p. 167) and has based many of its claims on professional authority.

EBP is a clinical decision-making process integrating the best current research evidence to achieve a particular outcome; client values, client circumstances, and clinical expertise to make decisions about what intervention to choose (Straus, Richardson, Glasziou, & Haynes, 2005). Empirical evidence is necessary, but not sufficient; rather, social workers should utilize an intervention that fits the client's expectations and circumstances (Starin, 2006). What do each of these terms mean?

- *Best current research evidence.* Practitioners should use knowledge derived from research studies that provide evidence that has been obtained through systematic tests of its accuracy (Gambrill, 1999), that is, reliable and valid. Although there is debate about what kinds of research constitute "evidence," you will learn that it includes "any systematically collected information relevant to practice" (Pollio, 2006, p. 225). Therefore, quantitative studies (e.g., randomized clinical trials), qualitative methods (e.g., case studies, focus groups), and practitioner-collected information (e.g., single-subject designs) all provide evidence. Such studies provide information that can test the accuracy of assessment tools or the effectiveness of different interventions.

- *Client values.* Clients bring their own preferences, concerns, and expectations for service and treatment (Haynes, Devereaux, & Guyatt, 2002; Straus et al., 2005). Client preferences may impact the type of intervention used. Clients may prefer individual interventions as opposed to group interventions, or they may prefer in-home services or interventions rather than going to a congregate site or an agency for services. This is not limited to individual clients but may include larger client systems. Community interventions require knowledge about what is acceptable in a particular community, just as organizational interventions require an understanding of what is acceptable given the culture of the organization.

- *Client circumstances.* You can imagine the variety of circumstances that bring clients to seek social services. Some clients may be facing a crisis, others a long-standing problem; they may be voluntary clients, or they may be court-ordered clients; they may live in rural areas, the suburbs, or urban communities. These are just some of the circumstances or situations that might be weighed in determining appropriate interventions.

- *Clinical expertise.* Clinical expertise involves using both past experiences with clients and clinical skills to assess and integrate the information learned from research studies, client values, and client circumstances (Haynes et al., 2002; Straus et al., 2005). Skilled social workers know how to find the relevant research literature, evaluate its accuracy, and determine its usefulness to a particular client or client system (Gambrill, 2001). They have communication skills needed to solicit client values and preferences, and, in turn, communicate to clients their options. Social workers are able to provide different interventions (or refer to appropriate providers) given a client's particular circumstances.

Another component of EBP is that social workers should provide clients with the information necessary to make decisions about services, including the effectiveness of the intervention, the client's role in the intervention, expectations of the client, and length of the intervention (Starin, 2006). Clients should be informed about the evidence, or lack of evidence, supporting a particular intervention. If there is no empirical evidence, social workers should provide the theoretical justification for the choice of service. Clients should also be told about alternative interventions and their relative effectiveness. With all of this information, clients can make informed decisions.

The EBP decision-making process includes five steps (Gray, Joy, Plath, & Webb, 2012; Straus, Richardson, Glasziou, & Haynes, 2011), though other authors have added a sixth step (Mullen, Bledsoe, & Bellamy, 2008) or reframed the steps by extending EBP beyond decision making to clinical practice (Drisko & Grady, 2012). The five steps adapted from Straus and her colleagues (2011, p. 3) are:

- *Step 1: Convert the need for information into an answerable question.* This step involves formulating the question based on what you learn through the client assessment process and might focus on assessment, intervention, or treatment (Mullin et al., 2008; Thyer, 2006). For example, you might ask, "Is a group home for mentally ill homeless individuals effective in retaining cognitive functioning?"

- *Step 2: Locate the best clinical evidence to answer the question.* A search for the best evidence might include finding research literature using the Internet, peer-review journals, and systematic reviews of treatment effectiveness. Your search may include clarifying diagnoses and the course of the problem (Drisko & Grady, 2012), but ultimately it will involve finding research about interventions and their effectiveness for a given problem.

- *Step 3: Critically evaluate the research evidence in terms of its validity, its clinical significance, and its usefulness.* You weigh the research designs used to produce the evidence, how much impact an intervention has on a particular outcome, and the applicability of the research to practice. As part of your evaluation, you must consider the similarity of the study participants to the characteristics of your clients.

- *Step 4: Integrate this critical appraisal of research evidence with one's clinical expertise and client values and circumstances.* In this stage, you should provide clients with the information necessary for the clients to make decisions regarding their preferences for treatment. This information includes what you have learned from the research about the relative effectiveness of different interventions, the client's role in the intervention process, and the length of the intervention (Starin, 2006).

- *Step 5: Evaluate one's effectiveness and efficiency in carrying out Steps 1 through 4 in order to improve one's efforts the next time.* You should reflect on the process identifying what went well and where there might be gaps in your ability to carry out the first four steps.

Although these steps may sound daunting, they are consistent with a social worker's ethical obligations as described in the National Association of Social Workers (2008) *Code of Ethics:* Enabling clients to make informed decisions is consistent with obtaining informed consent (1.03[a]); keeping up-to-date with relevant knowledge (4.01[b]);

utilizing interventions with an empirical basis (4.01[c]); and including evaluation and research evidence as part of professional practice (5.02[c]).

The challenge for social work researchers and social work practitioners is implementing evidence-based practice (Gray et al., 2012; Mullen et al., 2008; Proctor & Rosen, 2008). Mel Gray and colleagues' (2012) review of 11 studies of EBP implementation identified five barriers including (1) inadequate agency resources devoted to EBP, including time, funding, and access to research evidence; (2) inadequate skills and knowledge of research and EBP; (3) agency culture that required staff to follow agency guidelines; (4) nature of research and professional staff attitudes toward research; and (5) inadequate supervision.

Thomas Prohaska and Caryn Etkin (2010) expanded on these barriers, outlining some of the challenges in translating research to implementation in programs:

1. Researchers tend to focus on the effectiveness of the intervention in producing a desired outcome, with less consideration given to whether the effectiveness of the intervention translates to different settings. As a result practitioners wonder whether the findings have applicability to their setting.

2. Researchers often have specific criteria for selecting their participants and may even have criteria to exclude potential participants. Practitioners may conclude that the study population is unlike the clients they serve and, therefore, the findings are not applicable to their clients.

3. Researchers tend to focus on clinical outcomes. Practitioners and agency stakeholders are interested in achieving success with clinical outcomes, but they also have other factors to consider, including cost in achieving clinical outcomes as well as relationship to agency mission. Further, outcomes important to clients may differ from outcomes achieved in research studies.

4. Researchers suggest that there be treatment fidelity, in other words, that the delivery of the program follow a specific course of action. Practitioners may lack the documentation and materials to adequately implement the program as designed.

The translation of research findings to their application for practice cuts across disciplines and is not unique to social work. There are no easy answers to the implementation problem. We hope you are beginning to see the critical role that understanding the research process plays in providing services to client systems. You will need the skill to find relevant research literature and the ability to evaluate studies critically so that you can judge the findings and determine their usefulness to your practice and to your clients. Therefore, as you read this book, you will learn about research issues such as measurement, sampling, and research design; how to find research literature; and how to understand statistics. Each of these topics will contribute to your ability to carry out EBP.

回 Social Work Research in Practice

Although there are a great many studies of different phenomena, social conditions, impacts of different programs, and intervention methods, we can classify the purposes of these studies into four categories: description, exploration, explanation, and evaluation.

Descriptive Research

Defining and describing social phenomena of interest is a part of almost any research investigation, but descriptive research is often the primary focus of the initial research about some issue. **Descriptive research** typically involves the gathering of facts. Some of the central questions asked in research

Descriptive research Research in which social phenomena are defined and described.

on homelessness have been, Who is homeless? What are the needs of homeless people? and How many people are homeless? Measurement (the topic of Chapter 4) and sampling (Chapter 5) are central concerns in descriptive research. Survey research (Chapter 9) is often used for descriptive purposes.

Example: Who Are the Homeless?

For the last decade, Apt Associates and the University of Pennsylvania Center for Mental Health Policy and Services Research designed and implemented the *Annual Homeless Assessment Report* to address these questions (Solari, Cortes, Henry, Matthews, & Morris, 2014). One component of the study is to estimate the number of people who are homeless using emergency shelters, transitional housing, or permanent supportive housing during the 12-month period from October to September of the following year. To do so, they drew a nationally representative sample of communities participating in Continuums of Care (CoC). The data were retrieved from each setting's Homeless Management Information System, which was used to store data about individuals and families who were homeless. The estimate does not include individuals who remain unsheltered, reside in domestic violence shelters, or live in private or nonprofit long-term housing for people with a mental illness.

The design of the survey reinforces the importance of social scientific methods. Clear definitions were necessary, and the researchers had to carefully define many key concepts such as *continuums of care, homeless,* and *family.* The selection method had to ensure that the findings would be generalizable beyond the selected settings. Yet the findings could only be generalized to people found in residential assistance programs and not to other homeless individuals.

This study revealed the diversity among people who used a shelter program. In 2013, an estimated 1.42 million people used a shelter program; about 36% of people using a shelter were members of a shelter-using family; 63% were men; 22% were children under age 18; and 9.8% were veterans (Solari et al., 2014).

Exploratory Research

Exploratory research Seeks to find out how people get along in the setting under question, what meanings they give to their actions, and what issues concern them.

Exploratory research seeks to learn how people get along in the setting under question, what meanings they give to their actions, and what issues concern them. The goal is to learn "what is going on here" and to investigate social phenomena without explicit expectations. This purpose is associated with the use of methods that capture large amounts of relatively unstructured information. Research like this frequently involves qualitative methods, which are the focus of Chapter 10.

Example: How Do the Homeless Adapt to Shelter Life?

Among researchers interested in homelessness, one goal was to learn what it was like to be homeless and how homeless people made sense of their situation. In the past, homeless shelters were seen as temporary community solutions, but with homelessness growing, shelters were seen as necessary settings and, therefore, permanent. This change was accompanied by increased administrative oversight and rules to govern the residents. As a result of these changes, Sarah DeWard and Angela Moe (2010) wanted to learn about how the institutions operated and the ways residents adapted to administrative oversight. To answer these questions, DeWard and Moe conducted an exploratory study using observations and personal narratives of 20 women who were residents of a homeless shelter in a midwestern city. DeWard interviewed 20 women in private rooms in the shelter and spent about 100 hours over three months observing and interacting with staff and residents.

DeWard and Moe (2010) reported that the shelter had many rules and enforced a hierarchy between staff and residents. One rule was that any staff member could issue a point for violating the rules and residents receiving three points had to leave the shelter. This policy was a point of concern as expressed by one resident:

One girl got wrote up because she's got four kids. She's a single mom, and all her kids are too young to go to day camp. So, she's got four kids, and they wrote her up because a job that she went to didn't hire her—but she's got four kids, four small kids . . . where are her kids supposed to go? They of course not gonna hire her because she got four kids taggin' along with her to the interview. (p. 120)

The authority given to staff reinforced power differences and was often perceived to be misused. One resident noted that

[t]hey staff . . . they are something else! I think they pick and choose who they like and who let do certain stuff. . . . One woman got caught stealing . . . didn't nothing happen to her. Then somebody else bought take-out food and got written up. (p. 120)

DeWard and Moe (2010) found that the women choose one of four strategies to deal with the bureaucratic nature of the shelter. Some women simply submitted to the shelter, following the rules, accepting staff authority, and minding their own business. One woman, when asked if there was something she would change, commented that "I'm not going to say the [The Refuge] is perfect, but it is close to perfect" (p. 123). Other women adapted by emphasizing their spiritual self. They did not embrace the rules and structure but focused on their faith to guide their behavior. A third group adapted by creating a hierarchy among the residents—those who were homeless because of poor judgment or behavior and those who were houseless or temporarily homeless because of some event like losing a job. Finally, there were women who resisted the rules and authority of the staff, "I let them [staff] know they ain't gonna use none of that [rules and regulations] against me . . ." (p. 128). Such attitudes reinforced their desire to remain independent and autonomous even while living in the shelter.

DeWard and Moe (2010) concluded that the institutionalization of shelters had a negative impact on the residents. Women who were passive and more dependent were able to stay while women who tried to maintain their identities through resistance were terminated. Yet, for the women to ultimately return to the community successfully, they would need that self-sufficiency and sense of independence.

Explanatory Research

Many consider explanation the premier goal of any science. **Explanatory research** seeks to identify causes and effects of social phenomena and to predict how one phenomenon will change or vary in response to variation in some other phenomenon. Homelessness researchers adopted explanation as a goal when they began to ask such questions as Why do people become homeless? and Does the unemployment rate influence the frequency of homelessness? Explanatory research depends on our ability to rule out other explanations for our findings, to demonstrate a time order between two events, and to show that the two events are related to each other. Research methods used to identify causes and effects are the focus of Chapter 6.

> **Explanatory research** Seeks to identify causes and effects of social phenomena and to predict how one phenomenon will change or vary in response to variation in some other phenomenon.

Example: What Community-Level Factors Cause Homelessness?

Thomas Byrne and his colleagues (Byrne, Munley, Fargo, Montgomery, & Culhane, 2013) designed a study to understand why people become homeless. They were most interested in identifying what particular community-level structural factors caused homelessness. They were particularly interested in examining such factors as the housing market, local economic conditions, demographic composition of the community, adequacy of local safety net programs, local weather (climate) conditions, and the degree of residential mobility (transience). The researchers used data taken from the 2011 U. S. Department of Housing and Urban Development Annual Homeless Assessment; the sample comprised the count of people homeless or sheltered on a single night in the last 10 days of January 2009 across Continuums of Care (CoCs).

Their extensive analysis compared the metropolitan and rural CoCs separately. In metropolitan areas, the rate of people who were homeless was related to rent level, homeownership rate, population demographics like the proportion of single-parent households, Hispanic population, and baby-boomer population, and residential mobility. In rural areas, rents and unemployment rate were positively related to the rate of people homeless while the proportion of the African American population was negatively related. These findings lead to a straightforward explanation of homelessness: "Homelessness has its roots in housing market dynamics and particularly in the difficulty in obtaining affordable housing" (p. 621).

Evaluation Research

Evaluation research, frequently referred to as *program evaluation* or *practice evaluation,* involves searching for practical knowledge in considering the implementation and effects of social policies and the impact of programs. Carol Weiss (1998) defines *evaluation* as "the systematic assessment of the operation and/or the outcomes of a program or policy, compared

> **Evaluation research** Research that describes or identifies the impact of social programs and policies.

to a set of explicit or implicit standards, as a means of contributing to the improvement of the program or policy" (p. 4). Evaluation research uses research methods and processes for a variety of different tasks, such as describing the clients using a particular program, exploring and assessing the needs of different communities or population groups, evaluating the effectiveness of a particular program, monitoring the progress of clients, or monitoring the performance of staff. In general terms, evaluation research may be descriptive, exploratory, or explanatory. These same tools provide a standard by which we can also evaluate the evaluation.

Because evaluation research or program evaluation uses the same tools as other research, the two often become confused in the minds of readers and even researchers. The distinctions are important, particularly as they relate to the ethical conduct of research, which we discuss in Chapter 3, and, specifically, to institutional review processes to protect human subjects as required. The Centers for Disease Control and Prevention (2010) *Distinguishing Public Health Research and Public Health Non-Research*, provides a useful distinction between the two based on the intent of the activity. The intent of research is to develop or contribute to generalizable knowledge, with the beneficiaries of the research usually being society and perhaps the study participants. The intent of evaluation is to assess whether a program is achieving its objectives with a specific group as a means to monitor and improve the program; therefore, it is not research. The beneficiaries of the information are the program providers and/or the clients receiving the services. An evaluation becomes research when it is designed to test a new, previously untested, or modified intervention, or when the intent of the evaluation becomes an effort to generate generalizable knowledge.

Example: Should Housing or Treatment Come First?

The problem of homelessness spawned many new government programs and, with them, evaluation research to assess the impact of these programs. Should housing or treatment come first for homeless people with serious mental illness and, in particular, for those persons who use and/or abuse drugs and alcohol? Deborah Padgett, Leyla Gulcur, and Sam Tsemberis (2006) addressed this policy dilemma as part of a 4-year longitudinal study comparing housing-first and treatment-first programs. Participants were randomly assigned to one of the two groups: the *housing-first model*, in which the homeless are given immediate access to housing and offered an array of services, and abstinence is not a prerequisite, or the *treatment-first model*, in which housing is contingent on sobriety. People were randomly assigned to the two types of models so the researchers could be more confident that any differences found between the groups at the study's end had arisen after the subjects were assigned to the housing.

After 4 years, 75% of the housing-first clients were in a stable residence for the preceding 6 months, whereas only 50% of the treatment-first group had a stable residence. In addition, the researchers found that there were no statistically significant differences between the two groups on drug or alcohol use. The researchers concluded that the requirement for abstinence had little impact among mentally ill respondents whose primary concern was housing.

▣ Alternative Research Orientations

In addition to deciding on the type of research they will conduct, social work researchers must choose among alternative orientations to research. Some researchers adopt the same orientation in their research, but others vary their orientation based on the particular research question. It is also possible to combine these alterative orientations. We introduce three important questions that must be considered when you begin a research project: (1) Will the research use primary quantitative or qualitative methods, or some combination of the two? (2) Will your guiding philosophy in the research lean to *positivist*, with a focus on social realities, or lean to *constructivist*, with the focus on the meanings that people create? (3) What is the role of the researcher?

Quantitative and/or Qualitative Methods

Did you notice the difference between the types of data the studies used? The primary data collected in the study for HUD (Solari et al., 2014) were counts about the homeless population, how many had families, their gender, and other characteristics. These data were numerical, so we say that this study used **quantitative methods**. Byrne et al.'s (2012) study and the Padgett et al. (2006) study also used quantitative methods; they reported their findings as percentages and other statistics that summarized homelessness. In contrast, DeWard and Moe (2010) used personal narratives—original text—to understand life in a homeless shelter; because they used actual text, and not counts or other quantities, we say that their works used **qualitative methods**.

> **Quantitative methods** Methods such as surveys and experiments that record variation in social life in terms of categories that vary in amount. Data that are treated as quantitative are either numbers or attributes that can be ordered in terms of magnitude.
>
> **Qualitative methods** Methods such as participant observation, intensive interviewing, and focus groups that are designed to capture social life as participants experience it rather than in categories predetermined by the researcher. These methods typically involve exploratory research questions, inductive reasoning, an orientation to social context, human objectivity, and the meanings attached by participants to events.

The distinction between quantitative and qualitative methods involves more than just the type of data collected. Quantitative methods are most often used when the motives for research are explanation, description, or evaluation. Exploration is most often the motive for using qualitative methods, although researchers also use these methods for descriptive and evaluative purposes as well. The goals of quantitative and qualitative researchers may also differ. Whereas quantitative researchers generally accept the goal of developing an understanding that correctly reflects what is actually happening in the real world, some qualitative researchers instead emphasize the goal of developing an "authentic" understanding of a social process or social setting. An authentic understanding is one that reflects *fairly* the various perspectives of participants in that setting.

Studies that combine elements of quantitative methods and qualitative methods such as the manner in which data are collected or how the data are analyzed use **mixed methods** (Johnson, Onwuegbuzie, & Turner, 2007). In mixed-method studies, the data are both numerical and text. Mixed-methods research is used when researchers want to view the same phenomena from dif-

> **Mixed methods** The use of both qualitative and quantitative methods in a research study.

ferent perspectives, want both breadth and depth about a topic, seek additional information to elaborate or clarify what they have learned about a social process, or to explore new or understudied phenomena and then test the findings. Researchers using mixed methods tend to take a pragmatic view that neither objective reality nor a socially constructed reality alone explains social processes; rather there are interactions between the two types of reality (Biesta, 2010). A recent study of homeless young adults (Ferguson, Bender, Thompson, Maccio, & Pollio, 2012) was designed to identify predictors of employment status (quantitative study using a survey with 238 respondents) and to understand the challenges homeless youth face in finding employment and staying employed (qualitative study using focus groups with 20 homeless individuals).

Positivist or Constructivist Philosophies

A researcher's philosophical perspective on reality and on the appropriate role of the researcher will also shape methodological preferences. Researchers with a *positivist philosophy* believe that there is an objective reality that exists apart from the perceptions of those who observe it; the goal of science is to better understand this reality. This is the philosophy traditionally associated with natural science, with the expectation that there are universal laws of behavior, and with the belief that scientists must be objective and unbiased to see reality clearly (Weber, 1949).

Positivism The belief that there is a reality that exists quite apart from our own perception of it, that it can be understood through observation and that it follows general laws.

Postpositivism The belief that there is an empirical reality, but that our understanding of it is limited by its complexity and by the biases and other limitations of researchers.

Intersubjective agreement Agreement between social work researchers about the nature of reality; often upheld as a more reasonable goal of science than certainty about an objective reality.

Positivism asserts that a well-designed test of a theoretically based prediction—the test of the prediction that young adults with more education will be tolerant of other ethnic groups, for example—can move us closer to understanding actual social processes. Quantitative researchers are often guided by a positivist philosophy.

Postpositivism is a philosophy of reality that is closely related to positivism because it also assumes that there is an external, objective reality, but postpositivists acknowledge the complexity of this reality and the limitations of the researchers who study it (Guba & Lincoln, 1989). For example, postpositivists may worry that researchers, who are heavily oriented to a particular treatment modality, such as cognitive behavior therapy, might be biased in favor of finding positive results when evaluating it. As a result, postpositivists do not think we can ever be sure that scientific methods allow us to perceive objective reality. Instead, they believe that the goal of science is to achieve **intersubjective agreement** among scientists about the nature of reality (Wallace, 1983). We can be more confident in the ability of the community of social researchers to develop an unbiased account of reality than in the ability of any individual social scientist to do so (Campbell & Russo, 1999).

Qualitative research is often guided by a different philosophy: **constructivism**. Constructivist social scientists believe that social reality is socially constructed and that the goal of social scientists is to understand the meanings

Constructivism A perspective that emphasizes how different stakeholders in social settings construct their beliefs.

Interpretivism The belief that reality is socially constructed and that the goal of social scientists is to understand what meanings people give to that reality.

people give to reality, not to determine how reality works apart from these constructions. This philosophy rejects the positivist belief that there is a concrete, objective reality that scientific methods help us to understand (Lynch & Bogen, 1997); instead, constructivists believe that people construct an image of reality based on their own preferences and prejudices and their interactions with others and that this is as true of scientists as it is of everyone else.

Constructivism emphasizes that different stakeholders in a social setting construct different beliefs (Guba & Lincoln, 1989). It gives particular attention to the different goals of researchers and other participants in a research setting and seeks to develop a consensus among participants about how to understand the focus of inquiry (Sulkunen, 2008). The constructivist research report will highlight different views of the social program or other issue and explain how a consensus can be reached among participants. **Interpretivism** is a related research philosophy that emphasizes the importance of understanding subjective meanings people give to reality while believing that reality itself is socially constructed.

Here's the basic argument: All empirical data we collect come to us through our own senses and must be interpreted with our own minds. This suggests that we can never be sure that we have understood reality properly, that we can, or that our understandings can really be judged more valid than someone else's. Concerns like this have begun to appear in many areas of social science and have begun to shape some research methods. From this standpoint, the goal of validity becomes meaningless: "Truth is a matter of the best-informed and most sophisticated construction on which there is consensus at a given time" (Schwandt, 1994, p. 128).

Critical theory similarly focuses on examining structures, patterns of behavior, and meanings but rests on the premise that power differences, often manifested by discrimination and oppression, have shaped these structures and patterns. What is observed and described at a particular moment in time is the result of differential power relationships that have solidified over time. How people are socially located in a particular situation will construct their meanings and interests (Keenan, 2004). Researchers committed to this perspective see research as a way to challenge societal structures that reinforce oppression (Mertens, Bledsoe, Sullivan, & Wilson, 2010).

Critical theory A research focus on examining structures, patterns of behavior, and meanings but rests on the premise that power differences, often manifested by discrimination and oppression, have shaped these structures and patterns.

Feminist research is a term used to refer to a perspective on research that can involve many different methods (Reinharz, 1992). The feminist perspective on research includes the interpretivist and constructivist elements of concern with personal experience and subjective feelings and with the researcher's position and standpoint (Hesse-Biber, Nagy, & Leavy, 2007). The emphasis is on the importance of viewing the social world as complex and multilayered, of

> **Feminist research** Research with a focus on women's lives and often including an orientation to personal experience, subjective orientations, and the researcher's standpoint.

sensitivity to the impact of social differences—of being an "insider" or an "outsider," and of being concerned with the researcher's position. Patricia Hill Collins (2008) suggests that researchers who are sensitive to their outsider role within a social situation may have unique advantages: "Outsiders within occupy a special place—they become different people and their difference sensitizes them to patterns that may be more difficult for established sociological insiders to see" (p. 317).

Which philosophy makes the most sense to you? Do you agree with positivists and postpositivists that scientific methods can help us understand the social world as it is, not just as we would like to think it is? Does the constructivist focus on meanings sound like a good idea? What about integrating research with empowerment strategies of feminist research?

There is no easy answer to which is the correct philosophy. There has been an ongoing debate among social work researchers and educators about which is the appropriate philosophical approach. We argue that there is value to both of these approaches and there are good reasons to prefer a research philosophy that integrates some of the differences between these philosophies (Smith, 1991). Researchers influenced by a positivist philosophy should be careful to consider how their own social background shapes their research approaches and interpretations, just as constructivist researchers caution us to do. We also need to be sensitive to the insights that can be provided by other stakeholders in the settings we investigate. Researchers influenced more by a constructivist philosophy should be careful to ensure that they use rigorous procedures to check the trustworthiness of their interpretations of data (Riessman, 2008).

Researcher or Participatory Orientation

Whose prescriptions should specify how the research will be conducted? Much social work research is driven by the researcher who specifies the research question, the applicable theory or theories, and the variables to be investigated. The typical social science approach emphasizes the importance of the researcher's expertise and maintenance of autonomy.

Community-based participatory research (or *participatory action research*) encourages social work researchers to get out of the academic rut and bring values into the research process. Rosemary Sarri and Catherine Sarri (1992) suggest that participatory action research "seeks to reduce the distinction between the researcher and the researched by incorporating the latter in a collab-

> **Community-based participatory research** A type of research in which the researcher involves some community and/or organizational members as active participants throughout the study.

orative effort of knowledge creation that will lead to community betterment and empowerment" (p. 100). Therefore, the researcher involves as active participants members of the community or setting being studied, including designing questions, gathering information, analyzing data, making recommendations or conclusions, and/or disseminating the findings.

Hidenori Yamatani, Aaron Mann, and Patricia Wright (2000) used principles of participatory action research to conduct a needs assessment focused on unemployment in a working-class neighborhood in Pittsburgh. To conduct this study, the social work researchers knew they had to directly involve the community or their efforts would be unsuccessful. They chose to become research advisers assisting community members, who, in turn, defined the overall parameters of the study, designed the questionnaires, collected the data, coded the data, reviewed the findings to develop the report's recommendations, and reviewed and approved the written report. The researchers provided their advice on different steps in the research process, trained community members in various research-related tasks, analyzed the data, and wrote the report. The outcome was a report (and its recommendations) that had both community and organizational support.

回 Social Work Research in a Diverse Society

Social work research is conducted in an increasingly diverse society. In the past, diversity was primarily associated with race and ethnicity (National Association of Social Workers, 2001; Van den Berg & Crisp, 2004) but now includes "people of different genders, social classes, religious and spiritual beliefs, sexual orientation, ages, and physical and mental abilities" (National Association of Social Workers, 2001, p. 8). Although there is much that these groups share, there is also an increased awareness that there are distinct cultural, social, and historical experiences shaping and influencing group experiences. Just as social work practitioners are expected to engage in culturally competent practice, they must recognize that cultural norms impact the research process, whether it is the willingness to participate in research activities, the meaning ascribed to abstract terms and constructs, the way data are collected, or the interpretation of the findings. The failure by researchers to adequately address the cultural context impacts in different ways the research process and, ultimately, the validity and generalizability of research findings.

Historically, women and ethnic minorities have been underrepresented in research studies and, more specifically, in clinical studies testing the impact of health and mental health interventions. The reluctance of different groups to participate in research may be due to different reasons, such as distrust of the motives of the researchers (Beals, Manson, Mitchell, Spicer, & AI-SUPERPFP Team, 2003; Sobeck, Chapleski, & Fisher, 2003), historical experiences, not understanding the research process, not seeing any benefit to participation (Beals et al., 2003), and misuse of findings to the detriment of their communities (Sobeck et al., 2003). Inadequate representation makes it more difficult to conclude, for example, that the results from a primarily White sample can be generalized to other ethnic groups.

Cultural differences given to the meaning of different concepts, particularly psychological concepts, can also impact the validity of the research. Social work researchers use a variety of measurement instruments, but often people of color, women, low-income people, and other groups have not been adequately represented in the development or testing of these measurement instruments (Witkin, 2001). It is important to determine whether the concepts being measured have the same meaning and are manifested in the same way across different cultural groups.

Measurement bias can result in misidentifying the prevalence of a condition and result in group differences that may not actually exist. For example, some measures of depression have been criticized as inappropriate when used with older adults (Sharp & Lipsky, 2002), African Americans (Ayalon & Young, 2003; Zauszniewski, Fulton Picot, Debanne, Roberts, & Wykle, 2002), and women (Romans, Tyas, Cohen, & Silverstone, 2007; Sigmon et al., 2005). Because these measures may not be accurate, they may overestimate the prevalence of depression for each of these groups.

The quality of information obtained from surveys is in part dependent on the questions that are asked; there is an assumption that respondents share a common understanding of the meaning of the question and willingness or unwillingness to answer the question. Yet questions may have different meanings to different groups, may not be culturally appropriate, and even when translated into a different language may lack equivalent connotations (Pasick, Stewart, Bird, & D'Onofrio, 2001). For example, Rena Pasick and her colleagues (2001) found that the concept of *routine checkup* was unfamiliar to their sample of Chinese Americans, there was no similar concept in the Vietnamese language, and some Latina respondents did not understand the question, nor could they offer alternative language. The researchers had to find other ways to ask the question to get the information they desired.

Data must be analyzed carefully. Often ethnic and racial minorities are compared to the majority population; in doing so, we may be treating any differences as deficits when in fact they reflect cultural differences. In comparison studies, it is important to control for the impact of socioeconomic status given disparities in economic well-being. How data are reported must respect confidentiality. Beals and her colleagues (2003) noted that American Indian and Alaska Native communities had experienced research efforts that resulted in negative stereotypes and publicity for their communities; ensuring confidentiality is not limited to the individual respondent but also to the community.

As you can see from this brief introduction, the norms that develop within population subgroups have an impact that cuts across the research process. As you read each chapter, you will learn both the kinds of questions that researchers ask and the strategies they use to ensure that their research is culturally competent.

回 Conclusion

The studies we have highlighted in this chapter are only several of the dozens of large studies of homelessness done since 1980, but they illustrate some of the questions that social science research can address, several different methods that researchers can use, and ways that research can inform public policy. Each of the studies was designed to reduce the errors common in everyday reasoning:

- A clear definition of the population of interest in each study and the selection of a broad, representative sample of that population (e.g., Solari et al., 2014) increased the researchers' ability to draw conclusions without overgeneralizing findings to groups to which they did not apply.

- The use of surveys in which each respondent was asked the same set of questions (e.g., Padgett et al., 2006) reduced the risk of selective or inaccurate observation, as did careful and regular note taking by the field researchers (e.g., DeWard & Moe, 2010).

- The risk of illogical reasoning was reduced by carefully describing each stage of the research, clearly presenting the findings, and carefully testing the basis for cause-and-effect conclusions (e.g., Byrne et al., 2012; Padgett et al., 2006).

- Resistance to change was reduced by designing an innovative type of housing and making an explicit commitment to evaluate it fairly (e.g., Padgett et al., 2006).

Nevertheless, we would be less than honest if we implied that we enter the realm of beauty, truth, and light when we engage in social work research or when we base our opinions only on the best available social research. Research always has some limitations and some flaws (as does any human endeavor), and our findings are always subject to differing interpretations. Social work research permits us to see more, to observe with fewer distortions, and to describe more clearly to others the basis for our opinions, but it will not settle all arguments. Others will always have differing opinions, and some of those others will be social scientists and social workers who have conducted their own studies and drawn different conclusions. Are people encouraged to get off welfare by requirements that they get a job? Some research suggests that they are, other research finds no effect of work incentives, and one major study found positive but short-lived effects. More convincing answers must await better research, more thoughtful analysis, or wider agreement on the value of welfare and work.

However, even in areas of research that are fraught with controversy, where social scientists differ in their interpretations of the evidence, the quest for new and more sophisticated research has value. What is most important for improving understanding of the social world is not the result of any particular study, but the accumulation of evidence from different studies of related issues. By designing new studies that focus on the weak points or controversial conclusions of prior research, social scientists contribute to a body of findings that gradually expands our knowledge about the social world and resolves some of the disagreements about it.

We hope this first chapter has given you an idea of what to expect in the rest of the book. Social science provides a variety of methods to reduce the errors common in everyday reasoning. We explore different research methods to understand how they improve our ability to come to valid conclusions, which, in turn, can inform social work practice. Whether you plan to conduct your own research projects, read others' research reports, or just think about and act in the social world, knowing about research will give you greater confidence in your own opinions; improve your ability to evaluate others' opinions; and encourage you to refine your questions, answers, and methods of inquiry about the social world. Having the tools of research can guide you to improve the social programs in which you work, to provide better interventions with your clients, and to monitor their progress.

Key Terms

Adherence to authority   7
Community-based participatory
     research   17
Constructivism   16
Critical theory   16
Descriptive research   11
Evaluation research   14
Explanatory research   13

Exploratory research   12
Feminist research   17
Illogical reasoning   6
Inaccurate observation   5
Interpretivism   16
Intersubjective agreement   16
Mixed methods   15
Overgeneralization   5

Positivism   16
Postpositivism   16
Qualitative methods   15
Quantitative methods   15
Resistance to change   6
Selective observation   5
Social science   7

Highlights

- Social science research differs from the ordinary process of thinking about our experiences by focusing on broader questions that involve people outside our immediate experience and issues about why things happen.

- Social science is the use of logical, systematic, documented methods to investigate individuals, societies, and social processes, as well as the knowledge produced by these investigations.

- Five common errors in reasoning are overgeneralization, selective or inaccurate observation, illogical reasoning, resistance to change, and adherence to authority. These errors result from the complexity of the social world, subjective processes that affect the reasoning of researchers and the people they study, researchers' self-interest, and unquestioning acceptance of tradition or of those in positions of authority.

- Social science methods are used by social work researchers and practitioner-researchers to uncover the nature of a social condition, to test the accuracy of assumptions about the causes of the social condition, to identify populations at risk, and to test and

evaluate the effectiveness of interventions, programs, and policies designed to ameliorate the social condition.

- Social work research cannot resolve value questions or provide permanent, universally accepted answers.

- Quantitative and qualitative methods structure research in different ways and are differentially appropriate for diverse research situations. They may be combined in research projects.

- Positivism and postpositivism are research philosophies that emphasize the goal of understanding the real world; these philosophies guide most quantitative researchers.

- Constructivism emphasizes the importance of exploring and representing the ways in which different stakeholders in a social setting construct their beliefs. Interpretivism is a related research philosophy that emphasizes an understanding of the meaning people attach to their experiences.

- Cultural norms impact the research process from the willingness to participate in research, the meaning of terms, the way data are collected, or the interpretation of the findings.

Discussion Questions

1. Select a social issue that interests you. List four beliefs about this social issue, for example, its causes. What is the source of these beliefs? What type of policy, program, and intervention for helping resolve this social issue would be consistent with your beliefs?

2. Social work research using different methods can yield differing results about the same topic. Pick a social issue and describe how

quantitative, qualitative, and mixed methods might lead to different results.

3. Do you favor the positivist/postpositivist or interpretivist/constructivist philosophy as a guide for social work research? Explain your position.

Practice Exercises

1. Find a report of social work research in an article in a daily newspaper. What were the major findings? How much evidence is given about the measurement validity, generalizability, and causal validity of the findings? What additional design features might have helped to improve the study's validity?

2. Read the abstracts (initial summaries) of each article in a recent issue of a major social work journal. (Ask your instructor for some good journal titles.) On the basis of the abstract only, classify each research project represented in the articles as primarily descriptive, exploratory, explanatory, or evaluative. Note any indications that the research focused on other types of research questions.

Web Exercise

1. Prepare a 5- to 10-minute class presentation on the U.S. Department of Housing and Urban Development report *Homelessness: Programs and the People They Serve* (www.huduser.org/portal/ publications/homeless/homelessness/contents.html). Write up a brief outline for your presentation, including information on study design, questions asked, and major findings.

Developing a Research Proposal

Will you develop a research proposal in this course? If so, you should begin to consider your alternatives.

1. What topic would you focus on if you could design a social work–related research project without any concern for costs or time? What are your reasons for studying this topic? Develop four questions that you might investigate about the topic you just selected. Each question should reflect a different research motive: description, exploration, explanation, and evaluation. Be specific.

2. Which question most interests you? Would you prefer to attempt to answer that question with quantitative, qualitative methods or mixed methods? Why?

A Question of Ethics

Throughout the book, we discuss the ethical challenges that arise in social work research. At the end of each chapter, we ask you to consider some questions about ethical issues related to that chapter's focus. We introduce this critical topic formally in Chapter 3, but we begin here with some questions for you to ponder.

1. The chapter began with a brief description from a news article of a homeless person named Burt. We think stories like this can provide important information about the social problems that social workers confront. But what would *you* do if you were interviewing homeless persons and one talked of taking his own life out of despair? What if he was only thinking about it? Can you suggest some guidelines for researchers?

2. You read in this chapter that Deborah Padgett, Leyla Gulcur, and Sam Tsemberis (2006) found that their housing-first program enabled homeless persons to spend more time housed than those required first to undergo treatment for substance abuse. If you were these researchers, would you announce your findings in a press conference and encourage relevant agencies to eliminate abstinence requirements for homeless persons with substance abuse problems? When would you recommend that social work researchers urge adoption of new policies based on research findings? How strong do you think the evidence should be?

The Process of Social Work Research

Intimate partner violence continues to be major problem in our society. In a 2010 U. S. survey of 16,507 people sponsored by the Department of Justice and the Centers for Disease Control and Prevention, 35.6% of women and 28.5% of men said they had experienced rape, physical violence, or stalking by an intimate partner at some time in their lives (Black et al., 2011). Nearly 4.8 million women annually experience some form of physical violence (Breiding et al., 2014). In 2012, 1,487 women were killed by a male they knew; 924 were wives or intimate partners (Violence Policy Center, 2014). And the cost to society has been estimated to be as high as $8.3 billion (Max, Rice, Finkelstein, Bardwell, & Leadbetter, 2004).

Back in 1981, the Police Foundation and the Minneapolis Police Department began a landmark experiment to determine whether arresting accused spouse abusers on the spot would deter repeat incidents. The study's results, which were widely publicized, indicated that arrest did have a deterrent effect. In part because of this, the percentage of urban police departments that made arrest the preferred response to complaints of domestic violence rose from 10% in 1984 to 90% in 1988 (Sherman, 1992). Researchers in six other cities conducted studies like the Minneapolis experiment to determine whether changing the location would result in different outcomes. The Minneapolis Domestic Violence Experiment, the studies modeled after it, and the related controversies provide many examples for a systematic overview of the social research process.

In this chapter we introduce how you begin the process of social work research. We consider in some detail the techniques required to decide what to study: formulating research questions, finding information, and reviewing prior research. Next, we discuss the role of social theory and, when appropriate, formulating specific testable hypotheses. We then discuss different social research standards for social work research as a prelude to the details about these stages in subsequent chapters. By the chapter's end, you should be ready to formulate a research question, design a general strategy for answering this question, and critique previous studies that addressed this question.

回 Social Work Research Questions

A social work research question is a question that you seek to answer through the collection and analysis of firsthand, verifiable, empirical data. It is not a question about who did what to whom, but a question about people interacting with individuals, groups, or organizations; about tendencies in community change; or about the impact of different interventions. Think of the questions you might ask about intimate partner violence. How many women and men are victims of intimate partner violence? Are their age, gender, ethnicity, or income differences associated with intimate partner violence? Have rates of intimate partner violence changed since 1981? What are the causes of intimate partner violence? Do batterer intervention groups reduce subsequent battering? What are the costs of intimate partner violence to the United States? These questions are just a few of the many possible questions about domestic violence.

So many research questions are possible that it is more of a challenge to specify what does not qualify as a social work question. But that does not mean it is easy to specify a research question. Formulating a good research question can be surprisingly difficult. We can break the process into three stages: (1) identifying one or more questions for study, (2) refining the questions, and (3) evaluating the questions.

Identifying Social Work Research Questions

Social work research questions may emerge from your own experience. One experience might be membership in a youth group, another might be volunteering in a woman's shelter, or yet another might be a friend's death. You may find yourself asking questions like these: In what ways do adolescents benefit from youth group membership? Does domestic violence change a person's trust in others? What are effective methods of treating bereavement or loss?

Some research questions may emerge from your work or field practicum experiences. You might wonder about the effectiveness of the interventions used at your practicum site. You may ask yourself what causes some of the issues you see, such as what causes domestic violence or what family patterns seem related to school behavioral problems.

You also might begin to think about how social policies affect the clients your agency serves or the agency itself. Has the advent of managed care changed the kinds of services provided by mental health agencies? How do Temporary Assistance to Needy Families recipients who are going back to work manage their child-care needs?

Other researchers may pose interesting questions for you to study. Most research articles highlight unresolved issues and end with suggestions for additional research. The authors may suggest repeating the study with other samples in other settings or locations, or they may suggest that the research could have been improved by using a different design or instrument. They may suggest examining other variables to determine whether they explain a relationship. Any issue of a social work journal is likely to have articles with comments that point toward unresolved issues.

Some social work researchers find the source of their research questions in testing social theory. For example, you may find rational choice theory to be a useful approach to understanding diverse forms of social behavior because you feel that people seem to make decisions on the basis of personal cost-benefit calculations. You may ask whether rational choice theory can explain why some elderly people choose to participate in Supplemental Security Income and other eligible elderly people do not participate.

Finally, some research questions have very pragmatic sources. You may focus on a research question posed by someone else because it seems to be to your advantage to do so. Some social scientists conduct research on specific questions posed by a funding source in what is termed a *request for proposals* (RFP). Or you may learn that the social workers in the homeless shelter where you volunteer need help with a survey to learn about client needs, which becomes the basis for another research question.

Refining Social Work Research Questions

It is more challenging to focus on a problem of manageable size than it is to come up with an interesting question. We are often interested in much more than we can reasonably investigate with limited time and resources. Researchers may worry about staking a research project (and thereby a grant or a grade) on a single problem, so they address several research questions at once. Also, it might seem risky to focus on a research question that may lead to results discrepant with your own cherished assumptions. The prospective commitment of time and effort for some research questions may seem overwhelming, resulting in a certain degree of paralysis.

The best way to avoid these problems is to gradually develop the research question. Do not keep hoping that the perfect research question will just spring forth from your pen. Instead, develop a list of possible research questions as you go along. At the appropriate time, look through this list for the ones that appear more than once. Narrow your list to the most interesting, most workable candidates. Repeat this process as long as it helps to improve your research question.

Evaluating Social Work Research Questions

What makes a research question good? You should evaluate the best candidate in terms of three criteria: social importance, scientific relevance, feasibility given the time and resources available (G. King, Keohane, & Verba, 1994).

Social Importance

Social work research is not a simple undertaking, so it is hard to justify the expenditure of effort and resources unless we focus on a substantive area that is important. There are so many substantive areas related to social work that creating an all-encompassing list is difficult. You need to feel motivated to carry out the study; there is little point in trying to answer a question that does not interest you.

For most research projects, you should consider whether the research question is important to other people. Will an answer to the research question make a difference in improving the well-being of people? Social work research is not wanting for important research questions. A recent issue of *Research on Social Work Practice* included articles about the impact of an intervention on reducing children's aggressive behaviors; a summary of the effect of 15 interventions designed to reduce adolescent marijuana use; the effectiveness of a supervisor competency training on supervisory relationships with staff, job performance, and promoting professional development; and validating a scale to assess evidence-based practice research. All of these articles addressed research questions about social work interventions, and all raised new questions for additional research. Other social work journals address macro practice topics such as community building, organizational behavior, or policy research.

Scientific Relevance

Every research question should be grounded in both social work and social science literature. Whether we formulate a research question because we have been stimulated by an academic article or because we want to investigate a current social problem, we should turn to the literature to find out what has already been learned about this question. You can be sure that some prior study is relevant to almost any research question you can conceive.

The Minneapolis experiment was built on a substantial body of contradictory theorizing about the impact of punishment on criminality (Sherman & Berk, 1984). Deterrence theory predicted that arrest would deter individuals from repeat offenses; labeling theory predicted that arrest would make repeat offenses more likely. One prior experimental study of this issue was about juveniles; studies among adults had yielded inconsistent findings. Clearly, the Minneapolis researchers had good reason to conduct another study. Any new research question should be connected in this way to past research.

Feasibility

You must be able to conduct the study with the time and resources you have available. If time is short, questions that involve long-term change may not be feasible unless you can find data that have already been collected. For example, it is difficult to study the impact of antidrug education groups offered in middle school on subsequent adult drug use. Another issue is access to identified people or groups. It may be difficult to gain access to participants with particular characteristics. If you were interested in seeking people with a mental health diagnosis who live in your community, you might have to do an excessive amount of screening. Although you could turn to a mental health provider, the agency might not allow you access to its clients. You must consider whether you will have any additional resources, such as research funding or other researchers with whom to collaborate. Remember that there are severe limits on what one person can accomplish. However, you may be able to piggyback your research onto a larger research project. You also must take into account the constraints you face due to your schedules and other commitments, as well as your skill level.

The Minneapolis Domestic Violence Experiment shows how ambitious social research questions can be when a team of seasoned researchers secures the backing of influential groups. The project required hundreds of thousands of dollars, the collaboration of many social scientists and criminal justice personnel, and the volunteer efforts of 41 Minneapolis police officers. But many worthwhile research questions can be investigated with much more limited resources.

🏢 Consider Social Diversity When Formulating a Question

As you consider alternative research questions, it is important to remember that we live in a very diverse world. The language you use to conceptualize the research question may reflect age, gender, ethnic, or heterosexual bias or reinforce societal stereotypes. For example, questions about older adults sometimes reflect negative social stereotypes of the elderly, suggesting that aging is a problem by focusing on decline and deficits (Schaie, 1993). Terms like *old* or *elderly* may negatively affect attitudes toward older adults; neutral phrases such as "adults between 70 and 85 years of age" have less of a negative connotation (Polizzi & Millikin, 2002).

There are similar concerns when developing questions about ethnic groups. Sometimes questions about ethnic groups are characterized in terms of deficits as opposed to strengths, reinforcing negative stereotypes about ethnic groups. In research studies that compare ethnic groups, there is a tendency to phrase questions in ways that suggest the cultural superiority of one group in contrast to another group. Yet, these differences or gaps may reflect culturally appropriate responses.

While there has been a greater recognition of avoiding questions that reflect a heterosexist bias, such biases still persist (Phillips, Ingram, Smith, & Mindes, 2003). A heterosexist or genderist bias occurs when research questions "ignore the existence of LGBT people, devalue or stigmatize them, or assume that negative characteristics observed in them are caused by their sexual orientation or gender identity/expression" (J. I. Martin & Meezan, 2003, p. 195). For example, we think of a family as consisting of two parents of opposite genders, yet we know that families take on many different forms. Using a narrow definition of family reflecting societal stereotypes would certainly limit the cross-population generalizability of the findings. Language such as comparing lesbians or gay men to the "general population" marginalizes lesbians and gay men.

How we conceptualize our questions and the language we use are critical in the development of a research question. We must be attentive to the choice of language used. It is important to recognize that variables such as age, race, and gender are associated with many other variables such as power, status, or income that may explain group differences. The research question in the Minneapolis Domestic Violence Experiment reflected biases of the time, and by doing so limits the generalizability of the findings. The focus was only on males perpetrating violence on females. Yet we know that males may experience intimate partner violence and that there is intimate partner violence among same-sex intimate partners.

▣ Foundations of Social Work Research

How do we find prior research on a question of interest? You may already know some of the relevant material from prior coursework or your independent reading, but that will not be enough. You need to find reports of previous investigations that sought to answer the same research question that you wish to answer. If there have been no prior studies of exactly the same research question on which you wish to focus, you should seek to find reports from investigations of similar research questions. For example, you may be thinking about a study of the impact of cognitive-behavioral therapy on posttraumatic stress, but you cannot find any specific studies; you might turn to available research on cognitive-behavioral therapy with persons suffering from anxiety. Once you have located reports from prior research similar to the research you wish to conduct, you may expand your search to include studies about related topics or studies that used similar methods.

Searching the Literature

Conducting a thorough search of the research literature and then critically reviewing what you have found is an essential foundation for any research project. Fortunately, most of this information can be identified online and an increasing number of published journal articles can be downloaded directly to your own computer, depending on your particular access privileges. But just because there is a lot available does not mean that you need to find it all. Keep in mind that your goal is to find relevant reports of prior research investigations. You should focus on scholarly journals that publish articles that have been reviewed by other social scientists, a process known as *peer review*.

Newspaper and magazine articles may raise important issues or summarize research findings, but they are not acceptable sources for understanding the research literature. The Internet offers much useful material, including research reports from government and well-respected research centers, sites that describe social programs, and indexes of the published research literature. You may find copies of particular rating scales, reports from research in progress, and papers that have been presented at professional conferences. Web search engines will also find academic journal articles that you can access directly online, although usually for a fee. Rather than pay this fee, most of the published research literature will be available to you online through the website of your college or university library. However, the research information you find at various websites comes in a wide range of formats and represents a variety of sources, some of which may lead you astray, so be careful about the choices you make.

As with any part of the research process, your method for searching the literature will affect the quality of your results. Your search method should include the following steps:

Specify your research question. Your research question should be neither so broad that hundreds of articles are judged relevant nor so narrow that you miss important literature. "Is social support effective?" is probably too broad. "Does social support reduce rates of unnecessary use of assisted living residences by urban residing elderly?" may be too narrow. "Is social support effective in reducing unnecessary institutional living by the elderly?" is probably about right.

Identify appropriate bibliographic databases to search. Searching a computerized bibliographic database is by far the most efficient search strategy. Most academic libraries provide access to online databases that provide useful references for social work research such as Social Work Abstracts, PsycINFO or PsycArticles, EBSCO, and Web of Science. The search engine Google offers anyone with Internet connections access to Google Scholar. Do not limit yourself to one database as any one database may not provide a complete listing of relevant articles (Holden, Barker, Kuppens, Rosenberg, & LeBreton, 2015; McGinn, Taylor, McColgan, & McQuilkan, 2014).

Create a tentative list of keyword terms. List the question's parts and subparts and any related issues that you think might play an important role in the research: "social support," "informal support," "unnecessary institutionalization," "social support and the elderly." A good rule is to cast a net wide enough to catch most of the relevant articles with your key terms, but not so wide that it identifies many useless citations. Searching for "informal support" would be more useful than a search for "support." List the authors of relevant studies. Specify the most important journals that deal with your topic.

Narrow your search. The sheer numbers of references you find can be a problem. For example, searching for *elderly* retrieved 1,084 journal citations in Social Work Abstracts. Depending on the database you are working with and the purposes of your research, you may want to limit your search to English-language publications, to journal articles rather than conference papers or dissertations (both of which are more difficult to acquire), and to material published in recent years.

The way that words are entered into the search can lead to the retrieval of a different number of documents. A search for journal articles on *informal support* in Social Work Abstracts resulted in 147 journal citations. However, if we had searched for *informal* and *support*, we would have found 212 journal abstracts. The choice of keywords is also crucial in searching databases. If, instead of *elderly*, we had searched for *older adults*, only 561 documents would have been retrieved in Social Work Abstracts.

Use Boolean search logic. You can narrow your search by requiring that abstracts contain combinations of words or phrases. Using the Boolean connector *and* allows you to do this, while using the connector *or* allows you to find abstracts containing different words that mean the same thing. For example, searching for *elderly* and *informal support* in the same search reduced the number of documents to 37 while searching *older adult* and *informal support* retrieved 11 citations.

Use appropriate subject descriptors. Once you have an article that you consider to be appropriate, take a look at the "keywords" or "descriptors" field in the citation. You can redo your search after requiring that the articles be classified with some or all of these terms.

Check the results. Read the titles and abstracts to identify articles that appear to be relevant. In some databases, you are able to click on these article titles and generate a list of their references, as well as links to other articles that quoted the original article.

Locate the articles. Next, it is time to find the full text of articles of interest. You will probably find the full text of many articles available online, but this will be determined by the journals to which your library obtains online access.

Do not think of searching the literature as a one-time-only venture—something that you leave behind as you move on to your *real* research. You may encounter new questions or unanticipated problems as you conduct your research or as you burrow deeper into the literature. Searching the literature again to determine what others have found in response to these questions or what steps they have taken to resolve these problems can yield substantial improvements in your own research. There is so much literature on so many topics that it often is not possible to figure out in advance every subject you should search the literature for or what type of search will be most beneficial.

Another reason to make searching the literature an ongoing project is that the literature is always growing. During the course of one research study, whether it takes only one semester or several years, new findings will be published and relevant questions will be debated. Staying attuned to the literature and checking it at least when you are writing up your findings may save your study from being outdated.

Reviewing Research

If you have done your job well, you will have more than enough literature as background for your own research unless it is on a very obscure topic. At this point, your main concern is to construct a coherent framework in which to develop your research problem, drawing as many lessons as you can from previous research. You may use the literature to identify hypotheses to be reexamined, to find inadequately studied specific research questions, to explicate the disputes about your research question, to summarize the major findings of prior research, and to suggest appropriate methods of investigation.

Effective review of the prior research you find is an essential step in building the foundation for new research. You must assess carefully the quality of each research study, consider the implications of each article for your own plans, and expand your thinking about your research question to take account of new perspectives and alternative arguments. Through reviewing the literature and using it to extend and sharpen your own ideas and methods, you become a part of the social work research community.

Literature reviews appear in different formats. Some literature reviews are part of research proposals and accompany articles reporting research findings; most of the research articles that you find will include a short literature review on the specific focus of the research. Other literature reviews may be more extensive and are included in theses and dissertations. There are literature reviews that stand alone as a paper so as you search the literature, you may find that someone else has already searched the literature on your research question and discussed what they found in a special review article. For example, Lori Weeks and Kristal LeBlanc (2011) published a review of the research literature addressing older women and their experiences of intimate partner violence.

Regardless of your purpose in writing a literature review, a good literature review provides a synthesis about what is known about a particular topic and offers a critical assessment of the works reviewed. A literature review is not simply a summary of articles nor is it an annotated bibliography in which you summarize and evaluate article after article (Mongan-Rallis, 2014).

Reviewing the literature is really a two-stage process. In the first stage, you must describe and assess each article separately. The second stage of the review process is to assess the implications of the entire set of articles (and other materials) for the relevant aspects of your research question and procedures, and then to write an integrated review that highlights those implications. Although you can find literature reviews that consist simply of assessments of one published article after another—that never get beyond stage one in the review process—your understanding of the literature and the quality of your own work will be much improved if you make the effort to write an integrated review.

The first stage assessment includes both description and evaluation. You should organize your notes about each article that you read using standard sections: research question(s), theory, methods, findings, and conclusions. As you summarize the methods, you want to identify the study setting, the sample and the sampling method, measures and variables, and how data were collected. Further, you should summarize the limitations of the study; do not just rely on the limitations described in the article as you may find other limitations. A particularly easy way to summarize your notes is to create a table using the above section headings and completing details for each article (Galvan, 2013). The questions posed in these two appendices, *Questions to Ask About a Quantitative Research Article* (Appendix A) or *Questions to Ask About a Qualitative Research Article* (Appendix C) can help guide your review.

The goal of the second stage of the literature review process is to integrate the results of your separate article reviews. The literature review should accomplish several objectives:

1. Provide background for the social issue that led to the research question.

2. Summarize prior research. Your summary of prior research must focus on the particular research question that you will address with the intent of identifying the current state of knowledge about the question. The summary should be organized around themes or particular topics. Each paragraph should address a specific issue noted in the first sentence, and the subsequent sentences should summarize findings from several studies about that particular issue.

3. Critique prior research. Evaluate the strengths and weaknesses of the prior research. You might identify concerns such as gaps in the populations studied, issues related to sampling, measurement concerns, or the use of designs that limit conclusions.

4. Present pertinent conclusions. Conclude with the contribution your study will make given the knowledge gaps and your hypotheses if you are proposing a quantitative study or your specific research aims. Explain how the unanswered questions raised by prior research or the limitations of methods used in prior research make it important for you to conduct your own investigation (Fink, 2005).

These four objectives are evident in the literature review section of an article by Larry Bennett, Charles Stoops, Christine Call, and Heather Flett (2007; see Exhibit 2.1). The first paragraph briefly notes that domestic violence is a problem and that intervention efforts have had small effects. While the first two sentences of the second paragraph introduce possible reasons for the modest effects, it is the second that focuses on program dropout that is of particular interest; the rest of the paragraph provides information about what is known about those who failed to complete treatment. The third paragraph provides a critique of what is known, suggesting that the focus has been on only one or several programs but not on the unified system of programs in a community. The fourth paragraph describes the contribution the study will make: "*examining completion and re-arrest in a natural system of BIPS rather than a single program permits us to draw conclusions about a larger system rather than individual programs*" (p. 43.). The authors end this paragraph with the study's two specific research aims.

Implications for Evidence-Based Practice

Social work practitioners engaged in evidence-based practice must be able to find research evidence, and they must be able to critically appraise that evidence. In the past, this might have meant doing extensive literature searches or looking for reviews of the literature about the effectiveness of a treatment. Searching for individual articles is time consuming, and single studies have limited generalizability. Literature reviews of a treatment model generally describe the findings of a variety of studies about an intervention's effectiveness, but these reviews tend to be subjective, and the conclusions tend to be based on the reviewer's opinions about the evidence (Lipp, 2007).

As evidence-based practice has grown, there has been a greater emphasis on **systematic reviews** of research findings. A systematic review examines a research question using explicit methods to summarize and assess relevant research (Moher, Liberati, Tetzlaff, & Altman, 2009). A systematic review has a

> **Systematic reviews** Summary review about the impact of an intervention in which the analyst tries to account for differences in research design and participant characteristics, often using statistical techniques such as meta-analysis.

Exhibit 2.1 Literature Review Example

Research on the effectiveness of gender-specific batterer intervention programs (BIPs) is still in the early stages, with only four controlled experimental studies completed to date (Dunford, 2000; Feder & Dugan, 2002; Palmer, Brown, & Barrera, 1992; Taylor, Davis, & Maxwell, 2001). These studies, supported by more than 50 quasi-experimental and nonexperimental outcome studies, suggest BIPs have modest effects on recidivism. A recent meta-analysis of controlled BIP studies found that the effect size of batterer intervention programs is small but significant (Babcock, Green, & Robie, 2004). Given the high prevalence of domestic violence in our society, even small program effects may translate into a large reduction in the number of victimizations of partners of men receiving the intervention compared to victims of men who did not receive the intervention.

Reasons BIPs may have modest effects include unidentified and untreated substance abuse and mental disorders, poverty, cultural mismatch, "stake in conformity" issues, applying person-level interventions to a society-level problem, failure to sanction noncompliance, and inclusion of generally violent men in programs that are not designed to address general antisocial behavior. Another reason for the modest effects of BIPs is that on average, 50% of the participants never complete the program, regardless of whether they are court ordered (Daly & Pelowski, 2000). Recidivism rates for men who drop out of BIPs are greater than for men who complete the program (Cadsky, Hanson, Crawford, & Lalonde, 1996), so the "dosing" effect of keeping men in programs longer may have a direct effect on outcome after controlling for other differences between dropouts and completers. Gordon and Moriarty (2003) found that the number of sessions attended was an important predictor of recidivism and that successful completion of all treatment sessions reduced the likelihood of rearrest. One study of four well-established BIPs found that program completion reduced the risk of re-offense by 46% to 66% (Gondolf, 2002). Variables that have predicted program completion in other studies include age, education, employment, prior arrest, violence in the family of origin, substance abuse, power motivation, motivation to change, mental disorder, partner residence, number of children, and lack of court sanction (Bersani & Chen, 1988; DeHart, Kennerly, Burke, & Follingstad, 1999; DeMaris, 1989; Gondolf, 1999; Grusznski & Carrillo, 1988; Hamberger & Hastings, 1989; Pirog-Good & Stets, 1986; Saunders & Parker, 1989).

Almost all of the work on BIPs has examined either a single program or else compared a few different programs within a community. To date, there are no studies of larger systems of batterer programs operating under unifying conditions. There may be advantages to examining a larger, naturally occurring batterer intervention system (BIS), because such a system might include latent community level effects and therefore better represent actual conditions within which individual programs operate. In fact, most of the research on BIPs has been conducted not on psychotherapeutic interventions with known active components but rather on service delivery systems within communities with numerous unidentified influences. By *batterer intervention system* we refer to a community based intimate partner violence reduction project with some level of coordination. In this article, we define the BIS as a natural network of BIPs within a single court jurisdiction operating under a single set of state standards and utilizing a standardized definition of program completion.

The purpose of this article is to describe program completion and re-arrest for a BIS consisting of 30 BIPs linked to the misdemeanor probation unit of the Circuit Court of Cook County, Illinois. Examining completion and re-arrest in a natural system of BIPs rather than a single program permits us to draw conclusions about a larger system rather than individual programs. Furthermore, if that system is connected to a unit of government or policy-making body, study findings may be useful to similar units in other settings. In a county criminal justice system such as the one described in this article, findings can be applied by policy makers and program designers either implementing new BIPs or seeking to improve current programs, aiding the development of service protocols and standards. The specific questions that this evaluation addresses are (a) What predicts program completion and re-arrest? and (b) What is the effect of program completion on re-arrest?

Source: Bennett, L. W., Stoops, C., Call, C., & Flett, H. (2007). Program completion and re-arrest in a batterer intervention system. *Research on Social Work Practice, 17,* 42–54.

format typical of research studies: it begins with a research question and a rationale for the study, a methods section that describe how studies will be identified, selected, and synthesized, a results section, and a discussion section including limitations. The review tries to account for differences in design and participant characteristics, often using statistical techniques such as meta-analysis (which we describe in Chapter 7). Julia Littell (2005) suggests that such reviews provide better information about the impact of an intervention and how these impacts may vary.

Xiaoling Xiang's (2013) systematic review of interventions addressing substance abuse among homeless youth provides a good example of the degree of detail common to systematic reviews. She searched eight databases for published research as well as ongoing trials using a combination of keywords including: drug, substance alcohol, homeless youth, homeless adolescents, street youth, runaways, intervention, treatment, programs and services. Xiang reviewed the bibliographies of acceptable articles to determine if there were others that should be assessed. Xiang (2013) used clear and specific criteria to select studies; the result was that though the key words extracted 1,692 articles, only 18 articles (15 unique studies) met the inclusion criteria.

Although systematic reviews are believed to be objective, this does not mean that there are not controversies surrounding any particular review, including differences about the inclusion or exclusion of studies and what qualifies as a rigorous study design. The Preferred Reporting Items for Systematic Reviews and Meta-Analyses Group (PRISMA Group) provides a 27-item checklist for systematic reviews (Moher et al., 2009) at www.openmedicine.ca/article/view/285/247.

For systematic reviews to be used by social work practitioners, they have to be both easily accessible and understandable. The Internet has eased the access to such studies, and there are now both private and government-supported programs to produce and disseminate systematic reviews. We describe several such efforts next.

Campbell Collaboration and Cochrane Community

In 1999, evaluation researchers founded the Campbell Collaboration (www.campbellcollaboration.org) to publicize and encourage systematic review of evaluation research studies. The Campbell Collaboration encourages systematic reviews of research evidence on interventions and programs in education, criminal justice, social welfare, and research methods. These reviews are accessible to anyone with an Internet connection and can be used to provide evidence about different intervention techniques. For example, some of the 51 reviews (retrieved July 9, 2015) conducted about social welfare interventions address violence and include "Advocacy Interventions to Reduce or Eliminate Violence and Promote the Physical and Psychosocial Well-Being of Women Who Experience Intimate Partner Abuse" (Ramsay et al., 2009) and "Cognitive Behavioural Therapy for Men Who Physically Abuse Their Female Partner" (Smedslund, Clench-Aas, Dalsbo, Steiro, & Winsvold, 2011).

The Cochrane Community is a collaboration that provides systematic reviews (among many other related services) about health care and mental health. As of July 9, 2015, there were over 5,000 reviews in the Cochrane Library, which is accessed online at www.cochranelibrary.com.

Government-Supported Resources

A variety of government agencies have begun to provide registries of effective interventions. For example, the Substance Abuse and Mental Health Services Administration supports the National Registry of Evidence-Based Programs and Practices (NREPP; http://nrepp.samhsa.gov/aboutnrepp.aspx). This registry features reviews of different programs, including descriptive information about the intervention, ratings of the quality of the research, and ratings about the ease of implementing an intervention to an agency setting. The interventions are rated with respect to individual outcomes so that an intervention may be effective in treating one outcome, but less so with another outcome. Search terms in the NREPP database include areas of interest (such as co-occurring disorders), outcomes (e.g., violence, homelessness), geographic location (e.g., urban, rural, tribal), age, race, gender, and settings (e.g., inpatient, outpatient, residential).

NREPP provides one source of information, but there are other government-supported registries. For example, the Guide to Community Preventive Services (www.thecommunityguide.org) is supported by the Centers for Disease Control and Prevention. The Community Guide provides systematic reviews and interventions to promote community health on a range of topics such as mental health, sexual behavior, and violence. The Office of Juvenile Justice and Delinquency Prevention sponsors a registry of programs. The Model Program Guide (www.ojjdp.gov/mpg) provides ratings on a wide range of topics from prevention programs to reentry programs.

凹 Theory and Social Work Research

Many of us have general notions about how things work, what people are like, and so on, but much of social work practice draws from a more formal set of ideas embodied in social theory. A **theory** is a logically interrelated set of propositions that helps us make sense of many interrelated phenomena and predict behavior or attitudes that are likely to occur when certain conditions are met. Theories help us understand how social problems emerge; they guide us in the design of interventions to help individuals, families, groups, or communities; they are used to explain relationships within organizations as well as between organizations; and they are often used to design social policy. As members of an applied profession, social work practitioners and researchers often draw from theories developed in other academic disciplines, such as sociology, psychology, economics, or political science.

> **Theory** A logically interrelated set of propositions about reality.

A theory consists of concepts (or constructs), which are mental images that summarize a set of similar observations, feelings, or ideas; concepts have labels designed to describe some phenomenon. A theory includes propositions or statements about the relationships among the concepts. Exhibit 2.2a illustrates a simple model of stress theory. There are two concepts, *stressors* (such as individual, family, or work-related sources of stress) and *stress* (impacts on a person's well-being). The proposition is that the more stressors in a person's life, the more stress; this is a positive relationship as indicated by the + in Exhibit 2.2a. The theory might be expanded to include a third concept, *coping resources*, which may alter the relationship between stressors and stress. Based on this small model of stress theory, the stressors in one's life can lead to poor psychological outcomes, but this depends on the coping resources available to deal with the stressful event.

Some social work researchers use theory to examine the relationship between different phenomena. Stress theory led Sands and Goldberg-Glen (2000) to ask whether the availability of social supports (a type of coping resource) was associated with different levels of anxiety (a type of stress) for older adults who were raising a grandchild (a type of stressor). They thought that grandparents with social supports would experience less anxiety than grandparents without social supports would (see Exhibit 2.2b). Support for such a finding would suggest practical applications for this population.

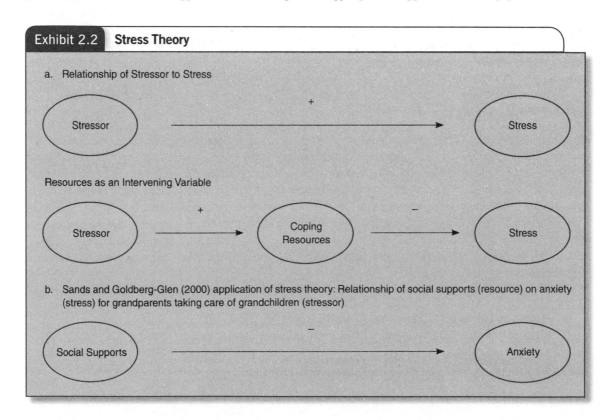

Exhibit 2.2 Stress Theory

a. Relationship of Stressor to Stress

Stressor —+→ Stress

Resources as an Intervening Variable

Stressor —+→ Coping Resources —−→ Stress

b. Sands and Goldberg-Glen (2000) application of stress theory: Relationship of social supports (resource) on anxiety (stress) for grandparents taking care of grandchildren (stressor)

Social Supports —−→ Anxiety

There is no one theory of social work practice as different models of social work practice draw from different broader theories often rooted in other disciplines. Some social work researchers are engaged in testing and building practice theory. For example, William Bradshaw (1997) evaluated an intervention based on cognitive-behavioral theory that was designed to improve the psychological functioning of mentally ill individuals while reducing their symptoms and frequency of hospitalization. He noted that "cognitive-behavioral treatments had been applied to a wide range of populations and problems" (p. 419), but not to those suffering with schizophrenia. As described by Payne (1997), cognitive-behavioral therapy is based on the following:

- *Behavior theory,* which suggests that behavior is learned through conditioning. Behavior is something that one does in response to a stimulus, such as a person or a situation. Conditioning occurs when a behavior becomes linked to a particular stimulus.

- *Cognition theory,* which "argues that behavior is affected by perception or interpretation of the environment during the process of learning" (Payne, 1997, p. 115). Therefore, if the response to a stimulus is an inappropriate behavior, the response was due to misperceptions or misinterpretations.

Based on these two theories, Bradshaw taught clients stress management and social skills, as well as techniques to replace negative thoughts.

Some researchers are interested in organizational behavior, both how organizations operate internally and how they relate to other organizations in their environment. For example, Jennifer Mosley (2010) used *resource mobilization theory* and *resource dependency theory* to understand what distinguishes nonprofit organizations' participation in policy advocacy. Other researchers are interested in both the development and critique of social policies and will use different theories to test and explain policy outcomes. Seefeldt and Orzol (2005) used *human capital theory* (the relationship of skills and knowledge to social status) to understand differences between short-term and long-term recipients of Temporary Assistance to Needy Families (TANF).

Most social work research is guided by some theory, although the theory may be only partially developed in a particular study or may even be unrecognized by the researcher. When researchers are involved in conducting a research project or engrossed in writing a research report, they may easily lose sight of the larger picture. It is easy to focus on accumulating or clarifying particular findings rather than considering how the study's findings fit into a general understanding of the social world.

Up to now, we have described the importance of theory in social work research. A competing view, expressed eloquently by Bruce Thyer (2001), suggests that social work researchers should not impose theory when engaged in studies of the effectiveness of interventions and programs in social service agencies. He does not discount the importance of theory, but suggests that we can learn from evaluation research studies not driven by a theoretical perspective.

As you can see, social theories do not provide the answers to the questions we pose as topics for research. Instead, social theories suggest the areas on which we should focus and the propositions that we should consider for a test.

▣ Alternative Research Strategies

When we conduct social work research, we are attempting to connect theory with empirical data—the evidence we obtain from the social world. Researchers use two alternative strategies to make this connection:

- **Deductive research** starts with a theory and then some of its implications are tested with data; it is most often the strategy used in quantitative methods.

- **Inductive research** starts with the researcher first collecting the data and then developing a theory that explains patterns in the data; the inductive process is typically used with qualitative methods.

> **Deductive research** The type of research in which a specific expectation is deduced from a general premise and is then tested.

A research project can use both deductive and inductive strategies. The two strategies have a two-way, mutually reinforcing relationship that can be represented by the research circle (see Exhibit 2.3). The research circle reflects the process of conducting research, moving from theory to data and back again, or from data to theory and back again. It comprises the three main research strategies: deductive research, inductive research, and descriptive research.

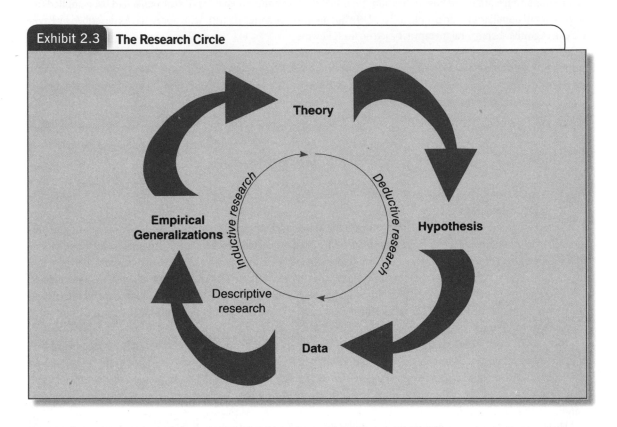

Exhibit 2.3   The Research Circle

Research In the News

For Further Thought ?

DOES MONEY BUY HAPPINESS?

According to a study of lawyers, high pay and working at prestigious law firms was unrelated to happiness and well-being. Even partners making the highest salaries were no happier than associates. Lawyers working in public service jobs and having the lowest salaries were most likely to report being happy. And lawyers in public service jobs drank less alcohol and were just as satisfied with their lives as the high paid lawyers.

1. What factors do you believe are associated with these findings?

2. Develop a theory that might explain these findings.

Source: Quenqua (2015, p. A19).

Deductive Research

In deductive research we start with a theory and from the theory derive a specific expectation; data are then collected to test the specific expectation (see Exhibit 2.3). For example, when people have more human capital, that is work-related skills and education, they are likely to have higher incomes. We can deduce from this relationship a hypothesis, or a more specific expectation, that persons who graduate from college (and therefore have greater human capital) should have a higher income than persons who do not graduate from college. Now that we have a hypothesis, we can collect data about level of education and income. We cannot always directly test the general theory, but we can test specific hypotheses that are deduced from it.

A **hypothesis** proposes a relationship between two or more **variables.** A variable is a characteristic or property that can vary. Variation in one variable is proposed to predict or cause variation in the other variable. In the above example, we are proposing that having a college degree or having less than a college degree will predict income level. "College graduate" as the proposed influence is called the **independent variable;** its effect or consequence, in this case income level, is the **dependent variable.**

A hypothesis derived from a theory does not just state that there is a connection between variables; it suggests that one variable actually influences another—that a change in the first one somehow predicts, influences, or causes a change in the second. It says that *if one* thing happens, *then* another thing is likely to happen.

Exhibit 2.4 presents several hypotheses with their independent and dependent variables and their "if–then" equivalents.

> **Hypothesis** A tentative statement about empirical reality, involving a relationship between two or more variables.
>
> *Example of a hypothesis:* The higher the poverty rate in a community, the higher the percentage of community residents who are homeless.
>
> **Variables** Characteristic or property that can take on different values or attributes.
>
> *Examples of a variable:* Poverty rate, percentage of homeless community residents.
>
> **Independent variable** A variable that is hypothesized to cause, or lead to, variation in another variable.
>
> *Example of an independent variable:* Poverty rate.
>
> **Dependent variable** A variable that is hypothesized to vary depending on or under the influence of another variable.
>
> *Example of a dependent variable:* Percentage of community residents who are homeless.

Exhibit 2.4 Examples of Hypotheses

Original Hypothesis	Independent Variable	Dependent Variable	IF-THEN Hypothesis	Direction of Association
1. As the number of stressors increase, the number of depressive symptoms increase.	Number of Stressors	Depressive symptoms	IF the number of stressor is higher, THEN the number of depressive symptoms is higher.	Positive
2. As years of education decrease, income decreases.	Years of Education	Income	IF years of education decreases THEN income decreases.	Positive
3. As social support increases, caregiver stress decreases.	Social support level	Caregiver stress	If social support is higher, THEN caregiver stress is less.	Negative
4. Depressive symptoms are higher for adolescents and older adults than for persons 20 to 65.	Age of person	Depressive symptoms	IF people are age 13 to 19 or 65 or.older, THEN the number of depressive symptoms is higher compared to people 20 to 65.	Curvilinear
5. Property crime is higher in urban areas than in suburban or rural areas.	Urbanization	Rate of property crimes	IF areas are urban, THEN property crime is higher compared to crime in suburban or rural areas.	Not Applicable

Direction of association A pattern in a relationship between two variables; the values of one variable tend to change consistently in relation to change in the value of the second variable.

Another feature of hypotheses is that they include the expected direction of the relationship, called the **direction of association** (see Exhibits 2.4 and 2.5). So an increase in the independent variable might lead to an increase in the dependent variable or an increase in the independent variable might predict a decrease in the dependent variable. When researchers hypothesize that one variable increases as the other variable increases, the direction of association is positive (Hypothesis 1); when one variable decreases as the other variable decreases, the direction of association is also positive (Hypothesis 2). But when one variable increases as the other decreases, or vice versa, the direction of association is negative, or inverse (Hypothesis 3). Some hypotheses, such as Hypothesis 4, are not linear

| Exhibit 2.5 | Direction of Association |

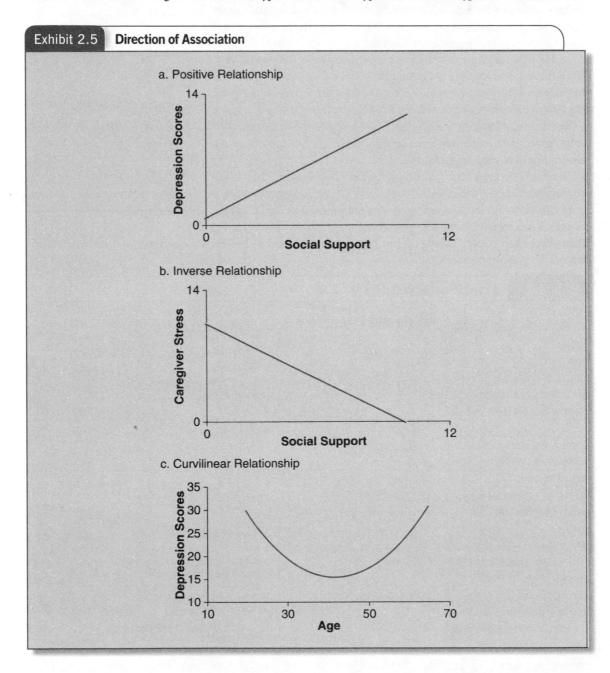

but rather curvilinear, meaning that the relationship does not reflect a straight line but a curve of some sort. Hypothesis 4 suggests that the percentage of people who are depressed is highest among teenagers and older adults whereas it is lower for people between the ages of 20 and 65. Hypothesis 5 is a special case in which the independent variable is categorical: It cannot be said to increase or decrease. In this case, the concept of direction of association does not apply, and the hypothesis simply states that one category of the independent variable is associated with higher values on the dependent variable.

Explanatory and evaluative research studies are types of deductive research. In both types of research, researchers explicitly state their hypotheses or their statements of expectations. The research is designed to test these expectations. Deductive researchers show their hand by stating their expectations in advance, and then by letting the "chips fall where they may," the researcher accepts the resulting data as a more or less objective picture of reality.

Domestic Violence and the Research Circle

The classic Sherman and Berk (1984) study of domestic violence is a good example of how the research circle works. In an attempt to determine ways to prevent the recurrence of spouse abuse, the researchers repeatedly linked theory and data, developing both hypotheses and empirical generalizations.

The first phase of Sherman and Berk's (1984) study was designed to test a hypothesis. According to deterrence theory, punishment will reduce recidivism or the propensity to commit further crimes. From this theory, Sherman and Berk deduced a specific hypothesis: Arrest for spouse abuse reduces the risk of repeat offenses. In this hypothesis, arrest is the independent variable, and the risk of repeat offenses is the dependent variable (it is hypothesized to depend on arrest).

Of course, in another study, arrest might be the dependent variable in relation to some other independent variable. For example, in the hypothesis, the greater the rate of layoffs in a community, the higher the frequency of arrest, the dependent variable is frequency of arrest. Only within the context of a hypothesis, or a relationship between variables, does it make sense to refer to one variable as dependent and the other as independent.

Sherman and Berk (1984) tested their hypothesis by setting up an experiment in which the police responded to complaints of spouse abuse in one of three ways designated by the researchers: arresting the offender, separating the spouses without making an arrest, or simply warning the offender. When the researchers examined their data (police records for the people in their experiment), they found that, of those arrested for assaulting their spouse, only 13% repeated the offense, compared with a 26% recidivism rate for those who were separated from their spouse by the police without any arrest. This pattern in the data, or **empirical generalization**, was consistent with the hypothesis that the researchers deduced from deterrence theory. The theory thus received support from the experiment (see Exhibit 2.6).

> **Empirical generalization** A statement that describes patterns found in data.

Because of their doubts about the generalizability of their results, Sherman, Berk, and new collaborators began to journey around the research circle again, with funding from the National Institute of Justice for replications (repetitions) of the experiment in six more cities. These replications used the same basic research approach, but with some improvements. The random assignment process was tightened up in most of the cities so that police officers would be less likely to replace the assigned treatment with a treatment of their own choice. In addition, data were collected about repeat violence against other victims, as well as against the original complainant. Some of the replications also examined different aspects of the arrest process to see whether professional counseling helped and whether the length of time spent in jail after arrest mattered at all.

By the time results were reported from five of the cities in the new study, a problem was apparent. In three of the cities—Omaha, Nebraska; Charlotte, North Carolina; and Milwaukee, Wisconsin—researchers were finding long-term increases in domestic violence incidents among arrestees. But in two—Colorado Springs, Colorado, and Dade County, Florida—the predicted deterrent effects seemed to be occurring (Sherman, Smith, Schmidt, & Rogan, 1992).

Sherman and his colleagues had now traversed the research circle twice in an attempt to answer the original research question, first in Minneapolis and then in six other cities. But rather than leading to more confidence in

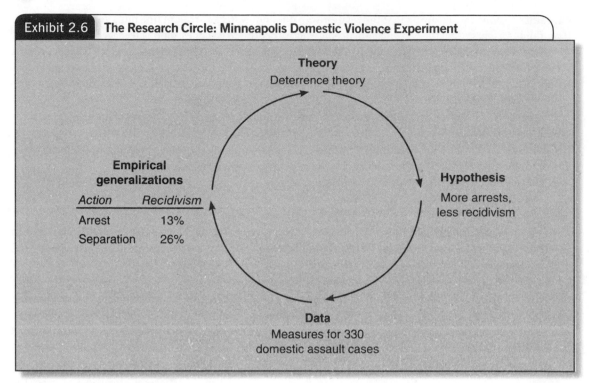

Exhibit 2.6   The Research Circle: Minneapolis Domestic Violence Experiment

Source: Data from Sherman & Berk, 1984, p. 267.

deterrence theory, the research results were calling it into question. Deterrence theory now seemed inadequate to explain empirical reality, at least as the researchers had measured this reality. So the researchers began to reanalyze the follow-up data from several cities to try to explain the discrepant results, thereby starting around the research circle once again (Berk, Campbell, Klap, & Western, 1992; Pate & Hamilton, 1992; Sherman et al., 1992).

Inductive Research

Inductive research begins with specific data, which are then used to develop (induce) a general explanation (a theory) to account for the data. One way to think of this process is in terms of the research circle (Exhibit 2.3): Rather than starting at the top of the circle with a theory, the researcher starts at the bottom of the circle with data and then develops the theory. Another way to think of this process is represented in Exhibit 2.7. In deductive research, reasoning from specific premises results in a conclusion that a theory is supported, while in inductive research, the identification of similar empirical patterns results in a generalization about some social process.

Inductive research The type of research in which general conclusions are drawn from specific data.

Inductive reasoning enters into deductive research when we find unexpected patterns in the data we have collected for testing a hypothesis. We call these patterns **serendipitous findings** or anomalous findings. Whether we begin by doing inductive research or add an inductive element later, the result of the inductive process can be new insights and provocative questions. But the adequacy of an explanation formulated after the fact is necessarily less certain than an explanation presented prior to the collection of data. Every phenomenon can always be explained in some way. Inductive explanations are thus more trustworthy if they are tested subsequently with deductive research.

Serendipitous findings Unexpected patterns in data that stimulate new ideas or theoretical approaches.

An Inductive Approach to Explaining Domestic Violence

The domestic violence research took an inductive turn when Sherman and his colleagues began trying to make sense of the differing patterns in the data collected in the different cities. Could systematic differences in the samples or implementation of arrest policies explain the differing outcomes? Or was the problem an inadequacy in the theoretical basis of their research? Was deterrence theory really the best way to explain the patterns in the data they were collecting?

The researchers had found that individuals who were married and employed were deterred from repeat offenses by arrest, but individuals who were unmarried and unemployed were actually more likely to commit repeat offenses if they were arrested. What could explain this empirical pattern? The researchers turned to control theory, which predicts that having a *stake in conformity* (resulting from inclusion in social networks at work or in the community) decreases a person's likelihood of committing crimes (Toby, 1957). The implication is that people who are employed and married are more likely to be deterred by the threat of arrest than those without such stakes in conformity. This is indeed what the data revealed.

Now the researchers had traversed the research circle almost three times, a process perhaps better described as a spiral (see Exhibit 2.8). The first two times, the researchers had traversed the research circle in a deductive,

Exhibit 2.7	Deductive and Inductive Reasoning
Deductive	
Premise 1:	All unemployed spouse abusers recidivate
Premise 2:	Joe is an unemployed spouse abuser
Conclusion:	*Joe will recidivate*
Inductive	
Observation 1:	Joe, an unemployed spouse abuser, recidivated
Observation 2:	Harold, an unemployed spouse abuser, recidivated
Observation 3:	George, an employed spouse abuser, did not recidivate
Conclusion:	*All unemployed spouse abusers recidivate*

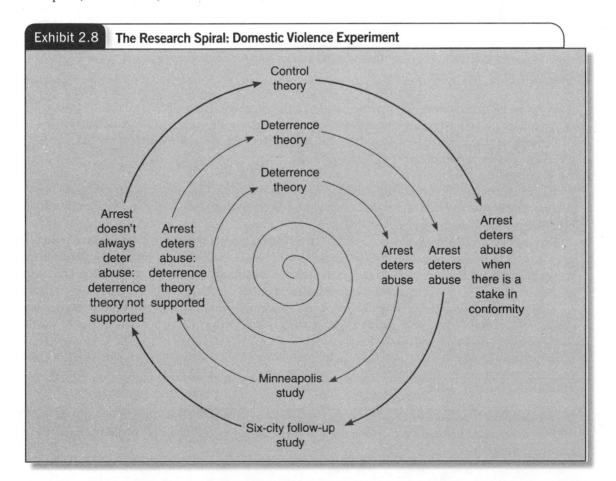

Exhibit 2.8   The Research Spiral: Domestic Violence Experiment

hypothesis-testing way. They started with theory and then deduced and tested hypotheses. The third time they were more inductive: They started with empirical generalizations from the data they had already obtained and then turned to a new theory to account for the unexpected patterns in the data. At this point, they believed that deterrence theory made correct predictions, given certain conditions, and that another theory, control theory, might specify what these conditions were.

This last inductive step in their research made for a more complex but also conceptually richer picture of the impact of arrest on domestic violence. The researchers seemed to have come closer to understanding how to inhibit domestic violence. But they cautioned that their initial question—the research problem—was still not completely answered. Employment and marital status do not solely measure the strength of social attachments; they also are related to how much people earn and the social standing of victims in court. So maybe social ties are not really what make arrest an effective deterrent to domestic violence. The real deterrent may be cost-benefit calculations ("If I have a higher income, jail is more costly to me") or perceptions about the actions of authorities ("If I am a married woman, judges will treat my complaint more seriously"). Additional research was needed (Berk et al., 1992).

Exploratory Research

One motivation for inductive research is exploration. The researchers begin by observing social interaction or interviewing social actors in depth and then develop an explanation for what has been found. The researchers often ask questions like "What is going on here?" "How do people interpret these experiences?" "Why do people do what they do?" Rather than test a hypothesis, the researchers are trying to make sense of some social phenomenon.

Angela Moe (2007) wanted to understand women's decisions to seek help after abuse experiences. Moe interviewed 19 women in a domestic violence shelter. In interviews lasting about 1 hour each, the women were able to discuss, in their own words, what they had experienced and how they responded. Moe then reviewed the interview transcripts carefully and identified major themes that emerged in the comments.

The following quote is from a respondent who had decided not to call the police to report her experience of abuse (Moe, 2007):

> I tried the last time to call the police and he ripped both the phones out of the walls . . . That time he sat on my upper body and had his thumbs in my eyes and he was just squeezing. He was going, "I'll gouge your eyes out. I'll break every bone in your body. Even if they do find you alive, you won't know to tell them who did it to you because you'll be in intensive care for so long you'll forget."

We can use this type of information to identify some of the factors behind the underreporting of domestic violence incidents. Moe or other researchers might design a survey of a larger to sample to determine how frequently each basis for underreporting occurs.

Explanations developed inductively from qualitative research can feel authentic because we have heard what people have to say "in their own words," and we have tried to see the social world "as they see it." Explanations derived from qualitative research will often be richer and more finely textured than the explanations resulting from quantitative research, but they are likely to be based on fewer cases from a limited area. We cannot assume that the people studied in this setting are like others or that other researchers would develop explanations similar to ours to make sense of what was observed or heard. Because we do not initially set up a test of a hypothesis according to some specific rules, another researcher cannot come along and conduct just the same test.

Descriptive Research

Some social work research is purely descriptive. Such research does not involve connecting theory and data, but it is still part of the research circle: It begins with data and proceeds only to the stage of making empirical generalizations based on those data (refer to Exhibit 2.3).

Valid description is important in its own right—in fact, it is a necessary component of all investigations. Much important research for the government and public and private organizations is primarily descriptive: How many poor people live in this community? Is the health of the elderly improving? Where do the uninsured go to obtain medical treatment? Simply put, good description of data is the cornerstone of the scientific research process and an essential component for understanding the social world. Good descriptive research can also stimulate more ambitious deductive and inductive research. Knowing the prevalence of a social condition such as homelessness motivated many researchers to examine the causes of homelessness and test interventions and programs to serve the homeless.

🔲 Social Research Standards

Social work researchers seek to develop an accurate understanding of empirical reality by conducting research studies that lead to valid knowledge about the world; we have reached the goal of validity when our statements or conclusions about empirical reality are correct. The purpose of social work research is not to come up with conclusions that people will like, to find answers that make our agencies look better, or that suit our own personal preferences. Rather, social work research is about (a) conducting research that leads to valid interpretations of the social world, (b) making useful conclusions about the impact of social policy, and (c) formulating valid conclusions about the effects of our practice with clients. Therefore, we are concerned with three standards of validity: measurement validity, generalizability, and causal validity. We will also focus on the standard of authenticity, a concern with reflecting fairly the perspectives of participants in a setting that we study.

Measurement Validity

Measurement validity is our first concern in establishing the validity of research results because if we have not measured what we think we measured, we really do not know what we are talking about. Problems with measurement validity can occur for many reasons. The phenomenon of interest may be

> **Measurement validity** Exists when a measure measures what we think it measures.

poorly defined or the definition may change, such as has occurred with the term *homelessness*. The nature of the questions may result in inaccurate responses or responses may be affected by the presence of other individuals. Even when we think we are using an accurate measure, the measure may not be appropriate and comparable for subgroups of the population

Suffice it to say at this point that we must be careful in designing our measures and in evaluating how well they have performed. Chapter 4 introduces several different ways to test measurement validity. We must be careful to ensure that the measures are comparable for diverse groups; we cannot just *assume* that measures are valid.

Generalizability

The generalizability of a study is the extent to which it can be used to inform us about people, places, or events that were not studied. Although most American cities have many shelters for homeless people and some homeless people sleep on the streets to avoid shelters, many studies of "the homeless" are based on surveys of individuals found in just one shelter. When these studies are reported, the authors state that their results are based on homeless people in one shelter, but then they go on to talk about "the homeless this" and "the homeless that," as if their study results represented all homeless people in the city or even in the nation. If every homeless person was like every other one, generalizations based on observations of one homeless person would be valid. But, of course, that is not the case. In fact, homeless people who avoid shelters tend to be different from those who use shelters, and different types of shelters may attract different types of homeless people.

Sample generalizability Exists when a conclusion based on a sample, or subset, of a larger population holds true for that population.

Cross-population generalizability Exists when findings about one group or population or setting hold true for other groups or populations or settings (see Exhibit 2.9).

There are two kinds of generalizability. **Sample generalizability** refers to the ability to take findings obtained from a sample, or subset, of a larger population and apply them to that population. This is the most common meaning of generalizability. A community organizer may study a sample of residents living in a particular neighborhood in order to assess their attitudes toward opening a homeless shelter in their neighborhood and then generalize the findings to all the residents of the neighborhood. The value of the findings is enhanced if what the community organizer learns is representative of all the residents and not just the residents who were surveyed. Sample generalizability is the focus of Chapter 5.

Cross-population generalizability refers to the ability to generalize from findings about one group or population or setting to other groups or populations or settings (see Exhibit 2.9). We discuss this more in Chapter 7. Cross-population generalizability occurs to the extent that the results of a study hold true for multiple populations; these populations may not all have been sampled or they may be represented as subgroups within the sample studied. Consider this when you read about an intervention to help homeless individuals obtain and maintain a permanent

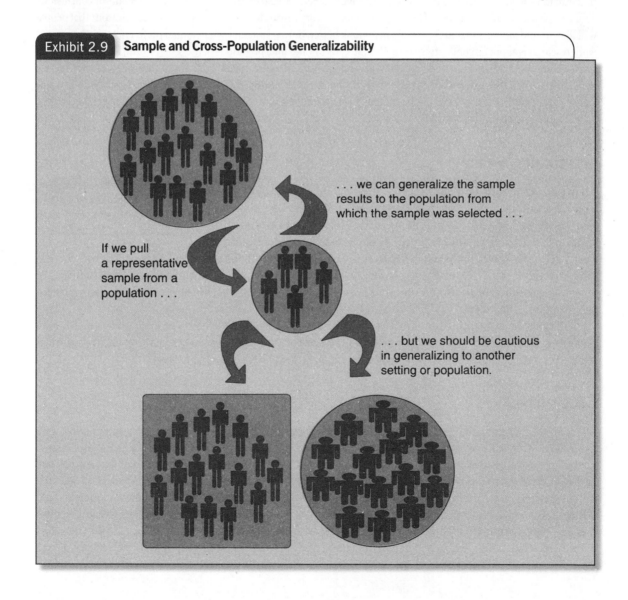

Exhibit 2.9 Sample and Cross-Population Generalizability

If we pull a representative sample from a population . . .

. . . we can generalize the sample results to the population from which the sample was selected . . .

. . . but we should be cautious in generalizing to another setting or population.

residence. It is likely that such a study is done in a particular agency, serving homeless individuals with particular characteristics, living in a particular community. Ideally, you would like to be able to implement that intervention with the hope of the same success in your agency, working with your particular clients, in your particular community. You will have greater confidence in implementing the intervention if there is evidence of cross-population generalizability.

Causal Validity

Most research seeks to determine what causes what, so social scientists frequently must be concerned with causal validity. **Causal validity**, also known as *internal validity*, refers to the accuracy of the assertion that A causes B. It is the focus of Chapter 6.

Causal validity Exists when a conclusion that A leads to or results in B is correct.

Many researchers seek to determine if a particular type of intervention causes desired changes in participants. For example, Russell Schutt (2011) asked whether independent apartments would be as effective as group homes for individuals who had been homeless and were diagnosed with serious mental illness. Schutt could have compared people who had lived in one of these two types of housing, but it is quite likely that such individuals who ended up living in independent apartments would differ in important ways from those who were living in group homes. Instead, Schutt designed an experiment in which individuals in need of housing were assigned randomly to either individual apartments or group homes (all the participants were assigned case managers). This procedure made it unlikely that people who were less sociable, more eager to live independently, less ill, younger, and so on were disproportionately placed in the independent apartments. Therefore, differences in housing outcomes were more likely to be due to the differences in the types of housing, rather than to differences in the types of people being housed. Participants in the group homes benefited more—in terms of housing retention and cognitive functioning—so Schutt (2011) concluded that group homes were more effective than independent apartments for homeless persons who are seriously mentally ill (see Exhibit 2.10).

Establishing causal validity can be quite difficult. You will learn in subsequent chapters how experimental designs and statistics can help us evaluate causal propositions, but the solutions are neither easy nor perfect: We always have to consider critically the validity of causal statements that we hear or read.

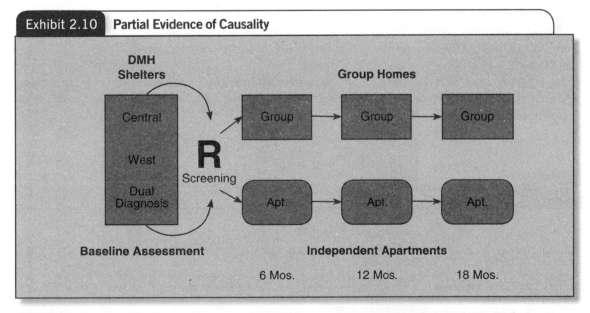

| Exhibit 2.10 | Partial Evidence of Causality |

Source: Reprinted by permission of the publisher from *Homelessness, Housing, and Mental Illness* by Russell K. Schutt, with Stephen M. Goldfinger. Cambridge, Mass.: Harvard University Press, Copyright © 2011 by the President and Fellows of Harvard College.

Authenticity

The goal of **authenticity** is stressed by researchers who focus attention on the subjective dimension of the social world. An authentic understanding of a social process or social setting is one that reflects fairly the various perspectives of participants in that setting (Gubrium & Holstein, 1997). Authenticity reflects a belief that those who study the social world should focus first and foremost on how participants view that social world rather than on developing a unique social scientist's interpretation of that world. Rather than expecting social scientists to be able to provide a valid mirror of reality, the perspective emphasizes the need for recognizing that what is understood by participants as reality is a linguistic and social construction of reality (Kvale, 2002). For example, Moe (2007) explained her basis for considering the responses of women she interviewed in the domestic violence shelter to be authentic: "Members of marginalized groups are better positioned than members of socially dominant groups to describe the ways in which the world is organized according to the oppressions they experience" (p. 682).

> **Authenticity** When the understanding of a social process or social setting is one that reflects fairly the various perspectives of participants in that setting.

▣ Conclusion

Selecting a worthy research question does not guarantee a worthwhile research project. The simplicity of the research circle presented in this chapter belies the complexity of the social research process. In the following chapters, we focus on particular aspects of that process.

As you encounter these specifics, don't lose sight of the basic guidelines that researchers need to follow to overcome the most common impediments to social work research. Owning a large social science toolkit is no guarantee of making the right decisions about which tools to use and how to use them in the investigation of particular research problems. More important, our answers to research questions are never complete or entirely certain. Thus, when we complete a research project, we should point out how the research could be extended and evaluate the confidence we have in our conclusions. Recall how the elaboration of knowledge about deterrence of domestic violence required sensitivity to research difficulties, careful weighing of the evidence, and identification of unanswered questions by several research teams.

You are now forewarned about the difficulties that any scientists, but social scientists in particular, face in their work. We hope that you will return often to this chapter as you read the subsequent chapters, when you criticize the research literature, and when you design your own research projects. To be conscientious, thoughtful, and responsible—this is the mandate of every researcher. If you formulate a feasible research problem, ask the right questions in advance, try to adhere to the research guidelines, and steer clear of the most common difficulties, you will be well along the road to fulfilling this mandate.

Key Terms

Authenticity   44
Causal validity   43
Cross-population generalizability   42
Deductive research   33
Dependent variable   35
Direction of association   36

Empirical generalization   37
Hypothesis   35
Independent variable   35
Inductive research   38
Measurement validity   41
Sample generalizability   42

Serendipitous findings   38
Systematic reviews   29
Theory   32
Variables   35

Highlights

- Research questions should be feasible (within the time and resources available), socially important, and scientifically relevant.

- Research questions should avoid reflecting a social bias or reinforcing societal stereotypes.

- Some social work researchers engage in testing and building practice theory. Often practice theory is derived from broader social theory developed by other disciplines.

- The type of reasoning in most research can be described as primarily deductive or inductive. Research based on deductive reasoning proceeds from general ideas, deduces specific expectations from these ideas, and then tests the ideas with empirical data. Research based on inductive reasoning begins with specific data and then develops general ideas or theories to explain patterns in the data.

- It may be possible to explain unanticipated research findings after the fact, but such explanations have less credibility than those that have been tested with data collected for the purpose of the study.

- The scientific process can be represented as circular, with a path from theory to hypotheses, to data, and then to empirical generalizations. Research investigations may begin at different points along the research circle and traverse different portions of it. Deductive research begins at the point of theory; inductive research begins with data, but ends with theory. Descriptive research begins with data and ends with empirical generalizations.

- The three components of validity are measurement validity, generalizability (from the sample to the population from which it was selected and from the sample to other populations), and causal validity.

Discussion Questions

1. Describe the steps involved in a comprehensive literature review. What should you look for in journal articles? What cautions should you bear in mind when conducting searches online?

2. Discuss the relationship of social theory with practice theory.

3. Describe the relationship between inductive and deductive research.

Practice Exercises

1. Select a social issue that is of interest to you. Draft three research questions about this issue. Refine one of the questions and evaluate it in terms of the three criteria for good questions.

2. Select a social issue that is of interest to you. Develop a theory that would explain the social issue using at least three concepts. Include a symbol to describe the relationship between concepts. Develop a hypothesis based on your theory.

3. Locate a research article on a particular social issue such as homelessness, poverty, domestic violence, or child welfare. Consider the following questions:

   a. What is the social condition under study? What is the basic research question, or problem? Try to state it in just one sentence.

   b. How did the author(s) explain the importance of the research question? Is the research question relevant to social work practice and/or social welfare policy?

   c. What prior literature was reviewed? Was it relevant to the research problem? To the theoretical framework? Does the literature review appear to be adequate? Are you aware of (or can you locate) any important omitted studies? Is the literature review up to date?

   d. Was a theoretical framework presented? If so, what was it? Did it seem appropriate for the research question addressed? Can you think of a different theoretical perspective that might have been used?

   e. Were any hypotheses stated? Were these hypotheses justified adequately in terms of the theoretical framework? In terms of prior research?

   f. What were the independent and dependent variables in the hypothesis or hypotheses? What direction of association was hypothesized? Were any other variables identified as potentially important?

Web Exercises

1. Try your hand at developing a hypothesis of your own. Pick a theorist from the wide range of personality theorists at http://webspace.ship.edu/cgboer/perscontents.html. Read some of what you find. On what social phenomena does this theorist focus? What hypotheses seem consistent with his or her theorizing? Describe a hypothetical research project to test one of these hypotheses.

2. Go to the National Registry of Evidence-Based Programs and Practices website (http://nrepp.samhsa.gov). Find a review of a mental health intervention for older African American adults that used an experimental design and had a quality of research rating of at least 3.0.

Developing a Research Proposal

Now it's time to start writing the proposal. These next exercises are very critical steps.

1. What is the problem for study? Why is this important for social workers to address? If you have not identified a problem for study, or if you need to evaluate whether your research problem is doable, a few suggestions should help to get the ball rolling and keep it on course:

   a. Jot down questions that have puzzled you in some area having to do with social issues or social work practice. These may be questions that have come to mind while reading textbooks or research articles or things you might have heard about in the news. Try to identify questions that really interest you.

   b. Now take stock of your interests, your opportunities, and the work of others. Which of your research questions no longer seem feasible or interesting? What additional research questions come to mind? Pick out a question that is of interest and seems doable.

2. What is known about the problem? Search the literature (and the Web) on the research question you identified. Try to identify recent citations to articles (with abstracts from Social Work Abstracts or other indexes). Get the articles, and remember to inspect their bibliographies for additional sources. Write a brief description of each article and website you consulted. As you read the literature, try to identify the theories used to explain the problem, the methodological approaches used to study the problem, and the results of the studies. What additions or changes to your thoughts about the research question are suggested by the various articles?

3. How does your proposed study build on the current literature? What will be the specific objective of your study?

4. Write out your research question in one sentence, and elaborate on it in one paragraph. Identify the specific aims or hypotheses that will be addressed by your study. List at least three reasons why it is a good research question for you to investigate.

CHAPTER 3

Ethical and Scientific Guidelines for Social Work Research

A study of the impacts of closing a mental health hospital on the former residents. The efficacy of problem-solving therapy in reducing depressive symptoms in older methadone clients. Improving educational outcomes in a high-poverty neighborhood. Preventing gambling-related problems among older adults. Cognitive enhancement therapy for young adults with autism spectrum disorder. Lesbian, gay, bisexual, transgender, and questioning youth in child welfare. Transitions to adulthood for child welfare–involved youth. These are just some of the research studies under way at a school of social work, and like other social work research, these studies include vulnerable participants. Other research may include historically oppressed populations such as people of color, women, or sexual minorities who have reasons to distrust research efforts despite the assurances of the researchers.

Every scientific investigation, whether in the natural or social sciences, has an ethical dimension to it. First and foremost, researchers have to ensure that the rights of their participants are protected. Furthermore, the scientific concern with validity requires that scientists be honest and reveal their methods. Researchers also have to consider the uses to which their findings will be put. By adhering to scientific guidelines about the conduct of research, social work researchers can avoid mistakes about understanding the social world and prevent their investigations from being nothing more than a reflection of their own beliefs. In this chapter, we describe the foundations for both ethical guidelines and scientific guidelines for the conduct of research. You will find in subsequent chapters a discussion of ethical issues specific to the chapter topic.

回 Research on People

Let's begin with a story (or a trip down memory lane, depending on your earlier exposure to this example). One spring morning as you are drinking coffee and reading the newspaper, you notice a small ad for a psychology experiment at the local university. "Earn money and learn about yourself," it says. Feeling a bit bored with your job as a high school teacher, you call and schedule an evening visit to the lab.

WE WILL PAY YOU $45 FOR ONE HOUR OF YOUR TIME

Persons Needed for a Study of Memory

You arrive at the assigned room at the university, ready for an interesting hour or so, and are impressed immediately by the elegance of the building and the professional appearance of the personnel. In the waiting room, you see a man dressed in a lab technician's coat talking to another visitor—a middle-aged fellow dressed in casual attire. The man in the lab coat turns and introduces himself and explains that, as a psychologist, he is interested in the question of whether people learn things better when they are punished for making a mistake. He quickly convinces you that this is a very important question for which there has been no adequate answer; he then explains that his experiment on punishment and learning will help answer this question. Then he announces, "I'm going to ask one of you to be the teacher here tonight and the other one to be the learner."

The experimenter (as we'll refer to him from now on) says he will write either *teacher* or *learner* on small identical slips of paper and then asks both of you to draw out one. Yours says *teacher*.

The experimenter now says, in a matter-of-fact way, "All right. Now, the first thing we'll have to do is to set the learner up so that he can get some type of punishment." He leads you both behind a curtain, sits the learner down, attaches a wire to his left wrist and straps both his arms to the chair so that he cannot remove the wire (see Exhibit 3.1). The wire is connected to a console with 30 switches and a large dial on the other side of the room. When you ask what the wire is for, the experimenter says he will demonstrate. He then asks you to hold the end of the wire, walks back to the control console, flips several switches and focuses his attention on the dial. You hear a clicking noise, see the dial move, and then feel an electric shock in your hand. When the experimenter flips the next switch on the console the shock increases.

Exhibit 3.1	Learner Strapped in Chair With Electrodes

*Source:*From the film OBEDIENCE. Copyright © 1968 by Stanley Milgram, copyright renewed 1993 by Alexandra Milgram and distributed by Alexander Street Press.

"Ouch," you say. "This is the punishment. Couldn't it cause injury?" The experimenter explains that the machine is calibrated so that it will not cause permanent injury, but acknowledges that when it is turned up all the way it is very, very painful and can result in severe, although momentary, discomfort (see Exhibit 3.1).

Now you walk back to the other side of the room (so that the learner is behind the curtain) and sit before the console. The experimental procedure has four simple steps:

1. You read aloud a series of word pairs, such as *blue box, nice day, wild duck,* and so on.

2. You read one of the first words from those pairs and a set of four words, one of which contains the original paired word. For example, you might say, "Blue: sky ink box lamp."

3. The learner states the word that he thinks was paired with the first word you read. If he gives a correct response, you compliment him and move on to the next word. If he makes a mistake, you flip a switch on the console. This causes the learner to feel a shock on his wrist.

4. After each mistake, you are to flip the next switch on the console, progressing from left to right. You note that there is a label corresponding to every fifth mark on the dial, with the first mark labeled *slight shock,* the fifth *moderate shock,* the tenth *strong shock,* and so on through *very strong shock, intense shock, extreme intensity shock,* and *danger: severe shock.*

You begin. At first, the learner gives some correct answers, but then he makes a few errors. Soon you are beyond the fifth mark (moderate shock) and are moving in the direction of more and more severe shocks (see Exhibit 3.2). As you turn the dial, the learner's responses increase in intensity from a grunt at the tenth mark (strong shock) to painful groans at higher levels, anguished cries of "Get me out of here" at the extreme intensity shock levels, to a silence at the highest level. You also know that as you proceed and indicate your discomfort at administering the stronger shocks, the experimenter tells you, "The experiment requires that you continue," or occasionally, "It is absolutely essential that you continue."

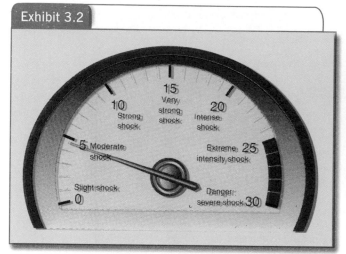

Exhibit 3.2

You may very well recognize that this thought experiment is a slightly simplified version of Stanley Milgram's obedience experiments, begun in 1960. What was the actual average level of shock administered by the 40 New Haven adults who volunteered for the experiment? A shock level of 24.53, or a level higher than extreme intensity shock and just short of the *danger: severe shock* level. Of Milgram's original 40 subjects, 25 (62.5%) complied with the experimenter's demands, all the way to the top of the scale (originally labeled simply as *XXX*). And judging from the subjects' own observed high stress and their subsequent reports they really believed that the learner was receiving actual, hurtful shocks. The same experiment was done with Yale undergraduates whose responses were similar to the nonstudent groups.

We introduce this small experiment not to discuss obedience to authority; instead, we want to introduce the topic of research ethics by encouraging you to think about research from the standpoint of the people who are the subjects of behavioral research. We refer to Milgram's famous research on obedience throughout this chapter, since it is fair to say that this research ultimately had as profound an influence on the way social scientists think about research ethics as it had on the way they understand obedience to authority.

Historical Background

Concern with ethical practice in relation to people who are in some respect dependent, whether as patients or research subjects, is not a new idea. Ethical guidelines for medicine trace back to Hippocrates in 5 BCE Greece (World Medical Association, 2011), and the American Medical Association (AMA) adopted the world's first formal professional ethics code in medicine in 1847 (AMA, 2011). Yet the history of medical practice makes it clear that having an ethics code is not sufficient to ensure ethical practice, at least when there are clear incentives to do otherwise.

A defining event occurred in 1946, when the Nuremberg War Crime Trials exposed horrific medical experiments conducted by Nazi doctors and others in the name of "science." However, as late as 1972, Americans learned from news reports that researchers funded by the U.S. Public Health Service had followed 399 low-income African American men with syphilis (and some without the disease) since the 1930s, collecting data to study the "natural" course of the illness (Exhibit 3.3). At the time, there was no effective treatment for the disease, but the men were told they were being treated for "bad blood," whether they had syphilis or not. Participants received free medical exams, meals, and burial insurance but were not asked for their consent to be studied. What made this research study, known as the Tuskegee Syphilis Experiment, so shocking was that many participants were not informed of their illness and, even after penicillin was recognized as an effective treatment in 1945 and in large-scale use by 1947, the study participants were not treated. The research was only ended after the study was exposed. In 1973, congressional hearings began and in 1974 an out-of-court settlement of $10 million was reached; it was not until 1997 that President Bill Clinton made an official apology (Centers for Disease Control and Prevention, 1997).

This study (and others) was an egregious violations of human rights and it made clear that formal review procedures were needed to protect research participants. The U.S. government established the National Commission for the Protection of Human Subjects of Biomedical and Behavioral Research and charged it with developing guidelines (Kitchner & Kitchner, 2009). The Commission's 1979 *Belmont Report* (U.S. Department of Health, Education, and Welfare, 1979) established three basic ethical principles for the protection of human subjects:

| Exhibit 3.3 | Tuskegee Syphilis Experiment |

*Source:*Tuskegee Syphilis Study Administrative Records. Records of the Centers for Disease Control and Prevention. National Archives—Southeast Region (Atlanta).

- *Respect for persons*: treating persons as autonomous agents and protecting those with diminished autonomy
- *Beneficence*: minimizing possible harms and maximizing benefits
- *Justice*: distributing benefits and risks of research fairly

The Department of Health and Human Services and the Food and Drug Administration translated these principles into specific regulations that were adopted in 1991 as the Federal Policy for the Protection of Human Subjects. This policy has shaped the course of social science research ever since, and you will have to take it into account as you design your own research investigations. Professional associations, including the National Association of Social Workers (NASW), university review boards, and ethics committees in other organizations, also set standards for the treatment of human subjects by their members, employees, and students, although these standards are all designed to comply with the federal policy. This section introduces these regulations.

Federal regulations require that every institution that seeks federal funding for biomedical or behavioral research on human subjects have an **institutional review board** (IRB) that reviews research proposals. IRBs at universities and other agencies apply ethical standards that are set by federal regulations but can be expanded or specified by the IRB itself (Sieber, 1992). To promote adequate review of ethical issues, the regulations require that IRBs include members with diverse backgrounds. The Office for Human Research Protections in the National Institutes of Health monitors IRBs, with the exception of research involving drugs (which is the responsibility of the Food and Drug Administration).

Belmont Report The 1979 report of the Commission for the Protection of Human Subjects of Biomedical and Behavioral Research.

Institutional review board A group of organizational and community representatives required by federal law to review the ethical issues in all proposed research that is federally funded, involves human subjects, or has any potential harm to subjects.

Research In the News

For Further Thought ?

IS IT ETHICAL SCIENCE?

A federal court case regarding the State of Michigan's constitutional ban on same-sex marriage heard research evidence that children of same-sex couples are worse off than children raised by married heterosexual couples. The research was funded by organizations opposed to same-sex marriage. Further, the research and its findings were criticized by other researchers as being flawed.

1. Under what conditions is it ethical to take money from organizations with a stake in the results?

2. When such situations arise, what might you recommend to ensure that standards of science are met?

Source: Eckholm (2014, p. A16).

🔳 Ethical Principles

The National Association of Social Workers (NASW) acknowledges the importance of social workers contributing to knowledge as well as monitoring and evaluating practice and policy implementation. Given that social workers may be actively engaged in evaluation and research, the NASW has incorporated the four guidelines listed below into its ethical code. The NASW (2008) *Code of Ethics* (which can be found at www.naswdc.org/pubs/code/code.asp) incorporates both practice standards and specific evaluation and research standards (see Exhibit 3.4).

Exhibit 3.4 | **NASW Code of Ethics, Evaluation and Research**

5.02 Evaluation and Research

(d) Social workers engaged in evaluation or research should carefully consider possible consequences and should follow guidelines developed for the protection of evaluation and research participants. Appropriate institutional review boards should be consulted.

(e) Social workers engaged in evaluation or research should obtain voluntary and written informed consent from participants, when appropriate, without any implied or actual deprivation or penalty for refusal to participate; without undue inducement to participate; and with due regard for participants' well-being, privacy, and dignity. Informed consent should include information about the nature, extent, and duration of the participation requested and disclosure of the risks and benefits of participation in the research.

(f) When evaluation or research participants are incapable of giving informed consent, social workers should provide an appropriate explanation to the participants, obtain the participants' assent to the extent they are able, and obtain written consent from an appropriate proxy.

(g) Social workers should never design or conduct evaluation or research that does not use consent procedures, such as certain forms of naturalistic observation and archival research, unless rigorous and responsible review of the research has found it to be justified because of its prospective scientific, educational, or applied value and unless equally effective alternative procedures that do not involve waiver of consent are not feasible.

(h) Social workers should inform participants of their right to withdraw from evaluation and research at any time without penalty.

(i) Social workers should take appropriate steps to ensure that participants in evaluation and research have access to appropriate supportive services.

(j) Social workers engaged in evaluation or research should protect participants from unwarranted physical or mental distress, harm, danger, or deprivation.

(k) Social workers engaged in the evaluation of services should discuss collected information only for professional purposes and only with people professionally concerned with this information.

(l) Social workers engaged in evaluation or research should ensure the anonymity or confidentiality of participants and of the data obtained from them. Social workers should inform participants of any limits of confidentiality, the measures that will be taken to ensure confidentiality, and when any records containing research data will be destroyed.

(m) Social workers who report evaluation and research results should protect participants' confidentiality by omitting identifying information unless proper consent has been obtained authorizing disclosure.

(n) Social workers should report evaluation and research findings accurately. They should not fabricate or falsify results and should take steps to correct any errors later found in published data using standard publication methods.

(o) Social workers engaged in evaluation or research should be alert to and avoid conflicts of interest and dual relationships with participants, should inform participants when a real or potential conflict of interest arises, and should take steps to resolve the issue in a manner that makes participants' interests primary.

Source: National Association of Social Workers. (2008). *Code of ethics of the National Association of Social Workers.* Copyrighted material reprinted with permission from the National Association of Social Workers, Inc.

Mostly, ethical issues in research are covered by four guidelines:

1. To protect research subjects

2. To maintain honesty and openness

3. To achieve valid results

4. To encourage appropriate application of the findings

Though Milgram was not a social worker, these guidelines are typical of other professional organizations and apply to his work, to which we will refer. As you read the discussion of his work, you will soon realize that there is no simple answer to the question: What *is* (or *is not)* ethical research practice?

Protecting Research Participants

The guidelines can be divided into three specific directions:

1. Avoid harming research participants.

2. Obtain voluntary, informed consent.

3. Maintain privacy and confidentiality.

Avoid Harming Research Participants

Although this standard may seem straightforward, it can be difficult to interpret in specific cases and harder yet to define in a way agreeable to all social scientists. Does it mean that subjects should not be harmed psychologically as well as physically at all? That they should feel no anxiety or distress whatsoever during the study or only after their involvement ends? Should the possibility of any harm, no matter how remote, deter research?

Before we address these questions with respect to Milgram's experiments, a verbatim transcript of one session will give you an idea of what participants experienced (Milgram, 1965, p. 67):

150 volts delivered.   You want me to keep going?

165 volts delivered.   That guy is hollering in there. There's a lot of them here. He's liable to have a heart condition. You want me to go on?

180 volts delivered.   He can't stand it! I'm not going to kill that man in there! You hear him hollering? He's hollering. He can't stand it. . . . I mean who is going to take responsibility if anything happens to that gentleman? *[The experimenter accepts responsibility.]* Alright.

195 volts delivered.   You see he's hollering. Hear that. Gee, I don't know. *[The experimenter says: "The experiment requires that you go on."]* I know it does, sir, but I mean—huh—he don't know what he's in for. He's up to 195 volts.

210 volts delivered.

225 volts delivered.

240 volts delivered.

This experimental manipulation generated "extraordinary tension" (Milgram, 1963, p. 372):

Subjects were observed to sweat, tremble, stutter, bite their lips, groan and dig their fingernails into their flesh. . . . Full-blown, uncontrollable seizures were observed for 3 subjects. [O]ne . . . seizure so violently convulsive that it was necessary to call a halt to the experiment [for that individual]. (Milgram, 1963, p. 375)

An observer (behind a one-way mirror) reported, "I observed a mature and initially poised businessman enter the laboratory smiling and confident. Within 20 minutes he was reduced to a twitching, stuttering wreck, who was rapidly approaching a point of nervous collapse" (Milgram, 1963, p. 377).

From critic Diana Baumrind's (1964) perspective, this emotional disturbance in subjects was "potentially harmful because it could easily effect an alteration in the subject's self-image or ability to trust adult authorities in the future" (p. 422). Milgram (1964) quickly countered that

momentary excitement is not the same as harm. As the experiment progressed there was no indication of injurious effects in the subjects; and as the subjects themselves strongly endorsed the experiment, the judgment I made was to continue the experiment. (p. 849)

Milgram (1963) also attempted to minimize harm to subjects with postexperimental procedures "to assure that the subject would leave the laboratory in a state of well-being" (p. 374). A friendly reconciliation was arranged between the subject and the victim, and an effort was made to reduce any tensions that arose as a result of the experiment. In some cases, the "dehoaxing" (or debriefing) discussion was extensive, and all subjects were promised (and later received) a comprehensive report (Milgram, 1964).

When Milgram (1964) surveyed the subjects in a follow-up, 83.7% endorsed the statement that they were "very glad" or "glad" "to have been in the experiment," 15.1% were "neither sorry nor glad," and just 1.3% were "sorry" or "very sorry" to have participated (p. 849). Interviews by a psychiatrist a year later found no evidence "of any traumatic reactions" (p. 850). Subsequently, Milgram (1977) argued that "the central moral justification for allowing my experiment is that it was judged acceptable by those who took part in it" (p. 21).

In a later article, Baumrind (1985) dismissed the value of the self-reported "lack of harm" of subjects who had been willing to participate in the experiment. She argued that research indicates most introductory psychology students (and some students in other social sciences) who have participated in a deception experiment report a decreased trust in authorities as a result—a tangible harm in itself. Many social scientists, ethicists, and others concluded that Milgram's procedures had not harmed the subjects and so were justified for the knowledge they produced, but others sided with Baumrind's criticisms (A. G. Miller, 1986). Perry's (2013) recent investigation found even more evidence of psychological harm, including feelings of shame that persisted since the experiment. Experimental records reveal that debriefing never occurred for some participants and was very limited for almost all (Perry, 2013).

What do you think? Would you ban experiments such as Milgram's because of the potential for harm to subjects? Does the fact that Milgram's experiments seemed to yield significant insights into the effect of a social situation on human behavior make any difference? Do you believe that this benefit outweighs the foreseeable risks?

Obtain Informed Consent

Informed consent is essential if we are truly reflecting respect for the potential participant in the research study. It is the process by which potential participants are given all the information they need to decide whether to participate in the study. Such information includes but it not limited to the purpose of the study, the procedures involved in the study, and the potential risks and benefits to participation. It means that agency clients who are being recruited for a study understand that there are no ramifications if they choose not to participate in the study.

The requirement of informed consent is more difficult to define than it first appears. To be informed, consent must be given by the persons who are competent in that they understand what they have been told, recognize the significance of the information, can adequately weigh the benefits and costs, and voluntarily consent to participate or not (Zayas, Cabassa, & Perez, 2005). Who is competent to give consent? What does *competent* mean? Are people with mental illness competent to give consent, or does the nature of their specific illness preclude their ability to comprehend the nature of the research, their rights as research participants, and the benefits and costs of participating in the research?

A consent form should illustrate the basics of informed consent:

1. The consent form must be written in such a way as to be understood by the person signing it. If the research population includes speakers of languages other than English, the researcher must prepare forms in every language included in the target population.

2. The consent form must state clearly who is doing the research, including affiliation with a university or other sponsoring organization.

3. The consent form must briefly describe the research, including any anticipated risks to the research subjects and the benefits expected to flow from it, and any compensation that will be offered.

4. The consent form should describe how confidentiality will be maintained, including what will happen to records at the completion of the project.

5. Consent must be freely given and can be withdrawn at any time without consequences.

The basic contents are illustrated in two consent forms. Consent Form A (Exhibit 3.5) was approved by a university IRB for a mailed survey about substance abuse among undergraduate students. It is brief and to the point. Consent Form B (Exhibit 3.6) reflects the requirements of a social work professor's use of Photovoice with older methadone clients. Because the potential participants were receiving treatment and vulnerable to many legal issues, as well as potentially taking pictures of illegal activity, there was the need for an extensive and detailed explanation of the study.

Children who have not attainted the legal age for consent to treatment or procedures cannot legally give consent to participate in research. To conduct research with children a parent or guardian must give **permission**, that is, agree to the child's participation. Children must **assent** to participate. Assent requires that

> **Permission** Parent or guardian agreement to a child's participation in a research study.
>
> **Assent** Requirement that a child provide affirmative agreement to participate in a research study.

Exhibit 3.5	Consent Form A

University of Massachusetts at Boston
Department of Sociology
(617) 287–6250
October 28, 1996

Dear:

The health of students and their use of alcohol and drugs are important concerns for every college and university. The enclosed survey is about these issues at UMass/Boston. It is sponsored by University Health Services and the PRIDE Program (Prevention, Resources, Information, and Drug Education). The questionnaire was developed by graduate students in Applied Sociology, Nursing, and Gerontology.

You were selected for the survey with a scientific, random procedure. Now it is important that you return the questionnaire so that we can obtain an unbiased description of the undergraduate student body. Health Services can then use the results to guide campus education and prevention programs.

The survey requires only about 20 minutes to complete. Participation is completely voluntary and anonymous. No one will be able to link your survey responses to you. In any case, your standing at the university will not be affected whether or not you choose to participate. Just be sure to return the enclosed postcard after you mail the questionnaire so that we know we do not have to contact you again.

Please return the survey by November 15. If you have any questions or comments, call the PRIDE program at 287-5680 or Professor Schutt at 287-6250. Also call the PRIDE program if you would like a summary of our final report.

Thank you in advance for your assistance.

Russell K. Schutt, PhD
Professor and Chair

children provide *affirmative* agreement, and failure to object does not constitute agreement (U.S.D.H.S., 2009). There are also special protections for other populations that are likely to be vulnerable to coercion—prisoners, pregnant women, persons with mental disabilities, and educationally or economically disadvantaged persons.

Consent must be given voluntarily without coercion, that is, without forcing people to participate. Coercion need not be explicit; rather, coercion may be subtle and implicit. Where there are differences in power between the researchers and the subjects, implicit coercion may be a problem. Clients in human service agencies may feel that they may be better served by the agency if they agree to participate, or they may worry that by refusing to participate in the research, their services will be altered. To the extent possible, clients must be reassured that there is no penalty or other consequence for refusing to participate in the research. Further, potential research participants must be informed that they have the right to withdraw from the study without any penalty. The researcher's actions and body language should help convey his or her verbal assurance that consent is voluntary.

Subject payments may also affect the voluntary nature of participation. Even small amounts of money may be sufficient to induce people with low income to participate in research activities that they might otherwise have refused. Payments should be kept to a level that acknowledges the subject's participation and inconvenience but will not serve to entice people to participate. If the payment is a significant amount in relation to the participants' normal income, it could lead people to set aside their reservations about participating in a project—even though they may have reservations (Fisher & Anushko, 2008). Payments, if offered, should be given even if the subject terminates participation without fully completing the research.

To give informed consent, potential research participants must have sufficient information to weigh the benefits and risks of participation. That is why it is so important to describe as completely as possible the kinds of risks the participant will face. Yet, by doing so, participant responses may change and result in biased findings. Experimental researchers, such as Milgram, whose research design requires some type of subject deception, try to get around this

Exhibit 3.6 **Consent Form B**

University [name]

Institutional Review Board

Approval Date:

Renewal Date:

IRB Number:

Informed Consent For Methadone Clients

CONSENT TO ACT AS A PARTICIPANT IN A RESEARCH STUDY

TITLE: Photovoice: A Community-Based Project to Involve Older Adult Methadone Clients in the Decisions that Affect Their Lives

PRINCIPAL INVESTIGATOR:

SOURCE OF SUPPORT:

Why is this research being done?

The . . . is conducting a research project on the needs of older adult methadone clients. Your participation is voluntary in this research study and is not linked to the services that you receive at [agency]. The information obtained in this research study will be used to help social workers better understand the service needs of African American methadone clients over the age of 50.

Who is being asked to take part in this research study?

African American men and women who are over the age of 50 and are current patients at the [agency] methadone clinic in the [community] area are being asked to participate in this research study.

What procedures will be performed for research purposes?

As a participant in this research project you will be involved in taking photographs of various topics relevant to your lives. The project will last for a maximum of 8 weeks and you will be asked to attend 1 training session and 5-7 group sessions, which will include individual interviews that will last approximately 15-30 minutes.

The first session is devoted to introducing the concepts of photovoice to participants including a discussion of the ethics of photographing others. The training session will be lead by research staff and mentor photographers. The mentor photographers are professional photographers from the community who have volunteered to offer their expertise to help introduce participants to photographic techniques and the ethics/norms of photography in a community setting.

After the initial training, each week you will be asked to take photographs surrounding a specific theme such as transformation or spirituality. These photos will be used to guide individual interviews and group discussions. During individual interviews you will be asked to identify the photographs that you consider most significantly related to that week's theme. Following these interviews, you will also be asked to participate in weekly group meetings with other study participants which will last approximately 1 hour. During group meetings, you will be asked to describe and discuss the meaning of your images with other project participants. Lastly, you will be asked to participate in a final presentation of the project. All interviews will be audio taped for future transcription. Audio tapes and photos will be identified with an Identification Number and your name will not be attached to any research records.

Page 1 of 4

Participant's Initials: _____

(Continued)

Exhibit 3.6 (Continued)

University [name]

Institutional Review Board

Approval Date:

Renewal Date:

IRB Number:

What are the possible risks, side effects, and discomforts of this research study?

There are no known risks associated with participating in this study. However, some questions or images discussed in the interview or group meetings may be upsetting to some respondents. Please be aware that you do not have to answer any questions that you are not comfortable answering. Any information obtained during the course of this research project will be kept as confidential as possible; however there is a risk of breaches of confidentiality.

What are possible benefits from taking part in this study?

You will likely receive no direct benefit from taking part in this research study. Should the research obtained from the study help improve services for older African American clients, it is possible that you may receive some benefit from the information obtained. However, such a benefit cannot be guaranteed.

Will I be paid if I take part in this research study?

You will be paid a total of $15 at the completion of each weekly interview for eight weeks. If you leave the study early, you will receive an appropriate amount based on your extent of participation.

Are there any costs to me if I participate in this study?

There are no costs to you for participating in this study.

Who will pay if I am injured as a result of taking part in this study?

[. . .] researchers and their associates who provide services at [medical setting] recognize the importance of your voluntary participation in their research studies. These individuals and their staffs will make reasonable efforts to minimize, control, and treat any injuries that may arise as a result of this research. If you believe that you are injured as a result of the research procedures being performed, please contact immediately the Principal Investigator or one of the co-investigators listed on the first page of this form.

Emergency medical treatment for injuries solely and directly related to your participation in this research study will be provided to you by the hospitals of . . . . It is possible that [hospital name] may bill your insurance provider for the costs of this emergency treatment, but none of these costs will be charged directly to you. If your research-related injury requires medical care beyond this emergency treatment, you will be responsible for the costs of this follow-up care unless otherwise specifically stated below. You will not receive any monetary payment for, or associated with, any injury that you suffer in relation to this research.

Who will know about my participation in this research study?

Research staff will only have access to information associated with your participation in this project and will not have access to any of [agency] records. Also, [agency] staff will not be able to access your information associated with this study.

Page 2 of 4

Participant's Initials: _____

University [name]

Institutional Review Board

Approval Date:

Renewal Date:

IRB Number:

All records pertaining to your involvement in this study are kept strictly confidential (private) and any data that includes your identity will be stored in locked files at all times. A number will be assigned to your information and your name will be separated from this coded information during storage. At the end of this study, any records that personally identify you including photographs and audio tapes will remain stored in locked files and will be kept for a maximum of 3 years. Your identity will not be revealed in any description or publications of this research without your consent.

Please be aware that we are legally required to report any photos revealing child/elder abuse or likely prospect of harm to self or others to the appropriate legal authorities.

In addition to research staff from the [university], authorized representatives of the [newspaper] and [magazine] may have access to identifiable information (which may include your identifiable information) related to your participation in this research study for the purposes of completing photography instruction associated with research study participation.

In unusual cases, your research records may be released in response to an order from a court of law. It is also possible that authorized representatives from the University [name] Research Conduct and Compliance Office, the University [name] IRB, or the sponsors of this research study (National Institutes of Mental Health) may review your data for the purpose of monitoring the conduct of this study. Also, if the investigators learn that you or someone with whom you are involved is in serious danger or potential harm, they will need to inform the appropriate agencies, as required by [state name] law.

Is my participation in this research study voluntary?

Your participation in this study is completely voluntary. You may refuse to take part in it, or you may stop participating at any time, even after signing this form. Whether or not you provide your consent for participation in this research study will have no effect on your current or future relationship with [agency] or the University [name]. If you decide not to take part in this research study, you will still receive the routine services offered by your methadone clinic. You are not under any obligation to participate in any research study in order to receive services or methadone at the clinic.

May I withdraw, at a future date, my consent for participation in this research study?

You may withdraw, at any time, your consent for participation in this research study, to include the use and disclosure of your identifiable information for the purposes described above.

Any identifiable research recorded for, or resulting from, your participation in this research study prior to the date that you formally withdrew your consent many continue to be used and disclosed by the investigator for the purposes described above.

To formally withdraw your consent for participation in this research study you should provide a written and dated notice of this decision to the Principal Investigator of this research study:

Additionally, research staff reserves the right to remove you from the research study for failing to comply with study protocol. An example of a situation in which you would be withdrawn from the project would be if you did not attend the weekly sessions and complete the projects for that week.

Page 3 of 4

Participant's Initials: _____

(Continued)

Exhibit 3.6 (Continued)

University [name]

Institutional Review Board

Approval Date:

Renewal Date:

IRB Number:

****

VOLUNTARY CONSENT

All of the above has been explained to me and all of my current questions have been answered. I understand that I am encouraged to ask questions about any aspect of this research study during the course of this study, and that such future questions will be answered by the researchers listed on the first page of this form.

Any questions that I have about my rights as a research participant will be answered by the Human Subject Protection Advocate of the IRB Office, University [name] [phone number].

By signing this form, I agree to participate in this research study. A copy of this consent form will be given to me.

_____   _____

Participant's Signature   Date

CERTIFICATION of INFORMED CONSENT

I certify that I have explained the nature and purpose of this research study to the above-named individual(s), and I have discussed the potential benefits and possible risks of study participation. Any questions the individual(s) have about this study have been answered, and we will always be available to address future questions as they arise.

_____   _____

Printed Name of Person Obtaining Consent   Role in Research Study

_____   _____

Signature of Person Obtaining Consent   Date

Page 4 of 4

Participant's Initials: _____

Source: Reprinted with permission from Daniel Rosen.

Debriefing A researcher's informing participants after an experiment about the experiment's purposes and methods and evaluating participants' personal reactions to the experiment.

problem by withholding some information before the experiment begins, but then debriefing subjects at the end. To conduct the study, the researcher must convince an IRB that the risks are minimal and the benefits of carrying out the study are substantial. In a **debriefing,** the researcher explains to the subject what happened in the experiment and why and then responds to their questions. A carefully designed debriefing procedure can help the research participants learn from the experimental research and grapple constructively with feelings elicited by the realization that they were deceived (Sieber, 1992).

In Milgram's experiment, deception seemed necessary because the subjects could not be permitted to administer real electric shocks to the "stooge," yet it would not have made sense to order the subjects to do something that they didn't find to be so troubling. Milgram (1992) insisted that the deception was absolutely essential. The results of the experiments would be worthless if subjects understood what was really happening to them while the experiment was in progress. Is this sufficient justification to allow the use of deception?

Maintain Privacy and Confidentiality

Maintaining privacy and confidentiality is another key ethical standard for protecting research participants, and the researcher's commitment to that standard should be included in the informed consent agreement (Sieber, 1992). This means that nobody but research personnel have access to information that could be used to link respondents to their responses. This is different from anonymity, which means that no one, including the researchers, can link information to a particular respondent.

Procedures to protect each participant's privacy, such as locking records and creating special identifying codes, must be created to minimize the risk of access by unauthorized people. The standard of confidentiality does not apply to observation in public places and information available in public records.

However, statements about confidentiality should be realistic: Laws allow research records to be subpoenaed and may require reporting child abuse; a researcher may feel compelled to release information if a health- or life-threatening situation arises and participants need to be alerted. The National Institutes of Health can issue a **Certificate of Confidentiality** to protect researchers from being legally required to disclose confidential information. Researchers who focus on high-risk populations or behaviors, such as crime, substance abuse, sexual activity, or genetic information, can request such a certificate. Suspicions of child abuse or neglect must still be reported, and in some states researchers may still be required to report crimes such as elder abuse (Arwood & Panicker, 2007).

> **Certificate of Confidentiality** The National Institutes of Health can issue this to protect researchers from having to disclose confidential information.

The Health Insurance Portability and Accountability Act (HIPAA) passed by Congress in 1996 created much more stringent regulations for the protection of health care data. As implemented by the U.S. Department of Health and Human Services in 2000 (and revised in 2002), the HIPAA Final Privacy Rule applies to oral, written, and electronic information that "relates to the past, present or future physical or mental health or condition of an individual." The HIPAA Rule requires that researchers have valid authorization for any use or disclosure of "protected health information" from a health care provider. Waivers of authorization can be granted in special circumstances (Cava, Cushman, & Goodman, 2007).

Honesty and Openness

The scientific concern with validity requires, in turn, that scientists be open in disclosing their methods and honest in presenting their findings. To assess the validity of researchers' conclusions and the ethics of their procedures, you need to know exactly how the research was conducted. This means that articles or other reports must include a detailed methodology section, perhaps supplemented by appendixes containing the research instruments, or websites or an address where more information can be obtained.

Milgram's research reports seemed to present an honest and open account of his methods. His initial 1963 article included a detailed description of study procedures, including the text of the general introduction, the procedures involved in the learning task—"shock generator," administration of the "sample shock," the shock instructions and the preliminary practice run, the standardized feedback from the "victim" and from the experimenter—and the measures used. Many more details, including pictures, were provided in Milgram's (1974) subsequent book.

The act of publication itself is a vital element in maintaining openness and honesty. Others can review and question study procedures and so generate an open dialogue with the researcher. Although Milgram disagreed sharply with Baumrind's criticisms of his experiments, their mutual commitment to public discourse in journals widely available to social scientists resulted in a more comprehensive presentation of study procedures and a more thoughtful discourse about research ethics. Almost 50 years later, this commentary continues to inform debates about research ethics (Cave & Holm, 2003).

Honesty obviously extends to your results, even if they were not what you expected. A few years ago, a *New York Times* article began with the following headline and opening sentence:

After 400 Years, A Challenge to Kepler: He Fabricated His Data, Scholar Says

Johannes Kepler, the father of modern astronomy, fabricated data in presenting his theory of how the planets move around the Sun, apparently to bolster acceptance of the insight by skeptics, a scholar has found. (Broad, 1990)

The scholar referenced in the article, William Donohue (1988), used the methods described by Kepler and could not replicate Kepler's reported findings. Upon further examination of Kepler's work, he found erasures of what must have been the original findings before they were changed to conform to his theory of how planets orbited the sun. It turned out that Kepler's theory was indeed correct; it simply could not be demonstrated at that time. Was Kepler right to change his numbers?

Conflicts of interest When researchers have a significant stake in the design or outcome of their own research.

Conflicts of interest may occur when a researcher has a significant financial stake in the design or outcome of the research. Receiving speaking fees, consulting fees, patents or royalties, and other financial benefits as a result of the way in which a research project is designed or the results that it obtains creates a pressure to distort decisions and findings in one's favor. Both federal research agencies and journal editors require disclosure of possible conflicts of interest so that others can scrutinize the extent to which these conflicts may have lessened researchers' honesty and openness (Fisher & Anushko, 2008). Unfortunately, experimental research suggests that disclosure does not reduce trust in advice from people who have disclosed a conflict of interest (Humphries, 2011).

Commitment to achieving valid results is necessary for ethical research practice. Simply put, we have no business asking people to answer questions, submit to observations, or participate in experimental procedures if we are simply seeking to verify our preexisting prejudices or convince others to take action on behalf of our personal interests. It is the pursuit of objective knowledge about human behavior that motivates and justifies our investigations and gives us some claim to the right to influence others to participate in our research. Knowledge is the foundation of human progress as well as the basis for our expectation that we can help people achieve a brighter future. If we approach our research projects objectively, setting aside our personal predilections in the service of learning a bit more about human behavior, we can honestly represent our actions as potentially contributing to the advancement of knowledge.

The details in Milgram's 1963 article and 1974 book on his obedience experiments make a compelling case for his commitment to achieving valid results—to learning how and why obedience influences behavior. In Milgram's (1963) own words,

it has been reliably established that from 1933–45 millions of innocent persons were systematically slaughtered on command. . . . Obedience is the psychological mechanism that links individual action to political purpose. It is the dispositional cement that binds men to systems of authority. . . . [F]or many persons obedience may be a deeply ingrained behavior tendency. . . . Obedience may [also] be ennobling and educative and refer to acts of charity and kindness, as well as to destruction. (p. 371)

Milgram (1963) then explains how he devised experiments to study the process of obedience in a way that would seem realistic to the subjects and still allow "important variables to be manipulated at several points in the experiment" (p. 372). Every step in the experiment was carefully designed to ensure that the subjects received identical stimuli and that their responses were measured carefully.

Milgram's (1963) attention to validity is also apparent in his reflections on "the particular conditions" of his experiment, for, he notes, "understanding of the phenomenon of obedience must rest on an analysis of [these conditions]" (p. 377). These particular conditions included the setting for the experiment at Yale University, its purported "worthy purpose" to advance knowledge about learning and memory, and the voluntary participation of the subject as well as of the learner—as far as the subject knew. The importance of some of these particular conditions (such as the location at Yale) was then tested in subsequent replications of the basic experiment (Milgram, 1965).

However, Baumrind (1964) rejected the claim for external validity—the generalizability—of the experiment. Because "the laboratory is unfamiliar as a setting and the rules of behavior ambiguous" (p. 421), the laboratory is not the place to study degree of obedience or suggestibility, as a function of a particular experimental condition. So "the parallel between authority-subordinate relationships in Hitler's Germany and in Milgram's laboratory is unclear" (p. 423).

Milgram (1964) quickly published a rejoinder in which he disagreed with (among other things) the notion that it is inappropriate to study obedience in a laboratory setting: "A subject's obedience is no less problematical because it occurs within a social institution called the psychological experiment" (p. 850). Milgram (1974) also pointed out that his experiment had been replicated in other places and settings with the same results, that there was considerable evidence that the subjects had believed that they actually were administering shocks, and that the essence of his experimental manipulation—the request that subjects comply with a legitimate authority—was shared with the dilemma faced by people in Nazi Germany, soldiers at the My Lai massacre in Vietnam, and even cultists who drank poison in Jonestown, Guyana, at the command of their leader, Jim Jones (A. G. Miller, 1986).

Baumrind (1985) was still not convinced. In a follow-up article in the *American Psychologist,* she argued that "far from illuminating real life, as he claimed, Milgram in fact appeared to have constructed a set of conditions so internally inconsistent that they could not occur in real life" (p. 171).

Do you agree with Milgram's assumption that obedience could fruitfully be studied in the laboratory? Do you find merit in Baumrind's criticism? We cannot answer these questions for you, but before you dismiss them as inappropriate when we are dealing with ethical standards for the treatment of human subjects, bear in mind that both Milgram and his strongest critic, Baumrind, buttressed their ethical arguments with assertions about the external validity (or invalidity) of the experimental results. It is hard to justify *any* risk for human subjects, or even *any* expenditure of time and resources, if our findings tell us nothing about human behavior.

The Uses of Research

Scientists must also consider the uses to which their research is put. Although many scientists believe that personal values should be left outside the laboratory, some feel that it is proper for scientists to concern themselves with the way their research is used. Social scientists who identify with a more critical tradition question the possibility of setting our values aside and instead urge researchers to use research to achieve goals that they believe are worthy.

Sometimes it is difficult to separate research and advocacy given the nature of many of the kinds of questions social work researchers pursue. Some social work research is conducted to evaluate the impacts of social legislation, for example, research to assess changes in health care policy or the effects of welfare reform. The findings from such studies are likely to be used to help shape changes in policy or to reinforce current policy. Regardless of whether the researchers enter into the research with an opinion, the methods they use should be objective, and their reporting of the data should be accurate and honest. This will lend credibility to the conclusions that they reported.

The potential of withholding a beneficial intervention from some subjects also is a cause for ethical concern. Differential outcomes in welfare-to-work experiments mean that some individuals might well have higher earnings in both the short and long run (Brock & Harknett, 1998). Experiments comparing treatment methods such as intensive family preservation services with traditional case management might mean that some children have less chance of being reunified with their parents (Walton, 2001). There are potentially serious consequences for the participants.

The justification for such study designs, however, is quite persuasive: The researchers do not know prior to the experiment what would be an appropriate response to battering, what would be a better method of a welfare-to-work program, or what would be a better treatment method. Just because an approach is new or different does not make it automatically a better approach. That is why it is being tested to begin with—to determine whether it is beneficial. The researchers are not withholding a known, successful treatment from some subjects. Because of such concerns, rather than withhold treatment, many social work intervention studies will compare a new intervention or modification of an intervention to *treatment as usual*, that is, the current practice or intervention.

Social work researchers who conduct research on behalf of specific organizations may face additional difficulties when the organization, instead of the researcher, controls the final report and the publicity it receives. If organizational leaders decide that particular research results are unwelcome, the researcher's desire to have findings used appropriately and reported fully can conflict with contractual obligations. Researchers can often anticipate such dilemmas in advance and resolve them when the contract for research is negotiated—or simply decline a particular research opportunity altogether. But often, such problems come up only after a report has been drafted, or the problems are ignored by a researcher who needs to have a job or needs to maintain particular personal relationships. These possibilities cannot be avoided entirely, but because of them, it is always important to acknowledge the source of research funding in reports and to consider carefully the sources of funding for research reports written by others.

🔲 Institutional Review Board Reviews

Earlier, we described the requirement that potential research studies must be reviewed by IRB committees. In this section, we briefly describe the criteria IRB committees use to determine whether a study is research that requires informed consent. IRB reviews generally fall into three categories: exempt status determination, expedited reviews, and full committee reviews. We briefly define these reviews, but details are available in the federal regulations at www.hhs.gov/ohrp/policy/ohrpregulations.pdf (U.S. Department of Health and Human Services, 2009) and your universities.

A study assigned **exempt status** involves minimal human subject involvement. Exempt status is conferred on the following:

1. Research conducted in established or commonly accepted educational settings, involving normal educational practices.

2. Research involving the use of educational tests (cognitive, diagnostic, aptitude, achievement), survey procedures, interview procedures, or observation of public behavior.

3. Research involving the collection or study of existing data, documents, records, pathological specimens, or diagnostic specimens, if these sources are publicly available or if the information is recorded by the investigator in such a manner that subjects cannot be identified, directly or through identifiers linked to the subjects. (U.S. Department of Health and Human Services, 2009)

Exempt status cannot be attained for studies with participants under age 18 unless they are studies of educational tests or observations of public behavior not observed directly by the researcher. Also, research on prisoners does not have exempt status. Exempt studies do not require a signed consent form, but those involving data collection other than observation do require an introductory statement that briefly describes the study, any risks or benefits, how confidentiality is protected, the voluntary nature of participation as well as the ability to stop at any time, and contact information. Exempt status is determined and confirmed by the IRB committee.

Expedited reviews are done for new or continuing studies that present minimal risk of harm to the participant. Generally, such reviews are done by

Exempt status IRB review for research studies that involve minimal human subject involvement.

Expedited review IRB review that is done for a new or continuing study that presents minimal risk of harm to the participant.

the IRB chair or one or two designees with experience in IRB reviews. There are three categories common to social work research:

1. Research involving materials (data, documents, records, or specimens) that have been collected or will be collected solely for nonresearch purposes (such as medical treatment or diagnosis). Some research in this category may be exempt.

2. Collection of data from voice, video, digital, or image recordings made for research purposes.

3. Research on individual or group characteristics or behavior (including, but not limited to, research on perception, cognition, motivation, identity, language, communication, cultural beliefs or practices, and social behavior), or research employing survey, interview, oral history, focus group, program evaluation, human factors evaluation, or quality assurance methodologies. Some research in this category may be exempt. (U.S. Department of Health and Human Services, 2009)

Informed consent requirements have to be met when the research is approved by an expedited review.

> **Full review** IRB review that is completed for a research study with vulnerable populations or when there is the potential for harm.

Full reviews involve all other forms of research as well as research on populations such as prisoners. These extensive reviews are conducted, vetted, and voted on by the full IRB committee. For example, one university has three reviewers (primary, secondary, and tertiary) with broad expertise in the area of study. At the committee meeting, they summarize the proposal and discuss issues of concerns related to the research and informed consent documents, recommendations about the risk, and recommendations with regard to approval, modification, or disapproval. The full committee continues the discussion and ultimately can reach a variety of conclusions, including actions such as approval, disapproval, asking for the investigator to appear, referral to other committees, and the like.

The IRB, representing a range of perspectives, is an important tool for making reasonable, ethical research decisions when confronted with ethical ambiguity. Exhibit 3.7 shows a portion of the complex flowchart developed by the U.S. Department of Health and Human Services to help researchers decide what type of review will be needed for their research plans.

🔲 Internet Research

The Internet is increasingly being used as both a tool for research, such as online surveys, online focus groups, and one-on-one interviews, and a setting for research studies, such as content studies of social media sites, chatrooms, blogs, discussions, and websites. The ethical guidelines of traditional research modes hold true for Internet research, Yet just as any researcher using a traditional research method (an offline method) must address particular ethical issues, so too must a researcher doing Internet-based research study (Eynon, Fry, & Schroeder, 2008; Markham & Buchanan, 2012). For example, the issues associated with an online survey of MSW program directors may differ from an analysis of the discussions taking place in a chatroom for caregivers of older relatives.

Several broad issues arise for researchers using the Internet. These issues include:

- *Public and private space.* Are discussion boards, chatrooms, social media public or private space (Convery & Cox, 2012; Markham & Buchanan, 2012)? This is particularly important because observational research in public space has exempt status and does not require informed consent. Often comments posted on a discussion board or in many chatrooms are publically available to anyone who might read them. Yet even though the comments may be publically available, conceivably the individuals making the comments may view their comments as private. If you have a Facebook page with 600 friends, is that your private page or a public document? Are these Internet research contexts such that "an individual can reasonably expect that no observation or recording is taking place . . . and an individual can reasonably expect will not be made public" (U.S. Department of Health and Human Services, 2009)?

Exhibit 3.7 U.S. Department of Health and Human Services Human Subjects Decision Flow Chart 4: For Tests, Surveys, Interviews, Public Behavior Observation

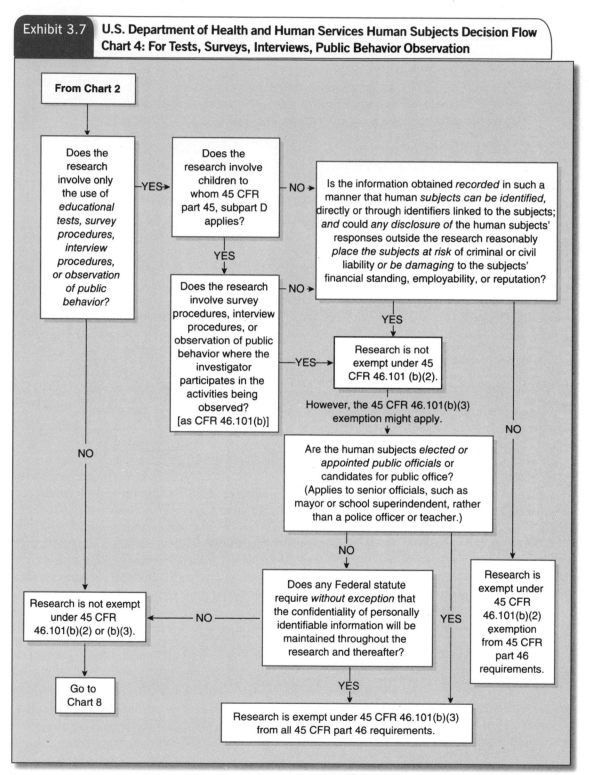

Source: U.S. Department of Health and Human Services. http://www.hhs.gov/ohrp/humansubjects/ guidance/decisioncharts.htm.

- *Confidentiality*. One possible risk is the breaching of confidentiality (Holmes, 2009). For some research, such as online surveys, the researcher may avoid asking for identifying information, keeping separate files of identifying information and survey responses, using encryption methods, and password protected computers on which to save the data (Eynon et al., 2008). For other forms of research, how the research is reported can lead to inadvertent breaches of confidentiality. Verbatim statements, even if left unidentified, could be traced back to an individual through the use of search engines. IP addresses can be traced to a particular computer.

- *Emotional harm*. The concern that questions or discussions evoke emotional distress is common to both Internet and traditional modes of research. The challenge is that it is more difficult for online researchers to determine if a participant is feeling distressed and /or how to address such feelings (Eynon et al., 2008; Holmes, 2009).

- *Informed consent*. Several particular issues arise when considering informed consent. When research is not conducted face-to-face, it is more challenging to respond to questions posed by the potential participant, can require additional time to obtain consent, and to assess whether the potential participant understands the research study (Eynon et al., 2008). Verifying whether the participant can legally consent is also a challenge. There are no foolproof methods, but the recruitment process may help in assuring with some certainty that a potential participant can legally provide informed consent.

Actually obtaining consent differs given the nature of the research. Online surveys may use buttons to agree or disagree to participation, forms may be sent via e-mail, or digital signatures may be acceptable. Informed consent may be more difficult to obtain when gathering data from chatrooms. The very act of collecting information may disrupt the chatroom and researchers may seek waivers from informed consent. Researchers might contact the chatroom owner/manager about seeking informed consent or post a notice asking for volunteers (Convery & Cox, 2012).

The very nature of the Internet and the speed of new technological advances will spur additional questions. Your university IRB is likely to have already encountered many Internet-related studies and may offer guidance about the growing range of ethical conundrums.

▣ Scientific Guidelines for Social Work Research

In the previous sections, we focused on the ethical guidelines that guide social work research. Some social work research addresses topics that challenge social conditions or social policy; other research will have treatment implications for clients. Therefore, there is an added burden on ensuring that the research is done well. The following are scientific guidelines that can be used to guide research (although qualitative researchers interpret some of the guidelines differently from quantitative researchers):

1. *Test ideas against empirical reality without becoming too personally invested in a particular outcome.* This guideline requires a commitment to testing, as opposed to reacting to events as they happen, being swayed by the popularity or status of others, or looking for what we want to see (Kincaid, 1996). When testing ideas, researchers have to recognize that what they find from their studies may not confirm what they had predicted the studies would find. Of course, qualitative researchers who question the utility of the concept of empirical reality don't follow this guideline literally, but they do try to be sensitive to the perspectives that shape how researchers and their subjects perceive reality.

2. *Plan and carry out investigations systematically.* Social work researchers have little hope of conducting a careful test of their ideas if they do not think through in advance how they should go about the test and then proceed accordingly. But a systematic approach is not always easy. Qualitative researchers may not be this systematic, but they remain careful in their use of particular methods and must maintain systematic procedures for recording and analyzing data.

3. *Document all procedures and disclose them publicly.* Social work researchers should disclose the methods on which their conclusions are based so that others can evaluate for themselves the likely soundness of these conclusions. Such disclosure is a key feature of science. The community of researchers, reacting to each other's work, provides the best guarantee against purely self-interested conclusions (Kincaid, 1996). Furthermore, by documenting procedures, other researchers will know how the study was completed and can replicate the study. Social work researchers using qualitative methods often include in their notes some comments about how they went about interviewing or observing.

4. *Clarify assumptions.* No investigation is complete unto itself; whatever the researcher's method, the research rests on some background assumptions. Research to determine whether arrest has a deterrent effect assumes that potential law violators think rationally and calculate potential costs and benefits prior to committing crimes. By definition, research assumptions are not tested, so we do not know for sure whether they are correct. By taking the time to think about and disclose their assumptions, researchers provide important information for those who seek to evaluate the validity of research conclusions. When using qualitative methods, researchers include in their notes comments about what they are thinking and how they are reacting when they interview or observe.

5. *Specify the meaning of all terms.* Words often have multiple or unclear meanings. *Alienation, depression, strengths, information and referral, welfare,* and so on can mean different things to different people. Of course, those using qualitative methods also give special attention to the meanings of the terms people use. Rather than using predetermined definitions of terms, the meanings of terms emerge from the voices of the respondents.

6. *Maintain a skeptical stance toward current knowledge.* The results of any particular investigation must be examined critically. A general skepticism about current knowledge stimulates researchers to improve the validity of current research results and expand the frontier of knowledge. Often, even in their own studies, researchers will conclude with a discussion of the limitations of their study designs. Interpretivist researchers see this issue somewhat differently. Different interpretations are viewed as each contributing to an overall understanding of how people view their situation.

7. *Replicate research and build social theory.* No one study is definitive by itself. We can't fully understand it apart from the larger body of knowledge to which it is related, and we can't place much confidence in it until it has been replicated. Theories organize the knowledge accumulated by numerous investigations into a coherent whole and serve as a guide to future inquiries. Different models of social work practice must be tested by repeated applications of a treatment modality with different subjects, in different settings, and with different types of concerns.

8. *Search for regularities or patterns.* Positivist and postpositivist scientists assume that the natural world has some underlying order of relationships, so that unique events and individuals can be understood at least in part in terms of general principles (Grinnell, 1992). Individuals are not unimportant to social scientists, but the goal of elaborating individual cases is to understand social patterns that characterize many individuals. Interpretivists are more oriented to the particulars of situations they have studied and to providing "thick" descriptions of them.

These general guidelines are ideals for much social work research, but no particular investigation is going to follow every guideline exactly. Real investigations by social work researchers do not always include much attention to theory, specific definitions of all terms, and so forth. Researchers guided by an interpretivist philosophy may even reject some of the guidelines. But it behooves any social researcher to study these guidelines and to consider the consequences of not following any with which he or she does not agree.

▣ Conclusion

The evaluation of ethical issues in a research project should be based on a realistic assessment of the overall potential for harm and benefit to research subjects rather than an apparent inconsistency between any particular aspect of a research plan and a specific ethical guideline. For example, full disclosure of "what is really going on" in an experimental study is unnecessary if subjects are unlikely to be harmed. Nevertheless, researchers should make every effort to foresee all possible risks and to weigh the possible benefits of the research against these risks. They should consult with individuals with different perspectives to develop a realistic risk–benefit assessment, and they should try to maximize the benefits to, as well as minimize the risks for, subjects of the research (Sieber, 1992).

Ultimately, these decisions about ethical procedures are not just up to you, as a researcher, to make. Your university's IRB sets the human subjects' protection standards for your institution and will require that researchers—even, in most cases, students—submit their research proposal to the IRB for review. So we leave you with the instruction to review the human subjects guidelines of the NASW, consult your university's procedures for the conduct of research with human subjects, consult with your agency, and then proceed accordingly.

Key Terms

Assent   55
Belmont Report   51
Certificate of Confidentiality   61
Conflicts of interest   62

Debriefing   60
Exempt status   64
Expedited review   64
Full review   65

Institutional review board (IRB)   51
Permission   55

Highlights

- Stanley Milgram's obedience experiments led to intensive debate about the extent to which deception could be tolerated in social science research and how harm to subjects should be evaluated.

- Egregious violations of human rights by researchers, including scientists in Nazi Germany and researchers in the Tuskegee syphilis study, led to the adoption of federal ethical standards for research on human subjects.

- The 1979 *Belmont Report* developed by a national commission established three basic ethical standards for the protection of

human subjects: (1) respect for persons, (2) beneficence, and (3) justice.

- In 1991 the U.S. Department of Health and Human Services adopted a Federal Policy for the Protection of Human Subjects. This policy requires that every institution seeking federal funding for biomedical or behavioral research on human subjects have an institutional review board to exercise oversight.

- Scientific research should maintain high standards for validity and be conducted and reported in an honest and open fashion.

Discussion Questions

1. Should social scientists be permitted to conduct replications of Milgram's obedience experiments? Can you justify such research as permissible by the current NASW ethical standards?

2. Why does unethical research occur? Is it inherent in science? Does it reflect "human nature"? What makes ethical research more or less likely?

3. Describe the differences between assent and permission.

4. Why does research with prisoners require a full IRB decision?

5. What policy would you recommend that researchers follow in reporting the results of their research? Should social scientists try to correct misinformation in the popular press about their research, or should they just focus on what is published in academic journals? Should researchers speak to audiences such as police conventions in order to influence policies related to their research results?

Practice Exercises

1. Pair up with one other student, and select one of the research articles you have reviewed for other exercises. Criticize the research in terms of its adherence to each of the ethical principles for research on human subjects as well as for the authors' apparent honesty, openness, and consideration of social consequences. Be generally negative but not unreasonable in your criticisms. The student with whom you are working should critique the article in the same way but from a generally positive standpoint, defending its adherence to the five guidelines, but without ignoring the study's weak points. Together, write a summary of the study's strong and weak points, or conduct a debate in the class.

2. Investigate the standards and operations of your university's IRB. Review the IRB website, record the composition of the IRB (if indicated), and outline the steps that faculty and students must take in order to secure IRB approval for human subjects research. In your own words, distinguish the types of research that can be exempted from review, that qualify for expedited review, and that require review by the full board. If possible, identify another student or a faculty member who has had a proposal reviewed by the IRB. Ask this person to describe the experience and how he or she feels about it.

3. Read one article based on research involving human subjects. What ethical issues did the research pose, and how were they resolved? Does it seem that subjects were appropriately protected?

Web Exercise

1. The Collaborative Institutional Training Initiative (CITI) offers an extensive online training course in the basics of human subjects protections issues. Go the public-access CITI site (www .citiprogram.org/rcrpage.asp?affiliation=100) and complete the course in social and behavioral research. Write a short summary of what you learn.

2. The U.S. Department of Health and Human Services maintains extensive resources concerning the protection of human subjects in research. Read several documents that you find on its website (www.hhs.gov/ohrp), and write a short report about them.

Developing a Research Proposal

Now it's time to consider the potential ethical issues in your proposed study and the research philosophy that will guide your research.

1. List the elements in your research plans that an IRB might consider to be relevant to the protection of human subjects. Rate each element from 1 to 5, where 1 indicates no more than a minor ethical issue and 5 indicates a major ethical problem that probably cannot be resolved.

2. Write one page for the application to the IRB that explains how you will ensure that your research adheres to each relevant NASW standard.

3. Draft a consent form to be administered to your subjects when they enroll in your research. Use underlining and margin notes to indicate where each standard for informed consent statements is met.

CHAPTER 4

Measurment

Alcohol abuse is a social problem of remarkable proportions. In 2012, 17 million Americans age 12 or older were alcohol abusers (Substance Abuse and Mental Health Services Administration [SAMHSA], 2012). Alcohol is involved in more than 30% of all fatal traffic crashes (National Highway Traffic Safety Administration, 2013), and almost 1.3 million arrests are made annually for driving under the influence (Federal Bureau of Investigation, 2013). Four in 10 full-time college students ages 18 to 22 binge drink (SAMHSA, 2012), and about 1 in 4 could be diagnosed as alcohol abusers or alcohol dependent (Slutske, 2005).

Whether your goal is to learn how society works, deliver useful services, design effective social policies, or even design your own study, at some point you might decide to read the research literature on that topic. If you are reading literature about alcohol abuse, you will have to answer three questions: (1) What is meant by *alcohol abuse* in this research (conceptualization)? (2) How is alcohol abuse measured (measurement)? and (3) Is the measurement method accurate and valid (reliability and validity)? These questions must be answered when we evaluate prior research and when we design new research. Only when we conclude that a study used valid measures of its key concepts can we have some hope that its conclusions are valid.

Measurement is a crucial component of social work practice and research. When you think of measurement in social work practice, you might think of assessment whereby you are collecting information about a client system; the assessment often includes key concepts and measures of those concepts. When evaluating a program's outcomes, broadly stated goals and objectives are translated into something that can be measured. What you learn from the assessment helps guide intervention decisions; what you learn about a program's outcomes influences the design or continuation of the program.

In this chapter, we describe the process of measurement—from taking an abstract concept and translating the concept to the point that we can assign some value to represent that concept. First we address the issue of conceptualization or how you define key terms, using alcohol abuse and other concepts as examples. We then focus on the characteristics, or levels of measurement, reflected in different measures. In the next section, we discuss different methods to assess the quality of measures, specifically the techniques used to assess reliability and validity. Finally, we discuss the importance of ensuring the cultural relevance of measures and the implications of measurement for evidence-based practice. By the chapter's end, you should have a good understanding of measurement and the crucial role it plays for social work practice and social work research.

▣ Concepts

Although the drinking statistics sound scary, we need to be clear about what they mean before we march off to a Temperance Society meeting. What, after all, is *binge drinking*? The definition SAMHSA (2013) used is "five or more drinks on the same occasion (i.e., at the same time or within a couple of hours of each other) on at least 1 day in the past 30 days." This is only one definition of binge drinking; other researchers suggest that while the definition is appropriate for men, it should be four drinks for women (Wechsler et al., 2002). The 5/4 definition is widely accepted by researchers, so when they use the term they can understand each other.

Is this what you call binge drinking? The National Institute on Alcoholism and Alcohol Abuse (NIAAA; n.d.) provides a more precise definition of binge drinking "as a pattern of drinking alcohol that brings blood alcohol concentration to 0.08 gram percent or above." Most researchers consider the 5/4 distinction to be a reasonable approximation of this precise definition. We cannot say that only one definition of *binge drinking* is correct or better. What we can say is that we need to specify what we mean when we use the term and that others know what definition we are using.

Binge drinking is a **concept**—a mental image that summarizes a set of similar observations, feelings, or ideas. To make that concept useful in research (and even in ordinary discourse), we have to define it. A challenge faced by social work researchers is that many of the topics they study involve abstract concepts or ideas that are not easily observable and not just simple objects. Some concepts, such as age or living arrangement, are straightforward, and there is little confusion about their meaning. When we refer to concepts like alcohol abuse, homelessness,

Concept A mental image that summarizes a set of similar observations, feelings, or ideas.

mental health, or poverty, we cannot count on others knowing exactly what we mean. Even the experts may disagree about the meaning of frequently used concepts. That's okay. The point is not that there should be only one definition of a concept but that we have to specify clearly what we mean when we use a concept, and we expect others to do the same.

Conceptualization in Practice

If we are to do an adequate job of **conceptualization**—working out what our key terms will mean in our research—we must do more than just think up some definition, any definition, for our concepts. We have to turn to social theory and prior research to review appropriate definitions. We may need to identify dimensions of the concept. We should understand how the definition we choose fits within the theoretical framework guiding the research and what assumptions underlie this framework.

Researchers start with a **nominal definition** of the concept; they define the concept in terms of other concepts. Nominal definitions are like those definitions found in dictionaries: You get an understanding of the word and its dimensions, but you still do not have a set of rules to use to measure the concept. For example, child abuse might be defined as evident when either severe physical or emotional harm is inflicted on a child or there is contact of a sexual nature. The nominal definition of child abuse includes concepts such as *severe harm*, *physical abuse*, and *emotional abuse*, but the definition does not provide the set of rules a researcher uses to identify the forms of abuse or distinguish between severe and not severe harm. The actual measure of child abuse should be consistent with the nominal definition.

Conceptualization The process of specifying what we mean by a term. In deductive research, conceptualization helps to translate portions of an abstract theory into testable hypotheses involving specific variables. In inductive research, conceptualization is an important part of the process used to make sense of related observations.

Nominal definition Defining a concept using other concepts.

Alcohal Abuse

What observations or images should we associate with the concept of alcohol abuse? Someone leaning against a building with a liquor bottle, barely able to speak coherently? College students drinking heavily at a party? Someone in an Alcoholics Anonymous group drinking one beer? A 10-year-old boy drinking a small glass of wine in an alley? A 10-year-old boy drinking a small glass of wine at the dinner table in France? Do all these images share something in common that we should define as alcohol abuse for the purposes of a particular research study? Do some of them? Should we take into account cultural differences? Gender differences? Age differences? Social situations? Physical tolerance for alcohol?

Many researchers now use the definition of *alcohol abuse* or *alcohol use disorder* contained in the American Psychiatric Association's (2013) *Diagnostic and Statistical Manual of Mental Disorders* (*DSM-5*): "a problematic pattern of alcohol use leading to clinically significant impairment or distress, as manifested by at least two of the following, occurring within a 12-month period:" (p. 490). Eleven symptoms or behaviors are listed with the number of presenting symptoms distinguishing between mild (2–3 symptoms), moderate (4–5 symptoms), and severe (6 or more symptoms) alcohol use disorder. Although a popular definition, we cannot judge the *DSM-5* definition of alcohol abuse as correct or incorrect. Each researcher has the right to conceptualize as he or she sees fit. However, we can say that the *DSM-5* definition of alcohol abuse is useful, in part, because it has been widely adopted. The definition is stated in clear and precise language that should minimize differences in interpretation and maximize understanding.

This clarity should not prevent us from recognizing that the definition reflects a particular theoretical orientation. *DSM-5* applies a medical "disease model" to alcohol abuse (as well as to mental illness). This theoretical model emphasizes behavioral and biological criteria, instead of the social expectations that are emphasized in a social model of alcohol abuse. How we conceptualize reflects how we theorize.

Just as we can connect concepts to theory, we can connect them to other concepts. What this means is that the definition of any one concept rests on a shared understanding of the terms used in the definition. So if our audience does not already have a shared understanding of terms such as *adequate social functioning*, *self-care functioning*, and *repeated use*, we must also define these terms before we are finished with the process of defining *alcohol abuse*.

Depression

Some concepts have multiple dimensions, bringing together several related concepts under a larger conceptual umbrella. One such concept is depression. Depression is unlike a normal emotional experience leading to sadness because it includes a range of symptoms, such as negative mood (sadness, loneliness, feelings of worthlessness) and somatic conditions (loss of interest in pleasurable activities, eating and sleeping problems, loss of energy, talking less). Depression is a combination of these different dimensions.

But even when there is agreement about the various dimensions that make up depression, there are still different approaches to measure the presence of depression. One approach assumes that the presence of psychological symptoms is not enough by itself, but these symptoms vary by intensity or severity (Dohrenwend & Dohrenwend, 1982). In the case of depression, it is not sufficient to look at whether the symptoms are present; rather, they have to be persistent, lasting for some time period. The symptoms must be so intense that they interfere with an individual's ability to function. So some researchers use scales that measure the intensity of the different items. For example, the Center for Epidemiologic Studies Depression (CES-D) scale asks respondents to rate the intensity (or severity) of each of the items; then the items are summed to represent a range on a continuum of intensity of depression.

The second approach to measuring depression is derived from the clinical case identification model used in assessment models such as the *DSM-IV-TR* and reflected in scales such as the Patient Health Questionnaire (PHQ-9; Kroenke & Spitzer, 2002). In the clinical diagnostic approach, researchers identify the presence of the various dimensions of depression during a specific time period, but they do not assess the intensity of the symptoms. Furthermore, researchers using this method gather additional information to assess whether the responses conform to criteria for a case of depression. Unlike the previous model, this approach identifies simply whether depression is present or absent.

Do these different perspectives really matter? Joy Newmann (1989) found that the relationship between age and depression depended on the type of assessment method. Studies using scales like the CES-D tended to show that highest depression scores occur among the youngest and oldest age groups, whereas studies using the clinical case method have found that the younger and older cohorts were less depressed than middle-age cohorts.

Poverty

Decisions about how to define a concept reflect the theoretical framework that guides the researchers. For example, the concept *poverty* has always been somewhat controversial because different conceptualizations of poverty result in different estimates of its prevalence and different social policies for responding to it.

Most of the statistics that you see in the newspaper about the poverty rate reflect a conception of poverty that was formalized by Mollie Orshansky, of the Social Security Administration, in 1965 and subsequently adopted by the federal government and many researchers. She defined poverty in terms of what is called an *absolute* standard, based on the amount of money required to purchase an emergency diet that is estimated to be nutritionally adequate for about 2 months. The idea is that people are truly poor if they can barely purchase the food they need and other essential goods. This poverty threshold is adjusted for household size and composition (number of children and adults), and the minimal amount needed for food is multiplied by three because a 1955 survey indicated that poor families spend about one third of their incomes on food (Orshansky, 1977). More recently, a governmental working group has developed a supplemental poverty measure that calculates income and poverty thresholds somewhat differently but is still based on minimum need (Garner, 2010).

Other social scientists reject this way of establishing an absolute standard and suggest an alternative method: the *basic needs budget* approach (Lin & Bernstein, 2008). This approach suggests that we need to establish the market cost of a basket of goods that each of us needs to meet basic needs. The cost of each category or good is estimated separately. This method also forces us to define what an *adequate amount* of that particular good is. Like the official poverty line, this definition requires adjustments for family size, but it also requires adjustments for the labor status of the parent, ages of the children, and geographic region of residence.

Some social scientists disagree with absolute standards and have instead urged adoption of a *relative* poverty standard. One such standard identifies the poor as those having some fraction of income such as whose incomes fall below

50% of the median household income (Wolff, 2009). The idea behind this relative conception is that poverty should be defined in terms of what is normal in a given society at a particular time.

Some social scientists prefer yet another conception of poverty. With the *subjective* approach, poverty is defined as what people think would be the minimal income they need to make ends meet. While some poverty researchers have argued that this approach is influenced too much by the different standards that people use to estimate what they "need," trends of poll responses to asking about the minimum income necessary for a family of four to get along in one's community tend to follow a path similar to changes in the median income (Blank, 2008).

What are the implications of these different approaches? If you are interested in determining the percentage of the population that is poor, a relative approach sets the percentage you consider poor based on income only. Basic needs approaches that attempt to specify the actual amount needed to meet basic needs tend to find three times as many poor in comparison to the multiplier approach used to calculate the Official Poverty Line (Lin & Bernstein, 2008). The different poverty thresholds based on these definitions are displayed on Exhibit 4.1. The differing poverty thresholds have implications for the number of people living in poverty and the types of policies that might be implemented to address poverty.

囗 From Concepts to Observations

After we define the concepts in a study, we must identify corresponding variables and develop procedures to measure them. To measure alcohol abuse we might use any number of variables: one variable might be the count of alcoholic drinks; another variable might involve asking about the presence of blackouts; a third variable may ask about binge drinking, and a fourth variable might reflect a score on a rating scale of 10 questions. Any of these variables could show low or high degrees of substance abuse.

Where do variables fit in the continuum from concepts to operational indicators? Think of it this way: Usually, the term *variable* is used to refer to some specific aspect of a concept that varies and for which we then have to select even more concrete indicators. Concepts vary in their level of abstraction, and this in turn affects how readily we can specify the variables pertaining to the concept. We may not think twice before we move from a conceptual definition

Exhibit 2.4	Poverty Thresholds Using Different Definitions 2013 for Selected Families (in dollars)		
Measure		**One Parent, One Child**	**Two Parents, Two Children**
Official Poverty Line[a]		16,057	23,624
Basic Needs Budget: Pittsburgh Metropolitan Region[b]		48,040	66,324
Basic Needs Budget: Boston Metropolitan Region[b]		67,924	86,502
Relative Poverty Line: National 50% definition[c]		26,125	26,125
Relative Poverty Line: Pittsburgh Metropolitan Region 50% definition[c]		25,646	25,646
Relative Poverty Line: Boston Metropolitan Region 50% definition[c]		36,454	36,454

Source: Economic Policy Institute; U.S. Census Bureau.

a *Source:* http://www.census.gov/hhes/www/poverty/data/threshld/index.html May 24, 2015.

b *Source:* Economic Policy Institute (2015), Family Budget Calculator http://www.epi.org/resources/budget.

b *Source:* Noss, A. (September 2014). Household income: 2013, American Community Survey Briefs. U.S. Census Bureau, U. S. Department of Commerce.

Research In the News

For Further Thought?

HOW TO MEASURE RACE AND ETHNICITY IN AMERICA?

The U.S. Bureau of the Census is considering how to best measure race and ethnicity for the 2020 Census. Increasing numbers of people are identifying multiple racial and ethnic categories, forced to respond to categories that they do not believe reflect their background, checking other race or other ethnicity, and/or switch categories from Census to Census.

1. How would you define race and ethnicity?

2. How would you operationalize race? ethnicity?

3. What does a "race" variable or "ethnicity" variable really measure?

Source: Vega, Tanzina. 2014. "Census Considers How to Measure a More Diverse America" *The New York Times*, July 1, 2014 [note downloaded from web site on 7-10-2014].

of *age* as time elapsed since birth to the variable *years since birth*. Binge drinking is also a relatively concrete concept, but it requires a bit more thought. We may define binge drinking conceptually as episodic drinking and select for our research on binge drinking the variable *frequency of five or more drinks in a row*. A single question is sufficient.

A more abstract concept like social support may have a clear role in theory but a variety of meanings in different social settings. For example, research on the concept of social support might focus on the variable *level of perceived support*. We might select as our variable the responses to a series of statements about social support, such as found in Zimet, Dahlem, Zimet, and Farley's (1988) "Multidimensional Scale of Perceived Social Support": "There is a special person around when I am in need."

Not every concept in a particular study is represented by a variable. If we were to study clients' alcohol abuse at an inpatient treatment unit, there is no variation; rather, all the clients are clients. In this case, client is called a constant; it is always the same and therefore is not a variable. Of course, this does not mean we cannot study gender differences among the clients. In this case, gender is the variable; the client is still a constant.

It is very tempting, and all too common, to simply try to measure everything by including in a study every variable we can think of that might have something to do with our research question. This haphazard approach will inevitably result in the collection of data that are useless and the failure to collect some data that are important. Instead, a careful researcher examines relevant theories to identify key concepts, reviews prior research to learn how useful different indicators have been, and assesses the resources available for measuring adequately variables in the specific setting to be studied.

Operationalization

Operationalization The process of specifying the operations that will indicate the value of cases on a variable.

Operational definition The set of rules and operations used to find the value of cases on a variable.

Once we have defined our concepts in the abstract—that is, we have provided a nominal definition—and we have identified the specific variables we want to measure, we must develop measurement procedures. The goal is to devise procedures to indicate the values of cases on a variable. **Operationalization** is the process of connecting concepts to observations.

Researchers provide an **operational definition**, which includes what is measured, how the indicators are measured, and the rules used to assign a value to what is observed and to interpret the value. Previously, we have provided a nominal definition of *alcoholism*. An operational definition might include the following content:

> The Michigan Alcoholism Screening Test (MAST) is a 24-item instrument that includes a variety of indicators of symptoms such as seeing drinking as a problem, seeking treatment for problem drinking, delirium tremens, severe shaking, hearing voices, complaints from others about drinking, memory loss from drinking, job loss due to drinking, social problems from drinking, arrests for drunk driving or for drunken behavior, guilt feelings about drinking, and ability to stop drinking. The scale may be administered orally or may be self-administered. Respondents respond yes or no to each item, and each item is given a weighted score ranging from 0 to 5. There are four items for which the alcoholic response is "no." The weighted item responses are summed, with a score of 0 to 3 indicating no problem with alcoholism, 4 considered to be suggestive of a problem, and 5 or above an indication of alcoholism.

As you can see from this definition, we are provided with the specific indicators included in the measure, the method(s) for data collection, specific scoring rules, and the interpretation of scale scores.

Exhibit 4.2 represents the operationalization process in three studies. The first researcher defines the concept, income, and chooses one variable, annual earnings, to represent it. This variable is then measured with responses to a single question or an item: What was your total income from all sources in 2015? The second researcher defines the concept, poverty, as having two aspects or dimensions: subjective poverty and absolute poverty. Subjective poverty is measured with responses to a survey question: Do you consider yourself poor? Absolute poverty is measured by comparing family income to the poverty threshold. The third researcher decides that the concept is defined by a position on three measured variables: income, education, and occupational prestige.

One consideration is the precision of the information that is necessary. The first researcher in Exhibit 4.2 is seeking information that is quite precise and assumes that respondents will be willing and able to accurately report

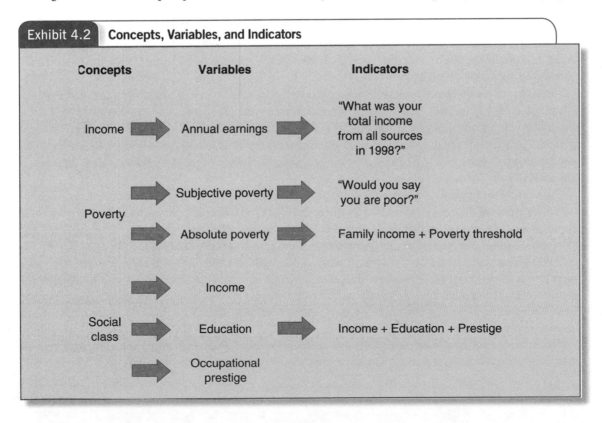

Exhibit 4.2 **Concepts, Variables, and Indicators**

Concepts	Variables	Indicators
Income	Annual earnings	"What was your total income from all sources in 1998?"
Poverty	Subjective poverty	"Would you say you are poor?"
	Absolute poverty	Family income + Poverty threshold
Social class	Income / Education / Occupational prestige	Income + Education + Prestige

the information. As an alternative, the question might have been: "Please identify the income category that includes your total income from all sources in 2015." This question will provide less exact information, but people might be more willing to respond to it. Generally, the decision about precision is based on the information that is needed for the research. It may also be based on what the researcher believes people can recall and the content people may be willing to report.

The variables and particular measurement operations chosen for a study should be consistent with the research question. Take the evaluative research question: Are self-help groups more effective in increasing the likelihood of abstinence among substance abusers than hospital-based treatments? We may operationalize the variable *form of treatment* in terms of participation in these two types of treatment. However, if we are answering the explanatory research question: What influences the success of substance abuse treatment? We should probably consider what it is about these treatment alternatives that is associated with successful abstinence. Prior theory and research suggest that some of the important variables that differ between these treatment approaches are level of peer support, beliefs about the causes of alcoholism, and financial investment in the treatment.

Scales to Measure Variables

When several questions are used to measure one concept, the responses may be combined by taking the sum or average of responses. A composite measure based on this type of sum or average is termed a **scale**. The idea is that idiosyncratic variation in response to particular questions will average out so that the main influence on the combined measure will be the concept on which all the questions focus. Each item is an indicator of the concept, but the item alone is often not a sufficient measure of the concept. A scale is a more complete measure of the concept than any single component question.

Scale A composite measure based on combining the responses to multiple questions pertaining to a common concept.

Creating a scale is not just a matter of writing a few questions that seem to focus on a concept. Questions that seem to you to measure a common concept might seem to respondents to concern several different issues. The only way to know that a given set of questions forms a scale is to administer the questions to people like those you plan to study. If a common concept is being measured, people's responses to the different questions should display some consistency.

Scales have been developed to measure many concepts, and some of these scales have been demonstrated to be accurate in a range of studies. It usually is much better to use such a scale to measure a concept than it is to try to devise questions to form a new scale. Use of a preexisting scale both simplifies the work involved in designing a study and facilitates comparison of findings to those obtained in other studies. Scales can be found in research articles; on the Internet, for example the ERIC/AE Test Locator (www.ericae.net/testcol.htm); or in compilations, such as *Measures for Clinical Practice and Research* (Fischer & Corcoran, 2013).

The Center for Epidemiologic Depression Scale (CES-D; see Exhibit 4.3) is a scale used to measure depression. The aspect of depression measured by the scale is the level (the frequency and number combined) of depressive symptoms. Given that depression consists of negative affect, lack of positive affect, and somatic behaviors, the developers of the scale designed questions to assess these dimensions. Many researchers in different studies have found that these questions form an accurate scale. Note that each question concerns a symptom of depression. People may have idiosyncratic reasons for having a particular symptom without being depressed; for example, people who have been suffering a physical ailment may say that they have a poor appetite. By combining the answers to questions about several symptoms, the scale score reduces the impact of this idiosyncratic variation.

The advantages of using scales rather than single questions to measure important concepts are clear, so surveys and interviews often include sets of multiple-item questions. However, several cautions are in order:

| Exhibit 4.3 | **Example of a Scale: The Center for Epidemiologic Studies Depression Scale (CES–D)** |

INSTRUCTIONS FOR QUESTIONS. Below is a list of the ways you might have felt or behaved in the past week.

Please tell me how often you have felt this way during the past week:

    Rarely or none of the time (less than 1 day)

    Some or a little of the time (1 to 2 days)

    Fairly often (3 to 4 days)

    Most or all of the time (5 to 7 days)

During the past week:

1. I was bothered by things that usually don't bother me.
2. I did not feel like eating; my appetite was poor.
3. I could not shake off the blues even with help from my family or friends.
4. I felt I was just as good as other people.
5. I had trouble keeping my mind on what I was doing.
6. I felt depressed.
7. I felt everything I did was an effort.
8. I felt hopeful about the future.
9. I thought my life had been a failure.
10. I felt fearful.
11. My sleep was restless.
12. I was happy.
13. I talked less than usual.
14. I felt lonely.
15. People were unfriendly.
16. I enjoyed life.
17. I had crying spells.
18. I felt sad.
19. I felt people disliked me.
20. I could not "get going."

Source: From Radloff, Lenore. 1977. "The CES-D Scale: A Self-Report Depression Scale for Research in the General Population" *Applied Psychological Measurement* 1:385–401.

1. *Our presupposition that each component question is indeed measuring the same concept may be mistaken.* Although we may include multiple questions in a survey to measure one concept, we may find that answers to the questions are not related to one another, so the scale cannot be created. Or we may find that answers to just a few of the questions are not related to the answers given to most of the others. Therefore, we may decide to discard these particular questions before computing the average that makes up the scale.

2. *Some questions in a scale may cluster together in subsets or subscales.* All the questions may be measuring the intended concept, but we may conclude that the concept actually has several different aspects; this results in a **multidimensional scale.** For example, the CES-D has some items that measure only negative affect, other questions that measure only lack of positive affect, and other questions measuring somatic symptoms. Each of these concepts is an indicator of depression. Researchers may choose to use a variable that summarizes the total scale or they may choose to use variables that summarize the subscale scores. Sometimes using the total scale score can obscure important differences among the subscale scores.

Multidimensional scale A scale containing subsets of questions that measure different aspects of the same concept.

3. *Sometimes particular questions are counted, or weighted, more than others in the calculation of the scale.* The individual items in the CES-D scale have equal weight; that is, each item makes the same contribution to

the depression score. Other scales have questions that are more central to the concept being measured than other questions and so may be given greater weight when computing the scale score. The MAST asks questions that are assigned different weights. A positive response to the question, "Have you ever been in a hospital because of your drinking?" is given 5 points (weighted higher) than a positive response to the question, "Do you feel you are a normal drinker?" which is assigned 2 points.

You will come across different kinds of scales, but several of the most popular types include Likert scales, semantic differential scales, and Guttman response scales.

- Likert scales use Likert-response categories and measure the extent to which respondents hold a particular attitude or feeling. The scores are summed or averaged.

- In a semantic differential scale, the concept of interest is described by a number of opposite pairs of words, with each pair being an adjective that captures some aspect of the concept. If you were interested in measuring mood, one pair might be *happy–sad*. Respondents then rate themselves on a 5- or 7-point scale for each of the paired opposite words. The scores are then summed to obtain a measure of the attitude. The challenge is to identify a set of adjectives that captures all the dimensions of the concept.

- Guttman scales are designed to capture different levels of the concept, where the different levels might be differences in the strength of an attitude, different intensity of services, or difficulty in answering the question. The assumption is that if you can answer the difficult question, then you are likely to answer the easier question. In a Guttman scale, there is a hierarchy from the easiest to the hardest or the most general to the most specific.

Treatment as a Variable

Frequently, social work researchers will examine the effectiveness of an intervention or compare two different intervention approaches. When an intervention is compared to no intervention or when two or more interventions are compared, the intervention becomes the independent variable. It is important for the researcher to provide a clear nominal definition of the intervention. It is not enough for the researcher to say that the study is comparing one method to another, such as traditional case management to intensive case management. Although the general meaning of such an approach may be familiar to you, the researcher should define what each approach involves. Case management may include full support so that the social worker working with the chronically mentally ill provides a variety of services and supports, including rehabilitation, social skill building, counseling, links to resources, identification of work and social opportunities, and money management, whereas another social worker may just assess the client, link the client to other services, and periodically reassess the client.

Nominal definitions of an intervention only provide the characteristics or components of the intervention, but fail to fully describe how the intervention was implemented. Researchers provide varying amounts of specificity regarding the actual operationalization of the intervention. Robert Newcomer, Taewoon Kang, and Carrie Graham (2006) evaluated a specialized case management (Providing Assistance to Caregivers in Transition; PACT) for nursing home individuals returning to the community. They specified the five components of the program and provided details about what each component included. In describing caregiver assessment and care management, they identified who carried out the task, where the assessment was completed, the topics covered in the assessment, the process for care planning, and the activities covered by case management. This amount of detail provides a much clearer sense of the nature of the intervention, but it would still not be possible to repeat the research or to use the intervention with clients without additional information. Without the actual description of the intervention and how the treatment model was implemented, you cannot adequately evaluate the research or replicate what was done if you want to implement the intervention at your agency.

Gathering Data

Social work researchers and practitioners have many options for operationalizing their concepts. We briefly mention these options here but go into much greater depth in subsequent chapters.

Researchers may use direct measures, such as visual or recorded observation or a physical measure such as a pulse rate. Although these methods are particularly useful for gauging behavior, they are typically intrusive. The very act of gathering the information may change people's behavior, thereby altering the accuracy of the obtained information. If a caseworker goes to a client's home to observe the client interacting with a child, the nature of the interactions may change because the parent knows the caseworker is present. The parent is likely to behave in a manner that is more socially acceptable to the caseworker. Similarly, self-monitoring of behavior may have the same effect. If a smoker is asked to monitor the number of cigarettes smoked in a day, the act of such monitoring may reduce the number of cigarettes smoked.

Data may be gathered by interviews or self-administered scales and questionnaires. These methods appear to be direct in that we gather the information directly from the respondent or the client. Yet what we are trying to do is infer behavior, attitudes, emotions, or feelings because we cannot observe these directly. These methods may also be quite intrusive, and the quality of the responses can be affected by the nature of the questions or the characteristics of the person asking the questions.

There are other sources of information from which measures can be operationalized. Many large data sets have been collected by the federal government, state governments, and nongovernmental sources. Many of these data sets have social indicators that are relevant to social services, such as employment, program participation, income, health, crime, mental health, and the like. A drawback to these data is that you are constrained by the way those who collected the data operationalized their measures.

Variables can be operationalized using written information in client records. The quality of these records depends on the recording accuracy of the individual staff. As with data collected by other sources, you are constrained by how variables were operationalized by the staff. Staff may not use common definitions, and these definitions may change over time, leading to inaccuracies in the data.

When we have reason to be skeptical of potential respondents' answers to questions, when we cannot observe the phenomena of interest directly, and when there are no sources of available data, we can use indirect or unobtrusive measures, which allow us to collect data about individuals or groups without their direct knowledge or participation (Webb, Campbell, Schwartz, & Sechrest, 2000).

Two types of unobtrusive measures are physical traces and content analysis. The physical traces of past behavior are most useful when the behavior of interest cannot be directly observed and has not been recorded in a source of available data. To measure the prevalence of drinking in college dorms or fraternity houses, we might count the number of empty bottles of alcoholic beverages in the surrounding trash bins. Content analysis studies are representations of the research topic in such media forms as news articles, chatrooms, and Twitter messages. An investigation of what motivates child abuse reporting might include a count of the amount of space devoted to newspaper articles in a sample of issues of the local newspaper or the number of television newscasters reporting on the maltreatment of children.

Combining Measurement Operations

The choice of a particular measurement method is often determined by available resources and opportunities, but measurement is improved if this choice also takes into account the particular concept or concepts to be measured. Responses to such questions as "How socially engaged were you at the party?" or "How many days did you use sick leave last year?" are unlikely to provide information as valid as direct observation or agency records. However, observations at social gatherings may not answer our questions about why some people do not participate; we may just have to ask people. If no agency is recording the frequency of job loss in a community, we may have to ask direct questions.

Triangulation—the use of two or more different measures of the same variable—can make for even more accurate measurement (Brewer & Hunter, 2005). When we achieve similar results with different measures of the same variable, particularly when the measures are based on such different methods as survey questions and field-based observations, we can be more confident in the validity of each measure. If results diverge with different measures, it may indicate that one or more of these measures is influenced by more measurement error than we can tolerate. Divergence between measures could also indicate that they actually operationalize different concepts.

Measurement in Qualitative Research

Qualitative research projects usually take an inductive approach to the process of conceptualization. In an inductive approach, concepts emerge from the process of thinking about what has been observed, compared with the deductive approach that we have described, in which we develop concepts on the basis of theory and then decide what should be observed to indicate that concept. Instead of deciding in advance which concepts are important for a study, what these concepts mean, and how they should be measured, qualitative researchers begin by recording verbatim what they hear in intensive interviews or what they see during observational sessions. This material is then reviewed to identify important concepts and their meaning for participants. Relevant variables may then be identified and procedures developed for indicating variation between participants and settings or variation over time. As an understanding of the participants and social processes develops, the concepts may be refined and the measures modified. Qualitative research often does not feature the sharp boundaries in quantitative research between developing measures, collecting data with those measures, and evaluating the measures.

You learn more about qualitative research in Chapter 9, but an example will help you understand the qualitative measurement approach. Darin Weinberg (2000) observed participants in three drug abuse treatment programs in Southern California. He was puzzled by the drug abuse treatment program participants' apparently contradictory beliefs—that drug abuse is a medical disease marked by "loss of control" but that participation in a therapeutic community can be an effective treatment. He discovered that treatment participants shared an "ecology of addiction" in which they conceived of being *in* the program as a protected environment, whereas being in the community was considered being *out there* in a place where drug use was inevitable—in "a space one's addiction compelled one to inhabit" (Weinberg, 2000, p. 609).

I'm doing real, real bad right now. . . . I'm havin' trouble right now staying clean for more than two days. . . . I hate myself for goin' out and I don't know if there's anything that can save me anymore. . . . I think I'm gonna die out there. (Weinberg, 2000, p. 609)

Participants contrasted their conscientiousness while in the program with the personal dissolution of those out in "the life."

So Weinberg developed the concepts of *in* and *out* inductively, in the course of the research, and he identified indicators of these concepts at the same time in the observational text. He continued to refine and evaluate the concepts throughout the research. Conceptualization, operationalization, and validation were ongoing and interrelated processes.

回 Levels of Measurement

The final part of operationalization is to assign a value or symbol to represent the observation. Each variable has categories of some sort, and we need to know how to assign a symbol—typically a number—to represent what has been observed or learned. We may have a discrete variable, whereby its symbol represents a separate category or a different status. The variable may be a continuous variable, for which the number represents a quantity that can be described in terms of order, spread between the numbers, and/or relative amounts.

When we know a variable's level of measurement, we can better understand how cases vary on that variable and so understand more fully what we have measured. Level of measurement also has important implications for the type of mathematical procedures and statistics that can be used with the variable. There are four levels of measurement: nominal, ordinal, interval, and ratio. Exhibit 4.4 depicts the differences among these four levels.

> **Level of measurement** The mathematical precision with which the values of a variable can be expressed. The nominal level of measurement, which is qualitative, has no mathematical interpretation; the quantitative levels of measurement—ordinal, interval, and ratio—are progressively more precise mathematically.

Nominal Level of Measurement

The **nominal level of measurement** identifies variables whose values have no mathematical interpretation; they vary in kind or quality, but not in amount. They may also be called categorical variables. In fact, it is conventional to refer to the values of nominal variables as attributes instead of values. The variable *ethnicity* can have several attributes (or categories or qualities): African American, Hispanic, Asian American, White, Native American, Other. We might indicate African American by the value 1, Hispanic by the value 2, and the like, but these numbers do not tell us anything about the difference between ethnic groups except that they are different. Hispanic is not one unit more of ethnicity than African American, nor is it twice as much ethnicity. The numbers simply represent a category.

> **Nominal level of measurement** Variables whose values have no mathematical interpretation: they vary in kind or quality, but not in amount.

Nominal-level variables are commonplace in social work research. Client characteristics such as marital status (e.g., Married, Widowed, Divorced,

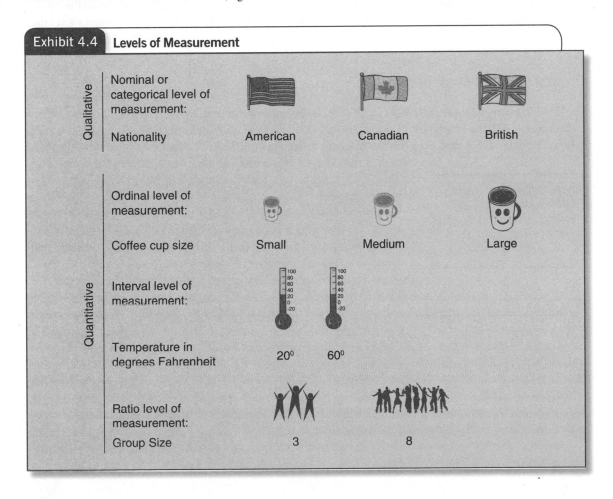

Exhibit 4.4 **Levels of Measurement**

Qualitative

Nominal or categorical level of measurement:

Nationality · American · Canadian · British

Quantitative

Ordinal level of measurement:

Coffee cup size · Small · Medium · Large

Interval level of measurement:

Temperature in degrees Fahrenheit · 20° · 60°

Ratio level of measurement:

Group Size · 3 · 8

Sepaated, Never Married) or mental health diagnosis (e.g., Mood Disorder, Personality Disorder, Other Disorder) are nominal-level variables. Program-related variables such as referral source or types of services used are nominal variables. In each case, the variables have a set of categories whose order has no meaning.

> **Mutually exclusive** A variable's attributes or values are mutually exclusive when every case can be classified as having only one attribute or value.
>
> **Exhaustive** Every case can be classified as having at least one attribute (or one value) for the variable.

Although the attributes of categorical variables do not have a mathematical meaning, they must be assigned to cases with great care. The attributes we use to categorize cases must be mutually exclusive and exhaustive:

- A variable's attributes or values are **mutually exclusive** if every case can have only one attribute.

- A variable's attributes or values are **exhaustive** when every case can be classified into one of the categories.

When a variable's attributes are mutually exclusive and exhaustive, every case corresponds to one and only one attribute. We know this sounds pretty straightforward, and in many cases it is. However, what we think of as mutually exclusive and exhaustive categories may really be so only because of social convention; when these conventions change, appropriate classification at the nominal level can become much more complicated. The Census Bureau has come to recognize that measuring "race" is not so straightforward (see *Research in the News*).

The only mathematical operation we can perform with nominal-level variables is a count. We can count how many clients last month were females and how many were males. From that count, we can calculate the percentage or proportion of females to males among our clients. If the agency served 150 women and 100 men, then we can say that 60% of the clients were female. But we cannot identify an average gender, nor can we add or subtract or compute any other kind of number.

Ordinal Level of Measurement

The first of the three quantitative levels is the **ordinal level of measurement.** At this level, the numbers assigned to cases specify only the order of the cases, permitting *greater than* and *less than* distinctions. The gaps between the various responses do not have any particular meaning. As with nominal variables, the different values of a variable measured at the ordinal level must be mutually exclusive and exhaustive. They must cover the range of observed values and allow each case to be assigned no more than one value.

> **Ordinal level of measurement** A measurement of a variable in which the numbers indicating a variable's values specify only the order of the cases, permitting greater than and less than distinctions.

The properties of variables measured at the ordinal level are illustrated in Exhibit 4.4 by the contrast among cup sizes at a coffee shop. You might choose between a small, medium, or large cup of coffee—that is ordinal measurement. The categories represent relative cup sizes but the gaps between the various responses do not have any particular meaning whether in quantity or in price.

A common ordinal measure used in social service agencies is a single question about client satisfaction. Often agencies will ask a client a global question about satisfaction with the services provided by the agency, using a rating system such as 4 = *very satisfied*, 3 = *satisfied*, 2 = *dissatisfied*, and 1 = *very dissatisfied*. Someone who responds *very satisfied*, coded as 4, is clearly more satisfied than someone who responds *dissatisfied*, coded as 2, but the person responding with a 4 is not twice as satisfied as the person responding with a 2. Nor is the person responding *very satisfied* (4) two units more satisfied than the person responding *dissatisfied* (2). We only know that the first person is more satisfied than the second person, and therefore the order has meaning. We can count the number of clients who fall into each category. We can also compute an average satisfaction, but the average is not a quantity of satisfaction; rather, the number summarizes the relative position of the group on the given scale.

Agencies sometimes use goal attainment scales to measure the progress of a client in achieving a particular goal. These scales are usually developed by describing the worst indicators, the best indicators, and several steps between.

The gap between the steps has no meaning, but the scoring represents the progress of the client. Exhibit 4.5 provides an example of a goal attainment scale to measure self-esteem and mother's attitude toward children. The social worker evaluates the extent to which there is improvement in self-esteem based on the nature of the verbal and nonverbal responses of the client. There is an order to the levels of achievement, and we can describe how many clients fall into each category.

Interval Level of Measurement

The values of a variable measured at the **interval level of measurement** represent fixed measurement units but have no absolute or fixed zero point. An interval level of measurement also has mutually exclusive categories, the categories are exhaustive, and there is an order to the responses. Further, the gaps between the numbers of the scale are meaningful; a one-unit difference is the same at any point in the scale. This level of measurement is represented in Exhibit 4.4 by the difference between two Fahrenheit temperatures. Because the gaps between numbers are equal, the gap between 60 degrees and 30 degrees is actually 30, but 60 in this case is not twice as hot as 30. Why not? Because heat does not begin at 0 degrees on the Fahrenheit scale. More broadly, the zero value on an interval scale does not indicate the complete absence of the measured variable.

> **Interval level of measurement** A measurement of a variable in which the numbers indicating a variable's values represent fixed measurement units but have no absolute, or fixed, zero point.

There are few true interval-level measures in social work, but many social work researchers treat scales created by combining responses to a series of ordinal-level variables as interval-level measures. Frequently, this is done because there are more mathematical operations associated with interval-level variables. For example, a scale of this sort could be created with responses to Attkisson's Client Satisfaction Questionnaire (CSQ; see Exhibit 4.6 for the CSQ-8). While each question is ordinal, researchers often treat the scores obtained from summing the eight items as an interval-level measure.

Exhibit 4.5	**Example of a Goal Attainment Scale**			
Problem Area	**Client Outcome Goal**	**No Achievement**	**Some Achievement**	**Major Achievement**
Self-esteem	To develop increased feeling of self-esteem	Makes only negative statements Does not identify strengths No verbal expression of confidence No sense of self-worth	Some positive statements Some negative statements Can identify some strengths but overly critical about self Emerging confidence Emerging self-worth	Makes many positive statements Few to no negative statements Can identify strengths without qualifying statements Is confident Has self-worth
Mother's attitude toward child	Less of a negative attitude toward child	Resists child's affection Constantly shows anger verbally and nonverbally Constantly shows frustration Constantly shows hostility Constantly inpatient	Occasional affection Occasional anger Occasional frustration Occasional hostility Occasional impatience	Accepts child's affection No verbal or nonverbal signs of anger, hostility, or frustration Patient

---

Exhibit 4.6 | **Example of an Interval-Level Measure: Client Satisfaction Questionnaire (CSQ-8)**

Circle your answer:

1. How would you rate the quality of service you have received?

4	3	2	1
Excellent	Good	Fair	Poor

2. Did you get the kind of service you wanted?

1	2	3	4
No, definitely	No, not really	Yes, generally	Yes, definitely

3. To what extent has our program met your needs?

4	3	2	1
Almost all of my needs have been met	Most of my needs have been met	Only a few of my needs have been met	None of my needs have been met

4. If a friend were in need of similar help, would you recommend our program to him or her?

1	2	3	4
No, definitely not	No, I don't think so	Yes, I think so	Yes, definitely

5. How satisfied are you with the amount of help you have received?

1	2	3	4
Quite dissatisfied	Indifferent or mildly dissatisfied	Mostly satisfied	Very satisfied

6. Have the services you received helped you to deal more effectively with your problems?

4	3	2	1
Yes, they helped a great deal	Yes, they helped	No, they really didn't help	No, they seemed to make things worse

7. In an overall, general sense, how satisfied are you with the service you received?

4	3	2	1
Very satisfied	Mostly satisfied	Indifferent or mildly dissatisfied	Quite dissatisfied

8. If you were to seek help again, would you come back to our program?

1	2	3	4
No, definitely not	No, I don't think so	Yes, I think so	Yes, definitely

Source: EVALUATION AND PROGRAM PLANNING by Daniel Larsen, C. Clifford Attkisson, William A. Hargreaves, Tuan D. Nguyen. Copyright 1979 by Elsevier Science & Technology Journals. Reproduced with permission of Elsevier Science & Technology Journals.

Ratio Level of Measurement

Ratio level of measurement A measurement of a variable in which the numbers indicating a variable's values represent fixed measuring unit and an absolute zero point.

The numbers indicating the values of a variable measured at the **ratio level of measurement** represent fixed measuring units with an absolute zero point; in this case, zero means absolutely no amount of whatever the variable indicates. Exhibit 4.4 displays an example of a variable measured at the ratio level. The number of people in the first group is 3, and the number in the second group is 8. The ratio of the two groups' sizes is then 2:67, a number that mirrors the relationship between the sizes of the groups. Note that there does not actually have to be any group with a size of 0; what is important is that the numbering scheme begins at an absolute zero—in this case, the absence of any people.

Ratio-level variables are common in social work practice and research. We can report to supervisors the number of clients in a program, the time spent providing counseling, or the number of hot meals delivered to homebound elderly. We can describe a community by the number of community development organizations, the number of abandoned buildings, or the number of afterschool programs. In each case, the answer zero is meaningful, representing the complete absence of the variable.

Researchers often treat the interval and ratio levels of measurement as equivalent. In addition to having numerical values, both the interval and ratio levels also involve continuous measures: The numbers indicating the values of variables are points on a continuum, not discrete categories. Despite these similarities, there is an important difference between variables measured at the interval and ratio levels. On a ratio scale, 10 is 2 points higher than 8 and is also 2 times greater than 5. Ratio numbers can be added and subtracted; because the numbers begin at an absolute zero point, they can be multiplied and divided (so ratios can be formed between the numbers). For example, people's ages can be represented by values ranging from 0 years (or some fraction of a year) to 120 or more. A person who is 30 years old is 15 years older than someone who is 15 years old ($30 - 15 = 15$) and is twice as old as that person ($30/15 = 2$). Of course, the numbers also are mutually exclusive, are exhaustive, have an order, and there are equal gaps.

The Case of Dichotomies

Dichotomies, variables having only two values, are a special case from the standpoint of levels of measurement. The values or attributes of a variable such as depression clearly vary in kind or quality, not in amount. Thus, the variable is categorical—measured at the nominal level. Yet in practical terms, we can think of the variable in a slightly different way, as indicating the presence of the attribute *depressed* or *not depressed*. Viewed in this way, there is an inherent order: A depressed person has more of the attribute (it is present) than a person who is not depressed (the attribute is not present). We are likely to act given the presence or absence of that attribute; we intervene or refer to treatment a depressed client, whereas we would not do so with a client who was not depressed. Nonetheless, although in practical terms there is an order empirically we treat a dichotomous variable as a nominal variable.

Types of Comparisons

Exhibit 4.7 summarizes the types of comparisons that can be made with different levels of measurement, as well as the mathematical operations that are legitimate. Each higher level of measurement allows a more precise mathematical comparison to be made between the values measured at that level compared with those measured at a lower level. However, each comparison between cases measured at lower levels can also be made about cases measured at higher levels. Thus, all four levels of measurement allow researchers to assign different values to different cases. All three quantitative measures allow researchers to rank cases in order.

Researchers choose levels of measurement in the process of operationalizing the variables; the level of measurement is not inherent in the variable. Many variables can be measured at different levels with different procedures. A variable to describe alcoholic drinking can be measured by asking respondents to identify how many alcoholic drinks they had in the last week, a ratio variable, or answer the same question by checking *None, 1 to 4, 5 to 9, or 10 or more*, an ordinal variable. A nominal variable about drinking could be created by simply asking, Did you consume any alcoholic drink in the last week" with response categories *yes* or *no*.

It is a good idea to try to measure variables at the highest level of measurement possible if doing so does not distort the meaning of the concept that is to be measured. The more information available, the more ways we have to compare cases. There are more possibilities for statistical analysis with quantitative than with qualitative variables. Further, you

| Exhibit 4.7 | Properties of Measurement Levels | | | | |

Examples of comparison statements	Appropriate math operations	Relevant level of measurement			
		Nominal	Ordinal	Interval	Ratio
A is equal to (not equal to) B	= . . .	o	o	o	o
A is greater than (less than) B	> (<)		o	o	o
A is two more than (less than) B	+ (−)			o	o
A is twice (half) as large as B	× (÷)				o

can create ordinal or nominal variables from ratio-level variables, but you cannot go in the reverse direction. If you know the actual number of alcoholic drinks, you can combine the reports into categories at a later time, but if you ask respondents to check the category, you cannot later modify that variable to reflect the actual number of drinks consumed.

Be aware that other considerations may preclude measurement at a high level. For example, many people are reluctant to report their exact incomes even in anonymous questionnaires. So asking respondents to report their income in categories (e.g., less than $10,000, $10,000–19,999, $20,000–29,999) will result in more responses, and thus more valid data, than asking respondents for their income in dollars.

Oftentimes, researchers treat variables measured at the interval and ratio levels as comparable. They then refer to this as the interval-ratio level of measurement. You will learn in Chapter 14 that different statistical procedures are used for variables with fixed measurement units, but it usually does not matter whether there is an absolute zero point.

⊞ Measurement Error

No matter how carefully we operationalize and design our measures, no measure is perfect, and there will be some error. It might be that the measurement instrument needs to be corrected or reevaluated. Sometimes people are simply inconsistent in the way that they respond to questions. For example, the U.S. Census Bureau's Survey of Income and Program Participation 1984 Panel included data collected nine times, with 4 months between interviews. Using this data set, Engel (1988) completed a study on poverty and aging. One of the questions dealt with marital status, seemingly an easy question to answer and one that should provide consistent responses. It turned out that a portion of the sample, primarily women, kept moving from divorced to widow and sometimes back to divorced. On reflection, this made sense because, among members of this cohort of older adults (born between 1900 and 1919), divorce was a less acceptable social status than being a widow.

In gathering data, we get a response from the participant, this response being the reported score. The reported score is not necessarily the true score or the true response because of the imperfections of measurement. The true response differs from the reported response because of measurement error, of which there are two types: systematic error and random error.

Systematic error is generally considered to be a predictable error, in that we can predict the direction of the error. Think about weighing yourself on a scale each day. If you put a scale on a particular part of the floor in your house, you will always weigh less (reported score) than you actually do (true score). The direction of the error is predictable; your scale will always underreport your true weight.

Systematic error Error due to a specific process that biases the results.

There are different forms of systematic error, some of which we detail in later chapters, but each of these forms of systematic error reflects some bias:

- *Social desirability*. Social desirability bias occurs when respondents wish to appear most favorable in the eyes of the interviewer or researcher. For example, in the 1980s, polling information about elections between African American Democratic candidates and White Republican candidates typically showed larger victory margins anticipated for the Democratic candidate than actually occurred in the election. One factor was the unwillingness of White Democrats to admit they were unwilling to vote for an African American, even of the same political party, as this would have made the respondents appear less favorable in the eyes of the interviewer.

- *Acquiescence bias*. There is a tendency for some respondents to agree or disagree with every statement, regardless of whether they actually agree.

- *Leading questions*. Leading questions have language that is designed to influence the direction of a respondent's answer. There are many different ways in which this might be done. You might encounter words that have a negative connotation in society (regardless of the reason). For example, during the 1980s, the use of the words *liberal* and *welfare* began to take on negative connotations. So a question like "Do you support the liberal position on . . . ?" is meant to lead people to disagree with the position. Another form of a leading question is to use the names of controversial people in the question. A third way of evoking certain responses is simply to include some responses to a question in the actual question, but not all the responses.

- *Differences in subgroup responses according to gender, ethnicity, or age*. Differences in cultural beliefs or patterns, socialization processes, or cohort effects may bias findings from what otherwise might be a set of neutral questions.

To avoid systematic error requires careful construction of scales and questions and the testing of these questions with different population groups. We explore these methods in depth in Chapter 9.

> **Random error** Errors in measurement that are due to chance and are not systematic in any way.

Unlike systematic error, **random error** is unpredictable in terms of its effects. Random error may be due to the way respondents are feeling that particular day. Respondents may be fatigued, bored, or not in a cooperative mood, or they may be having a great day. Respondents may also be affected by the conditions of the testing. The lighting may be bad, the room may be noisy, the seating may be cramped, the lack of walls in the cubicle may mean other people can hear, there may be other people in the room, or they may not like the looks of the person gathering the information.

Another form of random error is *regression to the mean*. This is the tendency of people who score very high on some measure to score less high the next time or for people who score very low to score higher. What might have influenced the high or low score on the first test may not operate in the second test.

Random error might occur when researchers rating behaviors are not adequately trained to do the rating. For example, two people grading an essay test might come up with different grades if they have not discussed the grading criteria beforehand. A field supervisor and a student might assess a client differently given the variation in their years of experience.

As we have already said, the effects of random error cannot be predicted: Some responses overestimate the true score, whereas other responses underestimate the true score. Many researchers believe that if the sample size is sufficiently large, the effects of random error cancel each other out. Nonetheless, we want to use measurement scales and questions that are stable to minimize the effects of random error as much as possible.

⊞ Assessing Measurement Accuracy

Do the operations to measure our variables provide stable or consistent responses—are they *reliable?* Do the operations developed to measure our concepts actually do so—are they *valid?* Why are these questions important? When we test the effectiveness of two different interventions or when we monitor a client's progress, we want the changes we observe to be due to the intervention and not to the instability or inaccuracy of the measurement instrument. We also want to know that the measure we use is really a measure of the outcome and not a measure of some other outcome. We cannot have much confidence in a measure until we have empirically evaluated its reliability and validity.

Reliability

Reliability means that a measurement procedure yields consistent or equivalent scores when the phenomenon being measured is not changing. If a measure is reliable, it is affected less by random error or chance variation than if it is unreliable. Reliability is a prerequisite for measurement validity: We cannot really measure a phenomenon if the measure we are using gives inconsistent results. In fact, because it usually is easier to assess reliability than validity, you are more likely to see an evaluation of measurement reliability in a research report than an evaluation of measurement validity.

> **Reliability** A criterion to assess the quality of scales based on whether the procedure yields consistent scores when the phenomenon being measured is not changing.

Test-Retest Reliability

When researchers measure a phenomenon that does not change between two points separated by an interval of time, the degree to which the two measurements are related to each other is the **test–retest reliability** of the measure. If you take a test of your research methodology knowledge and retake the test 2 months later, the test is performing reliably if you receive a similar score both times—presuming that nothing happened during the 2 months to change your research methodology knowledge. We hope to find a correlation between the two tests of about .7 and prefer even a higher correlation, such as .8.

> **Test–retest reliability** It is demonstrated by showing that the same measure of a phenomenon at two points in time is highly correlated, assuming that the phenomenon has not changed.
>
> **Testing effect** Measurement error related to how a test is given; the conditions of the testing, including environmental conditions; and acclimation to the test itself.

Of course, if events between the test and the retest have changed the variable being measured, then the difference between the test and retest scores should reflect that change. As the gap in time between the two tests increases, there is a greater likelihood that real change did occur. This also presumes that you were not affected by the conditions of the testing: a **testing effect**. The circumstances of the testing, such as how you were given the test, or environmental conditions, such as lighting or room temperature, may impact test scores. A testing effect may extend to how you felt the first time you took the test; because you did not know what to expect the first time, you may have been very nervous, as opposed to the second time, when you knew what to expect.

Radloff's (1977) initial effort to evaluate the test–retest reliability of the CES-D highlights the difficulties that may emerge from the testing and that make interpreting the scores problematic. A probability sample of households was taken in one county; within each household, one person 18 years or older was randomly chosen to participate in an interview. Each person was also asked to complete and mail back a CES-D scale either 2, 4, 6, or 8 weeks after the initial interview. Only 419 of the initial 1,089 respondents sent back mail questionnaires. The test–retest correlations were moderately high, ranging from .51 at 2 weeks to .59 at 8 weeks. Radloff offered a variety of explanations about the moderate correlations, which included such methodological problems as the bias introduced by nonresponse (maybe those who responded differed from those who did not respond), the problem of using an interview at Time 1 and a self-administered questionnaire for the follow-up (perhaps people responded differently to the interviewer than to the questionnaire), and the effects of being tested twice. Furthermore, she noted that the CES-D was meant to capture depressive symptoms in a 1-week period, and perhaps there had been real changes. This example illustrates how test–retest reliability scores may potentially be affected by real change or by the effect of testing.

Internal Consistency

When researchers use multiple items to measure a single concept, they are concerned with **internal consistency**. For example, if the items composing the CES-D (like those in Exhibit 4.3) reliably measure depressive symptoms, the answers to the questions should be highly associated with one another. The stronger the association among the individual items and the more items that are included, the higher the reliability of the scale.

One method to assess internal consistency is to divide the scale into two parts, or **split-half reliability**. We might take a 20-item scale, such as the CES-D, and sum the scores of the first 10 items, sum the scores of the second 10 items (items 11–20), and then correlate the scores for each of the participants. If we have internal consistency, we should have a fairly high correlation, such as .8 or .9. This correlation typically gets higher the more items there are in the scale. So what may be considered a fairly high split-half reliability score for a 6-item scale might not be considered a high score for a 20-item scale.

There are countless ways in which you might split the scale, and in practical terms, it is nearly impossible to split the scale by hand into every possible combination. The speed of computers allows us to calculate a score that indeed splits the scale in every combination. A summary score, such as **Cronbach's alpha coefficient**, is the average score of all the possible split-half combinations. In Radloff's (1977) study, the Cronbach's alpha coefficients of different samples were quite high, ranging from .85 to .90.

> **Internal consistency** An approach to reliability based on the correlation among multiple items used to measure a single concept.
>
> **Split-half reliability** Reliability achieved when responses to the same questions divided into two randomly selected halves are about the same.
>
> **Cronbach's alpha** A statistic commonly used to measure internal reliability. It is the average correlation of all the possible ways to divide a scale in half.

Alternate-Forms Reliability

Researchers are testing **alternate-forms reliability** (or parallel-forms reliability) when they compare subjects' answers to slightly different versions of survey questions (Litwin, 1995). A researcher may reverse the order of the response choices in a scale, modify the question wording in minor ways, or create a set of different questions. The two forms are then administered to the subjects. If the two sets of responses are not too different, alternate-forms reliability is established. You might remember taking the SATs or ACTs when you were in high school. When you compared questions with your friends, you found that each of you had taken different tests. The developers had assessed the tests using alternate-forms reliability to ensure that the different forms were equivalent and comparable.

> **Alternate-forms reliability** A reliability procedure in which participants' answers are compared with participants' responses to slightly different versions of the questions.

Interrater Reliability

When researchers use more than one observer to rate the same people, events, or places, **interrater reliability** is their goal. If observers are using the same instrument to rate the same phenomenon, their ratings should be similar. If they are similar, we can have much more confidence that the ratings reflect the phenomenon being assessed rather than the orientations of the observers.

Assessments of interrater reliability may be based on the correlation of the rating between two raters. Two raters could evaluate the quality of play between five teenage mothers and their children on a 10-point scale. The correlation would show whether the direction of the raters' scores was similar as well as how close the agreement was for the relative position for each of the five scores. One rater may judge the five mothers as 1, 2, 3, 4, and 5, whereas the second rater scores the mothers as 6, 7, 8, 9, and 10. The correlation would be quite high—in fact, the correlation would be perfect. But as demonstrated by this example, the agreement about the quality of the interactions was quite different. So an alternative method is to estimate the percentage of exact agreement between the two raters. In this case, the rater agreement is zero.

> **Interrater reliability** The degree of agreement when similar measurements are obtained by different observers rating the same people, events, or places.

Assessing interrater reliability is most important when the rating task is complex. Consider a commonly used measure of mental health, the Global Assessment of Functioning Scale (GAF). The rating task seems straightforward, with clear descriptions of the subject characteristics that are supposed to lead to high or low GAF scores. However, the judgments that the rater must make while using this scale are complex. They are affected by a wide range of subject characteristics, attitudes, and behaviors, as well as by the rater's reactions. As a result, interrater agreement is often low on the GAF unless the raters are trained carefully.

Intrarater Reliability

Intrarater reliability occurs when a single observer is assessing an individual at two or more points in time. It differs from test–retest reliability in that the ratings are done by the observer as opposed to the subjects. Intrarater reliability is particularly important when you are evaluating a client's behavior or making judgments about the client's progress. Although the GAF has been found to have low interobserver reliability, it has been found to have pretty high intraobserver reliability. It turns out that although different raters disagree, a single rater tends to provide consistent reports about an individual.

> **Intrarater reliability** Consistency of ratings by an observer of an unchanging phenomenon at two or more points in time.

Measurement Validity

Validity refers to the extent to which measures indicate what they are intended to measure. Technically, a valid measure of a concept is one that is (a) closely related to other apparently valid measures of the concept, (b) closely related to the known or supposed correlates of that concept, and (c) not related to measures of unrelated concepts (adapted from Brewer & Hunter, 2005). Measurement validity is assessed with four different approaches: face validation, content validation, criterion validation, and construct validation.

Face Validity

Researchers apply the term **face validity** to the confidence gained from careful inspection of a measure to see whether it is appropriate "on its face." A measure is face valid if it obviously pertains to the meaning of the concept being measured more than to other concepts (Brewer & Hunter, 2005). For example, a count of how many drinks people consumed in the past week would be a face-valid measure of their alcohol consumption.

> **Face validity** The type of validity that exists when an inspection of items used to measure a concept suggests that they are appropriate "on their face."

Although every measure should be inspected in this way, face validation does not provide convincing evidence of measurement validity. The question, "How much beer or wine did you have to drink last week?" looks valid on its face as a measure of frequency of drinking, but people who drink heavily tend to underreport the amount they drink. So the question would be an invalid measure in a study that includes heavy drinkers.

Content Validity

Content validity establishes that the measure covers the full range of the concept's meaning. To determine that range of meaning, the researcher may solicit the opinions of experts and review literature that identifies the different aspects or dimensions of the concept.

An example of an alcoholism measure that covers a wide range of meaning is the MAST. The MAST includes 24 questions representing the following subscales: recognition of alcohol problems by self and others; legal, social, and work problems; help seeking; marital and family difficulties; and liver pathology (Skinner & Sheu, 1982). Many experts familiar with the direct consequences of substance abuse agree that these dimensions capture the full range of possibilities. Thus, the MAST is believed to be valid from the standpoint of content validity.

> **Content validity** The type of validity that exists when the full range of a concept's meaning is covered by the measure.

Content validity is an important step in developing measures and assessing measures. However, like face validity, content validity is a subjective assessment of validity and, therefore, is a weaker form of validity than the next two types of validity, which are based on empirical assessments.

Criterion Validity

Criterion validity is established when the scores obtained on one measure are similar to scores obtained with a more direct or already validated measure of the same phenomenon (the criterion). The criterion that researchers select can be measured either at the same time as the variable to be validated or after that time. **Concurrent validity** exists when a measure yields scores that are closely related to scores on a criterion measured at the same time. A measure of blood-alcohol concentration or a urine test could serve as the criterion for validating a self-report measure of drinking as long as the questions we ask about drinking refer to the same period. A measure of walking speed based on mental counting might be validated concurrently with a stop watch. **Predictive validity** is the ability of a measure to predict scores on a criterion measured in the future. For example, SAT or ACT scores could be compared to academic success in college. In each of these cases, the measure is being compared to some criterion believed to measure the same construct.

Criterion validation is well worth the effort because it greatly increases confidence that the measure is measuring what was intended. It is a stronger form of validity than face or content validity as it is based on empirical evidence rather than subjective assessment.

> **Criterion validity** The type of validity established by comparing the scores obtained on the measure being validated to scores obtained with a more direct or already validated measure of the same phenomenon (the criterion).
>
> **Concurrent validity** The type of validity that exists when scores on a measure are closely related to scores on a criterion measured at the same time.
>
> **Predictive validity** The type of validity that exists when a measure predicts scores on a criterion measured in the future.

Construct Validity

Construct validity is demonstrated by showing that a measure is related to a variety of other measures as specified in a theory. This theoretical construct validation process relies on using a deductive theory with hypothesized relationships among the constructs (Koeske, 1994). The measure has construct validity (or theoretical construct validity) if it "behaves" as it should relative to the other constructs in the theory. For example, Danette Hann, Kristin Winter, and Paul Jacobsen (1999) compared subject scores on the CES-D to a number of indicators that they felt from previous research and theory should be related to depression: fatigue, anxiety, and global mental health. The researchers found that individuals with higher CES-D scores tended to have more problems in each of these areas, giving us more confidence in the CES-D's validity as a measure.

A somewhat different approach to construct validation is **discriminant validity**. In this approach, scores on the measure to be validated are compared to scores on another measure of the same variable and to scores on variables that measure different but related concepts. Discriminant validity is achieved if the measure to be validated is related most strongly to its comparison measure and less so to the measures of other concepts. The CES-D would demonstrate discriminant validity if the scale scores correlated strongest with the Beck Depression Inventory (a validated scale to measure depression) and correlate lower with the Beck Anxiety Inventory (a validated scale to measure anxiety).

Convergent validity is achieved when you can show a relationship between two measures of the same construct that are assessed using different methods (Koeske, 1994). For example, we might compare the CES-D scale scores to clinical judgments made by practitioners who have used a clinical protocol. The CES-D scores should correlate with the scores obtained from the clinical protocol.

> **Construct validity** The type of validity that is established by showing that a measure is related to other measures as specified in a theory.
>
> **Discriminant validity** An approach to construct validity; the scores on the measure to be validated are compared to scores on another measure of the same variable and to scores on variables that measure different but related concepts. There is discriminant validity if the measure to be validated is related most strongly to the comparison measure and less strongly to the measures of other concepts.
>
> **Convergent validity** The type of validity achieved when one measure of a concept is associated with different measures of the same concept.

Known-groups validity Demonstrating the validity of a measure using two groups with already-identified characteristics.

Factorial validity A form of construct validity used to determine if the scale items relate correctly to different dimensions of the concept.

Another approach to construct validity is referred to as **known-groups validity**. In this method, we might have two groups with known characteristics, and we compare our measure across these two groups. We would expect that our measure should score higher with the group that it is related to and lower with the unrelated group. For example, we might give the CES-D to a group of people who have been clinically diagnosed as depressed and to a group that does not have a clinical diagnosis of depression. We would expect the CES-D scores to be higher among those clinically depressed than those who have no clinical diagnosis.

Finally, another method that has become associated with construct validity is **factorial validity**. This approach relies on factor analysis and, in many ways, is simply an empirical extension of content analysis. This procedure is usually applied when the construct of interest has different dimensions. In the analysis, we look to see whether the items thought to be measuring the same dimension are more highly related to each other than to items measuring other dimensions. The CES-D scale has been hypothesized to have four dimensions: negative affect, positive affect (lack), somatic symptoms, and interpersonal. Several items are associated with each dimension. Therefore, a factor analysis would test whether the items measuring negative affect are more highly related to each other than to items measuring somatic symptoms. Negative affect items such as *feeling blue, sad, depressed*, and the like should have stronger relationships to each other than to items measuring somatic symptoms such as *overeating, sleeping too much*, or *difficulty concentrating*. A test of factorial validity would assess the expected internal theoretical relationships of the construct.

The distinction between criterion and construct validation is not always clear. Opinions can differ about whether a particular indicator is indeed a criterion for the concept that is to be measured. Koeske (1994) suggests that a key difference is simply that with criterion validity, "the researcher's primary concern is with the criterion in a practical context, rather than with the theoretical properties of the construct measure" (p. 50). What if you want to validate a question-based measure of the amount of social support that people receive from their friends? Should you just ask people about the social support they have received? Could friends' reports of the amount of support they provided serve as a criterion? Are verbal accounts of the amount of support provided adequate? What about observations of social support that people receive? Even if you could observe people in the act of counseling or otherwise supporting their friends, can an observer be sure that the interaction is indeed supportive? There is not really a criterion here, just related concepts that could be used in a construct validation strategy.

What construct and criterion validation have in common is the comparison of scores on one measure to scores on other measures that are predicted to be related. It is not so important that researchers agree that a particular comparison measure is a criterion rather than a related construct. But it is very important to think critically about the quality of the comparison measure and whether it actually represents a different view of the same phenomenon.

Ways to Improve Reliability and Validity of Existing Measures

A reliable measure is not necessarily a valid measure, as Exhibit 4.8 illustrates. This discrepancy is a common flaw of self-report measures of substance abuse. Most respondents answer questions in a consistent way, so the scales are reliable. However, a number of respondents will not admit to drinking even though they drink a lot. Their answers to the questions are consistent, but they are consistently misleading. So the scales based on self-report are reliable, but invalid. Unfortunately, many measures are judged to be worthwhile on the basis only of a reliability test.

The reliability and validity of measures in any study must be tested after the fact to assess the quality of the information obtained. If it turns out that a measure cannot be considered reliable and valid, little can be done to save the study. Hence, it is important to select in the first place measures that are likely to be reliable and valid. Consider the different strengths of different measures and their appropriateness to your study. Conduct a pretest in which you use the measure with a small sample and check its reliability. Provide careful training to ensure a consistent approach if interviewers or observers will administer the measure. However, in most cases, the best strategy is to use measures that have been used before and whose reliability and validity have been established in other contexts. But the selection of

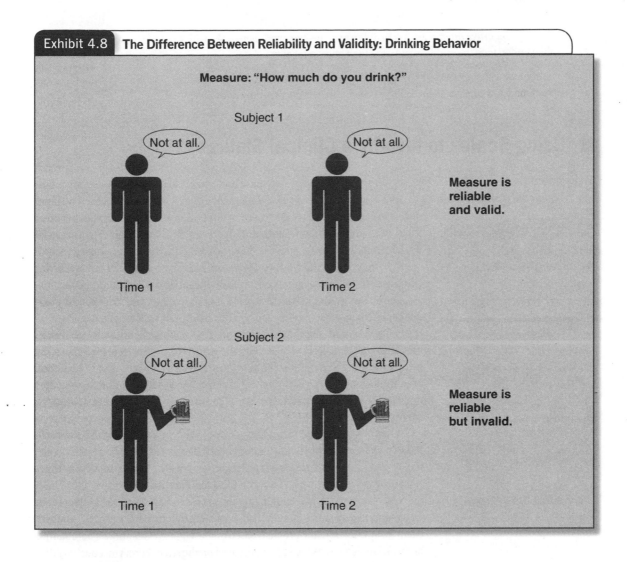

Exhibit 4.8 The Difference Between Reliability and Validity: Drinking Behavior

tried and true measures still does not absolve researchers from the responsibility of testing the reliability and validity of the measure in their own studies.

When the population studied or the measurement context differs from that in previous research, instrument reliability and validity may be affected. So the researchers must take pains with the design of their study. For example, test–retest reliability has proved to be better for several standard measures used to assess substance use among homeless people when the interview was conducted in a protected setting and when the measures focused on factual information and referred to a recent time interval (Drake, McHugo, & Biesanz, 1995). Subjects who were younger, female, recently homeless, and less severely afflicted with psychiatric problems were also more likely to give reliable answers.

If the research focuses on previously unmeasured concepts, new measures will have to be devised. Researchers can use one of three strategies to improve the likelihood that new question-based measures will be reliable and valid (Fowler, 1995):

1. *Engage potential respondents in group discussions about the questions to be included in the survey.* This strategy allows researchers to check for consistent understanding of terms and to hear the range of events or experiences that people will report.

2. *Conduct cognitive interviews.* Ask people a test question, and then probe with follow-up questions about how they understood the question and what their answer meant.

3. *Audiotape test interviews during the pretest phase of a survey.* The researchers then review these audiotapes and systematically code them to identify problems in question wording or delivery.

⊞ Using Scales to Identify a Clinical Status

Many scales do not just measure the range or intensity of some phenomenon, but are also used as screening methods to make educated guesses about the presence or absence of some clinical condition. The CES-D has been used not only to measure the level of depressive symptoms, but also to determine whether someone might suffer from depression. Scores on the CES-D scale can range from 0 to 60; people with scores above 16 may be classified as depressed, whereas people below 16 may be classified as not depressed. This score a called a **cut-off score** and is used to define the presence or absence of a particular condition.

Cut-off scores should be as accurate as possible. If not, we risk expending limited resources on what may turn out to be an inaccurate assessment, we risk missing individuals with the condition, and we risk labeling clients with a condition they might not actually have. Typically, the validity of a cut-off score is assessed by comparing the scale's classifications to an established clinical evaluation method or to an already-known condition. For example, the MAST cut-off score might be evaluated against a urinalysis. The CES-D cut-off score might be compared with a clinical diagnosis using the *DSM-5*.

A summary of the analysis of the validity of a cut-off is presented in Exhibit 4.9. If the cut-off score provides an accurate assessment, there should be a high proportion of cases classified as either a **true negative** (cell a) or a **true positive** (cell d). A true negative occurs when, based on the scale, the client is assessed as not having a problem and really does not have the problem. A true positive occurs when it is determined from the obtained scale score that the client has a problem and the client really does have the problem based on the clinical evaluation. There should be few **false negatives** (cell b) when, based on the scale score, you conclude that the client does not have the problem, but the client really does have the problem, and few **false positives** when you conclude from the scale score that the client does have a significant problem, but in reality that person does not have the problem.

Researchers use different measures to establish the validity of the cut-off score. **Sensitivity** describes the true positive cell. It is a proportion based on the number of people who are assessed as having the condition (d) relative to the number of people who actually have the condition, (b + d); that is, d/(b + d). **Specificity** describes the true negative cell. It is a proportion based on the number of people assessed as not having a condition (cell a) relative to the number who really do not have the condition (a + c); its mathematical formula is a/(a + c). False-negative rates and false-positive rates are similarly calculated.

Ideally, we would like both the sensitivity and specificity of the scale's cut-off scores to be very high so that we make few mistakes. Yet there are trade-offs. To identify all the true positives, the cut-off score would need to be eased; in the case of the CES-D, it would need to be lowered. This will increase sensitivity, but will also likely result in more false positives, which means a lower specificity. Making it

Cut-off score A score used in a scale to distinguish between respondents with a particular status and respondents who do not have that status.

True negative When it is determined from a screening instrument score that the participant does not have a particular status and the participant really does not have the status based on a clinical evaluation.

True positive When it is determined from a screening instrument score that the participant does have a particular status and the participant really does have the status based on a clinical evaluation.

False negative The participant does not have a particular problem according to a screening instrument, but the participant really does have the problem based on a clinical evaluation.

False positive The participant has a particular problem according to a screening instrument but in reality does not have the problem based on a clinical evaluation.

Sensitivity The proportion of true positives based on the number of people assessed as having a diagnosis by a screening instrument to the number of people who actually have the diagnosis.

Specificity The proportion of true negatives based on the number of people assessed as not having a diagnosis by a screening instrument relative to the number of people who really do not have the diagnosis.

Exhibit 4.9	**Outcomes of Screening Scale Versus Clinical Assessment**			
	Actual Diagnosis for the Clinical Condition			
Screening Scale Result	Client does not have clinical condition	Client has clinical condition	Total	
Assessed as not having condition	True negative (a)	False negative (b)	a + b	
Assessed as having the condition	False positive (c)	True positive (d)	c + d	
Total	a + c	b + d		

more difficult to test positive, for example, by setting a higher cut-off score, will increase the specificity, but will produce more false negatives, and the sensitivity score will decline.

Two other types of estimates you will see are the positive predictive value and the negative predictive value. The positive predictive value is the proportion of people who actually have the condition (d) compared to the number who were assessed by the screening tool as having the condition (c + d); that is, d/(c + d). The negative predictive value is the proportion of all those who actually do not have the condition (a) compared to all those who were assessed as having the condition (a + b); that is, a/(a + b). The ability to predict accurately is useful when we decide to use a screening scale to get some sense of how prevalent a particular condition is in the community. So if we wanted to assess how common depression is in the community, we would want high predictive values.

🏛 Measurement in a Diverse Society

Throughout this chapter, we have suggested that measurement is crucial not just for research, but for every aspect of social work practice. Whether a researcher is examining the prevalence of alcohol abuse in the community or a social worker is assessing substance abuse with a client, it is important to use the best available method. Although it is crucial to have evidence of reliability and validity, it is important that such evidence cut across the different populations served by social workers. Often people of color, women, the poor, and other groups have not been adequately represented in the development or testing of various measurement instruments (S. Witkin, 2001). Just because a measure appears valid does not mean that you can assume cross-population generalizability.

It is reasonable to consider whether the concepts we use have universal meaning or differ across cultures or other groups. C. Harry Hui and Harry C. Triandis (1985) suggest that four components must be evaluated to determine whether a concept differs across cultures:

1. *Conceptual equivalence.* The concept must have the same meaning, have similar precursors and consequences, and relate to other concepts in the same way.

2. *Operational equivalence.* The concept must be evident in the same way so that the operationalization is equivalent.

3. *Item equivalence.* Items used must have the same meaning to each culture.

4. *Scaler equivalence.* The values used on a scale mean the same in intensity or magnitude.

Take the concept *self-esteem.* Bae and Brekke (2003) note that cross-cultural research has found that Asian Americans typically have lower self-esteem scores than other ethnic groups. They hypothesized that Korean

Americans would have lower scores on positively worded items than other ethnic groups but would have similar scores on negatively worded items. They suggested that this response pattern would be due to culture: "Giving high scores on the positive items is intrinsically against their collective culture in which presenting the self in a self-effacing and modest manner is regarded as socially desirable behavior to maintain social harmony" (p. 28). Bae and Brekke did find that overall self-esteem scores were lower among Korean Americans and that it was due to Korean Americans scoring lower on the positively worded items while scoring the same or higher than other ethnic groups on the negatively worded items.

Similar concerns have been noted for scales measuring depression. For example, Joy Newmann (1987) has argued that gender differences in levels of depressive symptoms may reflect differences in the socialization process of males and females. She suggests that some scales ask questions about items such as crying, being lonely, and feeling sad, which are more likely to be responded to in the affirmative by women and not by men because men are socialized to not express such feelings. More recent studies have found similar gender differences in response patterns (S. R. Cole, Kawachi, Maller, & Berkman, 2000; Sigmon et al., 2005). Similarly, Debra Ortega and Cheryl Richey (1998) note that people of color may respond differently to questions used in depression scales. Some ethnic groups report feelings of sadness or hopelessness as physical complaints and therefore have high scores on these questions, but low scores on emotion-related items. Different ethnic groups respond differently to "how do you feel" questions and "what do you think" questions. Ortega and Richey also note that some items in depression scales, such as suicidal ideation, are not meaningful to some ethnic groups. The elderly are more likely to endorse some items that also measure physical changes as opposed to changes brought about by depression (Sharp & Lipsky, 2002).

Scores impacted by response bias can result in practical problems. For example, many scales include cut-off scores to demonstrate the presence or absence of a condition. If there is a response bias, the result could be the treatment of a condition that does not exist or not identifying a condition that does exist (Bae & Brekke, 2003). The failure to measure correctly may affect the ability to identify effective interventions. The relationship of different phenomena may be distorted because of measurement bias. Therefore, it is important to assess the samples used for validation and to use measures that have been validated with the population group to whom it will be administered.

🔲 Measurement Implications for Evidence-Based Practice

Measurement is an essential ingredient in social work practice, whether it is your assessment of a client or your monitoring and evaluation of your practice. Further, the studies you review depend, in part, on the quality of the measurement; systematic errors can negate the validity of a particular study (Johnston, Sherer, & Whyte, 2006). You need to be confident that the evidence presented is due to the intervention and not the instability of the measurement instrument.

What should you consider when you examine the efficacy of a measure for your agency? In the previous sections, we have stressed the importance of measurement reliability and validity. That alone is insufficient because there should be evidence of the appropriateness of the measure for the population with whom it will be used. Therefore, when you review research about the reliability and validity of a measure, you need to look at the samples that were used in the studies. Too often these studies are done without consideration of gender, race, ethnicity, or age. It may be that the samples used in the studies look nothing like the population you are serving. If that is the case, the instrument may not be appropriate for your agency or setting.

The same holds true for scales that can be used for diagnostic purposes; there should be statistical evidence that the scale is accurate in its determination of correct diagnoses (true positives and true negatives) with few incorrect diagnoses (false positives and false negatives; Warnick, Weersing, Scahill, & Woolston, 2009). Earlier, we described the CES-D as a commonly used scale with a more or less acceptable cut-off score of 16. On further inspection, researchers found that this score was too low to be useful with the elderly. Some item reports in the CES-D can be due to physical conditions that are common among the elderly. As a result, an appropriate cut-off score for elderly people with physical ailments has been determined to be 20 (Schein & Koenig, 1997). The bottom line is to take nothing for granted about cut-off scores described in the literature.

Of course, you should also keep in mind practical considerations in selecting a measurement scale. These considerations include:

- *Administration of the scale.* Different methods of administration require different amounts of time to complete, as well as skill to gather the data. For example, self-report takes less time than interviewing the client.

- *Cost.* The instrument should be affordable. Many useful measures and scales can be found in the public domain, but many other scales have to be purchased, and sometimes you must also pay for their scoring.

- *Sensitivity to change.* The measure you use should be sufficiently sensitive to pick up changes in the desired outcome and there should be a sufficient number of items that you are able to identify changes.

- *Reactivity.* To the extent possible, you want nonreactive measures, that is, measures that do not influence the responses that people provide.

- *Acceptability.* The measures have to be accepted by staff as measures that will provide valid information

All of these were considerations we had to take into account when we were asked by a family service agency's senior adult unit to recommend a short and simple screen for pathological gambling. The agency uses a 25- to 30-minute psychosocial assessment at intake, screening for a variety of social, economic, health, and mental health concerns, so it did not want something that would add terribly to the length of the assessment. At the same time, the agency wanted something that would be accurate, easy to use, and not offend its older clients. Ultimately, we found a reliable and valid two-item screen that could be added to the intake assessment.

Just as there are systematic reviews of intervention research, you may find systematic reviews of different measurement and screening instruments. For example, Henry O'Connell and his colleagues (2004) recently reviewed self-report alcohol screening instruments for older adults, and Warnick and colleagues (2009) reviewed measures to predict youth mental health.

As you read intervention research or other types of research studies or you develop a research proposal, there are important questions for you to consider. You should identify the major concepts in the study and assess whether the measure is clearly defined. Next, you should examine how the concepts are operationalized. Is the operational definition sufficient to capture the various dimensions of the concept? When scales are used, is there evidence of reliability and validity as well as the scale's appropriateness for the specific study population? Our confidence in the measure is enhanced when the author reports methods used to enhance reliability of the measure, such as the specific training in collecting the information, or using multiple measures.

▣ Conclusion

Remember always that measurement validity is a necessary foundation for social work research. Gathering data without careful conceptualization or conscientious efforts to operationalize key concepts often is a wasted effort. The difficulties of achieving valid measurement vary with the concept being operationalized and the circumstances of the particular study.

Planning ahead is the key to achieving valid measurement in your own research; careful evaluation is the key to sound decisions about the validity of measures in others' research. Statistical tests can help to determine whether a given measure is valid after data have been collected, but if it appears after the fact that a measure is invalid, little can be done to correct the situation. If you cannot tell how key concepts were operationalized when you read a research report, don't trust the findings. If a researcher does not indicate the results of tests used to establish the reliability and validity of key measures, remain skeptical.

Key Terms

Highlights

- Conceptualization plays a critical role in research. In deductive research, conceptualization guides the operationalization of specific variables; in inductive research, it guides efforts to make sense of related observations.

- Concepts may refer to either constant or variable phenomena. Concepts that refer to variable phenomena may be similar to the actual variables used in a study, or they may be much more abstract.

- Concepts should have a nominal definition and an operational definition. A nominal definition defines the concept in terms of other concepts, whereas the operational definition provides the specific rules by which you measure the concept.

- The intervention is often a variable requiring an operational definition that describes the intervention in detail.

- Scales measure a concept by combining answers to several questions and thereby reducing idiosyncratic variation. Several issues should be explored with every intended scale: Does each question actually measure the same concept? Does combining items in a scale obscure important relationships between individual questions and other variables? Is the scale multidimensional?

- Measures are not perfect, and there may be two types of measurement error. Systematic error refers to predictable error and should be minimized. Random error is unpredictable in terms of effect on measurement.

- Level of measurement indicates the type of information obtained about a variable and the type of statistics that can be used to describe its variation. The four levels of measurement can be ordered by complexity of the mathematical operations they permit: nominal (least complex), ordinal, interval, and ratio (most complex). The measurement level of a variable is determined by how the variable is operationalized. Dichotomies, a special case, may be treated as measured at the nominal level.

- Measurement reliability is a prerequisite for measurement validity, although reliable measures are not necessarily valid. Reliability can be assessed through a test–retest procedure, in terms of interitem consistency, through a comparison of responses to alternate forms of the test, or in terms of consistency among observers and in one observer over time.

- The validity of measures should always be tested. There are four basic approaches: face validation, content validation, criterion validation (either predictive or concurrent), and construct validation. Criterion validation provides strong evidence of measurement validity, but there often is no criterion to use in validating social science measures.

- Some scales are used to screen for the presence or absence of a clinical condition and, therefore, use cut-off scores. The accuracy of cut-off scores is assessed using measures of sensitivity and specificity.

- In examining studies of measurement reliability and validity, it is important to look at the samples to ensure that there is evidence of reliability and validity for different population subgroups.

Discussion Questions

1. Describe the relationship between a nominal definition and an operational definition of a concept. How are these two types of definitions related?

2. What does "global assessment of functioning" mean to you? What behaviors would you look for to assess global assessment of functioning? Identify two such behaviors. What questions would you ask to measure global assessment of functioning? Create a scale by writing five questions with response choices. How would you assess the reliability and validity of your scale?

3. If you were given a questionnaire right now that asked you about your use of alcohol and illicit drugs in the past year, would you disclose the details fully? How do you think others would respond? What if the questionnaire was anonymous? What if there was a confidential ID number on the questionnaire so that the researcher could keep track of who responded? What criterion validation procedure would you suggest for assessing measurement validity?

Practice Exercises

1. a. Provide nominal and operational definitions for any of the following concepts: self-esteem, school stress, child abuse, and alcohol abuse.

    b. Write down two observable behaviors that you believe would provide feasible measures of the concept you have chosen.

    c. Develop a scale by generating some questions that could serve as indicators for the concept you have chosen.

    d. Outline a plan to assess the validity and reliability of the behavior measures and the scale.

2. Find a research study that uses a scale to measure some concept. How does the author justify the reliability and validity of the scale? Does the author convince you that the scale can be applied to the sample in the study?

3. In the study chosen in Exercise 2, what are the variables? What is the level of measurement for each variable?

Web Exercises

1. How would you define alcoholism? Write a brief definition. Based on this conceptualization, describe a method of measurement that would be valid for a study of alcoholism.

2. Now go to the American Council for Drug Education and read some facts about alcohol (www.acde.org/common/alcohol2.pdf). Is this information consistent with the definition you developed for Question 1?

Developing a Research Proposal

At this point, you can begin the process of conceptualization and operationalization.

1. Identify the concepts you will use in the study. Provide a nominal definition for each concept. When possible, this definition

should come from the existing literature—either a book you have read for a course or a research article.

2. How will the concepts be operationalized? Identify the variables you will use to study the research question. Which of

these are independent or dependent variables? What is the level of measurement for each variable? How will these variables be coded?

3. Develop measurement procedures, or identify existing instruments that might be used. If you are using a new measure, what procedures will you use to determine the reliability and validity of the measure? If you are using an existing instrument, report the evidence for the instrument's reliability and validity.

A Question of Ethics

1. Why is it important that the reliability and validity of any scale be evaluated with different populations?

CHAPTER 5

Sampling

A common technique in journalism is to put a "human face" on a story. For instance, a reporter for the *New York Times* went to an emergency assistance unit near Yankee Stadium to ask homeless mothers about new welfare policies that require recipients to work. One woman with three children suggested, "If you work a minimum wage job, that's nothing. . . . Think about paying rent, with a family." In contrast, another mother with three children remarked, "It's important to do it for my kids, to set an example."

These are interesting comments, but we do not know whether they represent the opinions of most homeless people in the United States, in New York City, or even in the emergency assistance unit near Yankee Stadium. Even if the reporter had interviewed 10 homeless single mothers with children, we would not know how representative their opinions were. Because we have no idea whether these opinions are widely shared or unique, we cannot really judge what they tell us about the impact of welfare reform on single mothers. We would not want to develop programs to help single mothers based on these two comments alone. In other words, we do not know whether these comments are generalizable.

This same concern applies to social work research. Perhaps you read a research study about the effectiveness of a cognitive-behavioral treatment for adolescent boys with depression and you wonder whether the treatment might work with the adolescent boys in your unit. Perhaps your agency collects information from key community stakeholders about the most prevalent community needs, and you think that residents might have a different perspective. These are issues of generalizability. How we choose people from whom to gather information (or households, organizations, or even something as mundane as client records) has ramifications for the conclusions that we make. Are the findings true for only those who provided the information, or can the findings from some sample be generalized to the population from which the sample was drawn? This is really the most basic question to ask about a sample.

Although we think of sampling as something limited to research, it is an important part of the overall functioning and evaluation of social service programs. When an agency is trying to demonstrate the effectiveness of services to a funding organization such as the United Way, the director may choose to use a smaller group of clients to make the case. When a community organizer is trying to learn about the needs of older adults in a particular neighborhood, he or she may ask different people in the neighborhood, but probably will not ask everybody; therefore, a sample of some sort is being used.

In this chapter, you will learn about sampling methods—the procedures that primarily determine the generalizability of research findings. We first review the rationale for using sampling in social work research. Next, we describe specific sampling methods and when they are most appropriate. We introduce the concept of sampling distribution and explain how it helps in estimating our degree of confidence in statistical generalizations. Finally, we discuss strategies for recruiting diverse populations. By the chapter's end, you should understand the questions you need to ask to evaluate the generalizability of a study as you consider the evidence base of the findings as well as the choices you need to make when designing a sampling strategy.

⊞ Sample Planning

You have encountered the problem of generalizability in each of the studies you have read about in this book. Whether we are designing a sampling strategy or evaluating the generalizability of someone else's findings, we have to understand how and why researchers decide to sample and what the consequences of these decisions are for the generalizability of the findings.

Although sampling is common in research, it is not always necessary. Often the decision to take a sample of a population depends on the size of that population and/or the purpose of the study. If the population is small and it is feasible to contact everyone in the population, there is no need to sample. If a program in an agency saw only 100 clients and the director wants feedback about client satisfaction, there is no need to take a sample. The population is sufficiently small that it would not take a great deal of time or the expenditure of a large amount of resources to try to obtain the information from all 100 clients. In addition, if there is no desire or interest in generalizing the findings to a broader population, there is no need to take a sample.

Define Sample Components and the Population

Let's say that we are designing a study of a topic that involves a lot of people (or other entities such as households, agencies, or communities). We often do not have the time or resources to study the entire **population**, that is, the entire set of individuals (or other entities) in which we are interested. Therefore, we decide to study a **sample**, a subset of the population of interest. The individual members or other entities of the sample are called **elements**.

In many studies, we sample directly from the elements in the population of interest. We may survey a sample of the entire population of students at a school based on a list obtained from the registrar's office. This list from which the elements of the population are selected is termed the **sampling frame**. The students who are selected and interviewed from that list are the elements. Sampling frames or lists come from a variety of sources, such as state maltreatment report registries (Leiter, 2007), Temporary Assistance for Needy Families recipients registered by the state (Sullivan, Larrison, Nackerud, Risler, & Bodenschatz, 2004), social workers licensed by a state department (D. Cole, Panchanadeswaran, & Daining, 2004), or social service agencies compiled by a human service consortium (Engel, Rosen, Weaver, & Soska, 2010).

In some studies, it is not easy to access the elements from which we want information, but we can find a group that includes those elements. For example, we may have a list of households in a town but not a list of its entire adult population, even though the adults are the elements we actually want to sample. In this situation, we could draw a sample of households and then identify the adult individuals in these households. The households are termed **enumeration units**, and the adults in the households are the elements (Levy & Lemeshow, 2008).

> **Population** The entire set of individuals or other entities to which study findings are to be generalized.
>
> **Sample** A subset of a population that is used to study the population as a whole.
>
> **Elements** The individual members of the population whose characteristics are to be measured.
>
> **Sampling frame** A list of all elements or other units containing the elements in a population.
>
> **Enumeration units** Units that contain one or more elements and that are to be listed in a sampling frame.
>
> **Sampling units** Units listed at each stage of a multistage sampling design.

Sometimes the individuals or other entities from which we collect information are not actually the elements in our study. For example, a researcher who wants to obtain information about child welfare programs might sample child welfare agencies for a survey and then interview a sample of staff within each of the sampled organizations. The child welfare agencies and the staff are both termed **sampling units** because we sample from both (Levy & Lemeshow, 2008). The child welfare agencies are selected in the first stage, so they are the *primary sampling units*, and in this case they are also the elements in the study. The staff are *secondary sampling units*, but they are not elements, although they do provide information about the entire organization (see Exhibit 5.1).

It is important to know how the population is defined. Surveys of older adults may reasonably be construed as including individuals over the age of 65, but always be alert to ways in which the population may have been narrowed or expanded by the sample selection procedures. If a researcher used a list provided by the American Association for Retired Persons, *older* would be defined as ages 50 and above. In other surveys, older adults living in institutions such as skilled nursing homes or personal care homes are often excluded. Sometimes age is capped so that only people ages 65 to 84 are surveyed. In each survey, the sample is based on a somewhat different population. The population for a study is the aggregation of elements that we actually focus on and sample from, not some larger aggregation that we really wish we could have studied.

Some populations, such as the homeless, are not identified by a simple criterion such as a geographic boundary or an organizational membership. If we are interested in the needs of homeless people we would require a clear definition of *homeless*. Such a definition is difficult, but quite necessary, since anyone should be able to determine just what population was actually studied. However, studies of homeless people in the early 1980s "did not propose definitions, did not use screening questions to be sure that the people they interviewed were indeed homeless, and did not make major efforts to cover the universe of homeless people" (Burt, 1996, p. 15). The result was "a collection of studies that could not be compared" (Burt, 1996, p. 15). Several studies of homeless people in urban areas addressed the problem by employing a more explicit definition of the population: "People are homeless if they have no home or permanent place to stay of their own (renting or owning) and no regular arrangement to stay at someone else's place" (Burt, 1996, p. 18). Even this

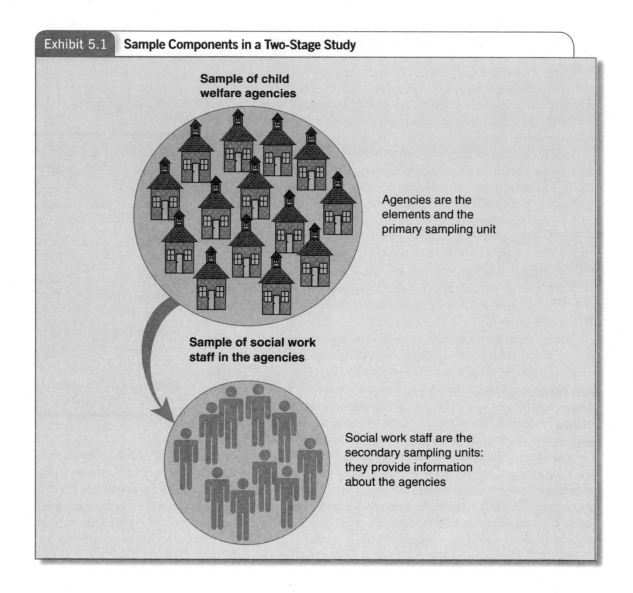

Exhibit 5.1   Sample Components in a Two-Stage Study

Sample of child welfare agencies

Agencies are the elements and the primary sampling unit

Sample of social work staff in the agencies

Social work staff are the secondary sampling units: they provide information about the agencies

more explicit definition is insufficient as it requires answers to: What is a *regular arrangement*? How permanent does a *permanent place* have to be?

Evaluate Generalizability

Once we have defined clearly the population from which we will sample, we need to determine the scope of the generalizations we will seek to make from our sample. Do you recall from Chapter 1 two different meanings of *generalizability*?

- *Can the findings from a sample of the population be generalized to the population from which the sample was selected*? Did Solari and colleagues' (2014) findings apply to all homeless? This type of generalizability was defined as sample generalizability.

- *Can the findings from a study of one population be generalized to another, somewhat different population*? Are homeless people in Pittsburgh similar to those in other states? This type of generalizability was defined as cross-population generalizability.

Sample generalizability depends on sample quality, which is determined by the amount of **sampling error**—the differences between the characteristics of a sample and the characteristics of the population from which it was selected. The larger the sampling error, the less representative the sample—and thus, the less generalizable the findings. To assess sample quality when you are planning or evaluating a study, ask yourself these questions:

> **Sampling error** Any difference between the characteristics of a sample and the characteristics of a population.
>
> **Target population** A set of elements larger than or different from the population sampled and to which the researcher would like to generalize study findings.

- From what population were the cases selected?

- What method was used to select cases from this population?

- Do the cases that were studied represent, in the aggregate, the population from which they were selected?

Cross-population generalizability involves quite different considerations. Researchers are engaged in cross-population generalizability when they project their findings onto groups or populations much larger than, or simply different from, those they have actually studied. The **target population** is a set of elements larger than or different from the population that was sampled and to which the researcher would like to generalize any study findings. When we generalize findings to target populations, we must be somewhat speculative. We must carefully consider the validity of claims that the findings can be applied to other subgroups of the population, geographic areas, cultures, or times.

Assess the Diversity of the Population

Sampling is unnecessary if all the units in the population are identical. Physicists do not need to select a representative sample of atomic particles to learn about basic physical processes. They can study a single atomic particle because it is identical to every other particle of its type. Similarly, biologists do not need to sample a particular type of plant to determine whether a given chemical has toxic effects on that particular type.

What about people? The social world and the people in it are just too diverse to be considered identical units. In the past, researchers assumed that psychological and social processes were similar and generalizations could be made. The problem with this assumption is that there is no way to know for sure whether the processes being studied are identical across all people. Generalizing the results of single experiments and intervention studies is risky because such research often studies a small number of people who do not represent any particular population.

The larger point is that social work researchers as well as other social scientists rarely can skirt the problem of demonstrating the generalizability of their findings. If a small sample has been studied in a particular agency, in an experiment, or in a field research project, the study should be replicated in different settings or, preferably, with a **representative sample** of the population to which generalizations are sought (see Exhibit 5.2). Community- and agency-based studies have produced good social work research, but they need to be replicated in other settings with other subjects in order to claim generalizability.

> **Representative sample** A sample that "looks like" the population from which it was selected in all respects that are potentially relevant to the study. The distribution of characteristics among the elements of a representative sample is the same as the distribution of those characteristics among the total population. In an unrepresentative sample, some characteristics are overrepresented or underrepresented.

Sampling Methods

Certain features of samples make them more or less likely to represent the population from which they are selected. The most important distinction to be made is whether the samples are based on a probability or nonprobability sampling method. Probability sampling methods allow us to know in advance how likely it is that any element of a population will be selected for the sample. Sampling methods that do not let us know the likelihood in advance are termed nonprobability sampling methods.

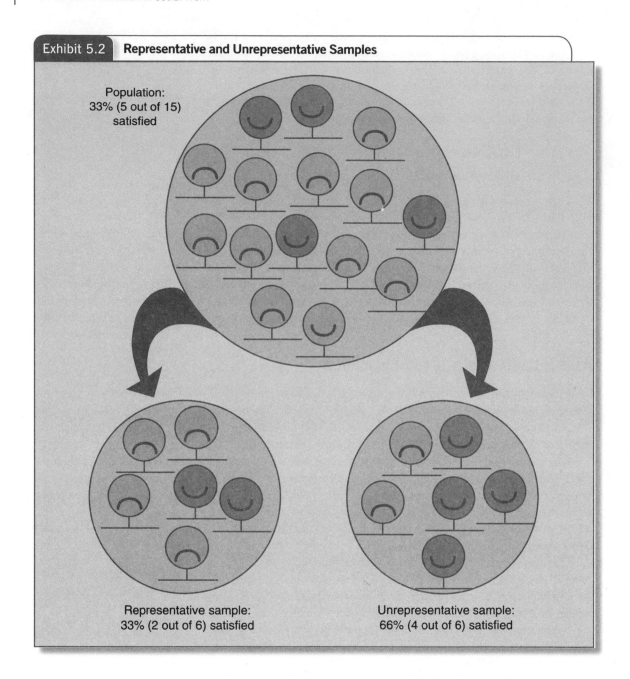

Exhibit 5.2 **Representative and Unrepresentative Samples**

Population:
33% (5 out of 15)
satisfied

Representative sample:
33% (2 out of 6) satisfied

Unrepresentative sample:
66% (4 out of 6) satisfied

Probability Sampling

Probability sampling methods are used when we want to be able to generalize the results to the broader population. Because these methods are based on probability theory, we can estimate the extent to which the sample is actually representative of the broader population.

Probability sampling methods rely on **random sampling**, that is, a random selection procedure in which elements are selected only on the basis of chance. In principle, it is the same as flipping a coin to decide which of two people wins and which one loses. Heads and tails are equally likely to turn up

Random sampling A sampling method that relies on a random or chance selection method so that every element of the sampling frame has a known probability of selection.

Research In the NEWS

For Further Thought **?**

WHAT ARE THE BEST PRACTICES FOR SAMPLING VULNERABLE POPULATIONS?

In the 1950s, Perry Hudson studied the effectiveness of early prostate screening in reducing cancer. He sampled 1,200 alcoholic homeless men from the flophouses of Lower Manhattan. His research was funded and supported by the National Institutes of Health, but he did not properly inform participants of the risks associated with prostate screening. Many men who participated endured a painful prostate biopsy and no medical follow-up if they screened positive for cancer. Robert Aronowitz, a medical historian, looks back at this ethical tragedy as a "convenient population" used in the name of science.

1. Since this time, research standards have been changed to protect vulnerable populations, In what circumstances do you think that it is ethical to draw samples for research from prisoners, patients, students, and other "captive" populations that are convenient to study?

2. Should samples of large populations, exclude person who suffer from mental illness, addiction, extreme poverty, limited literacy, or other conditions that might make them less likely to make a fully informed decision about participation in research? Are there any risks with such exclusions?

Source: Kolata (2013, p. A1).

in a coin toss, so both people have an equal chance to win. That chance, their **probability of selection**, is 1 out of 2, or .5.

Flipping a coin is a fair way to select one of two people because the selection process harbors no **systematic bias**; nothing but chance determines which elements are included in the sample. You might win or lose the coin toss, but you know that the outcome was due simply to chance, not to bias. For the same reason, a roll of a six-sided die is a fair way to choose one of six possible outcomes (the odds of selection are 1 out of 6, or .17). Dealing out a hand after shuffling a deck of cards is a fair way to allocate sets of cards in a card game (the odds of each person getting a particular outcome, such as a full house or a flush, are the same). Similarly, state lotteries use a random process to select winning numbers. Thus, the odds of winning a lottery, the probability of selection, are known, although they are much smaller (perhaps 1 out of 1 million) than the odds of winning a coin toss.

There is a tendency to confuse the concept of random sampling, in which cases are selected only on the basis of chance, with a *haphazard* method of sampling. Leaving things up to chance seems to imply not exerting any control over the sampling method. But to ensure that nothing but chance influences the selection of cases, the researcher must proceed methodically, leaving nothing to chance except the selection of the cases. The researcher must follow carefully controlled procedures if a purely random process is to occur.

When reading about sampling methods in research journals or papers, do not assume that a random sample was obtained just because the researcher used a random selection method at some point in the sampling process. Two particular problems are issues of concern: selecting elements from an incomplete list of the total population and failing to obtain an adequate response rate.

Probability of selection The likelihood that an element will be selected from the population for inclusion in the sample. In a census of all the elements of a population, the probability that any particular element will be selected is 1.0. If half the elements in the population are sampled on the basis of chance (say, by tossing a coin), the probability of selection for each element is one half, or .5. As the size of the sample as a proportion of the population decreases, so does the probability of selection.

Systematic bias Overrepresentation or underrepresentation of some population characteristics due to the method used to select the sample.

If the sampling frame is incomplete, a sample selected randomly from that list will not really be a random sample of the population. You should always consider the adequacy of the sampling frame. Even for a simple population like a university's student body, the registrar's list is likely to be at least a bit out of date at any given time. For example, some students will have dropped out, but their status will not yet be officially recorded. Although you may judge the amount of error introduced in this particular situation to be negligible, the problems are greatly compounded for a larger population. The sampling frame for a city, state, or nation is always likely to be incomplete because of constant migration into and out of the area. Omissions from the sampling frame can bias a sample against particular groups within the population.

An inclusive sampling frame may still yield systematic bias if many sample members cannot be contacted or refuse to participate. Nonresponse is a major hazard in survey research because nonrespondents are likely to differ systematically from those who take the time to participate. You should not assume that findings from a randomly selected sample will be generalizable to the population from which the sample was selected if the rate of nonresponse is considerable (certainly not if it is much above 30%).

Probability Sampling Methods

Probability sampling methods are those in which the probability of selection is known and is not zero, so there is some chance of selecting each element. These methods randomly select elements and therefore have no systematic bias; nothing but chance determines which elements are included in the sample. This feature of probability samples makes them much more desirable than nonprobability samples when the goal is to generalize to a larger population.

> **Probability sampling methods** Sampling methods that rely on a random or chance selection method so that the probability of selection of population elements is known.

Although a random sample has no systematic bias, it will certainly have some sampling error due to chance. The probability of selecting heads is .5 in a single toss of a coin and in 20, 30, and however many tosses of a coin you like. But it is perfectly possible to toss a coin twice and get heads both times. The random sample of the two sides of the coin is selected in an unbiased fashion, but it still is unrepresentative. Imagine selecting randomly a sample of 10 clients from an agency program that includes 50 men and 50 women. Just by chance, you find that these 10 clients include 7 women and only 3 men. The sample was selected in an unbiased fashion but is unrepresentative of the population. Fortunately, we can determine mathematically the likely degree of sampling error in an estimate based on a random sample (as we discuss later in this chapter)—assuming that the sample's randomness has not been destroyed by a high rate of nonresponse or by poor control over the selection process.

In general, both the size of the sample and the homogeneity (sameness) of the population affect the degree of error due to chance. Specifically

- *The larger the sample, the more confidence we can have in the sample's representativeness.* If we randomly pick five people to represent the entire population of our city, our sample is unlikely to be representative of the entire population in terms of age, gender, race, attitudes, and so on. But if we randomly pick 100 people, the odds of having a representative sample are much better; with a random sample of 1,000, the odds become very good indeed.

- *The more homogeneous the population, the more confidence we can have in the representativeness of a sample of any particular size.* Let's say we plan to draw samples of 50 from each of two communities to estimate mean family income. One community is diverse, with family incomes varying from $12,000 to $85,000. In the other, more homogeneous community, family incomes are concentrated in a narrow range, from $41,000 to $64,000. The estimated mean family income based on the sample from the homogeneous community is more likely to be representative than is the estimate based on the sample from the more heterogeneous community. With less variation to represent, fewer cases are needed to represent the homogeneous community.

- *The fraction of the total population that a sample contains does not affect the sample's representativeness unless that fraction is large.* The number of cases is more important than the proportion of the population represented by the sample. We can regard any sampling fraction less than 2% with about the same degree of confidence (Sudman, 1976). In fact, sample representativeness is not likely to increase much until the sampling fraction is quite a bit higher. Other things being equal, a sample of 1,000 from a population of 1 million (with a sampling fraction of 0.001, or 0.1%) is much better than a sample of 100 from a population of 10,000 (although the sampling fraction is 0.01, or 1%, which is 10 times higher). The size of the sample is what makes representativeness more likely, not the proportion of the whole that the sample represents.

Polls to predict presidential election outcomes illustrate both the value of random sampling and the problems that it cannot overcome. In most presidential elections, pollsters have predicted accurately the outcome of the actual vote by using random sampling and, these days, phone interviewing to learn which candidate likely voters intend to vote for. Exhibit 5.3 shows how close these sample-based predictions have been in the past 10 contests. In the 2012 presidential

| Exhibit 5.3 | Election Outcomes: Predicted[1] and Actual | |

Winner/Year	Final Poll	Result
Kennedy (1960)	51%	50%
Johnson (1964)	64%	61%
Nixon (1968)[2]	43%	43%
Nixon (1972)	62%	62%
Carter (1976)	48%	50%
Reagan (1980)[2]	47%	51%
Reagan (1984)	59%	59%
Bush (1988)	56%	54%
Clinton (1992)[2]	49%	43%
Clinton (1996)[2]	52%	50%
Bush, G. W. (2000)[2]	48%	50%
Bush, G. W. (2004)[2]	49%	51%
Obama (2008)	55%	53%
Obama (2012)	49%	51%

Source: Gallup Poll (2013). Election Polls—Accuracy Record in Presidential Elections. Retrieved August 5, 2013, from www.Gallup.com/poll/9442/Election-Polls-Accuracy-Record-Presidential-Elections.aspx.

[1] Final Gallup poll prior to the election.

[2] There was also a third-party candidate.

election, the final poll came within 2% of the vote for President Obama. The exceptions to accurate prediction were the 1980 and 1992 elections, when third-party candidates had an unpredicted effect. Otherwise, the small discrepancies between the votes predicted through random sampling and the actual votes can be attributed to random error.

Nevertheless, election polls have produced some major errors in prediction. The reasons for these errors illustrate some of the ways in which unintentional systematic bias can influence sample results. In 1936, a *Literary Digest* poll predicted that Alfred M. Landon would defeat President Franklin D. Roosevelt in a landslide, but instead, Roosevelt took 63% of the popular vote. The problem? The *Digest* mailed out 10 million mock ballots to people listed in telephone directories, automobile registration records, voter lists, and so on. But in 1936, the middle of the Great Depression, only relatively wealthy people had phones and cars, and they were more likely to be Republican. Furthermore, only 2,376,523 completed ballots were returned, and a response rate of only 24% leaves much room for error. Of course, this poll was not designed as a random sample, so the appearance of systematic bias is not surprising. Gallup was able to predict the 1936 election results accurately with a randomly selected sample of just 3,000 (Bainbridge, 1989).

In 1948, pollsters mistakenly predicted that Thomas E. Dewey would beat Harry S. Truman based on the random sampling method that George Gallup had used successfully since 1934. The problem? Pollsters stopped collecting data several weeks before the election, and in those weeks, many people changed their minds (Kenney, 1987). So the sample was systematically biased by underrepresenting shifts in voter sentiment just before the election.

Because they do not disproportionately exclude or include particular groups within the population, random samples that are successfully implemented avoid systematic bias in the selection process. However, when some types of people are more likely to refuse to participate in surveys or are less likely to be available for interviews, systematic bias can still creep into the sampling process. In addition, random error will still influence the specific results obtained from any random sample.

The likely amount of random error will also vary with the specific type of random sampling method as we explain in the next sections. The four most common methods for drawing random samples are (1) simple random sampling, (2) systematic random sampling, (3) stratified random sampling, and (4) cluster sampling.

Simple Random Sampling

Simple random sampling requires some procedure that generates numbers or otherwise identifies cases strictly on the basis of chance. As you know, flipping a coin and rolling a die both can be used to identify cases strictly on the basis of chance, but these procedures are not efficient tools for drawing a sample. A **random numbers table**, like the one in Exhibit 5.4 simplifies the process considerably. The researcher numbers all the elements in the sampling frame and then uses a systematic procedure for picking corresponding numbers from the random numbers table. (Practice Exercise 1 at the end of this chapter explains the process step by step.) Alternatively, a researcher may use a lottery procedure. Each case number is written on a small card, and then the cards are mixed up and the sample selected from the cards.

Simple random sampling A sampling method in which every sample element is selected only on the basis of chance through a random process.

Random numbers table A table containing lists of numbers that are ordered solely on the basis of chance; it is used for drawing a random sample.

When a large sample must be generated, these procedures are cumbersome. For a large sample, a computer program can easily produce a random sample of any size by generating a random selection of numbers within the desired range. Random number generators may also be found on the Internet simply by searching using *random numbers generator*.

Organizations that conduct phone surveys often draw random samples with an automated procedure called **random digit dialing** (RDD). A machine dials random numbers within the phone prefixes corresponding to the area in which the survey is to be conducted. Random digit dialing is particularly useful when a sampling frame is not available. The researcher simply replaces any inappropriate numbers (e.g., those that are no longer in service or that are for businesses) with the next randomly generated phone number.

Random digit dialing The random dialing by a machine of numbers within designated phone prefixes, which creates a random sample for phone surveys.

RDD has become more complex, as the fraction of the population that has only cell phones has increased (40% in 2013); it is essential to explicitly sample cell

Exhibit 5.4		**Random Numbers Table**											
(1)	(2)	(3)	(4)	(5)	(6)	(7)	(8)	(9)	(10)	(11)	(12)	(13)	(14)
10480	15011	01536	02011	81647	91646	69179	14194	62590	36207	20969	99570	91291	90700
22368	46573	25595	85393	30995	89198	27982	53402	93965	34095	52666	19174	39615	99505
24130	48360	22527	97265	76393	64809	15179	24830	49340	32081	30680	19655	63348	58629
42167	93093	06243	61680	07856	16376	39440	53537	71341	57004	00849	74917	97758	16379
37570	39975	81837	16656	06121	91782	60468	81305	49684	60672	14110	06927	01263	54613
77921	06907	11008	42751	27756	53498	18602	70659	90655	15053	21916	81825	44394	42880
99562	72905	56420	69994	98872	31016	71194	18738	44013	48840	63213	21069	10634	12952
96301	91977	05463	07972	18876	20922	94595	56869	69014	60045	18425	84903	42508	32307
89579	14342	63661	10281	17453	18103	57740	84378	25331	12566	58678	44947	05585	56941
85475	36857	43342	53988	53060	59533	38867	62300	08158	17983	16439	11458	18593	64952
28918	69578	88231	33276	70997	79936	56865	05859	90106	31595	01547	85590	91610	78188
63553	40961	48235	03427	49626	69445	18663	72695	52180	20847	12234	90511	33703	90322
09429	93969	52636	92737	88974	33488	36320	17617	30015	08272	84115	27156	30613	74952
10365	61129	87529	85689	48237	52267	67689	93394	01511	26358	85104	20285	29975	89868
07119	97336	71048	08178	77233	13916	47564	81056	97735	85977	29372	74461	28551	90707
51085	12765	51821	51259	77452	16308	60756	92144	49442	53900	70960	63990	75601	40719
02368	21382	52404	60268	89368	19885	55322	44819	01188	65255	64835	44919	05944	55157
01011	54092	33362	94904	31273	04146	18594	29852	71585	85030	51132	01915	92747	64951
52162	53916	46369	58586	23216	14513	83149	98736	23495	64350	94738	17752	35156	35749
07056	97628	33787	09998	42698	06691	76988	13602	51851	46104	88916	19509	25625	58104

Source: CRC Handbook of Tables for Probability and Statistics, 1979 Edition by William Beyer.

phone numbers as well as landline phone numbers (McGeeney & Keeter, 2014). Those who use cell phones only tend to be younger, more male, more single, and more likely to be African American or Hispanic compared with those who have a landline phone. As a result, failing to include cell phone numbers in a phone survey can introduce bias (Christian, Keeter, Purcell, & Smith, 2010).

The key characteristic of a true simple random sample is that the probability of selection is equal for each element. In the case of an agency audit, if a sample of 40 files is selected from a population of 600 (i.e., a sampling frame of 600), then the probability of selection for each element is 40/600, or .0667. Every element has an equal chance of being selected, just like the odds in a toss of a coin (1/2) or a roll of a die (1/6). Thus, simple random sampling is an equal probability of selection method (EPSEM).

Simple random sampling can be done either with or without replacement sampling. In replacement sampling, each element is returned to the sampling frame after it is selected so that it may be sampled again. In sampling without replacement, each element selected for the sample is then excluded from the sampling frame. In practice, it makes no difference whether sampled elements are replaced after selection as long as the population is large and the sample is to contain only a small fraction of the population. Random sampling with replacement is, in fact, rarely used.

Christopher Cambron, Christina Gringeri, and Mary Beth Vogel-Ferguson (2014) wanted to learn whether childhood experiences with emotional, physical, and sexual health was associated with subsequent physical and mental health. To answer this question, they drew a random sample of participants in a Temporary Assistance for Needy Families (TANF) program in Utah. The participants were currently active cash assistance cases who had been receiving assistance between two and nine months, and had a required employment plan. Sixty-five percent of the sample responded, and using administrative data the authors found that there were no demographic differences between respondents and nonrespondents.

Let's assess the sample quality using the questions posed earlier in the chapter:

- *From what population were the cases selected?* There is a clearly defined population: adult participants in a TANF program who met specific criteria.

- *What method was used to select cases from this population?* A random selection procedure is used so there are no systematic biases.

- *Do the cases that were studied represent, in the aggregate, the population from which they were selected?* Based on the analysis comparing respondents and nonrespondents it appears that the sample represented the population, but there may be undetermined differences particularly around the study's key variables (childhood abuse, mental and physical health). Further, any conclusions would need to be limited to participants in this particular program and to Utah alone as TANF policies vary by state.

We must also consider the findings in light of cross-population generalizability: Do findings from this sample have implications for any larger group beyond the population from which the sample was selected? Cambron and colleagues (2014) acknowledge the lack of cross-population generalizability, noting that TANF policies vary by state.

Systematic Random Sampling

Systematic random sampling is a variant of simple random sampling. The first element is selected randomly from a list or from sequential files and then every *n*th element is selected. This is a convenient method for drawing a random sample when the population elements are arranged sequentially. It is particularly efficient when the elements are not actually printed (i.e., there is no sampling frame), but instead are represented by folders in filing cabinets.

Systematic random sampling requires three steps:

> **Systematic random sampling** A sampling method in which sample elements are selected from a list or sequential files, with every nth element being selected after the first element is selected randomly with the first interval.
>
> **Sampling interval** The number of cases from sampled case to another in a systematic random sample.

1. The total number of cases in the population is divided by the number of cases required for the sample. This division yields the **sampling interval**, the number of cases between one sampled case and another. If 50 cases are to be selected out of 1,000, the sampling interval is 20; every 20th case is selected.

2. A number from 1 to 20 (or whatever the sampling interval is) is selected randomly. This number identifies the first case to be sampled, counting from the first case on the list or in the files. Alternatively, a number is selected randomly using the entire range; in this case, from 1 to 1,000. In either method, a random numbers table or a random number generator can be used to decide on a starting number.

3. After the first case is selected, every *n*th case is selected for the sample, where *n* is the sampling interval. If the sampling interval is not a whole number, you may round, but whatever the decimal is, you must round up even if the interval is 30.1. Rounding down precludes some elements from having any chance of being selected. Alternatively you may vary the size of the sampling interval to yield the proper number of cases for the sample. For example, if the sampling interval is 30.5, the sampling interval alternates between 30 and 31.

In almost all sampling situations, systematic random sampling yields what is essentially a simple random sample. The exception is a situation in which the sequence of elements is affected by *periodicity*—that is, the sequence varies in some regular, periodic pattern. For example, the houses in a new development that has the same number of houses on each block

Exhibit 5.5   The Effect of Periodicity on Systematic Random Sampling

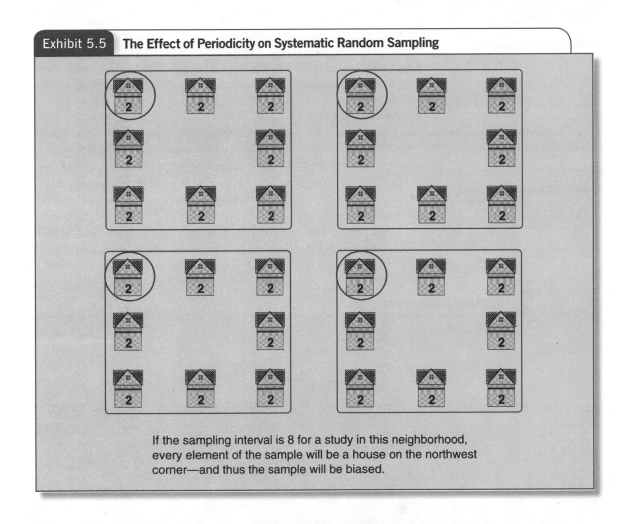

If the sampling interval is 8 for a study in this neighborhood, every element of the sample will be a house on the northwest corner—and thus the sample will be biased.

(eight, for example) may be listed by block, starting with the house in the northwest corner of each block and continuing clockwise. If the sampling interval is 8, the same as the periodic pattern, all the cases selected will be in the same position (see Exhibit 5.5). Some couples' research suffered from this problem when the couples were listed systematically by gender and an even number was used for the sampling interval. But in reality, periodicity and the sampling interval are rarely the same.

Stratified Random Sampling

Stratified random sampling uses information known about the total population prior to sampling to make the sampling process more efficient. First, all elements in the population (i.e., in the sampling frame) are distinguished according to their value on some relevant characteristic. This characteristic forms the sampling strata. For example, race may be the basis for distinguishing individuals in some population of interest. Next, elements are sampled randomly from within these strata; so within each racial category, individuals are randomly sampled. Of course, using this method requires more information prior to sampling than is the case with simple random sampling. Each element must belong to one and only one stratum and the size of each stratum in the population must be known.

> **Stratified random sampling** A method of sampling in which sample elements are selected separately from population strata that are identified in advance by the researcher.

This method is more efficient than drawing a simple random sample because it ensures appropriate representation of elements across strata. Imagine that you plan to draw a sample of 500 from an ethnically diverse neighborhood. The neighborhood population is 15% Black, 10% Hispanic, 5% Asian, and 70% White. If you drew a simple random sample, you might end up with disproportionate numbers of each group. But if you created sampling strata based on race and

Proportionate stratified sampling Sampling method in which elements are selected from strata in exact proportion to their representation in the population.

ethnicity, you could randomly select cases from each stratum: 75 Blacks (15% of the sample), 50 Hispanics (10%), 25 Asians (5%), and 350 Whites (70%). By using **proportionate stratified sampling**, you would eliminate any possibility of error in the sample's distribution of ethnicity. Each stratum would be represented exactly in proportion to its size in the population from which the sample was drawn (see Exhibit 5.6).

This was the strategy Kim Jones and Brent Benda (2004) used in a study of the factors associated with alcohol use by adolescents with non-resident fathers. Of the 21,540 students enrolled in school in a midwestern state, 33% attended schools in urban districts and 67% attended schools in rural districts. Jones and Benda (2004) stratified by rural and urban and selected participants in proportion to the population: One third of the sample came from urban settings, and two thirds came from rural settings.

Disproportionate stratified sampling Sampling in which elements are selected from strata in different proportions from those that appear in the population.

In **disproportionate stratified sampling**, the proportion of each stratum that is included in the sample is intentionally varied from what it is in the

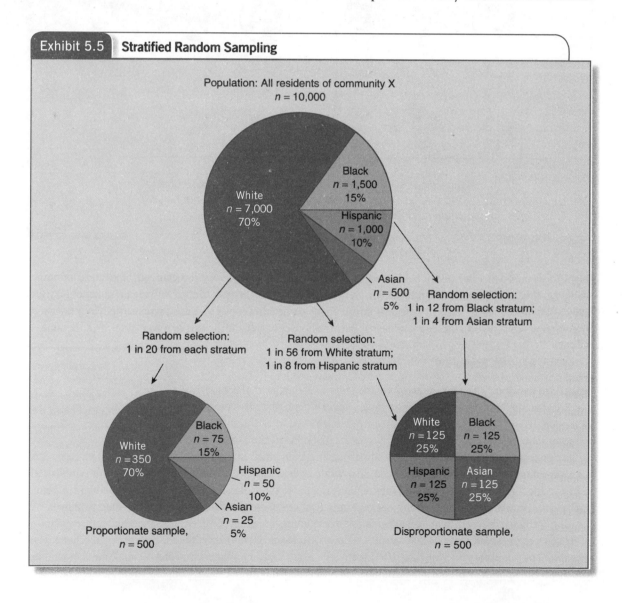

Exhibit 5.5 | Stratified Random Sampling

population. In the case of the sample stratified by ethnicity, you might select equal numbers of cases from each racial or ethnic group: 125 Blacks (25% of the sample), 125 Hispanics (25%), 125 Asians (25%), and 125 Whites (25%). In this type of sample, the probability of selection of every case is known but unequal between strata. You know what the proportions are in the population, and so you can easily adjust your combined sample statistics to reflect these true proportions. For instance, if you want to combine the ethnic groups and estimate the average income of the total population, you would have to weight each case in the sample. The weight is a number you multiply by the value of each case based on the stratum it is in. For example, you would multiply the incomes of all Blacks in the sample by 0.6 (75/125), the incomes of all Hispanics by 0.4 (50/125), and so on. Weighting in this way reduces the influence of the oversampled strata and increases the influence of the undersampled strata to just what they would have been if pure probability sampling had been used.

Why would anyone select a sample that is so unrepresentative in the first place? The most common reasons are to ensure that cases from smaller strata are included in the sample in sufficient numbers to allow separate statistical estimates, to have an adequate number to reflect subgroup differences or heterogeneity, and to facilitate comparisons between strata. Remember that one of the determinants of sample quality is sample size. The same is true for subgroups within samples. If a key concern in a research project is to describe and compare the incomes of people from different racial and ethnic groups, then it is important that the researchers base the mean income of each group on enough cases to be a valid representation. If few members of a particular minority group are in the population, they need to be oversampled. Such disproportionate sampling may also result in a more efficient sampling design if the costs of data collection differ markedly between strata or if the variability (heterogeneity) of the strata differs.

Michael Hendryx and his colleagues (2012) used disproportionate stratified sampling to assess the impact of increased premiums, increased copayments, setting deductibles, and raising the maximum out-of-pocket cost-sharing on enrollment in a state health insurance program. They divided the population using two strata: enrollment status (stayers and leavers) and income category (3 groups). These created six sampling strata (two enrollment groups by three income groups). They sought 190 completed responses per group providing a total sample of 1,140 participants. They used this strategy to ensure that there were sufficient people represented in each income group.

Cluster Sampling

Cluster sampling is useful when a sampling frame is not available, as is often the case for large populations spread out across a wide geographic area or among many different organizations. A **cluster** is a naturally occurring mixed aggregate of elements of the population, with each element appearing in one and only one cluster. Schools could serve as clusters for sampling students, blocks could serve as clusters for sampling city residents, counties could serve as clusters for sampling the general population, and agencies could serve as clusters for sampling social work staff.

Cluster sampling is at least a two-stage procedure. First, the researcher draws a random sample of clusters. A list of clusters should be much easier to obtain than a list of all the individuals in each cluster in the population. Next, the researcher draws a random sample of elements within each selected cluster. Because only a fraction of the total clusters is involved, obtaining the sampling frame at this stage should be much easier.

Cluster sampling Sampling in which elements are selected in two or more stages, with the first stage being the random selection of naturally occurring clusters and the last stage being the random selection of elements within clusters.

Cluster A naturally occurring mixed aggregate of elements of the population.

For example, in a needs assessment of residents of a particular neighborhood, blocks could be the first-stage clusters. Someone could walk around each selected block and record the addresses of all occupied dwelling units (see Exhibit 5.7). In a cluster sample of students, a researcher could contact the schools selected in the first stage and make arrangements with the registrar to obtain lists of students at each school. Cluster samples often involve multiple stages, with clusters within clusters, as when a national sample of middle school students involves first sampling states, then counties, then schools, and finally students in each selected school.

How many clusters and how many individuals within clusters should be selected? As a general rule, cases in the sample will be closer to the true population value if the researcher maximizes the number of clusters selected and

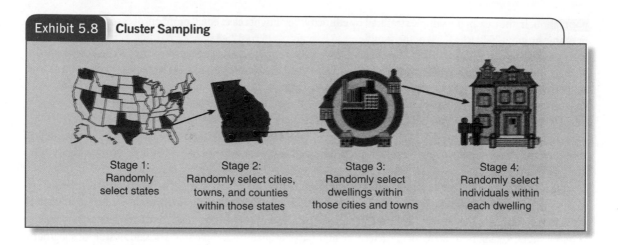

Exhibit 5.8 | **Cluster Sampling**

Stage 1: Randomly select states

Stage 2: Randomly select cities, towns, and counties within those states

Stage 3: Randomly select dwellings within those cities and towns

Stage 4: Randomly select individuals within each dwelling

minimizes the number of individuals within each cluster. Unfortunately, this strategy also maximizes the cost of the sample for studies using in-person interviews. The more clusters selected, the higher the travel costs. It also is important to take into account the homogeneity of the individuals within clusters—the more homogeneous the clusters, the fewer cases needed per cluster.

Cluster sampling is a popular method among survey researchers, but it has one drawback: Sampling error is greater in a cluster sample than in a simple random sample. This error increases as the number of clusters decreases, and it decreases as the homogeneity of cases per cluster increases.

Many surveys use cluster sampling. Israel Colon and Brett Marston (1999) wanted to evaluate "not in my back yard" attitudes toward a proposed residential home for HIV-positive individuals in a community. A local agency had wanted to provide such housing, but at hearings extreme opposition was found. Although the residence was ultimately built, the authors wanted to understand the source(s) of the opposition. Was it homophobia? Fear of AIDS? Concern about property values? Proximity to the housing? Colon and Marston listed all the blocks in the community and then took a 10% random sample of the blocks. They then tried to interview a member of each household in the selected blocks.

Random digit dialing is often used for cluster sampling. When using random digit dialing to contact households in a community, the telephone exchanges (the first three numbers) are often used as the clusters. Once clusters are selected, sometimes four-digit numbers are randomly selected to complete the phone number. Sometimes a multistage random digit dialing method is used. The exchanges are chosen, then the next two numbers are chosen, and finally the remaining two numbers are chosen.

Probability Sampling Methods Compared

Exhibit 5.8 summarizes the key features of these different types of sampling. Can you see why researchers often prefer to draw a stratified random sample or a cluster sample rather than a simple random sample? Sometimes, professionally designed surveys use combinations of clusters and stratified probability sampling methods.

Nonprobability Sampling Methods

Nonprobability sampling methods Sampling methods in which the probability of selection of population elements is unknown.

Nonprobability sampling methods do not use a random selection procedure, and therefore, elements within the population do not have a known probability of being selected. We cannot expect a sample selected using a nonprobability sampling method to yield a representative sample. The findings cannot be generalized to the broader population of interest.

Exhibit 5.8   **Features of Probability Sampling Methods**

Feature	Simple	Systematic	Stratified	Cluster
Unbiased selection of cases	Yes	Yes	Yes	Yes
Ensures representation of key strata	No	No	Yes	No
Uses natural grouping of cases	No	No	No	Yes
Reduces sampling costs	No	No	No	Yes
Sampling error compared with simple random sample	—	Same	Lower	Higher

Nonprobability sampling methods are often used in qualitative research. In qualitative research, a focus on one setting or a very small sample allows a more intensive portrait of activities and actors. In quantitative research, these methods are useful when random sampling is not possible, with a research question that does not concern a large population or require a random sample or for a preliminary pilot study. These methods are often applied to experimental studies testing the effectiveness of different treatment or intervention methods or with program evaluations conducted in agencies. There are four commonly used nonprobability sampling methods: (1) availability sampling, (2) quota sampling, (3) purposive sampling, and (4) snowball sampling. Because nonprobability sampling methods do not use a random selection procedure, we cannot expect a sample selected with any of these methods to yield a representative sample.

Availability Sampling

Elements are selected for **availability sampling** (or *convenience sampling*) because they are available or easy to find. There are many ways to select elements for an availability sample: standing on street corners and talking to whoever walks by, asking questions of employees who come to pick up their paychecks at a personnel office and who have time to talk to a researcher, or approaching

> **Availability sampling** Sampling method in which elements are selected on the basis of convenience.

particular individuals while observing activities in a social setting. To study sexual risk taking among homeless youth in Minneapolis, Linda Halcón and Alan Lifson (2004) hired experienced street youth outreach workers who approached youth known or suspected to be homeless and asked whether they would be willing to take part in an interview. To describe why women become homeless and how these reasons might differ from male homelessness, Tara Richards and her colleagues (T. N. Richards, Garland, Bumphus, & Thompson, 2010) went to homeless shelters, soup kitchens, and a shelter to find participants.

An availability sample is often appropriate in social work research—for example, when a researcher is exploring a new setting and trying to get some sense of prevailing attitudes or when a survey researcher conducts a preliminary test of a new set of questions. Availability samples are also common techniques used in different aspects of agency-based evaluative research, such as evaluating the effectiveness of one of its programs. For example, Kinnevy, Healey, Pollio, and North (1999) studied the effectiveness of a task-centered structured group program with low-income, high-risk youth. The program, called BicycleWORKS, was based in a community agency and was designed to teach participants how to build and repair bicycles during six group sessions as well as accumulate points to earn a bicycle. Participants signed a conduct pledge and had to pass a test to graduate from the program. It was hoped that the program would have a positive impact on the self-esteem of the participants and their ability to work with others while reducing problematic behaviors. The subjects were those participants who were available and people on the agency wait list.

Availability sampling often masquerades as a more rigorous form of research. Popular magazines periodically survey their readers by printing a questionnaire for readers to fill out and mail in. A follow-up article then appears in the magazine under a title such as "What You Think About Intimacy in Marriage." If the magazine's circulation is large, a large sample can be achieved in this way. The problem is that usually only a tiny fraction of readers return the questionnaire, and these respondents are probably unlike other readers, who did not have the interest or time to participate. So the survey is based on an availability sample. Although the follow-up article may be interesting, we have no basis for thinking that the results describe the readership as a whole—much less the population at large.

Do you see why availability sampling differs so much from the different probability sampling methods, which require that "nothing but chance" affects the actual selection of cases? What makes availability sampling haphazard is precisely that a great many things other than chance can affect the selection of cases. To truly leave the selection of cases up to chance, we have to design the selection process very carefully so that other factors are not influential.

Quota Sampling

Quota sampling is intended to overcome the most obvious flaw of availability sampling—that the sample will consist of only whoever or whatever is available, without any concern for its similarity to the population of interest. The distinguishing feature of **quota sampling** is that quotas are set to ensure that the sample represents certain characteristics in proportion to their prevalence in the population.

> **Quota sampling** A nonprobability sampling method in which elements are selected to ensure that the sample represents certain characteristics in proportion to their prevalence in the population.

Suppose that you wish to sample adult residents of a city in a study of support for building a casino. You know from the city's annual report what the proportions of the residents are in terms of gender, employment status, age, and race. You think that each of these characteristics might influence support for building a casino, so you want to be sure that the sample includes men, women, people who work, people not in the labor force, older people, younger people, and various ethnic groups in proportion to their numbers in the town population.

This is where quotas come in. Let's say that 48% of the city's adult residents are men and 52% are women and that 60% are employed, 5% are unemployed, and 35% are out of the labor force. These percentages and the percentages corresponding to the other characteristics become the quotas for the sample. If you plan to include a total of 500 residents in your sample, 240 must be men (48% of 500), 260 must be women, 300 must be employed, and so on. You may even set more refined quotas, such as certain numbers of employed women, employed men, unemployed women, and so on. With the quota list in hand, you (or your research staff) can now go out into the community looking for the right number of people in each quota category. You may go door to door or bar to bar, or you can just stand on a street corner until you have surveyed 240 men, 260 women, and so on.

The problem is that even when we know that a quota sample is representative of the particular characteristics for which quotas have been set, we have no way of knowing whether the sample is representative of any other characteristics. In Exhibit 5.9, for example, quotas have been set for gender only. Under the circumstances, it's no surprise that the sample is representative of the population only in terms of gender, not in terms of race; a random sample was not taken of the population. A problem with quota sampling is that interviewers may avoid potential respondents with menacing dogs in the frontyard or only interview people who look like they would be easy to interview. Realistically, researchers can set quotas for only a small fraction of the characteristics relevant to a study, so a quota sample is really not so much better than an availability sample (although following careful, consistent procedures for selecting cases within the quota limits always helps).

This last point leads to another limitation of quota sampling: You must know the characteristics of the entire sample to set the right quotas. Sharon Kirkpatrick and Valerie Tarasuk (2011) were able to use census tract data to determine the relative proportion of families living in subsidized and market rental apartments; they went door to door and recruited participants to match these percentages. Yet, in most cases, researchers know what the population looks like in terms of no more than a few of the characteristics relevant to their concerns. In some cases, they do not have any information about the entire population.

Exhibit 5.9   Quota Sampling

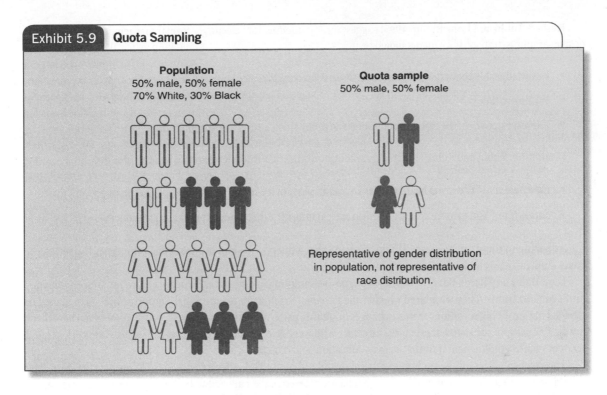

Does quota sampling remind you of stratified sampling? It is easy to understand why, since both methods involve selecting sample members based, in part, on one or more key characteristics. Exhibit 5.10 summarizes the differences between quota sampling and stratified random sampling. Of course, the essential difference is quota sampling's lack of random selection, and therefore you cannot generalize the findings.

Purposive Sampling

In **purposive sampling**, each sample element is selected for a purpose usually because of the unique position of the sample elements. Purposive sampling may involve studying the entire population of some limited group (directors of shelters for homeless adults) or a subset of a population (mid-level managers with a reputation for efficiency). Purposive sampling may be used to examine the effectiveness of some intervention with a set of subjects or clients who have particular characteristics, such as a specific diagnosis. A purposive sample may be a *key informant survey*, which targets individuals who are particularly knowledgeable about the issues under investigation.

Purposive sampling A sampling method in which elements are selected for a purpose, usually because of their unique position.

Exhibit 5.10   Comparison of Stratified and Quota Sampling Methods

Feature	Stratified	Quota
Unbiased (random) selection of cases	Yes	No
Sampling frame required	Yes	No
Ensures representation of key strata	Yes	Yes
Generalizable to the population	Yes	No

Herbert Rubin and Irene Rubin (1995) suggest three guidelines for selecting informants when designing any purposive sampling strategy. Informants should be

- Knowledgeable about the cultural arena or situation or experience being studied

- Willing to talk

- Represent[ative of] the range of points of view (p. 66)

In addition, Rubin and Rubin (1995) suggest continuing to select interviewees until you can pass two tests:

- *Completeness.* "What you hear provides an overall sense of the meaning of a concept, theme, or process" (p. 72).

- *Saturation.* "You gain confidence that you are learning little that is new from subsequent interview[s]" (p. 73).

Adhering to these guidelines will help to ensure that a purposive sample adequately represents the setting or issues studied.

Leon Haley and Ralph Bangs (2000) used purposive sampling in a study of the impact of welfare reform on non-profit organizations. They wondered whether the Personal Responsibility and Work Opportunities Act enacted in 1996 led nonprofit organizations to make changes in staffing patterns, budgets, and services provided, given new client needs. The sample consisted of executive directors who were selected because their agencies provide work-related services such as employment training, literacy, education, and day care.

The executive directors were chosen with Rubin and Rubin's (1995) criteria in mind: (a) As agency directors, they should be knowledgeable about the changes that have occurred in their agencies; (b) they are willing to participate in the interviews, suggesting a willingness to talk; and (c) they represent a range of services, are located in different communities and neighborhoods, and serve different demographic groups. The findings of this study are not generalizable to all agencies providing such services or to all agencies providing work-related services in the communities served by the sampled agencies. Any conclusions are limited to the set of respondents.

Snowball Sampling

For **snowball sampling**, you identify one member of the population and speak to him or her; you ask that person to identify others in the population and speak to them; you ask them to identify others, and so on. The sample thus "snowballs" in size. Snowball sampling is useful for hard-to-reach or hard-to-identify, interconnected populations (at least some members of the population know each other), such as drug users, parents with small children, participants in Alcoholics Anonymous groups or other peer support groups, and informal organizational leaders. For example, Suk-Young Kang and his colleagues (Kang, Domanski, & Moon, 2009) used snowball sampling to learn about depression among Korean older adult immigrants who did not reside in ethnic enclaves. Because there was no sampling frame, they sought participants from a Korean church and then asked those whom they had recruited to refer other older adult Koreans to the study. However, researchers using snowball sampling normally cannot be confident that their sample represents the total population of interest.

Snowball sampling A sampling method in which sample elements are selected as they are identified by successive informants or interviewees.

One caveat when using a snowball sampling technique is that you are asking people to identify other people with a similar status without the knowledge or consent of the people being identified. The people who are identified may not wish others to know that they have a particular status. This is particularly a concern when snowball sampling is used to identify subgroups of the population who may experience oppression or discrimination because they hold a particular status. In class, we often use a sampling exercise that requires students to identify a nonprobability sampling technique to gather information from gay and lesbian members of the community with the purpose of identifying their social service needs. Often students will suggest snowball sampling without realizing that what they are doing is asking people to "out" their acquaintances without permission of those being identified.

Nonprobability Sampling, Qualitative Research, and Generalizability

Qualitative research often focuses on populations that are hard to locate or very limited in size. Therefore, nonprobability sampling methods such as purpose, availability, and snowball sampling are frequently used. However, this does not mean that generalizability should be ignored in qualitative research, or that a sample should be studied simply because it is convenient (Gobo, 2008). Two different ways to increase the generalizability of the samples obtained in such settings include the following (Schofield, 2002):

- *Studying the Typical.* Choosing sites on the basis of their fit with a typical situation is far preferable to choosing on the basis of convenience (p. 181).

- *Performing Multisite Studies.* A finding emerging repeatedly in the study of numerous sites would appear to be more likely to be a good working hypothesis about some as yet unstudied site than a finding emerging from just one or two sites . . . . Generally speaking, a finding emerging from the study of several very heterogeneous sites would be more . . . likely to be useful in understanding various other sites than one emerging from the study of several very similar sites (p. 184).

Another approach is to select a case because it is atypical or deviant; investigating social processes in a situation that differs from the norm will improve understanding of how social processes work in typical situations (Gobo, 2008).

Some qualitative researchers question the value of generalizability, as most researchers understand it. The argument is that understanding the particulars of a situation in depth is an important object of inquiry itself (Schofield, 2002).

▣ Sampling Distributions

The use of probability sampling methods does not guarantee that a sample is representative of the population from which it was selected even when we have avoided the problems of nonresponse. Random sampling (probability-based selection techniques) is an unbiased method of sample selection and so minimizes the odds that a sample is unrepresentative, but there is always some chance that the sample differs substantially from the population. Random samples are subject to sampling error due just to chance. To deal with that problem, social researchers take into account the properties of a **sampling distribution,** a hypothetical distribution of a statistic across all the random samples that could be drawn from a population. Any single random sample can be thought of as just one of an infinite number of random samples that, in theory, could have been selected from the population.

> **Sampling distribution** The hypothetical distribution of a statistic across all the random samples that could be drawn from a population.

What does a sampling distribution look like? Because a sampling distribution is based on some statistic calculated for different samples, we need to choose a statistic. Let's focus on the arithmetic average, or mean. To calculate a mean, you add up the values of all the cases and divide by the total number of cases. Let's say you draw a random sample of 500 families and find that their average (mean) family income is $58,239. Imagine that you then draw another random sample. That sample's mean family income might be $60,302. Imagine marking these two means on graph paper, drawing more random samples, and marking their means on the graph. The resulting graph would be a sampling distribution of the mean.

Exhibit 5.11 demonstrates what happened when we did something similar to what was just described—not with an infinite number of samples and not from a large population, but through the same process—using the 2012 General

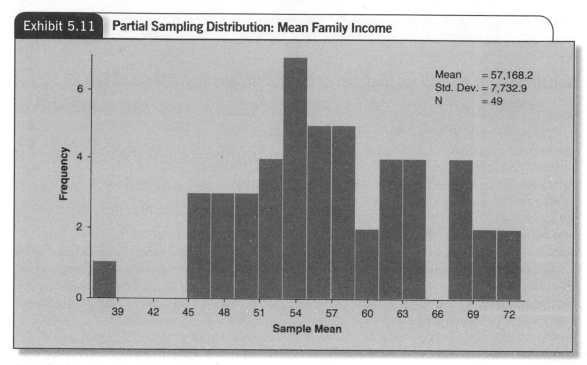

Exhibit 5.11 | Partial Sampling Distribution: Mean Family Income

Mean = 57,168.2
Std. Dev. = 7,732.9
N = 49

Source: Data from General Social Survey, 1996.

Social Survey (GSS) sample as if it were a population. First, we drew 49 different random samples, each consisting of 30 cases, from the GSS. (The standard notation for the number of cases in each sample is $n = 30$.) Then we calculated for each random sample the approximate mean family income (approximate because the GSS does not record actual income in dollars). We then graphed the means of the 49 samples. Each bar in Exhibit 5.11 shows how many samples had a family income in each $2,000 category between $37,000 and $75,000. The mean for the population (the total GSS sample) is $58,238, and you can see that many of the samples in the sampling distribution are close to this value with the mean for the sampling distribution being $57,168.20—almost identical to the population mean. However, although many of the sample means are close to the population mean, some are quite far from it (the lowest is actually $37,508 while the highest is $72,930). If you had calculated the mean from only one sample, it could have been anywhere in this sampling distribution. But that one mean is *unlikely* to have been far from the population mean—that is, unlikely to have been close to either end (or *tail*) of the distribution.

Estimating Sampling Error

We do not actually observe sampling distributions; researchers just draw the best sample they can—one sample, not a distribution of samples. A sampling distribution is a theoretical distribution. However, we can use the properties of sampling distributions to calculate the amount of sampling error that was likely with the random sample used in a study. **Inferential statistics** is a mathematical tool for estimating how likely it is that a statistical result based on data from a random sample is representative of the population from which the sample is assumed to have been selected.

Sampling distributions for many statistics, including the mean, have a *normal shape*. A graph of a normal distribution looks like a bell, with one hump in the middle, centered on the population mean, and the number of cases tapering off on both sides of the mean. Note that a normal distribution is symmetric: If you folded

Inferential statistics Mathematical tools for estimating how likely it is that a statistical result based on data from a random sample is representative of the population from which the sample is assumed to have been selected.

it in half at its center (at the population mean), the two halves would match perfectly. This shape is produced by random sampling error—variation due purely to chance. The value of the statistic varies from sample to sample because of chance, so higher and lower values are equally likely.

The partial sampling distribution in Exhibit 5.11 does not have a completely normal shape because it involves only a small number of samples (49), each of which has only 30 cases. Exhibit 5.12 shows what the sampling distribution of family incomes would look like if it formed a perfectly normal distribution—if, rather than 49 random samples, thousands of random samples had been selected.

The properties of a sampling distribution facilitate the process of statistical inference. In the sampling distribution, the most frequent value of the **sample statistic**—the statistic (such as the mean) computed from sample data— is identical to the **population parameter**—the statistic computed for the entire population. In other words, we can have a lot of confidence that the value at the peak of the bell curve represents the norm for the entire population. A population parameter also may be termed the *true value* for the statistic in that population. A sample statistic is an estimate of a population parameter.

Sample statistic The value of a statistic, such as a mean, computed from sample data.

Population parameter The value of a statistic, such as a mean, computed using the data for the entire population.

In a normal distribution, a predictable proportion of cases also falls within certain ranges. Inferential statistics takes advantage of this feature and allows researchers to estimate how likely it is that, given a particular sample, the true population value will be within some range of the statistic. For example, a statistician might conclude from a sample of 30 families that we can be 95% confident that the true mean family income in the total population is between $39,037 and $89,997. The interval from $39,037 to $89,997 would then be called the 95% *confidence interval for the mean*. The lower ($39,037) and upper ($89,997) bounds of this interval are termed the *confidence limits*. Exhibit 5.12 marks such confidence limits, indicating the range that encompasses 95% of the area under the normal curve; 95% of all sample means would fall within this range, as does the mean of our hypothesized sample of 30 cases.

Although all normal distributions have these same basic features, they differ in the extent to which they cluster around the mean. A sampling distribution is more compact when it is based on larger samples. If the sample size had

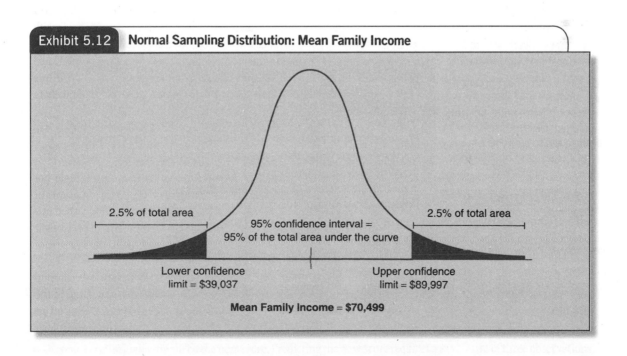

Exhibit 5.12 Normal Sampling Distribution: Mean Family Income

2.5% of total area

95% confidence interval = 95% of the total area under the curve

2.5% of total area

Lower confidence limit = $39,037

Upper confidence limit = $89,997

Mean Family Income = $70,499

been greater than 30 families, the sampling distribution would have been more compact. Stated another way, we can be more confident in estimates based on larger random samples because we know that a larger sample creates a more compact sampling distribution. For instance, the 95% confidence interval for a sample of 100 families was $53,109 and $83,563, which is narrower than the confidence level for the 30 families.

Determining Sample Size

You have learned that more confidence can be placed in the generalizability of statistics from larger samples, so you may be eager to work with random samples that are as large as possible. Unfortunately, researchers often cannot afford to sample a large number of cases. Therefore, they try to determine during the design phase of their study how large a sample they must have to achieve their purposes. They have to consider the degree of confidence desired, the homogeneity of the population, the complexity of the analysis they plan, and the expected strength of the relationships they will measure:

- The less sampling error desired, the larger the sample size must be.

- Samples of more homogeneous populations can be smaller than samples of more diverse populations. Stratified sampling uses prior information on the population to create more homogeneous population strata from which the sample can be selected, so it can be smaller than if simple random sampling were used.

- If the only analysis planned for a survey sample is to describe the population in terms of a few variables, a smaller sample is required than if a more complex analysis involving sample subgroups is planned. If much of the analysis will focus on estimating the characteristics of subgroups within the sample, it is the size of the subgroups that must be considered, not the size of the total sample (Levy & Lemeshow, 2008).

- When the researchers will be testing hypotheses and expect to find strong relationships among the variables, they will need a smaller sample to detect these relationships than if they expect weaker relationships.

Researchers can make more precise estimates of the sample size required through a method termed *statistical power analysis* (Cohen, 1988). Statistical power is increasingly used to identify the sample size necessary to identify treatment effects. Statistical power analysis requires a good advance estimate of the strength of the hypothesized relationship in the population. Statistical power analysis has become an essential component for federally submitted research proposals and is part of the institutional review board consideration of research propriety.

Exhibit 5.13 shows the results of a power analysis conducted to determine the sample size required to estimate a proportion in the population, when the null hypothesis is that the proportion is .50. For the sake of simplicity, it is assumed that the researcher wants to be 90% confident that the actual population differs from the null hypothesis of .50; in other words, he wants a sample size that will identify a difference from .5 that is significant at the .05 level. You can see that if the true proportion in the population is actually .55, a sample larger than 800 will be needed to detect this difference at the .05 level of significance. However, if the true proportion in the population is .60, then a random sample of only 200 cases is necessary. The required sample size falls off gradually beyond this point, as the actual proportion in the population rises beyond .60.

It should be clear from Exhibit 5.13 that you must have a good estimate of the true population value of the statistic you are going to calculate. You also have to decide what significance level (such as .05) you want to be achieved in your statistical test. Both of these factors can have a major impact on the number of cases you need to obtain.

You can obtain some general guidance about sample sizes from the current practices of social scientists. For professional studies of the national population in which only a simple description is desired, professional social science studies typically have used a sample size of between 1,000 and 1,500, with up to 2,500 being included if detailed analyses are planned. Studies of local or regional populations often sample only a few hundred people, in part because these studies

Exhibit 5.13   **Power Graph**

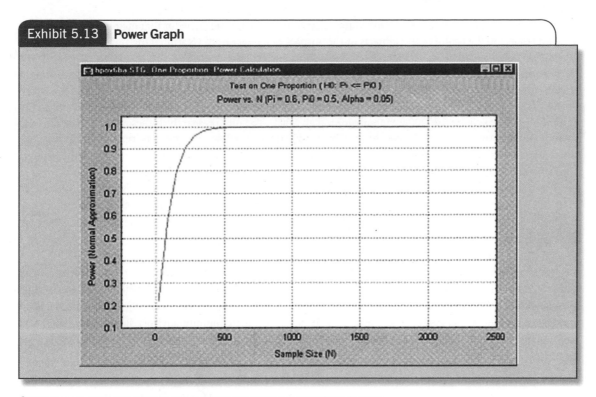

Source: Power Table from StatSoft's Electronic Statistics Textbook: www.statsoft.com/textbook.

lack sufficient funding to draw larger samples. Of course, the sampling error in these smaller studies is considerably larger than in a typical national study (Sudman, 1976).

Recruitment Strategies With Diverse Populations

One goal for social work researchers is to ensure the representation of diverse populations in research studies. Different subgroups of the population, whether categorized by gender, ethnicity, age, class, or sexual orientation, have been underrepresented in research efforts. Given that social work research can inform treatment effectiveness, intervention methods, and policy directions, it is important that what is learned pertains to and is useful to all segments of society (Miranda, Azocar, Organista, Munoz, & Lieberman, 1996).

Therefore, it is important to recruit diverse groups for all types of studies whether the studies involve surveys, testing interventions, or observations. Adequate representation is necessary to ensure that a study's findings are applicable to diverse groups. With sufficient representation, researchers can do analyses or present findings by groupings such as gender, ethnicity, or age; such analyses are important in demonstrating that a result is applicable to various populations (Yancey, Ortega, & Kumanyika, 2006).

The problems of exclusion or omission have been sufficiently problematic that Congress required the National Institutes of Health (NIH) to establish guidelines to ensure the inclusion of women and ethnic minorities in clinical research when it passed the NIH Revitalization Act of 1993 (PL 103-43). Now NIH-supported biomedical and behavioral research projects must include women and minorities unless a "clear and compelling rationale and justification establishes to the satisfaction of the relevant Institute/Center Director that inclusion is inappropriate with respect to the health of the subjects or the purpose of the research" (National Institutes of Health, 1994, "Policy" section, para.1).

A common response is that it is hard to recruit minorities to participate in research. There are legitimate reasons for minority communities to distrust research efforts, whether it is the exploitation of African American participants in the Tuskegee experiments on syphilis or the misuse of findings to the detriment of minority communities (Bates & Harris, 2004; Moreno-John et al., 2004). Too often research studies have not benefited the participating communities, and by couching comparative studies as evidence of deficits, researchers have sometimes stigmatized ethnic communities (George, Duran, & Norris, 2014). Language barriers can further inhibit recruitment (George et al., 2014)

When appropriate efforts are made, people of color do participate at high rates in research activities (Ofstedal & Weir, 2011; E. Thompson, Neighbors, Munday, & Jackson, 1996; Yamatani, Mann, & Wright, 2000). Because of cultural and historical differences, there is "no one-size fits all" (Sood & Stahl, 2011, p. 6) to address recruitment, but there are some general themes emerging in the literature (George et al., 2014; Yancey et al., 2006):

- *Involve key community members and organizations to obtain credibility and gain acceptance.* Ilena Norton and Spero Manson (1996) describe the importance of first gaining the approval of the tribe before seeking individual permission of Native Americans to participate in research. To recruit elderly African American participants, Reed and colleagues (Reed, Foley, Hatch, & Mutran, 2003) established a community advisory board whose members were tied to the community and key organizations; the board, in turn, identified churches with whom relationships should be established.

- *Use culturally adapted procedures.* Often recruitment seems to be centered in the wrong locations. For example, African Americans and Latinos have lower rates of usage of mental health provider services, and therefore recruitment should be at settings that they frequent, such as community hospitals or primary care providers. There is a preference for recruitment by ethnically matched research staff as that facilitates trust. Having materials and information in the appropriate language as well as research staff conversant in the appropriate language enhances recruitment efforts (George et al., 2014; Yancey et al., 2006).

- *Demonstrate that there is a benefit to the community.* Many ethnic communities have seen research efforts that not only have not helped the community but have had adverse impacts on the community. Yet, different ethnic groups shared a common desire to help their families, community, and to increase scientific knowledge (George et al., 2014).

- *Understand cultural barriers.* As a general rule, it is important that the research effort take into account cultural considerations. Miranda et al. (1996) identify several cultural norms among Latinos that may preclude or facilitate participation in treatment research, including importance of family, respect toward older adults, respect toward professionals, and warmth in interactions between professionals/researchers and clients/participants. They suggest that recruitment procedures that are too informal or cold will fail, whereas success comes from "treating older Latinos with respect using formal titles, while being warm and personable" (p. 870).

- *Understanding cultural differences is important in decisions about the choice of and training of interviewers.* In a multistage cluster study of an African American neighborhood, Hide Yamatani, Aaron Mann, and Pat Wright (2000) achieved a high response rate, in part, by using local members of the community to conduct the interviews. Dilworth-Anderson and Williams (2004) in a study of caregivers recruited interviewers who understood African American family culture and traditions and emphasized these dynamics in their interviewer training.

Difficulties of recruitment are not limited to people of color. Other population groups have legitimate fears of being stigmatized and facing discrimination if they are identified. For example, there has been recent discussion of how to recruit gay males and lesbians to research studies. Silvestre (1994) describes a brokering technique that was used to recruit nearly 3,000 gay and bisexual men (as of 1994) to an ongoing longitudinal epidemiological study of HIV among gay and bisexual men. The process included the following:

- Hiring a community organizer and having publicly known leaders in the gay community participate in the search.

- Establishing a community advisory board reflecting the diversity of interests in the community.

- Engaging in the exchange of goods and services between the researchers and the formal and informal gay leadership. Researchers provided things such as access to the most recent information about HIV; access to university facilities for meetings and community events; public discourse and development of HIV-related public policy; protocols that both protect confidentiality and provide education to participants; participation in study decisions; and a clinic with supportive and qualified staff, referrals, and the like. Gay leadership provided statements of public support; facilities and time to present information, distribute questionnaires, and the like at their organizations or businesses; distribution of flyers, posters, and newsletters; advice; introductions to other key community members; and person-to-person communications.

In subsequent work to recruit gay males of color, Silvestre and his colleagues (2006) followed these guidelines as well as added two other guidelines:

- Having recruitment staff that was knowledgeable and culturally competent to work with minority men having sex with men.

- Locating the research site in areas that were seen as accessible and safe by the participants. In one site, they used a mobile clinic in a nearby town because participants were concerned about being seen by people who knew them.

Recruitment should use multiple approaches and different approaches may be more effective with subgroups of gay and bisexual men (Barresi et al., 2010; McKee, Picciano, Roffman, Swanson, & Kalichman, 2006). These approaches include advertising in a variety of media, recruiting at clubs and bars, snowball recruiting in which enrollees encouraged participation, clinic outreach and street outreach.

Roffman, Picciano, Wickizer, Bolan, and Ryan (1998) describe a different effort to recruit gay and bisexual males to an intervention and research project. Potential participants were given the choice of enrolling by a confidential option or anonymously. Those enrolling through the confidential option were asked for a phone number and instructions about the type of message that could be left; they were interviewed over the phone. To enroll anonymously, participants were asked to rent a postal box using a real name or a pseudonym, and they were sent a money order to pay for the postal box with no name written on the payee line. All subsequent communications about treatment, data collection, and incentive payments were conducted through the postal box. The project enrolled a large number of participants, and the researchers found differences between those who used the confidential versus anonymous approach.

To recruit and retain research participants requires an understanding of why some groups fail to participate in research, as well as the cultural backgrounds of different groups. As you can see by the examples described previously, recruitment and retention may require creative approaches.

▣ Implications for Evidence-Based Practice

There are several lessons for evidence-based practice implicit in the evaluations of the sampling methods. Remember, our goal is to make conclusions about a measure, a treatment, or a policy finding and to determine its appropriateness for practice. Therefore, it is important that what is learned pertains to and is useful to all segments of society (Miranda et al., 1996). Because issues of sampling cut across various research topics, we summarize these lessons in this chapter, but we will return to these lessons in other chapters.

We cannot evaluate the quality of a sample if we don't know what population it is supposed to represent. If the population is unspecified because the researchers were never clear about just what population they were trying to sample, then we can safely conclude that the sample is no good. We can't evaluate the generalizability of a sample if we don't know how cases in the sample were selected from the population. If the method was specified, we then need to know whether cases were selected in a systematic fashion and on the basis of chance.

Sample quality is determined by the sample actually obtained, not just by the sampling method. Even if we have chosen to sample in the best possible way, if many of the people selected for our sample are nonrespondents or people (or other entities) who do not participate in the study, although they have been selected for the sample, the quality of our sample is undermined. Those who chose to participate may be unlike those who chose not to participate in ways that limit the generalizability of the findings. Therefore, the response rate, the percentage of the sample that actually responds, is critically important. We return to this issue in Chapter 9.

We need to be aware that even researchers who obtain good samples may talk about the implications of their findings for some group that is larger than or just different from the population they actually sampled—what we have described as cross-population generalizability. As you evaluate their claims, you must consider the relevance of the population sampled to your own practice context—the particular setting, the location, or the type of clients. For example, findings from a representative sample of students in one university often are discussed as if they tell us about university students in general. Maybe they do; we just do not know.

The sample size may influence statistical conclusions about the findings. The sample size may lack statistical power—that is, be too small to find a statistically significant relationship even when there appears to be a relationship. However, as we expand in Chapter 14, many statistical tests are influenced by sample size. A large sample may produce a statistically significant relationship even if that relationship is trivial or not clinically significant.

▣ Conclusion

Sampling is a powerful tool for social work research. Probability sampling methods allow researchers to use the laws of chance or probability to draw samples from which population parameters can be estimated with a high degree of confidence. When probability sampling methods are used, findings from a small number of cases can be generalized to a much larger population. Many researchers rely on these techniques when they are interested in describing population groups, understanding the impacts of different social welfare policies, or learning about community needs or attitudes.

There are many different research questions that are not easily answered by a probability sampling technique, particularly as we seek answers about questions from vulnerable populations. The experience of Kathryn Edin and Laura Lein (1997), described in *Making Ends Meet*, offers a telling example. They wanted to know how single mothers on Aid to Families with Dependent Children or working in low-wage jobs survived economically each month. Edin started out with a survey by phone and in person of respondents who had been randomly selected for the 1983–1985 Chicago Survey of Poverty and Material Hardship. This effort failed to produce accurate information because respondents did not trust her, "had no personal introduction to her and therefore suspected she was 'checking up' on them in some official capacity" (p. 9). She turned to a snowball technique that would facilitate personal introduction from a trustworthy individual, a technique that ultimately proved successful in gathering accurate information.

Most studies of the impact of a practice intervention rely on nonprobability sampling techniques. As a result, replication studies at both the same and different agencies are required for social workers to be confident that they have the best evidence.

Ultimately, whether designing or evaluating a study, it is important to consider the type of sampling and the conclusions that might be made from the method of sampling. Can generalizations be made? To what population or population subgroups can the results be generalized? Are there characteristics about the setting that limit the generalizability of the results? Is the sample size too small? Should all elements have been studied? Is the response rate sufficiently high? Each of these questions is a consideration when thinking about applying research findings.

Social work researchers and other social scientists often seek to generalize their conclusions from the population that they studied to some larger target population. The validity of generalizations of this type is necessarily uncertain because having a representative sample of a particular population does not at all ensure that what we find will hold true in other populations. Nonetheless, the accumulation of findings from studies based on local or otherwise unrepresentative populations can provide important information about broader populations.

Key Terms

Availability sampling 119
Cluster 117
Cluster sampling 117
Disproportionate stratified
   sampling 116
Elements 105
Enumeration units 105
Inferential statistics 124
Nonprobability sampling methods 118
Population 105
Population parameter 125

Probability of selection 109
Probability sampling methods 110
Proportionate stratified sampling 116
Purposive sampling 121
Quota sampling 120
Random digit dialing 112
Random numbers table 112
Random sampling 108
Representative sample 107
Sample 105
Sample statistic 125

Sampling distribution 123
Sampling error 107
Sampling frame 105
Sampling interval 114
Sampling units 105
Simple random sampling 112
Snowball sampling 122
Stratified random sampling 115
Systematic bias 109
Systematic random sampling 114
Target population 107

Highlights

- Sampling theory focuses on the generalizability of descriptive findings to the population from which the sample was drawn. It also considers whether statements can be generalized from one population to another.

- Sampling is unnecessary when the elements that would be sampled are identical, but the complexity of the social world makes it difficult to argue very often that different elements are identical.

Conducting a complete census of a population also eliminates the need for sampling, but the resources required for a complete census of a large population are usually prohibitive.

- Nonresponse undermines sample quality: The obtained sample, not the desired sample, determines sample quality.

- Probability sampling methods rely on a random selection procedure to ensure no systematic bias in the selection of elements. In a probability sample, the odds of selecting elements are known, and the method of selection is carefully controlled.

- A sampling frame (a list of elements in the population) is required in most probability sampling methods. The adequacy of the sampling frame is an important determinant of sample quality.

- Simple random sampling and systematic random sampling are equivalent probability sampling methods in most situations. However, systematic random sampling is inappropriate for sampling from lists of elements that have a regular, periodic structure.

- Stratified random sampling uses prior information about a population to make sampling more efficient. Stratified sampling may be either proportionate or disproportionate. Disproportionate stratified sampling is useful when a research question focuses on a stratum or on strata that make up a small proportion of the population.

- Cluster sampling is less efficient than simple random sampling but is useful when a sampling frame is unavailable. It is also useful for large populations spread out across a wide area or among many organizations.

- Nonprobability sampling methods can be useful when random sampling is not possible, when a research question does not concern a larger population, and when a preliminary exploratory study is appropriate. However, the representativeness of nonprobability samples cannot be determined.

- The likely degree of error in an estimate of a population characteristic based on a probability sample decreases when the size of the sample and the homogeneity of the population from which the sample was selected increases. Sampling error is not affected by the proportion of the population that is sampled, except when that proportion is large. The degree of sampling error affecting a sample statistic can be estimated from the characteristics of the sample and knowledge of the properties of sampling distributions.

- To ensure the representation of diverse populations in research studies, a variety of different methods can and should be used to encourage participation of people of color, women, older adults, and sexual minorities.

Discussion Questions

1. Underrepresentation of different subgroups can significantly limit the generalizability of social work research findings and their subsequent applications. Suppose you were conducting a study of barriers to health care access in urban areas. What are some of the strategies you might employ to encourage minority participation in your research project?

2. A State Department of Aging representative used a nonprobability sampling method to audit an agency's case records. Discuss the potential weaknesses of this approach in reaching a conclusion about the entire agency's filing compliance. Identify instances in which the use of an availability sample might be more appropriate or required.

3. Although probability-based selection techniques minimize the odds of sample unrepresentativeness, there remains a chance that the sample does differ substantially from the population. What do confidence limits tell us about the statistic we have derived from our sample and the likelihood of it being true for the population? How is the confidence interval impacted by sample size?

4. What ethical issues might you confront when using snowball sampling?

Practice Exercises

1. Select a random sample using the table of random numbers in Exhibit 5.4. Compute a statistic based on your sample, and compare it to the corresponding figure for the entire population. Here's how to proceed:

   a. First, go to www.census.gov/hhes/www/hlthins/data/children/uninsured_low-income.html to find rates of low-income uninsured children by state. Click on the table for 2010, 2011, and 2012.

b. The next step is to create your sampling frame, a numbered list of all the elements in the population. When using a complete listing of all elements, as from a U.S. Census Bureau publication, the sampling frame is the same as the list. Just number the elements by writing a number next to the name of each state.

c. Now calculate the average value of the percentage of children at or below 200% of the poverty level for the total population of states. You do this by adding the values for each state in that column and dividing by the number of states.

d. Decide on a method of picking numbers out of the random numbers table in Exhibit 5.4, such as taking every number in each row, row by row (or you may move down or diagonally across the columns). Use only the first (or last) digit in each number if you need to select 1 to 9 cases or only the first (or last) two digits if you want fewer than 100 cases.

e. Pick a starting location in the random numbers table. It's important to pick a starting point in an unbiased way, perhaps by closing your eyes and then pointing to some part of the page.

f. Record the numbers you encounter as you move from the starting location in the direction you decided on in advance, until you have recorded as many random numbers as the number of cases you need in the sample. If you are selecting states, 10 might be a good number. Ignore numbers that are too large (or small) for the range of numbers used to identify the elements in the population. Discard duplicate numbers.

g. Calculate the average value in your sample by adding up the values of the percentage of children at or below 200% of the poverty level for each of the states (elements) in the sample you have just selected and dividing by the number of elements in the sample.

h. How close is the sample average to the population average you calculated in Step c?

i. Guesstimate the range of sample averages that would be likely to include 90% of the possible samples of the same size.

2. A survey found that 4 in 10 college students endure stress often (Fram & Tompson, 2008). Propose a probability sampling design to study this issue at your university that combines stratification and clustering. What challenges would you confront in implementing your design?

3. Draw a snowball sample of people who are involved in Ultimate Frisbee. Ask friends or find a campus organization that can get you a contact. Call, e-mail, or visit this person and ask for names of others. Stop when you have identified a sample of 10. Review the problems you encountered and consider how you would proceed if you had to draw a larger sample.

4. Identify one article at the book's study site that used a survey research design. Describe the sampling procedure. What type was it? Why did the author(s) use this method? To what population are the results generalizable, if any?

Web Exercise

1. Research on health care concerns has increased in recent years as health care costs have risen. Search the Web for sites that include the term *medically uninsured* and see what you find. You might try limiting your search to those that also contain the word *census*. Pick a site, and write a paragraph about what you learned from it.

2. Check out the People and Households section of the U.S. Bureau of the Census website: www.census.gov. Based on some of the data you find there, write a brief summary of some aspect of the current characteristics of the American population.

Developing a Research Proposal

1. Propose a sampling design that would be appropriate for your research study. Define the population, identify the sampling frame (if any), and specify the elements. Indicate the exact procedure for selecting people to be included in the sample.

Specify any specific selection criteria. How many subjects will you need?

2. Develop appropriate procedures for the recruitment of human subjects in your study. Include a recruitment form with these procedures.

A Question of Ethics

Silvestre (1994) recruited nearly 3,000 gay and bisexual men to an ongoing longitudinal epidemiological study of HIV among gay and bisexual men. Do you believe that the researchers had any ethical obligation to take any action whatsoever when they learned that a respondent was currently engaging in risky sexual practices? Are any of the ethical guidelines presented in Chapter 3 relevant to this situation? How would a decision to take action to reduce the risk of harm to others affect the promise to preserve the anonymity of respondents?

Causation and Research Design

I dentifying causes—figuring out why things happen—is the goal of most social science research. Unfortunately, valid explanations of the causes of social phenomena do not come easily. Why did the poverty rate for children under age 6 stay relatively stable in the 1970s, increase in the 1980s and early 1990s, begin to decline in 1993, and then recently begin to increase (see Exhibit 6.1)? Variations in the economy? Changes in public policy? Barriers to employment? Changing demographic patterns? To distinguish these possibilities, we must design our research strategies carefully.

But identifying causes is just one goal for social work practice and social policy. We want to be able to rule out ineffective interventions and policies while utilizing those interventions that produce predetermined outcomes (S. Witkin & Harrison, 2001). Understanding the relationship of different research designs to attributing causality is a critically important component necessary to assess the evidence about a particular intervention or social policy. We start by reviewing research design alternatives. After reviewing these design considerations, we review the criteria for achieving explanations that are causally valid from a nomothetic perspective and the meaning of causality from an idiographic perspective. By the end of the chapter, you should have a good grasp of the meaning of causation and be able to ask the right questions to determine whether causal inferences are likely to be valid as you review and evaluate the evidence base of social work interventions.

⊡ Research Design Alternatives

We begin this chapter by discussing three key elements of research design: the design's unit of analysis, its use of cross-sectional or longitudinal data, and whether methods are primarily quantitative or qualitative. Whenever we design research, we must decide whether to use individuals or groups as our units of analysis and whether to collect data at one or several points in time. The decisions that we make about these design elements will affect our ability to draw causal conclusions in our analysis. Whether the design is primarily quantitative or qualitative also affects the type

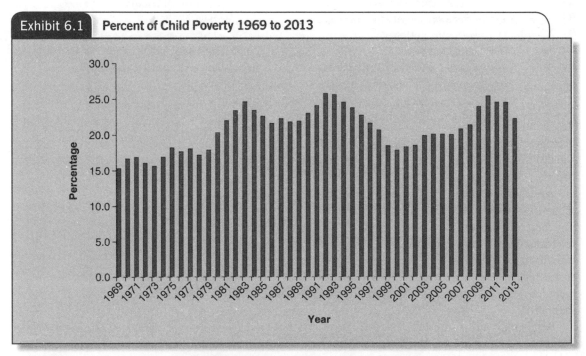

Exhibit 6.1 | **Percent of Child Poverty 1969 to 2013**

Source: U.S. Bureau of the Census, Current Population Survey, Annual Social and Economic Supplements.

of causal explanation that can be developed: Quantitative projects lead to nomothetic causal explanations, whereas qualitative projects that have a causal focus can lead to idiographic explanations.

Units of Analysis and Errors in Causal Reasoning

We can easily come to invalid conclusions about causal influences if we do not know what **units of analysis** the measures in our study refer to—that is, the level of social life on which the research question is focused, such as individuals, families, households, groups, neighborhoods, or communities. We point out the possible errors in causal reasoning associated with misidentifying the unit of analysis.

> **Units of analysis** The level of social life on which a research question is focused.

Individual and Group Units of Analysis

In many social work studies the units of analysis are individuals. The researcher may collect survey data from individuals, analyze the data, and then report on, say, how many individuals felt socially isolated and whether substance abuse by individuals was related to their feelings of social isolation.

The units of analysis may be groups of some sort, such as families, households, schools, human service organizations, neighborhoods, towns, or states. For example, a researcher may want to learn about the relationship between the degree of cohesiveness in neighborhoods and the crime rate, thinking that more cohesive neighborhoods will have a lower crime rate; in this case, neighborhood is the unit of analysis.

It is important to distinguish the concept, units of analysis from the **units of observation**. In many studies, the units of observation and the units of analysis are the same. Yet there are occasions when the two are different. In studies of economic well-being, household income is often collected from individual household members—the unit of observation—but the data are used to describe the household, the unit of analysis. Whether we are drawing conclusions from data or interpreting others' conclusions, it is important to be clear about the relationship to which we refer.

> **Units of observation** The cases from which measures or information are obtained in a sample.

We also have to know the units of analysis to interpret statistics appropriately. Measures of association tend to be stronger for group-level than for individual-level data because measurement errors at the individual level tend to cancel out at the group level (Bridges & Weis, 1989).

The Ecological Fallacy and Reductionism

Researchers should make sure that their causal conclusions reflect the units of analysis in their studies. Conclusions about processes at the individual level should be based on individual-level data; conclusions about group-level processes should be based on data collected about groups. When this rule is violated, we can be misled about the association between two variables.

A researcher who draws conclusions about individual-level processes from group-level data is making what is termed an **ecological fallacy** (see Exhibit 6.2). The conclusions may or may not be correct, but we must recognize that group-level data do not describe individual-level processes. For example, the term *underclass* first referred to neighborhoods or communities with certain characteristics

> **Ecological fallacy** An error in reasoning in which the incorrect conclusions about individual-level processes are drawn from group-level data.

such as high rates of unemployment, poverty, out-of-wedlock births, welfare recipiency, and lower educational attainment. The term began to be misused when the individuals living in such communities were described as members of the underclass.

Bear in mind that conclusions about individual processes based on group-level data are not necessarily wrong. We just do not know for sure. Say that we find communities with higher average incomes have lower crime rates. The only thing special about these communities may be that they have more individuals with higher incomes, who tend to

Reductionist fallacy An error in reasoning that occurs when an incorrect conclusion about group-level processes is based on individual-level data.

Causal effect (*nomothetic perspective*) The finding that change in one variable leads to change in another variable, other things being equal.

Causal effect (*ideographic perspective*) The finding that a series of events following an initial set of conditions leads in a progressive manner to a particular event or outcome.

commit fewer crimes. Although we collected data at the group level and analyzed them at the group level, they reflect a causal process at the individual level.

When data about individuals are used to make inferences about group-level processes, a problem occurs that can be thought of as the mirror image of the ecological fallacy: the **reductionist fallacy,** or reductionism (see Exhibit 6.2). For example, William Julius Wilson (1987) notes that we can be misled into concluding from individual-level data that race has a **causal effect** on violence because there is an association at the individual level between race and the likelihood of arrest for violent crime. However, community-level data reveal that almost 40% of poor African Americans lived in extremely poor areas in 1980, compared with only 7% of poor Whites. The concentration of African Americans in poverty areas, not the race or other characteristics of the individuals in these areas, may be the cause of higher rates of violence. Explaining violence in this case requires community-level data.

The fact that errors in causal reasoning can be made should not deter you from conducting research with group-level or aggregate data nor make you unduly critical of researchers who make inferences about individuals on the basis of aggregate data. When considered broadly, many research questions point to relationships that could be manifested in many ways and on many levels. Sampson's (1987) study of urban violence is a case in point. His analysis involved only aggregate data about cities, and he explained his research approach as in part a response to the failure of other researchers to examine this problem at the structural, aggregate level. Moreover, Sampson argued that the rates of joblessness and family disruption in communities influence community social processes, not just the behavior of the specific individuals who are unemployed or who grew up without two parents. Yet Sampson suggests that the experience of joblessness and poverty is what tends to reduce the propensity of individual men to marry and that the experience of growing up in a home without two parents in turn increases the propensity of individual juveniles to commit crimes. These conclusions about the behavior of individuals seem consistent with the patterns Sampson found in his aggregate, city-level data, so it seems unlikely that he is committing an ecological fallacy when he proposes them.

The solution is to know what the units of analysis and units of observation were in a study and to take these into account in weighing the credibility of the researcher's conclusions. The goal is not to reject out of hand conclusions that refer to a level of analysis different from what was actually studied. Instead, the goal is to consider the likelihood that an ecological fallacy or a reductionist fallacy has been made when estimating the causal validity of the conclusions.

Cross-Sectional and Longitudinal Designs

Do you want to know the percentage of homeless people who are single parents with children or do you want to know whether the percentage of homeless people who are single parents has changed over the last several years? Do you want to know the characteristics of people who presently use mental health services or do you want to know whether the composition of those using mental health services has changed in the last 10 years? If you want to describe or understand social phenomena in the present or at one time point, you will employ a **cross-sectional research design**. However, if you want to track changes over time, you will

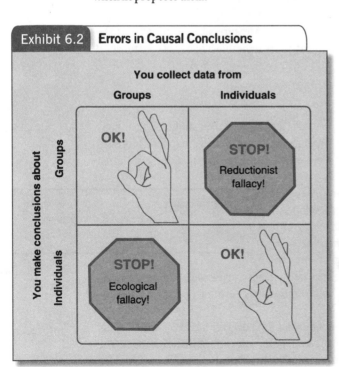

Exhibit 6.2   Errors in Causal Conclusions

need to collect data from the entire period you are studying; in this case you will use a **longitudinal research design**.

Therefore, the research question determines whether a researcher needs to collect cross-sectional or longitudinal data. If the research question only concerns the here and now, there is no need for longitudinal data. However, it is also important to recognize that any research question involving a causal analysis—about what causes what—creates an issue about change over time. Identifying the time order of effects, what happened first, is critical for developing a causal analysis, but can be an insurmountable problem with a cross-sectional design. In longitudinal research designs, identification of the time order of effects can be quite straightforward.

> **Cross-sectional research design** A study in which the data are collected at only one point in time.
>
> **Longitudinal research design** A study in which data are collected that can be ordered in time; research in which data are collected at two or more points in time.

Cross-Sectional Designs

In a cross-sectional research design, all of the data are collected at one point in time. It is like taking a still photo snapshot as you see a picture of what exists at that point in time but not what came before or after. Cross-sectional designs do not allow you to examine the impact of time on a variable. For instance, you might find that in a sample of adolescent girls those who had given birth had also dropped out of school. What you do not know is which event came first: Did the girls drop out and then become pregnant? Or did the girls become pregnant and then drop out of school? You cannot determine the time order of events, so you do not know what causes what. You might think the time order is not important, but if you are designing programs, it does become important. Do you provide outreach to those who have dropped out and offer programs to prevent pregnancy? Do you provide school-based child care to enable girls to continue in school? As a result, cross-sectional designs do not let you determine the impact of one variable on another variable.

Christopher Gjesfjeld, Catherine Greeno, Kevin Kim, and Carol Anderson (2010) used a cross-sectional survey design to study the relationship of economic stress, social support, and depressive symptoms. Their sample included 336 mothers with at least one child who received mental health services. Their theoretical framework was based on stress theory, or the idea that stressors such as individual or family changes generate stress in people's lives, but the extent or nature of that stress may be altered by the resources available to the individual or family (see Exhibit 6.3). One type of resource that varies among individuals or families is social support. They hypothesized that economic stress would have a direct effect on depression but that part of the effect would be the result of reduced social support. They used a model of social support deterioration to support their hypothesis that economic stress would negatively impact social support.

Gjesfjeld and colleagues (2010) confirmed their hypotheses. Economic stress was related to depressive symptoms; economic stress was also related to reduced social support and less social support was also related to higher levels of depressive symptoms. Although stress theory suggested the time order of events, their design could not establish directly that the variation in depression occurred after variation in social support. Maybe people who are depressed may find that their social support network wants to be less involved in their lives. It is difficult to discount such a possibility when only cross-sectional data are available.

As a general rule, cross-sectional designs do not allow you to establish time order. There are four special circumstances in which cross-sectional data can reasonably be used to infer the time order of effect (R. Campbell, 1992):

1. *The independent variable is fixed at some point prior to the variation in the dependent variable.* So-called demographic variables that are determined at birth—such as sex, race, and age—are fixed in this way. So are variables such as education and marital status, if we know when the value of cases on these variables was established and if we know that the value of cases on the dependent variable was set some time later. For example, say we hypothesize that education influences the type of job individuals have. If we know that respondents completed their education before taking their current jobs, we would satisfy the time order requirement even if we were to measure education at the same time we measure type of job. However, if some respondents possibly went back to school as a benefit of their current job, the time order requirement would not be satisfied.

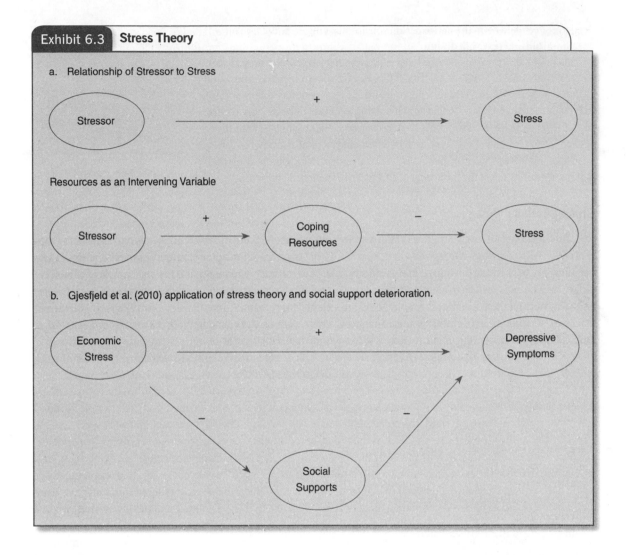

Exhibit 6.3 Stress Theory

a. Relationship of Stressor to Stress

Stressor → (+) → Stress

Resources as an Intervening Variable

Stressor → (+) → Coping Resources → (−) → Stress

b. Gjesfjeld et al. (2010) application of stress theory and social support deterioration.

Economic Stress → (+) → Depressive Symptoms

Economic Stress → (−) → Social Supports → (−) → Depressive Symptoms

2. *We believe that respondents can give us reliable reports of what happened to them or what they thought at some earlier point in time.* Julie Horney, D. Wayne Osgood, and Ineke Haen Marshall (1995) provide an interesting example of the use of such retrospective data. The researchers wanted to identify how criminal activity varies in response to changes in life circumstances. They interviewed 658 newly convicted male offenders sentenced to a Nebraska state prison. In a 45- to 90-minute interview, they recorded each inmate's report of his life circumstances and of his criminal activities for the preceding 2 to 3 years. They then found that criminal involvement was related strongly to adverse changes in life circumstances, such as marital separation or drug use. Retrospective data are often inadequate for measuring variation in past psychological states or behaviors, however, because what we recall about our feelings or actions in the past is likely to be influenced by what we feel in the present (Elliot, Holland, & Thompson, 2008). People cannot report reliably the frequency and timing of many past events, from hospitalization to hours worked. However, retrospective data tend to be reliable concerning major, persistent experiences in the past, such as what type of school someone went to or how a person's family was structured (R. Campbell, 1992).

3. *Our measures are based on records that contain information on cases in earlier periods.* Government, agency, and organizational records are an excellent source of time-ordered data after the fact. However, sloppy record keeping and changes in data collection policies can lead to inconsistencies that must be taken into account. Another

weakness of such archival data is that they usually contain measures of only a fraction of the variables that we think are important.

4. *We know that cases were equivalent on the dependent variable prior to the independent variable.* For example, we may hypothesize that a training program (independent variable) improves the English-speaking abilities (dependent variable) of a group of recent immigrants. If we know that none of the immigrants could speak English prior to enrolling in the training program, we can be confident that any subsequent variation in their ability to speak English did not precede exposure to the training program. This is one way that traditional experiments establish time order: Two or more equivalent groups are formed prior to exposing one of them to some treatment.

Longitudinal Designs

In longitudinal research, data are collected that can be ordered in time. By measuring the value of cases on an independent variable and a dependent variable at each of these different times, the researcher can determine whether change in the independent variable precedes change in the dependent variable. This design strategy enables researchers to test hypotheses that the independent variable does in fact come before changes in the dependent variable. Using a cross-sectional design you cannot be sure which came first, but in a longitudinal design you can measure the independent variable and then see at a later time the effect on the dependent variable. Following the same group of high school girls over several years would clarify whether dropping out precedes or follows becoming an adolescent mother.

It is more difficult to collect data at two or more points in time than at one time, and often researchers simply cannot, or are unwilling to, delay completion of a study in order to collect follow-up data. Still, many research questions really should involve a much longer follow-up period. The value of longitudinal data is so great that every effort should be made to develop longitudinal research designs when they are appropriate for the research question asked.

In some longitudinal designs, the same sample (or panel) is followed over time; in other designs, sample members are rotated or completely replaced. The frequency of measurement can vary including just two points of time to studies in which various indicators are measured every month for many years. The three major types of longitudinal designs are trend studies, panel designs, and cohort designs (see Exhibit 6.4).

Trend Studies. Also known as repeated cross-sectional studies, **trend studies** involve gathering data at two or more points in time from different samples of the same population. For example, we are used to hearing reports of monthly rates of unemployment and labor force participation as well as annual poverty rates. These reports generally come from the Current Population Survey (CPS), which

> **Trend studies** A longitudinal study in which data are collected at two or more points in time from different samples of the same population.

is a monthly survey jointly conducted by the Census Bureau and the Bureau of Labor Statistics of 50,000 households designed to represent the civilian, noninstitutional population. Each survey represents a different sample of households. In general, trend studies involve the following:

1. Drawing a sample from a population at Time 1 and collecting data from the sample

2. As time passes, some people leave the population and others enter it

3. At Time 2, drawing a different sample from this population

Trend studies are appropriate when the goal is to determine whether a population has changed over time. Has the rate of child poverty changed since 1996? The data reported in Exhibit 6.1 come from the CPS. In another trend study, Katherine Magnuson, Marcia Meyers, and Jane Waldfogel (2007) used CPS surveys from 1992 to 2000 to determine whether increased public funding for child care led to increased enrollment in formal child care by low-income families. Note that these questions concern changes in the population as whole or in defined populations, not changes in individuals within the population.

Panel study A longitudinal study of the same individuals.

Panel Designs. These are used when we want to know whether individuals within the population have changed, we use a **panel study**. To conduct a panel study,

1. a sample (called a panel) is drawn from a population at Time 1, and data are collected from the sample.

2. a Time 2, data are collected from the same people as at Time 1 (the panel)—except for those people who cannot be located.

Because a panel design follows the same individuals, it is better than a trend study for testing causal hypotheses. For example, Yiran Li, Bradford Mills, George Davis, and Elton Mykerezi (2014) used a panel design to investigate the relationship of child food insecurity and participation in the Supplemental Nutrition Assistance Program (SNAP). Using data from the Core Food Security Model of the Panel Study of Income Dynamics, they were able to track monthly food insecurity for a set of households. They learned that child food insecurity starts several months before receiving food stamps; that in months in which food stamps were received, child food insecurity was only partially eased; and that after being in the program for four months, child food insecurity returned to a pre-participation level.

Despite their value in establishing time order of effects, panel studies are a challenge to implement successfully. There are two major difficulties:

1. *Expense and attrition.* It can be difficult and expensive to keep track of individuals over a long period, and inevitably the proportion of panel members who can be located for follow-up will decline over time. Panel studies often lose more than one quarter of their members through attrition (D. Miller & Salkind, 2002). However, subject attrition can be reduced substantially if sufficient staff can be used to keep track of panel members. A high rate of subject attrition may result in the follow-up sample no longer being representative of the population from which it was drawn. It helps to compare the baseline characteristics of those who are interviewed at follow-up with the characteristics of those lost to follow-up. If these two groups of panel members were not very different at baseline, it is less likely that changes had anything to do with the characteristics of the missing panel members.

2. *Subject fatigue.* Panel members may grow weary of repeated interviews and drop out of the study, or they may become so used to answering the standard questions in the survey that they start giving stock answers, rather than actually thinking about their current feelings or actions (R. Campbell, 1992).

Cohort study A type of longitudinal study in which data are collected at two or more points in time from individuals or groups with a common stating point.

Because panel studies are so useful, researchers have developed increasingly effective techniques for keeping track of individuals and overcoming subject fatigue. But when resources do not permit use of these techniques to maintain an adequate panel, repeated cross-sectional designs usually can be employed at a cost that is not a great deal higher than that of a one-time-only cross-sectional study.

Cohort Studies. In a **cohort study** (also known as event-based designs), the follow-up samples (at one or more times) are selected from the same cohort—people who all have experienced a similar event or a common starting point. Some examples include

- Birth cohorts—those who share a common period of birth (those born in the 1940s, 1950s, 1960s, etc.)

- Seniority cohorts—those who have worked at the same place for about 5 years, about 10 years, and so on

- School cohorts—incoming kindergarteners

A cohort study can be either a type of trend design or a type of panel design. In a trend design, separate samples are drawn from the same cohort at two or more different times. In a cohort panel design, the same individuals from

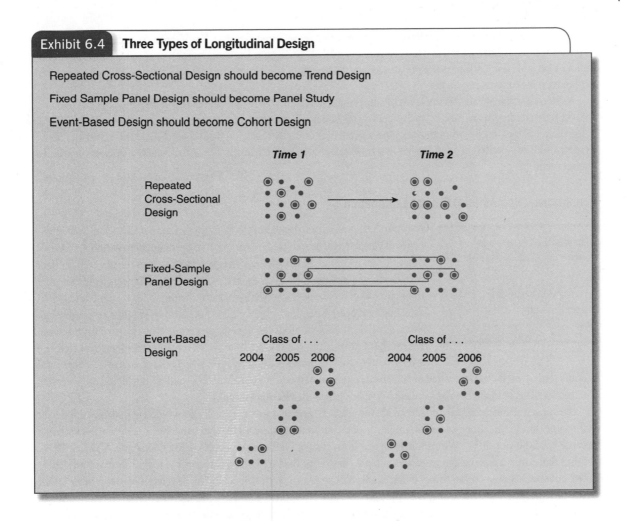

Exhibit 6.4 | **Three Types of Longitudinal Design**

Repeated Cross-Sectional Design should become Trend Design

Fixed Sample Panel Design should become Panel Study

Event-Based Design should become Cohort Design

the same cohort are studied at two or more different times. Comparing findings between different cohorts can help reveal the importance of the social or cultural context that the different cohorts experienced (Elliott et al., 2008).

Some of you may have been or are currently involved in a unique research project called *Monitoring the Future* (www.monitoringthefuture.org/purpose.html). This project was designed to study changes in the beliefs and attitudes of high school–age people across the United States. The project has evolved to include all three types of longitudinal designs. It started in 1975 as a trend study in which each year a sample of 12th graders was surveyed; in later years, 8th and 10th graders were added. Starting in 1976, a panel design was added. Every year, a random sample of each 12th-grade class is taken, and these subsamples are interviewed every 2 years. Differences in cohorts can be examined, for example, by comparing the 1976 panel with the 1986 panel, the 1996 panel, and the 2006 panel.

Quantitative or Qualitative Causal Explanations

A cause is an explanation for some characteristic, attitude, or behavior of groups, individuals, or other entities (such as families, organizations, or communities) or for events. Some social work researchers test the assumption that interventions cause changes in client status. Other social work researchers seek to explain the causes of social conditions. For instance, some researchers seek to identify the causes of poverty so that they can recommend policy changes that would deal with the identified causes. One explanation for poverty is that it is the result of differences in human capital—that is, differences in the skills and education that people bring to the marketplace. If that is the case, then social policy should emphasize programs to increase human capital. You should recognize that there is a hypothesis here: Adults with less education are more likely to be poor than adults with more education. The independent variable (education) is the presumed cause of the dependent variable (poverty status). This type of causal explanation is termed *nomothetic*.

A different type of cause is the focus of some qualitative research (see Chapter 10). In this type of causal explanation, termed *idiographic*, individual events or the behaviors of individuals are explained with a series of related, prior events. For example, you might explain a particular crime as resulting from several incidents in the life of the perpetrator that resulted in a tendency toward violence, coupled with stress resulting from a failed marriage and a chance meeting.

Quantitative (Nomothetic) Causal Explanation

Nomothetic causal explanation An explanation that identifies common influences on a number of cases or events.

Counterfactual The situation as it would have been in the absence of variation in the independent variable.

A **nomothetic causal explanation** involves the belief that variation in an independent variable will be followed by variation in the dependent variable, when all other things are equal. In this perspective, researchers who claim a causal effect have concluded that the value of cases on the dependent variable differs from what their value would have been in the absence of variation in the independent variable. For instance, researchers might claim that income is higher for people who went to college than it would be if those same people only finished high school. Researchers examining the impact of an intervention might suggest that the level of depressive symptoms is less for people who received cognitive-behavioral therapy than it would be if they had not received cognitive-behavioral therapy. The situation as it would have been in the absence of variation in the independent variable is called the **counterfactual**.

Of course, the fundamental difficulty with this perspective is that we never really know what would have happened at the same time to the same people (or families, groups, communities, etc.) if the independent variable had not varied—because it did (Shrout, 2011). We cannot rerun real-life scenarios for the same people (G. King, Keohane, & Verba, 1994).

But there are ways to design research to create conditions that are indeed comparable so that we can confidently assert our conclusions—other things being equal. We can examine the impact on the dependent variable of variation in the independent variable alone, even though we will not be able to compare the same people at the same time in exactly the same circumstances except for the variation in the independent variable. By knowing the ideal standard of comparability, we can improve our research designs and strengthen our causal conclusions.

Quantitative researchers test nomothetic causal explanations with experimental or nonexperimental research designs. However, the way in which experimental and nonexperimental designs attempt to identify causes differs quite a bit. It is hard to meet some of the criteria for achieving valid nomothetic causal explanations using a nonexperimental design. Most of the rest of this chapter is devoted to a review of these causal criteria and a discussion of how experimental and nonexperimental designs can help establish them.

Qualitative (Idiographic) Causal Explanation

An **idiographic causal explanation** is one that identifies the concrete, individual sequence of events, thoughts, or actions that resulted in a particular outcome for a particular individual or that led to a particular event (Hage & Meeker, 1988). An idiographic explanation also may be termed a *narrative* or *case-oriented explanation*.

Idiographic causal explanation An explanation that identifies the concrete, individual sequence of events, thoughts, or actions that resulted in a particular outcome for a particular individual or that led to a particular event.

A causal effect that is idiographic includes statements of initial conditions and then relates a series of events at different times that led to the outcome or causal effect. This narrative or story is the critical element in an idiographic explanation, which may therefore be classified as narrative reasoning (Richardson, 1995). Idiographic explanations focus on particular social actors, in particular social places, at particular social times (Abbott, 1992). Idiographic explanations are also typically concerned with context—with understanding the particular outcome as part of a larger set of interrelated circumstances.

The rich detail about events and processes that field research generates (see Chapter 10) can be the basis for a convincing idiographic, narrative account of why things happened. Elijah Anderson's (1990) field research in a poor urban community produced a narrative account of how drug addiction often resulted in a downward slide into residential instability and crime:

> When addicts deplete their resources, they may go to those closest to them, drawing them into their schemes. . . . The family may put up with the person for a while. They provide money if they can. . . . They come to realize that the person is on drugs. . . . Slowly the reality sets in more and more completely, and the family becomes drained of both financial and emotional resources. . . . Close relatives lose faith and begin to see the person as untrustworthy and weak. Eventually the addict begins to "mess up" in a variety of ways, taking furniture from the house [and] anything of value. . . . Relatives and friends begin to see the person . . . as "out there" in the streets. . . . One deviant act leads to another. (pp. 86–87)

An ideographic explanation can also be developed from the narration of an individual. For example, Carole Cain interviewed Alcoholics Anonymous (AA) members about their experience to learn how they construct their identities as alcoholics. In one interview, excerpted by Catherine Kohler Riessman (2008), "Hank" describes some of his experiences with drinking:

> One morning he found he could not get up even after several drinks. . . . When he did get up, he found AA, although he cannot remember how he knew where to go. . . . From the morning when he contacted AA, he did not drink again for over five years. . . . Life improved, he got himself in better shape and got back together with his wife. After several years, the marriage broke up again, and in anger with his wife, he went back to drinking for another five years.

Research In the News

For Further Thought ?

WHY IS CHILD POVERTY SO HIGH?

Christopher Ingraham reported that the United States has one of the highest rates of child poverty among wealthy nations, noting that one third of U.S. children live in households below 60% of the national median income. Yet, the United States is the richest nation in the world. And the report notes that there are wide differences by state as poverty rates tend to be higher in the South and lower in New England and the Northcentral part of the country.

1. Why do you think poverty is so high in the United States?

2. What reasons might explain regional differences?

3. Propose a study that would examine the causes of the extent of child poverty. How might this study differ from one that looks at regional differences?

Source: Ingraham (2014).

An idiographic explanation like Anderson's or Cain's pays close attention to time order and causal mechanisms. Nonetheless, it is difficult to make a convincing case that one particular causal narrative should be chosen over an alternative narrative (Abbott, 1992). Does low self-esteem result in vulnerability to the appeals of drug dealers, or does a chance drug encounter precipitate a slide in self-esteem? Did drinking lead Hank to go to AA, or did he start drinking more because he knew it would push him to go to AA? Did his drinking start again because his marriage broke up, or did his orientation lead to his wife to leave and to his renewed drinking? The prudent causal analyst remains open to alternative explanations.

Idiographic explanation is deterministic, focusing on what caused a particular event to occur or what caused a particular case to change. As in nomothetic explanations, idiographic causal explanations can involve counterfactuals, by trying to identify what would have happened if different circumstances had occurred. But unlike in nomothetic explanations, in idiographic explanations the notion of a probabilistic relationship, an average effect, does not really apply. A deterministic cause has an effect in every case under consideration.

回 Criteria for Quantitative (Nomothetic) Causal Explanations

How a research project is designed influences our ability to draw causal conclusions. Three criteria must be considered when deciding whether a causal connection exists. Many times researchers have to leave one or more of the criteria unmet and therefore are left with some important doubts about their causal conclusions, if they even make any causal assertions. These three criteria are generally considered the most important bases for identifying a nomothetic causal effect: (1) empirical association, (2) appropriate time order, and (3) nonspuriousness. The features of experimental research designs are particularly well suited to meeting these criteria and for testing nomothetic causal explanations. However, we must consider the degree to which these criteria are met when evaluating nonexperimental research that is designed to test hypotheses.

Two other criteria—identifying a causal mechanism and specifying the context in which the effect occurs—can considerably strengthen causal explanations. They are not necessary for establishing a causal connection, but they help us better understand the causal connection. A causal mechanism helps us understand more fully *why* a causal connection exists. Identifying the context helps us understand *when* or *under what conditions* the causal effect occurs. Providing information about both mechanism and context can strengthen causal explanations (Hammersley, 2008).

In the following subsections, we describe how researchers attempt to meet the criteria with a study using an experimental design and a study using a nonexperimental design. Catherine Reich and Jeffrey Berman's (2015) study of the impact of financial literacy classes on financial knowledge and behavior illustrates how an experimental approach can be used to meet the criteria for establishing causal relations. Illustrations of nonexperimental design features will be based on the study by Gjesfjeld and colleagues (2010) described earlier.

Reich and Berman (2015) recruited participants from a transitional housing program for homeless families. To be considered for the housing program, families had to be homeless and include a child under age 17. The applicant had to be employed or employable and pass both a background check and drug screen. Sixty-one residents agreed to participate in the study but only 33 actually followed through; 17 were assigned to the experimental group, and 16 were assigned to the comparison group. Information about financial knowledge (percentage of responses to 12 questions), negative financial events (percentage of 16 behaviors such as missing bill payments, taking cash advances, borrowing money from friends, and positive behaviors (sum of 8 behaviors such as putting money into a savings account, paying bills on time, storing information in a secure place, and packing lunch) were collected before and after the conclusion of the intervention.

Residents in the experimental group participated in a 5-week financial literacy course adapted from the Money Smart program developed by the Federal Deposit Insurance Corporation (Reich & Berman, 2015). The course taught information about budgeting, loan repayment, use of checking accounts and credit, and the nature of loans and the repayment of debt. Participants learned about guarding against identity theft and reading credit reports. The comparison group members were placed on a wait list.

Did the intervention make any difference? Participants had higher scores on the financial knowledge test and were more likely to engage in positive behaviors. There were no differences in negative behaviors.

Association

The first criterion for identifying a causal effect is an empirical (or observed) **association** (sometimes a *correlation*) between the independent and dependent variables. This means that when the independent variable changes, the dependent variable also changes; if there is no association between two variables, there cannot be a causal relationship. Reich and Berman (2015) found a relationship between participation in the financial literacy group and knowledge and behaviors. An empirical association is typically demonstrated by using statistical techniques to show that the relationship between an independent and dependent variable is not due to chance.

> **Association** A criterion for establishing a nomothetic causal relationship between two variables: variation in one variable is related to variation in another variable.

We can determine whether an association exists between the independent and dependent variables in a true experiment because there are two or more groups that differ in terms of their value on the independent variable. One group receives some treatment, such as intensive, in-home, family-based services, which is a manipulation of the value of the independent variable. This group is termed the *experimental group*. In a simple experiment, there may be one other group that does not receive the treatment; it is termed the *control group*. In social work research, it is common for the other group to receive what is routinely provided (sometimes referred to as *treatment as usual*) so it is getting some form of treatment; this second group is termed the *comparison group*. Reich and Berman (2015) compared two groups; other experiments may compare more groups, which represent multiple values of the independent variable or even combinations of the values of two or more independent variables. An empirical association was demonstrated by comparing the two groups using statistical techniques to show that the differences were not due to chance.

In nonexperimental research, the test for an association between the independent and dependent variables is like that used in experimental research—seeing whether values of cases that differ on the independent variable tend to differ in terms of the dependent variable. The difference with nonexperimental research designs is that the independent variable is not a treatment to which the research assigns some individuals. Gjesfjeld and colleagues (2010) were able to show that there was a statistical relationship between variation in the level of economic stress (independent variable), social support (intervening variable), and depressive symptoms (dependent variable).

Time Order

Association is a necessary criterion for establishing a causal effect, but it is not sufficient. We must also ensure that the variation in the dependent variable occurred after the variation in the independent variable. This is the criterion of **time order**. The research design determines whether time order is achieved.

> **Time order** A criterion for establishing a causal relation between two variables. The variation in the presumed cause (the independent variable) must occur before the variation in the presumed effect (dependent variable).

In a true experiment, the researcher determines the time order. Reich and Berman (2015) gathered baseline information prior to the start of the financial literacy class. As you can imagine, we cannot be so sure about time order when we use a cross-sectional research design to test a causal hypothesis. While Gjesfjeld and colleagues (2010) were able to show that there were statistical relationships among the variables, the research design does not lend itself to knowing which came first. This is a limitation that they noted in their study, and they recommended that a future study should implement a longitudinal design.

Nonspuriousness

Nonspuriousness is another essential criterion for establishing the existence of a causal effect of an independent variable on a dependent variable. We say that a

> **Nonspuriousness** A criterion for establishing a causal relation between two variables; when a relationship between two variables is not due to variation in a third variable.

> **Spurious relationship** When the relationship between two variables is actually caused by a third variable.

relationship between two variables is not spurious when it is not due to variation in a third variable. A causal relationship requires that we can rule out all alternative explanations that might explain the relationship. This is why correlation is not sufficient for causation, because an association between two variables might be caused by something other than an effect of the presumed independent variable on the dependent variable. This is called a **spurious relationship**.

Do storks bring babies? If you believe that correlation establishes causation, then you might think so. The more storks that appear in certain districts in Holland, the more babies are born. But the association in Holland between the number of storks and the number of babies is spurious. In fact, both the number of storks and the birth rate are higher in rural districts than in urban districts. The rural or urban character of the districts (the extraneous variable) causes variation in the other two variables.

If you think this point is obvious, consider a social science example. Do schools with better resources produce better students? Before you answer the question, consider the fact that parents with more education and higher income tend to live in neighborhoods that spend more on their schools. These parents are also more likely to have computers and books in the home and provide other advantages for their children. Does the economic and educational status of the parents cause variation in both school resources and student performance? If so, there would be an association between school resources and student performance that was at least partially spurious.

Randomization

A true experiment like Reich and Berman's (2015) study of financial literacy classes uses a technique called **randomization** to reduce the risk of spuriousness. If subjects were assigned to only two groups, a coin toss could have been used (see Exhibit 6.5). The participants in their experiment were randomly assigned to either the experimental group or the comparison group. This means that chance determined into which group a resident would be placed.

> **Randomization** Placing participants into an experimental or control group using some chance method such as by the toss of a coin.
>
> **Random assignment** A procedure using chance to assign each research participant to an experimental or comparison group.

Random assignment ensures that the residents' other characteristics could not influence which of the treatment methods they received. As a result, the different groups are likely to be equivalent in all respects at the outset of the experiment. The greater the number of cases assigned randomly to the groups, the more likely that the groups will be equivalent in all respects. Whatever the preexisting sources of variation among the families, these could not explain why the group that received the financial literacy intervention had increased their financial knowledge and engage in more positive behaviors than the residents in the comparison group.

Statistical Control

A nonexperimental study like Gjesfjeld and colleagues' (2010) cannot use random assignment to comparison groups to minimize the risk of spurious effects. We cannot randomly assign people to many of the social conditions they experience, such as having a child receiving mental health services or living in a particular neighborhood. Instead, nonexperimental researchers commonly use an alternative approach to try to achieve the criterion of nonspuriousness. The technique of **statistical control** allows researchers to determine whether the relationship between the independent and dependent variables still occurs while we hold constant the values of other variables. If it does, the relationship could not be caused by variation in these other variables.

> **Statistical control** A method in which one variable is held constant so that the relationship between two or more other variables can be assessed without the influence of variation in the control variable.

Gjesfjeld and colleagues (2010) designed their study to control for other factors that might explain the relationships among economic stress, social support, and depression. They evaluated age, race, and number of children and found no relationship to depression. They included marital status and working outside the home in their overall analysis and found that controlling for their impacts did not change their findings.

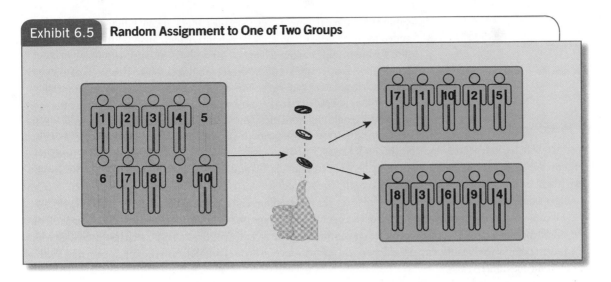

| Exhibit 6.5 | Random Assignment to One of Two Groups |

We can strengthen our understanding of nomothetic causal connections and increase the likelihood of drawing causally valid conclusions by considering two additional criteria: causal mechanism and causal context. These two criteria are emphasized in the definition of idiographic causal explanation, with its attention to the sequence of events and the context in which they happen, but here we limit our discussion to research oriented toward nomothetic causal explanations.

Mechanism

A causal **mechanism** is some process that creates the connection between variation in an independent variable and the variation in the dependent variable (Cook & Campbell, 1979; Marini & Singer, 1988). In social work research, this might involve understanding the theoretical components of the intervention model or it might be to understand the underlying process, the essential actions, that led to the desired change.

> **Mechanism** A discernible process that creates a causal connection between two variables.

Figuring out some aspects of the process by which the independent variable influenced the variation in the dependent variable should increase confidence in our conclusion that there was a causal effect (Costner, 1989). However, there may be many components to the causal mechanism, and we cannot hope to identify them all in one study.

Our confidence in causal conclusions based on nonexperimental research also increases with identification of a causal mechanism (Shrout, 2011). Such mechanisms, termed **intervening variables** in nonexperimental research, help us understand how variation in the independent variable results in variation in the dependent variable. One such variable is a **mediating variable.** In this case, the independent variable impacts the mediating variable, and the mediating variable affects the dependent variable. The effect of the independent variable on the dependent variable becomes zero. This is different from a spurious relationship. When the relationship is spurious, the independent variable and the third variable also have no relationship; with a mediating variable, change in the independent variable is associated with change in the mediating variable. Rarely is there a true mediating variable in social science and social work research; rather, variables have a partial mediating effect. Gjesfjeld and colleagues (2010) found that social

> **Intervening variable** Variables that are influenced by independent variables and in turn influence variation in a dependent variable, thereby helping to explain the relationship between the independent and dependent variables.
>
> **Mediating variable** The independent variable impacts the mediating variable, and the mediating variable affects the dependent variable. The effect of the independent variable on the dependent variable becomes zero.

Moderator variable A third variable that interacts with the independent variable.

Context A focus of idiographic causal explanation; a particular outcome is understood as part of a larger set of interrelated circumstances.

support was a partial mediating variable (refer back to Exhibit 6.3). When they added the mediating variable, social support to their analysis, they found that the direct relationship between economic stress and depressive symptoms weakened but did not disappear; part of the direct relationship was the result of high economic stress reducing social supports and its impact on depressive symptoms.

A different kind of third variable may *moderate* the relationship of the independent variable and the dependent variable. A **moderator variable** affects the relationship between independent variable and dependent variable because it interacts with the independent variable (Baron & Kenny, 1986). For example, Gjesfjeld and colleagues (2010) might have proposed that age moderates the relationship between economic stress and depressive symptoms. The specific hypothesis might be that given the same level of economic stress, older women are more likely to experience stress than are younger women. Economic stress still is related to depressive symptoms, but the impact of social support differs by age.

Of course, identification of one (or two or three) intervening variables does not end the possibilities for clarifying the causal mechanisms. This process could go on and on. The point is that identification of a mechanism through which the independent variable influences the dependent variable increases our confidence in the conclusion that a causal connection does indeed exist.

Context

No cause has its effect apart from some larger **context** involving other variables. For whom, when, and in what conditions does this effect occur? Do the causal relationships differ among different groups of people? Neighborhoods? Organizations? Regions? Over time? When relationships among variables differ across groups or geographic regions, researchers say there is a contextual effect. Identification of the context in which a causal relationship occurs can help us understand the relationship. A cause is really one among a set of interrelated factors required for the effect (Hage & Meeker, 1988; Papineau, 1978). Identification of the context in which a causal effect occurs is not a criterion for a valid causal conclusion, and it is not always attempted, but it does help us understand the causal relationship.

An example of how effects can vary across groups occurred in the Reich and Berman (2015) study. They noted an interesting outcome in their findings. Overall, experimental participants reported higher positive behaviors than did participants assigned to the comparison group. Within the experimental group there were differences as well. Participants with few positive behaviors at baseline tended not to increase their positive behaviors; conversely, participants with higher positive behaviors at baseline did increase the number of positive behaviors. They suggested that the intervention should be modified for persons with few positive behaviors.

Specifying the context in which causal effects occur is no less important in nonexperimental than in experimental research. Nonexperimental research is well suited to exploring the context in which causal effects occur. Administering surveys in many different settings and to different types of individuals is usually much easier than administering experiments in different ways.

▣ Comparing Research Designs

The central features of the basic social research designs you will study in detail in the next chapters—true experiments, quasi-experiments, nonexperiments, single-subject designs, surveys, and qualitative methods—provide distinct perspectives even when used to study the same social processes. Comparing subjects randomly assigned to a treatment and to a comparison group, looking at how subjects differ when subjects cannot be randomly assigned, evaluating changes in a single participant, asking standard questions of the members of a random sample, or observing while participating in a natural social setting involve markedly different decisions about measurement, causality, and generalizability. As you can see in Exhibit 6.6 none of these research designs can be reasonably graded as superior to the others in all respects, and each varies in its suitability to different research questions and goals. Choosing among them for a particular investigation requires consideration of the research problem, opportunities and resources, prior research, philosophical commitments, and research goals.

True experimental designs are strongest for testing nomothetic causal hypotheses and are most appropriate for studies of treatment effects. Random assignment reduces the possibility of preexisting differences between treatment and comparison groups to small, specifiable, chance levels, so many of the variables that might create a spurious association are controlled. But despite this clear advantage, an experimental design requires a degree of control that cannot always be achieved in other settings. It can be difficult to ensure in real-world settings that a treatment was delivered as intended and that other influences did not intrude. As a result, what appears to be a treatment effect or non-effect may be something else altogether. Community- or agency-based experiments thus require careful monitoring of the treatment process. Researchers may be unable to randomly assign participants to groups or have too few participants to assign to groups, and unfortunately, most field experiments also require more access arrangements and financial resources than can often be obtained. In lieu of these difficulties, quasi- and nonexperimental designs are used but at the cost of causal validity.

True experiments permit much more control over conditions, but at the cost of less generalizable findings. People must volunteer for group experimental designs, and so there is a good possibility that experimental subjects differ from those who do not volunteer. Ethical and practical constraints limit the types of treatments that can be studied experimentally. The problem of generalizability in an experiment using volunteers lessens when the object of investigation is an orientation, behavior, or social process that is relatively invariant among people, but it is difficult to know which orientations, behaviors, or processes are so invariant. If a search of the research literature on the topic identifies many prior experimental studies, the results of these experiments will suggest the extent of variability in experimental effects and point to the unanswered questions about these effects.

Single-subject designs are particularly useful for building social work practice knowledge and are more easily applied to agency-based research. Systematic measurement in both the baseline and intervention phases reduces the chances that there are other explanations for the findings, although this does not eliminate all sources of uncertainty about the findings. Generalizability of the findings has less to do with representativeness, but rather whether the findings about the intervention can be repeated in different settings, with different clients or communities, and other related problems.

| Exhibit 6.6 | Comparing Research Methods |

Design	Measurement Validity	Generalizability	Type of Casual Assertions	Causal Validity
Group Experiments				
• True Experiments	+	−	Nomothetic	+
• Quasi-experiments	+	−	Nomothetic	+/− [a]
• Nonexperiments	+	−	Nomothetic	−
Single Subject	+	−	Idiographic	+/−[a]
Surveys	+	+	Nomothetic	+/−[b]
Qualitative	+/−[c]	−	Idiographic	−

[a] Quasi-experiments and single-subject designs differ in their utility for establishing causality.

[b] Surveys are a weaker design for identifying causal effects than true experiments, but use of statistical controls can strengthen causal arguments.

[c] Reliability is low compared to surveys, and systematic evaluation of measurement validity is often not.

Surveys, experiments, and single-subject designs typically use standardized, quantitative measures of attitudes, behaviors, or social processes. Closed-ended questions and scales are most common and are well suited for the reliable measurement of variables that have been studied in the past and whose meanings are well understood. Of course, surveys often include measures of many more variables than are included in an experiment or in a single-subject design, but this feature is not inherent in these designs. Phone surveys may be quite short, whereas some experiments can involve lengthy sets of measures. The level of funding for a survey often determines which type of survey is conducted and thus how long the questionnaire is.

Many surveys rely on random sampling for their selection of cases from some larger population, and this feature makes them preferable for descriptive research that seeks to develop generalizable findings. However, survey questionnaires can only measure what respondents are willing to report; they may not be adequate for studying behaviors or attitudes that are regarded as socially unacceptable. Surveys are also often used to test hypothesized causal relationships. When variables that might create spurious relationships are included in the survey, they can be controlled statistically in the analysis and thus eliminated as rival causal influences.

Qualitative methods presume an intensive measurement approach in which indicators of concepts are drawn from direct observation or in-depth commentary. This approach is most appropriate when it is not clear what meaning people attach to a concept or what sense they might make of particular questions about it. Qualitative methods are also suited to the exploration of new or poorly understood social settings when it is not even clear what concepts would help to understand the situation. Further, these methods are useful in uncovering the process of a program or the implementation of an intervention. They may also be used instead of survey methods when the population of interest is not easily identifiable or seeks to remain hidden. For these reasons, qualitative methods tend to be preferred when exploratory research questions are posed or when new groups are investigated. But, of course, intensive measurement necessarily makes the study of large numbers of cases or situations difficult, resulting in the limitation of many field research efforts to small numbers of people or unique social settings. The individual field researcher may not require many financial resources, but the amount of time required for many field research projects serves as a barrier to many would-be field researchers.

When qualitative methods can be used to study several individuals or settings that provide marked contrasts in terms of a presumed independent variable, it becomes possible to evaluate nomothetic causal hypotheses with these methods. However, the impossibility of taking into account many possible extraneous influences in such limited comparisons makes qualitative methods a weak approach to hypothesis testing. Qualitative methods are more suited to the elucidation of causal mechanisms. In addition, qualitative methods can be used to identify the multiple successive events that might have led to some outcome, thus identifying idiographic causal processes.

▣ Implications for Evidence-Based Practice

In Chapter 1, we noted that one of the pillars of evidence-based practice is knowledge gained from research findings about the effectiveness or ineffectiveness of different interventions. A key consideration in weighing research evidence is the type of research design used to test the intervention. As you have learned from this chapter, the strength of a conclusion that an intervention leads to some predefined outcome differs depending on the type of research design employed.

Randomized experimental designs (also known as randomized clinical trials) such as Reich and Berman's study typically represent research designs that provide strong evidence that the intervention is effective for a particular problem (American Psychological Association, 2006; Gambrill, 2006; Johnston, Sherer, & Whyte, 2006). Ideally, there are a number of randomized experimental trials of the intervention's effectiveness relative to a particular outcome. But many social work interventions have not been tested using randomized experimental designs, and therefore, we must rely on evidence based on other types of research designs. These designs may account for only one or two of the criteria for causality, or even none of the criteria.

Some guidelines (e.g., American Psychological Association, 2006; Johnston et al., 2006) offer a hierarchy of different designs based on the extent to which the designs control for some aspects of causality. For example, quasi-experimental designs (one of the subjects of Chapter 7) control for only one or two criteria and therefore do not provide evidence as strong as randomized experimental designs about an intervention's effectiveness. Other research designs also fail to control for the necessary criteria.

We want to emphasize that, although this evidence is important and necessary for decision making about choosing an intervention, it is not the sole criterion. Evidence about the clinical utility of a particular intervention is important, but evidence about the applicability of the intervention in a particular setting or with particular clients is also an important consideration. As you learn in Chapter 7, although randomized experimental designs meet the criteria to establish causality, they are not perfect, and the generalizability of the findings is harder to establish. So, for example, evidence derived from clinical studies in a rural outpatient clinic may not translate to an urban, inpatient clinic.

🔲 Conclusion

Causation and the means for achieving causally valid conclusions in research is the last of the three legs on which the validity of research rests. In this chapter, you have learned about the two main meanings of causation (nomothetic and idiographic). You have learned that our ability to meet the criteria for causality is shaped by research design features such as the use of a cross-sectional or longitudinal design and the use of randomization or statistical control to deal with problems of spuriousness. You have also seen why the distinction between experimental and nonexperimental designs has so many consequences for how and how well we are able to meet nomothetic criteria for causation.

We should reemphasize that the results of any particular study are part of an always changing body of empirical knowledge about social reality. Thus, our understandings of causal relationships are always partial. Researchers always wonder whether they have omitted some relevant variables from their controls or whether their experimental results would differ if the experiment were conducted in another setting. But by using consistent definitions of terms and maintaining clear standards for establishing the validity of research results—and by expecting the same of others who do research—social researchers can contribute to a growing body of knowledge that can reliably guide social policy and social understanding.

When you read the results of a social scientific study, you should now be able to evaluate critically the validity of the study's findings. If you plan to engage in social research, you should now be able to plan an approach that will lead to valid findings. With a good understanding of the three dimensions of validity (measurement validity, generalizability, and causal validity) under your belt, you are ready to focus on the four major methods of research design used by social scientists.

Key Terms

Highlights

- Units of analysis refer to the level of social life about which we can generalize our findings and include such levels as individuals, groups, families, communities, or organizations.

- Invalid conclusions about causality may occur when relationships between variables measured at the group level are assumed to apply at the individual level (the ecological fallacy) and when relationships between variables measured at the level of individuals are assumed to apply at the group level (the reductionist fallacy). Nonetheless, many research questions point to relationships at multiple levels and may profitably be answered by studying different units of analysis.

- Longitudinal designs are usually preferable to cross-sectional designs for establishing the time order of effects. Longitudinal designs vary in terms of whether the same people are measured at different times, how the population of interest is defined, and how frequently follow-up measurements are taken. Panel designs provide the strongest test for the time order of effects, but they can be difficult to carry out successfully because of their expense and subject attrition and fatigue.

- Causation can be defined in either nomothetic or idiographic terms. Nomothetic causal explanations deal with effects on average. Idiographic causal explanations deal with the sequence of events that led to a particular outcome.

- The concept of nomothetic causal explanation relies on a comparison. The value of cases on the dependent variable is measured after they have been exposed to variation in an independent variable. This measurement is compared to what the value of cases on the dependent variable would have been if they had not been exposed to the variation in the independent variable. The validity of nomothetic causal conclusions rests on how closely the comparison group comes to the ideal counterfactual.

- From a nomothetic perspective, three criteria are generally viewed as necessary for identifying a causal relationship: association between the variables, proper time order, and nonspuriousness of the association. In addition, the basis for concluding that a causal relationship exists is strengthened by identification of a causal mechanism and the context.

- Association between two variables is in itself insufficient evidence of a causal relationship. This point is commonly made with the expression "Correlation does not prove causation."

- Experiments use random assignment to make comparison groups as similar as possible at the outset of an experiment to reduce the risk of spurious effects due to extraneous variables.

- Nonexperimental designs use statistical controls to reduce the risk of spuriousness. A variable is controlled when it is held constant so that the association between the independent and dependent variables can be assessed without being influenced by the control variable.

- Longitudinal designs are usually preferable to cross-sectional designs for establishing the time order of effects. Longitudinal designs vary in terms of whether the same people are measured at different times, how the population of interest is defined, and how frequently follow-up measurements are taken. Panel designs provide the strongest test for the time order of effects, but they can be difficult to carry out successfully because of their expense and subject attrition and fatigue.

- Idiographic causal explanations can be difficult to identify because the starting and ending points of particular events and the determination of which events act as causes in particular sequences may be ambiguous.

Discussion Questions

1. Discuss the utility of cross-sectional research designs. How might we address the problem of time order in cross-sectional designs?

2. Compare and contrast the nomothetic and idiographic explanations of causation. How do the approaches or goals of each vary? How might these perspectives be applied to studies on child poverty?

3. Develop an explanation of the relationship between juvenile delinquency and the poverty rate by specifying intervening variables that might link the two. Is your proposed causal mechanism more compatible with a "culture of poverty" explanation of this relationship or with a conflict theory explanation? Explain your answer.

Practice Exercises

1. Review articles in several newspapers, copying down all causal assertions. These might range from assertions that the increasing divorce rate is due to women's liberation from traditional gender roles to explanations about why welfare rates are decreasing or child abuse reports are increasing. Inspect the articles carefully, noting all evidence used to support the causal assertions. Are the explanations nomothetic, idiographic, or a combination of both? Which criteria for establishing causality in a nomothetic framework are met? How satisfactory are the idiographic explanations? What other potentially important influences on the reported outcome have been overlooked?

2. Search Social Work Abstracts for several articles on studies using any type of longitudinal design. You will be searching for article titles that use words such as *longitudinal, panel, trend,* or *over time.* How successful were the researchers in carrying out the design? What steps did the researchers who used a panel design take to minimize panel attrition? How convinced are you by those using repeated cross-sectional designs that they have identified a process of change in individuals? Did any researchers use retrospective questions? How did they defend the validity of these measures?

Web Exercise

1. Go to Current Population Survey Historical Poverty Tables website, http://www.census.gov/hhes/www/poverty/data/historical/index.html. Pick a table and see if you can identify the trend with regard to the report that you see.

2. What are the latest trends in crime? Write a short statement after inspecting the FBI's Uniform Crime Reports at www.fbi.gov.

Developing a Research Proposal

How will you try to establish your hypothesis about causal effects?

1. Identify at least one hypothesis involving what you expect is a causal relationship.

2. Identify key variables that should be controlled to increase your ability to avoid arriving at a spurious conclusion about the

hypothesized causal effect. Draw on relevant research literature and social theory to identify these variables.

3. Review the criteria for establishing a causal effect, and discuss your ability to satisfy each one.

A Question of Ethics

1. Walton and colleagues' (1993) conducted a child welfare experiment and found a positive impact of intensive in-home, family-based services on improving rates of family reunification. After this positive result, would you consider it ethical to conduct additional experiments with such families in which some do not receive intensive services? Are there any situations in which you would not approve of such research? Any types of at-risk families you would exclude from such research?

2. Federal regulations require special safeguards for research on persons with impaired cognitive capacity. Special safeguards are also required for research on prisoners and on children. Do you think special safeguards are necessary? Why or why not? Do you think it is possible for individuals in any of these groups to give "voluntary consent" to research participation? What procedures might help make consent to research truly voluntary in these situations?

Group Experimentlal Designs

A challenge for social work researchers is to demonstrate that different treatment modalities and interventions are effective and to examine accurately the impact of social policy changes. All too often in the past, evidence demonstrating the effectiveness of interventions and policy changes was based on research designs that did not meet the criteria for causality described in Chapter 6. More recently, there has been a trend among funders of programs, such as the United Way, to require evidence that a funded program is producing the kinds of outcomes that were promised. The level of evidence may not be so stringent that causality must be demonstrated, but evidence of an association is required.

We begin this chapter by discussing in greater detail validity and experimental research designs. The ability to demonstrate internal validity provides the framework by which we then discuss three different types of group designs that social work researchers and agencies use to test or demonstrate treatment effectiveness and to show the impact of policy changes. Although the examples we use in this chapter relate specifically to research and evaluation in social work practice and social policy, the same principles apply to research in other disciplines. The independent variable in many of the examples is an intervention or a social policy, but the independent variable could just as easily be "the amount of exposure to violence in television" or "presence of seatbelt laws."

🏛 Threats to the Validity of Group Experimental Designs

Group experimental designs, like any research design, must be evaluated for their ability to yield valid conclusions. Remember there are three kinds of validity: (1) internal validity (nonspuriousness), (2) external validity (generalizability), and (3) measurement. In Chapter 4, we discussed measurement validity and that group experimental designs offer no special advantages or disadvantages in measurement. Therefore we will focus on internal and external validity, that is, alternative explanations that may explain the effects of the independent variable on the dependent variable and external validity or the ability to generalize the findings beyond the experimental conditions.

Internal Validity

An experiment's ability to yield valid conclusions about internal validity is determined by the comparability of its experimental and comparison groups. First, a comparison group must be created. Second, this comparison group must be so similar to the experimental group that it shows what the experimental group would be like if it had not received the experimental treatment, that is, if the independent variable had not varied. In Chapter 6, we referred to the process of establishing comparable groups as randomization or random assignment; the process of assigning individuals into a group by chance so that the experimental and comparison groups are more or less equal in their composition at the onset of the experiment. The following sections discuss threats to the internal validity that may occur (see Exhibit 7.1).

Threat to Internal Validity Reduced by Randomization

The purpose of randomization, or random assignment to the experimental and comparison groups, is to equate the two or more groups at the start of the experiment. The goal is to eliminate the effect of **selection bias**.

1. *Selection bias.* The lack of similarity between groups may offer an alternative explanation for an experiment's findings as opposed to the effect of the independent variable on the dependent variable. Selection bias occurs when a comparison group and experimental group are initially different; selection bias is related to the methods used to assign subjects to the groups. When subjects are assigned randomly (by chance) to treatment and comparison groups, the threat of selection bias is reduced. However,

> **Selection bias** The lack of similarity between groups may offer an alternative explanation for an experiment's findings as opposed to the effect of the independent variable on the dependent variable.

Exhibit 7.1   Summary of Threats to Internal Validity

Threat to Internal Validity Reduced by Randomization

- *Selection bias* Two groups are different at the start of the experiment. Less of a problem with random assignment, more of a problem when random assignment is not used,

Threats to Internal Validity Reduced by a Comparison Group

- *History* An event outside the experiment that participants are exposed to
- *Testing* Respondents learn from the pretest: reduced anxiety from having taken the test or learning content on their own
- *Instrumentation* Use of measures lacking reliability.
- *Maturation* Respondents change as part of the natural process of the passing of time.
- *Statistical regression* Respondents improve or get worse because their initial scores may reflect a "bad day" as opposed to their true score.
- *Secular drift* Broader societal trends that impact on the desired outcomes of the experiment.

Threats to Internal Validity Requiring Attention While the Experiment Is in Progress

- *Mortality* Group composition changes due to dropping out during the experiment.
- Contamination When the comparison or control group is affected by the treatment group. This includes

  o *Compensatory rivalry* Comparison group aware that they are denied some advantage increase their efforts to succeed.

  o *Resentful demoralization* Comparison group aware that they are denied some advantage reduce their efforts to succeed.

  o *Diffusion of treatment* When groups interact and the nature of the treatment becomes known to the control group.

- *Compensatory equalization of treatment* Staff provide more than expected to comparison group.
- *Placebo effect* when subjects received a treatment they consider likely to be beneficial and improve because of that expectation.

---

when subjects are assigned using other methods besides random assignment, the threat of selection bias is great even if the researcher selects a comparison group that matches the treatment group on important variables (e.g., demographic characteristics). Imagine assigning highly motivated participants to one group and less motivated participants to a second group. The highly motivated participants are apt to perform better than are the less motivated participants. Randomization should result in similar group characteristics, although with some possibility for error due to chance. The likelihood of difference due to chance can be identified with appropriate statistics.

Threats to Internal Validity Reduced by a Comparison Group

The types of problem that can largely be eliminated by having a comparison group as well as a treatment group are those that arise during the study period itself (D. Campbell & Stanley, 1966). There are six such threats:

1. *History*. External events during the experiment (things that happen outside the experiment) can change participants' outcome scores. For example, a new cook is hired at a nursing home, and the food improves at the same time a researcher is evaluating a group intervention to improve the morale of residents. In an experiment in which participants go to a particular location for the treatment and the control group participants do not, something in that location unrelated to the treatment could influence the experimental subjects.

History A source of causal invalidity that occurs when something other than the treatment influences outcome scores; also called an effect of external events.

2. *Testing*. Taking a pretest can influence posttest scores. Participants may learn something or may be sensitized to an issue by the pretest and, as a result, respond differently the next time they are asked the same questions on the posttest. Just taking a test the first time often reduces anxiety provoked by the unknown, and participants will be more comfortable with subsequent testing. This is one reason that SAT courses involve frequent testing; the providers want the students to acclimate to the test and reduce the unknown associated with the test.

3. *Instrumentation*. When the same method of measurement is used for the pretest and posttest, the measures must be stable (demonstrate measurement reliability); otherwise, the findings may reflect the instability of the measurement and not the effect of the treatment. When different methods of measurement are used, such as a paper measure for the pretest and behavioral observations for the posttest, the two methods must be equivalent (again, measurement reliability); otherwise, any changes might be due to the lack of equivalency.

> **Instrumentation** A problem that occurs in experimental designs when the measurement methods are not stable or equivalent.
>
> **Maturation** A threat to internal validity; changes that naturally occur with the passage of time.
>
> **Statistical regression** People experience cyclical or episodic changes that result in different scores with repeated measurement.
>
> **Secular drift** A type of contamination in true experimental and quasi-experimental designs that occurs when broader social or economic trends impact the findings of a study.

4. *Maturation*. Changes in outcome scores during experiments that involve a lengthy treatment period may result from maturation. Participants may age, gain experience, or grow in knowledge as part of a natural maturational experience and therefore respond differently on the posttest than on the pretest. The passing of time often results in changes such as after the death of a family member or friend, feelings of depression and sadness become less intense.

5. *Statistical regression*. People experience cyclical or episodic changes that result in different posttest scores, a phenomenon known as statistical regression. Participants who are chosen for a study because they received low scores on a test may show improvement in the posttest simply because some of the low scorers were having a bad day.

6. *Secular drift*. Broader social or economic trends may impact on the findings of a study. For example, trends in the economy may impact on the findings of the efficacy of a job training program. You might have a comparison group and an experimental group and end up with no group differences if the economy is in a severe recession (members of both groups have difficulty finding jobs) or no group differences if the economy is in a period of growth (members of both groups find jobs). The impact of eliminating the cash program Aid to Families with Dependent Children and replacing it with the Temporary Assistance for Needy Families (TANF) program in 1996 was deemed successful in reducing the number of people on cash assistance. Yet this trend had already started prior to 1996. Was the reduction in the number of people on cash assistance due to the policy change, or did the reduction reflect a trend that had already begun as the economy improved?

Threats to Internal Validity Requiring Attention While the Experiment Is in Progress

Even in a research design that involves a comparison group and random assignment, the experimental and comparison groups can become different.

7. *Differential attrition.* This problem (also known as mortality) occurs if the groups become different after the experiment begins because more participants drop out of one of the groups than out of the other group. There are different reasons why participants drop out including: (a) the study is too lengthy; (b) participants in the experimental group may become more motivated than members of the comparison group to continue in the study; or (c) participants receiving some advantageous program benefit are more likely to stay in the study than participants who are not receiving the program benefits.

> **Differential attrition** A problem that occurs in experiments when comparison groups become different because subjects are more likely to drop out of one of the groups for various reasons.

Contamination A source of causal invalidity that occurs when either the experimental or the compassion group is aware of the other group and is influenced in the posttest as a result.

Compensatory rivalry A type of contamination in true experimental and quasi-experimental designs that occurs when control group members are aware that they are being denied some advantage and so increase their efforts by way of compensation.

Resentful demoralization This problem for experimental designs occurs when comparison group members perform worse than they otherwise might have because they feel that they have been left out of a valuable treatment.

Diffusion of treatment A type of contamination in experimental and quasi-experimental designs that occurs when treatment and comparison groups interact and the nature of the treatment becomes known to the comparison group.

Compensatory equalization of treatment A threat to internal validity. When staff providing a treatment to a comparison group feel that it is unfair that the group is not getting the experimental treatment, the staff may work harder or do more than if there were no experiment.

Double-blind procedures An experimental method in which neither the subjects nor the staff delivering the experimental treatments know which subjects are getting the treatment and which are receiving a placebo.

Placebo effect A source of treatment misidentification that can occur when subjects who receive a treatment that they consider likely to be beneficial improve because of that expectation rather than because of the treatment itself.

8. *Contamination.* Contamination occurs in an experiment when the comparison group is in some way affected by, or affects, the treatment group. This problem arises from failure to control adequately the conditions of the experiment. There are three forms of contamination. When comparison group members are aware that they are being denied some advantage, they may increase their efforts to compensate, creating a problem termed **compensatory rivalry** (Cook & Campbell, 1979). Comparison group members may become demoralized, called **resentful demoralization**, if they feel that they have been left out of some valuable treatment and perform worse than they would have outside the experiment. Therefore, the treatment may have appeared to have a more beneficial effect than it actually did. Both compensatory rivalry and demoralization may distort the impact of the experimental treatment. Another form of contamination may occur when treatment and control (comparison) groups interact, and the nature of the treatment becomes known to the control group. This problem, called **diffusion of treatment**, may result in the control group sharing in the benefits of the treatment.

9. *Expectancies of experimental staff.* Change among experimental subjects may be due to the positive expectations of the experimental staff who are delivering the treatment, rather than the treatment itself. Even well-trained staff may convey their enthusiasm for an experimental program to the subjects in subtle ways. Such positive staff expectations create a self-fulfilling prophecy. Because social programs are delivered by human beings, such expectancy effects can be difficult to control in field experiments. Staff providing services to the comparison group may feel that it is unfair and, therefore, work harder or do more than they might have if there had been no experiment. This effect is called **compensatory equalization of treatment**. To counter this effect, some researchers use **double-blind procedures**; neither staff delivering the treatments nor participants know which group is the treatment group or comparison group.

10. *Placebo effect.* A placebo effect may occur when participants receive a treatment that they consider likely to be beneficial and improve because of that expectation, rather than because of the treatment itself. Medical research, where the placebo is often a chemically inert substance that looks like the experimental drug but actually has no effect, indicates that the placebo effect produces positive health effects in two thirds of patients suffering from relatively mild medical problems (Goleman, 1993). Placebo effects can also occur in social work research. One way to reduce this threat to internal validity is to provide the comparison group with something that should not impact the dependent variable.

Generalizability

The need for generalizable findings can be thought of as the Achilles' heel of group experimental designs. The design components that are essential to minimize the threats to internal validity make it more difficult to achieve sample generalizability (being able to apply the findings to some clearly defined larger population) and cross-population generalizability (generalizing across subgroups and to other populations and settings).

Sample Generalizability

Participants who can be recruited for a laboratory experiment, randomly assigned to a group, and kept under carefully controlled conditions for the study's duration are unlikely to be a representative sample of any large population of interest to social work researchers. Can they be expected to react to the experimental treatment in the same way as members of the larger population?

Researchers can take steps both before and after an experiment to increase a study's generalizability. Participants can be selected randomly from the population of interest, and thus, the researchers can achieve results generalizable to that population. Some studies of the effects of income supports on the work behavior of poor people have randomly sampled people in particular states before randomly assigning participants to experimental and comparison groups. But in most experiments, neither random selection from the population nor selection of the entire population is possible. Potential subjects must make a conscious decision to participate—probably resulting in an unrepresentative pool of volunteers.

When random selection is not feasible, the researchers may be able to increase generalizability by selecting several sites for conducting the experiment that offer marked contrasts in key variables of the population. As a result, although the findings are not statistically generalizable to a larger population, they do give some indication of the study's general applicability (Cook & Campbell, 1979). Ultimately, generalizability is enhanced through replication of the study with different groups, in different settings, and in different communities.

External Validity

Researchers are often interested in determining whether treatment effects identified in an experiment demonstrate cross-population generalizability, that is, hold true for subgroups of subjects and across different populations, times, or settings. This type of validity is called **external validity**. Of course, determining that a relationship between the treatment and the outcome variable holds true for certain subgroups does not establish that the relationship also holds true for these subgroups in the larger population, but it suggests that the relationship might have external validity.

> **External validity** See cross-population generalizability.
>
> **Reactivity** Changes in an individual or group behavior due to the nature of the experimental conditions or process of measurement.

Evidence of an overall sample effect does not mean that the effect holds true for subgroups within the study. For example, Roger Roffman et al. (1997) examined the effectiveness of a 17-session HIV prevention group with gay and bisexual males. The researchers found that those in the treatment group had better outcomes than those in the control group. But within the treatment group, outcomes were better for exclusively gay males than for bisexual males. This study shows how an interaction effect limits the generalizability of the findings.

Multiple sites can help researchers address both generalizability and external validity. For example, in 2001 the National Institute on Aging and the National Institute of Nursing Research funded the Resources for Enhancing Alzheimer's Caregiver Health II, a five-site study to test the effectiveness of an intervention for caregivers for family members with dementia. By having multiple sites, the researchers were able to test the intervention's impact in five different locations. Further, they were able to increase the ethnic heterogeneity of the sample participants, which would not have been possible if the research had been limited to any one site (Belle & REACH II Investigators, 2006).

Reactivity

A variant on the problem of external validity, called **reactivity**, occurs when the experimental treatment has an effect only when the particular conditions created by the experiment occur. Without the experimental conditions, there would be no effect. This is a problem as social work providers try to translate research findings into practice. The agency does not want to have to re-create the experimental conditions in order to provide an effective treatment. Reactivity takes several different forms:

- *Interaction of testing and treatment.* One such problem occurs when the treatment has an effect only if subjects have had the pretest. The pretest sensitizes the subjects to some issue so that when they are exposed to the treatment, they react in a way they would not have reacted if they had not taken the pretest. In other words, testing and treatment interact to produce the outcome. For example, answering questions in a pretest about anti-Semitism may sensitize subjects so that when they are exposed to the experimental treatment, seeing a film about prejudice, their attitudes are different than they would have been if they had not answered the pretest questions. In this situation, the treatment truly had an effect, but it would not have had an effect if it were repeated without the sensitizing pretest.

- *Reactive effects of experimental arrangement.* Members of the treatment group change in terms of the dependent variable because their participation in the study makes them feel special. Experimental group members could feel special simply because they are in the experiment. This is called a *Hawthorne Effect*, named after a famous productivity experiment at the Hawthorne electric plant outside Chicago. No matter what conditions researchers changed, and whether the goal was to improve or diminish productivity, the workers seemed to work harder simply because they were part of a special group.

- *Interaction of selection and treatment.* This effect occurs when the results are related to selection biases in who receives the treatment and who serves in the comparison group. For example, voluntary clients often do better than involuntary clients. If the treatment group consists of voluntary clients and the comparison group consists of involuntary clients, the findings of the study are likely to be influenced by the biased assignment.

- *Multiple treatment interference.* This refers to clients or participants who have been exposed to other interventions prior to the experiment. The questions of multiple treatment interference are, Was the intervention successful on its own, or was it successful because of the participant's cumulative experience with other treatments or interventions? For example, individuals who are chronically mentally ill are likely to have had past treatment experiences, both in the community and perhaps in an institutional setting. If multiple treatment interference is a problem, the generalizability of the findings may be limited to a population having experienced a similar treatment pattern.

We have described in detail the problems of internal validity and generalization because they provide a framework by which group designs can be compared. Group designs fall into three categories—true experimental designs, quasi-experimental designs, and nonexperimental designs—that are distinguished by the extent to which threats to internal validity are controlled.

🏛 Features of True Experiments

True experimental research designs (or randomized clinical trials) provide the most powerful designs for testing causal hypotheses, because they allows us to confidently establish the first three criteria for causality: association, time order, and nonspuriousness. True experimental research designs are used when a social work researcher wants to show that an intervention (independent variable) caused a change in an outcome (the dependent variable). **True experiments** have three features that help provide the strongest evidence about an intervention's effectiveness including

True experiments Group designs that are used to test the causal relationship between the independent and dependent variables. These designs enable the researcher to show that the independent variable occurs prior to the change in the dependent variable, that there is a statistical association, and that other explanations (internal validity) can be ruled out.

1. Two comparison groups (in the simplest case, an experimental and a control group) to establish an association

2. Random assignment to the two (or more) comparison groups to establish internal validity

3. Variation in the independent variable before assessment of change in the dependent variable to establish time order

The combination of these features permits us to have much greater confidence in the validity of causal conclusions than is possible in other research designs. Confidence in the validity of an experiment's findings is further enhanced by two things:

- Identification of the causal mechanism
- Control over the context of an experiment

Experimental and Comparison Groups

To establish an association between an independent variable and a dependent variable, true experimental designs have at least two groups. One group, called the **experimental group,** receives some treatment or manipulation of the independent variable. The second group, the **control group**, does not receive the treatment, or as is often the case in social work research, the second group is a **comparison group**, which typically receives the traditional intervention (**treatment as usual**). Providing the intervention to the comparison group also helps recruit participants because they receive something for their participation. Finally, because they receive treatment, subjects in the comparison group are less likely to drop out. The experimental group and control group scores on the outcome or dependent variable are compared in order to establish an association.

A study can have more than one experimental group if the goal is to test several versions of the treatment (the independent variable) or several combinations of different treatments. For example, a researcher testing different interventions for depression might include a control group, a group receiving medication, a group receiving counseling, and a group receiving both medication and counseling. But there is still a comparison group either not receiving any treatment or receiving treatment as usual.

> **Experimental group** In an experiment, the group that receives the treatment or experimental manipulation.
>
> **Control group** A comparison group that receives no treatment.
>
> **Comparison group** The group that is exposed to the traditional treatment, rather than the experimental treatment.
>
> **Treatment as usual** The comparison group in an experiment receives the intervention that is normally given.

Randomization

It is crucial that the groups be more or less equal at the beginning of the study. **Randomization**, or random assignment, is used to make the experimental group and the control group similar at the beginning of the study; it provides a powerful tool for identifying the effects of the treatment. A randomized control group can provide a good estimate of the counterfactual—the outcome that would

> **Randomization** Placing participants into an experimental or control group using some chance method such as by the toss of a coin.

have occurred if the subjects who were exposed to the treatment actually had not been exposed, but otherwise had the same experiences (Mohr, 1992). A researcher would not be able to accurately determine what the unique effects of the treatment were if the comparison group differed from the experimental group in any way besides not receiving the treatment (or receiving a different treatment).

There are different ways that random assignment into groups can be done. Because assignment to a group is by chance, you can toss a coin, pull names out of a hat, use a table of random numbers, or generate random numbers with a computer (see Exhibit 7.2). In any case, the participants should not be free to choose the group nor should you (the researcher) be free to put subjects into whatever group you want.

Assigning subjects randomly to the experimental and comparison groups ensures that systematic bias does not affect the assignment of subjects to groups. Of course, random assignment cannot guarantee that the groups are perfectly identical at the start of the study. Random assignment removes bias from the assignment process but only by relying on chance, which can result in some intergroup differences. Fortunately, researchers can use statistical methods to determine the odds of ending up with groups that differ on the basis of chance, and these odds are low even for groups of moderate size. The larger the group, the less likely it is that even modest differences will occur on the basis of chance and the more possible it becomes to draw conclusions about causal effects from relatively small differences in the outcome.

Note that the random assignment of subjects to experimental and comparison groups is not the same as random sampling of individuals from some larger population (see Exhibit 7.3). In fact, random assignment does not help at all to ensure that the research subjects are representative of some larger population; instead, representativeness is the goal of random sampling. What random assignment does—create two (or more) equivalent groups—is ensure internal validity, not generalizability.

Why is random assignment useful for ensuring internal validity? The underlying assumption of random assignment is that if chance is used to determine who goes into a particular group, equivalent groups are created. The groups are believed not only to be more or less equal in demographic makeup and to have similar scores on the dependent variable (something we can check) but also to be more or less equal with regard to the impact of alternative explanations. For example, some people in a bereavement group might be susceptible to a maturation effect. Through the use of random assignment, such people are believed to be more or less equally distributed between the experimental group and the control group; therefore, the effects of maturation will cancel each other out. Similarly, some people are highly motivated, whereas others are less motivated; random assignment distributes these individuals into the two groups so that motivation for change does not explain away the treatment's effects. It is difficult to control conditions when research about treatment is occurring in community-based settings. When research participants are randomly assigned to groups, the home and community environments during the treatment period should be the same on average.

Although these methods should result in similar groups, *matching* is sometimes used to better equate the experimental and comparison groups. In individual matching, individuals are matched in pairs (see Exhibit 7.4). You start by identifying important characteristics that might impact the study, and then you match pairs of individuals with similar or identical characteristics. For example, in a study of older adults you might match subjects by gender and age. These two characteristics are important for the elderly given that gender and increasing age are associated with a wide variety of differences among the elderly, such as health, marital status, and economic well-being. In this study, you might match a 75-year-old female with a 76-year-old female. Once the pairs have been identified, you would then use a random assignment procedure to determine which one of the pair would go into the experimental group and which one would go into the control group. This method eliminates the possibility of differences due to chance in the gender and age composition of the groups.

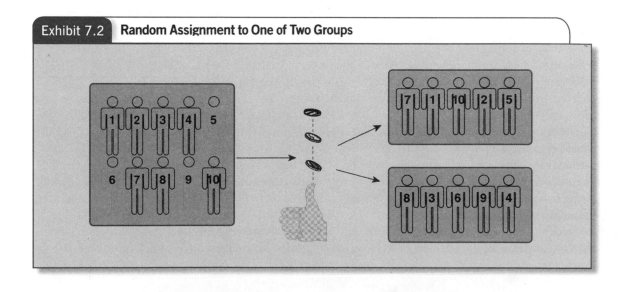

| Exhibit 7.2 | Random Assignment to One of Two Groups |

| Exhibit 7.3 | **Random Sampling Versus Random Assignment** |

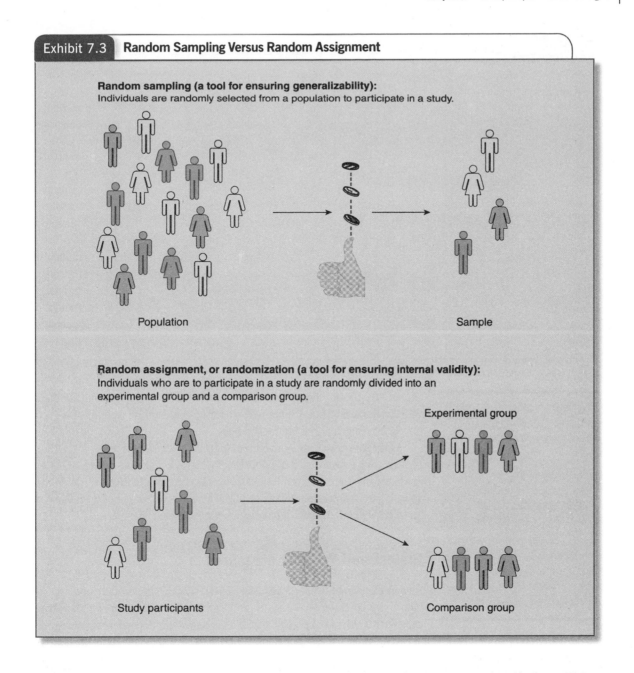

Random sampling (a tool for ensuring generalizability):
Individuals are randomly selected from a population to participate in a study.

Population

Sample

Random assignment, or randomization (a tool for ensuring internal validity):
Individuals who are to participate in a study are randomly divided into an
experimental group and a comparison group.

Experimental group

Study participants

Comparison group

The basic problem is that, as a practical matter, individuals can be matched on only a few characteristics; unmatched differences between the experimental and comparison groups may still influence outcomes. However, matching combined with randomization can reduce the possibility of differences due to chance. A second problem occurs when one of the matched pair drops out of the study, unbalancing the groups. In this case, researchers will often exclude the findings of the individual who remained in the study.

Block matching is used when participants are grouped by their characteristics. A gerontologist might group older adults by age and gender, creating a group of men between the ages of 65 and 74, a second group between the ages of 75 and

> **Block matching** A form of matching that groups individuals by their characteristics. Within each group, members are randomly assigned to the experimental and control groups.

Exhibit 7.4 Experimental Design Combining Matching and Random Assignment

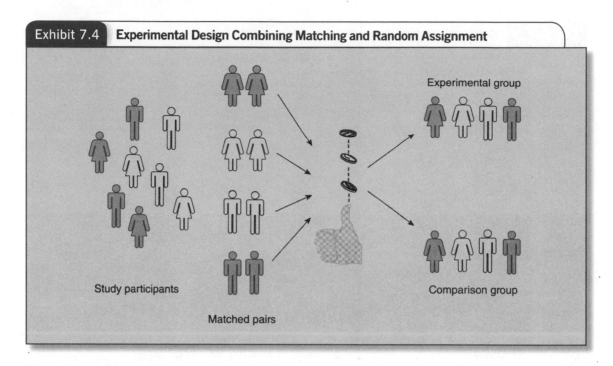

Study participants

Matched pairs

Experimental group

Comparison group

Aggregate matching Two or more groups, such as classes, are matched and then randomly assigned to the experimental and control conditions.

Posttest In experimental research, the measurement of an outcome (dependent variable) after an experimental intervention or after a presumed independent variable has changed for some other reason.

Pretest In experimental research, the measurement of an outcome (dependent variable) prior to an experimental intervention or change in a presumed independent variable.

84, and a third group ages 85 and older. The same grouping by age would be done with female participants. Within each group, the members are randomly assigned into the experimental and treatment groups.

Aggregate matching is matching by group. Older adults living in a senior high-rise might be grouped by floor. The floor and not the individual is assigned randomly into the experimental and comparison groups. In this case, randomly assigning the floors assumes that the mix of residents on each floor is similar and that there are no systematic differences among the floors.

Pretest and Posttest Measures

All true experiments have a **posttest**, that is, measurement of the outcome in both groups after the experimental group has received the treatment. Many true experiments also have a **pretest**, that is, a measure of the dependent variable prior to the experimental intervention. Usually, the pretest measurement of the dependent variable is exactly the same as the posttest measurement of the dependent variable. We say *usually* because sometimes the measurement methods used for the pretest and posttest differ, although both methods must be equivalent measures of the same concept. One researcher might use the same children's behavior checklist scale for the pretest and posttest. Another researcher might use the checklist scale for the pretest, but observe actual behavior for the posttest. This is appropriate as long as the two methods have measurement equivalence.

Strictly speaking, a true experiment does not require a pretest. When researchers use random assignment, the groups' initial scores on the dependent variable and all other variables are likely to be similar. Any difference in outcome between the experimental and comparison groups should be due to the intervention (or to other processes occurring during the experiment), and the likelihood of a difference just on the basis of chance can be calculated. The advantage of having a pretest score is that the researcher can verify that the randomization did produce similar groups.

🔲 Types of True Experimental Designs

We focus on three particular true experimental designs as well as several variations of these designs. Other designs, such as using placebos, are common in other disciplines such as medical or pharmaceutical research, but are quite rare in social work research. Furthermore, there are additional variations that we do not describe in detail, such as incorporating multiple measures or taking measures during the course of treatment. To describe the designs, we use abbreviations and symbols that are displayed in Exhibit 7.5.

Exhibit 7.5	Design Abbreviations
R	Random assignment
O	Observation taken for dependent or outcome variable
X	Intervention or Treatment
X_e	Experimental or new intervention
X_t	Traditional intervention
A, B etc	Group A, Group B, etc.

Pretest–Posttest Control Group Design

A common true experimental design is the *Pretest–Posttest Control Group Design* (Classical Experimental Design; Randomized Before/After Control Group Design).

$$RA \quad O_{1a} \quad X_e \quad O_{2a}$$
$$RB \quad O_{1b} \quad \quad O_{2b}$$

As you can see from the design, the steps involved include (a) random assignment into two groups (A and B), (b) taking an observation of the dependent/outcome variable prior to the intervention, (c) implementing the intervention in Group A, and (d) taking a second observation after the intervention. A variation on this design is to use a comparison group so that Group A receives the new intervention, whereas Group B receives the traditional or alternative intervention.

$$RA \quad O_{1a} \quad X_e \quad O_{2a}$$
$$RB \quad O_{1b} \quad X_t \quad O_{2b}$$

What can we say about causality with these two designs? First, we can establish *time order* given that the treatment precedes the second observation. Second, we can statistically evaluate whether there is a relationship between the treatment variable and change, so we can establish an *association*. You can make two different comparisons to demonstrate the association. If you want to assume that the Time 1 observations are more or less equal, you only need to compare O_{2a} with O_{2b}. But in this case, you are making an assumption that really is not necessary; instead, it is common to compare the change between observations in Group A (Δ_A) with the change in Group B (Δ_B).

Because there is random assignment, different *threats to internal validity* may be ruled out. History, maturation, instrumentation, and statistical regression can be ruled out because we would expect those threats to apply equally to both groups, and, therefore, they would cancel each other out. In principle, we should be able to rule out selection bias, but if you are at all nervous about selection bias, the design allows you to compare Time 1 observations on the dependent variable to determine whether they are more or less equal. The weakness of this design is that there might be a testing effect; that is, the pretest measurement might affect the posttest scores. It is possible that the test might sensitize respondents to the treatment and therefore make the treatment more effective than it would have been without the test. Or, it is possible that a test effect might explain a finding of no differences between the two groups.

Zvi Gellis and his colleagues (2008) used a *Pretest–Posttest Comparison Group Design* to evaluate the impact of problem-solving therapy (PST) for older adults with minor depression who were receiving home care (see Exhibit 7.6). Using PST was based on the idea that if clients have improved problem-solving skills, the likelihood that they might become depressed given their illness could be reduced. Participants in the experimental group would receive PST designed to teach problem-solving skills for 6 weeks in their home. The comparison group received treatment as usual (TAU) that included acute home health care services and referrals to their physicians regarding their minor depression plus educational literature on facts about depression and its treatment; the TAU group were contacted weekly for 6 weeks to assess their potential need for additional referrals. Participants were randomly assigned using a computer-generated random allocation table into the PST group or the TAU comparison group. Time 1 interviews were conducted prior to treatment, with follow-up interviews immediately at the end of treatment, 3 months, and 6 months. The researchers found that PST group members had lower depression scores than did TAU group members.

Variations on the Pretest–Posttest Control Group Design can be quite complex. The following example (Exhibit 7.6), illustrates one variation as well as a model that allowed for the examination of the *causal mechanisms* leading to differences. Thomas Brock and Kristen Harknett (1998) used this design with multiple measures to compare the effectiveness of two welfare-to-work case management models in helping recipients get off the TANF program. In the traditional case management model, income maintenance and employment services were separated into two different jobs performed by two different staff members. They compared the traditional model to an integrated model in which both income maintenance and employment services were provided by the same person. The researchers believed that this would result in speedier job placement and lower payments of cash assistance.

Brock and Hartnett (1998) randomly assigned 6,912 single parents whose youngest child was age 3 or older into three groups: a group receiving the traditional services, a group receiving integrated services, and a control group in which members received cash assistance but no employment service assistance by a case manager. Baseline measures were taken, assignment was made, and then repeated measures were taken for 2 years. Brock and Harknett then took a random sample of each group and did a series of comparisons. They found that subjects in the integrated model group participated in more job-related activities, were less likely to be referred for sanctioning for nonparticipation, and received less cash assistance from welfare benefits. In contrast, the researchers found no differences in employment earnings between the integrated and traditional model subjects. Both treatment groups did better than the control group on all of these measures.

Brock and Harknett (1998) were intrigued by the finding that, despite differences in cash benefits, there were no differences in employment and earnings between the two case-management model groups. This finding was contrary to what they had expected. To understand the cause or explanation for this unexpected finding, they interviewed welfare department staff. They found that when the income maintenance and Job Opportunities and Basic Skills training program (JOBS) staff positions were combined (integrated model), the case manager was able to detect unreported income. When the functions were separate (traditional model), the income maintenance workers did not pursue unreported income and JOBS compliance. From this example, you can see why it is important to try to understand the underlying *mechanism* for different findings.

Posttest-Only Control Group Design

The weakness of the Pretest–Posttest Control Group Design is that there may be a testing effect. To safeguard the reactive effects of testing, a second research design, the Posttest-Only Control Group Design (Randomized Control Group After-Only Design) can be used. Like the preceding design, this one may use a comparison group as opposed to a control group.

$$RA \quad X_e \quad O_{2a} \quad \text{or} \quad RA \quad X_e \quad O_{2a}$$
$$RB \quad \quad O_{2b} \quad \phantom{\text{or}} \quad RB \quad X_t \quad O_{2b}$$

The process is the same except that no baseline measurement is taken. The only comparison made is between O_{2a} and O_{2b}. In this case, the researcher assumes that the baseline measures would be more or less equal because random assignment is used. But because random assignment is based on probability, there is the possibility that unequal groups were formed. Because of the structure of this design, it is impossible to check whether the groups are equivalent initially, and, therefore, the internal validity threat of selection bias is a possibility.

Exhibit 7.6	**Examples of Pretest–Posttest Group Designs**

Pretest–Posttest Comparison Group Design:

Randomized Controlled Trial of Problem-Solving Therapy for Minor Depression in Home Care (Gellis, et al. 2011)

Subjects	Random Assignment	O_1	X	O_2
Older adults with minor depression and receive home care	Group A	Depressive symptom scores	Problem-solving therapy	Depressive symptom scores
	Group B	Depressive symptom scores	Treatment as usual: Acute services Referral for depression Literature about depression	Depressive symptom scores

Pretest–Posttest Comparison Group Design With Repeated Measurements:

A comparison of two welfare-to-work case management models (Brock & Harknett, 1998)

Subjects	Random Assignment	O_1	X	$O_2 O_3 O_4, \ldots, O_{24}$ (Posttests Monthly for 2 Years)
Single parents, AFDC recipients, youngest child 3 years or older	Group A	AFDC income and employment related data	Traditional: Income Maintenance worker; JOBS case manager	AFDC income and employment-related data; JOBS participation data
	Group B	AFDC income and employment related data	Integrated: Single case manager; Sanctions	AFDC income and employment-related data; JOBS participation data
	Group C	AFDC income and employment related data	Control: On their own	AFDC income and employment-related data

Janna Heyman and Irene Gutheil (2010) used the Posttest-Only Comparison Group Design to assess the effectiveness of three different methods for helping older Latinos with end-of-life planning (see Exhibit 7.7). They chose this design as they were concerned that a pretest measure might influence the posttest responses. The participants were clients of a home care agency. Participants were randomly assigned into three groups: One group received a state developed information form and instruction booklet (treatment as usual); another group received treatment as usual and a one-on-one discussion about the topics provided in the information form (Conversación A); and the third group received treatment as usual and intensive one-on-one discussion about specific themes developed in focus groups with adult children and Latino elders (Conversación B). The outcomes of interest were attitudes toward end-of-life planning and comfort with discussing end-of-life planning. The interventions were provided by trained bilingual social workers in the participants' homes. To avoid any treatment contamination, social workers providing Conversación A were unaware of the added substance of Conversación B. The posttest interview was conducted by a second social worker two weeks after the intervention.

The researchers compared the three groups on a variety of health and demographic variables and concluded that the three groups were similar except for living arrangements. They controlled for this difference in their analysis. Overall, they found that both Conversación A and Conversación B had a similar, positive impact on attitudes toward end-of-life planning but that only Conversación A had a positive impact on comfort with end-of-life planning.

Exhibit 7.7	Posttest Only Group Design

Posttest-Only Control Group Design:
Older Latinos' attitudes toward and comfort with end-of-life planning (Heyman & Gutheil, 2010)

Subjects	Random Assignment	O_1	X	O_2
Older Latino adults who were clients of a home care agency	Group A		Conversación A: information form and instruction book AND one-one-one discussion about topics in the information form.	Attitudes toward end-of-life planning Comfort with discussing end-of life planning
	Group B		Conversación B: information form and instruction book AND one-one-one discussion about end-of-life topics developed by a focus group.	Attitudes toward end-of-life planning Comfort with discussing end of life planning
	Group C		Treatment as Usual: Information form and instruction book	Attitudes toward end-of-life planning Comfort with discussing end of life planning

Solomon Four Group Design

Sometimes researchers want to test whether there is a test–treatment interaction and do so by combining both designs, conducting a *Solomon Four Group Design*. If testing and treatment do interact, the difference in outcome scores between the experimental and comparisons groups will be different for subjects who took the pretest compared with those who did not.

$$RA \quad O_{1a} \quad X_e \quad O_{2a}$$

$$RB \quad O_{1b} \quad \quad O_{2b}$$

$$RC \quad \quad X_e \quad O_{2c}$$

$$RD \quad \quad \quad O_{2d}$$

Remember why this interaction is problematic. When social workers apply research findings to their practice, they do not want to have to re-create the research conditions. The interaction of testing and treatment might be an exception to this concern. It is common for clients to receive an initial test—one that we might refer to as an *initial assessment* or even a *follow-up assessment*. The testing effect may be beneficial if it adds to the effectiveness of the intervention. It depends on the test and an agency's ability to adapt the test as part of the assessment process.

"Difficulties" in True Experiments in Agency-Based Research

If true experimental designs are powerful tools to demonstrate causality, why are they typically the province of social work researchers and used less often by agencies to evaluate their programs? Implementing true experimental designs requires expertise, sufficient numbers of clients, and plenty of time. In addition, there are real and imagined criticisms:

Research In the News

For Further Thought ?

HOW TO ARRIVE AT THE BEST HEALTH POLICIES

A randomized controlled study on the impact of health insurance led to some surprising results that ran contrary to what many policy makers had hypothesized. In 2008, Oregon randomly assigned low-income residents to two groups: one group getting health insurance through Medicaid and one group remaining uninsured. Contrary to expectation, persons with Medicaid had a greater use of emergency rooms, found doctors more easily, and they were more likely to be admitted to the hospital.

1. What more would you need to know to establish the generalizability of the results?

2. How would you design this study in your state?

Source: Sanger-Katz (2014).

- The program cannot change during the course of the experiment or evaluation (Weiss, 1998). This poses a problem because managers want continual improvement. Weiss (1998) recommends that if there are program changes, the timing of the changes be noted and to assess outcomes at the time when a program changes.

- Even if the program or treatment does not change, implementation depends on staff with different skill levels, such as ability to engage clients or provide services. This is less likely to be a problem if the sample is large because variations should cancel out; in contrast, with small numbers of clients, differences may be magnified (Weiss, 1998).

- The more controlled the conditions under which the treatment or program is provided, the less generalizable it will be to other times or locations. This is certainly a concern and points to the importance of being able to describe the context and conditions under which the research is undertaken. One solution is to replicate the intervention in different sites and with different samples.

- Threats to professional judgment may arise. Posavac and Carey (1997) refer to these problems as "I know what is best for my client" (p. 184). This concern manifests itself in two ways. One concern is about random assignment. Typically, social workers choose clients for treatment based on need or when someone comes to seek help. Many social workers (including our students) object to letting chance (randomization) dictate who gets help and who will have to wait; rather, they want to base their decisions on their professional judgment. The second concern is that an experiment defines the intervention provided to clients and how the intervention is provided. Some social workers believe this threatens their ability to make decisions about how to best meet their clients' needs.

- Some staffers might feel that "if the experimental approach is believed to be so good, I want all my clients to get it." The reason for trying a new method is based on some belief—whether anecdotal or theoretical—that suggests that the model is indeed better. Staff want their clients to receive the best service, so they argue, "Why delay implementing what we know should work?" Yet social workers have an ethical responsibility to have evidence that the new intervention is better before it is widely implemented.

- Clients may say, "Don't experiment on me" (Posavac & Carey, 1997, p. 183). People are suspicious of experimentation, and clients, who are particularly vulnerable, may be even more suspicious of experimentation. This makes recruitment and retention more difficult. With proper human subject protections, such as the use of informed consent, these fears can be mitigated.

The Limits of True Experimental Designs

The distinguishing features of true experiments—experimental and comparison groups, pretests and posttests, and randomization—do not help researchers identify the mechanisms by which treatments have their effects. Often the question of causal mechanism is not addressed in experimental research. The hypothesis test does not require any analysis of mechanism; if the experiment is conducted under carefully controlled conditions during a limited span of time, the causal effect (if any) may seem to be quite direct. But attention to causal mechanisms can augment experimental findings. One may measure the intermediate outcomes that lead to the change that is the program's primary focus. For example, in a job training program designed to ultimately result in employment, researchers might assess whether the program increased job seeking skills and work-related skills if they are precursors to landing a job.

True experimental designs also do not guarantee that the researcher has been able to maintain control over the conditions to which subjects are exposed after they are assigned to the experimental and comparison groups. If these conditions begin to differ, the variation between the experimental and comparison groups will not be that which was intended. Such unintended variation is often not much of a problem in laboratory experiments, where the researcher has almost complete control over the conditions (and can ensure that these conditions are nearly identical for both groups). But control over conditions can become a big concern for field- or agency-based experiments in real-world settings.

▣ Quasi-Experimental Designs

Sometimes using a true experimental design to test hypotheses about the impact of service delivery, the effectiveness of a treatment modality, or the manner in which services are offered, is not feasible with the desired participants and in the desired setting. A true experimental design may be too costly or take too long to carry out, it may not be ethical to randomly assign subjects to different conditions, or it may be too late to do so. As practitioners respond to the demands for outcome accountability and monitoring of practice, true experimental designs are often unnecessary. Researchers use quasi-experimental designs that retain some components of experimental designs; agency directors and program evaluators may use these designs for outcome evaluation.

Quasi-experimental design A research design in which at least some threats to internal validity may be ruled out.

A **quasi-experimental design** is one in which we may be able to rule out at least some threats to internal validity. We discuss three types of quasi-experimental designs (others can be found in Cook & Campbell, 1979; Mohr, 1992): nonequivalent control group designs, time series designs, and ex-post facto designs.

Nonequivalent Control Group Designs

The nonequivalent control group design is exactly like the Pretest–Posttest Control Group Design except that there is no random assignment into the groups; rather the experimental and comparison group participants are assigned before the treatment occurs without random assignment.

$$A \quad O_{1a} \quad X_e \quad O_{2a} \quad \text{or} \quad A \quad O_{1a} \quad X_e \quad O_{2a}$$
$$B \quad O_{1b} \quad \quad O_{2b} \quad\quad\quad\quad B \quad O_{1b} \quad X_t \quad O_{2b}$$

There are two groups: One is exposed to the independent variable, whereas the other is not exposed to the independent variable. Researchers also may use this design to compare two (or more) interventions.

In this type of quasi-experimental design, a comparison group is selected as similar as possible to the treatment group. Two selection methods can be used:

- *Individual matching.* Individual cases in the treatment group are matched with similar individuals in the comparison group. In some situations, this can create a comparison group that is similar to the experimental group. However, in many studies, it may not be possible to determine in advance the important variables or to match on the most important variables.

- *Aggregate matching.* In most situations, when random assignment is not possible, the second method of matching makes more sense: identifying a comparison group that matches the treatment group in the aggregate, rather than trying to match individual cases. This means finding a comparison group that has similar distributions on key variables: the same average age, the same percentage female, and so on. For this design to be considered even quasi-experimental, however, individuals may not choose which group to join or where to seek services.

Where are matches to be found? One potential source for finding matches is an agency waiting list. People on the waiting list are not yet receiving services from the agency and, therefore, are a comparison group that is likely to be similar to the treatment group. Another alternative is locating similar individuals in the community who are willing to serve as a control group. A third option is to compare client outcomes in one agency with client outcomes in another agency, assuming, of course, that the second agency is serving a similar population group.

Different strategies were used in studies by James Moran and Marian Bussey (2007), Christopher Mitchell (1999), and Nora Wikoff, Donald Linhorst, and Nicole Morani (2012). Moran and Bussey (2007) used a similar community to establish a matched group for their study of an alcohol prevention program with urban American Indian youth (see Exhibit 7.8). The intervention was carried out with youth living in the Denver metropolitan area. The nonintervention urban area chosen was Colorado Springs as it was the second-largest metropolitan area with the second-largest number of American Indians in Colorado. Concerned that group differences in selection and attrition might impact the findings, they compared the two groups' demographic composition and scores on various measures at the start of the study; they also examined the impact of attrition on the group composition. Finding only two differences at pretest and no differences in attrition, they were confident that the two groups were similar and that their characteristics were not related to the observed group differences on the outcome measures.

Christopher Mitchell's (1999) study of the impact of an 8-week cognitive-behavioral group treatment on treating panic disorders illustrates the use of a waiting list to create a matched group (see Exhibit 7.8). Mitchell wanted to examine whether medication and the cognitive-behavioral therapy group would reduce anxiety to a lower level than medication only. The sample included 56 people seeking treatment at an HMO. Comparisons were made between the 30 participants who received medications and participated in therapy groups and 26 people who were on the waiting list for the group therapy or who had declined therapy but were receiving medication.

Wikoff and colleagues (2012) assessed the effectiveness of a reentry program for prisoners in limiting recidivism (see Exhibit 7.8). Unable to use random assignment, they compared released prisoners who voluntarily entered the reentry program to prisoners released at the same time who opted not to participate in the program. They acknowledged in their limitations that self-selection and, therefore, motivation was a potential problem (Wikoff et al., 2012). They noted that the groups differed in age, education, and gender but the groups were similar by race and other risk factors such as substance abuse, mental health, or adjustment to prison. They were unsure as to whether the several differences contributed to the outcomes.

Nonequivalent control or comparison group designs are particularly useful for researchers (and evaluators). Because of the pretest and posttest, both *time order* and a *statistical association* can be demonstrated, suggesting that even if not causal, there is a correlation between the treatment and outcome. Further, if the selection process appears sound, you might rule out other explanations such as the effects of history, maturation, testing, and instrumentation. The key is whether you are convinced that the matched comparison group has been chosen and

Exhibit 7.8　Nonequivalent Group Designs

Nonequivalent Control Group Design:

Results of an alcohol prevention program with urban American Indian youth (Moran & Bussey, 2007)

Subjects	O_1	X	O_2 and 1 year followup
Group A: American Indian youth living in Metropolitan Denver	Demographics Impact of alcohol use Locus of control Depression Self-concept Perceived social support Decision-making skills Indian identify	Culturally designed 13 week after school program AND Six sessions 6 months later	Impact of alcohol use Locus of control Depression Self-concept Perceived social support Decision-making skills Indian identify
Group B: American Indian youth living in Colorado Springs	Demographics Impact of alcohol use Locus of control Depression Self-concept Perceived social support Decision-making skills Indian identify		Impact of alcohol use Locus of control Depression Self-concept Perceived social support Decision-making skills Indian identify

Nonequivalent Comparison Group Design:

Treatment of anxiety in a managed care setting (Mitchell, 1999)

Subjects	O_1	X	O_2
Group A: willing to be treated	Anxiety measures	Medication Eight weeks cognitive behavioral therapy	Anxiety measures
Group B: unwilling to be treated	Anxiety measures	Medication only	Anxiety measures

Nonequivalent Comparison Group Design:

Recidivism among participants of a reentry program for prisoners released without supervision (Wickoff, Linhorst, & Morani, 2012)

Subjects	O_1	X	O_2
Group A: *Participants* Recruited inmates released from prison from March 1, 2007 to February 2008 plus some released from June 6, 2006 to January 30, 2007.	Demographics Severity of Crime Institutional risk Substance Abuse Mental Health	Reentry Program: Case management 6-month monetary support in form of bus passes, grocery, and clothing gift cards	Recidivism: Conviction resulting in state-level crime to October 2009 resulting in prison time or probation. Did not include fine or jail term.
Group B: *Refusal Group* Inmates released from prison March 1, 2007 to February 2008	Demographics Severity of Crime Institutional risk Substance Abuse Mental Health	Housing Substance abuse treatment Job training programs	Recidivism: Conviction resulting in state-level crime to October 2009 resulting in prison time or probation. Did not include fine or jail term.

evaluated in such a way that you are willing to accept the comparability between the two groups despite the lack of random assignment. As you can see from the three examples, the researchers tried to find as close a comparison group as possible and to the extent possible reported the comparability of the groups as well as the similarity of scores on the dependent variables.

Time Series Designs

A time series design is unlike the other research designs we have described up until now in that no control or comparison group is needed. A time series design typically involves only one group for which multiple observations of data have been gathered both prior to and after the intervention. Although many methodologists distinguish between repeated measures panel designs, which include several pretest and posttest observations, and time series designs, which include many (preferably 30 or more) such observations in both pretest and posttest periods, we do not make that distinction here.

A common design is the *Interrupted Time Series Design,* in which three or more observations are taken before and after the intervention.

$$A \quad O_1 \quad O_2 \quad O_3 \quad X \quad O_4 \quad O_5 \quad O_6$$

Like other designs, there are variations on this basic design, including time series designs with comparison or control groups and time series designs in which observations are also gathered during the course of the intervention.

One advantage of a time series design is that there is only one group, so a second group need not be created. A second advantage is that, depending on the question, both the pretest and posttest observations need not occur prospectively and therefore a variety of issues ranging from changes in social policy to changes in agency administrative practices to changes in agency programs can be assessed using data already collected. Time series designs can answer questions like the following: (a) Did the number of families receiving cash assistance change after the implementation of welfare reform? (b) Did community employment increase after the creation of empowerment zones? (c) Did the number of phone calls to an information and referral line increase after a period of extensive outreach? (d) Did absenteeism rates decline after a stress-reduction program was put into place?

A time series design is based on the idea that, by taking repeated measures prior to an intervention or programmatic change, you have the opportunity to identify a pattern. A pattern may show a trend reflecting an ongoing increase or decline, or it may simply stay flat at either too high or too low a level. The pattern may be seasonal, with differences based on time of year; use of a homeless shelter may decline in the summer while peaking in the winter. Having identified the preintervention pattern, the question then is whether an intervention or program altered the nature of the pattern to what is considered to be a more favorable state. Furthermore, by taking repeated measures after the intervention, you can determine whether the impact of the intervention persisted.

The analysis of time series data can become quite complex statistically, but to start, it is best to graph the observations. Dattalo (1998) describes methods that might be used when it is difficult to identify a pattern, such as graphing 3-month moving averages, as well as statistical techniques that can be used to analyze the patterns.

What can we say about causality when using a time series design to test an intervention? The pretest and posttest measurements enable us to establish a *time order* and an *association.* If we are looking at a treatment's impact, we should be able to rule out several threats to internal validity, such as maturation, regression, testing, and instrumentation. Any changes due to these threats would have been observed during the course of the pretest observations. The major threat to internal validity is history; it is possible that shifts may be due to some extraneous event happening during the period of treatment, that is, an event happening between the last observation of the pretest period and the first observation of the posttest period.

Hyunkag Cho and Dina Wilke (2005) used an interrupted time-series design to assess the effect of the Violence Against Women Act on the incidence of domestic violence, reporting to the police, perpetrator arrest, and contact with other authorities such as a prosecutor or court officer. They hypothesized that the incidence of domestic violence would decline while the rates of the other three outcomes would increase. They used quarterly data from the National Crime Victimization Survey beginning in 1992 and ending in 2003. Since the VAWA was enacted in September 1994, they had nine quarters of pretest measures and 35 post-enactment measures. While the overall trends reflected declines in incidence rates and increased rates of reporting, arrest, and contact, the unique effect of the VAWA was related only to contact with other authorities. Other efforts (events) such as state or local legislation or the role of social services might explain the improving trends in incidences of domestic violence and rates of reporting and arrest.

Ex Post Facto Control Group Designs

The *ex post facto* (after the fact) control group design appears to be similar to the nonequivalent control group design, and the two are often confused. The ex post facto design meets fewer of the criteria to demonstrate causality than other quasi-experimental designs. Like nonequivalent control group designs, this design has experimental and comparison groups that are not created by random assignment. But unlike the groups in nonequivalent control group designs, the groups in ex post facto designs are designated after the treatment has occurred. The problem with this is that if the treatment takes any time at all, people with particular characteristics may select themselves for the treatment or avoid it. However, the particulars will vary from study to study; in some circumstances, we may conclude that the treatment and control groups are so similar that causal effects can be tested (Rossi & Freeman, 1989).

Joseph Walsh's (1994) study of social support outcomes for participants in assertiveness community treatment used an ex post facto design (see Exhibit 7.9). He compared clients at two agencies that provide assertiveness community treatment programs. In one agency, clients received a variety of on-site group interventions and individualized case management services, whereas at the second agency, clients received just the individualized case management. Both agencies were located in the same county, and the staff had a common philosophy of care.

Walsh (1994) found that the self-reported size of personal social support networks was higher for the clients receiving the group intervention than for clients receiving just individualized case management. However, there were no differences in the number of social support clusters (such as family, recreation, and friends), perceived support from friends, or perceived support from family. Nonetheless, the finding that the size of the social support network is larger is important, as network size is a predictor of overall social integration.

What distinguishes this study design from a quasi-experimental design is the fact that the programs were already operating. These two teams were chosen from 23 county teams because they represented different treatment approaches while serving demographically similar mental health clients. Walsh (1994) was aware that he could not rule out other explanations, noting that "it is also difficult to rule out individual case manager effects unrelated to the basic intervention format" (p. 461).

Exhibit 7.9 | Ex Post Facto Control Group Design

Social Support Resource Outcomes (Walsh, 1994)			
Subjects	**Pretest**	**Intervention**	**Posttest**
Experimental group	Measures of social support	Group interventions and individualized case management	Measures of social support
Comparison group	Measures of social support	Individualized case management only	Measures of social support

🁢 Nonexperimental Designs

A third set of designs, described as nonexperimental or pre-experimental research designs, are classified as such because they provide little to no control over internal threats to validity. To the extent that social work researchers are trying to demonstrate that different treatment modalities cause a change, a glaring weakness is the lack of control over internal threats to validity. This weakness often leads researchers, evaluators, and consumers of research to discount the utility of these designs and the findings from studies using these designs. Yet these designs have utility for research, and we point out how the designs might be used. The simplicity of these designs also makes them useful for evaluating agency programs.

Types of Nonexperimental Designs

The *One-Group Pretest–Posttest Design* (Before-After One-Group Design) is characterized by the absence of a comparison group; unlike the time series design, it lacks repeated pretest measures. All cases are exposed to the experimental treatment. The basis for comparison is provided by the pretreatment measures in the group.

$$A \qquad O_{1a} \qquad X \qquad O_{2a}$$

Because there is a pretest and a posttest, it is possible to demonstrate a *time order* and statistical analyses can be conducted to determine whether there is an *association* between the independent and dependent variables. The weakness of this design is that there are many different threats to the internal validity of the design. History, maturation, testing, instrumentation, statistical regression, and selection bias, as well as the interactions of selection and history or testing cannot be ruled out.

This is a popular form of design for program evaluation both for its ease of use and for the types of questions that one might answer. It is far simpler to implement than are group designs because no comparison group is needed. The design flows from a typical practice model of assessment, intervention, and evaluation of the impact of the intervention (follow-up assessment). The conformity to a practice model is more easily understood and accepted by agency directors and practitioners.

This design provides answers to a variety of questions of interest to researchers and social service providers. Using this design, you can demonstrate whether improvement occurred, how much change occurred, and how many individuals improved. It can be used to determine how well clients are functioning and the number of clients who have achieved some minimum standard of functioning at the end of the program.

John McNamara, Kevin Tamanini, and Suzanne Pelletier-Walker (2008) used a pretest–posttest design to study the effectiveness of brief counseling with women at a domestic violence shelter. The social work counselors, with a feminist treatment orientation, drew from treatment models such as cognitive-behavior, solution-focused, and family or systems tailored to the individual client needs. They were interested in determining if clients who had received at least three counseling sessions would have improvements in coping ability, life functioning, symptom measures, interpersonal relationships, and carrying out social roles. McNamara and colleagues selected this design as they felt that the shelter's crisis-oriented services were not amenable to using a random assignment to a comparison group. The researchers did find improvements in each of the assessed areas.

A less rigorous one-group design is the *After-Only Design* (Posttest-Only; A Cross-Sectional Group; One-Shot Only):

$$A \qquad X \qquad O_2$$

This design is characterized by only one group without a control or comparison group, and it includes no pretest observations, so there are no benchmarks to which the posttest scores can be compared. As a result, the After-Only Design has little utility for researchers trying to establish an intervention's effectiveness. Because there is no pretest, both *time order* and *association* cannot be determined. The researcher does not know whether the final outcomes are higher, lower, or equal to the preintervention level. Furthermore, it is impossible to rule out other explanations.

This design does offer some benefit to social work researchers. It is useful for piloting and developing measures, developing hypotheses about relationships that then require more rigorous designs, and providing information about attrition related to the treatment.

The After-Only Design is also used to provide factual information for agency-based program evaluation. It has been used to describe participant functioning at the end of the program, answering questions such as, How many clients are no longer depressed? How many are no longer abusing alcohol? and How many are employed after a job training program? But as we have said, changes in depression, alcohol abuse, or employment cannot be attributed solely to the program. This is also the typical design used to assess client satisfaction. Although it may be argued that client satisfaction should be monitored during the program, most agencies still examine satisfaction only after completion of the program.

Sometimes when it has been impossible to do a pretest, evaluators and researchers may try to construct a baseline so that the design looks more like the One Group Pretest–Posttest Design. There are different ways that a baseline might be constructed. One way is to look at initial intakes or initial assessments. Another way is to ask clients to recall what their status was prior to the intervention. Both of these mechanisms suffer from the reliability of the data collected. Another method to improve this design is to create a comparison group by comparing people at different stages of the intervention. In this case, the scores of people who have completed the intervention might be compared to the scores of those currently receiving the intervention.

A third nonexperimental design is the *Static-Group Design*. It includes two groups without random assignment: One group gets the treatment, whereas the other does not receive the treatment, and there is no pretest or baseline. This design is frequently used when a program has already begun and baseline information cannot be obtained.

$$A \quad X \quad O_{2a}$$
$$B \quad \quad O_{2b}$$

The central issue of this design is finding a comparable group. If an agency waiting list is used, perhaps an argument might be made about the comparability of Group B. Or one might find nonparticipants who are eligible for the program to use as a comparison group. The problem persists that, without a pretest, the comparability of the groups cannot be tested. Without such a test, it is a leap of faith to say that comparing posttest scores provides evidence of a time order and an association, let alone controls for internal threats to validity.

One alternative to modify this design is to compare program methods or intensity. The *Comparative Intensity Design* compares two groups receiving intervention. The two groups may be receiving different services within the same agency or across two agencies. While the selection problem persists, a potential argument (although a weak argument) is that clients having the same difficulty probably are alike.

$$A \quad X_{t1} \quad O_{2a}$$
$$B \quad X_{t2} \quad O_{2b}$$

One way that the usefulness of nonexperimental designs can be enhanced is replication. Conducting a single After-Only Design provides limited information. But repeating this design systematically and following similar procedures provides additional support for suggesting the program may be related to the outcome, if consistently positive results are found.

⊞ Implications for Evidence-Based Practice

The types of designs described throughout this chapter provide varying degrees of evidence to support the notion that a particular intervention resulted in the desired change in some outcome. There is a hierarchy among these group designs based on the three criteria for causality. True experimental designs (or randomized clinical trials) are commonly accepted as the gold standard in offering evidence about the efficacy of an intervention because they are organized to meet the criteria of association, time order, and internal validity (APA, 2006; Gambrill, 2006; Johnston et al., 2006). Ideally, there are a number of randomized experimental trials of the intervention's effectiveness relative to a particular outcome. Quasi-experimental and nonexperimental designs provide less conclusive evidence about the effectiveness of the intervention.

But we do not mean to suggest that you need not look critically at the evidence learned from a true experiment, let alone quasi-experimental and nonexperimental designs. Throughout this chapter, we have suggested that there are specific issues you should consider as you read the results of research studies:

- *Randomization process.* Many authors report using random assignment of participants to the experimental and comparison groups without clarifying how the actual assignment was made. This is important information for assessing the findings' internal validity.

- *Sample size.* In Chapter 5, we briefly mentioned the concept of statistical power; the study needs to have a sample size that is sufficient to detect a statistically significant difference. With small samples, the chances of finding no treatment effect are greater than with a larger sample size; in other words, there may indeed be a treatment effect, but the sample size may be too small to detect the impact of the treatment.

- *Attrition.* It is likely that some participants will drop out of the study, and there may be differential rates of attrition for the experimental and comparison groups. You should consider how attrition is handled in the analysis. Participants who drop out may not be any different than participants who remain but too often authors fail to examine the effect on the composition of the two groups.

Even after you are convinced that the results are meaningful, and not the outcome of a poor process of random assignment, small sample size, or attrition, you will have to address the external validity of the findings. Remember you are taking research-derived knowledge and applying that knowledge to your individual clients. Ted McNeill (2006) notes that "clinical expertise is indispensable for deciding whether external evidence applies to an individual client and, if so, how it should be integrated into treatment" (p. 151). Will the treatment's effects hold true for your clients who, for example, may differ by race, gender, social class, or sexual orientation from the people in the intervention studies? Do the study's setting and location impact the findings? These are all considerations in determining an appropriate intervention.

Meta-Analysis

Of course, the findings from one experimental study may be suggestive of a positive result but alone may not be convincing. **Meta-analysis** is a quantitative method for identifying patterns in findings across multiple studies of the same research question (Cooper & Hedges, 1994). Unlike a traditional literature review, which describes previous research studies verbally, meta-analyses treat previous studies as cases whose features are measured as variables and are then analyzed statistically. It is like conducting a survey in which the respondents are previous studies. Meta-analysis shows how evidence about interventions varies

> **Meta-analysis** The quantitative analysis of findings from multiple studies.

across research studies. If the methods used in these studies varied, then meta-analysis can be used to describe how this variation affected study findings. If social contexts or demographic characteristics varied across the studies, then a meta-analysis can indicate how social context or demographic characteristics affected study findings. Meta-analysis often accompanies systematic reviews that summarize what we know about the effectiveness of a particular intervention. By integrating different study samples and controlling for social context and demographic characteristics, meta-analysis enhances the generalizability of the findings.

Meta-analysis can be used when a number of studies have attempted to answer the same research question with similar experimental designs. It is not typically used for evaluating results from multiple studies that used different methods or measured different dependent variables. It is also not very sensible to use meta-analysis to combine study results when the original case data from these studies are available and can actually be combined and analyzed together (Lipsey & Wilson, 2001). Meta-analysis is a technique to combine and statistically analyze the statistical findings in published research reports.

After a research problem is formulated based on the findings of prior research, the literature must be searched systematically to identify the entire population of relevant studies. Typically, multiple bibliographic databases are used; some researchers also search for related dissertations and conference papers. Eligibility criteria must be specified carefully to determine which studies to include and which to omit as too different. Mark Lipsey and David Wilson (2001) suggest that eligibility criteria include the following:

- *Distinguishing features.* This includes the specific intervention tested and perhaps the groups compared.

- *Research respondents.* The pertinent characteristics of the research respondents must be similar to the population to which generalization is sought.

- *Key variables.* These must be sufficient to allow tests of the hypotheses of concern and controls for likely additional influences.

- *Research methods.* Apples and oranges cannot be directly compared, but some trade-off must be made between including the range of studies about a research question and excluding those that are so different in their methods as not to yield comparable data.

- *Cultural and linguistic range.* If the study population is going to be limited to English language publications, or limited in some other way, this must be acknowledged and the size of the population of relevant studies in other languages should be estimated.

- *Time frame.* Social processes relevant to the research question may have changed for such reasons as historical events or new technologies, so temporal boundaries around the study population must be considered.

- *Publication type.* It must be determined whether the analysis will focus only on published reports in professional journals, or include dissertations and/or unpublished reports.

Once the studies are identified, their findings, methods, and other features are coded (e.g., sample size, location of sample, strength of the association between the independent and dependent variables). Statistics are then calculated to identify the average effect of the independent variable on the dependent variable, as well as the effect of methodological and other features of the studies (Cooper & Hedges, 1994). The effect size statistic is the key to capturing the association between the independent and dependent variables across multiple studies. The effect size statistic is a standardized measure of association—often the difference between the mean of the experimental group and the mean of the control group on the dependent variable, adjusted for the average variability in the two groups (Lipsey & Wilson, 2001).

The meta-analytic approach to synthesizing research results can result in more generalizable findings than those obtained with just one study. Methodological weaknesses in the studies included in the meta-analysis are still a problem; it is only when other studies without particular methodological weaknesses are included that we can estimate effects with some confidence. In addition, before we can place any confidence in the results of a meta-analysis, we must be confident that all (or almost all) relevant studies were included and that the information we need to analyze was included in all (or most) of the studies (Matt & Cook, 1994).

One of the challenges of meta-analysis is that the authors of the articles to be reviewed may not always report sufficient information. For example, the study reports (whether a journal article or an unpublished report) may not contain information about participant characteristics, an especially important variable if we are to consider the generalizability of the results to different population groups. Littell (2005) noted that to conduct her meta-analysis of Multisystemic Therapy, she had to contact principal investigators to obtain more information about participant characteristics, interventions, and outcomes.

Case Study Meta-Analysis: Do Parent Training Programs Prevent Child Abuse?

Brad Lundahl, Janelle Nimer, and Bruce Parsons (2006) were interested in the effect of parent training and parent education programs on reducing risk factors associated with child abuse. They included only studies that met these eligibility criteria: the training was conducted with families in which there were no parent or child developmental or cognitive delays; the training was directed to preventing physical abuse, child neglect, or emotional abuse and not sexual abuse; there was actual training; and pretests and posttests were given to at least five participants. Using three keywords (*child abuse, child neglect,* and *parent training*) the researchers searched three databases (ERIC, PsycINFO, and Social Work Abstracts) for any articles published between 1970 and 2004. Of 186 studies, they found 23 that met the eligibility criteria. They coded outcome measures including parents' emotional adjustment, child-rearing attitudes, child-rearing behaviors, and documented abuse as well as moderating and independent variables including participant characteristics, parent training program characteristics, and the methodological rigor of the studies.

Overall, Lundahl et al. (2006) found that parent training had a moderate effect and was effective in changing parental beliefs and attitudes towards children (effect size = .60), improving parental emotional well-being (.53), altered child-rearing behaviors (.51), and reducing documented abuse (.45). They also found that specific program characteristics influenced these outcomes. For example, programs that included home visitors had a greater impact than programs without home visitors, and programs that did training in both the home and the office were more effective than programs that limited training to one site.

▣ Diversity, Group Design, and Evidence-Based Practice

In Chapter 5, we described how historically racial minorities and women had not been adequately represented in research studies. Under the provisions of the NIH Revitalization Act of 1993 (PL 103-43), women and minorities must be included in clinical research supported by the National Institutes of Health. We also described recruitment strategies in Chapter 5. In this section, we want to highlight the link between adequate representation in research and evidence-based practice.

The most important consideration is the external validity of the findings from group research designs. For what population groups has the intervention been determined to be effective? Although social work research extends to many different areas, the evidence about the inclusion of people of color and women is probably best developed in the evaluations of mental health studies. Jeanne Miranda, Richard Nakamura, and Guillermo Bernal (2003) found that, between 1986 and 1997, in studies using true experimental designs to test the effectiveness of treatment for depression, bipolar disorder, schizophrenia, and attention deficit hyperactivity disorder, few minorities were included. Using the studies' reports of ethnicity, of nearly 10,000 participants, Miranda and her colleagues could only identify 561 African Americans, 99 Latinos, 11 Asian Americans and Pacific Islanders, and no American Indians or Alaska Natives (Miranda et al., 2003; U.S. Department of Health and Human Services, 2001). Another analysis of 379 National Institutes of Mental Health–funded studies by Winnie Mak, Rita W. Law, Jennifer Alvidrez, and Eliseo J. Perez-Stable (2007) reported that women were adequately included across studies, whereas, of ethnic groups, only Whites and African Americans were adequately represented.

Representation alone is insufficient because there needs to be a sufficient number of participants so that subgroups can be analyzed. Researchers often fail to do an analysis just for women in their sample or just for African Americans in their sample. Rather, the results are often only analyzed for the entire sample; different treatment effects for women or people of color may not be reported or observed. Miranda et al. (2003) reported finding no studies that included an analysis by racial or ethnic group. In an updated analysis of articles published between 2001 and 2010, Santiago and Miranda (2014) found increasing numbers of racial and ethnic representation but still few studies reporting analyses by racial or ethnic group.

Therefore, as you review the available research and try to answer the "for whom" question, it is necessary to identify the characteristics of those who participated in the research. This is likely to be challenging because many of the studies described by Miranda et al. (2003), Mak et al. (2007), and Santiago and Miranda (2014) included no information about ethnicity or lumped all those who were not White into a single category.

A group of scholars (Lewis-Fernandez et al., 2013) suggest that even knowing the characteristics of participants is insufficient in reporting findings. They are testing a 16-item list, GAP-REACH, which can be used to assess reporting of race, ethnicity, and culture in mental health journals. The items are organized around sections commonly found in research articles, including the overall article (e.g., inclusion in the title or abstract), introduction/background, methods, results, and discussion.

Finally, the broad categories we use to depict racial or ethnic groups tend to imply that all African Americans, all Latinos, or all Asian Americans share the same cultural, social, and historical legacies. Yet within these groups, there are differences in cultural definition, language, history, and immigration experience. For example, William Vega and his colleagues (1998) found that Mexican immigrants have lower rates of depression than do Mexican Americans born in the United States. You can see that even within what seems like a narrowly defined ethnic group—Mexican Americans—there can be significant differences, in this case based on birthplace. Given that there can be so many variations, evaluating the evidence becomes even more difficult. Therefore, any intervention should at least have a theoretical base, and there is some evidence to link that theoretical base to culture (Miranda et al., 2003).

⊞ Ethical Issues in Experimental Research

Experimental evaluations of social programs pose ethical dilemmas because they require researchers to withhold possibly beneficial treatment from some of the subjects just on the basis of chance. While rarely a concern for much social work research social science experiments may involve subject deception. Primarily because of this feature, some experiments have prompted contentious debates about research ethics. In this section, we give special attention to the problems of the distribution of benefits in experimental research and deception.

Selective Distribution of Benefits

One ethical issue that is somewhat unique to field experiments is the distribution of benefits: How much are subjects harmed by the way treatments are distributed in the experiment? For example, participation in the Brock and Harknett (1998) study of different models of case management for TANF recipients had serious implications. The requirements of TANF impose a lifetime limit on participation, so people receiving a potentially less adequate method of case management could lose valuable time. Furthermore, it was thought that one method would help people find work faster and that those people would earn more from employment than would participants receiving the other method.

Is it ethical to give some potentially advantageous or disadvantageous treatment to people on a random basis? Random distribution of benefits is justified when the researchers do not know whether some treatment actually is beneficial—and, of course, it is the goal of the experiment to find out. Chance is as reasonable a basis for distributing the treatment as any other. If insufficient resources are available to fully fund a benefit for every eligible person, distribution of the benefit on the basis of chance to equally needy people is ethically defensible (Boruch, 1997).

Deception

Deception occurs when subjects are misled about research procedures in order to determine how they would react to the treatment if they were not research subjects. Deception is a critical component of many social experiments, although it occurs less frequently in social work research. One reason deception is used is because of the difficulty of simulating real-world stresses and dilemmas in a laboratory setting. The problem with deception is that potential participants are not given the information they need to make an informed decision and may give consent to participate in research that they otherwise would not have agreed to with full information.

You read in Chapter 3 about Milgram's (1965) use of deception in his study of obedience to authority. Volunteers were recruited for what they were told was a study of the learning process, not a study of "obedience to authority." The experimenter told the volunteers that they were administering electric shocks to a "student" in the next room, when there were actually neither students nor shocks. Whether or not you believe that you could be deceived in this way, you are not likely to be invited to participate in an experiment such as Milgram's. Current federal regulations preclude deception in research that might trigger such upsetting feelings.

The overarching question is, "Is there sufficient justification to allow the use of deception?" The NASW Code of Ethics does not explicitly discuss deception in research, but it does allude to deception in discussing informed-consent:

> 5.02(g) Social workers should never design or conduct evaluation or research that does not use consent procedures, such as certain forms of naturalistic observation and archival research, unless rigorous and responsible review of the research has found it to be justified because of its prospective scientific, educational, or applied value and unless equally effective alternative procedures that do not involve waiver of consent are not feasible.

To ensure that there no harm is caused to participants, researchers use a procedure is called debriefing. Debriefing involves explaining the true nature of the research to participants after the experiment and to address any issues that might have arisen as a result of their participation.

▣ Conclusion

True experiments play two critical roles in social work research. First, they are the best research designs for testing causal hypotheses. Even when conditions preclude use of a true experimental design, many research designs can be improved by adding some experimental components. Second, true experiments also provide a comparison point for evaluating the ability of other research designs to achieve causally valid results.

Despite their obvious strengths, true experiments are used infrequently to study many of the research problems that interest social work researchers. There are three basic reasons.

The experiments required to test many important hypotheses require far more resources than most social scientists have at their disposal. Most of the research problems of interest to social work researchers simply are not amenable to experimental designs for reasons ranging from ethical considerations to the limited possibilities for randomly assigning people to different conditions in the real world. Finally, the requirements of experimental design usually preclude large-scale studies and so limit generalizability to a degree that is unacceptable to many social scientists.

Just because it is possible to test a hypothesis with an experiment does not mean it will always be desirable to do so. When a social program is first being developed and its elements are in flux, it is not a good idea to begin a large evaluation study that cannot possibly succeed unless the program design remains constant. Researchers should wait until the program design stabilizes somewhat. It also does not make sense for researchers engaged in program evaluation to test the impact of programs that cannot actually be implemented or to test programs that are unlikely to be implemented in the real world because of financial or political problems (Rossi & Freeman, 1989).

Many forms of social work research, particularly research and evaluation done in agencies, will require design decisions about what is feasible. As you can see from the contents of this chapter, there are many components and factors to consider in choosing a group design. Regardless of the design used, it is important to understand the limits of the conclusions that can be made, both in terms of the internal validity of the design and the generalizability of the findings.

Key Terms

Aggregate matching   166
Block matching   165
Comparison group   163
Compensatory equalization of
   treatment   160
Compensatory rivalry   160
Contamination   160
Control group   163
Differential attrition   159
Diffusion of treatment   160

Double-blind procedures   160
Experimental group   163
External validity   161
History   158
Instrumentation   159
Maturation   159
Meta-analysis   179
Placebo effect   160
Posttest   166
Pretest   166

Quasi-experimental design   172
Randomization   163
Reactivity   161
Resentful demoralization   160
Secular drift   159
Selection bias   157
Statistical regression   159
Treatment as usual   163
True experiments   162

Highlights

- Causal explanation relies on a comparison. The value of cases on the dependent variable is measured after they have been exposed to variation in an independent variable. This measurement is compared to what the value of cases on the dependent variable would have been if they had not been exposed to the variation in the independent variable.

- Three criteria are necessary to identify a causal relationship: association between the variables, proper time order, and nonspuriousness of the association. In addition, the basis for concluding that a causal relationship exists is strengthened by identification of a causal mechanism and the context.

- True experimental research designs have three essential components: (1) use of at least two groups of subjects for comparison, (2) measurement of the change that occurs as a result of the experimental treatment, and (3) use of random assignment.

- Random assignment of subjects to experimental and comparison groups eliminates systematic bias in group assignment. The odds of a difference between the experimental and comparison groups on the basis of chance can be calculated.

- Random assignment involves placing participants into two or more groups on the basis of chance. Matching can improve the comparability of groups when it is used to supplement randomization.

- The independent variable in an experiment is represented by a treatment or other intervention. Some subjects receive one type of treatment; others may receive a different treatment or no treatment.

- Causal conclusions derived from experiments can be invalid because of selection bias, endogenous change, external events, cross-group contamination, or treatment misidentification. In true experiments, randomization should eliminate selection bias and bias due to endogenous change. External events, cross-group contamination, and treatment misidentification can threaten the validity of causal conclusions in both true experiments and quasi-experiments.

- The external validity of causal conclusions is determined by the extent to which they apply to different types of individuals and settings. When causal conclusions do not apply to all the subgroups in a study, they are not generalizable to corresponding subgroups in the population—and so they are not externally valid with respect to those subgroups. Causal conclusions can also be considered externally invalid when they occur only under the experimental conditions.

- Quasi-experimental group designs control for some threats to internal validity, while nonexperimental group designs tend to control for few or no threats to internal validity. It is common to find both types of designs in agency settings.

- A common ethical problem is selective distribution of benefits. Random assignment may be the fairest way of allocating treatment when treatment openings are insufficient for all eligible individuals and when the efficacy of the treatment is unknown.

Discussion Questions

1. A program has recently been funded to provide casework intensive services to the homeless. The mission of the program is to provide skills that will lead to self-sufficiency and employment. Develop a research study using the following:

   True experimental design

   Quasi-experimental design

   Nonexperimental design

   Be specific in describing the procedures you would have to do to implement your design. This may mean specifying how you will assign clients to groups (if you have more than one group) or where you would find clients for your control/comparison groups (if you have such groups). Identify the benefits and weaknesses of each of the specific designs you chose.

2. Describe individual matching, block matching, and aggregate matching. What is the rationale for using these techniques, and what are their limitations?

3. The three broad approaches to research design covered in this chapter are true experimental, quasi-experimental, and nonexperimental. How would you rate these approaches (i.e., "+", strength/ "−", weakness) on the following four criteria: (1) external validity, (2) internal validity, (3) random assignment, and (4) use of control/comparison group.

Practice Exercises

1. Go to the book's study site, www.sagepub.com/engelprsw4e, and choose two research articles that include some attention to causality (as indicated by a check in that column of the article matrix). For each article describe the following:

   a. What type of design was used? How does the author describe the design? Was it suited to the research question posed and the specific hypotheses tested, if any? Why do you suppose the author chose that particular design?

   b. Did the design eliminate threats to internal validity? If so, how did it do this? Are you satisfied with the internal validity conclusions stated by the author? Why or why not?

   c. What is the setting for the study? Does the setting limit the generalizability of the results to other similar settings or to the broader population? Is reactivity a problem? Are there other threats to external validity?

2. Search for a research study using a true experimental design to examine the effects of hospice care. Diagram the experiment using the exhibits in this chapter as a model. How generalizable do you think the study's results are to the population from which cases were selected? To other populations? To specific subgroups in the study? To other settings? How thoroughly do the researchers discuss these issues?

Web Exercise

1. Try out the process of randomization. Go to the Research Randomizer website (www.randomizer.org). Type numbers into the randomizer for an experiment with two groups and 20 individuals per group. Repeat the process for an experiment with four groups and 10 individuals per group. Plot the numbers corresponding to each individual in each group. Does the distribution of numbers within each group truly seem to be random?

2. Participate in a social psychology experiment online. Go to www.socialpsychology.org/expts.htm, pick an experiment in which to participate, and follow the instructions. After you finish, write up a description of the experiment and evaluate it using the criteria discussed in the chapter.

Developing a Research Proposal

If you are planning to use a group design:

1. What specific design will you use? How long will the study last? At what time points will data be collected? How will the data be collected?

2. If you are using a design with more than one group, describe how participants are assigned to each group.

3. Discuss the extent to which each source of internal validity is a problem in the study.

4. How generalizable would you expect the study's findings to be? What can be done to improve generalizability?

5. Develop appropriate procedures for the protection of human subjects in your study. Include in these procedures a consent form.

A Question of Ethics

1. Randomization and double-blind procedures are key features of experimental design that are often used by studies to investigate the efficacy of new treatments for serious and often incurable, terminal diseases. What ethical issues do these techniques raise in studies of experimental treatments for incurable, terminal diseases?

2. Under what conditions do you think that randomized assignment of subjects to a specific treatment is ethical in social work research? Was it ethical for Brock and Hartnett (1998) to randomly assign individuals to receive higher payments than others?

Single-Subject Design

Jody was a 40-year-old married White female who had been ill since 22 years of age. She had multiple hospitalizations including 1 year in the state hospital. In the past year, she had six hospitalizations. She suffered from hallucinations, delusions, psychomotor retardation, apathy, flat affect, and avoidance of people and social situations. She was suicidal, inactive, and unable to do minimal self-care. She lived with her husband, who took care of her. She was a high school graduate and had attended 1 year of training as a dental assistant before her illness forced her to drop out of school. She took neuroleptic medications interspersed with brief periods of noncompliance due to paranoid ideas about the medicine. (Bradshaw, 1997, p. 438)

It is not unusual for social work practitioners to have clients such as Jody who have a mental health condition such as schizophrenia. As practitioners, we often think we know when a client is improving. Yet, when we use our own subjective conclusions, we are prone to human error. In this chapter, you learn how single-subject designs can be used to systematically test the effectiveness of a particular intervention as William Bradshaw did with Jody and subsequently with other participants (Bradshaw 1997, 2003; Bradshaw & Roseborough, 2004), as well as how it can be used to monitor client progress.

Single-subject (sometimes referred to as single-case or single-system) designs offer an alternative to the group designs described in Chapter 7. The focus is on a single participant whether that participant is an individual, a group, or a community, and yet, as we will illustrate, single-subject designs can be used with groups. The structure of these designs, which are easily adapted to social work practice, makes them useful for research on interventions in direct and community practice. The process of assessment, establishing intervention goals and specific outcomes, providing the intervention, and evaluating progress prior to termination, parallels the process of using single-subject designs, which depend on identifying the focus of the intervention, taking preintervention measures, providing the intervention, taking additional measures, and making decisions about the efficacy of the intervention. Because of these parallels, single-subject designs can be used not just for research but also adapted to evaluating practice and monitoring client progress.

Contrast this design with group designs. In Chapter 7, we noted that group designs do not naturally conform to practice, particularly when the practice involves interventions with individuals. The analysis of these designs typically refers to the "group's average change score" or "the number of subjects altering their status." By describing the group, we miss each individual's experience with the intervention. Once a group design is implemented, it is difficult to change the nature of the treatment, yet individual participants within the group may not respond to the particular type of treatment offered.

In this chapter, we begin by taking you through the basic features of single-subject designs. Next, we describe ways to measure changes in the case that is the target of the intervention. We then describe different designs and connect them to their uses for social work research, practice evaluation, and client monitoring. Finally, we end the chapter with a discussion about the implications of single-subject designs for evidence-based practice and the ethical issues associated with single-subject designs.

▣ Foundations of Single-Subject Design

The underlying principle of a single-subject design as a social work research method is that if an intervention with a client, a group of clients, an agency, or a community is effective, it should be possible to see a change in status from the period prior to intervention to the period during and after the intervention. At a minimum, single-subject research designs include

- repeated measurements to identify a client's status,

- the baseline phase or the time period prior to the start of the intervention, and

- the treatment phase or the time period during the intervention.

Furthermore, the baseline and treatment phase measurements are usually displayed using graphs.

Repeated Measurement

Single-subject designs require the repeated measurement of a dependent variable, that is, the target or the focus of the intervention such as a status, condition, or problem. The target is measured at regular time intervals such as hours, days, weeks, or months, prior to the intervention and during the intervention. The preferred method is to take measures of the target with the client prior to implementing the intervention, for example, during the assessment process, and then continue during the course of the intervention. Gathering information may mean withholding the intervention until the repeated measures can be taken. Alternatively, repeated measures of the dependent variable can begin when the client is receiving an intervention for other concerns. For example, a child may be seen for behavioral problems, but eventually communication issues will be a concern. The repeated measurement of the communication issues could begin prior to that specific intervention focus.

Sometimes it is not possible to delay the intervention either because there is a crisis or because to delay would be unethical. Yet you may still be able to construct a set of preintervention measures using data already collected or by asking about past experiences. Client records may have information from which a baseline can be constructed, although you are limited to the information that is available on the record. Some client records, such as report cards, may have complete information, but other client records, such as case files, may or may not. Another option is to ask the client or, if permission is granted, ask significant members of the client's network about past behaviors. Trying to construct measures by asking clients or family members assumes that the information is both remembered and reported accurately. Generally, behaviors and events are easier to recall than moods or feelings, yet the recall of even behaviors or events becomes more difficult with the passage of time and probably should be limited to the preceding month. Although recognizing the limits of these retrospective data collection methods is important, the limitations should not preclude using the information if that is all that is available, particularly for evaluating practice.

There are other times when using retrospective data is feasible. Agencies often collect quite a bit of data about their operations, and these data can be used to obtain repeated measurements. For example, if an agency director was trying to find an outreach method that would increase the number of referrals, previous monthly referral information could be used and the intervention begun immediately. Or if an organizer was interested in the impact of an empowerment zone on levels of employment in a community, the preintervention employment data are likely to exist.

Baseline Phase

The **baseline phase** (abbreviated by the letter A) represents the period in which the intervention to be evaluated is not offered to the respondent. During the baseline phase, repeated measurements of the dependent variable are taken or reconstructed. These measures reflect the status of the client (or agency or community) on the dependent variable prior to the intervention. The baseline phase measurements provide two aspects of control analogous to a control group in a group design. First, in a group design, we expect the treatment group to have different scores than the control group after the intervention. In a single-subject design, the subject serves as the control as the repeated baseline measurements establish the pattern of scores that we expect the intervention to change. Without the intervention, researchers assume that the baseline pattern of scores would continue its course. Second, in a control group design, random assignment controls for threats to internal validity. In a single-subject design, the repeated baseline measurements allow the researcher to discount most threats to the internal validity of the design.

> **Baseline phase** The initial phase of a single-subject design, typically abbreviated by the letter A; it represents the period in which the intervention to be evaluated is not offered to the subject. During the baseline phase, repeated measurements of the dependent variable are taken or constructed.

Patterns

In the baseline phase, measurements are taken until a *pattern* emerges. You have found a pattern when you can predict with some certainty what might be the next score. Predicting the next score requires a minimum of three observations in the baseline stage. When there are only two measures, as shown in Exhibit 8.1a, can you predict the next score with any certainty? The next data point could be higher, lower, or the same as the previous data points (see Exhibit 8.1b). With three measures, your certainty increases about the nature of the pattern. But even three measures might not be enough depending on the pattern that is emerging. In the graph shown in Exhibit 8.1c, is the pattern predictable? You probably should take at least two more baseline measures, but three or four additional measures may be necessary to see

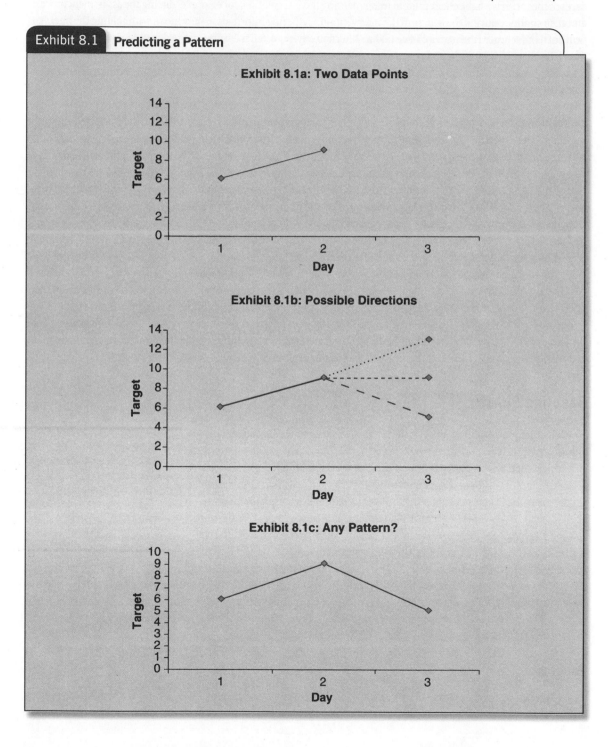

Exhibit 8.1 **Predicting a Pattern**

Exhibit 8.1a: Two Data Points

Exhibit 8.1b: Possible Directions

Exhibit 8.1c: Any Pattern?

a pattern emerge. As a general rule, the more data points, the more certain you will be about the pattern; it takes at least three consecutive measures that fall in some pattern for you to have confidence in the shape of the baseline pattern.

The three common types of patterns are a stable line, a trend line, and a cycle. A **stable line** (see Exhibit 8.2a) is a relatively flat line, with little variability in the scores so that the scores fall in a narrow band. This kind of line is desirable because changes can easily be detected, and it is likely that there are few problems of testing, instrumentation, statistical regression, and maturation in the data. A wider band or range of scores (see Exhibit 8.2b) is more difficult to interpret than a stable line with little variation.

A **trend** occurs when the scores may be either increasing or decreasing during the baseline period. When there is a linear trend (see Exhibit 8.2c), the scores tend to increase (or decrease) at a more or less constant rate over time. A trend may also be curvilinear (see Exhibit 8.2d) so that the rate of change is accelerating over time rather than increasing or decreasing at a constant rate.

Stable line A line that is relatively flat, with little variability in the scores so that the scores fall in a narrow band.

Trend An ascending or descending line.

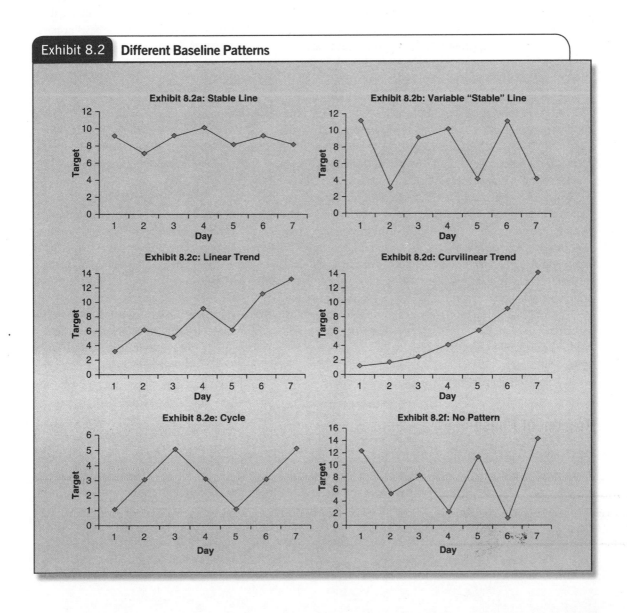

Exhibit 8.2 | **Different Baseline Patterns**

Cycle A pattern reflecting ups and downs depending on time of measurement.

A **cycle** (see Exhibit 8.2e) is a pattern in which there are increases and decreases in scores depending on the time of year (or week or month) when the measures are taken. For example, homeless shelter occupancy varies by the time of year with increased use in winter months and decreased use in summer months.

There are times when no pattern emerges (see Exhibit 8.2f). With such baseline patterns, it is important to consider the reasons for the variability in scores. Is it due to the lack of reliability of the measurement process? If so, then an alternative measure might be sought. The client may be using a good measure, but not reporting information consistently, such as completing a depression scale at different times of day. Or the variability in scores may be due to some changing circumstance in the life of the client.

Internal Validity

Findings of causality depend on the internal validity of the research design. Identifying patterns by taking repeated baseline measurements can control for several threats to the internal validity of single-subject designs. Specifically, problems of maturation, instrumentation, statistical regression, and testing may be evaluated because patterns illustrative of these threats to internal validity should appear in the baseline. When the measurement in the baseline phase is reconstructed from existing data or memory, these threats to internal validity are problematic.

When baseline measures are stable lines, these threats may be ruled out, but it is more difficult to rule out some threats if the pattern is a trend, particularly if the trend is in the desired direction. For example, if maturation is a problem, you would expect to find a trend line and not a horizontal line. Perhaps you have a client who has suffered a loss and you are measuring sadness. At the first baseline measurement, you find a high degree of sadness. At the second baseline measurement a week later, you find a lower level of sadness, and a third baseline measurement finds sadness has declined below the level of the second week. This pattern suggests that there may be a maturation effect as improvement is in the desired direction and occurs before the intervention. This does not mean that an intervention would not be effective, but it may be more difficult to demonstrate its effectiveness.

If statistical regression and testing effects occur, the impact is likely to appear initially in the baseline measures. A high score obtained from a measurement may be lower in a second measurement because of statistical regression or because of the respondent's acclimation to the measurement process. If there were only one or two baseline measures, the line might reflect these effects. But with multiple measures, the effect of statistical regression should occur in the beginning of measurement, and continued measurement should produce a baseline pattern. The testing effect should be observable early in the baseline measurement process, as the subject adjusts to the testing requirements, and not with subsequent measurement.

The most significant threat to internal validity is history. Repeated measurement in a baseline will not control for an extraneous event (history) that occurs between the last baseline measurement and the first intervention measurement. The longer the time period between the two measurement points, the greater the possibility that an event might influence the participant's scores. At the end of the study, the researcher should check with participants to determine whether some other event may have influenced the results.

Treatment Phase

The **treatment phase** (signified by a B) represents the time period during which the intervention is implemented. During the treatment phase, repeated measurements of the same dependent variable using the same measures are

Treatment phase The intervention phase of a single-subject design.

obtained. Ultimately, the patterns and magnitude of the data points are compared to the data points in the baseline phase to determine whether a change has occurred. The length of the treatment phase should be as long as the baseline phase (Barlow, Nock, & Hersen, 2009; Tripodi, 1994).

Graphing

The phases of a single-subject design are usually summarized on a graph. Graphing the data facilitates monitoring and evaluating the impact of the intervention. The y-axis represents the scores of the dependent variable, whereas the x-axis represents a unit of time, such as an hour, day, week, or month. Although you may make your graph by hand, both statistical software and spreadsheet software have the capacity to present data on graphs. For example, Deochand and colleagues (2015) provide simple instructions to using Microsoft Excel 2013 to create graphs for single-subject designs.

Care in graphing is important as the act of graphing can create visual distortions that can lead to inaccurate conclusions. When making a graph, it is important to make the axes as proportionate as possible in order to minimize distortions. You want to ensure that the graph will visually represent small but meaningful changes.

回 Measuring Targets of Intervention

Three questions to answer about measurement are (1) what target to measure, (2) how to measure the target, and (3) who will do the measuring. With each decision, there are important issues to consider. There should be some certainty based on theoretical literature, empirical support, or practice experience to suggest that the chosen intervention is an appropriate method to address the target.

What to Measure

The dependent variable in a single-subject design is the target, that is, the concern or issue that is the focus of the intervention. The target and intervention are usually established as part of the research project and specified prior to any client interaction. In contrast, social work practitioners using single-subject design methods to evaluate practice or monitor their work typically arrive at the target problem through their interaction with clients or client systems. Clients may start with some general problem or need that, through the processes of assessment and discussion, becomes narrowed to a specific set of treatment goals. Similarly, a community organizer may identify the general needs of a community, and through discussion and meetings, specific outcomes are identified.

The target may focus on one specific concern or different aspects of that concern. For example, with an adolescent who is having behavioral problems in school, you may decide to measure the frequency of the behavioral problems. Or you may hypothesize that the adolescent's behavioral problems are caused by poor family communication and low self-esteem, so you may choose to measure all three concerns. The target problems can be measured simultaneously or sequentially.

Single-subject design is applicable to other systems as well, such as agencies and communities. An agency director may decide to evaluate the efficacy of different methods to improve agency functioning or examine the extent to which a community-based program produces changes in the community. The choice of the target becomes a question of determining the information that is important to the agency or community.

How to Measure

Once the target or outcome of the intervention has been identified, you must determine how you will measure it. Generally, in a research study, operationalization occurs prior to the beginning of the study; when practitioners evaluate practice or monitor clients, operationalization takes place through client and practitioner discussion. For example, if you are evaluating the impact of positive parenting techniques on altering a child's behavior, you would identify jointly with the parents a behavior such as tantrums. You would then guide the parents to be able to distinguish a tantrum from other behaviors or verbal expressions. This engagement is particularly important because there may be gender and ethnic differences in how a general problem may manifest itself (Nelson, 1994).

Measures of, status, or functioning are often characterized in four ways: frequency, duration, interval, and magnitude:

- **Frequency** refers to counting the number of times a behavior occurs or the number of times people experience different feelings within a particular time period. Based on the prior example, you could ask the parents to count the number of tantrums their child had each week. Frequency counts are useful for measuring targets that happen regularly, but counting can be burdensome if the behavior occurs too often. However, if the behavior happens only periodically, the counts will not be meaningful.

- **Duration** refers to the length of time an event or some symptom lasts and usually is measured for each occurrence of the event or symptom. Rather than counting the number of tantrums in a week, the parents could be asked to time the length of each tantrum. The parents would need a clear definition as to what constitutes the beginning and end of a tantrum. A measure of duration requires fewer episodes than do frequency counts of the target.

- The **interval**, or the length of time between events, may be measured. Using a measure of interval, the parents in our example would calculate the length of time between tantrums. Just as a clear operational definition was necessary for the duration measure, the parents would need a clear definition when measuring the interval between tantrums. This kind of measure may not be appropriate for events or symptoms that happen frequently unless the intent of the intervention is to delay their onset.

- The **magnitude** or intensity of a particular behavior or psychological state can be measured. A scale might be used by the parents to rate or score the intensity of the tantrum—how loud the screaming is, whether there is rolling around on the floor or hitting, and the like. Often magnitude or intensity measures are applied to psychological symptoms or attitudes such as measures of depressive symptoms, quality of peer interactions, or self-esteem.

Frequency In a single-subject design, counting the number of times a behavior occurs or the number of times people experience different feelings within a particular period.

Duration The length of time an event of some symptom lasts; usually it is measured for each occurrence of the event or symptom.

Interval Used in single-subject design, a measure of the length of time between events, behaviors, or symptoms.

Magnitude Measuring the intensity of a particular behavior or psychological state.

Social work researchers and practitioners have a variety of alternative methods available to measure the target problem. Standardized scales cover a wide range of psychological dimensions, family functioning, individual functioning, and the like. Another option is to collect data based on clinical observations. Observations are particularly useful when the target problem involves a behavior. A third option is to develop measures within the agency, such as a goal attainment scale. Regardless of how the data are collected, the measures should be reliable and valid. In particular, the reliability and validity of the instruments should have been tested on subjects of the same age, gender, and ethnicity as the client who is the focus of the single-subject design (Nelson, 1994).

Who Should Measure

It is important to consider who will gather the data and to understand the potential consequence of each choice. Participants or clients can be asked to keep logs and to record information in the logs. Participants can complete instruments at specified time points, either through self-administration or an interview; or the social work researcher may choose to observe the participant's behavior.

A particular problem in gathering the data is the issue of reactivity. You do not want the process of collecting data to influence a subject's behavior. If you ask a subject to keep a log and record each time a behavior occurred, the act of keeping the log may reduce the behavior. Observing a father interacting with his children might change the way he behaves with them. Staff, knowing that supervisors are looking for certain activities, may increase the number of those activities. Changes due to reactivity may be short in duration and observable in the baseline, so repeated measurements in the baseline might mitigate this problem (Tripodi, 1994). Nonetheless, it is important to recognize that there might be reactivity and to choose methods that limit reactivity.

Yet reactivity is not always a problem for either research or practice. If you were testing an intervention to improve a father's interaction skills with his children and you decided to observe the interactions, reactivity is likely to occur. The father, knowing that he is under observation, is likely to perform at his best. But in this case, reactivity is useful for the researcher who wants to see what the father thinks is the best way to interact with his children. It could be that the "best" is not very good, and the intervention would work on improving those skills.

Reactivity may have clinical utility for practice interventions. If keeping a log enhances the impact of the intervention, then this finding could be integrated into the actual intervention. But we would still have to test whether different methods of gathering data produce different outcomes.

Another measurement concern is the feasibility of the measurement process. Repeatedly taking measures can be cumbersome, inconvenient, and difficult. Is it going to be possible to use the method time and time again? Is the method too time-consuming for the subject and/or the researcher or practitioner? Will continuous measurements reduce the incentive of the subject to participate in the research or treatment?

The choice of measurement must be sensitive enough to detect changes. If the measuring scale is too global, it may be impossible to detect incremental or small changes, particularly in such target problems as psychological status, feelings, emotions, and attitudes. In addition, whatever is measured must occur frequently enough or on a regular basis so that repeated measurements can be taken. Unless the research is designed to last a long time, it will be impractical to take repeated measures of infrequent events or behaviors.

To assess the influence of cognitive-behavioral therapy with Jody and other participants, Bradshaw (1997) measured three outcomes simultaneously: symptomatology, psychosocial functioning, and hospitalizations. The symptoms measure was based on the severity of the symptoms (magnitude), the psychosocial functioning measure had behavioral anchors and was characterized by magnitude, and hospitalizations were the actual number that occurred in each month (frequency). The rating scales had been evaluated previously for their reliability and validity. To assure reliability and validity, the ratings were done by a psychotherapist and two case managers trained to use the measures. Each client was rated by two observers (usually the psychotherapist and one case manager), providing a measure of interrater reliability. Information about the hospitalizations was obtained from the clients. Consistent with a focus on practice, Bradshaw (1997) measured outcomes specific to the client; in Jody's case, he measured social supports, employment, and her comfort with her sexuality.

⌗ Analyzing Single-Subject Designs

How might we analyze data from a single-subject design? One option is to use a statistical technique such as the two-standard deviation-band, chi-square analysis, or time series to analyze the data (see Barlow et al., 2009; Bloom, Fischer, & Orme, 2009; Borckardt et al., 2008). Charles Auerbach and Wendy Zeitlin Schudrich (2013) have developed open-source software, SSD for R, incorporating visual graphic display capacity and a range of statistical tests for single-subject designs. In this chapter, we concentrate on visual analysis.

Visual Analysis

Visual analysis is the process of looking at a graph of the data points to determine whether the intervention has altered the subject's preintervention pattern of scores. Three concepts that help guide visual inspection are level, trend, and variability.

Level

Level relates to the amount or magnitude of the target variable. Has the amount of the target variable changed from the baseline to the intervention period? Changes in level are used when the observed scores fall along relatively stable lines. The

> **Level** Flat lines reflecting the amount or magnitude of the target variable; used in a single-subject design.

simple method is to inspect the actual data points to see if the intervention data points differ from the baseline points. In Exhibit 8.3a, it appears that the actual amount of the target variable—anxiety—has decreased.

Alternatively, the level of the phase scores may be summarized by drawing a line at the typical score for each phase separately. For example, the level may be summarized into a single observation using the mean (the average of the observations in the phase) or the median (the value at which 50% of the scores in the phase are higher and 50% are lower). The median is typically used in place of the mean when there are outliers or one or two extreme scores that greatly alter the mean. The mean of the baseline scores is calculated, and a horizontal line is drawn across the baseline phase at the mean. Then the mean of the intervention scores is calculated, and a horizontal line is drawn at the mean score across the intervention phase (see Exhibit 8.3b). The summary line for the baseline phase is compared to the summary line for the intervention phase.

Changes in level are typically observations that fall along relatively stable flat lines and are not used when the baseline pattern is either ascending or descending. Imagine the case, displayed in Exhibit 8.3c, where there is an ascending trend in the baseline phase and a descending trend in the intervention phase. As you can see, the direction has changed, but the mean for each phase may not have changed or may have changed only insignificantly.

Trend

When the baseline data points reflect trend lines, there are two different questions depending on the nature of the lines in the treatment phase. The first question is, Has the intervention altered the direction of the trend? If the baseline trend line is ascending, is the trend line descending in the treatment phase? When the direction does not change, you may be interested in whether the rate of increase or decrease in the trend has changed. You might ask the second question: Does the intervention alter the slope, that is, the rate of increase or decrease of the line?

Visually inspecting the lines might provide an answer but trends can also be represented by summary lines. One approach is to use ordinary least squares (OLS) regression to calculate a regression line that summarizes the scores in the baseline and another regression line to summarize the scores in the intervention phase. The baseline OLS regression line is extended into the intervention phase, and the two lines are visually examined to determine whether the trend has changed (see Exhibit 8.4a). The increasing level of anxiety reflected in the baseline has stopped and the level of anxiety has dropped. Since the calculation is quite complicated, statistical software can be used to produce OLS regression lines.

William Nugent (2000) suggests a simpler approach to represent the trend in a phase. When the trend is linear (as opposed to curvilinear), draw a straight line connecting the first and last data points in the baseline phase with an arrow at the end to summarize the direction. A similar line would then be drawn for the points in the intervention phase. These two lines could then be compared. In the case of an outlier, the line should be drawn either from the second point to the last point if the first point is the outlier or from the first point to the second to last point if the last point is the outlier. The same methods can be used to summarize nonlinear trends except that two lines are drawn, one representing the segment of the first point to the lowest (or highest) point and the second line from the lowest (or highest point) to the last data point.

Exhibit 8.4b illustrates the use of Nugent's method. A line was drawn through the first and last time points in the baseline; this line was extended into the intervention phase. A similar line was drawn through the first and last time points in the intervention phase. A comparison of the lines suggests that the level of anxiety was no longer increasing, but had stabilized at a much lower score.

Variability

Variability The extent to which cases are spread out through the distribution or clustered in just one location.

The **variability** of scores, or how different the scores are within the baseline and intervention phases, may be evaluated. Widely divergent scores in the baseline make the assessment of the intervention more difficult, as do widely different scores in the intervention phase. There are some conditions for which the lack of stability is the

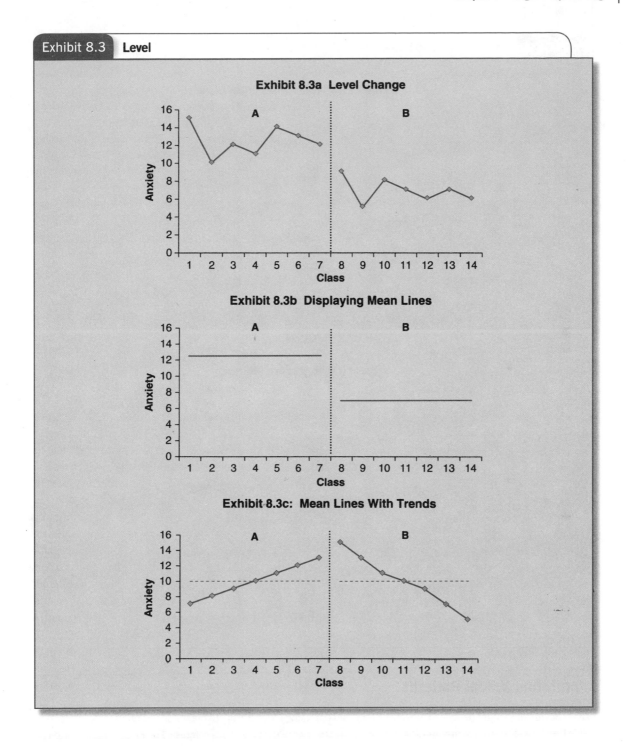

Exhibit 8.3 Level

Exhibit 8.3a Level Change

Exhibit 8.3b Displaying Mean Lines

Exhibit 8.3c: Mean Lines With Trends

problem, so creating stability may represent a positive change. One way to summarize variability with a visual analysis is to draw range lines (see Exhibit 8.5). Whether the intervention had an effect depends on what goal was established with the client. As you can see in this graph, the only change has been a reduction in the spread of the points. But this does not mean that the intervention has not been effective because it depends on the goal of the intervention.

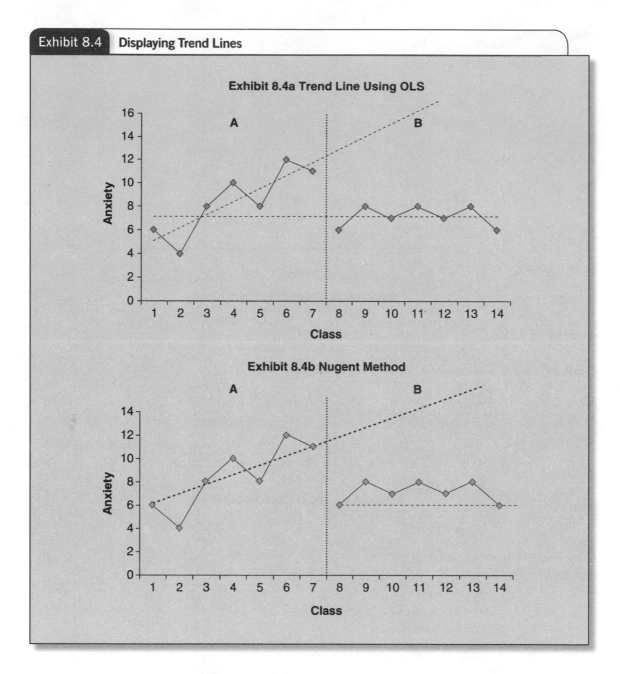

Exhibit 8.4 Displaying Trend Lines

Exhibit 8.4a Trend Line Using OLS

Exhibit 8.4b Nugent Method

Interpreting Visual Patterns

What conclusions might be made from level and trend patterns? Exhibit 8.6a displays a situation in which there is a stable line (or a close approximation of a stable line), so the *level* of the target is of interest. The target in this exhibit is the amount of anxiety, with lower scores being desired. For Outcome A, the intervention has only made the problem worse, for Outcome B the intervention has had no effect, and Outcome C suggests that there has been an improvement, although the effects of history may explain the change. Exhibit 8.6b illustrates outcomes of a stable baseline and a trend line in the treatment phase. Outcome D represents a deteriorating trend, while Outcome E reflects an improving trend.

Exhibit 8.5 | **Variability and Range Bars**

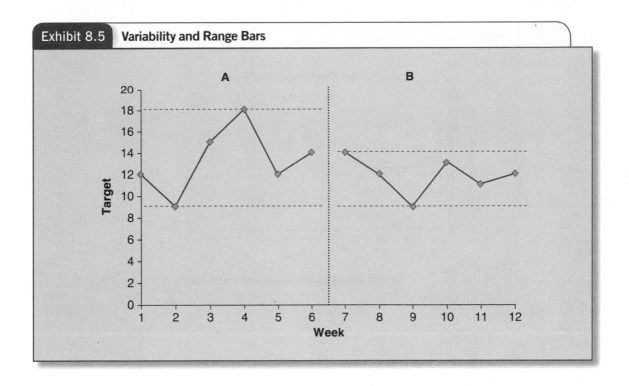

Exhibit 8.6c displays common patterns when there is a trend in the baseline; the baseline phase is marked by an increase in anxiety from week to week. In the case of Outcome F, the intervention had no effect on the level of anxiety. For Outcome G, there was no change in the direction of the trend, but the rate of increase of anxiety has slowed, suggesting that the intervention has had some effect, but has not alleviated it. Outcome H represents the situation in which the intervention has improved the situation only to the extent that it is not getting worse. Finally, for Outcome I, the intervention has resulted in an improvement in the subject's status.

Regardless of whether you use visual inspection or one of these statistical approaches, the overriding issue is the clinical significance (or practical significance) of the findings. Has the intervention made a meaningful difference in the well-being of the subject? Although clinical significance at times is subjective, there are several principles you might apply to reduce the uncertainty:

- *Setting criteria.* One simple method is to establish with the client or community the criteria for success. If the intervention reaches that point, then the change is meaningful.

- *Cut-off scores.* A second method, particularly useful for psychological symptoms, is whether the intervention has reduced the problem to a level below a clinical cut-off score. For example, if you are using the Center for Epidemiologic Studies Depression scale (described in Chapter 4), you would determine whether the depressive symptom scores fall below the cut-off score for depression for that particular scale. Visual inspection or a statistical test may lead you to conclude that the intervention did reduce the number of reported symptoms of depression, but the number did not fall below a cut-off score for depression. Is it a clinically meaningful change if the client is still depressed?

- *Costs and benefits.* A third way to view practical significance is to weigh the costs and benefits to produce the change. Do efforts to increase employment in a community result in sufficient change to be worth the cost and effort to produce the improvement in employment?

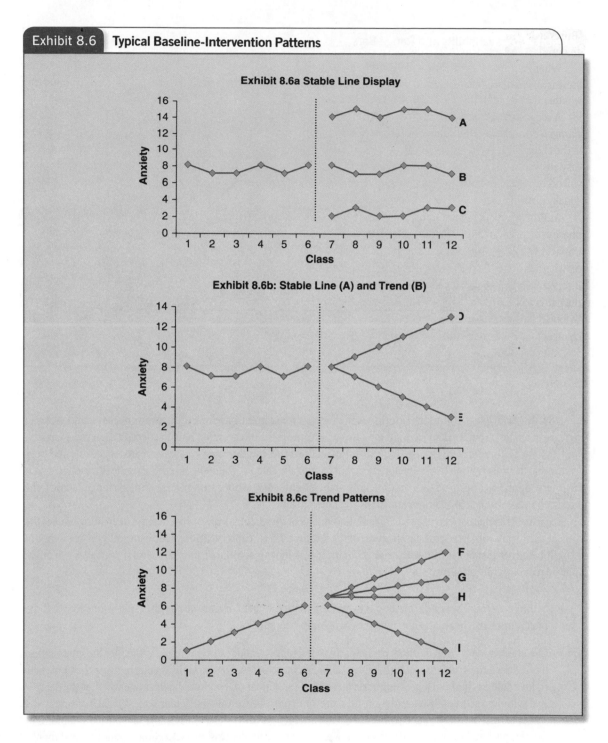

Exhibit 8.6 | **Typical Baseline-Intervention Patterns**

Exhibit 8.6a Stable Line Display

Exhibit 8.6b: Stable Line (A) and Trend (B)

Exhibit 8.6c Trend Patterns

Problems of Interpretation

The examples presented up to now have been quite neat, but when you are engaged in real practice research or evaluation, you are less likely to obtain such clear patterns. Because you are relying on visual judgment, there is the real possibility of coming to the wrong conclusion even if you are using systematic approaches like those suggested by Nugent

(Borckardt, Murphy, Nash, & Shaw, 2004). There are several possible concerns that make conclusions from visual analysis less certain including (1) discrepant scores, (2) delayed change, and (3) improvement in the baseline.

When scores in the baseline widely differ (discrepant scores; see Exhibit 8.2f), it is harder to determine whether there is any pattern. Measures used to create a summary line may poorly represent the data points. Therefore, judging whether the intervention has made a difference becomes more difficult.

A second issue is how to interpret changes in the intervention phase that are not immediately apparent (*delayed change*). For example, the changes in anxiety displayed in Exhibit 8.7 take place several weeks into the intervention. Is the change due to the intervention or some extraneous event or factor unrelated to the intervention? There is no easy answer to this question. It may depend on the nature of the intervention and when it is hypothesized that change will occur. The alternative interpretation that "something extraneous happened" (i.e., history) to produce the effect is equally plausible.

Another difficult judgment occurs when there is improvement in the target problem scores during the baseline phase even prior to the onset of the intervention. This improvement may occur for a variety of reasons, including the impact of an event or the passage of time (i.e., maturation). The effectiveness of the intervention may then depend on whether there is a shift in level or in the rate of the improvement. In Exhibit 8.8a, you see a pattern in which the intervention had no impact, as the improvement continues unchanged after the intervention has begun. Based on the pattern of scores in Exhibits 8.8b and 8.8c, there may have been an intervention effect on the target problem. In Exhibit 8.8b, there was a shift in level, whereas in Exhibit 8.8c, the rate of improvement has accelerated. Of course, these changes may still be due to an event occurring between the last baseline measure and the first intervention measure.

田 Types of Single-Subject Designs

Single-subject designs may be used for research, as a method to assess practice outcomes, or as a tool to monitor client progress. There are more constraints when using a single-subject design for research purposes than when using it for practice evaluation; monitoring client progress has even fewer constraints.

The goal of a research experiment is to test the efficacy of an intervention on a particular target and, therefore, to enhance social work knowledge about what works. The intervention has already been specified, as has the target(s) that

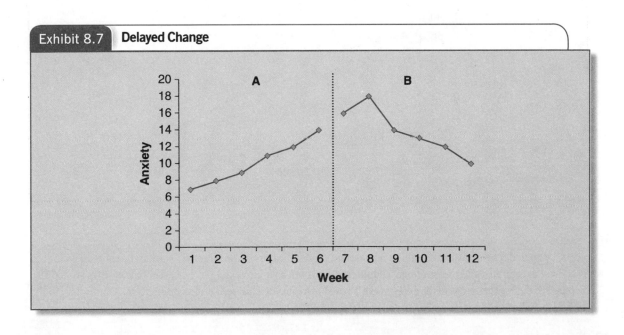

Exhibit 8.7 **Delayed Change**

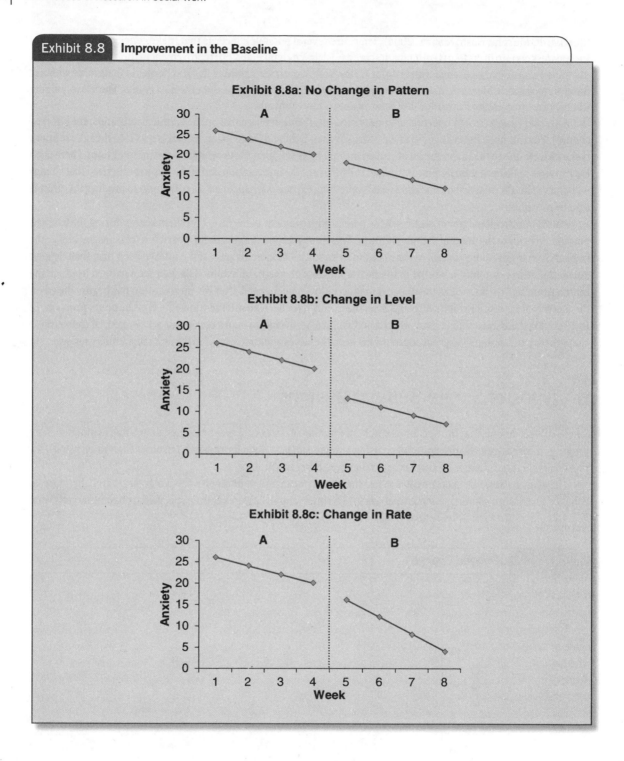

Exhibit 8.8   Improvement in the Baseline

Exhibit 8.8a: No Change in Pattern

Exhibit 8.8b: Change in Level

Exhibit 8.8c: Change in Rate

will be evaluated. The measures should be reliable and valid indicators of the target(s). The baseline should include at least three data points, and measurement should continue until a pattern emerges. The baseline measures should also be collected during the course of the experiment. To establish causality, the design should control for all internal validity threats, including history.

The focus of practice evaluation is to describe the effectiveness of the program or particular intervention approach. Increasing knowledge about a particular treatment approach may be a goal, but that is secondary to the overall purpose of evaluation. Practice or program evaluation is conducted to provide feedback about the program to agency staff and funders, making demonstrating a causal relationship less important. The specific target and the appropriate intervention emerge from the interaction of the social worker with the client rather than being established before the interaction. As in a research study, the measures should be reliable and valid indicators of the target. Ideally, the baseline should include at least three measures and be characterized by a stable pattern, but this may not be possible; only one or two measures may be available. Unlike the case in a research design, the baseline measures may be produced through the recollection of the client, significant others, or client records. Finally, controlling for causality is less important.

The purpose of monitoring is to systematically track a client's progress. Monitoring provides ongoing feedback that may be more objective than just relying on the practitioner's impressions. The information can be used by the social worker to determine whether the intervention should continue without change or whether the intervention should be modified. As with practice evaluation, the target problem and intervention are not specified in advance; rather, they emerge through the client–social worker interaction. Ideally, the measures are reliable and valid indicators. There may not be any baseline, or the baseline may be limited to a single assessment. When the techniques are used to monitor a client's progress, threats to internal validity are not a concern.

Keep these distinctions in mind as you read about the various designs. Some designs can be used for both research and practice evaluation, while other designs are more suited for monitoring.

Basic Design: A-B

The *A-B design* is the basic single-subject design and is used for all three purposes: research, evaluation, and client monitoring. It includes a baseline phase with repeated measurements and an intervention phase continuing the same measures. Bradshaw (1997), in his work with Jody and three other clients who also had schizophrenia, used an A-B design to test the effectiveness of cognitive-behavioral therapy (CBT). Bradshaw collected 3 months of baseline data on symptomatology, role functioning, and psychosocial functioning using standardized scales. This was followed by 18 months of intervention, with data collected monthly. As a research study, Bradshaw (a) set the length of the study and the particular outcomes prior to contact with the participants, (b) used standardized measures for which there was evidence of reliability and validity, and (c) had a minimum of three baseline measures.

The results for Jody's role functioning scores are presented in Exhibit 8.9. The three baseline scores did result in a stable line; subsequently there is a delayed change but after an additional four months, role functioning shows improvement. Based on the evidence of just this graph (remember Bradshaw had three other subjects), you could argue that the intervention had a positive effect on role functioning, but you could also plausibly suggest that some event (history) might have occurred after month seven that resulted in a positive change.

This example points to the limits of the A-B design. The design cannot rule out history, so it is impossible to conclude that the treatment *caused* the change. It is important that the participant and the researcher debrief to review whether any events transpired that might offer an alternative explanation for the results. The A-B design provides evidence of an association between the intervention and the change, and given that some threats to internal validity are controlled, it is analogous to a quasi-experimental design.

The A-B design can also be used to monitor a client's progress. Consider a case in which a social worker is meeting with the parents who are having problems with their 17-year-old daughter. They note that for several months their daughter has been squabbling constantly with her brother and being rude and sarcastic with her parents. The social worker suggests an intervention based on negative rewards may lead to a behavioral change. The parents agree to use a point system, with points being accrued for poor behavior. Once a certain number of points are attained, the child will begin to lose certain privileges. The parents are instructed to count and record the total number of rude and sarcastic comments, as well as sibling arguments begun by the daughter, every 3 days over a 15-day period. The intervention begins on the 16th day, with the parents explaining how she might get negative points and face the consequences of accumulating points.

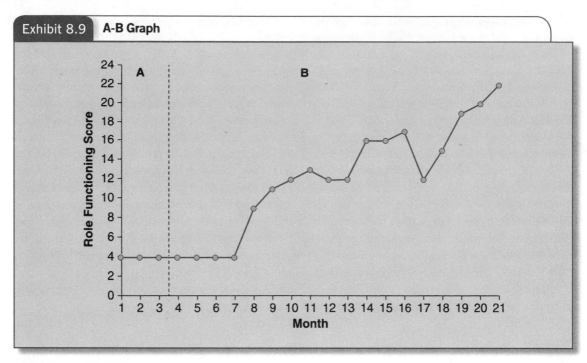

Exhibit 8.9   A-B Graph

Source: Bradshaw, W. (1997). Evaluating cognitive-behavioral treatment of Schizophrenia: Four single-case studies. *Research on Social Work Practice, 7,* 419–445.

Withdrawal Designs

There are two withdrawal designs: the *A-B-A design* and the *A-B-A-B design*. By withdrawal, we mean that the intervention is concluded (A-B-A design) and there is a planned, systematic follow-up or the intervention is stopped for some period of time before it is restarted (A-B-A-B design). The premise is that if the intervention is effective, the target problem should improve only during the course of intervention, and the target scores should worsen when the intervention is removed. If this assumption is correct, then the impact of an extraneous event (history) between the baseline and intervention phase would not explain the change.

However, this premise is problematic for social work research. Ideally, the point of intervention is to reduce or eliminate the target problem without the need for ongoing intervention. We would like the impact of the intervention to be felt long after the client has stopped the intervention. Practice theories, such as behavioral or cognitive-behavioral treatment, are based on the idea that the therapeutic effects will persist. This concern, referred to as the **carryover effect**, may inhibit the use of these designs. To be used for research, the implementation of each of the withdrawal designs may necessitate limiting the length of the intervention and ending it prematurely. Or the design can be used to test the assumption that the impact of the treatments persists after it is discontinued. If the designs are being used for evaluation, it is unnecessary to prematurely withdraw the intervention; rather, the second baseline provides important follow-up information.

> **Carryover effect** The impact of an intervention persists after the end of the treatment process.

A-B-A Design

The A-B-A design builds on the A-B design by integrating a posttreatment follow-up that would typically include repeated measures. This design answers the question left unanswered by the A-B design: Does the effect of the intervention persist beyond the period in which treatment is provided? Depending on the length of the follow-up period, it may also be possible to learn how long the effect of the intervention persists.

The follow-up period should include multiple measures until a follow-up pattern emerges. This arrangement is built into a research study. For practice evaluation, the practicality of this depends on whether the relationship with the client extends beyond the period of the actual intervention and on the ease of collecting information. For example, the effect of an intervention designed to reduce problem behaviors in school might be amenable to repeated measurement after the end of the intervention given that the client is likely to still be in school. Some involuntary clients are monitored after the end of the intervention period. The effects of community practice interventions or organizational changes are more amenable to follow-up repeated measurements.

However, a voluntary client who has come to a family service agency for treatment of depression might be more difficult to locate or might be unwilling to go through repeated follow-up measurements. Nevertheless, do not be dissuaded from trying to obtain follow-up measures. Some clients may not find the continued monitoring cumbersome, particularly if they understand that they may benefit. The methods of collecting data may be simplified and adapted to further reduce the burden on ex-clients, such as using phone interviews rather than face-to-face interviews.

Claire O'Connor and colleagues (O'Connor, Smith, Nott, Lorang, & Mathews, 2011) explored the effectiveness of a video-simulated family member presence on reducing resistance to care (RTC) and increased participation in a variety of tasks with a nursing resident with dementia. The two A phases involved treatment as usual with staff operating as they might typically do with a resident. The intervention used during the B phase involved playing one of several very brief videos with a family member encouraging the relative to comply with staff and participate in taking medicine, eating, and the like; the video was played right before the staff came to interact with the participant. The baseline period included 12 data points over 10 days, the intervention was conducted for 14 days to get 12 data points, and the withdrawal period covered 15 days to obtain 12 data points. The results are graphed on Exhibit 8.10; RTC was reduced during the intervention period and increased when the video was withdrawn while participation increased during the intervention phase and slightly worsened with withdrawal of the intervention.

A-B-A-B Design

The A-B-A-B design builds in a second intervention phase. The intervention in this phase is identical to the intervention used in the first B phase. The replication of the intervention in the second intervention phase makes this design useful for social work practice research. For example, if, during the follow-up phase, the effects of the intervention began to reverse (see Exhibit 8.11a), then the effects of the intervention can be established by doing it again. If there is a second improvement, the replication reduces the possibility that an event or history explains the change.

Just as with the A-B-A design, there is no guarantee that the effects will be reversed by withdrawing the intervention. If the practice theory holds, then it is unlikely that the effects will actually be reversed. So it may be that this first intervention period has to be short and ended just as evidence of improvement appears. Even if the effect is not reversed during the follow-up, reintroducing the intervention may demonstrate a second period of additional improvement, as displayed in Exhibit 8.11b. This pattern suggests that the changes between the no-treatment and treatment phases are due to the intervention and not the result of history.

Kam-fong Monit Cheung (1999) used an A-B-A-B design to evaluate the effectiveness of a combination of massage therapy and social work treatment on six residents in three nursing homes. Measurements included an assessment of activities of daily living and the amount of assistance received. Each phase took 7 weeks, with the massage therapy applied in Weeks 8 through 14 and Weeks 22 through 28. In the first 7 weeks (the A phase), residents received their usual social work services; in the second 7 weeks (the B phase), residents received massage therapy and social work services. In the third 7-week period (the second A phase), residents received just social work services; in the fourth 7-week period (the second B phase), massage therapy resumed. The measurements at the baseline were retrospectively constructed from client, nursing aide, and social work assessments. Subsequent measurements were taken from logs and reported behavior by the clients.

Exhibit 8.10 A-B-A Design

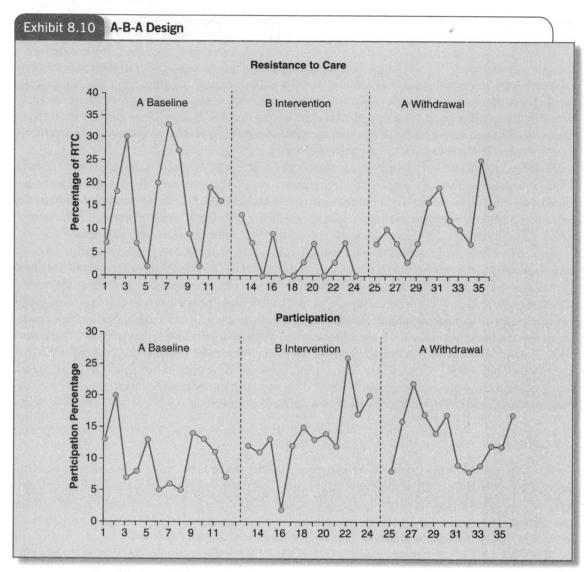

Source: O'Connor, C. M., Smith, R., Nott, M. T., Lorang, C., & Mathews, R. M. (2011). Using video simulated presence to reduce resistance to care and increase participation of adults with dementia. *American Journal of Alzheimer's Disease & Other Dementias, 26,* 312–325.

Multiple Baseline Designs

In the previous designs, the individual baseline scores serve as the control for the impact of the intervention. Yet the withdrawal designs suffer from the problem that often the target behavior cannot be reversed, and it may not be ethical to withdraw treatment early. A solution to these problems is to add additional subjects, target problems, or settings to the study. This method provides social work researchers with a feasible method of controlling for the effects of history.

The basic format is a *concurrent multiple baseline design*, in which a series of A-B designs (A-B-A or A-B-A-B designs) is implemented at the same time for at least three cases (clients, target problems, or settings). While the data are collected at the same time, the unique feature of this design is that the length of the baseline phase is staggered (see Exhibit 8.12) to control for history across the three cases. The baseline phase for the second case extends until the intervention data points for the first case become more or less stable. Similarly, the intervention for the third case does not

Exhibit 8.11   A-B-A-B Designs

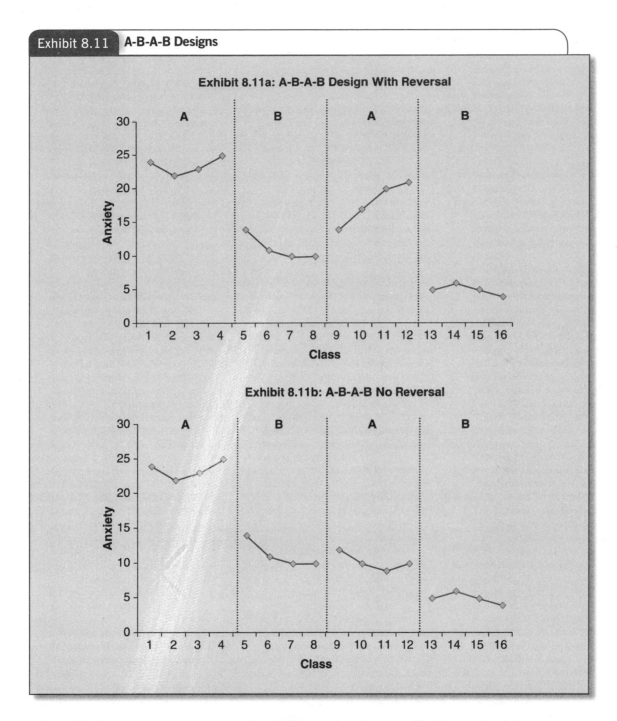

Exhibit 8.11a: A-B-A-B Design With Reversal

Exhibit 8.11b: A-B-A-B No Reversal

begin until the data points in the intervention phase for the second case become stable. The second and third cases act as a control for history in the first case, and the third case acts as a control for the second case.

One problem with a design requiring that all subjects start at the same time is having enough available subjects. An alternative that has been used is a *nonconcurrent multiple baseline design*. In this case, the researcher decides on different lengths of time for the baseline period. Then as clients or subjects meeting the selection criteria become available, they are randomly assigned into one of the baseline phases. For example, Matthew Jarrett and Thomas Ollendick (2012) used the nonconcurrent multiple baseline design to evaluate the impact of a treatment integrating parent management

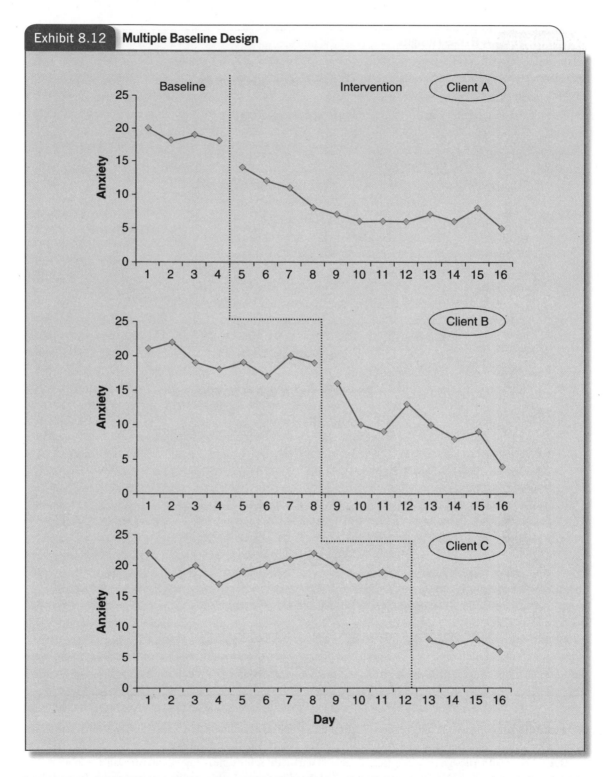

Exhibit 8.12 **Multiple Baseline Design**

training and cognitive behavioral therapy on anxiety with children with attention-deficit/hyperactivity disorder. They randomly assigned clients to a baseline phase of 2, 3, or 4 weeks.

Multiple baseline designs have features for establishing causality. The design introduces two replications so that if consistent results are found, the likelihood that history is causing the change is reduced. If history does impact on all three cases, the effect of the event may be picked up by the control cases. The pattern of change in Exhibit 8.13 suggests that something occurred that affected not only Client A but also simultaneously Clients B and C, as they reported changes and improvement even before they received the intervention.

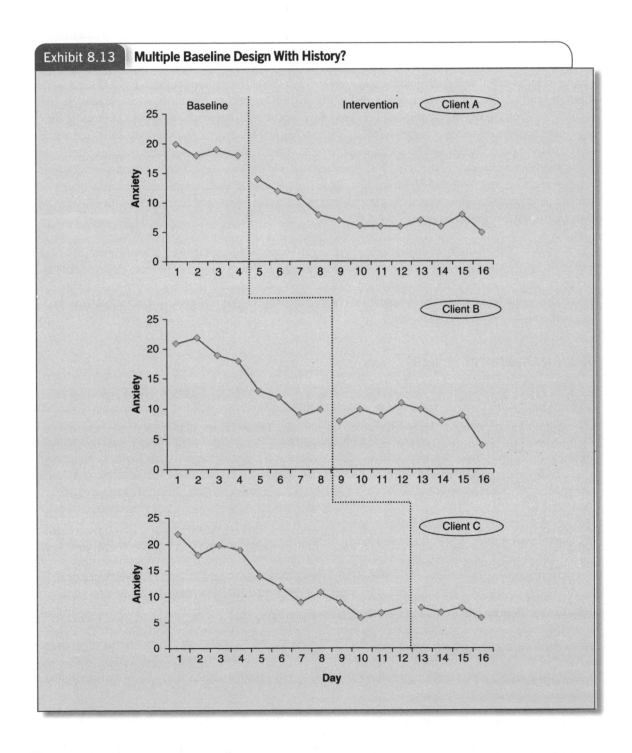

Exhibit 8.13 **Multiple Baseline Design With History?**

Across subjects. When a multiple baseline is used across subjects, each subject receives the same intervention sequentially to address the same target problem. After Bradshaw's 1997 study, he tested the effectiveness of CBT with schizophrenia with seven participants using a concurrent multiple baseline A-B design (Bradshaw, 2003). All participants started the program at the same time. The baseline phase lasted 6 months for two participants, 9 months for two participants, and 12 months for the remaining three participants. During the baseline phase, all participants received treatment as usual.

Across target problems. In this case there is one client, and the same intervention is applied to different but related problems or behaviors. The application of the intervention as it relates to the target problems or behaviors is staggered. For example, Christina Johnson and Jeannie Golden (1997) used a multiple baseline design to examine whether an intervention using both prompting and reinforcement would have a positive impact on different aspects of peer interactions for a child with language delays. The three behaviors measured were social response (verbal or nonverbal efforts to join in play with another child), approach behavior (approaching another child using vocal expressions or gestures), and play organizer (the child organizing play by specifying an activity, its rules, or inviting another child to play). The baseline period for social response lasted 3 sessions, the baseline for approach behavior overlapped these 3 sessions and continued for 7 more sessions, and the baseline for play organizer overlapped the above two baselines and continued for 4 more sessions, lasting 14 sessions. Measuring these different behaviors for different periods allowed Johnson and Golden to determine which behaviors were influenced by the intervention while controlling for external events.

Across different settings. Multiple baseline designs can be applied to test the effect of an intervention as it is applied to one client, dealing with one behavior but sequentially applied as the client moves to different settings. You might imagine a client with behavioral problems in school, at home, and at play with friends. A behavioral intervention might be used, with the application of rewards introduced sequentially across the three settings, starting with home, then school, and then play.

Multiple Treatment Designs

In a multiple treatment design, the nature of the intervention changes over time, and each change represents a new phase of the design. One type of change that might occur is the intensity of the intervention. For example, you might be working with a family that is having communication problems. The actual amount of contact you have with the family may change over time, starting with counseling sessions twice a week, followed by a period of weekly sessions, and concluding with monthly interactions. In this case, the amount of contact declines over time. *Changing intensity designs* are characterized by $A\text{-}B_1\text{-}B_2\text{-}B_3$.

Another type of changing intensity design is when, during the course of the intervention, you add additional tasks to be accomplished. For example, older adults who lose their vision in later life need to relearn how to do different independent activities of daily living taking into account their vision loss. The intervention is learning independent self-care. The B_1 may involve walking safely within the house, the B_2 may add methods for using a checkbook, the B_3 may add a component on cooking, and the like.

In an *alternative treatment design* (A-B-C-D), the actual intervention changes over time so that each phase represents a different intervention. For example, a student designed a study to determine the effectiveness of outreach efforts on the number of phone calls received by a help line (information and referral). The baseline period represented a time in which there was no outreach; rather, knowledge about the help line seemed to spread by word of mouth. The B phase represented the number of calls after the agency had sent notices about its availability to agencies serving older adults and families. During the C phase, the agency ran advertisements using radio, TV, and print media. Finally, during the D phase, agency staff went to a variety of different gatherings, such as community meetings or programs run by different agencies, and described the help line.

Exhibit 8.14 **Multiple Treatment Design**

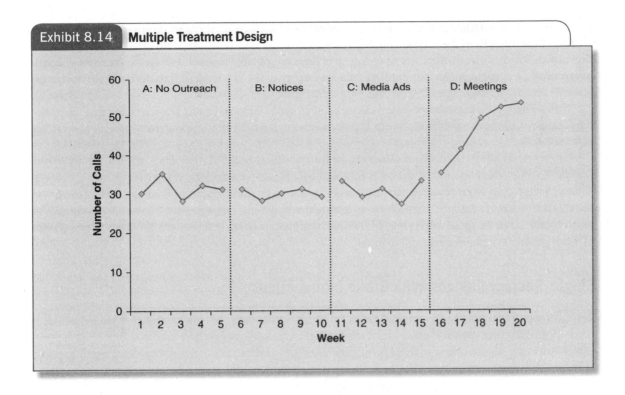

The student found (see Exhibit 8.14) that the number of phone calls did not increase appreciably after notices were sent to other professionals or after media efforts, but calls did increase dramatically in the final phase of the study. This graph demonstrates how tricky the interpretation of single-subject data can be since only adjacent phases can be compared. One plausible explanation for the findings is that sending notices to professionals and media efforts at outreach were a waste of resources in that the notices produced no increase in the number of calls relative to doing nothing, and advertising produced no increase relative to the notices. Only the meetings with community groups and agency-based presentations were effective, at least relative to the advertising. An alternative interpretation of the findings is that the *order* of the activities was essential. There might have been a carryover effect from the first two efforts that added legitimacy to the third effort. In other words, the final phase was effective only because it had been preceded by the first two efforts. If the order had been reversed, the impact of the outreach efforts would have been negligible. A third alternative is that history or some other event occurred that might have increased the number of phone calls.

Multiple treatment designs might also include interactions where two treatments are combined. An interaction design often parallels experiences with clients or agency activities in which interventions are combined or done simultaneously. In the previous example, the agency outreach effort might have included its baseline (A), notices to agencies (B), media efforts (C), and then a combination of the two (B-C phase).

Monitoring Client Progress

When monitoring a client's progress, the A-B design is recommended for the baseline information it provides. But there are times when establishing a baseline is not possible, other than to have a single point based on an initial assessment. Nonetheless, to ascertain whether a client is making progress, a form of monitoring should be done. Therefore, a social worker might use a B or a B-A design.

The *B design* (see Exhibit 8.15a) has only an intervention phase; during the course of the intervention, the social worker takes repeated measurements. This design can be used to determine whether the client is making progress in the desired direction. If the client is not making progress, the social worker may decide to change the type of intervention or the intensity of the intervention. For example, if you were working with a client who had symptoms of depression, but after 4 weeks there was no reduction in these symptoms, you would change the intensity or type of intervention. Or it might be that the symptoms reduced somewhat, but then leveled off at a level still above a cut-off score. As a result, you might again alter the nature of the intervention.

With a B design, the actual improvement cannot be attributed to the intervention. There is no baseline, and therefore, changes might be due to different threats to internal validity, reactivity to the measurement process, or reactivity to the situation.

If a period of follow-up measurements can be introduced, then a *B-A design* is a better alternative (see Exhibit 8.15b). The intervention period is followed by a period of no intervention for the specific target. Although it is harder to get repeated measurements of a client after the intervention has concluded, if treatment about other concerns continues, then follow-up measures are possible. Having reduced depressive symptoms to an acceptable level, the social worker may address social support network building with the client. Measurement of the depressive symptoms might still continue.

Single-Subject Designs With Group Interventions

Though it appears that single subject designs are meant for treatments and interventions targeted to individuals, all of these designs have been applied to group interventions. Single subject designs have been used to assess both group processes such as attendance, cohesion, verbal participation, and group interactions and treatment outcomes (Macgowan & Wong, 2014). For example, James Hall and colleagues (Hall, Dineen, Schlesinger, & Stanton, 2000) evaluated the efficacy of a social skills training group on improving different social skills with six developmentally disabled adults. To assess the influence of the intervention, they used a multiple baseline design across skills gathering data for 8 weeks plus a 1 year follow-up. The intervention was provided in a group format, four times a week for 1 hour per session over 6 weeks. Baseline information was collected three times in week one for all six skills with the onset of intervention for a particular skill staggered throughout subsequent weeks. Subsequent data were collected once a week. So the baseline for social conversation consisted of three data points collected in Week 1; the baseline for social invitations included these three data points plus the fourth data point. The intervention was provided during Weeks 2 through 8. The results were provided in a series of graphs, one for each participant.

🏛 Implications for Evidence-Based Practice

Single-subject designs offer a range of evidence to assess the impact of different interventions. The most rigorous designs control for threats to internal validity, while monitoring designs demonstrate client outcomes but without the ability to suggest it was the intervention that mattered. Therefore, understanding the differences in these designs is crucial to weighing the evidence derived from such studies.

One benefit of single-subject design is the focus on the individual as opposed to a group as an aggregate. The evidence derived from single-subject designs differs from that of group designs in that the question of interest is different (Johnston, Sherer, & Whyte, 2006). In a single-subject design, the question is, Does an intervention work for an individual? In contrast, the questions in a group design are, Does the group average change? Does the treatment group average differ in comparison to a second group? In a group design, the impact on any one individual is obscured by the impact on the group.

This different focus is particularly important for social workers because much of their practice involves interventions with individuals or with groups of individuals. Given the focus on the individual, cultural and other contextual variables are considered in evaluating outcomes (Arbin & Cormier, 2005). Single-subject designs are likely to give greater consideration to client characteristics such as gender, age, ethnicity, sexual orientation, or class. Therefore, the evidence may be quite compelling because it reflects more accurately findings from actual practice.

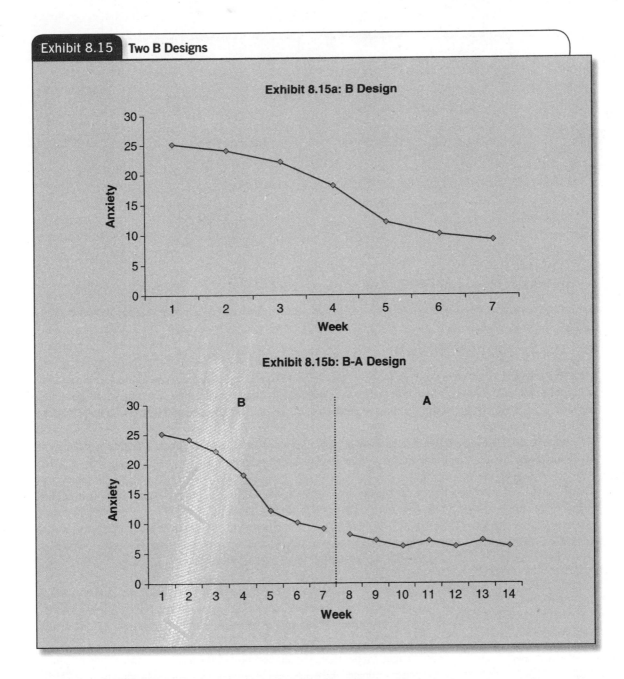

Exhibit 8.15 Two B Designs

Exhibit 8.15a: B Design

Exhibit 8.15b: B-A Design

However, the strength of single-subject designs with their focus on an individual is also suggested to be their weakness. How are we to judge findings about a single individual? How is evidence about that single individual relevant to other clients? We can think about this criticism as a statistical problem and/or as a problem about building the generalizability of the findings. The statistical problem is being addressed by statisticians who are developing meta-analytic methods to assess single-subject design research; these methods are designed to take the findings of many single-subject design studies and aggregate them (Jenson, Clark, Kircher, & Kristjansson, 2007).

The problem of generalizability of single-subject design research is not unlike that of group design research—it is an issue of external validity. Ideally, we want to take what has been tested in one research context and apply the findings to different settings, clients, or communities; to other providers; and even to other

Research In the News

For Further Thought

EXERCISE YOUR BRAIN?

Katie Hafner (2008) reported on the many exercises that baby boomers are taking up to keep their brains active, to reduce forgetfulness, and, it is hoped, to lessen the risk of Alzheimer's disease. These include video games, on-line cognitive behavioral training, and taking on new brain stimulation challenges like learning to play the piano.

1. Design a single-subject study to test the impact of one of these brain exercise games on a friend. What indicators could you use to track the impact of the game?

Source:Hafner (2008).

problems related to the target concern of the research. To do so when the sample consists of a single subject engaged in a particular intervention provided by a particular individual is challenging. To demonstrate the external validity of single-subject design requires replication of the research conditions and to extend the assessment to other targets and settings.

Barlow et al. (2009) suggest that three sequential replication strategies be used to enhance the external validity of single-subject design: direct replication, systematic replication, and clinical replication.

Direct replication. **Direct replication** involves repeating the same procedures, by the same researchers, including the same providers of the treatment, in the same setting, and in the same situation, with different clients who have similar characteristics (Barlow et al., 2009). The strength of the findings is enhanced by having successful outcomes with these other clients. When the results are inconsistent, differences in the clients can be examined to identify characteristics that may be related to success or failure.

Systematic replication. The next step is **systematic replication,** which involves repeating the experiment in different settings, using different providers and other related behaviors (Barlow et al., 2009). Systematic replication also increases the number and type of clients exposed to the intervention. Through systematic replication, the applicability of the intervention to different conditions is evaluated. Like direct replication, systematic replication helps to clarify conditions in which the intervention may be successful and conditions in which the intervention may not be successful.

Clinical replication. The last stage is **clinical replication,** which is defined as combining different interventions into a clinical package to treat multiple problems (Barlow et al., 2009). The actual replication takes place in the same setting and with clients who have the same types of problems. In many ways, findings from practice evaluation can enhance clinical replications.

Direct replication Used to enhance the generalizability of a single-subject design; the single-subject design is repeated using the same procedures by the same researchers and the same providers, in the same setting, and in the same situation with different clients.

Systematic replication Repeating a single-subject design in different settings, using different providers and other related behaviors to increase generalizability.

Clinical replication Used to enhance generalizability of single-subject designs; clinical replication involves combining different interventions into a clinical package to treat multiple problems.

For any replication effort to be successful, the treatment procedures must be clearly articulated, identified, and followed. Failing to adhere to the treatment procedures changes the intervention, and therefore, there is not a true replication of the experiment.

Bradshaw's efforts at demonstrating the effectiveness of CBT to treat schizophrenia represent the contribution such systematic research makes to advancing practice-related knowledge. His 1997 study was completed with four participants who had been referred for outpatient therapy after discharge from psychiatric hospitalizations. His 2003 study included 10 participants (3 did not complete the study) randomly selected from a county mental health system. In this study, the intervention period was twice as long as in the first study, but followed the same model of CBT. Finally, in collaboration with David Roseborough, Bradshaw reported findings from a third study of 30 clients (8 left the study) who received CBT for 18 months. The ongoing replication and findings of positive results has provided support for this intervention with clients with schizophrenia.

Social work practitioners can be active in building this evidence as part of their ongoing practice. Integrating systematically single-subject designs can provide additional clinical evidence for practice. You can become your own researcher!

回 Single-Subject Design in a Diverse Society

Throughout this chapter, we have noted instances when special attention must be paid to issues of diversity. These issues are not unique to research, but are relevant to practice. That is no surprise because single-subject design is so closely aligned to a practice model (Staudt, 1997). Researchers and practitioners must understand that how problems are identified and defined may depend on client characteristics such as gender, ethnicity, sexual orientation, and class. Measures must be acceptable and applicable (reliable and valid) to different population subgroups. Similarly, issues regarding informed consent are relevant for all population subgroups (J. Martin & Knox, 2000; Nelson, 1994).

Single-subject designs may be useful methods for engaging diverse groups that have been underrepresented in research and in particular experimental group designs or clinical research trials. Because they are often practice based, they may more easily mitigate distrust of the researcher. Because they focus on the individual, as opposed to the group, single-subject designs can more easily incorporate cultural factors and test for cultural variation (Arbin & Cormier, 2005).

回 Ethical Issues in Single-Subject Design

Like any form of research, single-subject designs require the informed consent of the participant. The structure of single-subject designs for research involves particularly unique conditions that must be discussed with potential participants. All aspects of the research, such as the purpose, measurement, confidentiality, and data collection, are a part of the information needed for informed consent. In particular, the need for repeated baseline measurements and the possibility of premature withdrawal of treatment are particularly unique to single-subject design research.

Participants must understand that the onset of the intervention is likely to be delayed until either a baseline pattern emerges or some assigned period elapses. Until this condition is met, a needed intervention may be withheld. Furthermore, the length of the baseline also depends on the type of design. In a multiple baseline design, the delay in the intervention may be substantial. The implications of this delay must be discussed as part of obtaining informed consent.

When a withdrawal or reversal design is used, there are additional considerations. The structure of such designs means that the intervention may be withdrawn just as the research subject is beginning to improve. The risks associated with prematurely ending treatment may be hard to predict. If there is a carryover effect, the subject's condition may not worsen, but it is possible that the subject's condition or status may indeed worsen. Given this possibility, the use of an A-B-A-B design as opposed to the A-B-A design is preferable for the purpose of research.

Obtaining informed consent may not be limited to the use of single-subject design for research purposes. As we noted in Chapter 3, the National Association of Social Workers (NASW; 2008) *Code of Ethics* does not distinguish between the need for informed consent in research and the need for informed consent for practice evaluation:

5.02(e) Social workers engaged in evaluation or research should obtain voluntary and written informed consent from participants, when appropriate, without any implied or actual deprivation or penalty for refusal to participate; without undue inducement to participate; and with due regard for participants' well-being, privacy, and dignity. Informed consent should include information about the nature, extent, and duration of the participation requested and disclosure of the risks and benefits of participation in research.

Others suggest that informed consent may not be necessary. For example, Royse, Thyer, Padgett, and Logan (2006) suggest that written informed consent is not necessarily required for practice evaluation because the intent is not to provide generalized knowledge or publish the results.

Even if written informed consent is not required when using these tools for practice evaluation and monitoring, social workers using these tools should be guided by practice ethics. According to the NASW (2008) *Code of Ethics*, social work practitioners should, as a part of their everyday practice with clients,

provide services to clients only in the context of a professional relationship based, when appropriate, on valid informed consent. Social workers should use clear and understandable language to inform clients of the purpose of the services, risks related to the services, limits to services because of the requirements of a third-party payer, relevant costs, reasonable alternatives, clients' right to refuse or withdraw consent, and the time frame covered by the consent. (Section 1.03[a])

Therefore, if such techniques are going to be used as part of the overall intervention, clients should be aware of the procedures.

▣ Conclusion

Single-subject designs are useful for doing research, evaluating practice, and monitoring client progress. Single-subject designs have been underutilized as a research tool by social work researchers. Yet researchers using these designs can make a unique contribution to social work practice knowledge because so much of practice is with individuals. Done systematically, the success or failure of different interventions can be evaluated with distinct clients and under differing conditions. Furthermore, single-subject designs may be useful for understanding the process of change and how change occurs with particular clients.

Applying these techniques to your own practice can be of benefit to your clients. As Aaron Rosen (2003) warns, "uncertainty regarding the effectiveness of any intervention for attaining any outcome pervades all practice situations, regardless of the extent and quality of empirical support" (p. 203). Therefore, if you monitor what you do, you will add to your own clinical experience, which enhances your future work with clients.

Key Terms

Baseline phase 189	Duration 194	Stable line 191
Carryover effect 204	Frequency 194	Systematic replication 214
Clinical replication 214	Interval 194	Treatment phase 192
Cycle 192	Level 195	Trend 191
Direct replication 214	Magnitude 194	Variability 196

Highlights

- Single-subject designs are tools for researchers and practitioners to evaluate the impact of an intervention on a single system such as an individual, community, or organization.

- Single-subject designs have three essential components: the taking of repeated measurements, a baseline phase (A), and a treatment phase (B).

- Repeated measurements control for many of the potential threats to internal validity. The period between the last baseline measure and the first treatment measure is susceptible to the effect of history.

- The baseline phase typically continues, if practical, until there is a predictable pattern. To establish a pattern requires at least three measurements. The pattern may include a stable line, an increasing or decreasing trend line, or a cycle of ups and downs dependent on time of measurement.

- Researchers often measure behaviors, status, or level of functioning. These measures are typically characterized by frequency (counts), duration (length of time), interval (time between events), or magnitude (intensity).

- Reactivity to the process of measurement may impact the outcomes, and efforts to limit reactivity are important.

- Data analysis typically involves visually inspecting graphs of the measurements. A researcher may look for changes in level (magnitude), rate or directional changes in the trend line, or reductions in variability. The most important criterion is whether the treatment has made a practical (or clinical) difference in the subject's well-being.

- Generalizability from single-subject designs requires direct replication, systematic replication, and clinical replication.

Discussion Questions

1. Visual analysis is used to communicate the impact of an intervention in visual form. What are the three primary ways that the pattern of scores established during a baseline or intervention stage may be viewed? When is each of them best used? What information is conveyed, and what information may be omitted by choosing each one of them over the others?

2. Single-subject designs lack the inclusion of additional subjects serving as controls to demonstrate internal validity. How do the measurements during the baseline phase provide another form of control?

3. Social work research seeks to confirm an intervention's effectiveness by observing scores when clients no longer receive the intervention. Yet the carryover effect may necessitate using a withdrawal design—ending a treatment prematurely—to do this successfully. Debate the merits of the withdrawal design in social work research. What are the advantages and disadvantages? Do the benefits outweigh the risks or vice versa?

Practice Exercises

1. Go to the book's study site (www.sagepub.com/engelprsw4e), and choose two research articles that include some attention to causality (as indicated by a check in that column of the article matrix). For each article describe the following:

   a. What type of design was used? How does the author describe the design? Was it suited to the research question posed and the specific hypotheses tested, if any? Why do you suppose the author chose the particular design?

   b. Did the design eliminate threats to internal validity? How did the design do this? Are you satisfied with the internal validity conclusions stated by the author? Why or why not?

   c. What is the setting for the study? Does the setting limit the generalizability of the results to other similar settings or to the broader population? Is reactivity a problem? Are there other threats to external validity?

2. Stress is a common occurrence in many students' lives. Measure the frequency, duration, interval, and magnitude of school-related stress in your life in a 1-week period. Take care to provide a clear operational definition of stress and construct a meaningful scale to rate magnitude. Did you notice any issues of reactivity? Which of the measurement processes did you find most feasible? Finally, do you believe that your operational definition was sufficient to capture your target and detect changes?

3. Patterns detected in the baseline phase of single-subject designs also emerge in the larger population. Obtain a copy of a newspaper, and locate stories describing contemporary issues that can be described as having the pattern of a stable line, a trend, and a cycle. Is information provided about the number of observations made? If so, does this number seem sufficient to warrant the conclusion about what type of pattern it is?

Web Exercise

1. Visit the Northwest Regional Education Laboratory's website (http://educationnorthwest.org). Search for "School Improvement Research Series." Choose School Improvement Program Research Series Materials, then Series V, and finally, click on Close-Up #9 School Wide and Classroom Discipline. Select three of the techniques that educators use to minimize disruption in educational settings, and then suggest a single-subject design that could be used to evaluate the effectiveness of each technique. Bear in mind the nature of the misbehavior and the treatment. Which of the designs seems most appropriate? How would you go about conducting your research? Think about things such as operationalizing the target behavior, determining how it will be measured (frequency, duration, magnitude, etc.), deciding on the length of the baseline and treatment periods, and accounting for threats to internal validity.

2. Search Social Work Abstracts for articles describing single-subject designs. Try to identify the type of design used. Read over the article. How well did this design satisfy the need for internal validity?

Developing a Research Proposal

If you are planning to use a single-subject design,

1. What specific design will you use? How long will the study last? How will the data be collected? How often?

2. Discuss the extent to which each source of internal validity is a problem in the study. Will you debrief with participants to assess history?

3. Discuss the extent to which reactivity is a problem. How will you minimize the effects of reactivity?

4. How generalizable would you expect the study's findings to be? What can be done to improve generalizability?

5. Develop appropriate procedures for the protection of human subjects in your study. Include a consent form.

A Question of Ethics

1. Use of single-subject methodology requires frequent measurement of symptoms or other outcomes. Practitioners should discuss with clients before treatment begins the plan to use de-identified data in reports to the research community. Clients who do not consent still receive treatment—and data may still be recorded on their symptoms in order to evaluate treatment effects. Should the prospect of recording and publishing de-identified data on single subjects become a routine part of clinical practice? What would be the advantages and disadvantages of such a routine?

2. The A-B-A design is a much more powerful single-subject design than the A-B design because it reduces the likelihood that the researcher will conclude that an improvement is due to the treatment when it was simply due to a gradual endogenous recovery process. Yet the A-B-A design requires stopping the very treatment that may be having a beneficial effect. Under what conditions do you think it is safe to use an A-B-A design? Why do some clinicians argue that an A-B-A-B design lessens the potential for ethical problems? Are there circumstances when you would feel it is unethical to use an A-B-A-B design?

CHAPTER 9

Survey Research

"Education forms a unique dimension of social status, with qualities that make it especially important to health" (Mirowsky & Ross, 2003, p. 1). Mirowsky and Ross make this claim at the start of *Education, Social Status, and Health* and then present evidence to support it throughout the book. Most of their evidence comes from two surveys. Their decision to use surveys is a very common strategy employed throughout social sciences, social work research, and social work practice.

In this chapter, we introduce you to survey research methods. We explain the major steps in questionnaire design and consider the features of five types of surveys, highlighting the unique problems attending each one and suggesting some possible solutions. We next focus on issues of social diversity and the implications for evidence-based practice. In the last section, we discuss ethical issues related to survey research. By the chapter's end, you should be well on your way to becoming an informed consumer of survey reports and a knowledgeable developer of survey designs.

▣ Survey Research in Social Work

Survey research Research in which information is obtained from a sample of individuals through their responses to questions about themselves or others.

Survey research involves the collection of information from a sample of individuals through their responses to questions. As you probably have observed, a great many researchers—as well as newspaper editors, political pundits, and marketing gurus—make the same methodological choice. In fact, surveys have become such a vital part of our social fabric that we cannot assess much of what we read in the newspaper or see on TV without having some understanding of this method of data collection (Converse, 1984; Tourangeau, 2004).

Attractions of Survey Research

Survey research owes its continuing popularity to three features: versatility, efficiency, and generalizability. Each of these features is changing as a result of new technologies.

Versatility

First and foremost, survey methods are versatile. Although a survey is not the ideal method for testing interventions, let alone all hypotheses, a well-designed survey can enhance our understanding of just about any social issue. Social work researchers have used survey methods to investigate every field of social work practice, including (but not limited to) child welfare, gerontology, health, mental health, income maintenance, community building, and community development. If you have worked in an agency or you are in field practicum, you have probably noticed that the methods of survey research have been adapted by the agency for program evaluation and practice. Surveys are used in agencies to assess the impact of policy changes, identify community needs, track changes in community characteristics, monitor and evaluate program effectiveness, and assess client satisfaction with programs. Your supervisor or the agency executive director has probably responded to surveys sent by the state, accrediting boards, or funding agencies such as the United Way. At your agency, you have used, or will learn to use, intake forms and psychosocial assessments; these are another form of surveys.

Computer technology has made surveys even more versatile. Computers can be programmed so that different types of respondents are asked different questions. Short videos or pictures can be presented to respondents on a computer screen. An interviewer may give respondents a laptop or notebook computer on which to record their answers to sensitive questions (Tourangeau, 2004).

Efficiency

Surveys also are popular because data can be collected from many people at relatively low cost and, depending on the survey design, relatively quickly. Surveys also are efficient because many variables can be measured without substantially increasing the time or cost. Mailed questionnaires can include up to 10 pages of questions before respondents begin to balk. In-person interviews can be much longer, taking more than an hour (e.g., the 2012 General Social Survey included about 799 variables). The upper limit for phone surveys seems to be about 45 minutes.

Modern information technology has been a mixed blessing for survey efficiency. The Internet makes it easier to survey some populations, but it leaves out important segments. Caller ID and answering machines make it easy to screen out unwanted calls, but these tools also make it harder to reach people in phone surveys who choose not to answer. In addition, cellphones have replaced landlines as a growing percentage of households, 41%, use only cell phones (Blumberg & Luke, 2014).

Generalizability

Survey methods lend themselves to probability sampling from large populations. Thus, survey research is appealing when *sample generalizability* is a central research goal. In fact, survey research is often the only means available for developing a representative picture of the attitudes and characteristics of a large population. Surveys also are the method of choice when cross-population generalizability is a key concern because they allow a range of social contexts and subgroups to be sampled. The consistency of relationships can then be examined across the various subgroups.

Unfortunately (for survey researchers), the new technologies that are lowering the overall response rate to surveys are also making it more difficult to obtain generalizable samples. Although in 2013 only 14% of households did not have access to the Internet at home, work, or elsewhere, these households tended to be overrepresented by older adults, lower income people, and people with no more than a high school education (Pew Research Center, 2014). People who use only cell phones tend to be younger, Hispanic, and poorer (Blumberg & Luke, 2014). In addition, the growing size of the foreign-born population in the United States, 13.0% in 2012, requires either foreign-language versions of survey forms or acknowledging problems of generalizability (A. Brown & Patten, 2014)

Errors in Survey Research

It might be said that surveys are too easy to conduct. Organizations and individuals often decide that a survey would help to solve some important problem because it seems so easy to prepare a form with some questions and send it out. But without careful attention to sampling, measurement, and overall survey design, the effort is likely to be a flop. The responsible survey researcher must take the time to design surveys properly and convince sponsoring organizations that this time is worth the effort (Turner & Martin, 1984).

For a survey to succeed, it must minimize the risk of two types of error: poor measurement of cases that are surveyed (*errors of observation*) and omission of cases that should be surveyed (*errors of nonobservation*; Groves, 1989). Measurement error was a key concern in Chapter 4, but there is much more to be learned about how to minimize these errors of observation in the survey process. Potential problems that can lead to errors of observation stem from the way questions are written, the characteristics of the respondents who answer the questions, the way questions are presented in questionnaires, and the interviewers who ask the questions. The potential measurement errors that survey researchers confront in designing questions and questionnaires are summarized in Exhibit 9.1; we discuss each of these sources of error throughout this chapter.

There are three sources of errors of nonobservation:

- Coverage of the population can be inadequate due to a poor sampling frame.

- The process of random sampling can result in sampling error—differences between the characteristics of the sample members and the population that arise due to chance.

- Nonresponse can distort the sample when individuals refuse to respond or cannot be contacted. Nonresponse to specific questions can distort the generalizability of the responses to those questions.

We considered the importance of a good sampling frame and the procedures for estimating and reducing sampling error in Chapter 5; we only add a few more points here. In this chapter, we focus more attention on procedures for reducing nonresponse in surveys as unfortunately, nonresponse is an increasing concern for survey researchers.

We can anticipate problems that lead to survey errors and identify possible solutions if we take enough time to think about the issue theoretically. A well-designed survey will maximize the social rewards, minimize the costs for participating in the survey, and establish trust that the rewards will outweigh the costs. The next two sections focus on principles to develop a well-designed survey.

Exhibit 9.1 **Measurement Errors Associated With Surveys**

Question Wording Does the question have a consistent meaning to respondents. Problems can occur with

- *Lengthy wording* Words that are unnecessary long and complicated.
- *Length of question* The question is unnecessary too long.
- *Lack of specificity* It is not clear from the question what is the desired information.
- *Lack of frame of reference* The question does not specify to what reference comparisons should be made.
- *Vague language* Words and phrases can have different meanings to respondents.
- *Double negatives* Use of two or more negative phrases in the question.
- *Double barreled* Question actually asks two or more questions.
- *Using jargon and initials* Professional or academic discipline specific terms are used.
- *Leading questions* Question phrasing meant to bias the response.
- *Cultural differences in meaning* Phrases or words that have different meanings to different population subgroups.

Respondent Characteristics Characteristics of respondents may produce inaccurate answers. These include

- *Memory recall* Problems of remembering events or details about events.
- *Telescoping* Remembering events as happening more recently than when they really occurred.
- *Agreement of acquiescence bias* Tendency for respondents to "agree."
- *Social desirability* Tendency to want to appear in a positive light and therefore providing the desirable response.
- *Floaters* Respondents who choose a substantive answer when they really don't know.
- *Fence sitters* People who see themselves as being neutral so as not to give the wrong answer.
- *Sensitive questions* Questions deemed too personal.

Presentation of Questions The structure of questions and the survey instrument may produce error including

- *Open-ended questions* Response categories are not provided, left to respondent to provide.
- *Close-ended questions* Possible response categories are provided.
- *Agree-disagree* Tendency to agree when only two choices are offered.
- *Question order* The context or order of questions can effect subsequent responses as respondents try to remain consistent.
- *Response set* Giving the same response to a series of questions.
- *Filter questions* Questions used to determine if other questions are relevant.

Interviewer The use of an interviewer may produce error.

- Mismatch of interviewer–interviewee demographic characteristics
- Unconscious judgmental actions to responses

回 Designing Questionnaires

Survey questions are answered as part of a **questionnaire** (or **interview schedule**, as it's often called in interview-based studies), not in isolation from other questions. The context created by the questionnaire has a major impact on how individual questions are interpreted and whether they are even answered. As a result, survey researchers must give careful attention to the design of the questionnaire as well as to the individual questions that it includes.

> **Questionnaire** The survey instrument containing the questions in a self-administered survey.
>
> **Interview schedule** The survey instrument containing the questions asked by the interviewer in an in-person or phone survey.

The way a questionnaire should be designed varies with the specific survey method used and with other particulars of a survey project. There is no precise formula for a well-developed questionnaire. Nonetheless, some key principles should guide the design of any questionnaire, and some systematic procedures should be considered for refining it.

Maintain Consistent Focus

A survey should be guided by a clear conception of the research problem under investigation and the population to be sampled. Does the study seek to describe some phenomenon in detail, to explain some behavior, or to explore some type of social relationship? Until the research objective is formulated clearly, survey design cannot begin. Throughout the process of questionnaire design, this objective should be the primary basis for making decisions about what to include and exclude and what to emphasize or to treat in a cursory fashion. Moreover, the questionnaire should be viewed as an integrated whole, in which each section and every question serves a clear purpose related to the study's objective and is a complement to other sections or questions.

Surveys often include too many irrelevant questions and fail to include questions that, the researchers realize later, are crucial. One way to ensure that possibly relevant questions are asked is to use questions suggested by prior research, theory, experience, or by experts (including participants) who are knowledgeable about the setting under investigation. Of course, not even the best researcher can anticipate the relevance of every question. Researchers tend to try to avoid missing something by erring on the side of extraneous questions (Labaw, 1980).

Build on Existing Instruments

If another researcher already has designed a set of questions to measure a key concept and evidence from previous surveys indicates that this measure is reliable and valid, then by all means use that instrument. Your literature review can provide useful information about existing instruments. Resources like Delbert Miller and Neil Salkind's (2002) *Handbook of Research Design and Social Measurement* or Joel Fischer and Kevin Corcoran's (2013) *Measures for Clinical Practice and Research* can give you many ideas about existing instruments.

There is a trade-off. Questions used previously may not concern quite the right concept or may not be appropriate in some ways to your population. Scales developed much earlier may no longer be appropriate for your population as times change. A good rule of thumb is to use a previously designed instrument if it measures the concept of concern to you and if you have no clear reason for thinking it is inappropriate with your survey population.

Order the Questions

The order in which questions are presented will influence how respondents react to the questionnaire as a whole and how they may answer some questions. As a first step, the individual questions should be sorted into broad thematic categories, which then become separate sections in the questionnaire. Both the sections and the questions within the sections must then be organized in a logical order that would make sense in a conversation. Throughout the design process, the grouping of variables in sections and the ordering of questions within sections should be adjusted to maximize the questionnaire's overall coherence.

The first question deserves special attention, particularly if the questionnaire is to be self-administered. This question signals to the respondent what the survey is about, whether it will be interesting, and how easy it will be to complete it. For these reasons, the first question should be connected to the primary purpose of the survey, it should be interesting, it should be easy, and it should apply to everyone in the sample (Dillman, 2007). It is not the time to ask a sensitive question as this might turn off a potential respondent.

Question order can lead to **context effects** when one or more questions influence how subsequent questions are interpreted (Schober, 1999). Prior questions can influence how questions are comprehended, what beliefs shape responses, and whether comparative judgments are made (Tourangeau, 2004). The potential for context effects is greatest when two or more questions concern the same issue or closely related issues. The impact of question order also tends to be greater for general, summary-type questions; for example, a global question about one's overall health status might influence reports on specific health issues or responding to specific health issues might impact a subsequent response to a global health status question (Garbarski, Shaeffer, & Dykema, 2015).

> **Context effects** Occur in a survey when one or more questions influence how subsequent questions are interpreted.

Context effects can be identified empirically if the question order is reversed on a subset of the questionnaires (the so-called *split-ballot design*) and the results compared. However, knowing that a context effect occurs does not tell us which order is best. Reviewing the overall survey goals and any other surveys with which comparisons should be made can help to decide on question order. What is most important is to be aware of the potential for problems due to question order and to evaluate carefully the likelihood of context effects in any particular questionnaire.

Add Interpretive Questions

A survey researcher can include interpretative questions in the survey to help the researcher understand what respondents mean by their responses to a particular question. An example from a study of people with motor vehicle driving violations illustrates the importance of interpretive questions:

> When asked whether their emotional state affected their driving at all, respondents would reply that their emotions had very little effect on their driving habits. Then, when asked to describe the circumstances surrounding their last traffic violation, respondents typically replied, "I was mad at my girlfriend," or "I had a quarrel with my wife," or "We had a family quarrel," or "I was angry with my boss." (Labaw, 1980, p. 71)

Were these respondents lying in response to the first question? Probably not. More likely, they simply did not interpret their own behavior in terms of general concepts like "emotional state." But their responses to the first question were likely to be misinterpreted without the further detail provided by answers to the second.

Consider five issues when you develop interpretive questions—or when you review survey results and need to consider what the answers tell you:

- *What do the respondents know?* Answers to many questions about current events and government policies are almost uninterpretable without also learning what the respondents know. In a survey of social service utilization, you may find that respondents are aware that a particular social service or a service provider exists, but they do not know that the service applies to their needs or that they are eligible for the service (Krout, 1985).

- *What relevant experiences do the respondents have?* Such experiences undoubtedly color the responses. For example, opinions about the effectiveness of policies such as Temporary Assistance to Needy Families may be quite different for people who have received some form of government assistance than for people who have not received government aid.

- *How consistent are the respondents' attitudes, and do they express some larger perspective or ideology?* An employee who seeks more wages because she believes that all employer profits result from exploitation is expressing a different sentiment from one who seeks more wages because she really wants a more expensive car with which to impress her neighbors.

- *Are respondents' actions consistent with their expressed attitudes?* We probably should interpret differently the meaning of expressed support for gender equality from married men who help with household chores and from those who do not. Questions about behavior may also provide a better way to assess orientations than questions about attitudes.

- *How strongly are the attitudes held?* The attitudes of those with stronger beliefs are more likely to be translated into action than attitudes that are held less strongly. Just knowing the level of popular support for, say, abortion rights or gun control thus fails to capture the likelihood that people will march or petition their representatives on behalf of the cause; we also need to know what proportion of supporters feels strongly (Schuman & Presser, 1981).

Make the Questionnaire Attractive

An attractive questionnaire is more likely to be completed and less likely to confuse either the respondent or, in an interview, the interviewer. An attractive questionnaire also should increase the likelihood that different respondents interpret the same questions in the same way.

Printing a multipage questionnaire in booklet form usually results in the most attractive and simplest-to-use questionnaire. Printing on both sides of folded-over legal-size paper (8½ by 14 inches) is a good approach, although pages can be printed on one side only and stapled in the corner if finances are tight (Dillman, 2000). An attractive questionnaire does not look cramped; plenty of white space—more between questions than within question components—makes the questionnaire appear easy to complete. Response choices are distinguished clearly and consistently, perhaps by formatting them with light print (while questions are formatted with dark print) and keeping them in the middle of the page. Response choices are listed vertically rather than horizontally across the page.

The proper path through the questionnaire for each respondent is identified with arrows or other graphics and judicious use of spacing and other aspects of layout. Respondents should not be confused about where to go next after they are told to skip a question. Instructions should help to route respondents through skip patterns, and such skip patterns should be used infrequently. Instructions should also explain how each type of question is to be answered (such as by circling a number or writing a response)—in a neutral way that isn't likely to influence responses. Some distinctive type of formatting should be used to identify instructions.

The visual design of a questionnaire has more subtle effects on how respondents answer questions. Such seemingly minor differences as whether responses are grouped under headings or just listed, whether separate response choices are provided or just the instruction to write in a response from a list of choices, and how much space there is between response choices can all affect the distribution of responses to a question (Dillman & Christian, 2005).

Exhibit 9.2 contains portions of the questionnaire used in a phone survey of contemporary families. The exhibit illustrates three of the features that we have just reviewed: numeric designation of response choices, clear instructions, and an attractive open layout. Because this questionnaire was read over the phone, rather than self-administered, there was no need for more explicit instructions about the matrix question (Question 49) or for a more distinctive format for the response choices (Questions 45 and 48). A questionnaire designed to be self-administered also should include these additional features.

▣ Writing Questions

Writing Clear Questions

The centerpiece of survey research is asking people questions. Because the way they are worded can have a great effect on the way they are answered, selecting good questions is essential. All hope for achieving measurement validity is lost unless the questions in a survey are clear and convey the intended meaning to respondents.

Exhibit 9.2   A Page From Ross's Interview Schedule

45. In the past 12 months, about how many times have you gone on a diet to lose weight?

    Never   0

    Once   1

    Twice   2

    Three times or more   3

    Always on a diet   4

46. What is your height without shoes on?

    _____ ft.   _____ in.

47. What is your weight without clothing?

    _____ lbs.

48a. Do you currently smoke 7 or more cigarettes a week?

    Yes. . . . .   1 –> (Skip to Q. 49)

    No.   2

48b. Have you ever smoked 7 or more cigarettes a week?

    Yes.   1

    No.   2

49. How much difficulty do you have . . .

	A great deal of difficulty	Some difficulty	No difficulty
A. Going up and down stairs? Would you say	1	2	3
B. Kneeling or stooping?	1	2	3
C. Lifting or carrying objects less than 10 pounds like a bag of groceries?.	1	2	3
D. Using your hands or fingers?	1	2	3
E. Seeing, even with glasses?	1	2	3
F. Hearing?	1	2	3
G. Walking?.	1	2	3

*Source:*Ross, Catherine E. 1990: "Work, Family, and the Sense of Control: Implications for the Psychological Well-Being of Women and Men" (Proposal submitted to the National Science Foundation). Urbana: University of Illinois.

You may be thinking that you ask people questions all the time and have no trouble understanding the answers you receive, but you may also remember misunderstanding or being confused by some questions. Consider just a few of the differences between everyday conversations and standardized surveys:

- Survey questions must be asked of many people, not just one person.

- The same survey question must be used with each person, not tailored to the specifics of a given conversation.

- Survey questions must be understood in the same way by people who differ in many ways.

- You will not be able to rephrase a survey question if someone does not understand it because that would result in a different question for that person.

- Survey respondents do not know you and so cannot be expected to share the nuances of expression that help you and your friends and family to communicate.

Every question considered for inclusion in a survey must be reviewed carefully for its clarity and ability to convey the intended meaning. Questions that are clear and meaningful to one population may not be so to another. Nor can you simply assume that a question used in a previously published study was carefully evaluated. Adherence to a few basic principles will go a long way toward ensuring clear and meaningful questions.

Avoid Confusing Phrasing

What's a confusing question? Try this question sent by the Planetary Society in its National Priorities Survey, U.S. Space Program:

> The Moon may be a place for an eventual scientific base, and even for engineering resources. Setting up a base or mining experiment will cost tens of billions of dollars in the next century. Should the United States pursue further manned and unmanned scientific research projects on the surface of the Moon?
>
> _____ Yes   _____ No   _____ No opinion

Does a "yes" response mean that you favor spending tens of billions of dollars for a base or mining experiment? Does the "next century" refer to the 21st century or to the 100 years following the survey's distribution (which was in the 1980s)? Could you favor further research projects on the Moon but oppose funding a scientific base or engineering resources? Are engineering resources supposed to have something to do with a mining experiment? Does a mining experiment occur "on the surface of the Moon"? How do you answer if you favor unmanned scientific research projects but not manned projects?

In most cases, a simple direct approach to asking a question minimizes confusion. Use shorter rather than longer words: _brave_ rather than _courageous_, _job concerns_ rather than _work-related employment issues_ (Dillman, 2000, p. 52). Try to keep the total number of words in a sentence to 20 or fewer and the number of commas to three or fewer (Peterson, 2000). The longer the question, the more confusing it will be to the respondent. Lengthy questions may go unanswered or may be given only a cursory reading without much thought to the answer.

Avoid Vagueness

Questions should not be abbreviated in a way that results in confusion: To ask "In what city or town do you live?" is to focus attention clearly on a specific geographic unit, a specific time, and a specific person (you). The simple statement,

> Residential location: _____

does not do this. It is a general question when a specific kind of answer is intended. There are many different reasonable answers to this question, such as Pittsburgh (a city), Squirrel Hill (a neighborhood), and Forbes Avenue (a street). Asking "In what neighborhood of Pittsburgh do you live?" provides specificity so that the respondent understands the intent of the question.

It is important to avoid vague language. For example, the question

> How many times in the past year have you talked with a doctor?

has at least two words, _doctor_ and _talk_, that create ambiguity. Any kind of doctor (dentist, medical doctor, chiropractor)? What does talk mean—a conversation about a physical or social problem or a casual conversation? A conversation over the phone, in the doctor's office, at a hospital?

Some words are vague, and their meaning may differ from respondent to respondent. The question

> Do you usually or occasionally attend programs at the community center?

will not provide useful information because the meaning of "usually or occasionally" can differ for each respondent. A better alternative is to define the two terms, such as "_usually_ (2–3 times a week)" and "_occasionally_ (2–3 times a month)." A second option is to ask respondents how often they attend programs at the community center; the researcher can then classify the responses into categories.

Provide a Frame of Reference

A frame of reference provides specificity about how respondents should answer a question. The question

Overall, the performance of this caseworker is:

_____ Excellent
_____ Good
_____ Average
_____ Poor

lacks a frame of reference. In this case, the researcher does not know the basis of comparison the respondent is using. In formulating an answer, some respondents may compare the caseworker to other caseworkers, whereas some respondents may use a personal absolute scale about a caseworker's performance. To avoid this kind of confusion, the basis of comparison should be specifically stated: "Compared to other caseworkers with whom you are familiar, the performance of this caseworker is . . ."

Avoid Negative Words and Double Negatives

Try answering the question, "Do you disagree that juveniles should not be tried as adults if they commit murder?" Respondents have a hard time figuring out which response matches their sentiments. Such errors can easily be avoided with minor wording changes, but even experienced survey researchers can make this mistake unintentionally, perhaps while trying to avoid some other wording problem.

Avoid Double-Barreled Questions

Double-barreled questions A single survey question that actually asks two questions but allows only one answer.

Double-barreled questions produce uninterpretable results because they actually ask two questions but allow only one answer. For example, the question, "Do you support increased spending on social services and schools?" is really two questions—about support for social services and support for schools. It is perfectly reasonable for someone to support increased spending on schools but not social services. A similar problem can also show up in the response categories.

Avoid Jargon

Avoid using jargon or technical language related to a profession or academic discipline. Words like *social justice, empowering,* and *strengths* may appear in social work literature, but they do not necessarily have a shared meaning in the profession, let alone the broader community. Using initials to abbreviate phrases is also a form of professional jargon. For example, to some social work students (particularly those students specializing in gerontology), AAA refers to the Area Agency on Aging, but to other social work students and the general population, the initials are just as likely to refer to the Automobile Association of America.

Reduce the Risk of Bias

Leading questions Question phrasing meant to bias the response.

Specific words in survey questions should not trigger biases unless that is the researcher's conscious intent. Such questions are referred to as **leading questions** because they lead the respondent to a particular answer. Biased or loaded words and phrases tend to produce misleading answers. There are words, such as *welfare* or *liberal*, that have taken on meanings that stir reactions in at least some people. Surveys have found that support for "programs to assist the poor" is 39% higher than when the word *welfare* is used (T. Smith, 1987).

Responses can also be biased when response alternatives do not reflect the full range of possible sentiment on an issue. When people pick a response choice, they seem to be influenced by where they are placing themselves relative to the other response choices. A similar bias occurs when some but not all possible responses are included in the question, "What do you like about your community, such as the parks and schools?" focuses respondents on those categories, and other answers may be ignored. It is best left to the respondent to answer the question without such response cues.

If the response alternatives fall on a continuum from positive to negative sentiment of some type, it is important that the number of positive and negative categories be balanced so that one end of the continuum doesn't seem more attractive (Dillman, 2000). If you ask respondents, "How satisfied are you with the child care program here?" and include "completely satisfied" as the most positive possible response, then "completely dissatisfied" should be included as the most negative possible response.

Memory Questions

Some questions require respondents to try to remember an event. Remembering an event is affected by the length of time since the event occurred and how important the event was to the respondent. **Recall loss** occurs when a respondent does not remember an event or behavior or can remember only aspects of the event. The problem is not unusual. Events important to the respondent are likely to be remembered, even if they happened long ago, whereas events unimportant to the respondent, even if they happened recently, are likely to be forgotten.

> **Recall loss** Problems of remembering events or details about events.
>
> **Telescoping effect** Remembering an event as happening more recently than when it really occurred.

Researchers face a second issue called a **telescoping effect**, which occurs when an event is thought to have happened during a particular period when it actually happened before that period. Some things we remember "just like it happened yesterday" because they are so meaningful or important. Unfortunately, they can be reported that way, too.

Adding questions may improve memory about specific past events. Imagine the problem you might have identifying the correct response to the question, "How often did you receive help from classmates while preparing for exams or completing assignments during the past month? (very often, somewhat often, occasionally, rarely, or never)." Now imagine a series of questions that asks you to identify the exams and assignments you had in the past month and, for each one, inquires whether you received each of several types of help from classmates: study suggestions, study sessions, related examples, general encouragement, and so on. The more specific focus on particular exams and assignments should result in more complete recall.

Another method used to improve memory about life events is to use a *life history calendar* (Axinn, Pearce, & Ghimire, 1999). Life history calendars are used to help sequence the timing of personal events by using standardized visual cues, including years (or months) and other cues related to individual responses, such as births, job changes, or moves. Using such cues, the respondent is then asked about the events related to the study. In this way, respondents can focus on less important events using the important events as cues (Axinn et al., 1999). Recall of traumatic events is often difficult; Yoshihama, Gillespie, Hammack, Belli, and Tolman (2005) compared use of a life history calendar and a semistructured interview with a structured interview and found the former provided more recall of instances of intimate partner violence.

Closed-Ended and Open-Ended Questions

Questions can be designed with or without explicit response choices. When explicit response categories are offered, the type of question is a **closed-ended question**. For example, the following question asked in a survey of agencies

> **Closed-ended question** A survey question that provides preformatted response choices for the respondent to check or circle.

providing mental health and/or substance abuse service is closed-ended because the desired response categories are provided. Mental health providers were asked,

What type of mental health care does your organization provide?

_____ In-patient care only
_____ Out-patient care only
_____ Both

Most surveys of a large number of people contain primarily closed-ended questions, which are easy to process with computers and analyze with statistics. Including the response choices reduces ambiguity, and respondents are more likely to answer the question that the researcher really wants them to answer. However, closed-ended questions can obscure what people really think if the choices do not match the range of possible responses to the question. Respondents can become frustrated when they are not able to find a category to fit their desired answer. Some respondents will choose response choices that do not apply to them simply to give some sort of answer (Peterson, 2000).

Most important, response choices should be mutually exclusive and exhaustive so that every respondent can find one and only one choice that applies to him or her (unless the question is of the "Check all that apply" format). To make response choices exhaustive, researchers may need to offer at least one option with room for ambiguity. For example, mental health and substance abuse providers were asked about why they did not treat problem gambling. The list included six different reasons, but concluded with the category "Other (please specify _____)" because the researchers were not sure they had all the possible reasons on their list. If respondents do not find a response option that corresponds to their answer to the question, they may skip the question entirely or choose a response option that does not indicate what they are really thinking.

Open-ended questions are questions without explicit response choices, so that respondents provide their own answers in their own words. This type of question is usually used when there is little knowledge about a particular topic, and you want to learn as much as possible without limiting responses. For example, if you are interested in learning the perceptions of agency directors about potential problems brought out by the opening of a casino, you might ask,

> **Open-ended question** A survey question to which the respondent replies in his or her own words, by either writing or talking.

How has your agency responded to the opening of the new casino?

The information obtained from a question such as this could be used as response categories for closed-ended questions in future surveys.

> **Closed-ended question** A survey question that provides preformatted response choices for the respondent to check or circle.

Open-ended questions provide additional information that may not be available from a **closed-ended question**. For example, in a questionnaire dealing with psychiatric conditions, respondents were asked a yes/no question: "In the past 2 weeks, have you had thoughts that you would be better off dead or of hurting yourself in some way?" They were then asked, "Can you tell me about it?" The purpose of the second question was to expand on the first question and help the analyst determine whether there was a threat of suicide.

Although open-ended questions provide a wealth of information, they also require careful consideration. Administering, analyzing, and summarizing open-ended questions can be time-consuming and difficult. Some respondents do not like to write a lot and may find open-ended questions taxing. Interviewing is not necessarily the solution: The amount of information provided by a respondent may depend on the respondent's personality—some respondents may provide short or cursory answers, whereas other respondents may provide extensive answers with a great deal of relevant (and irrelevant) information.

Closed-Ended Questions and Response Categories

When writing response categories for closed-ended questions, there are several guidelines that might help improve the questions. We have already mentioned that it is important to ensure that the responses are mutually exclusive and that the list is exhaustive. We offer these additional guidelines to consider when designing questions.

Allow for Disagreement

People often tend to agree with a statement just to avoid seeming disagreeable. This is termed *acquiescence bias* (or agreement bias). Numerous studies of agreement bias suggest that about 10% of respondents will agree just to be agreeable, without regard to what they really think (Krosnick, 1999).

You can take several steps to reduce the likelihood of acquiescence bias. As a general rule, you should present both sides of attitude scales in the question (Dillman, 2000): "In general, do you believe that *individuals* or *social conditions* are more to blame for poverty in the United States?" The response choices should be phrased to make each one seem as socially approved, as "agreeable," as the others. You should also consider replacing a range of response alternatives that focus on the word *agree* with others. For example, "To what extent do you support or oppose the new health care plan?" (response choices range from "strongly support" to "strongly oppose") is probably a better approach than the question, "To what extent do you agree or disagree with the statement 'The new health care plan is worthy of support'?" (response choices range from *strongly agree* to *strongly disagree*).

Social Desirability

Social desirability is the tendency for individuals to respond in ways that make them appear in the best light to the interviewer. The error, in this case, is that respondents are not providing their true opinions or answers. Social desirability effects are likely to occur when discussing issues that are controversial or when expressing a view that is not popular. Some surveys include scales to determine whether a respondent is providing socially desirable responses.

> **Social desirability** The tendency for individuals to respond in ways that make them appear in the best light to the interviewer.
>
> **Fence-sitters** Survey respondents who see themselves as being neutral on an issue and choose a middle (neutral) response.
>
> **Floaters** Survey respondents who provide an opinion on a topic in response to a closed-ended question that does not include a *don't know* option but who will choose *don't know* if it is available.

Minimize Fence-Sitting and Floating

Two related problems in question writing also stem from people's desire to choose an acceptable answer. There is no uniformly correct solution to these problems; researchers have to weigh the alternatives in light of the concept to be measured and whatever they know about the respondents.

There are **fence-sitters,** who see themselves as being neutral and whose responses may skew the results if you force them to choose between opposites. Having an explicit neutral response option is generally a good idea: It identifies fence-sitters and tends to increase measurement reliability (Schaeffer & Presser, 2003).

Floaters are respondents who choose a substantive answer when they really do not know or have no opinion. Because there are so many floaters in the typical survey sample, the decision to include an explicit *Don't know* option for a question is important. This decision is particularly important with surveys of less educated populations because *Don't know* responses are offered more often by those with less education—except for questions that are really impossible to decipher, to which more educated people are likely to say they do not know (Schuman & Presser, 1981). Unfortunately, the inclusion of an explicit *Don't know* response choice leads some people who do have a preference to take the easy way out and choose *Don't know*.

There are several ways to phrase questions and response choices to reduce the risk of completely missing fence-sitters and floaters. One good idea is to include an explicit "no opinion" category after all the substantive responses; if neutral sentiment is a possibility, also include a neutral category in the middle of the substantive responses (such as *Neither agree nor disagree*; Dillman, 2000). Adding an open-ended question in which respondents are asked to discuss their opinions (or reasons for having no opinion) can help by shedding some light on why some choose *Don't know* in response to a particular question (T. Smith, 1984). Researchers who use in-person or telephone interviews (rather than self-administered questionnaires) may get around the dilemma somewhat by reading the response choices without a middle or *Don't know* alternative, but recording a noncommittal response if it is offered.

Filter questions A survey question used to identify a subset of respondents who are then asked other questions.

Skip patterns The unique combination of questions created in a survey by filter questions and contingency questions.

Contingency questions Questions asked of the more limited group of people.

Likert-type responses Response categories that generally ask respondents to indicate the extent to which they agree or disagree with statements.

Matrix questions A series of questions that concern a common theme and have the same response choices.

Use Filter Questions

The use of **filter questions** is important to ensure that questions are asked only of relevant respondents. If you ask questions about work, you first need to determine who is working and who is not working. These filter questions create **skip patterns**. Based on the response to a filter question, respondents will be asked to either skip one or more questions or answer those questions. The questions asked of the more limited group of people are referred to as **contingency questions.** Skip patterns should be indicated clearly with arrows or other direction in the questionnaire, as demonstrated in Exhibit 9.3.

Utilize Likert-Type Response Categories

Likert-type responses generally ask respondents to indicate the extent to which they agree or disagree with statements. The response categories list choices for respondents to select their level of agreement with a statement, from *strongly agree* to *strongly disagree*. The questions in Exhibit 9.4 have Likert-type response categories.

Matrix Questions

Some question formats lend themselves to be presented in a matrix format. **Matrix questions** are actually a series of questions that concern a common

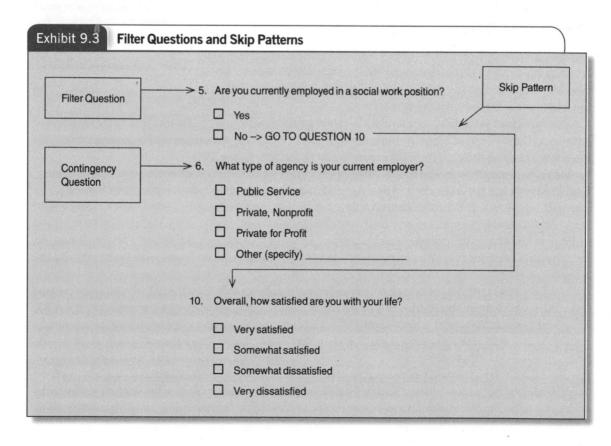

Exhibit 9.3   Filter Questions and Skip Patterns

Filter Question

Skip Pattern

5. Are you currently employed in a social work position?

☐ Yes

☐ No –> GO TO QUESTION 10

Contingency Question

6. What type of agency is your current employer?

☐ Public Service

☐ Private, Nonprofit

☐ Private for Profit

☐ Other (specify) _____

10. Overall, how satisfied are you with your life?

☐ Very satisfied

☐ Somewhat satisfied

☐ Somewhat dissatisfied

☐ Very dissatisfied

Exhibit 9.4	**Matrix Questions Using Likert-Type Responses**

15. In general, how well did: (Please circle one response for each question)

	Strongly agree				Strongly disagree
a. MSW classes prepared me for my social work position	1	2	3	4	5
b. Field education experiences prepare me for my social work position.	1	2	3	4	5
c. MSW classes prepare me for attaining a social work license.	1	2	3	4	5

theme and that have the same response choices. The questions are written so that a common initial phrase applies to each one (Exhibit 9.4). This format shortens the questionnaire by reducing the number of words that must be used for each question. It also emphasizes the common theme among the questions and so invites answering each question in relation to other questions in the matrix. It is important to provide an explicit instruction to "Circle one response on each line" in a matrix question, since some respondents will think that they have completed the entire matrix after they have responded to just a few of the specific questions.

Matrix questions are susceptible to a form of error called a **response set**. When scales are used (or a set of single questions, for that matter) with the same set of response categories, there is the possibility that, rather than reading and answering each question, the respondent simply circles the same response down the entire set of questions. To avoid this problem, researchers often phrase some questions in the opposite direction; if the questions were worded using positive language, they would ask some questions using negative language. The assumption is that if the respondent then answers all the questions with the same response, it is clear he or she was just circling them without thinking.

> **Response set** When a series of questions have the same set of response categories, there is the possibility that the respondent provides the same response for each question rather than reading the questions.

Sensitive Topics

Respondents may consider topics such as drug use, sexual activity, or use of mental health services as too sensitive or embarrassing to discuss. Some respondents will be reluctant to agree that they have ever engaged in such activities. In this situation, the goal is to write a question and response choices that will reduce the anxiety or threat of providing an answer. To do so may violate some of the guidelines we have mentioned.

One way is to make agreement seem more acceptable. For example, Dillman (2000) suggests that we ask, "Have you ever taken anything from a store without paying for it?" rather than "Have you ever shoplifted something from a store?" (p. 75). Asking about a variety of behaviors or attitudes that run the gamut from socially acceptable to socially unacceptable will also soften the impact of agreeing with those that are socially unacceptable. The behavior will also be softened by asking, "How often have you . . . ?" rather than using a filter and asking, "Have you ever . . . ?" and having "never" as one of the response categories.

▣ Refine and Test Questionnaires

Adhering to the preceding question-writing guidelines will go a long way toward producing a useful questionnaire. However, simply asking what appear to you to be clear questions does not ensure that people have a consistent understanding of what you are asking. Reviewing the relevant literature to find results obtained with similar surveys and comparable questions is also an important step to take if you have not already conducted such a review before writing your questions. Nonetheless, you need some external feedback.

One important form of feedback results from simply discussing the questionnaire content with others. People who should be consulted include expert researchers, key figures in the locale or organization to be surveyed (such as elected representatives or community leaders), and some individuals from the population to be sampled. Forming a panel of experts to review the questionnaire can help. Engel, Rosen, Weaver, and Soska (2010) formed a panel of service providers, addiction experts, and county representatives to provide feedback on a survey assessing social service capacity to treat problem and pathological gambling. Their feedback led to the addition of topics that they perceived could help their agencies in addressing problem gambling and, therefore, would be useful for a broader social service network.

Researchers are increasingly getting feedback from guided discussions among potential respondents. Such *focus groups* let you check for consistent understanding of terms and to identify the range of events or experiences about which people will be asked to report. By listening to and observing the focus group discussions, researchers can test their assumptions about what level of vocabulary is appropriate and what people are going to be reporting (Nassar-McMillan & Borders, 2002).

Researchers may choose to evaluate questions with **cognitive interviews**. Although the specifics vary, the interviewer asks people to *think aloud* as they answer a question by asking them what they were thinking about when they answered the question. The interviewer might further probe with follow-up questions to learn how the question was understood and whether its meaning varied for different respondents (Presser et al., 2004). Cognitive interviewing can identify many potential problems, particularly if the individuals interviewed reflect much of the diversity of the population to be surveyed.

Cognitive interview A technique to evaluate questions in which researchers ask people test questions, then probe with follow-up questions to learn how the repondents understood the questions and what their answers mean.

Another technique is **behavior coding**: A researcher observes several interviews or listens to taped interviews and codes according to strict rules the number of times that difficulties occur with questions. Such difficulties include respondents asking for clarification and interviewers rephrasing questions rather than reading them verbatim (Presser & Blair, 1994).

> **Behavior coding** The researcher categorizes according to strict rules the number of times certain behaviors occur.

No questionnaire should be considered ready for use until there has been a **pilot study**. Researchers may pretest their questions as well as their procedures in a pilot study. Prepare for the pilot study by completing the questionnaire yourself and then revising it. Next, try it out on some colleagues or other friends and then revise it. For the actual pilot study, draw a small sample of individuals from the

> **Pilot study** A small initial study to determine the quality of the data collection procedures that will be used in a larger study.

population you are studying or one similar to it, and carry out the survey procedures with them. This should include as many mailings as you plan for a mailed questionnaire and actual interviews if you are preparing to conduct in-person interviews. You may include in the pretest version of a written questionnaire some space for individuals to add comments on each key question or, with in-person interviews, audiotape the test interviews for later review.

Review the distribution of responses to each question, listen to the audiotapes, and/or read all the comments. Revise any questions that respondents do not seem to interpret as you had intended or that are not working well for other reasons. If the response rate is relatively low, consider whether it can be improved by some modifications in procedures.

Which pretesting method is best? Each has some unique advantages and disadvantages. Behavior coding, with its clearly specified rules, is the most reliable method across interviewers and repetitions, whereas pilot studies are the least reliable. However, focus groups and cognitive interviewing methods are better for understanding the bases of problems with particular questions. A review of questions by an expert panel is the least expensive method and identifies the greatest number of problems with questions (Presser & Blair, 1994).

Survey Design Alternatives

There are five basic social science survey designs: mailed, group-administered, phone, in-person, and electronic. Some researchers combine elements of two or more of these basic designs in *mixed-mode* research. Exhibit 9.5 summarizes the typical features of the five different survey designs. Each design differs from the others in one or more important features.

- *Manner of administration.* Mailed, group, and electronic surveys are completed by the respondents. During phone and in-person interviews, the researcher or a staff person asks the questions and records the respondent's answers.

- *Setting.* Most surveys are conducted in settings where only one respondent completes the survey at a time; most mailed and electronic questionnaires and phone interviews are intended for completion by only one respondent. The same is usually true of in-person interviews, although sometimes researchers interview several family members at once. A variant of the standard survey is a questionnaire distributed simultaneously to a group of respondents, who complete the survey while the researcher (or assistant) waits.

- *Questionnaire structure.* Survey designs differ in the extent to which the content and order of questions are structured in advance by the researcher. Most mailed, group, phone, and electronic surveys are highly structured, fixing in advance the content and order of questions and response choices. Some of these types of surveys, particularly mailed surveys, may include some open-ended questions. In-person interviews may be highly structured, but they may include many open-ended questions. Some interviews may proceed from an interview guide rather than a fixed set of questions. In these relatively unstructured interviews, the interviewer covers the same topics with respondents, but varies questions according to the respondent's answers to previous questions. Extra questions are added as needed to clarify or explore answers to the most important questions. Computers make it easy for researchers to use complex branching patterns since the computer can present different questions based on responses to prior questions (Tourangeau, 2004).

- *Cost.* In-person interviews are the most expensive type of survey. Phone interviews are much less expensive, although costs are increasing due to the need to make more calls to reach potential respondents. Surveying by mail is even cheaper. Electronic surveys are now the least expensive method because there are no interviewer costs, no mailing costs, and, for many designs, almost no costs for data entry. However, extra staff time and expertise are required to prepare an electronic questionnaire (Tourangeau, Conrad, & Couper, 2012).

Because of their different features, the five designs vary in the types of error to which they are most prone and the situations in which they are most appropriate. The rest of this section focuses on the various designs' unique advantages and disadvantages and identifies techniques for reducing error with each design.

Mailed Surveys

Mailed survey A survey involving a mailed questionnaire to be completed by the respondent.

A **mailed survey** is conducted by mailing a questionnaire to respondents, who then administer the survey themselves. The central concern in a mailed survey is maximizing the response rate. Even an attractive questionnaire full of clear questions will probably be returned by no more than 30% of a sample unless extra steps are taken to increase the rate of response. It is just too much bother for most potential recipients; in the language of social exchange theory, the costs of responding are perceived to be much higher than any anticipated rewards for doing so. Of course, a response rate of 30% is a disaster; even a response rate of 60% represents so much nonresponse error that it is hard to justify using the resulting data. Fortunately, the conscientious use of a systematic survey design method can be expected to lead to an acceptable 70% or higher rate of response to most mail surveys (Dillman, 2000).

Sending follow-up mailings to nonrespondents is the single most important requirement for obtaining an adequate response rate to a mailed survey. Follow-up mailings explicitly encourage initial nonrespondents to return a completed questionnaire; implicitly, they convey the importance of the effort. Dillman (2000) has demonstrated the effectiveness of a standard procedure for the mailing process that includes the following:

Exhibit 9.5   Typical Features of the Five Survey Designs

Design	Manner of Administration	Setting	Questionnaire Structure	Cost
Mailed survey	Self	Individual	Mostly structured	Low to moderate
Group survey	Self	Group	Mostly structured	Very low
Phone survey	Professional	Individual	Structured	Moderate
In-person interview	Professional	Individual	Structured or unstructured	High
Electronic survey	Self	Individual	Mostly structured	Low

1. A few days before the questionnaire is to be mailed, send a brief letter to respondents that notifies them of the importance of the survey they are to receive.

2. Send the questionnaire with a well-designed, personalized cover letter (see the next section), a self-addressed stamped return envelope, and, if possible, a token monetary reward. The materials should be inserted in the mail-out envelope so that they will all be pulled out together when the envelope is opened (Dillman, 2000). There should be no chance that the respondent will miss something.

3. Send a reminder postcard to all sample members 2 weeks after the initial mailing. The postcard is written to thank respondents and remind nonrespondents. The postcard should be friendly in tone and must include a phone number or e-mail address for those people who may not have received the questionnaire. It is important that this postcard be sent before most nonrespondents have discarded their questionnaires even though this means the postcard will arrive before all those who might have responded to the first mailing have done so.

4. Send a replacement questionnaire with a new cover letter only to nonrespondents 2 to 4 weeks after the initial questionnaire mailing. This cover letter should be a bit shorter and more insistent than the original cover letter. It should note that the recipient has not yet responded and stress the survey's importance. Of course, a self-addressed stamped return envelope must be included.

5. The final step is taken 6 to 8 weeks after the initial survey mailing. This step uses a different mode of delivery (either priority or special delivery) or a different survey design—usually an attempt to administer the questionnaire over the phone. These special procedures emphasize the importance of the survey and encourage people to respond.

The **cover letter** is critical to the success of a mailed survey since it sets the tone for the entire questionnaire. A carefully prepared cover letter should increase the response rate and result in more honest and complete answers to the survey questions; a poorly prepared cover letter can have the reverse effects (see Exhibit 9.6).

The cover letter or introductory statement must be

> **Cover letter** A letter sent with a mailed questionnaire; it explains the survey's purpose and auspices and encourages the recipient to participate.

- *Personalized.* The cover letter should include a personalized salutation (using the respondent's name, not just "Dear Student," for example), close with the researcher's signature (blue ballpoint pen is best because it makes it clear that the researcher has personally signed), and refer to the respondent in the second person ("Your participation . . .").

- *Credible.* The letter should establish that the research is being conducted by a researcher or organization that the respondent is likely to accept as a credible, unbiased authority. Research conducted by government agencies, university personnel, and recognized research organizations (such as Gallup or RAND) is usually credible in this sense, with government surveys getting the most attention.

- *Interesting.* The statement should interest the respondent in the contents of the questionnaire. Never make the mistake of assuming that what is of interest to you will also interest your respondents. Try to put yourself in their shoes before composing the statement, and then test your appeal with a variety of potential respondents.

- *Responsible.* Reassure the respondent that the information you obtain will be treated confidentially, and include a phone number to call if the respondent has any questions or would like a summary of the final report. Point out that the respondent's participation is completely voluntary. (Dillman, 2000)

Write an identifying number on each questionnaire so you can determine who nonrespondents are. This is essential for follow-up efforts. Of course, the identification must be explained in the cover letter.

| Exhibit 9.6 | Sample Questionnaire Cover Letter |

University of Massachusetts at Boston
May 24, 2003

Jane Doe

AIDS Coordinator

Shattuck Shelter

Dear Jane:

AIDS is an increasing concern for homeless people and for homeless shelters. The enclosed survey is about the AIDS problem and related issues confronting shelters. It is sponsored by the Life Lines AIDS Prevention Project for the Homeless—a program of the Massachusetts Department of Public Health.

As an AIDS coordinator/shelter director, you have learned about homeless persons' problems and about implementing programs in response to these problems. The Life Lines Project needs to learn from your experience. Your answers to the questions in the enclosed survey will improve substantially the base of information for improving AIDS prevention programs.

Questions in the survey focus on AIDS prevention activities and on related aspects of shelter operations. It should take about 30 minutes to answer all the questions.

Every shelter AIDS coordinator (or shelter director) in Massachusetts is being asked to complete the survey. And every response is vital to the success of the survey. The survey report must represent the full range of experiences.

You may be assured of complete confidentiality. No one outside of the university will have access to the questionnaire you return. (The ID number on the survey will permit us to check with nonrespondents to see if they need a replacement survey or other information.) All information presented in the report to Life Lines will be in aggregate form, with the exception of a list of the number, gender, and family status of each shelter's guests.

Please mail the survey back to us by Monday, June 4, and feel free to call if you have any questions.

Thank you for your assistance.

Yours sincerely,

Project Director   Project Assistant

Source: Russell Schutt.

If Dillman's procedures are followed and the guidelines for cover letters and questionnaire design also are adopted, the response rate is almost certain to approach 70%. The response rate may be higher with particular populations surveyed on topics of interest to them, and it may be lower with surveys of populations that do not have much interest in the topic.

There are other strategies to increase the response rate (Fowler, 1988; Mangione, 1995; D. Miller & Salkind, 2002). The individual questions should be clear and understandable to all the respondents because no interviewers will be on hand to clarify the meaning of the questions or to probe for additional details. There should only be a few open-ended questions, because respondents are likely to be put off by the idea of having to write out answers. Having a sponsor known to respondents may increase the response rate. Enclosing a token incentive such as a coupon or ticket worth $1 or $2 may help. Finally, include a stamped, self-addressed return envelope with the questionnaire.

When a survey has many nonrespondents, getting some ideas about their characteristics by comparing late respondents to early respondents can help to determine the likelihood of bias due to the low rate of response. If those who returned their questionnaires at an early stage are more educated or more interested in the topic of the questionnaire, the sample may be biased; if the respondents are not more educated or more interested than nonrespondents, the sample will be more credible.

If resources did not permit phone calls to all nonrespondents, a random sample of nonrespondents can be selected and contacted by phone or interviewed in person. It should be possible to secure responses from a substantial majority of these nonrespondents in this way. With appropriate weighting, these new respondents can then be added to the sample of respondents to the initial mailed questionnaire, resulting in a more representative total sample (Levy & Lemeshow, 2008).

Another concern for mailed surveys is the hazard of incomplete response. Some respondents may skip some questions or just stop answering questions at some point in the questionnaire. Fortunately, this problem does not occur often with well-designed questionnaires. Potential respondents who have decided to participate in the survey usually complete it. But there are many exceptions to this observation because questions that are poorly written, too complex, or about sensitive personal issues simply turn off some respondents. The revision or elimination of such questions during the design phase should minimize the problem. When it does not, it may make sense to impute values for the missing data. One imputation procedure would be to substitute the mean (arithmetic average) value of a variable for those cases that have a missing value on the variable (Levy & Lemeshow, 2008).

Finally, there is no control over the manner in which the respondent answers the questions. Despite efforts to create a meaningful order to the questions, the respondent can choose in what order the questions will be answered. The respondent can choose to answer all the questions at once or answer them over several days. The respondent may even discuss the questions with significant others, family, friends, and coworkers.

Group-Administered Surveys

A **group-administered survey** is completed by individual respondents assembled together. The response rate is not usually a major concern in surveys that are distributed and collected in a group setting because most group members will participate. The real difficulty with this method is that it is seldom feasible because it requires what might be called a captive audience. With the exception of students, employees, members of the armed forces, and some institutionalized populations, most populations cannot be sampled in such a setting.

> **Group-administered survey** A survey that is completed by individual respondents who are assembled in a group.

The person administering the survey to the group must be careful to minimize comments that might bias answers or that could vary between different groups in the same survey (Dillman, 2000). A standard introductory statement should be read to the group that expresses appreciation for their participation, describes the steps of the survey, and emphasizes (in classroom surveys) that the survey is not the same as a test. A cover letter like the one used in mailed surveys also should be distributed with the questionnaires. To emphasize confidentiality, respondents should be given an envelope in which to seal their questionnaire after it is completed.

A special concern with group-administered surveys is the possibility that respondents will feel coerced to participate and, as a result, will be less likely to answer questions honestly. Also, because administering a survey in this way requires approval of the setting's administrators—and this sponsorship is made quite obvious by the fact that the survey is conducted on the organization's premises—respondents may infer that the researcher is not at all independent of the sponsor. No complete solution to this problem exists, but it helps to make an introductory statement emphasizing the researcher's independence and giving participants a chance to ask questions about the survey. The sponsor should also understand the need to keep a low profile and to allow the researcher both control over the data and autonomy in report writing.

Telephone Surveys

In a **phone survey**, interviewers question respondents over the phone and then record respondents' answers. Phone interviewing is a popular method of

> **Phone survey** A survey in which interviewers question respondents over the phone and then record their answers.

conducting surveys in the United States because almost all families have phones. But two matters may undermine the validity of a phone survey: not reaching the proper sampling units and not getting enough complete responses to make the results generalizable.

Reaching Sampling Units

There are three different ways of obtaining a sampling frame of telephone exchanges or numbers: Phone directories provide a useful frame for local studies, a nationwide list of area code and exchange numbers can be obtained from a commercial firm (random digit dialing is used to fill in the last four digits), and commercial firms can provide files based on local directories from around the nation.

Most telephone surveys use random digit dialing to contact respondents. A machine calls random phone numbers within the designated exchanges regardless of whether the numbers are published. When the machine reaches an inappropriate household (such as a business in a survey that is directed to the general population), the phone number is simply replaced with another.

When households are contacted, the interviewers must ask a series of questions at the start of the survey to ensure that they are speaking to the appropriate member of the household. Exhibit 9.7 displays a phone interview schedule, the instrument containing the questions asked by the interviewer. This example shows how appropriate and inappropriate households can be distinguished so that the interviewer is guided to the correct respondent.

But the tremendous popularity of cellular telephones has made accurate coverage of random samples almost impossible for several reasons (Tavernise, 2011; Tourangeau, 2004): (1) cell phones are typically not listed in telephone directories, so they cannot be included in prepared calling lists; (2) laws generally forbid the use of automated dialers (RDD) to contact cell phones; (3) close to 27% of the U.S. population now has only a cell phone (no landline) and therefore cannot be reached by either RDD or many directories; and (4) about 44% of 18- to 30-year-olds have cell phones only.

| Exhibit 9.7 | Phone Interview Procedures for Respondent Designation |

868 Aging, Status, and the Sense of Control
Informant Questionnaire

Introduction and Selection of Respondent or Informant

[Not shown to interviewer, this is a check item]

[if contact attempts less than 15, the interviewer will go to >h101<.

Interviewers will only make a total of 20 attempts]

[if contact attempts greater than 15, the interviewer will go to >h102<]

YOU ARE CALLING [RNAM].

May I speak with [RNAM]?

   <1> YES, CONNECTED TO RESPONDENT

   <2> NOT AVAILABLE

   <3> NEVER ABLE TO INTERVIEW—TOO HARD OF HEARING, PERMANENTLY ILL, OR FOR SOME OTHER REASON

   <4> NO ONE THERE BY THAT NAME, OR NO LONGER LIVE THERE

   <5> LANGUAGE PROBLEM

   <6> DECEASED

   <7> OTHER

   <8> CHILD, NO ADULTS AVAILABLE

   <9> REFUSED

[if <1> go to expl] (Respondents go to main study questionnaire)

[if <2-9> go to wh02]

IF RESPONDENT IS NOT AVAILABLE AFTER SEVERAL ATTEMPTS OR YOU ARE UNABLE TO COMPLETE THE INTERVIEW WITH RESPONDENT, ATTEMPT TO UPDATE RESPONDENT'S ADDRESS AND TELEPHONE INFORMATION WITH AN INFORMANT.

(Introduction for a respondent)

My name is [Interviewer name] and I am calling from the University of Illinois. Approximately 2 years ago you participated in a telephone interview regarding health and different experiences pertaining to sense of control. We are calling to complete a follow-up survey that will take about 30 minutes.

<1>   YES, RESPONDENT IS AVAILABLE

<3>   RESPONDENT PREFERS CALLBACK-SET UP APPOINTMENT

<4>   NEVER ABLE TO INTERVIEW—TOO HARD OF HEARING, PERMANENTLY ILL, OR FOR SOME OTHER REASON

<5>   DUPLICATE

<6>   LANGUAGE PROBLEM

<7>   OTHER

<9>   REFUSED

(Introduction for an informant)

My name is [Interviewer name] and I am calling from the University of Illinois. Approximately 2 years ago [RNAM] participated in a telephone interview regarding health and different experiences pertaining to sense of control. We are calling to complete a follow-up survey with [RNAM]. Since [RNAM] is not available we would like to update (his or her) telephone and address information.

<1>   INFORMANT IS AVAILABLE

<3>   INFORMANT PREFERS CALLBACK-SET UP APPOINTMENT

<4>   NEVER ABLE TO INTERVIEW—TOO HARD OF HEARING, PERMANENTLY ILL, OR FOR SOME OTHER REASON

<5>   DUPLICATE

<6>   LANGUAGE PROBLEM

<7>   OTHER

<9>   REFUSED

. . .

YOU WILL VERIFY THE SPELLING OF THE RESPONDENT'S NAME AND ADDRESS.

Because this study is about how people may change during their lives, we may want to call [RNAM] again in a few years. I'd like to verify the information we have about [RNAM]. First, I would like to ask you about the spelling of [RNAM]'s name.

<1>   PROCEED [go to U1b]

<9>   REFUSED [go to U4]

   Is [RNAM]'s first name spelled [R First Name]?

<1>   Yes

<2>   No [go to U2]

<7>   NO CODED RESPONSE APPLICABLE

<8>   DON'T KNOW

<9>   REFUSED

. . .

(Continued)

Exhibit 9.7 (Continued)

Can [fill RNAM] still be reached at this phone number?

<1> Yes
<2> No
>U22<

What is the (correct) phone number to reach [fill RNAM]?
RECORD WHO YOU COMPLETED THE INTERVIEW WITH.
DID YOU SPEAK TO THE RESPONDENT OR INFORMANT? (DO NOT ASK.)

<1> RESPONDENT
<2> INFORMANT
<8> DON'T KNOW

Source: Ross, Catherine E. 1990: "Work, Family, and the Sense of Control: Implications for the Psychological Well-Being of Women and Men" (Proposal submitted to the National Science Foundation). Urbana: University of Illinois.

Maximizing Response to Phone Surveys

Social changes are lowering the response rate in phone surveys (Tourangeau, 2004). The Pew Research Center reports a decline in response rates based on all those sampled from 36% in 1997 to only 9% in 2012 (Kohut et al., 2012).

Four issues require special attention in phone surveys to maximize participant response. First, because people often are not home, multiple callbacks will be needed for many sample members. The number of callbacks needed to reach respondents by telephone has increased greatly in the past 20 years, with increasing numbers of single-person households, dual-earner families, and out-of-home activities. Survey research organizations have increased the usual number of phone contact attempts from just 4–8 to 20. The growth of telemarketing has created another problem for telephone survey researchers: Individuals have become more accustomed to "just say no" to calls from unknown individuals and organizations or to simply use their caller ID or answering machines to screen out unwanted calls (Dillman, 2000). Cell phone users are harder (and more costly) to contact in phone surveys because their numbers are not in published directories.

Second, researchers using phone surveys also must cope with difficulties due to the impersonal nature of phone contact. Visual aids cannot be used, so the interviewer must be able to convey verbally all information about response choices and skip patterns. Interviewers must know how to ask each question, how to answer questions posed by the respondent, and how to code responses. Exhibit 9.8 illustrates an example of interviewer instructions for a survey to measure symptoms of stress.

Third, interviewers must be prepared for distractions as the respondent is interrupted by other household members. Distractions are a special problem when respondents are called on a cell phone because they might be driving, in a restaurant or other crowded area, or otherwise involved in activities that make responding difficult and that would not occur in a survey using a landline in the home (American Association of Public Opinion Research [AAPOR], 2014). Sprinkling interesting questions throughout the questionnaire may help to maintain respondent interest. In general, rapport between the interviewer and the respondent is likely to be lower with phone surveys than with in-person interviews, so respondents may tire and refuse to answer all the questions (D. Miller & Salkind, 2002).

The fourth consideration is that careful interviewer training is essential for phone surveys. This is how one polling organization describes its training:

In preparation for data collection, survey interviewers are required to attend a two-part training session. The first part covers general interviewing procedures and techniques as related to the proposed survey. The second

Exhibit 9.8	Sample Interviewer Instructions

Question:

41. On how many of the past 7 days have you . . .

Number of days

  a. Worried a lot about little things?...................................... _____

  b. Felt tense or anxious?... _____

Instructions for interviewers:

Q41 For the series of "On how many of the past 7 days," make sure the respondent gives the numerical answer. If he/she responds with a vague answer like "not too often" or "just a few times," ask again "On how many of the past 7 days would you say?" Do NOT lead the respondent with a number (e.g., "would that be 2 or 3?"). If R says "all of them," verify that the answer is "7."

Question:

45. In the past 12 months about how many times have you gone on a diet to lose weight?

Never.. 0
Once.. 1
Twice... 2
Three times or more... 3
Always on a diet.. 4

Instructions for interviewers:

Q45 Notice that this question ends with a question mark. That means that you are not to read the answer categories. Rather, wait for R to respond and circle the appropriate number.

Source: Ross, Catherine E. 1990: "Work, Family, and the Sense of Control: Implications for the Psychological Well-Being of Women and Men" (Proposal submitted to the National Science Foundation). Urbana: University of Illinois.

entails in-depth training and practice for the survey. This training includes instructions on relevant subject matter, a question-by-question review of the survey instrument, and various forms of role-playing and practice interviewing with supervisors and other interviewers. (J. E. Blair, personal communication)

Procedures can be standardized more effectively, quality control maintained, and processing speed maximized when phone interviewers are assisted by computers using a computer-assisted telephone interview (CATI). In using CATI, the survey is programmed into the computer, including all relevant skip patterns; the interviewer reads the questions and enters the responses directly into the computer.

Computerized interactive voice response (IVR) technology allows even greater control over interviewer–respondent interaction. In a survey, respondents receive automated calls and answer questions by pressing numbers on their touch-tone phones or speaking numbers that are interpreted by computerized voice recognition software. These surveys can also record verbal responses to open-ended questions for later transcription. Although they present some difficulties when many answer choices must be used or skip patterns must be followed, IVR surveys have been used successfully with short questionnaires and when respondents are highly motivated to participate (Dillman, 2000). When these conditions are not met, potential respondents may be put off by the impersonal nature of this computer-driven method.

Phone surveying had for decades been the method of choice for relatively short surveys of the general population. Response rates in phone surveys traditionally tended to be high—often above 80%—because few individuals would hang up on a polite caller or stop answering questions (at least within the first 30 minutes or so). However, phone surveying is not a panacea and it should no longer be considered the best method to use for general purpose surveys. The long-term decline in response rates to household surveys is such a problem for survey researchers that they have devoted entire issues of major journals to it (E. Singer, 2006).

In-Person Interviews

In-person interview A survey in which an interviewer questions respondents face-to-face and records their answers.

What is unique to the **in-person interview**, compared with the other survey designs, is the face-to-face social interaction between interviewer and respondent. In-person interviewing has several advantages. Response rates are higher than with any other survey design. Questionnaires can be much longer than with mailed or phone surveys; the questionnaire can be complex, with both open- and closed-ended questions and frequent branching patterns; the order in which questions are read and answered can be controlled by the interviewer; the physical and social circumstances of the interview can be monitored; and respondents' interpretations of questions can be probed and clarified.

There are some special hazards due to the presence of an interviewer. Respondents should experience the interview process as a personalized interaction with an interviewer who is interested in the respondent's experiences and opinions. At the same time every respondent should have the same interview experience; that is, he or she should be asked the same questions in the same way by the same type of person, who reacts similarly to the answers. Therein lays the researcher's challenge—to plan an interview process that will be personal and engaging, yet consistent and nonreactive (and to hire interviewers who can carry out this plan). Careful training and supervision are essential because small differences in intonation or emphasis on particular words can alter respondents' interpretations of question meaning (Peterson, 2000). Without a personalized approach, the rate of response will be lower and answers will be less thoughtful and potentially less valid. Without a consistent approach, information obtained from different respondents will not be comparable, will be less reliable and less valid.

Adhering to some basic guidelines for interacting with respondents can help interviewers to maintain an appropriate balance between personalization and standardization:

- Project a professional image in the interview—that of someone who is sympathetic to the respondent, but nonetheless has a job to do.

- Establish rapport at the outset by explaining what the interview is about and how it will work and by reading the consent form. Ask the respondent whether he or she has any questions or concerns, and respond to these honestly and fully. Emphasize that everything the respondent says is confidential.

- During the interview, ask questions from a distance that is close, but not intimate. Stay focused on the respondent and make sure that your posture conveys interest. Maintain eye contact, respond with appropriate facial expressions, and speak in a conversational tone of voice.

- Be sure to maintain a consistent approach; deliver each question as written and in the same tone of voice. Listen empathetically, but avoid self-expression or loaded reactions.

- Repeat questions if the respondent is confused. Use nondirective probes—such as "Can you tell me more about that?"—for open-ended questions.

As with phone interviewing, computers can be used to increase control of the in-person interview. In a computer-assisted personal interviewing (CAPI) project, interviewers carry a laptop computer that is programmed to display the interview questions and to process the responses that the interviewer types in, as well as to check that these responses fall within allowed ranges (Tourangeau, 2004). Interviewers seem to like CAPI, and the quality of data obtained this way is at least as good as data from a noncomputerized interview (Shepherd, Hill, Bristor, & Montalvan,

1996; Smith & Kim, 2003). A CAPI approach also makes it easier for the researcher to develop skip patterns and experiment with different types of questions for different respondents without increasing the risk of interviewer mistakes (Couper et al., 1998).

The presence of an interviewer may make it more difficult for respondents to give honest answers to questions about socially undesirable behaviors such as drug use or sexual activity (Schaeffer & Presser, 2003). CAPI is valued for this reason, since respondents can enter their answers directly in the laptop without the interviewer knowing what their response is. Alternatively, interviewers can hand respondents a separate self-administered questionnaire containing the more sensitive questions. After answering these questions, the respondent then seals the separate questionnaire in an envelope so that the interviewer does not know the answers. The degree of rapport becomes a special challenge when survey questions concern issues related to such demographic characteristics as race or gender (Groves, 1989). If the interviewer and respondent are similar on these characteristics, the responses to these questions may differ from those that would be given if the interviewer and respondent differ on these characteristics.

Although in-person interview procedures are typically designed with the expectation that the interview will involve only the interviewer and the respondent, one or more other household members are often within earshot. It is reasonable to worry that this third-party presence will influence responses about sensitive subjects—even more so because the likelihood of a third party being present may correspond with other subject characteristics.

Even if the right balance has been struck between maintaining control over interviews and achieving good rapport with respondents, in-person interviews can still be problematic. Because of the difficulty of finding all the members of a sample, response rates may suffer.

Several factors affect the response rate in interview studies. Contact rates tend to be lower in central cities, in part because of difficulties in finding people at home and gaining access to high-rise apartments and in part because of interviewer reluctance to visit some areas at night, when people are more likely to be home (Fowler, 1988). In contrast, households with young children or elderly adults tend to be easier to contact, whereas single-person households are more difficult to reach (Groves & Couper, 1998).

Refusal rates vary with some respondent characteristics. People with less education participate somewhat less in surveys of political issues. Less education is also associated with higher rates of "Don't know" responses (Groves, 1989). High-income people tend to participate less in surveys about income and economic behavior (perhaps because they are suspicious about why others want to know about their situation). Unusual strains and disillusionment in society can also undermine the general credibility of research efforts and the ability of interviewers to achieve an acceptable response rate.

These problems can be lessened with an advance letter introducing the survey project and by multiple contact attempts throughout the day and evening, but they cannot entirely be avoided (Fowler, 1988; Groves & Couper, 1998). Making small talk to increase rapport and delaying asking a potential respondent to participate may reduce the likelihood of a refusal after someone first expresses uncertainty about participating (Maynard, Freese, & Schaeffer, 2010).

Electronic Surveys

Widespread use of e-mail and the Internet, increasingly with high speed connections and often through smartphones, creates new opportunities for survey researchers. Surveys can be e-mailed to respondents and returned in the same way; they can be posted on a website, and they can even be designed for completion on a smartphone.

Web surveys have become an increasingly useful survey method for two reasons: growth in the fraction of the population using the Internet and technological advances that make web survey design relatively easy. Many specific populations have very high rates of Internet use, so a web survey can be a good option for groups such as professionals, middle-class communities, members of organizations, and, of course, college students. Because of the Internet's global reach, web surveys also make it possible to conduct large, international surveys.

However, coverage remains a problem with many populations (Tourangeau et al., 2012). About one quarter of U.S. households are not connected to the Internet (File, 2013), so it is not yet possible to survey directly a representative sample of the U.S. population on the Web. Households without Internet access tend to be older, less educated, and poorer than those that are connected (File, 2013; Pew Research Center, 2013). Coverage problems are compounded in web surveys because of much lower rates of survey completion: It is just too easy to stop working on a web survey—much easier than it is to break off interaction with an interviewer (Tourangeau et al., 2012).

The extent to which the population of interest is connected to the Web is the most important consideration when deciding whether to conduct a survey through the Web. Other considerations that may increase the attractiveness of a web survey include the need for a large sample, for rapid turnaround, for collecting sensitive information that might be embarrassing to acknowledge in person, the availability of an e-mail list of the target population, and the extent to which the interactive and multimedia features will enhance interest in the survey (Sue & Ritter, 2012).

There are several different approaches to engaging people in web surveys, each with unique advantages and disadvantages and somewhat different effects on the coverage problem. Many web surveys begin with an e-mail message to potential respondents that contains a direct "hotlink" to the survey website (Gaiser & Schreiner, 2009). It is important that such e-mail invitations include a catchy phrase in the subject line as well as attractive and clear text in the message itself (Sue & Ritter, 2012). This particular approach is particularly useful when a defined population with known e-mail addresses is to be surveyed. The researcher can send e-mail invitations to a representative sample without difficulty. To ensure that the appropriate people respond to a web-based survey, researchers may require that respondents enter a personal identification number to gain access to it (Dillman, 2000; Sue & Ritter, 2012).

However, lists of unique e-mail addresses for the members of the defined populations generally do not exist outside of organizational settings. Many people have more than one e-mail address, and often there is no apparent link between an e-mail address and the name or location of the person it is assigned to. As a result, there is no available method for drawing a random sample of e-mail addresses for people from any general population, even if the focus is only on those with Internet access (Dillman, 2007).

Web surveys may instead be linked to a website that is used by the intended population, and everyone who visits that site is invited to complete the survey. Although this approach can generate a large number of respondents, the resulting sample will necessarily reflect the type of people who visit that website and thus be a biased representation of the larger population (Dillman, 2000). Some control over the resulting sample can be maintained by requiring participants to meet certain inclusion criteria (Van Selm & Jankowski, 2006).

Some web surveys are designed to reduce coverage bias by providing computers and Internet connections to those who do not have them. This design-based recruitment method begins by contacting people by phone and providing those who agree to participate with whatever equipment they lack. This approach considerably increases the cost of the survey, so it is normally used as part of creating the panel of respondents who agree to be contacted for multiple surveys over time. The start-up costs can then be spread across many surveys. Another approach to reducing coverage bias in web surveys is to recruit a volunteer panel of Internet users and then with the resulting sample to make it comparable to the general population in such demographics as gender, race, age, and education (Couper & Miller, 2009).

In contrast to problems of coverage, web surveys have some unique advantages (Tourangeau et al., 2012; Van Selm & Jankowski, 2006). Questionnaires completed on the Web can elicit more honest reports of illicit behavior and of victimization as compared with phone interviews (Kreuter, Presser & Tourangeau, 2008; Parks, Pardi, & Bradizza, 2006). Onoye, Geobert, and Nishimura (2012) found that conducting a survey on the Web increased self-reports of substance use compared with a paper-and-pencil survey. Web surveys are relatively easy to complete because respondents simply click on response boxes, and the survey can be programmed to move respondents easily through sets of questions, not presenting questions that do not apply to the respondent, thus leading to higher item completion rates (Kreuter et al., 2008).

Use of the visual, interactive web medium can also help. Pictures, sounds, and animation can be used as a focus of particular questions, and graphic and typographic variation can be used to enhance visual survey appeal. Definitions of terms can "pop up" when respondents scroll over them (Dillman, 2007). In these ways, a skilled Web programmer can generate a survey layout with many attractive features that make it more likely that respondents will give their answers and have a clear understanding of the question (Smyth, Dillman, Christian, & Stern, 2004). Responses can quickly be checked to make sure they fall within the allowable range. Because answers are recorded directly in the researcher's database, data entry errors are almost eliminated and results can be reported quickly.

Surveys are also now being conducted through social media such as Facebook, on smartphones, and via text messages (Sue & Ritter, 2012). Research continues into the ways that the design of web surveys can influence rates of initial response, the likelihood of completing the survey, and the validity of responses. At this point, there is reason enough to consider the option of a web survey for many studies, but proceed with caution and consider carefully their strengths and weaknesses when designing a web survey of any type and when analyzing findings from it.

Mixed-Mode Surveys

Survey researchers increasingly are combining different survey designs to improve the overall participation rate and to take advantage of the unique strengths of different methods. Mixed-mode surveys allow the strengths of one survey design to compensate for the weaknesses of another and they can maximize the likelihood of securing data from different types of respondents (Dillman, 2007; Van Selm & Jankowski, 2006). For example, a survey may be sent electronically to sample members who have e-mail addresses and mailed to those who do not. Phone reminders may be used to encourage responses to web or paper surveys, or a letter of introduction may be sent in advance of calls in a phone survey (Guterbock, 2008). Alternatively, nonrespondents to a mailed survey may be interviewed in person or over the phone. An interviewer may use a self-administered questionnaire to present sensitive questions to a respondent.

The mixed-mode approach is not a perfect solution. Respondents to the same questions may give different answers because of the survey mode, rather than because they actually have different opinions. Respondents to phone survey questions tend to endorse more extreme responses to scalar questions (which range from more to less) than respondents to mailed or web surveys (Dillman, 2007). When responses differ by survey mode, there is often no way to know which responses are more accurate (Kreuter et al., 2008; Peterson, 2000). However, the use of the same question structures, response choices, and skip instructions across modes substantially reduces the likelihood of mode effects, as does using a small number of response choices for each question (Dillman, 2000; Dillman & Christian, 2005). Web survey researchers are still learning the effect of visual appearance on the response to questions (Dillman, 2007).

A Comparison of Survey Designs

Which survey design should be used when? Group-administered surveys are similar in most respects to mailed surveys except that they require the unusual circumstance of having access to the sample in a group setting. We therefore do not need to consider this survey design by itself; what applies to mailed surveys applies to group-administered survey designs, with the exception of sampling issues. The features of mixed-mode surveys depend on the survey types that are being combined. Thus, we can focus our comparison on the four survey designs that involve the use of a questionnaire with individuals sampled from a larger population: mailed surveys, phone surveys, in-person surveys, and electronic surveys. Exhibit 9.9 summarizes the strong and weak points of each design.

The most important consideration is the response rate each design will likely generate. In this respect, mailed surveys must be considered the least-preferred survey design from a sampling standpoint. However, researchers may still prefer a mailed survey when they have to reach a widely dispersed population and do not have enough financial resources to hire and train interview staff or to contract with a survey organization that already has interview staff available in many locations.

Contracting with an established survey research organization for a phone survey is often the best alternative to a mailed survey. The persistent follow-up attempts that are necessary to secure an adequate response rate are much easier over the phone than in person. But the process requires an increasing number of callbacks, and rates of response have declined. Current federal law prohibits automated dialing of cell phone numbers, so it is very costly to include the growing number of cell phone only individuals in a phone survey. However, the declining rate of response to phone interview calls is reducing the advantages of the method. Phone surveys tend to be shorter and the question format less complex. Respondents tend to lose interest during the survey. They tend to offer responses that will complete the survey more quickly and they tend to be less trusting of the survey motives (Holbrook, Green, & Krosnick, 2003).

| Exhibit 9.9 | Advantages and Disadvantages of Four Survey Designs |

Characteristics of Design	Mail Survey	Phone Survey	In-Person Survey	Web Survey
Representative sample				
Opportunity for inclusion is known				
For completely listed populations	High	High	High	Medium
For incompletely listed populations	Medium	Medium	High	Low
Selection within sampling units is controlled (e.g., specific family members must respond)	Medium	High	High	Low
Respondents are likely to be located:				
If samples are heterogeneous	Medium	High	High	Low
If samples are homogeneous and specialized	High	High	High	High
Questionnaire construction and question design				
Allowable length of questionnaire	Medium	Medium	High	Medium
Ability to include:				
Complex questions	Medium	Low	High	High
Open questions	Low	High	High	Medium
Screening questions	Low	High	High	High
Tedious, boring questions	Low	High	High	Low
Ability to control question sequence	Low	High	High	High
Ability to ensure questionnaire completion	Medium	High	High	Low
Distortion of answers				
Odds of avoiding social desirability bias	High	Medium	Low	High
Odds of avoiding interviewer distortion	High	Medium	Low	High
Odds of avoiding contamination by others	Medium	High	Medium	Medium
Administrative goals				
Odds of meeting personnel requirements	High	High	Low	Medium
Odds of implementing quickly	Low	High	Low	High
Odds of keeping costs low	High	Medium	Low	High

Source: Dillman, D. A. (2007). *Mail and internet surveys: The tailored design method* (2nd ed.). Hoboken, NJ: Wiley & Sons.

In-person surveys are clearly preferable in terms of the possible length and complexity of the questionnaire, as well as the researcher's ability to monitor conditions while the questionnaire is being completed. Mailed surveys often are preferable for asking sensitive questions, although this problem can be lessened in an interview by giving respondents a separate sheet to fill out on their own. Although interviewers may distort results, either by changing the wording of questions or failing to record answers properly, this problem can be lessened by careful training, monitoring, and tape recording of the answers.

The advantages and disadvantages of electronic surveys must be weighed in light of the population to be surveyed and capabilities at the time that the survey is to be conducted. At this time, too many people lack Internet connections for general use of Internet surveying. But when the entire sample has access and ability, web-based surveys can be very effective.

These various points about the different survey designs lead to two general conclusions. First, in-person interviews are the strongest design and generally preferable when sufficient resources and trained interview staff are available; telephone surveys have many of the advantages of in-person interviews at much less cost, but response rates are an increasing problem. Second, the "best" survey design for any particular study must take the unique features and goals of the study into account.

⊞ Survey Research Design in a Diverse Society

Whether designing questions, constructing questionnaires, or choosing a data collection method, we must consider cultural differences and the impact of these differences. Although the term *culture* is often linked to ethnicity, shared belief systems may develop among members of different social groups (A. Stewart & Nápoles-Springer, 2000). Therefore, when we speak of culture, we include different population groups such as gender, ethnicity, age cohort, or socioeconomic class. When developing individual questions, we need to be careful about our choice of language; when constructing the questionnaire, we need to ensure that the format conveys the same meaning for all respondents; when deciding on a data collection method, particularly interviewing, we may find that responses to questions may be affected by interviewer–respondent characteristics.

Researchers would like to have all survey respondents attach the same meaning to a question; therefore, it is necessary to ensure that the question has the same meaning across different population subgroups. Although it is important that the wording be appropriate for different groups, it is also necessary to show that the concept being examined is equivalent across groups—that questions adequately reflect group values, traditions, and beliefs (Marin & Marin, 1991). For example, there can be wide variation in the meaning of the concept *family*. There are differences in both the boundaries used to establish membership in the family and the expectations and obligations of family members (Luna et al., 1996). The wording of a particular question and the available response categories would need to account for these differences.

In Chapter 4, we addressed the issue of measurement equivalence with a particular focus on methods to evaluate the equivalence of scales. Questions and measures should capture not only universal definitions of the concept, but also group-specific concerns and issues (A. Stewart & Nápoles-Springer, 2000). We return to some of the methods described in this chapter to illustrate how researchers examine the meaning of concepts, questions, and words and use what they learn to revise questions and instruments.

Anna Nápoles-Springer, Jasmine Santoyo-Olsson, Helen O'Brien, and Anita Stewart (2006) describe the process of using cognitive interviews in combination with behavioral coding and content analysis of the interviewer–respondent interaction to improve the wording and format of a health questionnaire. The cognitive interview included probes about the meaning of specific words, whether some questions were redundant, what respondents were thinking as they heard and answered questions, whether questions were offensive, and whether the items were culturally appropriate. Behavior coding of tapes and transcripts was done to assess the interview process and included problems such as an interviewer accidentally or purposefully skipping a question, reacting to a response, or changing the meaning of the question or a respondent not understanding the question, giving a response not on a scale, or not answering the question but telling an irrelevant story. For example, they found different interpretations for specific words such as *medical procedures* among Whites, African Americans, Latinos interviewed in English, and Latinos interviewed in Spanish and, therefore, had to provide different wording for each group.

Bonnie Green, Joyce Chung, Anahita Daroowalla, Stacey Kaltman, and Caroline DeBenedictis (2006) were concerned that a measure to screen for a history of traumatic events that had been developed with college women might not be effective with other population groups. They conducted focus groups with low-income African American women to learn about the kinds of events that were seen as stressful, why the events were stressful, whether they were traumatic, and how the events related to health and mental health. With a second group of African American women, they conducted cognitive interviews of their questionnaire, asking questions about the meaning of each question, the meaning of specific words, and the ease of remembering the questions. Finally, they reviewed past videotaped assessments to record how questions were asked by interviewers and questions requiring clarification. For the most part, they found that the language was appropriate, as was the meaning of the questions, but there were instances of difficulties with some words as well as question length. As a result, they revised the instrument.

Translating Instruments

For many potential respondents, English is not their first language, and many would prefer to use their native language as they do so in their daily life. In the United States in 2011, 15.8% of persons aged 18 years and older were foreign born, and more than half of these adults said they did not speak English very well (Motel & Patten, 2013). Although English becomes the primary language spoken by almost all children of immigrants, many first-generation immigrants are not fluent in English (Hakimzadeh & Cohn, 2007). As a result, they can only be included in a survey if it is translated into their native language.

So, survey researchers find increasingly that they must translate their questionnaires into one or more languages to represent the population of interest. This does not mean doing a literal translation; such a translation may not result in statements that are interpreted in the same way to non-English speakers. In translating instruments, researchers want to produce questions that mean the same across different language instruments. Five dimensions should be evaluated to achieve this goal:

1. *Content equivalence.* The content of each item is relevant to the phenomena of each culture being studied.

2. *Semantic equivalence.* The meaning of each item is the same in each culture after translation into the language and idiom of each culture.

3. *Technical equivalence.* The method of assessment (e.g., pencil and paper, interview) is comparable in each culture with respect to the data that it yields.

4. *Criterion equivalence.* The interpretation of the measurement of the variable remains the same when compared with the norm for each culture studied.

5. *Conceptual equivalence.* The instrument is measuring the same theoretical concept in each culture. (Flaherty et al., 1988, p. 258)

Compounding this problem is the likelihood of regional differences in a language. We are familiar enough with this problem with English: A hoagie in Philadelphia is a sub elsewhere, a bubbler in Boston is a water fountain in Pittsburgh, and a queue in England is a line in the United States. Marin and Marin (1991) offer these suggestions to deal with regional variations for Hispanics, but in many ways these suggestions are generalizable when a particular language is used in many different countries:

1. Use all appropriate variations of a word in a self-administered questionnaire.

2. Target vocabulary variations to each subgroup. When there are subgroups, alter the wording to conform to the vocabulary of that subgroup.

3. Avoid colloquialisms. Colloquialisms may differ from place to place and add to the confusion of a word's meaning.

4. Use alternate questions. (pp. 85–86)

Ligia Chavez, Leida Matías-Carrelo, Concepcion Barrio, and Glorisa Canino (2007) used a complex process to achieve content, semantic, and technical equivalence in their efforts to adapt a Youth Quality of Life scale for Latinos. The instrument included such domains as sense of self, social relationships, environment, and general quality of life, as well as contextual and behavioral items. They used an iterative process known as **decentering**, which means that both the original and translated instruments are modified to increase their equivalence (Chavez et al., 2007). The original English and Spanish versions were reviewed by a bilingual committee composed of clinicians and researchers from Puerto Rico and then a multinational bilingual committee for such changes as wording, syntax, and colloquial use. This revised version was then assessed by 10 focus groups: 5 in Puerto Rico and 5 in Los Angeles. These groups included adolescents, parents, and clinicians. The focus groups began with discussions of "quality of life," the meaning of each domain, the meaning and relevance of each item, and the format of the instrument, rating scales, and instructions. Their comments were reviewed by the bilingual committee, which modified items based on the focus group comments; these changes were sent to the multilingual committee, which made further modifications, found universal Spanish equivalents where possible, or integrated multiple words to reflect differences in Mexican American and Puerto Rican cultures.

> **Decentering** Method of making equivalent different language versions of an instrument; it involves modifying both the original instrument and the translated instrument to increase their equivalence.

Chavez and colleagues (2007) believed that content equivalence was achieved through the reviews and evaluations of content by the two expert committees. Semantic equivalence was achieved through the translation and retranslation efforts. Technical, criterion, and conceptual equivalence would ultimately require data collection.

To prepare questions and measures for a pilot study, Milagros Rosal, Elena Carbone, and Karin Goins (2003) used cognitive interviewing with five older Hispanics to assess Spanish versions of four instruments designed to measure knowledge of diabetes, quality of life, self-management, and depression. Depending on the item, they used one or more of three cognitive interviewing techniques, including asking respondents to clarify the answer as they asked participants the questions, asking participants after the interview was completed about some questions, and using paraphrasing or asking participants to repeat the question in their own words. Rosal et al. found that respondents would answer the question even when they did not understand the question. One of the specific problems they identified was that participants did not understand or recall general instructions. For example, participants forgot the instructions to answer the depression items (Center for Epidemiologic Studies Depression scale); therefore, Rosal et al. modified the questions so that each item began with the time frame and asked respondents to indicate the number of days. They changed "I felt depressed" to "During the past week, how many days did you feel depressed?" (p. 1012).

Other researchers use less involved methods to translate concepts. For example, in a survey of Russian-speaking elderly, Tran, Khatutsky, Aroian, Balsam, and Conway (2000) used a male and a female translator to modify a survey. The modifications were reviewed in a focus group by bilingual health experts. To develop an instrument to be used with a group of Cuban Americans, Morano (2003) had the instrument translated into Spanish and then retranslated back into English. After modifications were made, the newly translated version was pilot tested, accompanied by an interview with respondents.

Interviewer–Respondent Characteristics

Ideally, the interviewer has no impact on the responses respondents proffer. Any interviewer impact would simply be random and not affect responses in some systematic way leading to biased response. There are concerns that particular interviewer characteristics can impact on respondents' willingness to respond to a survey question, how they respond, and whether they provide accurate responses (Davis, Couper, Janz, Caldwell, & Resnicow, 2010). These concerns take three directions: (1) Do specific interviewer characteristics impact on responses to surveys? (2) Is there a difference when interviewers and respondents are matched on certain characteristics? and (3) Do respondents desire a matching of characteristics? And such concerns include not just face-to-face interviews but also telephone interviews as respondents use voice cues to perceptually identify the interviewer's characteristics (Davis et al., 2010).

Davis and colleagues (2010) reviewed public health survey studies dating back to the 1950s and reported several conclusions regarding these three questions including the following:

- Interviewer race did affect nonresponse and the type of response on sensitive topics such as substance abuse or physical abuse or attitudes related to race-related issues.

- Interviewer gender may have an impact on reports of certain health and mental health conditions, substance abuse, and gender-related attitudes.

- Such findings are found in both face-to-face and telephone interviews.

- There is insufficient research to draw conclusions about ethnic or gender matching.

- There is insufficient research evidence as to the preferences of respondents.

As you might surmise, there is still much for researchers to learn about interviewer effects.

🔲 Implications for Evidence-Based Practice

The survey research designs we have described in this chapter are typically not used to test the effectiveness of a particular intervention, although the methods described in this chapter are relevant to data gathering for any of the quantitative designs. Survey research designs can be used to evaluate the impact of social policies, and these designs often provide critical information about the need, availability, and utilization of various services.

In Chapter 6, we distinguished between cross-sectional and longitudinal designs. In a cross-sectional survey, data are collected at a single time point. Depending on the research question, it is possible to determine whether a program had an effect on participants assuming that data were collected on the relevant variables. For example, one of the desired outcomes of the Women and Infant Children's program (WIC) is the baby's birth weight. You can compare participants in WIC with eligible nonparticipants and determine whether the program made a difference. Statistical controls can enable you to evaluate the impact while holding other variables constant. Panel designs provide additional evidence that a program may have had an effect. Because data are collected over time with the same respondents, it is possible to see the impact of a program if the participation occurs during the course of the panel. Therefore, survey research can and does provide useful evidence.

Another use of survey research for evidence-based practice is that it provides information about the use or lack of use of various programs. Survey research can be used to address important questions such as these: What is the prevalence of a particular status or condition? Are services being used? What are the barriers to service use? What characteristics distinguish between those who use and those who do not use a service? Although these questions do not address specifically the effectiveness of a particular intervention or program, these data can be used to improve treatment delivery (Clark, Power, Le Fauve, & Lopez, 2008).

🔲 Ethical Issues in Survey Research

Survey research usually poses fewer ethical dilemmas than do experimental or field research designs. Potential respondents to a survey can easily decline to participate, and a cover letter or introductory statement that identifies the sponsors of and motivations for the survey gives them the information required to make this decision. The data collection methods are quite obvious in a survey, so little is concealed from the respondents. Only in group-administered survey designs might the respondents be, in effect, a captive audience (probably of students or employees), so special attention is required to ensure that participation is truly voluntary. (Those who do not wish to participate may be told they can just hand in a blank form.)

If the survey could possibly have any harmful effects for the respondents, these should be disclosed fully in the cover letter or introductory statement. The procedures used to reduce such effects should also be delineated, including how the researcher will keep interviews confidential or anonymous. Surveys that attempt to measure sensitive subject matter should have other protections in place. When asking respondents to recall sensitive topics, there is the possibility of causing respondents emotional harm. Respondents might be offered a phone number they can call if they are emotionally upset.

Many surveys include some essential questions that might in some way prove damaging to the subjects if their answers were disclosed. To prevent any possibility of harm to subjects due to disclosure of such information, it is critical to preserve subject **confidentiality**. Nobody but research personnel should have access to information that could be used to link respondents to their responses, and even that access should be limited to what is necessary for specific research purposes. Only numbers should be used to identify respondents on their questionnaires, and the names that correspond to these numbers should be kept in a safe location, unavailable to staff and others who might otherwise come across them. Follow-up mailings or contact attempts that require linking the ID numbers with names and

> **Confidentiality** Provided by research in which identifying information that could be used to link respondents to their responses is available only to designated research personnel for specific research needs.
>
> **Anonymity** Provided by research in which no identifying information is recorded that could be used to link respondents to their responses.

addresses should be carried out by trustworthy assistants under close supervision. For electronic surveys, encryption technology should be used to make information provided over the Internet secure from unauthorized people.

Few surveys can provide true **anonymity** so that no identifying information is ever recorded to link respondents with their responses. The main problem with anonymous surveys is that they preclude follow-up attempts to encourage participation by initial nonrespondents, and they prevent panel designs, which measure change through repeated surveys of the same individuals. In-person surveys rarely can be anonymous because an interviewer must in almost all cases know the name and address of the interviewee. However, phone surveys that are meant only to sample opinion at one point in time, as in political polls, can safely be completely anonymous. When no future follow-up is desired, group-administered surveys also can be anonymous. To provide anonymity in a mailed survey, the researcher should omit identifying codes from the questionnaire but could include a self-addressed, stamped postcard so the respondent can notify the researcher that the questionnaire has been returned without creating any linkage to the questionnaire (Mangione, 1995).

▣ Conclusion

Survey research is an exceptionally efficient and productive method for investigating a wide array of social research questions. In addition to the potential benefits for social science, considerations of time and expense frequently make a survey the preferred data collection method. One or more of the survey designs reviewed in this chapter can be applied to almost any research question. Surveys are one of the most popular research methods in social work. As use of the Internet increases, survey research should become even more efficient and popular.

The relative ease of conducting at least some types of survey research leads many people to imagine that no particular training or systematic procedures are required. Nothing could be further from the truth. But as a result of this widespread misconception, you will encounter a great many nearly worthless survey results. You must be prepared to examine carefully the procedures used in any survey before accepting its findings as credible. And if you decide to conduct a survey, you must be prepared to invest the time and effort required by proper procedures.

Key Terms

Highlights

- Surveys are the most popular form of social research because of their versatility, efficiency, and generalizability. Many survey data sets, like the Survey of Income and Program Participation or the General Social Survey, are available for social work researchers and students.

- Survey designs must minimize the risk of errors of observation (measurement error) and errors of nonobservation (errors due to inadequate coverage, sampling error, and nonresponse). The likelihood of both types of error varies with the survey goals.

- A survey questionnaire or interview schedule should be designed as an integrated whole, with each question and section serving some clear purpose and complementing the others.

- Questions must be worded carefully to avoid confusing respondents, encouraging a less-than-honest response, or triggering biases. Question wording should have the same meaning to all respondents regardless of race, ethnicity, gender, age, or class.

- Inclusion of Don't know choices and neutral responses may help, but the presence of such options also affects the distribution of answers. Open-ended questions can be used to determine the meaning that respondents attach to their answers. Answers to any survey questions may be affected by the questions that precede them in a questionnaire or interview schedule.

- Questions can be tested and improved through review by experts, focus group discussions, cognitive interviews, interpretive questions, and pilot testing. Every questionnaire and interview schedule should be pretested on a small sample that is like the sample to be surveyed.

- The cover letter for a mailed questionnaire should be credible, personalized, interesting, and responsible.

- Response rates in mailed surveys are typically well below 70% unless multiple mailings are made to nonrespondents and the questionnaire and cover letter are attractive, interesting, and carefully planned. Response rates for group-administered surveys are usually much higher.

- Phone interviews using random digit dialing allow fast turn-around and efficient sampling. Multiple call-backs are often required, and the rate of nonresponse to phone interviews is rising.

- In-person interviews have several advantages over other types of surveys: They allow longer and more complex interview schedules, monitoring of the conditions when the questions are answered, probing for respondents' understanding of the questions, and high response rates. However, the interviewer must balance the need to establish rapport with the respondent with the importance of maintaining control over the delivery of the interview questions.

- Electronic surveys may be e-mailed or posted on the Web. Interactive voice-response systems using the telephone are another option. At this time, use of the Internet is not sufficiently widespread to allow e-mail or web surveys of the general population, but these approaches can be fast and efficient for populations with high rates of computer use.

- The decision to use a particular survey design must take into account the particular features and goals of the study. In general, in-person interviews are the strongest but most expensive survey design.

- For survey data to be valid, question wording should convey the same meaning to different population groups. This may require translating and retranslating questions.

- Most survey research poses few ethical problems because respondents are able to decline to participate—an option that should be stated clearly in the cover letter or introductory statement. Special care must be taken when questionnaires are administered in group settings (to "captive audiences") and when sensitive personal questions are to be asked; subject confidentiality should always be preserved.

Discussion Questions

1. Why is survey research popular among social work researchers and social service agencies? Although popular, survey research is at risk for error. What are the two potential errors common in survey research? How can the researcher minimize the risk of error?

2. Thinking about the primary benefits and disadvantages of each of the five basic survey designs, which would you choose if you were interested in learning more about the caregiver burden experienced by parents raising young children younger than the age of 6? How would you try to ensure sample representativeness? What steps would you take to maximize the rate or response?

Practice Exercises

1. Develop 10 survey questions about social work students' beliefs about poverty. Did you use open- or closed-ended questions or both? What demographic information did you query? Did you attend to attractiveness? Is the instrument user-friendly?

2. After putting the survey you have developed for Practice Exercise 1 away for several days, review the questions for the following: confusing phrasing, vague language, double negatives, double-barreled questions, jargon, and leading questions. Once you have revised your survey instrument, pilot it with your classmates. Ask for their critical feedback.

3. Examine an existing instrument measuring beliefs about attitudes toward poverty. Would you consider using this instrument for your own research? Why or why not? How does the published instrument compare to yours? Is it measuring the same concept?

4. Design a survey experiment to determine the effect of phrasing a question or its response choices in different ways. Check recent issues of a local newspaper for a question used in a survey of attitudes about some social policy. Propose some hypothesis about how the wording of the question or its response choices might have influenced the answers people gave, and devise an alternative that differs only in this respect. Distribute these questionnaires to a large class (after your instructor makes the necessary arrangements) to test your hypothesis.

Web Exercise

1. Go to the Research Triangle Institute website (www.rti.org). Click on Survey Research & Services, and then Capabilities. Read about their methods under Data Collection Systems and then Cognitive Pretesting. What does this add to the treatment of these topics in this chapter?

2. Go to the Question Bank at http://surveynet.ac.uk/sqb/surveys .asp. Go to Topics and find a topic of interest to you. Click on the topic and then click on one of the listed surveys or survey sections that interest you. Review 10 questions used in the survey, and critique them in terms of the principles for question writing that you have learned. Do you find any question features that might be attributed to the use of British English? How might you change those features?

Developing a Research Proposal

These questions apply to survey research as well as to data collection in group and single-subject designs.

1. How will you gather the data? What specific data collection method will you use (e.g., mail, telephone interview, self-administered)?

2. Write questions for a one-page questionnaire that relate to your proposed research question. The questions should operationalize the variables on which you are focused.

3. Conduct a pretest of the questionnaire by conducting cognitive interviews with several respondents. For example, if you have closed-ended questions, ask respondents what they meant by each response or what came to mind when they were asked each question.

4. Polish up the organization and layout of the questionnaire following the guidelines in the chapter.

5. List the relative advantages and disadvantages to the way you will collect the data.

6. Develop appropriate procedures for the protection of human subjects in your study. Include a cover letter directed to the appropriate population that contains relevant statements about research ethics.

A Question of Ethics

1. How can researchers ameliorate the negative consequences that responding to a survey on experiences with trauma may have? What responsibility do researchers have in providing respondents with safety should they need it? Write a short statement in response to each question.

Qualitative Methods

"You have to look into a patient's eyes as much as you can, and learn to get the signals from there." This suggestion was made by a nurse explaining to future nursing home assistants how they were to deal with a dying patient. One of those future assistants, Timothy Diamond (1992), was also a researcher intent on studying work in nursing homes. For us, the statement he recorded has a dual purpose: It exemplifies qualitative methods, in which we learn by observing as we participate in a natural setting; it also reminds us that some features of the social world are ill suited to investigation with experiments or surveys.

In this chapter, you will learn how some of our greatest insights into the social processes that influence social work can result from what appear to be ordinary activities: observing, participating, listening, and talking. You will also learn that qualitative research is much more than just doing what comes naturally in social situations. Qualitative researchers must observe keenly, take notes systematically, question respondents strategically, and prepare to spend more time and invest more of their whole selves than often occurs with experiments or surveys. Moreover, if we are to have any confidence in the validity of a qualitative study's conclusions, each element of its design must be reviewed as carefully as we would review the elements of an experiment, single-subject design, or survey. The result of careful use of these methods can lead to insights that are ill suited to investigation with experiments or surveys and to social processes that defy quantification.

The chapter begins with an overview of the major features of qualitative research, as reflected in Diamond's (1992) study of nursing homes. The next section discusses the various approaches to participant observation research, which is the most distinctive qualitative method, and it reviews the stages of research using participant observation. Next, we review in some detail the issues involved in intensive interviewing before briefly describing focus groups, an increasingly popular qualitative method. The last three sections cover issues associated with evidence-based practice, diversity, and ethical issues that are of concern in qualitative research. By the chapter's end, you should appreciate the hard work required to translate "doing what comes naturally" into systematic research, be able to recognize strong and weak points in qualitative studies, and be ready to do some of it yourself.

▣ Fundamentals of Qualitative Methods

Qualitative methods refer to a variety of research techniques that share some basic features. First, we identify the features they have in common and then summarize how Timothy Diamond (1992) used qualitative methods to illuminate the inside of a nursing home and the attitudes and actions of staff. We conclude the section by providing more detail about several specific qualitative methods that exemplify the approach.

Features of Qualitative Methods

Although qualitative designs differ in many respects, they share several features that distinguish them from experimental and survey research designs (Denzin & Lincoln, 1994; Maxwell, 2005; Wolcott, 1995).

Collection primarily of qualitative rather than quantitative data. Any research design may collect both qualitative and quantitative data, but qualitative methods emphasize observations about natural behavior and artifacts that capture social life as it is experienced by the participants rather than in categories predetermined by the researcher.

Exploratory research questions, with a commitment to inductive reasoning. Qualitative researchers typically begin their projects seeking not to test preformulated hypotheses but to discover what people think, how they act, and why, in some social setting. Only after many observations do qualitative researchers try to develop general principles to account for their observations.

A focus on previously unstudied processes and unanticipated phenomena. Previously unstudied attitudes and actions cannot adequately be understood with a structured set of questions or within a highly controlled experiment. So qualitative methods have their greatest appeal when we need to explore new issues, investigate hard-to-study groups, or determine the meaning people give to their lives and actions. Diamond (1992) asked, "What was life like inside, day in and day out? Who lived in nursing homes, and what did they do there?" (p. 4).

An orientation to social context, to the interconnections between social phenomena rather than to their discrete features. The context of concern may be a program or organization, a case, or a broader social context. For example, Gary Stein, Nancy Beckerman, and Patricia Sherman (2010) wanted to learn about the concerns that gay and lesbian elders had about long-term care given their unique life experiences from those who were living this experience.

A focus on human subjectivity, on the meanings that participants attach to events and that people give to their lives. "Through life stories, people 'account for their lives.' . . . The themes people create are the means by which they interpret and evaluate their life experiences and attempt to integrate these experiences to form a self-concept" (Kaufman, 1986, pp. 24–25).

Use of idiographic rather than nomothetic causal explanation. With its focus on particular actors and situations and the processes that connect them, qualitative research tends to identify causes as particular events embedded within an unfolding, interconnected action sequence (Maxwell, 2005, pp. 20–21). The language of variables and hypotheses appears only rarely in the qualitative literature.

Reflexive research design, in which the design develops as the research progresses.

> Each component of the design may need to be reconsidered or modified in response to new developments or to changes in some other component. . . . The activities of collecting and analyzing data, developing and modifying theory, elaborating or refocusing the research questions, and identifying and eliminating validity threats are usually all going on more or less simultaneously, each influencing all of the others. (Maxwell, 2005, pp. 2–3)

J. Neil Henderson (1994) explains how a qualitative research design changed in a study of the involvement of ethnic minority elders in support groups. In the original plan, support group meetings were to be held at one African American church after publicity in other churches. After this approach failed to generate any participation, the researchers learned that the plan violated strong implicit "congregational loyalty boundaries." When the meetings were instead held in a neutral setting unaffiliated with any of the churches (a local public library), many community members attended.

Sensitivity to the subjective role of the researcher (reflexivity). Qualitative researchers recognize that their perspective on social phenomena will reflect in part their own background and current situation. Who the researcher is and "where he or she is coming from" can affect what the research finds. Some qualitative researchers believe that the goal of developing a purely objective view of the social world is impossible, but they discuss their own feelings about what they have studied so that others can consider how these feelings affected their findings.

> I was embarrassed and I did not know what to say. I had not bargained for this kind of experience when my research started. As I sat by his bed, my mind would be a confusing welter of thoughts and emotions. Sometimes I experienced anger. "Damn it. You can't die now. I haven't finished my research." Immediately I would be overtaken by feelings of self revulsion. Did our friendship mean only this? . . . Thus would I engage in the conflict between my human sensibilities and my scholarly purpose. (Rowles, 1978, p. 19)

William Miller and Benjamin Crabtree (1999) capture the entire process of qualitative research in a simple diagram (Exhibit 10.1). In this diagram, qualitative research begins with the qualitative researcher reflecting on the setting and the researcher's relation to it and interpretations of it. The researcher then describes the goals and means for the research. This description is followed by *sampling* and *collecting* data, *describing* the data, and *organizing* that data. Thus, the *gathering* and *analysis processes* proceed together, with repeated description and analysis of data as they are collected. As the data are organized, *connections* are identified between different data segments, and efforts are made to *corroborate* the credibility of these connections. This *interpretive process* begins to emerge in a written account that represents what has been done and how the data have been interpreted. Each of these steps in the research process informs the others and is repeated throughout the research process.

Making Gray Gold

You can get a better feel for qualitative methods by reading the following excerpts from Timothy Diamond's (1992) book about nursing homes, *Making Gray Gold*, and reasoning inductively from his observations. See if you can induce from these particulars some of the general features of field research. Ask yourself: What was the research question? How were the issues of generalizability, measurement, and causation approached? How did social factors influence the research? To conduct this study, Diamond became a nursing home assistant. In his own words:

Exhibit 10.1 Qualitative Research Process

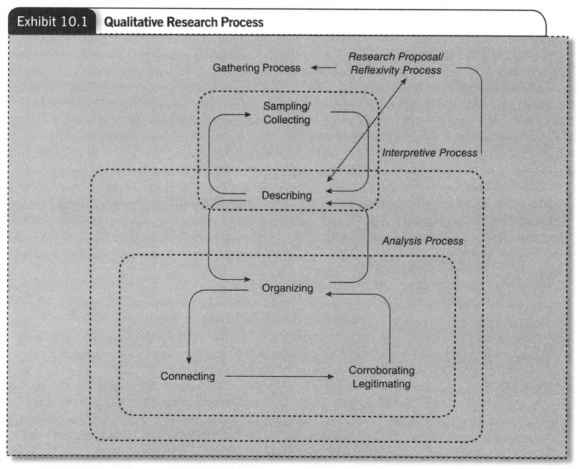

Source: Adapted from W. Miller and Crabtree (1999, p.16).

First I went to school for six months in 1982, two evenings a week and all day Saturdays, to obtain the certificate the state required [to work in a nursing home]. Then, after weeks of searching for jobs, I worked in three different nursing homes in Chicago for periods of three to four months each. (p. 5)

As this excerpt indicates, Diamond's research involved becoming a participant in the social setting that was the object of his study. Diamond spent more than a year gathering data as he worked full-time as an aide.

Diamond (1992) also describes the development of his research questions. His curiosity about health care for older people was piqued when he happened to become acquainted with Ina Williams and Aileen Crawford in a coffee shop across the street from the nursing home where they worked as assistants. He began to wonder:

How does the work of caretaking become defined and get reproduced day in and day out as a business? . . . How, in other words, does the everyday world of Ina and Aileen and their co-workers, and that of the people they tend, get turned into a system in which gray can be written about in financial journals as producing gold, a classic metaphor for money? What is the process of making gray gold? (p. 5)

With these exploratory research questions in mind, Diamond (1992) explains why he chose participant observation as his research method: "I wanted to collect stories and to experience situations like those Ina and Aileen had begun to describe. I decided that . . . I would go inside to experience the work myself" (p. 5).

The choice of participant observation precluded random sampling of cases, but Diamond (1992) did not ignore the need to generalize his findings. He went to considerable lengths to include three nursing homes that would represent a range of care-giving arrangements:

These [nursing] homes were situated in widely different neighborhoods of the city. In one of them residents paid for their own care, often with initial help from Medicare. In the other two, most of the residents were supported by Medicaid. . . . In the course of writing, I visited many homes across the United States to validate my observations and to update them in instances where regulatory changes had been instituted. (p. 6)

The data in Diamond's (1992) study were notes on the activities of the people as he observed and interacted with them. He did not use structured questionnaires and other formal data collection instruments, so his data are primarily qualitative rather than quantitative.

As for his method, it was inductive. First he gathered data. Then, as data collection continued, Diamond (1992) figured out how to interpret the data—how to make sense of the social situations he was studying. His analytic categories ultimately came not from social theory but from the categories by which people described one another and made sense of their social world. These categories seem to have broad applicability, suggesting the generalizability of the researcher's findings. For instance, the teachers Diamond encountered while earning his certificate passed along a distinct way of making sense of the caregiver's role in a nursing home:

The tensions generated by the introductory lecture . . . ideas of career professionalism were reflected in our conversations as we waited for the second class to get under way. Yet within the next half hour they seemed to dissolve. Mrs. Bonderoid, our teacher, saw to that. A registered nurse and nurse practitioner, an African American woman of about fifty, she must have understood a lot about classroom jitters and about who was sitting in front of her as well. "What this is going to take," she instructed, "is a lot of mother's wit." "Mother's wit," which connotes native intelligence irrespective of gender. She was talking about maternal feelings and skills. (p. 17)

Diamond (1992) did develop general conclusions about social life from his research. In the nursing home, he argues, "there were two kinds of narratives on caregiving: one formal, written, and shared by the professionals and administrators; another submerged, unwritten, and shared by the people who lived and worked on the floors" (p. 215).

To summarize, Diamond's (1992) research began with an exploratory question (to find out what was going on) and proceeded inductively throughout, developing general concepts to make sense of specific observations. Although Diamond, a White man, was something of an outsider in a setting dominated by women of color, he was able to share many participants' experiences and perspectives. His connecting sequences of events enabled him to construct plausible explanations about what seemed to be a typical group. He thus used qualitative research to explore human experiences in depth, carefully analyzing the social contexts in which they occur.

Basics of Qualitative Research

You can understand better how these different features make qualitative methods so distinct by learning the basics of specific qualitative methods and some of the insights those methods produced in leading section. We show how different qualitative research can produce insights about whole settings and cultures.

The Case Study

You can think of Diamond's research on the nursing home as representing a case study. **Case study** is not so much a single method as it is a way of thinking about what qualitative data analysis can, or perhaps should, focus on. The case may be an organization, community, social group, family, or even an individual, and as far as the qualitative analyst is concerned, it must be understood in its entirety. The idea is that the social world really functions as an integrated whole, so that the focus in quantitative research on variables and hypotheses "slices and dices" that whole in a way that can obscure how it actually functions.

Case Study A setting or group that the analyst treats as an integrated social unit that must be studied holistically and its particularity.

Educational researcher Robert Stake (1995) presents the logic of the case study approach:

> Case study is the study of the particularity and complexity of a single case, coming to understand its activity within important circumstances. . . . The qualitative researcher emphasizes episodes of nuance, the sequentiality of happenings in context, the wholeness of the individual. (pp. xi–xii)

Thick description A rich description that conveys a sense of what an experience is like from the standpoint of the natural actors in the setting.

Central to much qualitative case study research is the goal of creating a **thick description** of the setting studied, one that provides a sense of what it is like to experience that setting from the standpoint of the natural actors in that setting (Geertz, 1973). Stake's (1995) description of "a case within a case," a student in a school he studied, illustrates how a thick description gives a feel of the place and people within it:

> At 8:30 a.m. on Thursday morning, Adam shows up at the cafeteria door. Breakfast is being served but Adam doesn't go in. The woman giving out meal chits has her hands on him, seems to be sparring with him, verbally. And then he disappears. Adam is one of five siblings; all arrive at school in the morning with less than usual parent attention. Short, with a beautifully sculpted head. . . . Adam is a person of notice.

> At 8:55 he climbs the stairs to the third floor with other upper graders, turning to block the girls behind them and thus a string of others. Adam manages to keep the girls off-balance until Ms. Crain . . . spots him and gets traffic moving again. Mr. Garson . . . notices Adam, has a few quiet words with him before a paternal shove toward the room. (p. 150)

You will learn in the next sections how qualitative methodologists design research that can generate thick descriptions of particular cases.

Ethnography

Ethnography is the study of a culture or cultures that some group of people shares (Van Maanen, 1995). It is useful when one wants to understand *how* questions about social or economic processes evolve over time (Yin, 2003). As a method, it usually is meant to refer to the process by which a single investigator is immersed in the group for a long time (often 1 or more years), gradually establishing

> **Ethnography** The study of a culture or cultures that some group of people shares, using participant observation and/or interviewing over an extended period.

trust and experiencing the social world as do the participants (Madden 2010). Ethnographic research can be called *naturalistic*, because it seeks to describe and understand the natural social world as it is, in all its richness and detail. The goal is best achieved when an ethnographer is fluent in the local language and spends enough time in the setting to know how people live, what they say about themselves, what they actually do, and what they value (Armstrong, 2008).

There are no particular methodological techniques associated with ethnography, other than just "being there." The analytic process relies on the thoroughness and insight of the researcher to "tell it like it is" in the setting as he or she experienced it.

Code of the Street, Elijah Anderson's (1999) award-winning study of Philadelphia's inner city, captures the flavor of this approach:

> My primary aim in this work is to render ethnographically the social and cultural dynamics of the interpersonal violence that is currently undermining the quality of life of too many urban neighborhoods. . . . How do the people of the setting perceive their situation? What assumptions do they bring to their decision making? (pp. 10–11)

Like most traditional ethnographers, Anderson (1999) describes his concern with being "as objective as possible" and using his training as other ethnographers do "to look for and to recognize underlying assumptions, their own and those of their subjects, and to try to override the former and uncover the latter" (p. 11). From analysis of the data obtained in these ways, a rich description emerges of life in the inner city. Although we often do not "hear" the residents speak, we feel the community's pain in Anderson's (1999) description of "the aftermath of death":

> When a young life is cut down, almost everyone goes into mourning. The first thing that happens is that a crowd gathers about the site of the shooting or the incident. The police then arrive, drawing more of a crowd. Since such a death often occurs close to the victim's house, his mother or his close relatives and friends may be on the scene of the killing. When they arrive, the women and girls often wail and moan, crying out their grief for all to hear, while the young men simply look on, in studied silence. . . . Soon the ambulance arrives. (p. 138)

Anderson (1999) uses these descriptions as a foundation on which he develops the key concepts in his analysis, such as "code of the street":

> The "code of the street" is not the goal or product of any individual's actions but is the fabric of everyday life, a vivid and pressing milieu within which all local residents must shape their personal routines, income strategies, and orientations to schooling, as well as their mating, parenting, and neighbor relations. (p. 326)

Anderson's report on his related Jelly's Bar study illustrates how his understanding deepened as he became more socially integrated into the group. He thus became more successfully at "blending the local knowledge one has learned with what we already know sociologically about such settings" (Anderson, 2005 p. 51).

> I engaged the denizens of the corner and wrote detailed field notes about my experiences, and from time to time I looked for patterns and relationships in my notes. In this way, an understanding of the setting came

to me in time, especially as I participated more fully in the life of the corner and wrote my field notes about my experiences; as my notes accumulated and as I reviewed them occasionally and supplemented them with conceptual memos to myself, their meanings became more clear, while even more questions emerged. (Anderson, 2005, p. 41)

A good ethnography like Anderson's is only possible when the ethnographer learns the subtleties of expression used in a group and the multiple meanings that can be given to statements or acts (Armstrong, 2008). Good ethnographies also include some reflection by the researcher on the influence his or her own background has had on research plans, as well as on the impact of the research in the setting (Madden, 2010).

Netnography

Communities can refer not only to people in a common physical location, but also to relationships that develop online. Online communities may be formed by persons with similar interests or backgrounds, perhaps to create new social relationships that location or schedules did not permit, to supplement relationships that emerge in the course of work or school or other ongoing activities, or to provide peer support. Like communities of people who interact face-to-face, online communities can develop a culture and become sources of identification and attachment (Kozinets, 2010). And like physical communities, researchers can study online communities through immersion in the group for an extended period. **Netnography** is the use of ethnographic methods to study online communities.

Netnography The use of ethnographic methods to study online communities.

In some respects, netnography is similar to traditional ethnography. The researcher prepares to enter the field by becoming familiar with online communities and their language and customs, formulating an exploratory research question about social processes or orientation in that setting, and selecting an appropriate community to study. Unlike in-person ethnographies, netnographies can focus on communities whose members are physically distant and dispersed. The selected community should be relevant to the question, involve frequent communication among actively engaged members, and have a number of participants who, as a result, generate a rich body of textual data (Kozinets, 2010).

A netnographer must keep both observational and reflective field notes, but unlike a traditional ethnographer can return to review the original data—the posted text—long after it was produced. The data can then be coded, annotated with the researcher's interpretations, checked against new data to evaluate the persistence of social patterns, and used to develop a theory that is grounded in the data.

Photovoice

For about 150 years, people have been creating a record of the social world with photographs. This creates the possibility of observing the social world through photographs and of interpreting the resulting images as "text." For the most part, such visual imagery has captured social reality from the eyes of the researchers and therefore was being constructed by the researchers' interests, and not just what was depicted in the photographs. **Photovoice** builds on this history, but in the same way that other qualitative methods are designed to hear the voice of the respondents. Photovoice allows the participants to construct their social reality.

Photovoice A qualitative method in which participants both photograph meaningful scenes and interpret the photographs.

Carol Wang and Mary Ann Burris (1997) describe Photovoice as a method to enable people to "identify, represent, and enhance their community through a specific photographic technique" (p. 369). Therefore, Photovoice is a form of participatory research that can be used for community need assessment (Baker & Wang, 2006; Wang & Burris, 1997). Molloy (2007) suggests that this process is consistent with the empowerment tradition in social work by bringing groups together and enabling them to move to social action through their participation in the process. These are the goals of Photovoice:

1. Enable people to record and reflect on their community's strengths and concerns.

2. Promote critical dialogue and knowledge about personal and community issues through large and small group discussions of photographs.

3. Reach policy makers. (Wang & Burris, 1997, p. 369)

Photovoice includes the visual images provided by the photographs and is accompanied by narratives provided by the participants. Cameras are distributed to participants who share something in common, such as a social condition like homelessness or living in a particular community. There is a group facilitator who helps train the group members in using the cameras, serves as a resource for information, and enables the group to work together. The participants actively engage in the analysis of the photographs, choosing representative pictures, discussing their meaning, and developing themes and patterns.

Danny Rosen, Sara Goodkind, and Lindsey Smith (2011) used Photovoice to learn about the struggles and survival strategies, as well as the service needs and barriers to remaining abstinent, with 10 methadone clients over the age of 50. The project included a training session, eight weekly 2-hour group sessions, and brief individual interviews before each session. During the first 6 weeks, the discussions were centered on these questions: What are we seeing? What is happening? Why does this go on? How do you feel about this? The group sessions were also used by the participants to decide on a weekly theme about which they would take pictures during the week. The two remaining sessions were used for the participants to select the photographs that they felt most accurately represented their concerns, to tell stories about what the photographs meant, and to identify the themes they felt relevant.

With this picture (see Exhibit 10.2), a participant described his motivation for treatment:

This picture brings up memories of my addiction. I used to own a house that was in this spot. This picture broke me down . . . the house suffered neglect. My house is the only house that was torn down on this block. Because of my addiction.

Exhibit 10.2 Photovoice

Source: Daniel Rosen, Sara Goodkind & Mary Lindsey Smith (2011): Using Photovoice to Identify Service Needs of Older African American Methadone Clients, *Journal of Social Service Research*, 37:5, 526–538.

Participant observation A qualitative method for gathering data that involves developing a sustained relationship with people while they go about their normal activities.

Intensive interviewing A qualitative method that involves open-ended, relatively unstructured questioning in which the interviewer seeks in-depth information on the interviewee's feelings, experiences, and perceptions (Lofland & Lofland, 1984).

Focus groups A qualitative method that involves unstructured group interviews in which the focus group leader actively encourages discussion among participants on the topics of interest.

You can see how Photovoice can be a way to see and hear the voice of people. It has been used to explore social issues with such diverse topics and groups as Latino adolescents in rural North Carolina (Steng et al., 2004), parenting adolescents (Stevens, 2006), chronically mentally ill (N. Thompson et al., 2008), chronic pain in older adults (Baker & Wang, 2006), and employment-seeking behavior of people with HIV/AIDS (Hergenrather, Rhodes, & Clark, 2006).

It is now time to get into specifics. The specifics of qualitative methods can be best understood by reviewing three distinctive qualitative research techniques: **participant observation**, **intensive interviewing**, and **focus groups**. Participant observation and intensive interviewing are often used in the same project, whereas focus groups offer a unique data-collection strategy. These techniques often can be used to enrich experiments and surveys.

回 Participant Observation

Diamond (1992) carried out his study through participant observation. Participant observation is a method in which social processes are studied as they happen in their natural settings and left relatively undisturbed. It is a means of seeing the social world as the research participants see it, in its totality, and of understanding participants' interpretations of that world (Wolcott, 1995). By observing people and interacting with them in the course of their normal activities, participant observers seek to avoid the artificiality of experimental designs and the unnatural structured questioning of survey research (Koegel, 1987). This method encourages consideration of the context in which social interaction occurs, of the complex and interconnected nature of social relations, and of the sequencing of events (Bogdewic, 1999).

The term *participant observer* actually represents a continuum of roles (see Exhibit 10.3). A researcher may be a **complete** (*overt*) **participant** who is publically defined as a researcher and does not participate in group activities or the researcher may assume the role of **covert observer** in which the researcher neither participates in the activities nor self-identifies as a researcher. These two relatively passive roles contrast with the role of a researcher who participates actively in the setting. A **complete participant** (*covert participant*) acts just like other group members and does not disclose the research role while a **participant observer** (*overt participant*) engages in group activities and is known by the group to be a researcher.

Complete (covert) participant: A role in participant observation in which the researcher does not participate in group activities and is publicly identified as a researcher.

Covert observer: A role in field research in which the researcher does not reveal his or her identity as a researcher to those who are observed.

Participant observer: A qualitative method for gathering data that involves developing a sustained relationship with people while they go about their normal activities.

Choosing a Role

The first concern of every participant observer is to decide what balance to strike between observing and participating and whether to reveal their role as a researcher. These decisions must take into account the specifics of the social situation being studied, the researcher's own background and personality, the larger sociopolitical context, and ethical concerns. Which balance of participating and observing is most appropriate also changes during most projects. Moreover, the researcher's ability to maintain either a covert or an overt role will many times be challenged.

Covert Observation

In both observational roles, researchers try to see things as they happen without actively participating in these events. Although there is no fixed formula to guide the observational process, observers try to identify the who, what, when, where, why, and how of activities in the setting. Their observations will usually become more focused over time as observers develop a sense of the important categories of people and activities and gradually develop a theory that accounts for what is observed (Bogdewic, 1999).

In social settings involving many people, in which observing while standing or sitting does not attract attention, covert observation is possible and is unlikely to have much effect on social processes. You may not even want to call this covert observation, because your activities as an observer may be no different from those of others who are simply observing others to pass the time. However, when you take notes when you systematically check out the different areas of a public space or different people in a group, when you arrive and leave at particular times to do your observing, you are acting differently in important respects from others in the setting. When you write up what you have observed, you have taken something unique from the people in that setting. If you adopt such a covert observer role, you should always remember to evaluate your actions in the setting and your purposes for being there may affect the actions of others and your own interpretations.

Complete Observation

When you announce your role as a researcher observer, your presence is much more likely to alter the situation being observed. This is the problem of **reactive effects**. It is not natural in most social situations for someone who wants to record observations for research and publication purposes to be present, so individuals may alter their behavior. The complete observer is even more likely to have an impact when the social setting involves few people or if observing is unlike the usual activities in the setting. Observable differences between the observer and those being observed also increase the likelihood of reactive effects. For example, some Alzheimer's day-care staff members were aware of Karen Lyman's (1994) note-taking and staged interactions or monitored their speech "for the record":

> Some workers displayed frustration over the heads of clients (eyes rolling, sighs) or made humorous comments to clients about their personal quirks, clearly intended for me as the observer. . . . At one site a program aide caught himself midsentence: "They're all cra—." (p. 166)

However, in most situations, even complete observers find that their presence seems to be ignored by participants after a while and to have no discernible impact on social processes.

Exhibit 10.3 **The Participant Observation Continuum**

To study an activist group, you could take the role of a covert observer.

You could take the role of an overt observer:

You could take the role of a participant and observer:

You could take the role of a covert participant:

Reactive effects The changes in individual or group behavior that result from being observed or otherwise studied.

Participant Observation

Many field researchers adopt a role that involves some active participation in the setting. Usually, they inform at least some group members of their research interests, but then they participate in enough group activities to develop rapport with members and to gain a direct sense of what group members experience. Alison Cocks's (2008) study of children with learning disabilities in support agencies described her decision:

> I wanted to create relationships with the children based on honesty and friendship. I wanted to avoid non-participatory observation, as being observed is not an uncommon occurrence for the particular children who are continually monitored, assessed and judged by a wide range of professionals whose concern is with the progress of the child. I was keen to ensure that I would not be mistaken for another doctor, social worker, therapist or psychologist, who was going to give "an opinion" on the individual children. . . . Participation observation meant that I was open with the children about my purpose for visiting. (p. 168)

Participating and observing have two clear ethical advantages. Because group members know the researcher's real role in the group, they can choose to keep some information or attitudes hidden. By the same token, the researcher can decline to participate in unethical or dangerous activities without fear of exposing his or her identity.

Most field researchers who opt for disclosure get the feeling that after they have become known and at least somewhat trusted figures in the group, their presence does not have any palpable effect on members' actions. The major influences on individual actions and attitudes are past experiences, personality, group structure, and so on, so the argument goes, and these continue to exert their influence even when an outside observer is present. The participant observer can presumably be ethical about identity disclosure and still observe the natural social world. Of course, the argument is less persuasive when the behavior to be observed is illegal or stigmatized, so that participants have reason to fear the consequences of disclosure to any outsider.

Diamond (1992) describes how it can be difficult to maintain a fully open research role even in a setting without these special characteristics:

> During and after the fieldwork the first question many people asked was "Did you tell them?". . . I had initially hoped to disclose at every phase of the project my dual objective of working as a nursing assistant and writing about these experiences. In some instances it was possible to disclose this dual purpose, in others it was not. I told many nursing assistants and people who lived in the homes that I was both working and investigating. I told some of my nursing supervisors and some administrators. . . . The short answer is that as the study proceeded it was forced increasingly to become a piece of undercover research. (pp. 7–8)

Even when researchers maintain a public identity as researchers, ethical dilemmas arising from participation in the lives of their research subjects do not go away. In fact, social workers conducting qualitative research may obtain information that suggests some clinical intervention may be warranted to improve the life or health of a research participant, and then they must decide whether taking action would be consistent with research guidelines. When Jeanie Kayser-Jones and Barbara A. Koenig (1994) found that one of their elderly demented nursing home patients seemed to be dying from an untreated illness, they encouraged a nurse to override the wishes of the family to avoid any "heroic" measures and convinced the doctor on call to begin intravenous fluids. Such actions, whether right or wrong, whether taken to improve the health of some research participants or to remedy problems in group process, inherently create ethical dilemmas and heighten the potential for strains with other participants in the setting.

Experienced participant observers try to lessen some of the problems of identity disclosure by evaluating both their effect on others in the setting and the effect of others on the observers, writing about these effects throughout the time they are in the field, and while they analyze their data. They also are sure that while in the field to preserve some physical space and regular time when they can concentrate on their research and that they schedule occasional meetings with other researchers to review the fieldwork.

Covert Participation

To lessen the potential for reactive effects and to gain entry to otherwise inaccessible settings, some field researchers adopt the role of covert participant (or complete participant), keeping their research secret and trying their best to act like other participants in a social setting or group.

Although the role of covet participant lessens some of the reactive effects encountered by the complete observer, covert participants confront other problems:

- Covert participants cannot take notes openly or use any obvious recording devices. They must write notes based solely on memory and must do so at times when it is natural to be away from group members.

- Covert participants cannot ask questions that will arouse suspicion, so they often have trouble clarifying the meaning of other participants' attitudes or actions.

- The role is difficult to play successfully. Covert participants will not know how the regular participants would act in every situation in which the researchers find themselves. Regular participants have entered the situation from different social backgrounds and with goals different from that of the researchers. The researchers' spontaneous reactions to every event are unlikely to be consistent with those of the regular participants, thereby raising suspicion that the researcher is not "one of us" (R. Mitchell, 1993).

- Covert participants need to keep up the act at all times while in the setting under study. They may experience enormous psychological strain, particularly in situations where they are expected to choose sides in intragroup conflict or to participate in criminal or other acts. Of course, some covert observers may become so wrapped up in the role they are playing that they adopt not just the mannerisms but also the perspectives and goals of the regular participants—they "go native." At this point, they abandon research goals and cease to evaluate critically what they are observing.

Ethical issues have been at the forefront of debate over the strategy of covert participation. Kai Erikson (1967) argues that covert participation is, by its very nature, unethical and should not be allowed except in public settings. Researchers cannot anticipate the unintended consequences of their actions for research subjects. Furthermore, it is difficult to counter the interpretations offered by the research because the findings are not verifiable and the contextual nature of the research makes it more difficult to replicate the study (Herrera, 2003).

But a total ban on covert participation would "kill many a project stone dead" (Punch, 1994, p. 90). Studies of extreme or fringe political groups or of institutional malpractice would rarely be possible; "The crux of the matter is that some deception, passive or active, enables you to get at data not obtainable by other means" (Punch, 1994, p. 91). Therefore, some field researchers argue that covert participation is legitimate in some settings. If the researcher maintains the confidentiality of others, keeps commitments to others, and does not directly lie to others, some degree of deception may be justified in exchange for the knowledge gained (Punch, 1994).

Entering the Field

Entering the field, the setting under investigation, is a critical stage in a participant observation project because it can shape many subsequent experiences. Some background work is necessary before entering the field—at least enough to develop a clear understanding of what the research questions are likely to be and to review one's personal stance toward the people and problems likely to be encountered. Researchers must also learn in advance how participants dress and what their typical activities are so as to avoid being caught completely unprepared. Finding a participant who can make introductions is often critical (Rossman & Rallis, 1998), and formal permission may be needed in an organizational setting (Bogdewic, 1999). It can take weeks or even months until entry is possible.

Diamond (1992) tried to enter a nursing home twice, first without finding out about necessary qualifications:

> My first job interview . . . [t]he administrator of the home had agreed to see me on [the recommendation of two current assistants]. The administrator . . . probed suspiciously, "Now why would a white guy want to work for these kinds of wages?" . . . He continued without pause, "Besides, I couldn't hire you if I wanted to. You're not certified." That, he quickly concluded, was the end of our interview, and he showed me to the door. (pp. 8–9)

After taking a course and receiving his certificate, Diamond was able to enter the role of nursing assistant as others did.

When participant observing involves public figures or organizations that are used to or are seeking publicity, a more direct approach may secure entry into the field. Dorothy and David Counts (1996) simply wrote a letter to the married couple who led the Escapees RV Club describing their project and asking for permission to work with members. After a warm welcome from the leaders, the Counts were able to meet with Escapees at regular park gatherings and distribute questionnaires. They received few refusals, attributing this high rate of subject cooperation to members' desires to increase understanding of and appreciation for their lifestyle. Other groups have other motivations, but in every case, some consideration of these potential motives in advance should help smooth entry into the field.

In short, field researchers must be sensitive to the impression they make and the ties they establish when entering the field. This stage lays the groundwork for collecting data from people who have different perspectives and for developing relationships that researchers can use to surmount the problems in data collection that inevitably arise in the field. Researchers should be ready with a rationale for their participation and some sense of the potential benefits to participants. Discussion about these issues with key participants or gatekeepers should be honest and should identify what the participants can expect from the research, without necessarily going into detail about the researcher's hypotheses or research questions (Rossman & Rallis, 1998).

Developing and Maintaining Relationships

Researchers must be careful to manage their relationships in the research setting so they can continue to observe and interview diverse members of the social setting throughout the long period typical of participant observation (Maxwell, 2005). Every action the researcher takes can develop or undermine this relationship. Interaction early in the research process is particularly sensitive because participants do not know the researcher and the researcher does not know the routines. Dorothy and David Counts (1996) laid the foundation for their participant observation study of RVing seniors by joining the group they were to study and gaining trust from others as sympathetic observers. Eva Kahana, Boaz Kahana, and Kathryn Riley (1988) give some specific advice for those studying institutional settings:

> Prior to implementation of the project, it is useful for the research team to spend some time in the facility, familiarizing themselves with the staff and with the physical and social environment and becoming acceptable additions to the institutional setting. (p. 200)

Maintaining relationships can be challenging. Cocks (2008) encountered instances when the children in her study wanted her to use her authority as an adult to intervene in arguments and rough behavior. She described one such incident:

> In this incident I was asked to intervene by Jack, whose anxiety was increasing at the mounting tension. To intervene would have put me in an authoritarian adult role, but to have ignored his request would have broken the relationship we had achieved. Therefore, I limited my action to explaining why I would not do anything, using the term, "not allowed" purposely as it infers an adult-imposed restriction. (2008, p. 172)

Experienced participant observers recommend developing a plausible and honest explanation about yourself and your study and keeping the support of key individuals to maintain relationships in the field. They suggest that you be laid back and not be arrogant, showing off your expertise nor be too aggressive in questioning others. Do not fake your social similarity with your participants as they recognize the differences and you may limit self-disclosure. Finally, avoid giving or receiving money or tangible gifts (Bogdewic, 1999; Rossman & Rallis, 1998; Whyte, 1955; Wolcott, 1995).

Nonetheless, even the most careful strategies for maintaining relations can founder on unforeseen resentments, as when Boaz and Eva Kahana (1970) found that an order from administrators to cooperate in their research was resented as just another example of the administrators' insensitivity. Being adaptable and self-critical is essential.

Sampling People and Events

Sampling decisions in qualitative research are guided by the need to study intensively the people, places, or phenomena of interest. Therefore, most qualitative researchers limit their focus to just one or a few sites, programs, or specific types of people so they can focus all their attention on the social dynamics of those settings or the activities and attitudes of these people. This focus on a limited number of cases does not mean that sampling is unimportant. Researchers must be reasonably confident that they can gain access and that the site can provide relevant information. The sample must be appropriate and adequate for the study, even if it is not representative. Researchers may select one or more *critical cases* that are unusually rich in information pertaining to the research question, *typical cases* precisely because they are judged to be typical, and/or *deviant cases* that provide a useful contrast (Kuzel, 1999). Within a research site, plans may be made to sample different settings, people, events, and artifacts (see Exhibit 10.4).

Studying more than one case or setting almost always strengthens the causal conclusions and makes the findings more generalizable, particularly if the settings are different (G. King, Keohane, & Verba, 1994; Schofield, 2002). Diamond (1992) worked in three different Chicago nursing homes "in widely different neighborhoods" and with different fractions of residents supported by Medicaid; he then "visited many homes across the United States to validate my observations" (p. 5). J. Brandon Wallace (1994) encourages "efforts to include all kinds of people—African-Americans, Hispanics, males, females, rich and poor" (pp. 143–144)—to provide a more complete experience of aging in life history interview research.

Other approaches to sampling in field research are more systematic. You already learned in Chapter 5 about some of the nonprobability sampling methods that are used in field research. Purposive sampling can be used to identify opinion leaders and representatives of different roles. With snowball sampling, field researchers learn from participants about who represents different subgroups in a setting. Quota sampling also may be employed to ensure the representation of particular categories of participants.

Theoretical sampling is a systematic approach used when field researchers focus on particular processes that seem to be important and select new settings or individuals that permit comparisons to check their perceptions (Ragin, 1994; see Exhibit 10.5). Chung, Grogan, and Mosley (2012) used this approach when assessing resident's perceptions about effective community participation in local health decision making:

> **Theoretical sampling:** A sampling method recommended for field research; the sample is drawn in a sequential fashion, with settings or individuals selected for study as earlier observations or interviews indicate that these settings or individuals are influential.

We used a theoretical sampling strategy to create a set of dimensions along which the experiences and opinions concerning community representation would likely vary. These dimensions included socio-demographic characteristics such as age, gender, income level, education and employment status. Other key dimensions included length of time a resident lived in their neighborhood, renter versus owner status, and household composition. . . .

Overall, we screened 52 respondents and purposively sampled 14 to participate in the interviews. These 14 were purposively selected in order to attain maximum variation in the socio-demographic characteristics . . . and neighborhood of residence. (pp. 1654–1655)

Exhibit 10.4	Sampling Plan for a Participant Observation Project in Schools

Type of Information to be Obtained

Information Source*	Collegiality	Goals & Community	Action Expectations	Knowledge Orientation	Base
SETTINGS:					
Public places (halls, main offices)	X	X	X	X	X
Teachers' lounge	X	X		X	X
Classrooms		X	X	X	X
Meeting rooms			X	X	
Gymnasium or locker room		X			
EVENTS:					
Faulty meetings	X		X		X
Lunch hour	X				X
Teaching		X	X	X	X
PEOPLE:					
Principal		X	X	X	X
Teachers	X	X	X	X	X
Students		X	X	X	
ARTIFACTS:					
Newspapers		X	X		X
Decorations		X			

Source: Adapted from Marshall and Rossman (1999, pp. 75–76).

Taking Notes

Notes are the primary means of recording participant observation data (Emerson, Fretz, & Shaw, 1995). Many field researchers jot down partial notes while observing and then retreat to their computer to write up more complete notes on a daily basis. The computerized text can then be inspected and organized after it is printed out, or it can be marked up and organized for analysis using one of several computer programs designed especially for the task.

It is almost always a mistake to try to take comprehensive notes while engaged in the field—the process of writing extensively is just too disruptive. The usual procedure is to jot down brief notes about highlights of the observation period. These brief notes called **jottings** can serve as memory joggers when writing the actual **field notes** at a later session. It will also help to maintain a daily log in which

Jottings Brief nots written in the file about highlights of an observation period.

Field notes Notes that describe what has been observed, heard, or otherwise experienced in a participant observation study.

Exhibit 10.5 | **Theoretical Sampling**

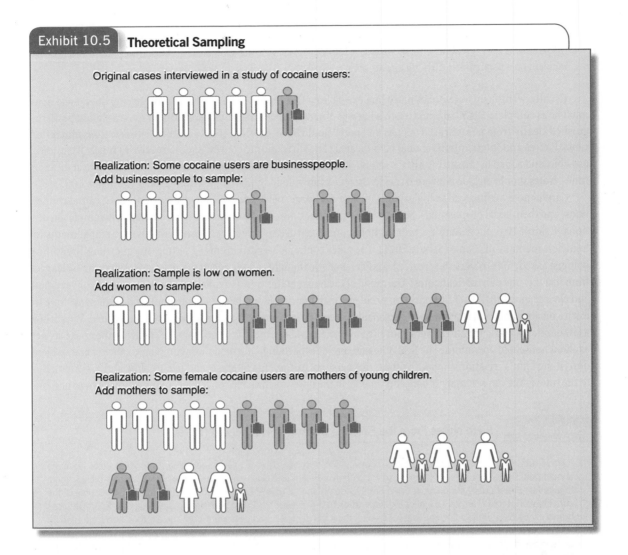

Original cases interviewed in a study of cocaine users:

Realization: Some cocaine users are businesspeople.
Add businesspeople to sample:

Realization: Sample is low on women.
Add women to sample:

Realization: Some female cocaine users are mothers of young children.
Add mothers to sample:

each day's activities are recorded (Bogdewic, 1999). With the aid of the jottings and some practice, researchers usually remember a great deal of what happened—as long as the comprehensive field notes are written immediately afterward or at least within the next 24 hours, and before they have been discussed with anyone else.

Taking notes was a challenge for Diamond (1992) because many people in the setting did not know that he was a researcher:

While I was getting to know nursing assistants and residents and experiencing aspects of their daily routines, I would surreptitiously take notes on scraps of paper, in the bathroom or otherwise out of sight, jotting down what someone had said or done. (pp. 6–7)

Lyman (1994) was able to take notes openly:

I took care to overcome the artificial barriers of note-taking through reassurances, humor, volunteered labor, food sharing, and casual conversations with the notepad conspicuously left on the table. . . . Note-taking was a daily reminder to all that I was an outsider, which at times created barriers to be overcome, but which also allowed me to extricate myself from what could have become all-consuming volunteer tasks when I felt the need to record something. One clear advantage of visible note-taking was that some people volunteered information they felt should be recorded. A social worker took me aside and . . . recounted an important incident on a particularly difficult day. (p. 167)

Usually, writing up notes takes much longer—at least three times longer—than the observing does. Field notes must be as complete, detailed, and true to what was observed and heard as possible. Direct quotes should be distinguished clearly from paraphrased quotes, and both should be set off from the researcher's observations and reflections. Pauses and interruptions should be indicated. The surrounding context should receive as much attention as possible, and a map of the setting always should be included, with indications of where individuals were at different times. Notes should include nonverbal cues as these cues provide additional context (Simpson & Cornelius, 2007).

Careful note taking yields a big payoff. On page after page, field notes will suggest new concepts, causal connections, and theoretical propositions. Social processes and settings can be described in rich detail, with ample illustrations. Exhibit 10.6, for example, contains field notes recorded by a researcher studying living arrangements for homeless mentally ill people (Schutt, 2011). The notes contain observations of the setting, the questions the anthropologist asked, the answers she received, and her analytic thoughts about one of the residents. What can be learned from just this one page of field notes? The mood of the house at this time is evident, with joking, casual conversation, and close friendships. "Dick" remarks on problems with household financial management, and at the same time we learn a bit about his own activities and personality (a regular worker who appears to like systematic plans). We see how a few questions and a private conversation elicit information about the transition from the shelter to the house, as well as about household operations. The field notes also provide the foundation for a more complete picture of one resident, describing "Jim's" relationships with others, his personal history, his interests and personality, and his orientation to the future. We can see analytic concepts emerge in the notes, such as the concept of "pulling himself together" and

---

Exhibit 10.6 | Field Notes From the Evolving Consumer Household (ECH)

I arrive around 4:30 P.M. and walk into a conversation between Jim and somebody else as to what color jeans he should buy. There is quite a lot of joking going on between Jim and Susan. I go out to the kitchen and find Dick about to take his dinner out to the picnic table to eat (his idea?) so I go ask if I can join him. He says yes. In the course of the conversation, I find out that he works 3 days a week in the "prevoc" program at the local day program, Food Services branch, for which he gets $10 per week. Does he think the living situation will work out? Yes. All they need is a plan for things like when somebody buys something and then everybody else uses it. Like he bought a gallon of milk and it was gone in two days, because everyone was using it for their coffee. I ask if he's gone back to the shelter to visit and he says "No. I was glad to get out of there." He came to the [ECH] from [a shelter] through homeless outreach [a Department of Mental Health Program]. Had been at [the shelter] since January. Affirms that [the ECH] is a better place to live than the shelter. Why? Because you have your own room and privacy and stuff. How have people been getting along with each other? He says, "Fine."

I return to the living room and sit down on the couch with Jim and Susan. Susan teases Jim and he jokes back. Susan is eating a T.V. dinner with M and M's for dessert. There is joking about working off the calories from the M and M's by doing sit-up's, which she proceeds to demonstrate. This leads to a conversation about exercise during which Jim declares his intention to get back into exercise by doing sports, like basketball.

Jim seems to have his mind on pulling himself together, which he characterizes as "getting my old self back." When I ask him what he's been doing since I saw him last, he says, "Working on my appearance." And in fact, he has had a haircut, a shave, and washed his clothes. When I ask him what his old self was like, he says, "you mean before I lost everything?" I learn that he used to work two jobs, had "a family" and was into religion." This seems to have been when he was quite young, around eighteen. He tells me he was on the street for 7–8 years, from 1978–1985, drinking the whole time. I ask him whether he thinks living at [the ECH] will help him to get his "old self back" and he says that it will "help motivate me." I observe that he seems pretty motivated already. He says yes, "but this will motivate me more."

Jim has a warm personality, likes to joke and laugh. He also speaks up—in meetings he is among the first to say what he thinks and he talks among the most. His "team" relationship with Bill is also important to him—"me and Bill, we work together."

of some house members working as a "team." You can imagine how researchers can go on to develop a theoretical framework for understanding the setting and a set of concepts and questions to inform subsequent observations.

Complete field notes must provide even more than a record of what was observed or heard. Notes also should include descriptions of the methodology: where researchers were standing or sitting while they observed, how they chose people for conversation or observation, and what counts of people or events they made and why. Sprinkled throughout the notes also should be a record of the researchers' feelings and thoughts while observing: when they were disgusted by some statement or act, when they felt threatened or intimidated, why their attention shifted from one group to another, and what ethical concerns arose. Notes like these provide a foundation for later review of the likelihood of bias or inattention to some salient features of the situation.

Notes may in some situations be supplemented by still pictures, videos, and printed material circulated or posted in the research setting. Such visual material can bring an entirely different qualitative dimension into the analysis and call attention to some features of the social situation and actors within it that were missed in the notes (Grady, 1996). Commentary on this material can be integrated with the written notes (Bogdewic, 1999).

Managing the Personal Dimensions

Because field researchers become a part of the social situation they are studying, they cannot help but be affected on a personal and emotional level. At the same time, those being studied react to researchers not just as researchers, but as personal acquaintances—often as friends, sometimes as personal rivals. Managing and learning from this personal side of field research is an important part of any project.

The impact of personal issues varies with the depth of researchers' involvement in the setting. The more involved researchers are in multiple aspects of the ongoing social situation, the more important personal issues become and the greater the risk of going native. Even when researchers acknowledge their role, "increased contact brings sympathy, and sympathy in its turn dulls the edge of criticism" (Fenno, 1978, p. 277).

The correspondence between researchers' social attributes—age, sex, race, and so on—and those of their subjects also shapes personal relationships, as Diamond (1992) noted:

> The staff were mostly people of color, residents mostly white. . . . Never before, or since, have I been so acutely aware of being a white American man. At first the people who lived in the homes stared at me, then some approached to get a closer look, saying that I reminded them of a nephew, a son, a grandson, a brother, a doctor. This behavior made more sense as time went on: except for the few male residents and occasional visitors, I was the only white man many would see from one end of the month to the next. (p. 39)

There is no formula for successfully managing the personal dimension of field research. It is much more art than science, and it flows more from the researcher's own personality and natural approach to other people than from formal training. But novice field researchers often neglect to consider how they will manage personal relationships when they plan and carry out their projects. Then suddenly they find themselves doing something they do not believe they should, just to stay in the good graces of research subjects, or juggling the emotions resulting from conflict within the group.

Systematic Observation

We would be remiss if we failed to note that observations can be made in a more systematic, quantitative design that allows systematic comparisons and more confident generalizations. A research study using **systematic observation** develops a standard form on which to record variation within the observed setting in terms of the variables of interest. Such variables might include the frequency of some behavior(s), the particular people observed, and environmental conditions.

Systematic observation: A strategy that increases the reliability of observational data using explicit rules that standardize coding practices across observers.

Janet Shapiro and Sarah Mangelsdorf (1994) used systematic observation and surveys to look for factors related to the parenting abilities of adolescent mothers. Participants first completed the survey, which consisted of a variety of measures such as self-efficacy, life events, self-concept, life stress, and demographic information. The participants were then videotaped engaging in three parenting activities: feeding, unstructured play, and structured play. Coders viewed the videotapes and, using standardized scales, rated the adolescent mothers on their parental sensitivity, expressiveness with the child, positive regard, negative regard, caretaking ability, and the extent to which the adolescents permitted their child autonomy, as well as child responsiveness to the interaction (Shapiro & Mangelsdorf, 1994).

Intensive Interviewing

Intensive or depth interviewing is a qualitative method of finding out about people's experiences, thoughts, and feelings. Qualitative researchers can employ intensive interviewing exclusively, without systematic observation of respondents in their natural setting or as part of their participant-observation design. It shares with other qualitative research methods a commitment to learn about people in depth, on their own terms, and in the context of their situation.

Unlike the more structured interviewing that may be used in survey research, intensive interviewing relies on open-ended questions. Rather than asking standard questions in a fixed order, intensive interviewers allow the specific content and order of questions to vary from one interviewee to another. Rather than presenting fixed responses that presume the range of answers that respondents might give, intensive interviewers expect respondents to answer questions in their own words.

What distinguishes intensive interviewing from less structured forms of questioning is consistency and thoroughness. The goal is to develop a comprehensive picture of the interviewee's background, attitudes, and actions in his or her own terms, to "listen to people as they describe how they understand the worlds in which they live and work" (Rubin & Rubin, 1995, p. 3). For example, Shadi Martin and colleagues (2010) sought through intensive interviewing to learn how culture and discrimination influenced the care-seeking behaviors of older African American men and women. The interviews took from 1.5 hours to 3 hours and were designed "to hear the voices, the concerns and the stories of elderly African Americans" (p. 311).

Intensive interview studies do not reveal as directly as does participant observation the social context in which action is taken and opinions are formed. Like participant observation studies, intensive interviewing engages researchers more actively with participants than does standard survey research. The researchers must listen to lengthy explanations, ask follow-up questions tailored to the preceding answers, and seek to learn about interrelated belief systems or personal approaches to things, rather than measure a limited set of variables. As a result, intensive interviews are often much longer than standardized interviews, sometimes as long as 15 hours, conducted in several different sessions. The intensive interview becomes more like a conversation between partners than between a researcher and participant.

Intensive interviewers actively try to probe understandings and engage interviewees in a dialogue about what they mean by their comments. To prepare for this active interviewing, the interviewer should learn in advance about the setting and people to be studied. Preliminary discussion with key informants, inspection of written documents, and even a review of your own feelings about the setting can all help (W. Miller & Crabtree, 1999). Robert Bellah, Richard Madsen, William Sullivan, Ann Swidler, and Steven Tipton (1985) elaborate on this aspect of intensive interviewing in a methodological appendix to their national best-seller about American individualism, *Habits of the Heart*:

> We did not, as in some scientific version of "Candid Camera," seek to capture their beliefs and actions without our subjects being aware of us. Rather, we sought to bring our preconceptions and questions into the conversation and to understand the answers we were receiving not only in terms of the language but also, so far as we could discover, in the lives of those we were talking with. Though we did not seek to impose our ideas on those with whom we talked, . . . we did attempt to uncover assumptions, to make explicit what the person we were talking to might rather have left implicit. The interview as we employed it was active, Socratic. (p. 304)

The intensive interview follows a preplanned outline of topics. It may begin with a few simple questions that gather background information while building rapport. These are often followed by a few general **grand tour questions** that are meant to elicit lengthy narratives (W. Miller & Crabtree, 1999). Some projects may use relatively structured interviews, particularly when the focus is on developing knowledge about prior events or some narrowly defined topic. But more exploratory projects, particularly those aiming to learn about interviewees' interpretations of the world, may let each interview flow in a unique direction in response to the interviewee's experiences and interests (Kvale, 1996; Rubin & Rubin, 1995; Wolcott, 1995). In either case, qualitative interviewers must adapt nimbly throughout the interview, paying attention to nonverbal cues, expressions with symbolic value, and the ebb and flow of the interviewee's feelings and interests. "You have to be free to follow your data where they lead" (Rubin & Rubin, 1995, p. 64). The interview guide becomes a tool for ensuring that key topics are covered, rather than a guide to the ordering or language of specific questions.

> **Grand tour question:** A broad question at the start of an interview that seeks to engage the respondent in the topic of interest.

Random selection is rarely used to select respondents for intensive interviews, but the selection method still must be carefully considered. If interviewees are selected in a haphazard manner, for example, by speaking to those who happen to be available at the time that the researcher is on site, the interviews are likely to be of less value than when a more purposive selection strategy is used. Researchers should try to select interviewees who are knowledgeable about the subject of the interview, who are open to talking, and who represent the range of perspectives (Rubin & Rubin, 1995). Selection of new interviewees should continue, if possible, at least until the **saturation point** is reached, the point when new interviews seem to yield little additional information (see Exhibit 10.7). As new issues are uncovered, additional interviewees may be selected to represent different opinions about these issues.

> **Saturation point:** The point at which subject selection is ended in intensive interviewing, when new interviews seem to yield little additional information.

Establishing and Maintaining a Partnership

Because intensive interviewing does not engage researchers as participants in subjects' daily affairs, the problems of entering the field are much reduced. However, the logistics of arranging long periods for personal interviews can still be pretty complicated. It also is important to establish rapport with subjects by considering in advance how they will

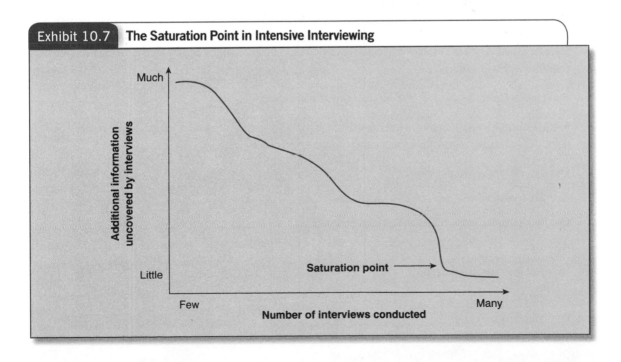

Exhibit 10.7 The Saturation Point in Intensive Interviewing

react to the interview arrangements and by developing an approach that does not violate their standards for social behavior. Interviewees should be treated with respect, as knowledgeable partners whose time is valued (among other things, that means you should avoid being late for appointments). A commitment to confidentiality should be stated and honored (Rubin & Rubin, 1995).

In the first few minutes of the interview, the goal is to show interest in the interviewee and to explain clearly the purpose of the interview (Kvale, 1996). During the interview, the interviewer should maintain an appropriate distance from the interviewee, one that doesn't violate cultural norms, and the interviewer should maintain eye contact and not engage in distracting behavior. An appropriate pace is also important; pause to allow the interviewee to reflect, elaborate, and generally not feel rushed (Gordon, 1992). When an interview covers emotional or otherwise stressful topics, the interviewer should give the interviewee an opportunity to unwind at the interview's end (Rubin & Rubin, 1995).

More generally, intensive interviewers must be sensitive to the broader social context of their interaction with the interviewee and to the implications of their relations in the way they ask questions and interpret answers. Tom Wengraf (2001) cautions new intensive interviewers to take account of their unconscious orientations to others based on past experience:

> Your [prior] experience of being interviewed may lead you to behave and "come across" in your interviewing . . . like a policeman, or a parent, a teacher or academic, or any "authority" by whom you have been interviewed and from whom you learnt a way of handling stress and ambiguity. (p. 18)

Asking Questions and Recording Answers

Intensive interviewers must plan their main questions around an outline of the interview topic. The questions should generally be short and to the point. More details can then be elicited through nondirective probes (such as "Can you tell me more about that?" or "Uh-huh," echoing the respondent's comment, or just maintaining a moment of silence). Follow-up questions can then be tailored to answers to the main questions.

Interviewers should strategize throughout an interview about how best to achieve their objectives while taking into account interviewees' answers. They must also be sensitive to the ways in which they shape the answers by their words, style of questioning, and personal characteristics:

> It is the combination of personal characteristics and expectations of the interviewer, the attitudes toward aging he or she indicates, and the conceptual grounding of the questions themselves that influence the topics informants choose to express and expand on as well as the topics they omit from discussion entirely. (Kaufman, 1994, p. 128)

Habits of the Heart (Bellah et al., 1985) provides a useful illustration:

[Coinvestigator Steven] Tipton, in interviewing Margaret Oldham [a pseudonym], tried to discover at what point she would take responsibility for another human being:

Q: So what are you responsible for?

A: I'm responsible for my acts and for what I do.

Q: Does that mean you're responsible for others, too?

A: No.

Q: Are you your sister's keeper?

A: No.

Q: Your brother's keeper?

A: No.

Q: Are you responsible for your husband?

A: I'm not. He makes his own decisions. He is his own person. He acts his own acts. I can agree with them, or I can disagree with them. If I ever find them nauseous enough, I have a responsibility to leave and not deal with it any more.

Q: What about children?

A: I . . . I would say I have a legal responsibility for them, but in a sense I think they in turn are responsible for their own acts. (p. 304)

Do you see how the interviewer actively encouraged the subject to explain what she meant by "responsibility"? This sort of active questioning undoubtedly did a better job of clarifying her concept of responsibility than a fixed set of questions would have.

The active questioning involved in intensive interviewing without a fixed interview script also means that the statements made by the interviewee can only be understood in the context of the interviewer's questions. Tom Wengraf (2001) provides an example of how the interviewer's statements and questions can affect the interview process:

Interviewer: Thank you for giving up this time for me.

Interviewee: Well, I don't see it as giving up the time, more as contributing . . .

Interviewer: Well, for giving me the time, contributing the time, thank you very much.

Wengraf: *Stay silent, let him clarify whatever the point is he wishes to make.*

Later,

Interviewer: Ok, so you're anonymous [repeating an earlier statement], so you can say what you like.

Wengraf: *Don't imply that he is slow on the uptake—it might be better to cut the whole sentence.*

Later,

Interviewee: I guess, it's difficult . . . being the breadwinner. Myself as a father, er . . . I'm not sure.

Wengraf: *He's uncertain, hoping to be asked some more about "being a father himself today."*

Interviewer [Slightly desperately]: Perhaps you could tell me a little about your own father.

Wengraf: *Interviewer ignores implied request but moves eagerly on to her intended focus on him as a son.*

You can see in this excerpt how, at every step, the interviewer is actively constructing with the interviewee the text of the interview that will be analyzed. Becoming a good intensive interviewer means learning how to "get out of the way" as much as possible in this process. Becoming an informed critic of intensive interviewing studies means, in part, learning to consider how the social interaction between the interviewer and interviewee may have shaped in subtle ways what the interviewee said and to look for some report on how this interaction was managed.

Tape recorders are commonly used to record intensive and focus group interviews. Most researchers who have tape-recorded interviews (including us) feel that they do not inhibit most interviewees and, in fact, are routinely ignored. The occasional respondent is concerned with his or her public image and may therefore speak for the tape recorder, but such individuals are unlikely to speak frankly in any research interview. There are now phone apps that allow you to record interviews that may be less intrusive. In any case, constant note taking during an interview prevents adequate displays of interest and appreciation by the interviewer and hinders the degree of concentration that results in the best interviews. If the tape recorder is inhibiting the interview, you can turn it off.

Research In the News

For Further Thought ?

CAN TAPING INTERVIEWS CAPTURE A TREND?

Eric Klinenberg used qualitative interviews to debunk assumptions about individuals who live alone. Klinenberg interviewed 300 people living alone over a 10-year period. What did he find? People who live alone are more social and less isolated. Intensive interviewing revealed older individuals expressing a desire for independence and single living. Economics greatly affect the ability to live alone and cultures all over the globe are seeing an increase in solo living.

1. Why might Klinenberg have used qualitative interviewing in this research rather than a quantitative survey? Explain why qualitative interviewing may have been more suited to identifying this misconception.

2. How could you design a study to explore this issue in different cultures? What interpretations could other cultures have of living alone?

Source: Klinenberg (2012, p. SR4).

回 Interviewing Online

Our social world now includes many connections initiated and maintained through e-mail and other web-based communication (known as computer-mediated communication), so it is only natural that interviewing has also moved online. Online interviewing can facilitate an interview with others who are separated by physical distance and is a means to conduct research with those who are only known through such online connections as a discussion group, an e-mail distribution list, or social media (James & Busher, 2009; Salmons, 2012). This method can reach isolated or socially stigmatized groups who might otherwise be ignored (McCoyd & Kerson, 2006).

Online interviews can be either synchronous—in which the interviewer and interviewee exchange messages as in online chatting or with text messages—or asynchronous—in which the interviewee can respond to the interviewer's questions whenever it is convenient, usually through e-mail but perhaps through a blog, wiki, or online forums (Salmons, 2012). Both styles of online interviewing have advantages and disadvantages (James & Busher, 2009). Synchronous interviewing provides an experience more similar to an in-person interview, thus giving more of a sense of obtaining spontaneous reactions, but it requires careful attention to arrangements and is prone to interruptions. Asynchronous interviewing allows interviewees to provide more thoughtful and developed answers, but it may be difficult to maintain interest and engagement if the exchanges continue over many days. The online asynchronous interviewer should plan carefully how to build rapport as well as how to terminate the online relationship after the interview is concluded (N. King & Horrocks, 2010). Adding video to the exchange can also increase engagement, whether through real-time videoconferencing or by sending video clips or podcasts (Salmons, 2012).

Allison Deegan (2012) initially tried synchronous interviewing in her study of teenage girls who had participated in the WriteGirl mentoring program. She had learned that most program alumnae used Facebook and so contacted them on Facebook and began to set up chat sessions. However, her first interviews turned out to be too slow and seemed jerky, so she instead began arranging asynchronous interviews by e-mail. Respondents could complete the interview questions and return the interview form when it was convenient for them. Deegan learned later that the problem with the pace of the chat sessions was due partly to the respondents doing multiple other tasks while they were in the chat sessions. So more (speed) does not necessarily result in a better interview.

Whether a synchronous or asynchronous approach is used, online interviewing can facilitate the research process by creating a written record of the entire interaction without the need for typed transcripts (McCoyd & Kerson, 2006). The relative anonymity of online communications can also encourage interviewees to be more open and honest about their feelings than they would be if interviewed in person (James & Busher, 2009). McCoyd and Kerson (2006) found that their e-mail interview participants gave thoughtful, and often emotional, responses exemplified by one respondent: "This is the hard part for me. I can never write this without feeling all that pain and loss just rush through my body" (p. 396). Further, e-mail interviews may provide more information than other types of interviews given a greater sense of anonymity, not having to deal with an interviewer's visual cues, being able to respond at one's convenience and/or in a safe environment (McCoyd and Kerson, 2006).

However, online interviewing lacks some of the most appealing elements of qualitative methods. The revealing subtleties of facial expression, intonation, and body language are lost. McCoyd and Kerson's (2006) participants did use "parentheticals such as '(crying now)' or symbols (:: indicated tears and ☹ and ☺) to indicate strong emotion" (p. 401), though this still does not substitute for visual cues. Establishing and maintaining rapport is more challenging and difficult and may require friendly, informal, and clearly written e-mails (McCoyd & Kerson, 2006). Further, those who are being interviewed have much greater ability to present an identity that is completely removed from their in-person persona; for instance, basic characteristics such as age, gender, and physical location can be completely misrepresented.

🔲 Focus Groups

Focus groups are groups of unrelated individuals that are formed by a researcher and then led in group discussion of a topic for 1 to 2 hours (Krueger & Casey, 2009). The researcher asks specific questions and guides the discussion to ensure that group members address these questions, but the resulting information is qualitative and relatively unstructured. Focus groups do not involve representative samples; instead, a few individuals who have the time to participate, have some knowledge pertinent to the focus group topic, and share key characteristics with the target population are recruited for the group.

Focus groups are used to collect qualitative data, with open-ended questions posed by the researcher (or group leader). Thus, a focused discussion mimics the natural process of forming and expressing opinions—and may give some sense of validity. No formal procedure exists for determining the generalizability of focus group answers, but the careful researcher should conduct at least several focus groups on the same topic and check for consistency in the findings. Some focus group experts advise conducting enough focus groups to reach the point of saturation, when an additional focus group adds little new information to that which already has been generated (J. Brown, 1999).

Most focus groups involve 6 to 12 people, a number that facilitates discussion by all in attendance; too few participants may produce a lackluster discussion and too many participants may hinder full participation on all topics (D. Stewart, Shamdasani, & Rook, 2007). Participants usually do not know one another, although some studies in organized settings may include friends or coworkers. Opinions differ on the value of using homogeneous versus heterogeneous participants. Homogeneous groups may be more convivial and willing to share feelings, but heterogeneous groups may stimulate more ideas (J. Brown, 1999). Of course, the characteristics of individuals that determine their inclusion are based on the researcher's conception of the target population for the study.

The focus group moderator must begin the discussion by generating interest in the topic, creating the expectation that all will participate, and that the moderator will not favor any particular perspective or participant. The group moderator uses an interview guide, but the dynamics of group discussion often require changes in the order and manner in which different topics are addressed (J. Brown, 1999). All questions should be clear, simple, and straightforward. The moderator should begin with easy-to-answer general questions; while the information itself is useful it will also help orient the participants to the group process and set the tone for the remaining time. About 15 to 20 minutes into the allotted time, the moderator should shift to key questions on specific issues. In some cases, discussion may be stimulated by asking participants to make a list of concerns or experiences, to rate predefined items, or to choose between alternatives. If the question flow is successful, the participants should experience the focus group as an engaging and friendly discussion and the moderator should spend more time after the introductory period listening and guiding the discussion rather than asking questions. Disagreements should be handled carefully so that no participants feel uncomfortable and the discussion should be kept focused on the announced topic (Smithson, 2008). The moderator may conclude the group discussion by asking participants for recommendations or their further thoughts that they have not had a chance to express (Krueger & Casey, 2009).

The interview guide usually consists of a maximum of 12 questions. The moderator generally will probe and further question to obtain more information. The first questions tend to be general while later questions are more specific (D. Stewart et al., 2007).

Berit Ingersoll-Dayton, Margaret Neal, Jung-hwa Ha, and Leslie Hammer (2003) provide an example of how focus groups can offer unexpected responses that produce new knowledge. They had organized 17 focus groups comprising adult children caring for parents or in-laws for at least 3 hours a week. The groups focused on caregiving and work, as well as caregiving and family responsibilities. "Although no specific questions about caregiving relationships among siblings were posed, participants initiated discussion of this topic in 16 of the 17 focus groups" (Ingersoll-Dayton et al., 2003, p. 55). Focusing on these responses, the researchers concluded,

> By examining caregiving from a collaborative perspective, this study revealed caregiving as a dynamic process. In fact, we found that sibling caregivers consciously switched from primary to secondary roles on a regular basis. As illustrated by the two sisters who planned to take turns caring for their dying father, siblings may purposefully vary their caregiving responsibilities. . . . Another important discovery is that aging parents can facilitate collaboration among adult siblings. . . . Our study shows how older parents can help their children cooperate by providing the same information or instructions to all of them. In so doing, siblings can concentrate their efforts on a similar goal rather than feeling confused and conflicted when parents provide contradictory instructions to different children. (p. 62)

Focus groups are now used extensively to identify social service needs and utilization patterns. For example, Caroline Rosenthal Gelman (2002) describes findings of a focus group with older Latinos. Service providers in a Massachusetts community asked for a needs assessment of elderly Latinos due to their low service utilization. A focus group with 10 elderly Latinos was used to discuss topics such as the needs of older Latinos, formal services, how they became aware of these services, and informal supports.

Focus group methods share with other field research techniques an emphasis on discovering unanticipated findings and exploring hidden meanings. They can be an indispensable aid for developing hypotheses and survey questions, for investigating the meaning of survey results, and for quickly assessing the range of opinion about an issue. Exhibit 10.8 offers guidelines for running focus groups.

回 Community-Based Participatory Research

Community-based participatory research (CBPR) or participatory action research is a collaborative approach to research in which the researcher involves as active participants and equal partners members of the community. The collaboration includes key stakeholders such as community residents, agency representatives, other organizational representatives, and researchers with each bringing different skills, knowledge, and expertise (Dulmus & Cristalli, 2012; Israel, Eng, Schulz, & Baker, 2005). The various members have shared input into all phases of the research from problem definition to dissemination and publication of the findings. Israel and her colleagues (2005) describe the aim of CBPR as "to increase knowledge and understanding of a given phenomenon and integrate the knowledge gained with interventions and policy and social change to improve the health and quality of life of community members" (p. 5).

Exhibit 10.8 | Keys to Running Focus Groups

- A great moderator—Is neutral and genuinely respects the participants, is a great listener who can draw people out, and creates a trusting environment.
- A great assistant—Is physically separated from the group, is responsible for recording, and taking notes about what is observed in group dynamics. The moderator should not be distracted with these tasks.
- Recording—Audio recording and observer notes is best.
- Setting—A location that is accessible and conducted in a space with minimal distractions (interesting paintings, large windows) as the goal is to have the group focused on the topic.
- Participants—Are homogenous by relevant category for comparisons, with no power differentials within the group. Group dynamics are an important consideration.
- Sampling—Is purposeful, representing the entire range of responses. Ideally participants in any group should be strangers to each other. Use reminders to attend with incentives.
- Analysis—Compare answers of different groups to different questions.
- Reporting—You are speaking for the participants. Lead with the big insights and answer the questions that were asked of the study. Interesting quotations get attention.
- Consider—Participants are helping you. Consider their needs with regard to transportation, need for child-care, food and the like.

Good focus groups get honest answers, on important topics from people who know.

Source: Adapted from Richard A. Krueger and Mary Anne Casey. (2000). *Focus Groups: A Practical Guide for Applied Research*, 3rd Edition. Thousand Oaks, CA: Sage.

CBPR is not itself a qualitative method, but these projects tend to use qualitative methods, which are more accessible to members of the community and which normally involve some of the same activities as in CBPR: engaging with individuals in their natural settings and listening to them in their own words. Those who engage in CBPR projects are making a commitment to "listen, learn from, solicit and respect the contributions of, and share power, information, and credit for accomplishments with the group that they are trying to learn about and help" (Horowitz, Robinson, & Seifer, 2009, p. 2634).

The emphasis on developing a partnership with the community is reflected in the principles presented in Exhibit 10.9; each principle identifies features of the researcher's relationships with the community. *Community* need not be a geographic area, but rather a community of identity, organized around groupings in which people have membership and which is defined by a common symbols, values, norms, shared interests, and commitment (Israel et al. 2005). These cultural aspects of community require *cultural humility* on the part of the researcher; to achieve cultural humility requires reflection, critique, and commitment to addressing power differences (Minkler, 2005).

The inclusive orientation of CBPR suggests that it is a feasible approach to working with at-risk and diverse population groups (Baffour, 2011; O'Toole, Aaron, Chin, Horowitz, & Tyson, 2003). The distrust such groups have about research may be mitigated by the shared decision making in the research process and commitment not just to scientific achievement but also to social action (Baffour, 2011).

Karen Hacker and colleagues (2008) collaborated with community partners in response to a public health emergency in a local community. After a series of youth suicides and overdoses from 2000 to 2005, a community coalition was formed with members from mental health service providers, school leaders, policy, and community parents. After reviewing multiple statistics, the coalition concluded that the deaths represented a considerable increase over previous years. However, when mental health professionals attempted to interview family members of adolescents who had committed suicide in order to investigate the background to the suicides, they were rebuffed; in contrast, family members were willing to talk at length with coalition members from their community. The coalition was then able to map out the relationships between the suicide victims. The process of using the results of this research to respond to the suicides

---

Exhibit 10.9 | **Principles of Community-Based Participatory Research (CBPR)**

1. CBPR acknowledges community as a unit of identity.
2. CBPR builds on strengths and resources within the community.
3. CBPR facilitates a collaborative, equitable partnership in all phases of research, involving an empowering and power-sharing process that attends to all inequalities.
4. CBPR fosters co-learning and capacity building among all partners.
5. CBPR integrates and achieves a balance between knowledge generation and intervention for the mutual benefit of all partners.
6. CBPR focuses on the local relevance of public health problems and on ecological perspectives that attend to the multiple determinants of health.
7. CBPR involves systems development using a cyclical and iterative process.
8. CBPR disseminates results to all partners and involves them in the wider dissemination of results.
9. CBPR involves a long-term process and commitment to sustainability

---

Source: Adapted from Israel, B. A., Eng, E., Schulz, A. J., & Parker, E. A. (2005). Introduction to methods in community-based participatory research for health. In B. A. Israel, E. Eng, A. J. Schulz, & E. A. Parker (Eds.), *Methods in community-based participatory research for health* (pp. 3-26). San Francisco, CA: Jossey-Bass.

included a candlelight vigil, a speak-out against substance abuse, the provision of crisis counseling, and programs to support families and educate the community. Subsequently, the suicide rate dropped back to its pre-2000 level.

Qualitative Research in a Diverse Society

Positivist research strategies and findings have been criticized as monocultural and Eurocentric (Kagawa-Singer, 2000; Stanfield, 1999) and gender focused (Griffin & Phoenix, 1994). Often the positivist view toward finding universal rules does not account for cultural differences; the theories and measures used in studies reflect one worldview. What is deemed as neutral and objective is not because the research is driven by that worldview (Stanfield, 1999). Qualitative research allows researchers to obtain a richer and more intimate view of the social world than more structured methods. These methods provide a greater voice to the people being studied than do the rigid structures imposed by quantitative methods. With a concern with not just behavior but also the meaning and interpretations ascribed to the behavior, qualitative methods are particularly useful for research with diverse population groups.

Qualitative research studies can enhance quantitative studies. We have described in Chapters 4 and 9 the need for questions and measures to be culturally equivalent. To do so requires the use of qualitative data collection techniques, such as intensive interviewing (such as cognitive interviewing), observing or listening (behavioral coding), and focus groups. These strategies are designed to improve the validity of the measures used in quantitative studies and, therefore, enhance the validity of the findings.

But qualitative studies go beyond just improving quantitative studies. Kagawa-Singer (2000) and Nápoles-Springer and Stewart (2006) suggest that health disparities and health care research have been too focused on the values and practices of Euro-Americans. A narrow approach to culture discounts how those with different worldviews define problems and precludes identifying alternative methods to deliver services that might be more effective. Therefore, a broader framework that encompasses both universal and cultural factors can improve outcomes for diverse and underserved populations (Kagawa-Singer, 2000; Nápoles-Springer & Stewart, 2006). Similar arguments can be made about different fields such as mental health, aging, or child welfare. These considerations have implications for evidence-based practice, as we discuss in the next section.

⌨ Implications for Evidence-Based Practice

The various qualitative methods described throughout this chapter provide important knowledge that is useful for evidence-based practice. Yet there is a fear that the experimental methods we have described up to this point will become the dominant research paradigm to provide evidence about the best practice. At the extreme, Norman Denzin (2005) suggests that "the evidence-based experimental science movement, with accompanying federal legislation, threatens to deny advances in critical qualitative inquiry, including rigorous criticisms of positivist research" (pp. 109–110).

Despite this extreme view, there appears to be general agreement that qualitative methods can and do provide useful research findings about practice effectiveness. As we have said in previous chapters, evidence-based practice involves integrating the best available research evidence with clinical expertise and client values and *not* just the application of empirically supported interventions (Gambril, 2006). This means that the best research evidence needs to be integrated with information about the client learned during the course of treatment and a client's characteristics, such as the way problems may be defined by the client or how they present to the social worker, developmental and life stage, social and cultural factors, family factors, environmental factors such as stressors, and personal preferences (American Psychological Association, 2006). To the extent that quantitative methods, and experimental designs in particular, fail to generalize across populations (i.e., lack external validity), qualitative methods are useful in shedding light on what is the most appropriate practice for a particular client, given a particular situation and given the context in which it is used (Plath, 2006).

There are various ways in which qualitative methods inform practice. Some of these ways include the following.

Qualitative methods can be used to assess the design and delivery of services. For example, Anderson-Butcher and her colleagues (Anderson-Butcher, Khairallah, & Race-Bigelow, 2004) recognized that, although much of the effort around welfare reform were strategies and interventions designed to get Temporary Assistance to Needy Families recipients to work, there were few interventions to support recipients over the long term. To understand how participation in a support group impacted group participants, nine participants were interviewed with open-ended, nondirective questions. They learned what made a group successful, including structural considerations (e.g., babysitting), facilitator characteristics (e.g., being a mediator), group composition, as well as the benefits for participants and their families. The findings can inform the design and delivery of services.

Qualitative methods are useful in uncovering the process and nature of service delivery. For example, although there is evidence to support Assertive Community Treatment (ACT) as a treatment approach with the chronically mentally ill, it has been criticized for being coercive and paternalistic in getting clients to adhere to treatment (Angell, Mahoney, & Martinez, 2006). To examine whether there was a coercive nature to ACT, Angell and colleagues (2006) identified an urban program and a rural program, observed 14 providers in interactions with clients, and subsequently conducted open-ended interviews with each of the participants. Through their study, they learned how ACT providers construct problems of nonadherence, how they promote adherence in their clients, and under what conditions the strategies vary. For example, there were differences between the rural and urban setting in whether and how coercive strategies were used. In some cases, workers compelled clients, whereas others used interpersonal influence strategies.

Qualitative methods can clarify clients' perceptions of interventions. Muriel Singer (2005) asked the question, "How do clients make sense of the experience of therapy?" She asked clients to write weekly case notes following a question guide, conducted taped interviews, and reviewed her own notes during the data collection period to understand the role of the client–therapist relationship in achieving outcomes.

These methods can help social workers understand why people in need of services do not seek help. Michael Lindsey and his colleagues (2006) wanted to learn about help-seeking behaviors and depression among African American adolescent boys. They conducted interviews with 18 urban youth recruited from community mental health centers and afterschool programs. Those in treatment had family members and school personnel who noted their depressive symptoms and facilitated their access to mental health services, whereas those youth not in treatment had family members who argued against seeking professional help.

Qualitative methods can be used to establish treatment fidelity in multisite studies. When interventions are tested at multiple sites, one concern is the degree to which implementation of the intervention follows the principles and procedures of the intervention model. Gary Bond and his colleagues (Bond, Drake, McHugo, Rapp, & Whitley, 2009) use both qualitative and quantitative methods to address this particular issue and to identify factors related to treatment fidelity. The qualitative component included observations recorded as field notes and in-depth interviews.

Therefore, the issue of establishing credible evidence should not be an argument for or against quantitative or qualitative methods. Evidence-based practice includes anything that provides systematically collected information that informs social work practice (Pollio, 2006).

▣ Ethical Issues in Qualitative Research

Qualitative research can raise some complex ethical issues. No matter how hard the field researcher strives to study the social world naturally, leaving no traces, the act of research imposes something unnatural on the situation. It is up to researchers to identify and take responsibility for the consequences of their involvement. The following main ethical issues arise.

Voluntary participation. Ensuring that subjects are participating in a study voluntarily is not often a problem with intensive interviewing and focus group research. When qualitative interviews are conducted in multiple sessions, the opportunity to withdraw consent should always be available to participants (N. King & Horrocks, 2010).

Maintaining the standard of voluntary participation can present more challenges in participant observation studies. Few researchers or institutional review boards are willing to condone covert participation because it offers no way to ensure that participation by the subjects is voluntary. However, interpreting the standard of voluntary participation can be difficult even when the researcher's role is more open. Practically, much field research would be impossible if the participant observer were required to request permission of everyone having some contact, no matter how minimal, with a group or setting being observed.

Process consent: An interpretation of the ethical standard of voluntary consent that allows participants to change their decision about participating at any point by requiring that the researcher check with participants at each stage of the project about their willingness to continue in the project.

Some researchers recommend adherence to a process consent standard to adjust the ideal of informed consent to the reality of the evolving nature of social relations and research plans in qualitative projects. **Process consent** allows participants to change their decision about participating at any point by requiring that the researcher check with participants at each stage of the project about their willingness to continue (Sieber & Tolic, 2013).

Subject well-being. Before beginning a new project, every field researcher should consider carefully how to avoid harm to participants. Direct harm to the reputations or feelings of particular individuals should be avoided at all costs. It will be difficult for others to counter the interpretations offered by participant observers since findings are not verifiable and the contextual nature of the research makes it more difficult to replicate the study (Herrera, 2003). The risk of such harm can be minimized by maintaining the confidentiality of research participants. Participant observers must also avoid adversely affecting the course of events while engaged in a setting.

The well-being of the group or community studied as a whole should also be considered in relation to the research and dissemination of findings. Some disadvantaged communities now require that researchers seek approval for all their procedures and request approval before releasing findings in order to prevent harm to the community (Lincoln, 2009). Researchers should spend time in local settings before the research plan is finalized in order to identify a range of community stakeholders who can then be consulted about research plans (Bledsoe & Hopson, 2009).

These problems are rare in intensive interviewing and focus groups, but even there, researchers should try to identify negative feelings and help distressed subjects cope with their feelings through debriefing or referrals for professional help. Online interviewing can create additional challenges for interviews in which respondents become inappropriately personal over time (N. King & Horrocks, 2010).

Identity disclosure. Current ethical standards require informed consent of research subjects, and most would argue that this standard cannot be met in any meaningful way if researchers do not disclose fully their identity. But how much disclosure about the study is necessary and how hard should researchers try to make sure that their research purposes are understood? In field research on Codependents Anonymous, Leslie Irvine (1998) found that the emphasis on anonymity and the expectations for group discussion made it difficult to disclose her identity. Less-educated subjects may not readily comprehend what a researcher is or be able to weigh the possible consequences of the research for themselves. The intimacy of the researcher–participant relationship in much qualitative research makes it difficult to inject reminders about the research into ongoing social interaction (Mabry, 2008).

Members of online communities can disguise their identities, so gaining informed consent creates unique challenges for netnography, yet the research should not proceed unless an effort is made to obtain informed and voluntary consent. Researchers conducting netnography should minimize the risks created by these uncertainties by making their own identities known, stating clearly their expectations for participation, and providing an explicit informed consent letter that is available as discussion participants come and go (Denzin & Lincoln, 2008).

Confidentiality. Field researchers normally use fictitious names for the characters in their reports, but doing so does not always guarantee confidentiality to their research subjects. Individuals in the setting studied may be able to identify those whose actions are described and may thus become privy to some knowledge about their colleagues or neighbors that had formerly been kept from them. Therefore, researchers should make every effort to expunge possible identifying material from published information and to alter unimportant aspects of a description when necessary to prevent identity disclosure. In any case, no field research project should begin if some participants clearly will suffer serious harm by being identified in project publications.

Focus groups create a particular challenge because the researcher cannot guarantee that participants will not disclose information that others would like to be treated as confidential. Cultures differ in their openness to dissent and their sensitivity to public discussion of personal issues, so focus groups can exacerbate the difficulty of establishing appropriate standards for confidentiality (Smithson, 2008). The risk can be reduced at the start of the focus group by reviewing a list of dos and don'ts with participants. Nevertheless, focus group methodology should not be used for very personally sensitive topics (Smithson, 2008).

With Photovoice the research participants are actively involved in gathering data as they take photos to address different topics. As part of the informed consent process, participants should be told that the researchers are legally required to report to legal authorities photos revealing child or elder abuse or the likely prospect of harm to oneself or to others. Participants might need to be discouraged from taking identifiable pictures of people, and if they do then they will need to learn about methods to obtain consent prior to taking the pictures. The participants should also know that the researcher legally owns the photographs, though part of the Photovoice process is that the researcher and the participants decide jointly which photographs to make public; nonetheless, ownership and publishing of the photos may become a source of conflict.

Online interviewing adds unique twists to these ethical issues. Confidentiality of e-mails and downloaded texts are concerns that require efforts to de-identify the source of the e-mail or other communication, protect the computer from viruses or hacking, and store information in password protected files (Hamilton & Bowers, 2006; McCoyd & Kerson, 2006)

Appropriate boundaries. This is an ethical issue that cuts across several of the others including identity disclosure, subject well-being, and voluntary participation. You probably are familiar with this issue in the context of guidelines for professional social work practice. Social workers must maintain appropriate boundaries with their clients. This is a special issue in qualitative research because it often involves *lessening* the boundary between the "researcher" and the "participant." Qualitative researchers may seek to build rapport with those they plan to interview by expressing an interest in their concerns and conveying empathy for their situation. The long-term relationships that can develop in participant observation studies can make it seem natural for researchers to offer tangible help to participants. These involvements can make it difficult to avoid becoming an advocate rather than an observer. Qualitative researchers need to be sensitive to the potential for these problems and respond flexibly and respectfully to the concerns of research participants.

These ethical issues cannot be evaluated independently. The final decision to proceed must be made after weighing the relative benefits and risks to participants. Few qualitative research projects will be barred by consideration of these ethical issues, however, except for those involving covert participation. The more important concern for researchers is to identify the ethically troublesome aspects of their proposed research and resolve them before the project begins and to act on new ethical issues as they come up during the project.

回 Conclusion

Qualitative research allows the careful investigator to obtain a richer and more intimate view of the social world than do more structured methods. The emphases in qualitative research on inductive reasoning and incremental understanding help to stimulate and inform other research approaches, too. Exploratory research to chart the dimensions of previously unstudied social settings and intensive investigations of the subjective meanings that motivate individual action are particularly well served by the techniques of participant observation, intensive interviewing, and focus groups.

The characteristics that make qualitative research techniques so appealing restrict their use to a limited set of research problems. It is not possible to draw representative samples for study using participant observation and, for this reason, the generalizability of any particular field study's results cannot really be known. Only the accumulation of findings from numerous qualitative studies permits confident generalization, but here again, the time and effort required to collect and analyze the data make it unlikely that many field research studies will be replicated.

Even if qualitative researchers made more of an effort to replicate key studies, their notion of developing and grounding explanations inductively in the observations made in a particular setting would hamper comparison of findings. Measurement reliability is thereby hindered, as are systematic tests for the validity of key indicators and formal tests for causal connections.

In the final analysis, qualitative research involves a mode of thinking and investigating different from that used in experimental and survey research. Qualitative research is inductive and idiographic; whereas experiments and surveys tend to be conducted in a deductive, quantitative, and nomothetic framework. Both approaches can help social scientists learn about the social world; the proficient researcher must be ready to use either. Qualitative data are often supplemented with counts of characteristics or activities. As you have already seen, quantitative data are often enriched with written comments and observations, and focus groups have become a common tool of survey researchers seeking to develop their questionnaires. Thus, the distinction between qualitative and quantitative research techniques is not always clear-cut, and combining methods is often a good idea. We will return to this in Chapter 12, on mixed methods.

Key Terms

Case study   262
Complete (covert)
    participant   266
Covert observer   266
Ethnography   263
Field notes   272
Focus groups   266

Grand tour questions   277
Intensive interviewing   266
Jottings   272
Netnography   264
Participant observation   266
Photovoice   264
Process consent   286

Reactive effects   267
Saturation point   277
Systematic observation   275
Theoretical sampling   271
Thick description   262

Highlights

- Qualitative methods are most useful in exploring new issues, investigating hard-to-study groups, and determining the meaning people give to their lives and actions. In addition, most social research projects can be improved in some respects by taking advantage of qualitative techniques.

- Qualitative researchers tend to develop ideas inductively, try to understand the social context and sequential nature of attitudes and actions, and explore the subjective meanings that participants attach to events. They rely primarily on participant observation, intensive interviewing, and focus groups.

- Case studies use thick description and other qualitative techniques to provide a holistic picture of a setting or group.

- Ethnographers attempt to understand the culture of a group.

- Netnographers use ethnographic techniques to study online communities.

- Participant observers may adopt one of several roles for a particular research project. Each role represents a different balance between observing and participating. Many field researchers prefer a moderate role, participating as well as observing in a group, but acknowledging publicly the researcher role. Such a role avoids ethical issues posed by covert participating while still allowing the insights into the social world derived from participating directly in it. The role that the participant observer chooses should be based on an evaluation of the problems likely to arise from reactive effects and the ethical dilemmas of covert participating.

- Field researchers must develop strategies for entering the field, developing and maintaining relations in the field, sampling, and recording and analyzing data. Selection of sites or other units to study may reflect an emphasis on typical cases, deviant cases, and/or critical cases that can provide more information than others. Sampling techniques commonly used within sites or in selecting interviewees in field research include theoretical sampling, purposive sampling, snowball sampling, quota sampling, and, in special circumstances, random selection.

- Recording and analyzing notes is a crucial step in field research. Jottings are used as brief reminders about events in the field, while daily logs are useful to chronicle the researcher's activities. Detailed field notes should be recorded and analyzed daily. Analysis of the notes can guide refinement of methods used in the field and of the concepts, indicators, and models developed to explain what has been observed.

- Intensive interviews involve open-ended questions and follow-up probes, with specific question content and order varying from one interview to another. Intensive interviews can supplement participant observation data.

- Focus groups use elements of participant observation and intensive interviewing. They can increase the validity of attitude measurement by revealing what people say when presenting their opinions in a group context, instead of the artificial one-on-one interview setting.

- Community-based participatory research uses an ongoing collaboration with community participants to define the problem for research, to conduct the research, and to develop research reports.

- Five main ethical issues in field research that should be given attention concern voluntary participation, subject well-being, identity disclosure, confidentiality, and boundaries.

Discussion Questions

1. Define and describe participant observation, intensive interviewing, and focus groups. What features do these research designs share? How are they different?

2. Discuss the relative merits of complete observation, participant observation, and covert participation. What are the ethical considerations inherent in each?

3. Compare and contrast intensive interviewing with interviews used in survey research. Under what circumstances might you choose intensive interviewing techniques? What are the potential difficulties of using this type of research?

Practice Exercises

1. Conduct a brief observational study in a public location on campus where students congregate such as a building lobby, lounge, or cafeteria. Sit and observe, taking notes unobtrusively, without violating any expectations of privacy. Observe for 30 minutes. Write up field notes, being sure to include a description of the setting and a commentary on your own behavior and your reactions to what you observed.

2. Develop an interview guide that focuses on a research question of interest to you. Using this guide, conduct an intensive interview with one person who is involved with the topic in some way. Take only brief notes during the interview, and then write up as complete a record of the interview as soon as you can immediately afterword.

3. Read and summarize one of the qualitative studies student website for this book, www.sagepub.com/engel prsw4e. Review and critique the study using the article review questions presented in Appendix A. What questions are answered by the study? What questions are raised for further investigation?

Web Exercise

1. You have been asked to do field research on the Web's impact on the socialization of children in today's world. The first part of the project involves writing a compare-and-contrast report on the differences between how you and your generation were socialized as children and how children today are being socialized. Collect your data by surfing the Web "as if you were a kid." Using any of the major search engines, explore the Web within the Kids or Children subject heading, keeping field notes on what you observe. Write a brief report based on the data you have collected. How has the Web affected child socialization in comparison to when you were a child?

Developing a Research Proposal

Choose to either conduct a qualitative study or add a qualitative component to your proposed study. Pick the method that seems most likely to help answer the research question for the overall project.

1. For a participant observation component, propose an observational plan that would answer your research question. Present in your proposal the following information about your plan:

   a. Choose a site, and justify its selection in terms of its likely value for the research.

   b. Choose a role along the participant observation continuum, and justify your choice.

   c. Describe access procedures and note any likely problems.

   d. Discuss how you will develop and maintain relations in the site.

   e. Review any sampling issues.

   f. Present an overview of the way in which you will analyze the data you collect.

2. For an intensive interview component, propose a focus for the intensive interviews that you believe will add the most to your research question. Present in your proposal the following information about your plan:

   a. Present and justify a method for selecting individuals to interview.

   b. Write out several introductory biographical questions and five "grand tour" questions for your interview schedule.

   c. List different probes you may use.

   d. Present and justify at least two follow-up questions for one of your grand tour questions.

A Question of Ethics

1. In journalism, paying for information is a "cardinal sin" because journalists are indoctrinated with the notion that they are observers. They are trained to report on situations, but not to influence a situation. This is what many scholars believe a researcher's role should be. Does paying for information unduly influence the truthfulness of the information being sought? Do you believe some people will say anything to earn money? What are your thoughts on paying for information? What if you were investigating the problems faced by families living below the poverty level and during an interview you noticed that the family refrigerator and cupboards were empty and the baby was crying from hunger? What is the ethical reaction? If you believe the most ethical response would be to provide food or money for food, is it fair that there is another family next door in the same condition that did not happen to be on your interview list? How should gratuities be handled?

2. Should any requirements be imposed on researchers who seek to study other cultures in order to ensure that procedures are appropriate and interpretations are culturally sensitive? What practices would you suggest for cross-cultural researchers to ensure that ethical guidelines are followed? (Consider the wording of consent forms and the procedures for gaining voluntary cooperation.)

3. Discuss the ethical issues you would face in creating a focus group consisting of agency clients. Develop a written statement to recruit participants.

CHAPTER 11

Qualitative Data Analysis

I was at lunch standing in line and he [another male student] came up to my face and started saying stuff and then he pushed me. I said . . . I'm cool with you, I'm your friend and then he push me again and calling me names. I told him to stop pushing me and then he push me hard and said something about my mom. And then he hit me, and I hit him back. After he fell I started kicking him.

—Morrill, Yalda, Adelman, Musheno, and Bejarano (2000, p. 521)

This statement was not made by a soap opera actor but by a student writing an in-class essay about conflicts in which he had participated. But then you already knew that such conflicts are common in many high schools, so perhaps it will be reassuring to know that this statement was elicited by a team of social scientists who were studying conflicts in high schools to better understand their origins and to inform prevention policies. Does it surprise you that the text excerpt above is data used in a qualitative research project? The first difference between qualitative and quantitative data analysis is that the data to be analyzed are texts, rather than numbers, at least when the analysis first begins. Does it trouble you to learn that there are no variables and hypotheses in this qualitative analysis by Morrill et al. (2000)? This, too, is another difference between the typical qualitative and quantitative approaches to analysis, although there are some exceptions.

In this chapter, we present the features that most qualitative data analyses share. You will learn that there is no one way to analyze textual data. To quote Michael Quinn Patton (2002),

Qualitative analysis transforms data into findings. No formula exists for that transformation. Guidance, yes. But no recipe. Direction can and will be offered, but the final destination remains unique for each inquirer, known only when—and if—arrived at. (p. 432)

We discuss some of the different types of qualitative data analysis before focusing on content analysis, an approach to analyzing text that relies on quantitative techniques. We illustrate how computer programs are used for qualitative data analysis and how they are blurring the distinctions between quantitative and qualitative approaches to textual analysis.

⚏ Features of Qualitative Data Analysis

The distinctive features of qualitative data collection methods that you studied in Chapter 10 are also reflected in the methods used to analyze the data. The focus on text—on qualitative data, rather than on numbers—is the most important feature of qualitative analysis, but that does not define qualitative data analysis. The text that qualitative researchers analyze is most often transcripts of interviews or notes from participant observation sessions, but text can also refer to pictures or images that the researcher examines.

What can the qualitative data analyst learn from a text? There are two kinds of answers to this question. Some researchers view textual analysis as a way to understand what participants really thought, felt, or did in some situation or at some point in time. The text becomes a way to get behind the numbers that are recorded in a quantitative analysis to see the richness of real social experience.

Other qualitative researchers have adopted a *hermeneutic* perspective on texts, that is, a perspective that views text as an interpretation that can never be judged true or false. The text has many possible interpretations (Patton, 2002). The meaning of a text is negotiated among a community of interpreters, and to the extent that some agreement is reached about meaning at a particular time and place, that meaning can only be based on consensual validation. From the hermeneutic perspective, a researcher is constructing a reality with the interpretations of a text provided by the subjects of research; other researchers, with different backgrounds, could come to markedly different conclusions.

One of the other important differences between qualitative and quantitative data analysis is in the priority given to the views of the study participants versus those of the researcher. Qualitative data analysts seek to describe their textual data in ways that capture the setting or people who produced this text in their own terms rather than in terms of predefined measures and hypotheses. What this means is that qualitative data analysis tends to be inductive—drawing from the data the analyst identifies important categories in the data, as well as patterns and relationships, through a process of discovery. There are often no predefined measures or hypotheses. Anthropologists term this an emic focus, which means representing the setting in terms of the participants, rather than an etic focus, in which the setting and its participants are represented in terms that the researcher brings to the study.

Good qualitative data analyses are also distinguished by their focus on the interrelated aspects of the setting or group, or person, under investigation; the focus is on the case as a whole rather than breaking the whole into separate parts. The whole is understood to be greater than the sum of its parts, and so the social context of events, thoughts, and actions becomes essential for interpretation. Within this framework, it does not really make sense to focus on two variables out of an interacting set of influences and test the relationship between just those two.

Qualitative data analysis is an iterative and reflexive process that begins as data are being collected rather than after data collection has ceased (Stake, 1995). Next to the field notes or interview transcripts, the qualitative analyst jots down ideas about the meaning of the text and how it might relate to other issues. This process of reading through the data and interpreting them continues throughout the project. When it begins to appear that additional concepts need to be investigated or new relationships explored the analyst adjusts the data collection process. This process is termed **progressive focusing** (Parlett & Hamilton, 1976).

Progressive focusing The process by which qualitative analysts interact with the data and gradually refine their focus.

> We emphasize placing an interpreter in the field to observe the workings of the case, one who records objectively what is happening but simultaneously examines its meaning and redirects observation to refine or substantiate those meanings. Initial research questions may be modified or even replaced in mid-study by the case researcher. The aim is to thoroughly understand [the case]. If early questions are not working, if new issues become apparent, the design is changed. (Stake, 1995, pp. 8–9)

In the 1970s, Elijah Anderson (2005) was interested in how people organized themselves and how this resulted in a local system of social stratification. He conducted an ethnographic study of life at Jelly's Bar, a street corner bar, where he observed 55 African American men. In his memoir about this study, Anderson describes the progressive focusing process:

> Throughout the study, I also wrote conceptual memos to myself to help sort out my findings. Usually no more than a page long, they represented theoretical insights that emerged from my engagement with the data in my field notes. As I gained tenable hypotheses and propositions, I began to listen and observe selectively, focusing on those events that I thought might bring me alive to my research interests and concerns. This method of dealing with the information I was receiving amounted to a kind of dialogue with the data, sifting out ideas, weighing new notions against the reality with which I was faced there on the streets and back at my desk. (p. 51)

Carrying out this process successfully is more likely if the analyst reviews a few basic guidelines when starting the process of analyzing qualitative data (W. Miller & Crabtree, 1999):

1. Know yourself, your biases, and preconceptions.

2. Know your question.

3. Seek creative abundance. Consult others, and keep looking for alternative interpretations.

4. Be flexible.

5. Exhaust the data. Try to account for all the data in the texts, then publicly acknowledge the unexplained and remember the next principle.

6. Celebrate anomalies. They are the windows to insight.

7. Get critical feedback. The solo analyst is a great danger to self and others.

8. Be explicit. Share the details with yourself, your team members, and your audiences. (pp. 142–143)

Qualitative Data Analysis as an Art

If you miss the certainty of predefined measures and deductively derived hypotheses, you are beginning to understand the difference between quantitative and qualitative data analysis. When it comes right down to it, the process of qualitative data analysis is even described by some as involving as much art as science—as a "dance," in the words of William Miller and Benjamin Crabtree (1999; see Exhibit 11.1):

> Interpretation is a complex and dynamic craft, with as much creative artistry as technical exactitude, and it requires an abundance of patient plodding, fortitude, and discipline. There are many changing rhythms; multiple steps; moments of jubilation, revelation, and exasperation. . . . The dance of interpretation is a dance for two, but those two are often multiple and frequently changing, and there is always an audience, even if it is not always visible. Two dancers are the interpreters and the texts. (pp. 138–139)

Miller and Crabtree (1999) identify the different modes of reading the text within the dance of qualitative data analysis:

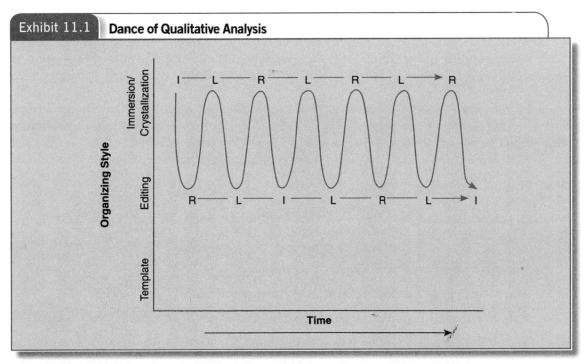

Exhibit 11.1 | **Dance of Qualitative Analysis**

Source: Miller & Crabtree, 1999b:139, Figure 7.1. Based on Addison, 1999.

1. When the researcher reads the text *literally* (L in Exhibit 11.1), the focus is on its literal content and form, so the text leads the dance.

2. When the researcher reads the text *reflexively* (R), the researcher focuses on how his or her own orientation shapes his or her interpretations and focus. Now, the researcher leads the dance.

3. When the researcher reads the text *interpretively* (I), the researcher tries to construct his or her own interpretation of what the text means.

Sherry Turkle's (2011) book *Alone Together: Why We Expect More From Technology and Less From Each Other* provides many examples of this analytic dance, although of course in the published book we are no longer able to see that dance in terms of her original notes. She often describes what she observed in classrooms. Here is an example of such a *literal* focus:

> In the summer of 1996, I met seven young researchers at the MIT Media Lab who carried computers and radio transmitters in their backpacks and keyboards in their pockets. . . . They called themselves "cyborgs" and were always connected to the Internet, always online, free from desks and cables. (p. 151)

Such literal reports are interspersed with *interpretative* comments about the meaning of her observations:

> The cyborgs were a new kind of nomad, wandering in and out of the physical real. . . . The multiplicity of worlds before them set them apart; they could be with you, but they were always somewhere else as well. (Turkle, 2011, p. 152)

And several times in each chapter, Turkle (2011) makes *reflexive* comments on her own reactions:

> I don't like the feeling of always being on call. But now, with a daughter studying abroad who expects to reach me when she wants to reach me, I am grateful to be tethered to her through the Net. . . . Even these small things allow me to identify with the cyborgs' claims of an enhanced experience. Tethered to the Internet, the cyborgs felt like more than they could be without it. Like most people, I experience a pint-sized version of such pleasures. (p. 153)

In this artful way, the qualitative data analyst reports on the notes from observing or interviewing, interprets those notes, and considers the reaction to the notes. These processes emerge from reading the notes and continue while editing the notes and deciding how to organize them, in an ongoing cycle.

Qualitative Compared to Quantitative Data Analysis

With these points in mind, let's review the ways in which qualitative data analysis differs from quantitative analysis (Denzin & Lincoln, 2000; Patton, 2002):

- A focus on meanings, rather than on quantifiable phenomena

- Collection of many data on a few cases, rather than few data on many cases

- Study in depth and detail without predetermined categories or directions, rather than emphasis on analyses and categories determined in advance

- Conception of the researcher as an instrument, rather than as the designer of the objective instruments to measure particular variables

- Sensitivity to context, rather than seeking universal generalizations

- Attention to the impact of the researcher's and others' values on the course of the analysis, rather than presuming the possibility of value-free inquiry

- A goal of rich descriptions of the world, rather than measurement of specific variables

Of course, even the most qualitative textual data can be transposed to quantitative data through a process of categorization and counting. Some qualitative analysts also share with quantitative researchers a positivist goal of better describing the world as it "really" is, but others have adopted a goal of trying to understand how different people see and make sense of the world, without believing there is any uniquely "correct" description.

🏛 Techniques of Qualitative Data Analysis

Many approaches to qualitative data analysis share five different techniques:

1. Documentation of the data and the process of data collection

2. Organization/categorization/condensation of the data into concepts

3. Examination and display of relationships between concepts

4. Corroboration/legitimization of conclusions by evaluating alternative explanations and disconfirming evidence and searching for negative cases

5. Reflection of the researcher's role

Some researchers suggest different or additional steps, such as developing propositions that reflect the relationships found and making connections with extant theories (Miles, Huberman, & Saldaña, 2014). Exhibit 11.2 highlights the key techniques and emphasizes the reciprocal relations between them. In qualitative data analysis, condensation of data into concepts may lead to some conclusions and to a particular form of display of

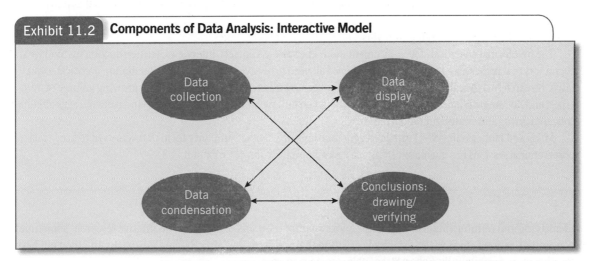

Exhibit 11.2 | **Components of Data Analysis: Interactive Model**

Source: Miles, M. B., Huberman, A. M., & Soldaña, J. (2014). *Qualitative data analysis: A methods sourcebook* (3rd ed.). Thousand Oaks, CA: Sage.

relationships between concepts, but the conclusions may then lead to some changes in conceptualization and display, an iterative process.

The analysis of qualitative research notes begins in the field, at the time of observation, interviewing, or both, as the researcher identifies problems and concepts that appear likely to help in understanding the situation. Simply reading the notes or transcripts is an important step in the analytic process. Researchers should make frequent notes in the margins to identify important statements and to propose ways of coding the data.

An interim stage may consist of listing the concepts reflected in the notes and diagramming the relationships among concepts (Maxwell, 2005). In large projects, weekly team meetings are an important part of this process. Susan Miller's (1999) research team met to go over their field notes, resolve points of confusion, and dialogue with other skilled researchers who helped to identify emerging concepts:

> The fieldwork team met weekly to talk about situations that were unclear and to troubleshoot any problems. We also made use of peer-debriefing techniques. Here, multiple colleagues, who were familiar with qualitative data analysis but not involved in our research, participated in preliminary analysis of our findings. (p. 233)

This process continues throughout the project and should assist in refining concepts during the report-writing phase long after data collection has ceased.

Documentation

The data for a qualitative study most often are notes jotted down in the field or during an interview—from which the original comments, observations, and feelings are reconstructed—or text transcribed from audiotapes. "The basic data are these observations and conversations, the actual words of people reproduced to the best of my ability from the field notes" (Diamond, 1992, p. 7). What to do with all this material? Many field research projects have slowed to a halt because a novice researcher becomes overwhelmed by the quantity of information that has been collected. A 1-hour interview can generate 20 to 25 pages of single-spaced text (Kvale, 1996). Analysis is less daunting, however, if the process is broken into smaller steps and the researcher maintains a disciplined transcription schedule.

> Usually, I wrote these notes immediately after spending time in the setting or the next day. Through the exercise of writing up my field notes, with attention to "who" the speakers and actors were, I became aware of the nature of certain social relationships and their positional arrangements within the peer group. (Anderson, 2005, p. 51)

You can see the analysis emerging from this simple process of taking notes.

The first formal analytical step is documentation. The various contacts, interviews, written documents, and whatever it was that preserves a record of what happened all need to be saved and listed. Documentation is critical to qualitative research for several reasons: It is essential for keeping track of what will be a rapidly growing volume of notes, tapes, and documents; it provides a way of developing an outline for the analytic process; and it encourages ongoing conceptualizing and strategizing about the text.

Miles and Huberman (1994) provide a good example of a contact summary form that was used to keep track of observational sessions in a qualitative study of a new school curriculum (see Exhibit 11.3).

Organization, Categorization, and Condensation

Identifying and refining important concepts is a key part of the iterative process of qualitative research. Sometimes conceptualization begins with a simple observation that is interpreted directly, "pulled apart," and then put back together more meaningfully. Robert Stake (1995) provides an example:

| Exhibit 11.3 | **Example of a Contact Summary Form** |

Contact type:

Visit ___X___

Phone _____

     (with whom)

Site: <u>Tindale</u>

Contact date: <u>11/28–29/79</u>

Today's date: <u>12/28/7</u>

1. What were the main issues or themes that struck you in this contact?

    Interplay between highly prescriptive, "teacher-proof" curriculum that is top-down imposed and the actual writing of the curriculum by the teachers themselves.

    Split between the "watchdogs" (administrators) and the "house masters" (dept. chairs & teachers) vis a vis job foci.

    District curric. coord'r as decision maker re school's acceptance of research relationship.

2. Summarize the information you got (or failed to get) on each of the target questions you had for this contact

Question	Information
History of dev. of innov'n	Conceptualized by Curric., Coord'r, English Chairman & Assoc.Chairman; written by teachers in summer; revised by teachers following summer with field testing data
School's org'l structure	Principal & admin'rs responsible for discipline; dep't chairs are educ'l leaders
Demographics	Racial conflicts in late 60's; 60% black stud. pop.; heavy emphasis on discipline & on keeping out non-district students slipping in from Chicago
Teachers' response to	Rigid, structured, etc. at first; now, they say they like it/NEEDS
innovation	EXPLORATION
Research access	Very good; only restriction: teachers not required to cooperate

3. Anything else that struck you as salient, interesting, illuminating, or important in this contact?

    Thoroughness of the innovation's development and training.

    Its embeddedness in the district's curriculum, as planned and executed by the district curriculum coordinator.

    The initial resistance to its high prescriptiveness (as reported by users) as contrasted with their current acceptance and approval of it (again, as reported by users).

4. What new (or remaining) target questions do you have in considering the next contact with this site?

    How do users really perceive the innovation? If they do indeed embrace it, what accounts for the change from early resistance?

    Nature and amount of networking among users of innovation.

    Information on "stubborn" math teachers whose ideas weren't heard initially—who are they? Situation particulars? Resolution?

    Follow-up on English teacher Reilly's "fall from the chairmanship."

    Follow a team through a day of rotation, planning, etc.

    CONCERN: The consequences of eating school cafeteria food for two days per week for the next four or five months... .

    <u>Stop</u>

Source: Miles & Huberman, 1994:53, Figure 4.1.

When Adam ran a push broom into the feet of the children nearby, I jumped to conclusions about his interactions with other children: aggressive, teasing, arresting. Of course, just a few minutes earlier I had seen him block the children climbing the steps in a similar moment of smiling bombast. So I was aggregating, and testing my unrealized hypotheses about what kind of kid he was, not postponing my interpreting. . . . My disposition was to keep my eyes on him. (p. 74)

The focus in this conceptualization "on the fly" is to provide a detailed description of what was observed and a sense of why that was important.

More often, analytic insights are tested against new observations, the initial statement of problems and concepts is refined, the researcher then collects more data, interacts with the data again, and the process continues. Anderson (2005) recounts how his conceptualization of social stratification at Jelly's Bar developed over a long period:

I could see the social pyramid, how certain guys would group themselves and say in effect, "I'm here and you're there." . . . I made sense of these "crowds" as the "respectables," the "non-respectables," and the "near-respectables." . . . Inside, such non-respectables might sit on the crates, but if a respectable came along and wanted to sit there, the lower status person would have to move. (pp. 42–43)

But this initial conceptualization changed with experience, as Anderson (2005) realized that the participants used other terms to differentiate social status: *winehead*, *hoodlum*, and *regular* (p. 46). What did they mean by these terms? "'The regulars' basically valued 'decency.' They associated decency with conventionality but also with 'working for a living,' or having a 'visible means of support'" (p. 47). In this way, Anderson progressively refined his concept as he gained experience in the setting.

Matrix A form on which to systematically record particular features of multiple cases or instances that a qualitative data analyst needs to examine.

A well-designed chart, or **matrix**, can facilitate the coding and categorization process. Exhibit 11.4 shows an example of a checklist matrix designed by Miles and Huberman (1994) to represent the extent to which teachers and teachers' aides ("users") and administrators at a school gave evidence of various supporting conditions that indicated preparedness for a new reading program. The matrix condenses data into simple categories, reflects further analysis of the data to identify "degree" of support, and provides a multidimensional summary that will facilitate subsequent more intensive analysis. Direct quotes still impart some of the flavor of the original text.

Examining and Displaying Relationships

Examining relationships is the centerpiece of the analytic process because it allows the researcher to move from simple description of the people and settings to explanations of why things happened as they did with those people in that setting. The process of examining relationships can be captured in a matrix that shows how different concepts are connected or perhaps what causes are linked with what effects.

Exhibit 11.5 displays a matrix used to capture the relationship between the extent to which stakeholders in a new program had something important at stake in the program and the researcher's estimate of their favorability toward the program. Each cell of the matrix was to be filled in with a summary of an illustrative case study. In other matrix analyses, quotes might be included in the cells to represent the opinions of these different stakeholders, or the number of cases of each type might appear in the cells. The possibilities are almost endless. Keeping this approach in mind will generate many fruitful ideas for structuring a qualitative data analysis.

The simple relationships that are identified with a matrix can be examined and then extended to create a more complex causal model (see Exhibit 11.6). Such a model represents the multiple relationships among the constructs identified in a qualitative analysis as important for explaining some outcome. A great deal of analysis must precede the construction of such a model, with careful attention to identification of important variables and the evidence that suggests connections between them.

Exhibit 11.4	**Example of Checklist Matrix**

Presence of Supporting Conditions		
Condition	**For Users**	**For Administrators**
Commitment	*Strong*—"wanted to make it work"	*Weak* at building level. Prime movers in central office committed; others not
Understanding	*"Basic"* ("felt I could do it, but I just wasn't sure how.") for teacher. *Absent* for aide ("didn't understand how we were going to get all this.")	*Absent* at building level and among staff. *Basic* for 2 prime movers ("got all the help we needed from developer.") *Absent* for other central office staff.
Materials	*Inadequate*: ordered late, puzzling ("different from anything I ever used"), discarded	N.A.
Front-end training	*"Sketchy"* for teacher ("it all happened so quickly"); no demo class. *None* for aide: ("totally unprepared. I had to learn along with the children.")	Prime movers in central office had training at developer site; none for others.
Skills	*Weak-adequate* for teacher. *"None"* for aide	One prime mover (Robeson) skilled in substance; others unskilled.
Ongoing inservice	*None*, except for monthly committee meeting; no substitute funds.	*None*
Planning, coordination time	*None*: both users on other tasks during day; lab tightly scheduled, no free time.	*None*
Provisions for debugging	*None* systematized; spontaneous work done by users during summer.	*None*
School admin. support	*Adequate*	N.A.
Central admin, support	*Very Strong* on part of prime movers.	Building admin. only acting on basis of central office commitment.
Relevant prior experience	*Strong* and useful in both cases: had done individualized instruction, worked with low achievers. But aide had no diagnostic experience.	*Present* and useful in central office, especially Robeson (specialist)

Source: Miles & Huberman, 1994:95, Figure 5.2.

Corroboration and Legitimization of Conclusions

No set standards exist for evaluating the validity or authenticity of conclusions in a qualitative study, but the need to consider carefully the evidence and methods on which conclusions are based is just as great as with other types of research. Individual items of information can be assessed in terms of at least three criteria (Becker, 1958):

Exhibit 11.5 | Coding Form for Relationships: Stakeholders' Stakes

Estimate of Various Stakeholders Inclination Toward the Program			
How high are the stakes for various primary stakeholders?	Favorable	Neutral of Unknown	Antagonistic
High			
Moderate			
Low			

*Source:*Patton (2002, p. 472).

*Note:*Construct illustrative case studies for each cell based on fieldwork.

Exhibit 11.5 | Example of a Causal Network Model

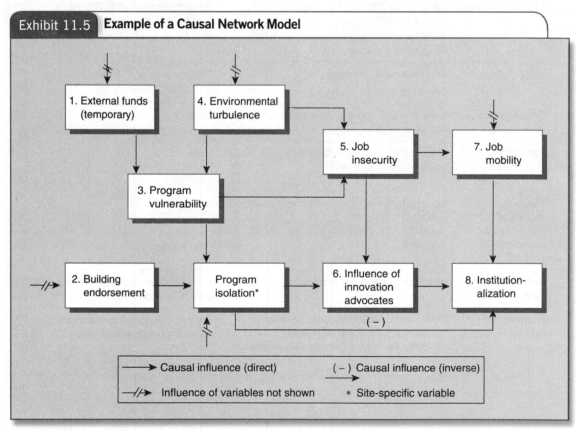

*Source:*Miles & Huberman, 1994:159, Figure 6.5.

1. *How credible was the informant?* Were statements made by someone with whom the researcher had a relationship of trust or by someone the researcher had just met? Did the informant have reason to lie? If the statements do not seem to be trustworthy as indicators of actual events, can they be used at least to help understand the informant's perspective?

2. *Were statements made in response to the researcher's questions or were they spontaneous?* Spontaneous statements are more likely to indicate what would have been said had the researcher not been present.

3. *How does the presence or absence of the researcher or the researcher's informant influence the actions and statements of other group members?* Reactivity to being observed can never be ruled out as a possible explanation for some directly observed social phenomenon. However, if the researcher carefully compares what the informant says goes on when the researcher is not present, what the researcher observes directly, and what other group members say about their normal practices, the extent of reactivity can be assessed to some extent.

A qualitative researcher's conclusions should also be assessed by his or her ability to provide a credible explanation for some aspect of social life. That explanation should capture group members' **tacit knowledge** of the social processes that were observed, not just their verbal statements about these processes. Tacit knowledge—"the largely unarticulated, contextual understanding that is often manifested in nods, silences, humor, and naughty nuances" (Altheide & Johnson, 1994, pp. 492–493)—is reflected in participants' actions as well as their words and in what they fail to state, but nonetheless feel deeply and even take for granted.

> **Tacit knowledge** In field research, a credible sense of understanding of social processes that reflects the researcher's awareness of participants' actions as well as their words, and of what they fail to state, feel deeply, and take for granted.

Comparing conclusions from a qualitative research project to those obtained by other researchers conducting similar projects can also increase confidence in their authenticity. Susan Miller's (1999) study of neighborhood police officers (NPOs) found striking parallels in the ways they defined their masculinity to processes reported in research about males in nursing and other traditionally female jobs:

> In part, male NPOs construct an exaggerated masculinity so that they are not seen as feminine as they carry out the social-work functions of policing. Related to this is the almost defiant expression of heterosexuality, so that the men's sexual orientation can never truly be doubted even if their gender roles are contested. Male patrol officers' language—such as their use of terms like "pansy police" to connote neighborhood police officers—served to affirm their own heterosexuality. . . . In addition, the male officers, but not the women, deliberately wove their heterosexual status into conversations, explicitly mentioning their female domestic partner or spouse and their children. This finding is consistent with research conducted in the occupational field. The studies reveal that men in female dominated occupations, such as teachers, librarians, and pediatricians, over-reference their heterosexual status to ensure that others will not think they are gay. (p. 222)

There are several other strategies qualitative researchers can use to address concerns about whether the findings and interpretations represent the researcher's biases and preconceived notions. These strategies include peer-debriefing, member checking, and triangulation.

Peer debriefing provides the opportunity for an objective second party to give feedback or ideas about the research; it involves discussions about the researcher's perspectives and analysis (Barusch, Gringeri, & George, 2011). Rather than an informal process, the qualitative researcher records the content of the discussion in notes. For example, Anderson was debriefed and questioned by his fellow students and friends at the University of Chicago and that their questions helped shape his analysis: "By relating my experiences to my fellow students, I began to develop a coherent perspective, or a 'story' of the place which complemented the accounts that I had detailed in my accumulating field notes" (p. 37). The outcome of Anderson's analysis of qualitative data resulted, in part, from the way in which he played his role as a researcher and participant, not just from the setting itself.

Member checking has been used to address researcher bias. **Member checking** involves going back to participants and seeking their input about the interviews, findings, and interpretations (Padgett, 2008). It may include asking participants to review their transcripts and making corrections or having

> **Peer debriefing** A qualitative researcher receives feedback from a second party like a colleague.
>
> **Member checking** When a qualitative researcher seeks input from participants about the interviews, findings, and interpretations.

discussions about the findings (Barusch et al., 2011). In a study of professional views of the quality of mental health services received by child welfare clients, J. Curtis McMillen and colleagues (McMillen, Fedoravicius, Rowe, Zima, & Ware, 2007) conducted four member checking groups with participants. They presented their findings and their story and participants were asked to correct and elaborate on the findings.

There is discussion about the utility of member checking beyond the difficulty in organizing participant reviews. In checking transcripts for content and omissions, participants may change their responses. Their interpretations or conclusions about the data may differ from the researcher's so the question is whose view of reality is "correct" (Barusch et al., 2011). Member checking can provide a deeper understanding and offers researchers the opportunity to further delve into their topics (Barusch et al., 2011).

Triangulation involves coming at different aspects of the research from different perspectives with the idea that multiple sources coming to similar conclusions adds to the legitimacy of the findings. Triangulation may come from using multiple theories to interpret data, using different methods of data collection (e.g., interviews, documents, observation), having more than one analyst, or having more than one person collecting data (Barusch et al., 2011; Padgett, 2008).

> **Triangulation** The use of multiple methods to study one research question.

Reflection on the Researcher's Role

Confidence in the conclusions from a field research study is also strengthened by an honest and informative account about how the researcher interacted with subjects in the field, what problems were encountered, and how these problems were or were not resolved. Such a natural history of the development of the evidence enables others to evaluate the findings. Such an account is important, first and foremost, because of the evolving and variable nature of field research: To an important extent, the researcher makes up the method in the context of a particular investigation, rather than applying standard procedures that are specified before the investigation begins.

Barrie Thorne (1993) provides a good example of this final element of the analysis:

Many of my observations concern the workings of gender categories in social life. For example, I trace the evocation of gender in the organization of everyday interactions, and the shift from boys and girls as loose aggregations to "the boys" and "the girls" as self-aware, gender-based groups. In writing about these processes, I discovered that different angles of vision lurk within seemingly simple choices of language. How, for example, should one describe a group of children? A phrase like "six girls and three boys were chasing by the tires" already assumes the relevance of gender. An alternative description of the same event—"nine fourth graders were chasing by the tires"—emphasizes age and downplays gender. Although I found no tidy solutions, I have tried to be thoughtful about such choices. . . . After several months of observing at Oceanside, I realized that my field notes were peppered with the words "child" and "children," but that the children themselves rarely used the term. "What do they call themselves?" I badgered in an entry in my field notes. The answer, it turned out, is that children use the same practices as adults. They refer to one another by using given names ("Sally," "Jack") or language specific to a given context ("that guy on first base"). They rarely have occasion to use age-generic terms. But when pressed to locate themselves in an age-based way, my informants used "kids" rather than "children." (pp. 8–9)

Qualitative data analysts display real sensitivity to how a social situation or process is interpreted from a particular background and set of values and not simply from the situation (Altheide & Johnson, 1994). Researchers are only human, after all, and must rely on their own senses and process all information through their own minds. By reporting how and why they think they did what they did, they can help others determine whether or how the researchers' perspectives influenced their conclusions. "There should be clear 'tracks' indicating the attempt [to show the hand of the ethnographer] has been made" (Altheide & Johnson, 1994, p. 493).

Anderson (2005) illustrates the type of tracks that an ethnographer makes, as well as how he can describe those tracks. After starting to observe at Jelly's, Anderson's tracks led to Herman:

> After spending a couple of weeks at Jelly's I met Herman and I felt that our meeting marked a big achievement. We would come to know each other well . . . something of an informal leader at Jelly's. . . . We were becoming friends. . . . He seemed to genuinely like me, and he was one person I could feel comfortable with. (p. 37)

So we learn that Anderson's (2005) observations were shaped, in part, by Herman's perspective.

🔳 Alternatives in Qualitative Data Analysis

The qualitative data analyst can choose from many interesting alternative approaches. Of course, the research question under investigation should shape the selection of an analytic approach, but the researcher's preferences and experiences inevitably also will have an important influence on the method chosen. The four alternative approaches presented here (ethnomethodology, conversation analysis, narrative analysis, and qualitative comparative analysis) give you a good sense of the different possibilities, but be forewarned that these four were selected from a long and growing list (Patton, 2002).

Ethnomethodology

Ethnomethodology focuses on the way that participants construct the social world in which they live—how they create reality—rather than on describing the social world itself. Actually, ethnomethodologists do not necessarily believe that we can find an objective reality; rather, the way that participants come to create and sustain a sense of reality is of interest. In the words of Jaber Gubrium and James Holstein (1997), in ethnomethodology, compared with the naturalistic orientation of ethnography (see Chapter 10),

> [t]he focus shifts from the scenic features of everyday life onto the ways through which the world comes to be experienced as real, concrete, factual, and "out there." An interest in members' methods of constituting their world supersedes the naturalistic project of describing members' worlds as they know them. (p. 41)

Unlike the ethnographic analyst, who seeks to describe the social world as the participants see it, the ethnomethodological analyst seeks to maintain some distance from that world. The ethnomethodologist views a code of conduct like that described by Anderson (2005) at Jelly's not as a description of a real normative force that constrains social action but as the way that people in the setting create a sense of order and social structure (Gubrium & Holstein, 1997). The ethnomethodologist focuses on how reality is constructed, not on what is.

The ethnomethodological focus on how the meaning of gender, ethnicity, and other categories are socially constructed leads to a concern with verbal interaction. In recent years, this has led ethnomethodologists and others to develop a more formal approach, called *conversation analysis*.

> **Ethnomethodology** A qualitative research method focused on the way that participants in a social setting create and sustain a sense of reality.
>
> **Conversation analysis** A qualitative method for analyzing the sequential organization and details of a conversation.

Conversation Analysis

Conversation analysis is a specific qualitative method for analyzing the sequential organization and details of conversation. Like ethnomethodology, from which it developed, conversation analysis focuses on how reality is constructed rather than on what it is. From this perspective, detailed analysis of conversational interaction is important as a "form of social organization through which the work of . . . institutions such as the economy, the polity, the family, socialization, etc." is accomplished (Schegloff, 1996).

It is through conversation that we conduct the ordinary affairs of our lives. Our relationships with one another, and our sense of who we are to one another is generated, manifest, maintained, and managed in and through our conversations, whether face-to-face, on the telephone, or even by other electronic means (Drew, 2005, p. 74).

Three premises guide conversation analysis (Gubrium & Holstein, 2000):

1. Interaction is sequentially organized, and talk can be analyzed in terms of the process of social interaction rather than in terms of motives or social status.

2. Talk, as a process of social interaction, is contextually oriented—it is both shaped by interaction and creates the social context of the interaction.

3. These processes are involved in all social interaction, so no interactive details are irrelevant to understanding it.

Consider these premises as you read the excerpt from Janne Solberg's (2011) analysis of how counselors frame questions that establish the expectation that clients are knowledgeable and how clients demonstrate accountability in their responses. In typical conversation analysis style, the text is broken into brief segments that capture shifts in meaning,

Exhibit 11.7	**Conversation Analysis Transcription Symbols**
	Examples of common conversation transcription symbols developed by Gail Jefferson.
(0.5)	The number in brackets indicates a time gap in tenths of a second.
(.)	A dot enclosed in a bracket indicates pause in the talk less than two tenths of a second.
.hh	A dot before an "h" indicates speaker in-breath. The more "h"s, the longer the in-breath.
hh	An "h" indicates an out-breath. The more "h"s the longer the breath.
(( ))	A description enclosed in a double bracket indicates a non-verbal activity. For example ((banging sound))
-	A dash indicates the sharp cut-off of the prior word or sound.
:::	Colons indicate that the speaker has stretched the preceding sound or letter. The more colons the greater the extent of the stretch.
° °	Degree signs are used to indicate that the talk that they encompass is noticeably quieter than the surrounding talk.
> <	More than and less than signs indicate that the talk they encompass was produced noticeably quicker than the surrounding talk.
↑↓	Pointed arrows indicate a marked falling or rising intonational shift. They are placed immediately before the onset of the shift.
CAPITALS	With the exception of proper nouns, capital letters indicate a section of speech noticeably louder than that surrounding it
Under	Underlined fragments indicate speaker emphasis.

Source: Adapted from Wooffitt, Robin. (2005). *Conversation Analysis and Discourse Analysis: A comparative and Critical Introduction.* Thousand Oaks, CA: Sage, p. 211.

changes in the speaker, pauses, nonspeech utterances and nonverbal actions, and emphases; the various symbols represent different language changes such as parentheses are pauses with the length of the pause (see Exhibit 11.7).

The following dialogue is between a vocational rehabilitation counselor and a client who is expected to prepare for work. The context of the dialogue is that this is a first-time meeting and the client had affirmatively responded to a question about feeling ready to "get going" (Solberg, 2011, p. 387):

58	Co:	he ha- have you thought anything about what that (.) what that could be?
59		(1.2)
60	Cl:	.h I do not really know what tha:t
61		(0.4)
62	Co:	°No.°
63		(1.6)
64	Cl:	I do know (.) sort of what I want to study like halfway and-
65		(.)
66	Co:	okay, mm.
67	Cl:	what I am interested in
68	Co:	mm,
69	Cl:	But:e-
70		(1.2)
71	Co:	>What is that then?<
72		(1.2)
73	Cl:	Eh:, (0.5) I don't know exactly what it is called but I feel like working with children and youth,

Can you see how the interaction reinforces the expectation that the client is knowledgeable? Here, in part, is how Solberg (2011) analyzes this conversation:

> Despite being introduced as a yes/no question (have or have not been thinking), the open design of this 'what' question doesn't truly invite a minimal response. Rather, it suggests that the client takes the floor and extends the topic. But we can already see from the gap in line 59 that the client has problems aligning to the counselor's expectation. Invoking the category of knowing in line 60, the client overtly orients to the elicitor as asking for information about possible actions. A possible no-knowledge claim is aborted, and the recycling of certain elements of the counselor's talk ("what that"), she might have been about to say "I don't really know what that should be." But the counselor's soft "no" [line 62] sends the ball back to the client. . . . Starting anew, the client now aligns, at least partly, with the assumption of her being knowledgeable on the topic. In line 64, the client makes a positive knowledgeable claim about knowing her study preferences and interests ("I do know"), though this is then mitigated ("sort of." "like halfway"). (p. 388)

Narrative Analysis

Narrative methods use interviews and sometimes documents or observations to "follow participants down their trails" (Riessman, 2008, p. 24). Unlike conversation analysis, which focuses attention on moment-by-moment interchange, narrative analysis seeks to put together the big picture about experiences or events as the participants understand them. Narrative "displays the goals and intentions of human actors; it makes individuals, cultures, societies,

Research In the News

For Further Thought?

WHAT'S IN A MESSAGE?

In response to the large number of military suicides, Attivo Inc., and military suicide experts are creating a qualitative coding scheme and searching through social media posts. Facebook and Twitter posts hold valuable information about a person's well-being; researchers are creating a way to analyze millions of posts. The program is called the Durkheim Project and aims to prevent suicides by systematically identifying at-risk soldiers or veterans.

1. What are the advantages and disadvantages that you see in using Facebook and Twitter posts to determine a person's well-being?

2. How do you think that analyzing online social interaction would compare as a research method to analyzing social interaction in person, through interviews, or observations? Which approach would be preferable in identifying at risk soldiers or veterans?

Source: Weintraub (2005, p. B5).

Narrative analysis A form of qualitative analysis in which the analyst focuses on how respondents impose order on their experiences and make sense of events and actions in which they have participated.

and historical epochs comprehensible as wholes" (Richardson, 1995, p. 200). **Narrative analysis** focuses on "the story itself" and seeks to preserve the integrity of personal biographies or a series of events that cannot adequately be understood in terms of their discrete elements (Riessman, 2002). The coding for a narrative analysis is typically of the narratives as a whole, rather than of the different elements within them. The coding strategy revolves around reading the stories and classifying them into general patterns.

For example, Cynthia Lietz (2006, 2007) conducted in-depth interviews with six families that were at high risk of poor family functioning, yet were functioning quite well, which she labeled as "resilience." She wanted to uncover the meaning of resilience from the stories these families told her. She identified five stages of reactions to difficulties (survival, adaptation, acceptance, growing stronger, and helping others) that families experienced but also learned that families could progress back and forth in these stages. In addition to these five stages, she found that there were 10 strengths that families relied on and that different strengths were associated with different stages.

Lietz (2007) defined survival as "a time at which these families took one day at a time just trying to figure out how to keep the family going" (p. 148). She describes an interview with parents whose son was diagnosed with leukemia:

The tough things in life hadn't hit us until really our daughter was a little bit older . . . but I think our son's the real kicker. That was real hard . . . it was touch and go on whether he was going to live. He had a bad case. . . . When I think about my son's thing . . . I learned how to get through life one day at a time. It was like, okay, well tomorrow we are going for treatment. Am I going to worry about this all night about what could of [*sic*] happened or can I go and get this done? (p. 149)

Lietz summarizes her classification of the stages of family resilience and their relationship with specific family strengths in a table (see Exhibit 11.8). How does such an analysis contribute to our understanding of family resilience? Much of the literature had suggested that the more risks a family faced, the poorer the functioning; therefore, social work interventions often focused on reducing risk factors (Lietz, 2007). But Lietz (2007) proposes that these findings suggest that teaching families to maximize their strengths and build new strengths may be an effective model of intervention.

Exhibit 11.8   **Family Resilience and Protective Factors/Family Strengths**

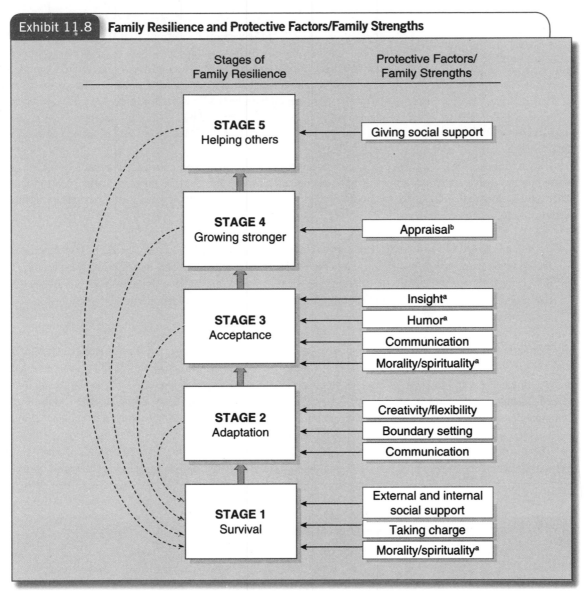

Source: Lietz, C. (2007). Uncovering stories of family resilience: A mixed methods study of resilient families, part 2. *Families in Society: Journal of Contemporary Social Services, 88*, 147–155. Reprinted with permission from *Families in Society* (www.familiesinsociety.org), published by the Alliance for Strong Families and Communities.

Qualitative Comparative Analysis

Daniel Cress and David Snow (2000) asked a series of specific questions about social movement outcomes in their study of homeless social movement organizations (SMOs). They collected qualitative data about 15 SMOs in eight cities. A content analysis of newspaper articles indicated that these cities represented a range of outcomes, and the SMOs within them were also relatively accessible to Cress and Snow due to prior contacts. In each of these cities, Cress and Snow used a snowball sampling strategy to identify the homeless SMOs and the various supporters, antagonists, and significant organizational bystanders with whom they interacted. They then gathered information from representatives of these organizations, including churches, other activist organizations, police departments, mayors' offices, service providers, federal agencies, and, of course, the SMOs.

Qualitative comparative analysis A systematic type of qualitative analysis that identifies the combination of factors that had to be present across multiple cases to produce a particular outcome.

To answer their research questions, Cress and Snow (2000) needed to operationalize each of the various conditions that they believed might affect movement outcomes using coding procedures that were much more systematic than those often employed in qualitative research. For example, Cress and Snow defined sympathetic allies operationally as "the presence of one or more city council members who were supportive of local homeless mobilization. This was demonstrated by attending homeless SMO meetings and rallies and by taking initiatives to city agencies on behalf of the SMO" (p. 1078; 7 of the 15 SMOs had such allies).

Cress and Snow (2000) also chose a structured method of analysis, **qualitative comparative analysis** (QCA), to assess how the various conditions influenced SMO outcomes. This procedure identifies the combination of factors that had to be present across multiple cases to produce a particular outcome (Ragin, 1987). Cress and Snow explain why this strategy was appropriate for their analysis:

> [Qualitative comparative analysis] is conjunctural in its logic, examining the various ways in which specified factors interact and combine with one another to yield particular outcomes. This increases the prospect of discerning diversity and identifying different pathways that lead to an outcome of interest and thus makes this mode of analysis especially applicable to situations with complex patterns of interaction among the specified conditions. (p. 1079)

Exhibit 11.9 summarizes the results of much of Cress and Snow's (2000) analysis. It shows that homeless SMOs that were coded as organizationally viable, used disruptive tactics, had sympathetic political allies, and presented a coherent diagnosis and program in response to the problem they were protesting were likely to achieve all four valued outcomes: representation, resources, protection of basic rights, and some form of tangible relief. Some other combinations of the conditions were associated with increased likelihood of achieving some valued outcomes, but most of these alternatives had positive effects less frequently.

The qualitative textual data on which the codes were based indicate how particular combinations of conditions exerted their influence. For example, one set of conditions that increased the likelihood of achieving increased protec-

---

Exhibit 11.9   Multiple Pathways to Outcomes and Level of Impact

Pathways	Outcomes	Impact
VIABLE * DISRUPT * ALLIES * DIAG * PROG	Representation, Resources, Rights, and Relief	Very strong
VIABLE * disrupt * CITY * DIAG * PROG	Representation and Rights	Strong
VIABLE * ALLIES * CITY * DIAG * PROG	Resources and Relief	Moderate
viable * DISRUPT * allies * diag * PROG	Relief	Weak
viable * allies * city * diag * PROG	Relief	Weak
viable * disrupt * ALLIES * CITY * diag * prog	Resources	Weak

Source: Cress, Daniel M. and David A. Snow. 2000. "The Outcomes of Homeless Mobilization: The Influence of Organization, Disruption, Political Mediation, and Framing." *American Journal of Sociology* 4: 1063–1104.

Note: Uppercase letters indicate presence of condition and lowercase letters indicate the absence of a condition. Conditions not in the equation are considered irrelevant. Multiplication signs (*) are read as "and."

tion of basic rights for homeless people included avoiding disruptive tactics in cities that were more responsive to the SMOs. Cress and Snow (2000) use a quote from a local SMO leader to explain this process:

> We were going to set up a picket, but then we got calls from two people who were the co-chairs of the Board of Directors. They have like 200 restaurants. And they said, "Hey, we're not bad guys, can we sit down and talk?" We had been set on picketing. . . . Then we got to thinking, wouldn't it be better . . . if they co-drafted those things [rights guidelines] with us? So that's what we asked them to do. We had a work meeting, and we hammered out the guidelines. (p. 1089)

We should note that QCA can also be used when the data are quantitative to start with, rather than converting qualitative data. For example, Dong-Ho Jang (2009) used QCA as a method for cross-national social policy analysis; Jang wanted to understand why there were differences in the combination of income transfers and social service spending in these countries. Rather than look at individual countries, Jang looked at four clusters of countries based on the percentage of gross domestic product attributed to income transfers and social service sending. The clusters represented (1) high income transfers and high services, (2) high income transfers and low services, (3) low income transfers and high services, and (4) low income transfers and low services. Jang was able to identify factors that distinguished between the clusters and differences within the clusters.

Grounded Theory

Theory development occurs continually in qualitative data analysis (Coffey & Atkinson, 1996). The goal of many qualitative researchers is to create **grounded theory**—that is, to build up inductively a systematic theory that is grounded in, or based on, the observations. The observations are summarized into conceptual categories, which are tested directly in the research setting with more observations. Over time, as the conceptual categories are refined and linked, a theory evolves (Glaser & Strauss, 1967; Huberman & Miles, 1994).

> **Grounded theory** Systematic theory developed inductively, based on observations that are summarized into conceptual categories, reevaluated in the research setting, and gradually refined and linked to other conceptual categories.

As observation, interviewing, and reflection continue, researchers refine their definitions of problems and concepts and select indicators. They can then check the frequency and distribution of phenomena: How many people made a particular type of comment? How often did social interaction lead to arguments? Social system models may then be developed, which specify the relationships among different phenomena. These models are modified as researchers gain experience in the setting. For the final analysis, the researchers check their models carefully against their notes and make a concerted attempt to discover negative evidence that might suggest that the model is incorrect.

Cecilia Ayón and Eugene Aisenberg (2010) used grounded theory to understand the role of cultural values and expectations in the development of a working relationship between Mexican American parents and child welfare workers. Parents were recruited from the waiting room of a public child welfare agency in Southern California; all the parents were of Mexican origin, were first or second generation in the United States, and were involved because of neglect and/ or physical abuse. Child welfare workers were recruited from the child welfare agency; to be eligible these workers had to have had a Mexican American family as a client within the preceding 6 months.

The analysis involved open coding and axial coding. Open coding involves "breaking down, examining, comparing, conceptualizing, and categorizing data" (Strauss & Corbin, 1990, p. 61). Ayón and Aisenberg (2010) described their open-coding process:

> The following example illustrates the process of open coding for the parent-worker relationship. . . . In the first reading of the interviews, each incident or idea was labeled based on the different aspects of the relationship that the parent or the worker was describing. Next, we categorized the major concepts. . . . Then, the properties and dimensions of the categories were examined. (p. 338)

Ayón and Aisenberg identified three factors perceived by parents and three factors perceived by workers. They also categorized workers' and parents' perceptions about the quality of the relationship (see Exhibit 11.10).

In the axial coding stage, Ayón and Aisenberg (2010) established links and connections between the categories. They constructed a model linking categories that promote or hinder the parent–worker relationship and outcomes of that relationship for workers' perceptions and parents' perceptions.

One factor from the parents' perspective helping or hindering their relationship with their workers was unannounced visits. Here is how Ayón and Aisenberg (2010) describe this factor:

Parents viewed such visits as a lack of trust and an invasion of their privacy.

One mother remarked:

One time I got upset. . . . I told [the in-home counselor] that I felt like I was being spied on because . . . [the worker] came without calling me. . . . I told the [in-home counselor] that I didn't like that. That's why I'm telling you that I feel more spied on than helped, because that made me feel bad.

Another mother previously had a worker who would arrive at her home unannounced. She stated that her current worker did not conduct unannounced visits and she regarded this as an act of respect.

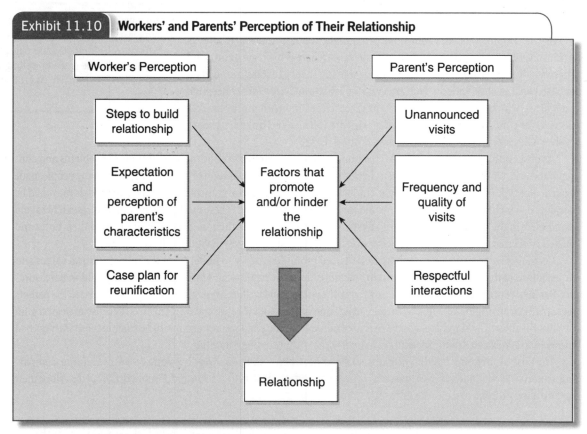

Exhibit 11.10 | **Workers' and Parents' Perception of Their Relationship**

Worker's Perception

Parent's Perception

Steps to build relationship

Expectation and perception of parent's characteristics

Case plan for reunification

Factors that promote and/or hinder the relationship

Unannounced visits

Frequency and quality of visits

Respectful interactions

Relationship

Source: Adapted from Ayón & Aisenberg, (2010), Negotiating cultural values and expectations within the public child welfare system: A look at familismo and personalismo. *Child & Family Social Work, 15,* 335–344.

He is respectful . . . he never shows up without letting me know, he's never at my door watching me, if I tell him that I'm going to school he's never checking up on me you know. I think that's being respectful . . . because other [workers] have done a lot of things like that. (p. 340)

As you can see, with procedures like these, the grounded theory approach develops general concepts from careful review of text or other qualitative materials and can then suggest plausible relationships among these concepts.

回 Content Analysis

Content analysis is a method for systematically analyzing and making inferences from text (R. Weber, 1985). You can think of a content analysis as a survey of some documents or other records of prior communication. In fact, a content analysis is a survey designed with fixed-choice responses so that it produces quantitative data that can be analyzed statistically.

> **Content analysis** A research method for systematically analyzing and making inferences from text.

As a form of textual analysis, content analysis is like qualitative data analysis. Like the analytic methods we have just been studying, it involves coding and categorizing text and identifying relationships among constructs identified in the text. However, as a quantitative procedure, content analysis overlaps with qualitative data analysis only at the margins—the points where qualitative analysis takes on quantitative features or where content analysis focuses on qualitative features of the text.

Jennifer Tichon and Margaret Shapiro's (2003) analysis of e-mail postings to an online support group for children whose siblings have special needs highlights both aspects of content analysis. Their qualitative analyses involved describing e-mail topics, the types of social support offered in the e-mails, and patterns of self-disclosure. The quantitative analysis provided both counts of different categories of topics, support, and patterns of self-disclosure and the relationship of types of social support to patterns of self-disclosure.

The units that are surveyed in a content analysis can include newspapers, journal articles, court decisions, books, videotapes, themes expressed in agency documents, or propositions made in different statements. Words or other features of these units are then coded to measure the variables involved in the research question. The content analysis proceeds through several stages (R. Weber, 1985):

1. Identify a population of documents or other textual sources for study. This population should be selected so that it is appropriate to the research question of interest. Perhaps the population will be all newspapers published in the United States, all agency annual reports, all U.S. Supreme Court decisions, or all articles in a particular journal.

2. Determine the units of analysis. These could be items such as newspaper articles, court decisions, research articles, or case records.

3. Select a sample of units from the population. The simplest strategy might be a simple random sample of documents. However, a stratified sample might be needed to ensure adequate representation of community newspapers in large and small cities. Sampling may be purposive, such as the use of three consecutive months of e-mail posting by Tichon and Shapiro (2003).

4. Design coding procedures for the variables to be measured. This requires deciding what unit of text to code, such as words, sentences, themes, or paragraphs. Then the categories into which the text units are to be coded must be defined. These categories may be broad, such as *client goal,* or narrow, such as *client improves behavior.*

5. Test and refine the coding procedures. Clear instructions and careful training of coders are essential.

6. Base statistical analyses on counting occurrences of particular words, themes, or phrases, and test relations between different variables. These analyses would use some of the statistics introduced in Chapter 14, including frequency distributions, measures of central tendency and variation, cross-tabulations, and correlation analysis.

Developing reliable and valid coding procedures is not an easy task. The meaning of words and phrases is often ambiguous. Homographs create special problems (words such as *mine* that have different meanings in different contexts), as do many phrases that have special meanings (such as *point of no return*; R. Weber, 1985). As a result, coding procedures cannot simply categorize and count words; text segments in which the words are embedded must also be inspected before codes are finalized. Because different coders may perceive different meanings in the same text segments, explicit coding rules are required to ensure coding consistency. Special dictionaries can be developed to keep track of how the categories of interest are defined in the study (R. Weber, 1985).

After coding procedures are developed, their reliability should be assessed by comparing different coders' codes for the same variables. Computer programs for content analysis can be used to enhance reliability (R. Weber, 1985). The rules the computer is programmed to use when coding text will be applied consistently. Validity can be assessed with a construct validation approach by determining the extent to which theoretically predicted relationships occur.

These various steps are represented in the flowchart in Exhibit 11.11. Note that each of these steps is comparable to the procedures in quantitative survey research; they overlap with qualitative data analysis techniques primarily at the point of developing coding schemes. Use this flowchart as a checklist when you design or critique a content analysis project.

▣ Computer-Assisted Qualitative Data Analysis

The analysis process can be enhanced in various ways by using a computer. Programs designed for qualitative data can speed up the analysis process, make it easier for researchers to experiment with different codes, test different hypotheses about relationships, and facilitate diagrams of emerging theories and preparation of research reports (Coffey & Atkinson, 1996; T. J. Richards & Richards, 1994). The steps involved in computer-assisted qualitative data analysis parallel those used traditionally to analyze text such as notes, documents, or interview transcripts: preparation, coding, analysis, and reporting. We use several of the most popular programs to illustrate these steps: HyperRESEARCH, QSR NVivo, and ATLAS.ti.

Text preparation begins with typing or scanning text into a word processor or, with NVivo, directly into the program's rich text editor. NVivo and ATLAS.ti can import text in a variety of forms including, text files, .doc files, PDF files, and rich text files. HyperRESEARCH requires that your text be saved as a text file (as ASCII in most word-processing programs) before you transfer it into the analysis program. HyperRESEARCH expects your text data to be stored in separate files corresponding to each unique case, such as an interview with one subject. These programs allow multiple files, including pictures and videos as well as text. Exhibit 11.12 displays the different file types and how they are connected in the organization of a project with ATLAS.ti.

Coding the text involves categorizing particular text segments. This is the foundation of much qualitative analysis. Either program allows you to assign a code to any segment of text (in HyperRESEARCH, you click on the first and last words to select text; in NVivo, you drag through the characters to select them). You can make up codes as you go through a document and assign to text segments codes that you have already developed. Exhibits 11.13a and 11.13b show the screens that appear in two programs at the coding stage when a particular text is "autocoded" by identifying a word or phrase that should always receive the same code or, in NVivo, by coding each section identified by the style of the rich text document—for example, each question or speaker (of course, you should carefully check the results of autocoding). The programs also let you examine the coded text "in context"—embedded in its place in the original document.

| Exhibit 11.11 | **Flowchart for the Typical Process of Content Analysis Research** |

1. *Theory and rationale: What* content will be examined and *why?* Are there certain *theories* or perspectives that indicate that this particular message content is important to the study? Library work is needed here to conduct a good literature review. Will you be using an integrative model, linking content analysis with other data to show relationships with source or receiver characteristics? Do you have *research questions? Hypotheses?*

↓

2. *Conceptualizations:* What *variables* will be used in the study, and how do you define them *conceptually* (i.e., with dictionary-type definitions)? Remember, you are the boss! There are many ways to define a given construct, and there is no one right way. You may want to screen some examples of the content you're going to analyze, to make sure you've covered everything you want.

↓

3. *Operationalizations (measures):* Your measures should match your conceptualizations ... What *unit of data collection* will you use? You may have more than one unit (e.g., by-utterance coding scheme and a by-speaker coding scheme). Are the variables measured well (i.e., at a high *level of measurement*, with categories that are *exhaustive and mutually exclusive*)? An *a priori* coding scheme describing all measures must be created. Both face validity and content validity may also be assessed at this point.

Human Coding   Computer Coding

4a. *Coding schemes:* You need to create the following materials:

  a. *Codebook* (with all variable measures *fully* explained)

  b. *Coding form*

4b. *Coding schemes:* With computer text content analysis, you still need a code book of sorts—a full explanation of your *dictionaries* and method of applying them. You may use standard dictionaries (e.g., those in Hart's program, *Diction*) or originally created custom dictionaries. When creating custom dictionaries, be sure to first generate a frequencies list from your text sample and examine for key words and phrases.

5. *Sampling:* Is a census of the content possible? (If yes, go to #6.) How will you *randomly sample* a subset of the content? This could be the time period, by issue, by page, by channel, and so forth.

6. *Training and pilot reliability:* During a training session in which coders work together, find out whether they can agree on the coding of the variables. Then, in an independent coding test, note the *reliability* on each variable. At each stage, *revise* the codebook or coding form as needed.

7a. *Coding:* Use at least two coders, to establish intercoder reliability. Coding should be done independently, with at least 10% overlap for the reliability test.

7b. *Coding:* Apply dictionaries to the sample text to generate per-unit (e.g., per news story) frequencies for each dictionary. Do some spot checking for validation.

Human Coding   Computer coding

8. *Final reliability:* Calculate a reliability figure (percent agreement, Scott's *pi,* Spearman's *rho,* or Pearson's *r,* for example) for each variable.

9. *Tabulation and reporting:* See various examples of content analysis results to see the ways in which results can be reported. Figures and statistics may be reported one variable at a time (univariate), or variables may be cross-tabulated in different ways (bivariate and multivariate techniques). Over-time trends are also a common reporting method. In the long run, relationships between content analysis variables and other measures may establish criterion and construct validity.

Source: Neuendorf, 2002:50–51.

Exhibit 11.12   File Types and Unit Structure in ATLAS.ti

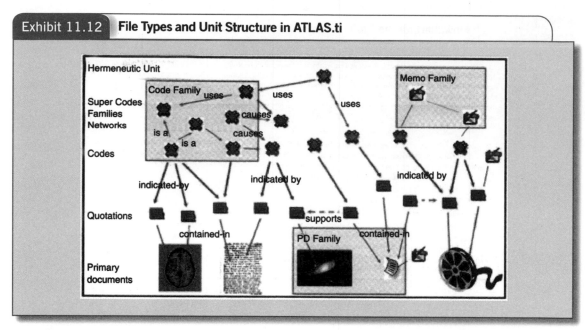

Source: Muhr and Friese, 2004, p. 29.

Exhibit 11.13a   HyperRESEARCH Coding Stage

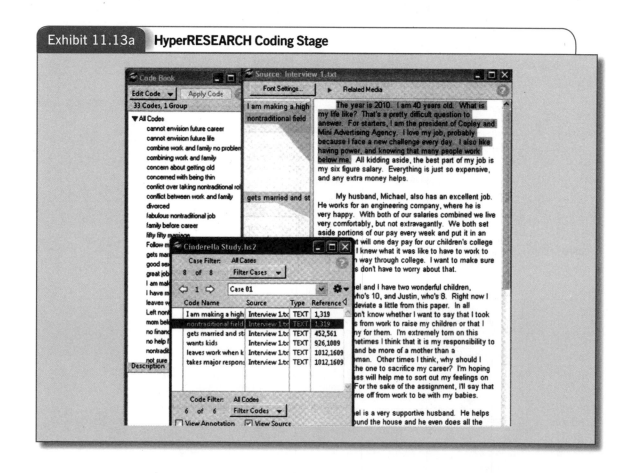

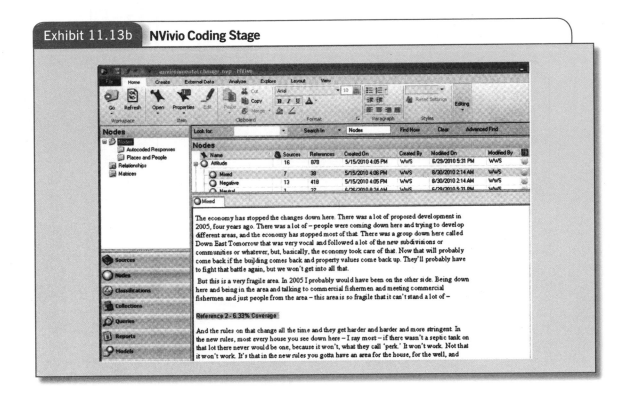

Exhibit 11.13b **NVivio Coding Stage**

In qualitative data analysis, coding is not a one-time-only or one-code-only procedure. Each program allows you to be inductive and holistic in your coding: You can revise codes as you go along, assign multiple codes to text segments, and link your own comments (memos) to text segments. In NVivo, you can work "live" with the coded text to alter coding or create new, more subtle categories. You can also insert hyperlinks to other documents in the project or any multimedia files outside it.

Analysis focuses on reviewing cases or text segments with similar codes and examining relationships among different codes. You may decide to combine codes into larger concepts. You may specify additional codes to capture more fully the variation among cases. You can test hypotheses about relationships among codes (see Exhibit 11.14).

Reports from all three programs can include text to illustrate the cases, codes, and relationships that you specify. You can also generate counts of code frequencies and then import these counts into a statistical program for quantitative analysis. However, the many types of analyses and reports that can be developed with qualitative analysis software do not lessen the need for a careful evaluation of the quality of the data on which conclusions are based.

Implications for Evidence-Based Practice

How might the analyses from several studies be combined so that we have more comfort with translating the findings to practice? **Meta-synthesis** is a method used to analyze and integrate findings from qualitative studies (S. Thorne, Jensen, Kearney, Noblit, & Sandelowski, 2004). This type of analysis requires not just aggregating findings from different qualitative studies but also reinterpreting the data once in aggregate form. James Forte (2010; see Case Study) examined mutual aid group studies and described the analysis plan as follows:

Meta-synthesis The qualitative analysis of findings from multiple studies.

Exhibit 11.14 | **A Free-Form Model in NVivo**

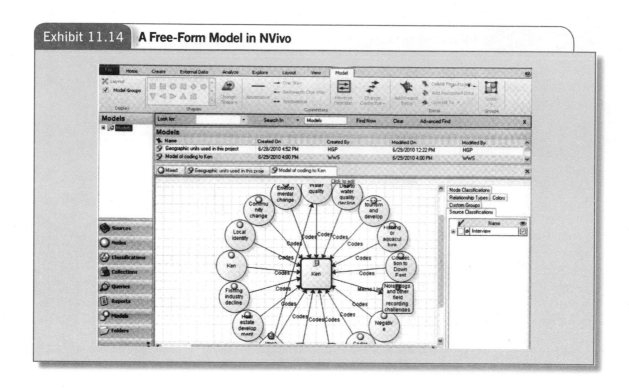

In the textual analysis reported in this article, the unit of analysis is the word and various word assemblies. I searched each research report for words, phrases, and passages including the researcher's findings about the change process. Each report, whether a journal or book, was analyzed line by line. Then, I assembled these findings and grouped them into notes organized by the change phase. Next, I translated the findings for each phase into relevant themes and metaphors. My translations used meaning that would be intelligible to practitioners. From these translations, I also generated inductively an integrative synthesis: a short summary in practitioners' terms of the interactionist phase conceptualization. Findings that did not fit were noted. Finally, I created a master or meta-synthesis of the entire set of interpretations across the phases of the planned change process; an attempt to capture in new words the SI [symbolic interactionist] stance to mutual aid group work. (p. 155)

Case Study Meta-Synthesis:
A Meta-Ethnographic Synthesis of Mutual Aid Groups

James Forte (2010) was interested in understanding the meanings and patterns of conduct in mutual aid group work. His goal was to translate the language of researchers into the language of practitioners to enhance their practice. Forte included ethnographic studies focused on symbolic interactionism and using either participant observation and/or in-depth interviewing. To find articles, Forte searched the table of contents of two journals: *Symbolic Interaction* (Fall 1977 to Fall 2007) and *Studies of Symbolic Interaction* (1978 to 2006). Forte then supplemented this list by searching the references of each chosen article. Twelve articles met the inclusion criteria. Forte synthesized and interpreted the researchers' interpretations of their data. He found the reviewed work did not provide metaphors or themes for translation in the engagement or evaluation phases of group development, but there were metaphors or themes describing the goal formulation, problem conceptualization, information gathering and assessment, and intervention phases.

🏛 Ethics in Qualitative Data Analysis

The qualitative data analyst is never far from ethical issues and dilemmas. Throughout the analytic process, the analyst must consider how the findings will be used and how participants in the setting will react. Miles and Huberman (1994) suggest several specific questions that should be kept in mind.

Privacy, confidentiality, and anonymity. In what ways will the study intrude, come closer to people than they want? How will information be guarded? How identifiable are the individuals and organizations studied? We have considered this issue already in the context of qualitative data collection, but it also must be a concern during the process of analysis. It can be difficult to present a rich description in a case study while not identifying the setting. It can be easy for participants in the study to identify each other in a qualitative description even if outsiders cannot.

Qualitative researchers should negotiate with participants early in the study the approach that will be taken to protect privacy and maintain confidentiality. Selected participants should also be asked to review reports or other products before their public release in order to gauge the extent to which they feel privacy has been appropriately preserved. Research with photographs that identify individuals raises special ethical concerns. Although legal standards are evolving, it is important not to violate an individual's expectations of privacy in any setting and to seek informed consent for the uses of images when privacy is expected. (Tinkler, 2013).

Intervention and advocacy. What do I do when I see harmful, illegal, or wrongful behavior on the part of others during a study? Should I speak for anyone's interests besides my own? If so, whose interests do I advocate? Maintaining what is called "guilty knowledge" may force the researcher to suppress some parts of the analysis so as not to disclose the wrongful behavior, but presenting "what really happened" in a report may prevent ongoing access and violate understandings with participants.

Research integrity and quality. Is my study being conducted carefully, thoughtfully, and correctly in terms of some reasonable set of standards? Real analyses have real consequences, so you owe it to yourself and those you study to adhere strictly to the analysis methods that you believe will produce authentic, valid conclusions. Visual images that demean individuals or groups should not be included in publications (Tinkler, 2013).

Ownership of data and conclusions. Who owns my field notes and analyses: me, my organization, my funders? Once my reports are written, who controls their diffusion? Of course, these concerns arise in any social research project, but the intimate involvement of the qualitative researcher with participants in the setting studied makes conflicts of interest between different stakeholders much more difficult to resolve. Researchers using qualitative methods in participatory action research/community based participatory research (PAR/CBPR) must work out data ownership agreements in advance of data collection to ensure there are no misunderstandings about retention of data and maintenance of confidentiality after the project ends (Hacker, 2013).

Use and misuse of results. Do I have an obligation to help my findings be used appropriately? What if they are used harmfully or wrongly? It is prudent to develop understandings early in the project with all major stakeholders that specify what actions will be taken to encourage appropriate use of project results and to respond to what is considered misuse of these results. PAR/CBPR projects are designed to help address local concerns, but harm might occur if results are not what were expected or if some findings cast some elements of the community in an unfavorable light. These possibilities should be addressed as the analysis progresses and resolved before they are publicized (Hacker, 2013).

▣ Conclusion

The variety of approaches to qualitative data analysis makes it difficult to provide a consistent set of criteria for interpreting their quality. Norman Denzin's (2002) interpretive criteria are a good place to start. Denzin suggests that, at the conclusion of their analyses, qualitative data analysts ask the following questions about the materials they have produced. Reviewing several of them serves as a fitting summary for our understanding of the qualitative analysis process:

- Do they illuminate the phenomenon as lived experience? In other words, do the materials bring the setting alive in terms of the people in that setting?

- Are they based on thickly contextualized materials? We should expect thick descriptions that encompass the social setting studied.

- Are they historically and relationally grounded? There must be a sense of the passage of time between events and the presence of relationships between social actors.

- Are they processual and interactional? The researcher must have described the research process and his or her interactions within the setting.

- Do they engulf what is known about the phenomenon? This includes situating the analysis in the context of prior research and also acknowledging the researcher's own orientation on starting the investigation.

When an analysis of qualitative data is judged as successful in terms of these criteria, we can conclude that the goal of authenticity has been achieved.

As a research methodologist, you must be ready to use both types of techniques, evaluate research findings in terms of both sets of criteria, and mix and match the methods as required by the research problem to be investigated and the setting in which it is to be studied.

Key Terms

Content analysis   313
Conversation analysis   305
Ethnomethodology   305
Grounded theory   311
Meta-synthesis   317

Matrix   300
Member checking   303
Narrative analysis   308
Peer debriefing   303
Progressive focusing   294

Qualitative comparative analysis   310
Tacit knowledge   303
Triangulation   304

Highlights

- Qualitative data analysts are guided by an emic focus on representing people in the setting on their own terms, rather than by an etic focus on the researcher's terms.

- Narrative analysis attempts to understand a life or a series of events as they have unfolded, in a meaningful progression.

- Grounded theory connotes a general explanation that develops in interaction with the data and is continually tested and refined as data collection continues.

- Special computer software can be used for the analysis of qualitative, textual, and pictorial data. Users can record their notes, categorize observations, specify links between categories, and count occurrences.

- Content analysis is a tool for systematic quantitative analysis of documents and other textual data. It requires careful testing and control of coding procedures to achieve reliable measures.

Discussion Questions

1. Describe the differences between quantitative and qualitative data analysis. What are the important guidelines to consider when analyzing qualitative data? Discuss the different modes of reading the text.

2. Identify and describe the five phases of qualitative data analysis. Discuss the importance of developing a matrix for coding the data.

3. What criteria should be used to evaluate a qualitative study's authenticity?

4. What are the advantages and disadvantages of using computer-assisted qualitative data analysis?

5. Describe the similarities and differences between content analysis and qualitative data analysis. Under what circumstances would you choose one mode of analysis over the other? Why?

Practice Exercises

1. Identify a social issue that is currently a hot topic nationally. Conduct a content analysis of the coverage of this issue on Internet discussion boards. What is your unit of analysis? Randomly sample these messages. What are the dominant themes? Evaluate these themes statistically.

2. Examine a qualitative study from a social work journal (e.g., *Affilia*). What techniques did the author employ to analyze the data? Critique the study with regard to the researcher's ability to authenticate the conclusions.

Web Exercise

1. *Qualitative Social Work* is an online journal about qualitative research. Inspect the table of contents for a recent issue at http://qsw.sagepub.com. Read one of the articles about issues pertaining to elders, and write a brief article review.

2. Be a qualitative explorer! Go to the "Qualitative Page" website at www.qualitativeresearch.uga.edu/QualPage and see what you can find that enriches your understanding of qualitative research. Be careful to avoid textual data overload.

Developing a Research Proposal

1. Which qualitative data analysis alternative is most appropriate for the qualitative data you proposed to collect for your project?

Using this approach, develop a strategy for using the techniques of qualitative data analysis to analyze your textual data.

A Question of Ethics

1. Robert Stake (1995) described behaviors of high school students that seemed likely to provoke violence in others. Should he have intervened directly to prevent escalation of conflicts? Should he have informed the school principal? What ethical guideline about intervention to prevent likely harm to others would you recommend?

2. In an innovative study of American Indian reservations, Bachman (1992) found high rates of homicide. She reported this and other important and troubling findings in her book, Death and Violence on the Reservation. In your opinion, do researchers have an ethical obligation to urge government officials or others to take action in response to social problems that they have identified? Why or why not?

CHAPTER 12

Secondary Data Analysis and Mixed Methods

In this chapter we describe two research methods, secondary data analysis and mixed methods. This is a unique chapter in that we describe two very different research methods, but each method emerges from the specific designs described in the previous chapters. Secondary data analysis is when researchers use preexisting data to answer a research question; the preexisting data may be derived from quantitative surveys or qualitative sources. Mixed methods utilize some combination of the quantitative and qualitative designs described in earlier chapters; a mixed-method design may even include a secondary data analysis. As you read this chapter, you will learn about the utility of secondary data analysis and mixed methods and their relative strengths and weaknesses.

回 Secondary Data Analysis

Richard Layte and Christopher Whelan sought to improve understanding of poverty in Europe. Rather than design their own data collection effort, they turned to five waves of data from the European Community Household Panel Survey, which were available to them from Eurostat, the Statistical Office of the European Communities (Eurostat, 2003). The data they obtained represented the years 1994 to 1998, thus allowing Layte and Whelan (2003) to investigate whether poverty tends to persist more in some countries than others and what factors influence the persistence in different countries. Their investigation of poverty dynamics found a tendency for individuals and households to be trapped in poverty, but this phenomenon varied with the extent to which countries provided social welfare supports.

Secondary data analysis is the method of using preexisting data in a different way or to answer a different research question than intended by those who collected the data. The most common source of **secondary data**—previously collected data that are used in a new analysis—are social science surveys and data collected by government agencies, often with survey research methods. It is also possible to reanalyze data that have been collected in experimental studies or with qualitative methods. Even a researcher's reanalysis of data that he or she collected qualifies as secondary analysis if it is employed for a new purpose or in response to a methodological critique.

> **Secondary data analysis** The method of using preexisting data to answer a research question.
>
> **Secondary data** Previously collected data are used in a new analysis.

Thanks to the data collected by social researchers, governments, and organizations over many years, secondary data analysis has become the research method used by many social work researchers to investigate important research questions. Why consider secondary data? (1) Data collected in previous investigations are available for use by other social researchers on a wide range of topics. (2) Available data sets often include many more measures and cases and reflect more rigorous research procedures than another researcher will have the time or resources to obtain in a new investigation. (3) Much of the groundwork involved in creating and testing measures with the data set has already been done. (4) Most funded projects collect data that can be used to investigate new research questions that the primary researchers who collected the data did not consider.

We first identify some sources for finding secondary data sets. We then give special attention to some easy-to-overlook problems with the use of secondary data. We introduce the concept of "Big Data," which involves the analysis of data sets of unprecedented size and has only become possible with the development of very powerful information storage and very fast computing facilities. At the end of this section, we conclude with some ethical cautions related to secondary data analysis.

Secondary Data Sources

With the advent of modern technology and the Internet, secondary data analysis has become an increasingly accessible research method for social work researchers. Literally thousands of large-scale data sets are now available for investigation, often with no more effort than the few commands required to download the data set; a number of important data sets can even be analyzed directly on the web by users who lack their own statistical software.

There are many sources of relevant secondary data available to social work researchers. These sources range from data compiled by governmental units and private organizations for administrative purposes, which are subsequently made available for research purposes, to data collected by researchers for one purpose that are then made available for other analyses. Many important data sets are collected for the specific purpose of facilitating secondary data analysis. Many social scientists who have received funding to study one research question have subsequently made the data they collect available to the broader social science community for investigations of other research questions. These data sets are sometimes available from a website maintained by the original research organization or placed in a data repository such as the University of Michigan's Inter-University Consortium for Political and Social Research (ICPSR).

Fortunately, you do not have to google your way around the Web to find all these sources on your own. Many websites provide extensive collections of secondary data. Chief among these is the ICPSR website at the University of Michigan. The University of California at Berkeley's Survey Documentation and Analysis (SDA) archive provides several data sets from national omnibus surveys, U.S. Census microdata, surveys on racial attitudes and prejudice, and several labor and health surveys. The National Archive of Criminal Justice Data is an excellent source of data in the area of criminal justice, although like many other data collections, including key data from the U.S. Census, it is also available through the ICPSR. Many of the statistical data collected by U.S. federal government agencies can be accessed through the consolidated FedStats website, http://fedstats.sites.usa.gov.

U.S. Census Bureau

The U.S. government has conducted a census of the population every 10 years since 1790; since 1940, this census has also included a census of housing. The decennial Census of Population and Housing is a rich source of information. The U.S. Census of Population and Housing aims to survey one adult in every household in the United States. The basic *complete-count* census contains questions about household composition as well as ethnicity and income. More questions are asked in a longer form of the census that is administered to a sample of households. A separate census of housing characteristics is conducted at the same time. Participation in the census is required by law, and confidentiality of the information obtained is mandated by law for 72 years after collection. Census data are reported for geographic units, including state, metropolitan areas, counties, census tracts (small, relatively permanent areas within counties), and even blocks. These different units allow units of analysis to be tailored to research questions.

The Census Bureau and Bureau of Labor Statistics' Current Population Survey (CPS) is a monthly employment and unemployment record for the United States, classified by age, sex, race, and other characteristics. The CPS uses a stratified random survey of about 60,000 households with separate forms for about 120,000 individuals. In addition, there is an annual supplement, the Current Population Survey Annual Social and Economic Supplement. The CPS annual supplement is a survey of about 68,000 households and 140,000 individuals. It provides information about work, income, program benefits, health insurance, and a variety of demographic characteristics.

The U.S. Census website (www.census.gov) provides much information about the nearly 100 surveys and censuses that the Census Bureau directs each year, including direct access to many statistics for geographic areas. The Census Bureau collects data on agriculture, manufacturing, construction and other business, foreign countries, and foreign trade. Some of the data sets gathered by the U.S. Census include the National Health Interview Survey (which looks at acute and chronic illness and health-related services), National Long-Term Care Survey (data on elderly individuals, including demographic characteristics and their ability to perform activities of daily living), and the Survey of Income and Program Participation (a series of panel studies of households providing data about source and amount of income, labor force participation, program participation, and program eligibility data (U.S. Census Bureau, 2015). The Census Bureau makes available interactive data retrieval systems for some surveys. For example, American FactFinder enables you to access data from the 2010 Census and American Community Survey (2001 to 2008); you can review its organization, create data tables, and download data at http://factfinder2.census.gov/main.html. You can create your own tables from the CPS Annual Social and Economic Supplement at the website, http://www.census.gov/cps/data/cpstablecreator.html. Many census files containing microdata—records from persons, households, or housing unites—are available online. You can download, install, and use DataFerrett (http://dataferrett.census.gov) to analyze and extract data from a number of data sets collected by other federal agencies.

Inter-University Consortium for Political and Social Research

Another major repository for secondary data is the University of Michigan's ICPSR. ICPSR houses the most extensive collection of social science data sets outside the federal government. Over 7,900 studies are represented in more than 500,000 files from 130 countries and from sources that range from U.S. government agencies such as the Census Bureau to international organizations such as the United Nations, social research organizations such as the National Opinion Research Center, and individual social scientists that have completed funded research projects.

The data sets archived by ICPSR are available for downloading directly from the ICPSR website (www.icpsr.umich .edu). ICPSR makes data sets obtained from the government sources available directly to the general public, but many other data sets are available only to individuals at the colleges and universities around the world that are members of the ICPSR consortium. The availability of some data sets is restricted because of confidentiality issues; to use these data sets, researchers must sign a contract and agree to certain conditions.

ICPSR contains surveys on a countless number of topics. In addition to the many surveys on economics, business, politics, and social relations, there are special archives related to health, mental health, aging, criminal justice, substance abuse, and child care. To find surveys, you can search by subject or by specific variables; each method produces a list of surveys on that subject or that used a particular variable.

ICPSR also catalogs reports and publications containing analyses that have used ICPSR data sets since 1962—67,068 citations were in this archive on August 4, 2015. This resource provides an excellent starting point for the literature search that should precede a secondary data analysis. In most cases, you can learn from detailed study reports a great deal about the methodology, including the response rate in a sample survey and the reliability of any indexes constructed. Published articles provide examples of how others have described the study methodology as well as research questions that have already been studied with the data and issues that remain to be resolved. You can search this literature at the ICPSR site simply by entering the same search terms that you used to find data sets or by entering the specific study number of the data set on which you have focused.

Qualitative Data Sources

Far fewer qualitative data sets are available for secondary analysis, but the number is growing. European countries, particularly England, have been in the forefront of efforts to promote archiving of qualitative data. The United Kingdom's Economic and Social Research Council established the Qualitative Data Archiving Resource Center at the University of Essex in 1994 (Heaton, 2008). Now part of the Economic and Social Data Service, UK Data Service Quali-Bank (2014) provides access to data from a large number of qualitative research projects. Researchers from outside the United Kingdom can apply to become users, though some data collections are available only to UK users.

In the United States, the ICPSR collection includes an expanding number of studies containing at least some qualitative data or measures coded from qualitative data. Studies range from transcriptions of original handwritten and published materials relating to infant and child care to transcripts of interviews with high school students involved in violent incidents. Harvard University's Institute for Quantitative Social Science has archived more than 400 studies that contain at least some qualitative data.

The University of Southern Maine's Center for the Study of Lives (http://usm.maine.edu/lifestorycenter/about.html) collects interview transcripts that record the life stories of people of diverse ages and backgrounds. As of July 2014, their collection included transcripts from more than 400 life stories, representing more than 35 different ethnic groups, experiences of historical events ranging from the Great Depression to the Vietnam War, and including reports on dealing with health problems.

International Data Sources

Comparative researchers and those conducting research in other countries can find data sets on the population characteristics, economic and political features, and political events of many nations. The European Commission administers the Eurobarometer Survey Series at least twice yearly across all the member states of the European Union. The survey monitors social and political attitudes and reports are published regularly online at www.gesis.org/en/services/data/survey-data/eurobarameter-data-service. Case-level data are stored at the ICPSR. The United Nations University

Research In the News

For Further Thought

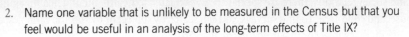

LONG-TERM IMPACT: HOW CAN RESEARCH MAKE THE CONNECTION?

Researchers are using quantitative data analysis to determine the long-term effects of Title IX—which required equal treatment for men and women in educational activities—on women's health and overall educational success. By controlling factors such as school size, income, and social differences, Betsey Stevenson was able to conclude that Title IX had a direct effect on female achievement. Robert Kaestner found that female athletes have a 7% lower risk of obesity years after participation in high school sports. These researchers compiled data on high school sports participation from the National Federation of State High School Associations and used census data to test their hypotheses.

1. What are some advantages of using census data to test hypotheses like this?

2. Name one variable that is unlikely to be measured in the Census but that you feel would be useful in an analysis of the long-term effects of Title IX?

Source: Parker-Pope (2010, p. D5).

makes available a World Income Inequality Database from ongoing research on income inequality in the developed, developing, and transition countries. ICPSR also maintains an International Data Resource Center that provides access to many other data sets from around the world.

Challenges for Secondary Data Analysis

The use of secondary data analysis has the following clear advantages for social work researchers (Rew et al., 2000):

- It allows analyses of social processes in other inaccessible settings.

- It saves time and money.

- It allows the researcher to avoid data collection problems.

- It facilitates comparison with other samples.

- It may allow inclusion of many more variables and a more diverse sample than otherwise would be feasible.

- It may allow data from multiple studies to be combined.

The secondary data analyst also faces some unique challenge. The easy availability of data for secondary analysis should not obscure the fundamental differences between a secondary and primary analysis of social science data. In fact, a researcher who can easily acquire secondary data may be tempted to minimize the limitations of the methods used to collect the data as well as insufficient correspondence between the measures in the data set and the research questions that the secondary data analyst wants to answer.

The greatest challenge faced in secondary data analysis results from the researcher's inability to design data collection methods best suited to answer the research question. The secondary data analyst also cannot test and refine the methods to be used on the basis of preliminary feedback from the population or processes to be studied. Nor is it possible to engage in the iterative process of making observations, developing concepts, or making more observations and refining concepts. This last problem is a special challenge for those seeking to conduct secondary analyses of qualitative data because an inductive process of developing research questions and refining observation and interview strategies is a hallmark of much qualitative methodology (Heaton, 2008).

These limitations mean that it may not be possible for a secondary data analyst to focus on the specific research question of original interest or to use the most appropriate sampling or measurement approach for studying the research question. Secondary data analysis inevitably involves a trade-off between the ease with which the research process can be initiated and the specific hypotheses that can be tested and methods that can be used. If the primary study was not designed to measure adequately a concept that is critical to the secondary analyst's hypothesis, the study may have to be abandoned until a more adequate source of data can be found. Alternatively, hypotheses or even the research question may be modified to match the analytic possibilities presented by the available data (Riedel, 2000).

Many of these problems can be lessened by reviewing data features and quality before deciding to develop an analysis of secondary data (Riedel, 2000) and then developing analysis plans that maximize the value of the available data. Replicating key analyses with alternative indicators of key concepts, testing for the stability of relationships across theoretically meaningful subsets of the data, and examining findings of comparable studies conducted with other data sets can each strengthen confidence in the findings of a secondary analysis.

Any secondary analysis will improve if the analyst—yourself or the author of the work that you are reviewing—answers several questions before deciding to develop an analysis of secondary data in the first place (Riedel, 2000; D. Stewart & Kamins, 1993):

1. What were the agency's or researcher's goals in collecting the data?

   The goals of the researcher or research sponsor influence every step in the process of designing a research project, analyzing the resulting data, and reporting results. Some of these goals will be stated quite explicitly, but others may only be implicit—reflected in the decisions made but not acknowledged in the research report or other publications. When you review a possible data set, you should consider whether your own research goals are similar to those of the original investigators and sponsors. The data collected are more likely to include what is necessary for achieving your own research goals if the original investigator had similar goals. When your research question or goals diverge, you should consider how this may have affected the course of the primary research project and whether this affects your ability to use the resulting data for a different purpose.

2. What data were collected, and what were they intended to measure?

   You should develop a clear description of how data enter the data collection system, for what purpose and how cases leave the system and why. Try to obtain the guidelines that were followed in processing cases and determine if there were any changes in the procedures (Riedel, 2000).

3. When was the information collected?

   Both historical and comparative analyses can be affected. There are issues of changing variables, changing response rates, and the like.

4. What methods were used for data collection? Who was responsible for data collection, and what were their qualifications? Are they available to answer questions about the data?

   Each step in the data collection process should be charted and the involved personnel identified. Copies of the forms used for data collection should be obtained, specific measures should be inspected, and the ways in which these data are processed should be reviewed.

5. How is the information organized (by date, individual, family, event, etc.)? Are there identifiers used to identify different types of data available?

   There are data sets such as the Survey of Income and Program Participation that provide information by different units of analysis (individual, family, and household). You will want to know how to link these different units of analysis if that is important to your research question.

6. What is known about the success of the data collection effort? How are missing data indicated and treated? What kind of documentation is available? How consistent are the data with data available from other sources?

The U.S. Census Bureau provides extensive documentation about data quality, including missing data and how they are treated, and it documents the efforts it makes to improve data quality. The degree to which information is available is not uniform, but the extent to which you can find answers will improve your use of the data set. The treatment of missing data is particularly important. Some data sets will leave the data as missing while other data sets may have an *imputed* response; that is, an operation was devised to insert a response. There are different imputation procedures so it is important to know the procedure used and the potential impact on the analysis.

Answering these questions helps ensure that you are familiar with the data that will be analyzed and can help identify any problems with it. It is unlikely that you or any secondary data analyst will be able to develop complete answers to these questions before starting an analysis, but it is still critical to attempt to assess what you know and do not know about data quality before deciding to use the data. If you uncover bases for real concern after checking documents, the other publications with the data, and information on websites, you have to decide to reject the analytic plan and instead search for another data set. If your answers to these six questions give sufficient evidence that the data can reasonably be used to answer your research question, you should still keep seeking to fill in missing gaps in your initial answers; through this ongoing process, you will develop the fullest possible understanding of the quality of your data. This will help you write a convincing description of the data set's advantages and limitations. Exhibit 12.1 contains the description of a data set available from the ICPSR. Read through it and see how many of the secondary data questions it answers.

Big Data

When do secondary data become what is now referred to as "Big Data"? Big Data involves data at an entirely different order of magnitude than what we are used to thinking about as large data sets. **Big Data** refers to massive amounts of data that are accessible in computer-readable form and are produced by people. The technology now exists to integrate data bases and to analyze these data.

There is a tendency to think about Big Data in the context of Facebook, YouTube, or Twitter. Facebook users upload more than 10 million photos every hour and leave a comment or click on a "like" button almost three billion times per day; YouTube users upload more than an hour of video every second; Twitter users were sending more than 400 million tweets per day. That is a lot of data! That is big! Yet these are not the only sources of Big Data; government agencies, private organizations, the electric company all have large amounts of data.

Big Data Massive data sets produced or accessible in computer-readable form that are produced by people and manageable with today's computers.

All this information would be of no more importance than the number of grains of sand on the beach or of stars in the sky except that these numbers describe information produced by people, available to social scientists, and manageable with today's computers. Already Big Data are being used to predict the spread of flu, the price of airline tickets, and the behavior of consumers.

Here is a quick demonstration. What contribution has social work and social welfare made to the social world? One way to answer that question is to see how frequently these two terms appear in all the books ever written. It may surprise you to learn that it is possible right now to answer that question, although with two key limitations: we can only examine books written in English and in several other languages and as of 2014 we were still limited to only a quarter of all books published (Aiden & Michel, 2013).

To check this out, go to the Google Ngrams site (https://books.google.com/ngrams), type in "social work, social welfare," and check the "case-insensitive" box and change the ending year to 2010. Exhibit 12.2 shows the resulting screen (if you do not obtain a graph, try using a different browser). Note that the height of a graph line represents the percentage of all words in books published in each year, so a rising line means greater relative interest in the word, not simply books being published. You can see that interest in both terms increased until the 1980s; since then "social welfare" has declined while "social work" has fluctuated but appears in decline.

Exhibit 12.1 ICPSR Data Set Description

Description—Study No. 4120

Bibliographic Description

ICPSR Study No.:	4120
Title:	Detroit Area Study, 1997: Social Change in Religion and Child Rearing
Principal Investigator(s):	Duane Alwin, University of Michigan
Series:	*Detroit Area Studies Series*
Bibliographic Citation:	Alwin, Duane. DETROIT AREA STUDY, 1997: SOCIAL CHANGE IN RELIGION AND CHILD REARING [Computer file]. ICPSR04120-v1. Ann Arbor, MI: Detroit Area Studies [producer], 1997. Ann Arbor, MI: Inter-university Consortium for Political and Social Research [distributor], 2005-06-02.
Scope of Study *Summary:*	For this survey, respondents from three counties in the Detroit, Michigan, area were queried about their work, health, marriage and family, finances, political views, religion, and child rearing. With respect to finances, respondent views were elicited on credit card purchases, recording expenditures, and savings and investments. Regarding political views, respondents were. . . .
Subject Term(s):	*abortion, Atheism, Bible, birth control, Catholicism, Catholics, child rearing, children, Christianity, church attendance, communism, Creationism, credit card use, divorce, drinking behavior, economic behavior, educational background, employment, ethnicity, families, . . .*
Geographic Coverage:	Detroit, Michigan, United States
Time Period:	1997
Date(s) of Collection:	1997
Universe:	Residents 21 years and older in the tri-county area (Wayne, Oakland, and Macomb) of Michigan.
Data Type:	survey data
Methodology *Sample:*	A random-digit dialing sample of residential telephone numbers in the Michigan counties of Wayne, Oakland, and Macomb. The sample was restricted to adults 21 years of age and older.
Mode of Data Collection:	telephone interview
Extent of Processing:	CDBK.ICPSR/ DDEF.ICPSR/ REFORM.DATA
Access & Availability	1 data file + machine-readable documentation (PDF) + SAS setup file + SPSS setup file + Stata *Extent of Collection:* setup file
Data Format:	Logical Record Length with SAS, SPSS, and Stata setup files, SPSS portable file, and Stata system file
Original ICPSR Release:	2005-06-02

ICPSR Description of Detroit Area Studies

Detroit Area Studies Series

- View studies in the series
- Related Literature

The Detroit Area Studies series was initiated in 1951 at the University of Michigan and has been carried out nearly every year till the present. The Department of Sociology and the Survey Research Center of the Institute for Social Research are associated with the development of the series. It was initially supported by funds from the Ford Foundation, but since 1988 the University of Michigan has provided primary financial support for the series, with supplemental funding obtained frequently from outside sources. The purpose of these surveys is to provide practical social research training for graduate students and reliable data on the Greater Detroit community. Each survey probes a different aspect of personal and public life, economic and political behavior, political attitudes, professional and family life, and living experiences in the Detroit metropolitan area. The different specific problems investigated each year are selected by the executive committee of the project.

Source: From *Detroit Area Study, 1997: Social Change in Religion and Child Rearing.* Inter-university Consortium for Political and Social Research.

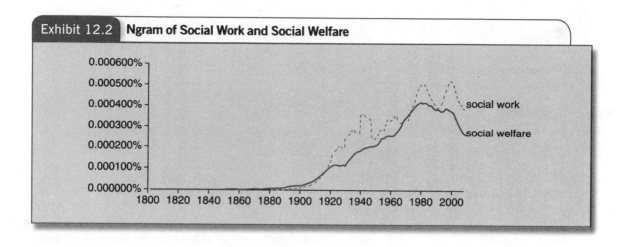

Exhibit 12.2 — Ngram of Social Work and Social Welfare

Access to Big Data also provides another method for investigating the social world and it is being used to address important questions. For example, the health sector is exploring how Big Data might predict health outcomes, treatment needs, and health care use. The Centers for Medicare and Medicaid Services (CMS) is the largest payer for health care services and has massive amounts of data, including medical service claims, assessments from nursing homes, skilled nursing facilities, inpatient rehabilitation, or home health services, consumer surveys, quality-related data, and prescription data (Brennan, Oelschlaeger, Cox, & Tavenner, 2014). CMS is now able to link these disparate sources of information:

> One example of the leading-edge analytics being conducted at the CMS is the use of Medicare data for real-time analysis of changes in clinical and economic features of the health care delivery system. Historically, CMS generated Medicare program performance metrics, such as per beneficiary spending, with a one-to-two year delay. (Brennan et al., 2014, p. 1197)

Some of the specific uses at CMS include predicting program metrics like hospital readmission rates, modeling and detecting fraud, monitoring health status and outcomes, and using information for competitive bidding.

Using Big Data is not a research method in itself, but the availability of Big Data and technologies for its analysis mean that researchers can apply standard research methods in exciting new ways. Big Data now permits researchers investigating some issues to forgo drawing samples in favor of analyzing data from an entire population (Mayer-Schönberger & Cukier, 2013).

The sources of Big Data are increasing rapidly. CMS has made aggregated data available in machine-readable form to the public and is sharing additional information to researchers through the CMS Virtual Research Data Center found at http://www.resdac.org/cms-data/request/cms-virtual-research-data-center. One billion people use Facebook, thereby creating digital records that can, with appropriate arrangements, be analyzed to better understand social behavior (Aiden & Michel, 2013). Big Data are generated by smartphones, wristband health monitors, student postings, and student online education programs (Mayer-Schönberger & Cukier, 2013). All sorts of organizations are collecting data about their consumers.

The availability of Big Data also makes possible the analysis of data from samples of a size previously unimaginable—even when limited research resources prevent the analysis of data from an entire population. Angela Bohn, Christian Buchta, Kurt Hornik, and Patrick Mair, in Austria and at Harvard, analyzed records of 438,851 users to explore the relation between friendship patterns and access to social capital (Bohn et al., 2014). They started their analysis with data on 1,712 users—because they did not have the computer power to analyze more data—who were selected randomly over a 2-month period. One of their findings was that having more communication partners increased social capital as indicated by responses received to their postings, but only up to 130 partners. Users with more than 130 partners tended to receive fewer postings (Bohn et al., 2014).

Ethical Issues in Secondary Data Analysis and Big Data

Analysis of data collected by others does not create the same potential for harm as does the collection of primary data, but neither ethical nor related political considerations can be ignored. Because in most cases the secondary researchers did not collect the data, a key ethical obligation is to cite the original, principal investigators, as well as the data source, such as the ICPSR.

Subject confidentiality is a key concern when original records are analyzed. Whenever possible, all information that could identify individuals should be removed from the records to be analyzed so that no link is possible to the identities of living respondents or their living descendants (Huston & Naylor, 1996). When you use data that have already been archived, you need to find out what procedures were used to preserve subject confidentiality. The work required to ensure subject confidentiality probably will have been done for you by the data archivist. For example, staff at ICPSR examines carefully all data deposited in the archive for the possibility of disclosure risk. All data that might be used to identify respondents are altered to ensure confidentiality, including removal of information such as birth dates or service dates, specific incomes, or place of residence that could be used to identify respondents indirectly. When these data cannot be removed without diminishing the data set quality, ICPSR restricts access to the data and requires that investigators agree to conditions of use that preserve subject confidentiality.

The institutional review board (IRB) for the protection of human subjects at your institution has the responsibility to decide whether they need to review and approve proposals for secondary data analysis. The federal regulations are not entirely clear on this point, so the acceptable procedures may vary between institutions based on what their IRBs have decided.

Data quality is always a concern with secondary data, even when the data are collected by an official government agency. Researchers who rely on secondary data inevitably make trade-offs between their ability to use a particular data set and the specific hypotheses they can test. If a concept that is critical to a hypothesis was not measured adequately in a secondary data source, the study might have to be abandoned until a more adequate source of data can be found. Alternatively, hypotheses or even the research question may be modified to match the analytic possibilities presented by the available data (Riedel, 2000).

Big Data also create some new concerns about research ethics. When enormous amounts of data are available for analysis, the procedures for making data anonymous no longer ensure that it stays that way. In 2006, AOL released for research purposes 20 million search queries from 657,000 users, after all personal information had been erased and only a unique numeric identifier remained to link searches. However, staff of the *New York Times* conducted analyses of sets of search queries and were able to quickly identify a specific individual user by name and location, based on their searches. The collection of Big Data also makes possible surveillance and prediction of behavior on a large scale. Crime control efforts and screening for terrorists now often involve developing predictions from patterns identified in Big Data. Without strict rules and close monitoring, potential invasions of privacy and unwarranted suspicions are enormous (Mayer-Schönberger & Cukier, 2013).

🔲 Mixed Methods

Do internal community assets, including elective leadership, community cohesion, and mental health, help a community rebuild after a natural disaster? Intae Yoon (2009) was concerned that no single method would reveal the breadth of internal community assets and their role in community rebuilding, nor could lay respondents fully assess the role of the community leadership and their interactions with each other and their interactions with other government agencies. As a result, Yoon adopted a mixed-methods approach to answering this research question. The quantitative component of the study involved mailing structured questionnaires to all 700 occupied housing units in the community; the survey was designed to measure respondent perceptions about the quality of elected officials' leadership, community cohesion, depressive symptoms, financial recovery, and emotional status. The qualitative component of the study included semistructured interviews with key informants and document reviews of government and nongovernment publications. The interviews were designed to elicit responses about elected officials' communications with other governmental agencies and to identify unknown community assets while documents were reviewed to learn about the community's responses to the disaster and the rebuilding process. While Yoon had several conclusions based on the mixed methods, one implication in particular stood out:

> First, flexible thinking in identifying assets is necessary in any disaster rebuilding process. High poverty and low education levels of Princeville predicted that the town was more likely to disappear. Contradictory to this anticipation, the town was able to survive. As suggested in the community assets perspective, the poverty-stricken community had its special assets. The most precious asset of the town was its symbolic meaning. . . . Any assets in a disaster-stricken community, including invisible symbolic meanings of the community, should not be ignored in the rebuilding process. (p. 26)

Intae Yoon's (2009) decision was not unique. An increasing number of social work researchers are turning to mixed methods to answer more sophisticated research questions that may not be answered by a single method. In this chapter, we first introduce the logic of mixed methods and different ways of combining qualitative and quantitative methods. We then review the strengths and limitations of the methods we have discussed; this review will help you choose the most appropriate research design for a particular investigation and decide when a combination of methods is most useful.

Philosophy of Mixed Methods

Should researchers consider combining qualitative and quantitative methods in single studies? For many years there was disagreement between researchers who took a positivist approach and researchers who took a constructivist approach. And to some extent, the debates persist; what has emerged is a third approach, pragmatism. You might remember these three broad approaches from Chapter 1; nonetheless, we start with a brief review.

A researcher who accepts a positivist philosophy believes that there is a reality that exists apart from our perceptions or interpretations of it. Researchers test ideas about the real world to see if the evidence obtained from quantitative methods indicates that the real world is consistent with their ideas about it. Researchers need to be objective, to ensure that their view is not distorted by finding what they want to find. If the evidence indicates that their ideas were wrong, then the ideas need to be revised accordingly (Morgan, 2014).

By contrast, a researcher who accepts a constructivist philosophy believes that the reality experienced by different people differs because reality exists only in relation to each individual's unique perspective. As researchers learn about others' experiences and beliefs, they interpret what was learned with their theories but there is no single reality that is used to test ideas. The evidence enables researchers to understand others' perspectives and to develop an understanding of larger social contexts, but it does not allow them to conclude that their perspective is correct (Morgan, 2014).

You can see how the two contrasting philosophies provide for disagreement among researchers who hold one view or the other view. Therefore, if the logic of quantitative methods necessarily reflects a positivist philosophy and the logic of qualitative methods necessarily reflects a constructivist philosophy, there is little basis for combining these methods in one project.

Researchers who seek to combine the strengths of qualitative and quantitative methods in one research project take a different approach. Some sidestep the conflicting philosophy debate using what seems to work best for answering a given research question (Onwuegbuzie & Combs, 2010). For example, Ryan Brown and his colleagues (2013) were guided by this approach when they sought to learn why most health intervention strategies with homeless adults have had limited effect:

> Properly addressing such complexity and interdependency requires agile research strategies that can not only assess causal factors at multiple levels but also flexibly incorporate new information as it arises during the research process. This means enabling creative and productive conversation between qualitative and quantitative measurement and analytic modalities—a mixed-methods approach. (p. 329)

Other researchers turn to a different philosophy to justify the use of mixed methods. Rather than the alternative perspectives of positivism and constructivism, they adopt the principle of **pragmatism**: "knowledge comes from taking action and learning from the outcomes" (Morgan, 2014, p. 7). They do not worry about the nature of reality; instead, they investigate the consequences that follow from taking action in particular situations. Marcus Weaver-Hightower (2013) explained the basis for pragmatic rejection of the positivist–constructivist debate:

> **Pragmatism** A philosophy that emphasizes the importance of taking action and learning from the outcomes to generate knowledge.

> Both qualitative and quantitative methods do have limitations for studying policy influence; qualitative methods can have difficulty establishing the extent of influence while quantitative methods can have difficulty in providing the whys, hows, and so whats. Rather than succumb to paralysis from competing claims for methodological incompleteness, I used mixed-methods to ameliorate each approach's limitations. (p. 6)

Types of Mixed-Methods Designs

Qualitative methods may be used at the same time as quantitative methods or they may be used before or after quantitative methods; that is, the sequencing of the two approaches can differ. In addition, one method may be given priority in a project or qualitative and quantitative methods may be given equal priority. Creswell (2010) has helped popularize a simple notational system for distinguishing different ways of mixing quantitative and qualitative methods. The basic conventions used are

- The primary method used in a mixed-methods project is written in all caps (QUAN or QUAL).

- The secondary method is written in lowercase letters (quan or qual)

- If both methods are of equal importance, they are both written in all caps.

- If the two methods are used at the same time (concurrently) and they have equal priority, the relation between the two methods is indicated with a +: QUAL + QUAN.

- If two methods are used concurrently, but one has priority the secondary method is said to be "embedded" in the primary method. This is indicated as follows: QUAL(quan) or QUAN(qual).

- If one method is used before the other, the sequence is indicated with an arrow (QUAL → quan, qual → QUAN, QUAN → QUAL, etc.)

The different types of mixed methods that result from these distinctions in priority and sequence are represented in Exhibit 12.3. These different types represent only research projects in which each method is used only once; more complex mixed-methods projects may involve combinations of these types, either at the same time or in sequence.

Sometimes researchers will develop a study flowchart to describe the mixed-methods process and sequence of events. Exhibit 12.4 summarizes the study plan for Townsend, Floersch, and Findling's (2010) assessment of the Drug Attitude Inventory for Youth. Both the quantitative and qualitative aspects have equal weight, as reflected by the QUAN and QUAL. The qualitative and quantitative data are collected at the same time. Though the data are analyzed separately, the integration of the methods begins when the data are merged to compare and contrast the findings. The mixing continues with interpretations of the combined findings.

Some examples will help to clarify the reasons for using different types of mixed-methods designs. A common reason for mixing both quantitative and qualitative methods in one research project is to take advantage of the unique strengths of each methodological approach when engaged in different stages of the research process (Teddlie & Tashakkori, 2010). Yoon's (2009) research followed such a process in answering the question, What internal (invisible) community assets helped a community rebuild? The quantitative investigation looked at the assets that according to the

Exhibit 12.3 **Types of Mixed Methods**

		Priority	
		Prioritized	Equal
Sequence	Sequential	Staged Method qual → QUAN quan → QUAL QUAL → quan QUAN → qual	Research Program QUAL → QUAN QUAN → QUAL
	Concurrent	Embedded Method QUAN(qual) QUAL(quan)	Integrated Method QUAN + QUAL

Exhibit 12.4 **Flowchart of a Study Plan**

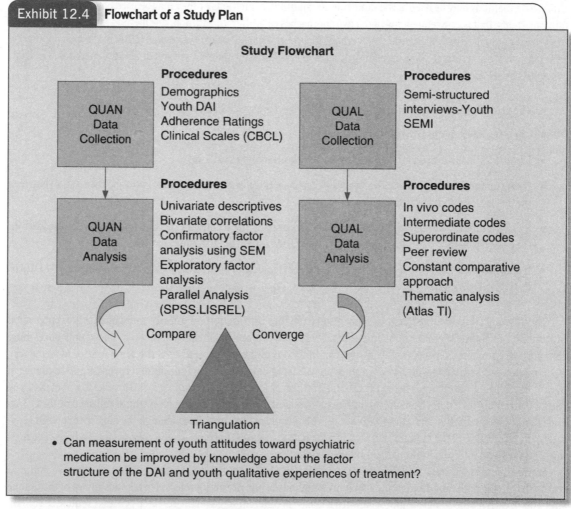

Study Flowchart

Procedures

QUAN Data Collection

Demographics
Youth DAI
Adherence Ratings
Clinical Scales (CBCL)

Procedures

QUAL Data Collection

Semi-structured
interviews-Youth
SEMI

Procedures

QUAN Data Analysis

Univariate descriptives
Bivariate correlations
Confirmatory factor
analysis using SEM
Exploratory factor
analysis
Parallel Analysis
(SPSS.LISREL)

Procedures

QUAL Data Analysis

In vivo codes
Intermediate codes
Superordinate codes
Peer review
Constant comparative
approach
Thematic analysis
(Atlas TI)

Compare   Converge

Triangulation

- Can measurement of youth attitudes toward psychiatric
  medication be improved by knowledge about the factor
  structure of the DAI and youth qualitative experiences of treatment?

Source: Townsend, Lisa, Jerry Floersch, and Robert L. Findling. 2010. "The Conceptual Adequacy of the Drug Attitude Inventory for Measuring Youth Attitudes Toward Psychotropic Medications: A Mixed Methods Evaluation." *Journal of Mixed Methods Research*, p. 36.

literature should have an effect, while the qualitative investigation tried to both shed light on one asset (leadership) and uncover other, unknown community assets. This project reflected a QUAL + QUAN method.

Another reason for mixing methods is to add unique insights about the intervention process that cannot easily be obtained from the primary method used in an investigation. Christiaan Abildso and colleagues (Abildso, Zizzi, Gilleland, Thomas, & Bonner, 2010) wanted to understand why a 12-week cognitive-behavioral weight management program might result in weight loss and improvement in psychosocial measures. The quantitative investigation focused on baseline and 12-week differences in a variety of weight-related measures and standardized measures of psychosocial factors while the subsequent qualitative investigation was designed to identify factors associated with program adherence, program success, and program strengths and weaknesses. This study used an integrated model, QUAN → qual.

Researchers may choose to use mixed methods when they want to explore new or understudied phenomena and then test findings from the qualitative research. Rogers and his colleagues (Rogers, Yancey, & Singletary, 2005) wanted to better understand faith-based social services and, in particular, the role of faith in service delivery, models of collaboration and factors that impact collaboration, and effective service delivery. They used a two-step process, beginning with a qualitative phase. The next step was to develop a questionnaire based "on the core networks and core codes from the qualitative data" (p. 195). The survey, consisting of 55 closed-ended questions, was sent to 15,000 faith-based nonprofit organizations and congregations (Garland, Rogers, Singletary, & Yancey, 2005). This would be a QUAL → QUAN design.

Sometimes mixed methods are used to develop a scale or to assess whether a scale is appropriate for a particular population. You learned in Chapter 9 that qualitative methods such as focus groups or cognitive interviewing can be used to refine questions for a quantitative scale. Having developed the scale, the researcher would use the quantitative component to test the quality of the scale, that is, the scale's validity and reliability. This would be a qual → QUAN design; one method precedes the other in time and one method has priority over the other method.

In this section, we discuss in more depth examples of research projects using integrated, embedded, and staged methods. When qualitative and quantitative methods are combined in these ways, researchers must make key decisions about how best to mix methods to achieve their study purposes.

Integrated Designs

In an **integrated design**, qualitative and quantitative methods are used concurrently and both are given equal importance. Findings produced from these methods are then integrated and compared during the analysis of project data. This is the QUAL + QUAN design. Susan McCarter (2009) extended prior research on juvenile justice processing with an integrated investigation of case processing and participant orientations in Virginia. Her hope was to use the results of the two methods to triangulate the study's findings; that is, to show that different methods lead to similar conclusions and therefore become more credible.

> **Integrated design** Qualitative and quantitative methods are used concurrently and both are given equal importance.

The large quantitative data set McCarter used in her research was secondary data collected on 2,233 African American and Caucasian males in Virginia's juvenile justice system:

> The quantitative data set (n = 2,920) is a disproportionate, stratified, random sample of juvenile cases from all 35 Virginia Court Service Units (CSU) where each CSU was treated as a separate stratum. These data were collected by the Joint Legislative Audit and Review Commission (JLARC) in an examination of court processing and outcomes of delinquents and status offenders in Virginia.
>
> JLARC collected data on the juveniles' previous felonies; previous misdemeanors; previous violations of probation/parole; previous status offenses; recent criminal charges, intake action on these charges, predisposition(s) of those charges, court disposition(s) of those charges; and demographics such as sex, race, data of birth, CSU, and geotype (urban, suburban, rural). For a subset of these cases, data included information from the youth's social history, which required judicial request. (p. 535)

Qualitative data were obtained from 24 in-depth interviews with juvenile judges, the commonwealth's attorneys, defense attorneys, police officers, juveniles, and their families (McCarter, 2009):

> The juvenile justice personnel were from six Court Service Units across the state, including two urban, two suburban, two rural. . . . Participants from each CSU were chosen to provide maximum diversity in perspectives and experiences, and thus varied by race, sex, and age; and the justice personnel also varied in length of employment, educational discipline and educational attainment (p. 536)

> . . . . The youth and their families were all selected from one Court Service Unit (CSU) located in an urban geotype with a population of approximately 250,000 (p. 536).

> The sample of youth and their families was comprised of all male juveniles, five mothers, and one father. Four of the six families were African American and two were Caucasian. (p. 540)

The in-depth interviews included open- and closed-ended questions. The open-ended responses were coded into categories that distinguished how participants perceived the role of race in the juvenile justice system (McCarter, 2009). The responses to a question about how common they believed instances of racial or ethnic bias occurred supported quantitative findings that race mattered in the juvenile justice system:

> Juvenile justice professionals as well as youth and their families cited racial bias by individual decision makers and by the overall system, and noted that this bias was most likely to occur by the police during the Alleged Act or Informal Handling stages. However, although race was considered a factor, when compared to other factors, professionals did not think race played a dominant role in affecting a youth's treatment within the juvenile justice system. . . . Eighteen of the juvenile justice professionals stated that they felt a disparity [between processing of African American and white juveniles] existed, four did not feel that a disparity existed, and two indicated that they did not know. (McCarter, 2009, p. 540)

In this way, the qualitative and quantitative findings were integrated. The study's key conclusion about race-based treatment was strengthened because it was based on triangulated identification (McCarter, 2009).

Embedded Designs

Testa, Livingston, and VanZile-Tamsen (2011) supplemented their quantitative study of violence against women with a qualitative component because violence against women is "a complex multifaceted phenomenon, occurring with a social context that is influenced by gender norms, interpersonal relationships, and sexual scripts" and "understanding of these experiences of violence is dependent on the subject meaning for the woman and cannot easily be reduced to a checklist" (p. 237). This was an **embedded design** using a QUAN(qual) sequence.

Embedded design Qualitative and quantitative methods are used concurrently in the research, but one is given priority.

Victims' responses to structured questions indicated an association between alcohol and rape, but when victims elaborated on their experiences in qualitative interviews, their comments led to a new way of understanding this quantitative association. Although this association has often been interpreted as suggesting "impaired judgement" about consent by intoxicated victims, the women interviewed by Testa et al. (2011) revealed that they had had so much to drink that they were unconscious or at least unable to speak at the time of the rape. Testa and her colleagues (2011) concluded that the prevalence of this type of incapacitated rape required a new approach to the problem of violence against women:

> Qualitative analysis of our data has resulted in numerous "a-ha" types of insights that would not have been possible had we relied solely on quantitative data analysis (e.g., identification of incapacitated rape and sexual precedence, heterogeneity in the way that sexual assaults arise) and also helped us to understand puzzling

quantitative observations. . . . These insights, in turn, led to testable, quantitative hypotheses that supported our qualitative findings, lending rigor and convergence to the process. We never could have anticipated what these insights would be and that is what is both scary and exhilarating about qualitative data analysis, particularly for a scientist who has relied on quantitative data analysis and a priori hypothesis testing. (p. 245)

Staged Designs

Christaan Abildso and colleagues (2010) wanted to understand why some people in a 12-week cognitive-behavioral weight loss program succeeded in completing the program and losing weight and other people failed to either complete the program or lost only a moderate amount of weight. The researchers chose for this purpose a staged design using the QUAN → qual sequence, in which a quantitative assessment of findings with 55 participants preceded and was the basis for qualitative telephone interviews with 11 participants.

Staged design Qualitative and quantitative methods are used in sequence in the research.

Abildso and colleagues (2010) identified four research aims:

1. Examine physical and psychosocial differences at baseline between completers of and dropouts from a 12-week weight management program;

2. Assess the physical, behavioral, and psychosocial impact on program completers;

3. Compare the psychosocial changes of high and moderate weight losers; and

4. Qualitatively explore factors associated with program adherence and weight loss (p. 3).

The researchers explained their use of mixed methods:

To our knowledge, this is the first mixed methods evaluation focusing on mechanisms of physical activity behavior change among overweight and obese adults in an insurance sponsored weight management program. The qualitative data provided additional depth of understanding to the quantitative outcomes, and as such, future researchers are encouraged to add qualitative elements to their randomized, controlled trials or other structured quantitative designs. Benefits of adopting mixed methods designs in this context include identifying the critical reasons why people change and why interventions work. (p. 13)

The quantitative component included physical measures (e.g., weight, height, body fat, and Body Mass Index) and scales to measure exercise thoughts (excuses for not exercising), exercise self-efficacy (confidence in overcoming barriers to exercising), barriers to exercise (items that interfered with or prevented exercise), and recent mood (positive and negative affect). They found that 73% completed the program and that 55% lost 15 or more pounds (high weight loss). There were no differences between people who completed the program and people who dropped out. People who were in the high weight loss category had greater improvements in physical outcomes and were more likely to report greater decreases in negative thoughts about exercise, barriers to exercise, and exercise self-efficacy (Abildso et al., 2010). The qualitative phase began with the random selection of participants for an in-depth telephone interview. They created four subgroups stratifying by completion status and weight loss category to ensure that there were interviewees in every condition:

A structured telephone interview script was developed by the investigators in conjunction with the insurance agency's health promotions director to determine factors associated with program adherence and success. Open-ended questions were used to gather feedback about programmatic components, assess 12-week results and post 12-week program impact, and identify strengths, weaknesses, and suggestions for the program. (p. 6)

Abildso conducted and transcribed the interviews (Abildso et al., 2010). The transcripts were reviewed by two independent reviewers and were independently coded with discrepancies discussed until agreement was achieved.

Four themes emerged that differentiated more successful and less successful participants: (1) staff accountability and personal attention, (2) perceived effort, (3) redefining success to both ongoing weight loss and two other tangible physical benefits, and (4) cognitive flexibility or using positive cognitive coping strategies when dealing with barriers.

Complex Designs

Miriam Stewart and her colleagues (2008) used a mixed-methods design in their study of the impact of socio-economic status on social exclusion and social isolation and how these concepts are related to health. This study used a **complex design** as it involved multiple phases of data collection. The study included three phases reflecting a QUAL → QUAN → QUAL design. The first phase use was qualitative employing individual and group interviews to explore isolation, belonging, inclusion, and exclusion and their relationship to socioeconomic status and health. The second phase, a quantitative phase, involved a telephone survey. The final phase was again qualitative and focused on learning from two small groups of policy makers and planners whether the results reflected their own experiences and to discuss the implications of the findings.

Complex design Qualitative and quantitative methods are combined in a research project that uses more than one of the four basic types of mixed-methods designs or that repeats at least one of those basic types.

The qualitative research began with a purposive sample of 119 people. Individual, face-to-face audiotaped interviews were conducted with high- and low-income respondents. The researchers reviewed the interview transcripts and using thematic content analysis, developed themes and subthemes.

The next phase, the quantitative phase, included a randomly selected sample of 1,671 respondents; the telephone survey instrument included 110 items, some of which came from validated self-rating scales while other items were developed by the researchers given responses from the qualitative study:

> Responses from these initial interviews were used to guide item development for most of Phase II survey questions. For example, six items were designed to elicit participants' level of satisfaction with their neighborhood infrastructure (e.g., shopping facilities, community agencies, housing, transportation), cited as major concerns in low-income participants' narratives in Phase I. More specifically, key challenges preventing people from participating in activities (i.e. 'enough money', 'lack of time', 'feeling unwelcome at events') identified in Phase I interviews, prompted us to develop three items (e.g., "People with low incomes do not have enough money to participate in community events and recreational activities") in the follow-up survey measure. (M. Stewart, Makwarimba, Barnfather, Letourneau, & Neufeld, 2008, p. 1408)

The third phase included two group interviews with 23 policy planners and policy makers. This phase focused on learning whether the results from the first two phases reflected their own experiences and to discuss the implications of the findings.

The researchers (M. Stewart et al., 2008) noted the value of their strategy in gaining a more comprehensive assessment in contrast to using only one approach:

> The mixture or sequential use of qualitative (individual and group interviews of low- and higher-income people) and quantitative (survey of low- and higher-income people) methods, followed by qualitative methods (group interviews of policy makers), yielded credible and comprehensive data demonstrating the same pattern of effect of income on exclusion/inclusion, isolation/belonging, and health. Quantitative data helped to generalize findings from the qualitative phases to a wider population of vulnerable people. The richness of the data reinforces the value of using mixed methods triangulating multiple sources (e.g., low-income people, higher-income people, service providers and managers, policy influencers of data. (p. 1410)

Strengths and Limitations of Mixed Methods

Combining qualitative and quantitative methods within one research project can strengthen the project's design by enhancing measurement validity, generalizability, causal validity, or authenticity. At the same time, combining methods creates challenges that may be difficult to overcome and ultimately limit the extent to which these goals are enhanced.

Measurement validity is enhanced when questions to be used in a structured quantitative survey are first refined through qualitative cognitive interviewing or focus groups. After quantitative measures are used, qualitative measures can be added to clarify the meaning of numerical scores. Alternatively, quantitative measures can provide a more reliable indicator of the extent of variation between respondents that has already been described based on naturalistic observations or qualitative interviews. Measurement validity is also enhanced when measures using different methods result in a similar picture. If people are observed to do what they say they do, then the validity of a self-report measure is strengthened by measurement triangulation.

But what if different measures do not reinforce each other? Did some respondents forget what they have done, or are they purposely not disclosing their activities? Are interview respondents trying to look good in interviews by offering socially desirable responses? Mixed methods enable further review of divergent outcomes using the different methods.

The most common way that causal, or internal, validity is strengthened with a mixed-methods design is when qualitative interviews or observations are used to explore the mechanism involved in a causal effect. You read about this earlier in the study by Abildso and colleagues (2010) who used the qualitative findings to shed light on why some people were successful and other people were not successful in weight management.

A mixed-methods design can improve external validity when a quantitative study is repeated in different contexts. Qualitative comparisons between the different contexts can then help make sense of the similarities and differences between outcomes across these contexts and thus identify the conditions for the effects. Schutt (2011) was able to demonstrate this in a study evaluating enhanced housing and services for reducing homelessness among homeless people diagnosed with serious mental issues. Enhanced housing reduced the time spent homeless in four of the five projects. It turned out that the one project that was an exception moved persons off the streets into a shelter, which while an improvement in residential status, still counted as being homeless (Schutt, 2011).

Mixed methods also facilitate achieving the goal of authenticity within a research project that also seeks to achieve measurement validity, generalizability, or causal validity. M. Stewart et al.'s (2008) complex mixed-method study of social inclusion and poverty leads to a conclusion that seems much more authentic than would have been the case if they had used just one method. They went beyond simply confirming hypotheses to substantiating them with policy makers and program planners who, in turn, made recommendations about how to improve social inclusion.

It is naïve to think of mixed methods as simply overcoming problems that can occur when a research design is limited to one method. It is not always clear how best to compare qualitative and quantitative findings or how to interpret discrepancies that arise after such comparison (Morgan, 2014). We cannot be certain that differences in findings mean that deficits have been uncovered in one method—some substance abusers do not disclose their abuse in answer to questions—or that the two methods are really answering different research questions.

Mixed methods also create challenges for researchers because different types of expertise are required for effective use of quantitative and qualitative methods. Recruiting multiple researchers for a project who then work as a team from conception to execution for the project may be the best way to overcome this limitation. The researchers also have to acknowledge in planning the study timetable that the time required for collection, coding, and analysis of qualitative data can challenge a quantitative researcher's expectation of more rapid progress.

Ethics and Mixed Methods

Researchers who combine methods must be aware of the ethical concerns involved in using each of the separate methods, but there are also some ethical challenges that are heightened in mixed-methods projects. One special challenge is defining the researcher's role in relation to the research participants. Every researcher creates an understanding about his or her role with research participants (Mertens, 2012). Researchers using quantitative methods often define themselves as outside experts who design a research project and collect research data using objective procedures that are best carried out without participant involvement. By contrast, qualitative researchers often define themselves as engaging in research in some type of collaboration with the community or group they are studying, with much input from their research participants into the research design and the collection and analysis of research data.

A researcher using mixed methods cannot simply adopt one of these roles: A researcher needs some degree of autonomy when designing quantitative research plans, but a researcher will not be able to collect intensive qualitative data if participants do not accord some degree of trust to the researcher as an insider. The challenge is compounded by the potential for different reactions of potential participants to the different roles. Authorities who control access to program clients or to community members may be willing to agree to a structured survey but not to a long-term engagement with researchers as participant observers so that a mixed-methods project that spans programs, communities, or other settings may involve a biased sampling for the qualitative component. Weighing both roles and the best combination of them is critical at the outset of a mixed-methods project, although the dilemma will be lessened if a project uses different researchers to lead the quantitative and qualitative components.

Complex mixed-methods projects in which quantitative surveying is interspersed with observational research or intensive interviews may also require renegotiation of participant consent to the particular research procedures at each stage:

> Different stages and different components of research may require the negotiation of different types of consent, some of which may be more explicit than others. Sampling, contact, re-contact, and fieldwork can be underpinned by different conceptualization and operationalization of informed consent. This behooves researchers to move away from the position of treating consent-seeking as an exercise that only occurs at certain points in the research process or only for certain types of research. Consent seeking should not be thought of merely as an event. (Sin, 2005, p. 290)

▣ Conclusion

As we noted at the beginning of this chapter, secondary data analysis and mixed methods are quite distinct but as you can also see, they build on kinds of designs that we have described in earlier chapters. Both offer opportunities for social work researchers to address a variety of research questions.

The easy availability of secondary analyses of data sets collected in thousands of social science investigations is one of the most exciting features of social science research in the 21st century. You can often find a previously collected data set that is suitable for testing new hypotheses or exploring these new issues of interest. Moreover, the research infrastructure that has developed at ICPSR and other research consortia, both in the United States and internationally, ensures that a great many of these data sets have been carefully checked for quality and archived in a form that allows easy access.

A research project that is designed to answer multiple research questions and investigate a complex social setting often requires a mixed-methods design. Of course, to some extent, the complexity of the social world always exceeds what can be captured successfully with one method, but the challenges increase as our questions become more numerous and our social settings more complex. No matter what your methodological preference is at this point, increased understanding of these issues in mixed methods will improve your own practice and your ability to critique the research of others.

Key Terms

Big Data   328
Complex design   338
Embedded design   336

Integrated design   335
Pragmatism   333
Secondary data   323

Secondary data analysis   323
Staged design   337

Highlights

- Secondary data analysts should have a good understanding of the research methods used to collect the data they analyze. Data quality is always a concern, particularly with older data.

- Secondary data are available from many sources. The ICPSR provides the most comprehensive data archive.

- Collection of massive sets of Big Data permits analysis of large-scale social patterns and trends.

- Researchers use mixed methods because a single method may not represent adequately the complexity of the social work that they are trying to understand.

- The paradigm disagreement between those who favor qualitative and quantitative methods emerged from inflexibly linking

positivist philosophy to quantitative methods and constructivist philosophy to qualitative methods.

- Pragmatism is a philosophy based on the belief that the meaning of actions and beliefs is found in their consequences.

- Mixed methods combine qualitative and quantitative methods in a systematic investigation of the same or related research questions.

- Types of mixed methods can be distinguished by the priority given to one method or the other, with the basic distinction being between designs that give equal priority to the two methods and those that prioritize one method over the other. Types of methods can also be distinguished by sequencing, with sequential designs using one method before the other and concurrent designs using both methods at the same time.

Discussion Questions

1. Discuss the strengths and weaknesses of secondary data analysis. Do you think it's best to encourage researchers to try to address their research questions with secondary data if at all possible?

2. In a world of limited resources and time constraints, should social work researchers be required to include in their proposals to collect new data an explanation of why they cannot investigate their proposed research question with secondary data? Such a requirement might include a systematic review of data that already are available at ICPSR and other sources. Discuss the

merits and demerits of such a requirement. If such a requirement were to be adopted, what specific rules would you recommend?

3. Testa et al. (2011) argued that mixed methods was a particularly appropriate approach for the study of violence against women. What makes mixed methods more appropriate for this concern in their opinion? What about your own opinion?

4. Discuss other social work areas that you think are more suited to the use of mixed methods.

Practice Exercises

1. Select one report by the U.S. Census Bureau about the U.S. population or some segment of it. Outline the report and list all the tables included in it. Summarize the report in two paragraphs. Suggest a comparative or historical study for which this report would be useful.

2. Think of a possible social work practice research question. Now think of at least two methods, one quantitative and one qualitative, that could be combined in a research design to explore this question.

Web Exercise

1. Go to the American FactFinder website and extract a report about your community.

2. Go to the CPS Annual Social and Economic Supplement Table Creator at the website (http://www.census.gov/cps/data/cpstablecreator.html). Extract a table that shows age, gender, and ethnic differences in health insurance coverage.

3. Go to the website for the online *Journal of Mixed Methods Research* (http://mmr.sagepub.com/). On the home page, click the link to Current Issue. When the table of contents for the current issue comes up, click on the abstracts for three of the articles. For each of these articles, write down the two or more methods that the authors used to conduct their research. Did any methods occur more than once? Were there any methods you had never heard of before?

4. Go back to the home page of the *Journal of Mixed Methods Research*. Find the box listing the "Most Read" articles. At the button for Article Statistics, click on "Most Read." Read the abstracts for the top five articles. What themes or main points do you see running through these articles? Based on the top five abstracts, write a paragraph or two describing the most important issues currently being discussed or investigated by mixed-method researchers.

Developing a Research Proposal

If you plan a *secondary data analysis* research project, you will have to revisit at least one of decisions about research design (see Exhibit 15.1 in Chapter 15 of this book).

1. Convert your proposal for research using survey data, in Chapter 9, into a proposal for a secondary analysis of survey data. Begin by identifying an appropriate data set available through ICPSR or the government. Be sure to include a statement about the limitations of your approach, in which you note any differences between what you proposed to study initially and what you are actually able to study with the available data.

2. At the ICPSR site, review the variables measured in the survey you will analyze and specify the main concepts they indicate. Specify the variables you would consider as an independent and dependent variable in your analysis. What variables should be used as control variables?

If you plan a *mixed-methods* approach,

1. Add a component involving a second method to your research proposal. If you already developed alternative approaches in answer to the exercises in earlier chapters, just write a justification for these additions that points out the potential benefits.

2. Consider the possible influences of educational context factors on the variables pertinent to your research question. Write a rationale for including a test for contextual influences in your proposed research.

3. Describe a method for studying the contextual influences in Question 2.

A Question of Ethics

1. What would be a reasonable IRB statement for secondary data? Would you exempt all secondary analyses from IRB review, just some of them, or none of them? Explain your reasoning.

2. Should separate consent forms and processes be used for the qualitative and quantitative components of a mixed-methods project? What would be the advantages and drawbacks of this approach?

CHAPTER 13

Evaluation Research

The Drug Abuse Resistance Education (D.A.R.E.) program is offered in elementary schools, middle schools, and high schools across the United States and internationally. D.A.R.E. has grown to include 15,000 police officers and as many as 75% of U.S. school districts (Berman & Fox, 2009). For parents worried about drug abuse among youth, or for any concerned citizens, the program has immediate appeal. It brings a special police officer into the schools once a week to speak with classes about the hazards of drug abuse and to establish a direct link between local law enforcement and young people. You only have to check out bumper stickers or attend a few PTA meetings to learn that it's a popular program.

But does it work? Do students who participate in the D.A.R.E. empowerment program become more resistant to the use of illicit drugs? Are they less likely to use illicit drugs while they are enrolled in the program or, more importantly, in the years after they have finished the program? Do students benefit in other ways from participation in D.A.R.E.? Are there beneficial effects for schools and communities? Although the idea of providing students with information about the harmful effects of substance abuse has intuitive appeal, the history of evaluation research about D.A.R.E. drives home an important point: To know whether social programs work, and to understand how they work, we have to evaluate them systematically and fairly, whether we personally think the program sounds like a good idea or not.

The first series of studies using experimental or quasi-experimental designs found that D.A.R.E. had no effect on drug or alcohol use at the time students completed D.A.R.E., although it led to a small reduction in tobacco use (Ringwalt et al., 1994; West & O'Neal, 2004). D.A.R.E. participants did improve their knowledge about substance use, as well as their social skills related to resisting substance abuse, attitudes toward the police, attitudes about drug use, and self-esteem, but these positive attitudinal effects were less than those identified in evaluations of other types of substance abuse programs. A 6-year randomized field experiment of D.A.R.E.'s effectiveness in a sample of Illinois also found no long-term beneficial effect (Rosenbaum & Hanson, 1998). As a result, some school districts stopped using D.A.R.E. (Rosenbaum, 2007)

Yet this was not the end of the story. The Robert Wood Johnson Foundation provided funding for the development of a new educational approach and its evaluation (Berman & Fox, 2009). The new program, Take Charge of Your Life, actually led to increased use of alcohol and cigarettes and no change in marijuana use (Sloboda et al., 2009). So D.A.R.E. administrators rejected that approach, adopted a different model ("keepin' it REAL"), and retooled once again (Toppo, 2002; West & O'Neal, 2004).

Of course, the new D.A.R.E. is now being evaluated, too. Sorry to say, one early quasi-experimental evaluation in 17 urban schools, funded by D.A.R.E. America, found no effect of the program on students' substance use (Vincus et al., 2010). Some researchers have concluded that the program should simply be ended, while others have concluded that some communities have good reasons for continuing to offer the program (Berman & Fox, 2009; Birkeland, Murphy-Graham, & Weiss, 2005).

This may seem like a depressing way to begin a chapter on evaluation research. D.A.R.E. is a very appealing program with an important message. But that should help to drive home the key point: Government agencies and other bodies that fund social programs should invest the necessary resources to evaluate their effectiveness, no matter how appealing. And this message is not limited to funders. Agencies should engage in evaluating their efforts, not just to satisfy funders but to ensure that programs are effective; evaluation offers agencies the opportunity to see what works and to modify interventions or programs when they are not working well.

In this chapter, we describe the distinctive features of evaluation research. You will learn a different vocabulary to understand agency-related processes and to integrate these into a model to describe these processes. We then turn to the kinds of questions often asked in an evaluation and the design alternatives to address these questions.

▣ Evaluation Basics

So what is evaluation research or *program evaluation*? It is not a method of data collection, like survey research or experiments, nor is it a unique component of research designs, like sampling or measurement. Instead, evaluation research is social work research that is conducted for a distinctive purpose: to assess social programs (such as substance abuse treatment programs, welfare programs, mental health programs, or employment and training programs). For each project, an evaluation researcher must select a research design and method of data collection that are useful for answering the particular evaluation questions posed and appropriate for the particular program investigated. So you can see why this chapter comes after those on experiments, single-subject designs, surveys, qualitative methods, mixed methods, and secondary data analysis; any one or more of these research designs may be appropriate to answer a particular evaluation question. When you review or plan evaluation research, you have to think about the research process as a whole and how different parts of that process can best be combined.

Exhibit 13.1 illustrates the process of evaluation research as a simple systems model. You will notice that this model treats programs like machines, with people functioning as raw materials to be processed. Clients, customers, students, or some other people or units enter the program as **inputs**. Families may begin structured family therapy, Temporary Assistance to Needy Families recipients may enroll in a new job training program, or people with schizophrenia may be sent to a community mental health center. We can think of clients or participants as necessary resources for the program to operate. Their characteristics should reflect the population for whom the program was intended. Besides clients, social programs require other inputs, that is, resources such as staff with certain types of expertise and knowledge and resources such as money, supplies, and equipment.

Next, some service or treatment is provided to the clients or consumers. The service may be a research class, assistance with independent living, counseling about family issues, residential housing, or special cash benefits. The **program process** is the mix of activities that constitute the actual program or intervention; it is these activities that are designed to have some impact on the clients.

The direct product of the program's service delivery process is its **output**. Program outputs may include clients served, case managers trained, food parcels delivered, or child abuse reports investigated. While the program outputs may be

desirable, they primarily serve to indicate that the program is operating. Notice that with each of these outputs, there is no mention as to whether the clients improved, whether the case managers actually acquired the skills, whether the food enhanced the health of the recipients, or whether the child was placed in a safe environment.

Program **outcomes** indicate the impact of the program on the recipients of the activities. Outcomes can range from improved social functioning or improved job-seeking skills to fewer substantiated child abuse reports and lower rates of poverty. Any social program is likely to have multiple outcomes, some intended and some unintended, some positive and others that are viewed as negative.

Variation in both outputs and outcomes influences the inputs to the program through a *feedback* process (see Exhibit 13.1). If too few clients are being served,

> **Inputs** The resources, raw materials, clients, and staff that go into a program.
>
> **Program process** The complete set of activities that constitute the service or intervention.
>
> **Outputs** The direct product of the program's activities.
>
> **Outcomes** The impact of the program process on the recipients.

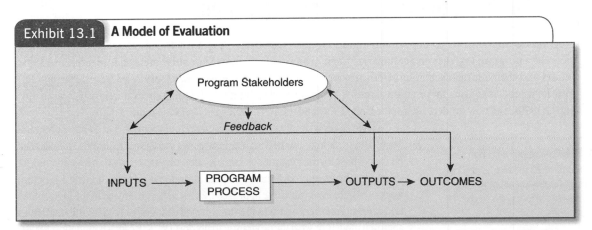

Exhibit 13.1   A Model of Evaluation

Source: Adapted from Martin, Lawrence L., and Peter M. Kettner. (2009).

resources may be devoted to the recruitment of new clients. If staff members lack the skills to implement the program, they may need to attend training workshops or the agency might hire new staff. If the program fails to achieve its outcomes, the agency might modify or terminate the program. If a program does not appear to lead to improved outcomes, clients may go elsewhere. Evaluation research is a systematic approach to feedback: It strengthens the feedback loop through credible analyses of program operations and outcomes.

Carol Weiss (1998) suggests that this feedback can describe a successful program in contrast to an unsuccessful program. In a successful program, the inputs (resources) are sufficient and appropriate to carry out the specific activities of the program, which set into motion a causal process (based on some practice theory) that produces the desired outcome. Programs may fail to achieve their desired outcomes for different reasons. The inputs may not be sufficient to carry out the program activities (input failure); the inputs may be sufficient, but the actual activities may be incomplete, insufficient, or poorly designed so that they do not set into motion the causal process (program failure); or the inputs may be sufficient and the program activities appropriate, but the causal process does not produce the desired outcomes (theory failure).

Stakeholders Individuals and groups who have some basis of concern with the program.

Evaluation research also broadens this loop to include connections to parties outside of the program. The evaluation process as a whole and feedback in particular can be understood only in relation to the interests and perspectives of program stakeholders. **Stakeholders** are individuals and groups that have some interest in the program. They might be clients, staff, agency executives, funders, or the public. The board of a program or agency, the parents or spouses of clients, the foundations that award program grants, the auditors who monitor program spending, and the members of Congress—each is a potential stakeholder, and each has an interest in the outcome of any program evaluation. Some may fund the evaluation, some may provide research data, and some may review or even approve the research report (L. Martin & Kettner, 2010). Who the program stakeholders are and what role they play in the program evaluation will have tremendous consequences for the research.

Can you see the difference between evaluation research and traditional social science research (Posavac & Carey, 2010)? Evaluation research is not designed to test the implications of a social theory; the basic issue often is "What is the program's impact?" Process evaluation often uses qualitative methods in the same way that traditional social science does. But unlike exploratory research, the goal is not to induce a broad theoretical explanation for what is discovered, instead, the question is, "How does the program do what it does?" Unlike social science research, evaluation studies take into account the information needs of program stakeholders. But there is no sharp boundary between social science research and evaluation studies. In their attempt to explain how and why the program has an impact and whether the program is needed, evaluation researchers often bring theories into their projects, but for immediately practical aims.

▣ Describing the Program: The Logic Model

Program assumptions. Target populations. Inputs. Outputs. Outcomes. Program activities. How can we put all these pieces of a program together and summarize them in an easy fashion? One popular method is to develop a **logic model**—a schematic representation of the various components that comprise a social service program. The popularity of logic models as a tool for program planning, program implementation, and program evaluation, increased during the 1990s, and now funders such as the United Way and the W. K. Kellogg Foundation require them.

Logic model A schematic representation of the various components that make up a social service program, including the assumptions underlying the program, inputs, activities, outputs, and outcomes.

A logic model is simply a chart of the different components that go into a program. There is no single logic model design; the categories you choose to include often depend on the purpose for the logic model. Logic models may describe (a) theory and its link to change (theory approach model), where attention is on how and why a program works; (b) outcomes (outcome approach model), where the focus of the logic model is to connect resources and activities to expected changes; or (c) activities (activities approach model), or what the program actually does (W. K. Kellogg Foundation, 2004).

Some funders use a logic model that also asks about community outcomes or community impact; in other words, what difference does the program make for the broader community? This type of logic model goes beyond the impact of the program on its participants and describes the impact of the program on the wider community.

We describe the basic components of the logic model (see Exhibit 13.2) using a partial hospitalization program to treat children with psychiatric problems. Partial hospitalization programs are an alternative to complete hospitalization in that the child is not completely removed from the community and the program provides for a transition to outpatient services. These programs often provide therapeutic services and educational classes to their clients (Kotsopoulos, Walker, Beggs, & Jones, 1996).

The first component of a logic model is to identify the *social problem*. Programs are designed to address a social condition deemed undesirable or to enhance a desirable condition. The range of social conditions is vast and might include social isolation among the elderly, child abuse, lack of income, drug use, homelessness, or employee productivity. The specific program may not address the entire social problem but only an aspect of the problem. In this example, the social problem is that children with moderate or severe psychiatric disorders have difficulty functioning in the community and therefore are at risk of placement in a full-time hospital environment.

The first column (For Whom) identifies the *target population* for the program. The evaluator identifies the criteria used to define an appropriate recipient of the service. There is a wide range of possible criteria to describe the target population, such as age group, income status, geographic residence, presence of specific physical or mental health condition, or status such as being unemployed. In this example, the target population has been defined by age (6–12), residence (in a particular county), and the presence of severe psychiatric disorders.

Because programs are designed to impact social conditions, the program design is based on assumptions about: (1) the causes of the social condition and (2) the appropriate intervention method to address the social condition. This suggests that two agencies might address the same social condition, but each may design different programs designed to produce different outcomes. For example, adolescent use of alcohol and other drugs may be due to the lack of knowledge about their consequences, and intervention would be designed to provide this knowledge. Another program might be based on the assumption that adolescents use drugs because they lack self-esteem and need strategies to cope with peer pressure; a group intervention to teach coping skills might be used. While most program logic models do not have an assumption column, we find it useful to include as the two types of assumptions relate directly to a program's outcomes and activities.

The partial hospitalization program (see Exhibit 13.2), is based on the assumption that the risk of institutionalization is due to several problems, including failure to control psychiatric symptoms, problems in anger management, behavioral problems, lack of coping and communication skills, poor self-esteem, and lack of parental knowledge. Based on practice research, the providers believed that the best treatment incorporates both cognitive-behavioral therapy and medication management.

The next component of the logic model is to identify the *inputs* required to run the program. We have already defined inputs as clients, staff, and resources. The logic model description of inputs is more specific, identifying the type of staff, their number, and their expertise. Inputs also include material resources such as equipment or space. The inputs for the partial hospitalization program reflect this degree of specificity (see Exhibit 13.2).

The fourth column identifies the specific *activities* (the program process) that comprise the program. Activities include actions taken directly with the client, such as assessment, counseling, or family meetings and activities that may not directly involve the client but are necessary for the program, such as treatment planning or team meetings. In the case of the partial hospitalization program, there are a range of activities, including group therapy and individual counseling.

Programs produce two types of *outputs*: (1) intermediate outputs reflecting units of service; and (2) final outputs called *service completions* (L. Martin & Kettner, 2010). Units of service describe activities undertaken by the program staff; such units of service are often described in terms of frequency or number, time or duration, or tangible good. For example, the outputs of one-on-one counseling sessions might be described as the number of individual counseling sessions, the amount of time spent in providing counseling, or the number of counseling sessions lasting a certain amount of time. Units of service reflect the aggregation of activities completed with clients during a specific period. You might find an agency's units of service on staff activity reporting forms.

Exhibit 13.2 Program Logic Model: Partial Hospitalization Program

Social Problem: Inability to function independently in the community

For Whom	Assumptions	Inputs	Activities	Outputs	Outcomes
Children age 6 to 12, living in the county who display moderate to severe psychiatric disorders and are at risk of inpatient hospitalization.	The inability to function independently in the community is due to: a. increased psychiatric symptoms b. lack of anger management skills c. behavioral problems d. lack of problem solving skills e. lack of communication skills f. poor coping skills g. low self-esteem h. parental lack of knowledge Treatment Model: Multiple interventions including Cognitive Behavioral Therapy Medication management	3 MSW level therapists 1 child psychiatrist 1 nurse M.Ed. in special education space chairs, desks educational materials computers money	Assessment Treatment planning Individual counseling Group therapy Family meetings Team meetings Discharge planning Discharge Educational classes	Intermediate: # of assessments completed/month # of hours of individual counseling provided/month # of group therapy sessions held/month # of hours of family meetings # of team meetings # of hours of discharge planning # of discharges Service Completion: Child attends 80% of individual and group counseling sessions and Family attends all family meetings	Intermediate: 1. Reduction in psychiatric symptoms 2. Increased anger management skills 3. Fewer behavioral problems 4. Improved problem solving skills 5. Improved communication skills 6. Improved coping skills 7. Increased self-esteem 8. Parents have more knowledge about diagnosis and symptoms Final: Child can function independently in school, home, and community.

Service completions refer to the agency's definition of a client who has received the full package of services, as opposed to someone who began the program but dropped out prematurely (L. Martin & Kettner, 2010). Service completions are often defined as encompassing a mix of services. For example, clients in the partial hospitalization program have completed the full range of services if they attended 80% of their assigned groups, participated in 80% of their scheduled individual counseling sessions, and attended all family meetings. Another way of defining a service completion is by using some measure of time. In the partial hospitalization program, client reviews are completed every 30 days; if it made sense to the agency administrator, a service completion might have been defined using this unit of time. A client could have 12 service completions during the course of a year.

Defining a service completion is particularly important for evaluations that examine program impact on the clients. A client should have the full dose of activities if improvements are to occur, or else why provide the various activities? It is similar to your doctor who, when prescribing an antibiotic for an ear infection warns that if you do not take the antibiotic for the full 12 days, you will not get better. When evaluators do studies of *client change*, they want to do them with those persons who have received the full mix of program activities.

The last column identifies the program's expected outcomes. These are the kinds of changes in a participant that are expected to occur as the result of the program. There are initial outcomes and final outcomes. Initial outcomes are the changes in the client that are necessary before the final outcome might occur. In the example, the initial outcomes include improved anger management skills, fewer behavioral problems, fewer psychiatric symptoms, improved communication skills, improved problem-solving skills, improved coping skills, better self-esteem, and parents knowing more about the diagnosis and symptoms. If these are achieved, then the final outcome of the child functioning independently in the school, home, and community should be more likely.

Some funders use a logic model that also asks about community outcomes or community impact; in other words, what difference does the program make for the broader community? Will the program reduce unemployment? Illiteracy? What difference does the partial hospitalization program make to the community? Will it reduce health care costs? Typically, these are more challenging to demonstrate given the many other factors that might affect community outcomes.

You might notice that there is a relationship between the assumptions about the factors related to the social problem and the initial outcomes. The activities in the program are intended to improve upon each of the areas identified in the assumptions; the initial outcomes reflect the desired changes in each of these areas. In the example, one problem is increased psychiatric symptoms; therefore, an initial outcome is a reduction in psychiatric symptoms. Each of the factors listed in the assumptions has a parallel intermediate outcome. The same is true with the overall social problem; if the problem is the inability of children to function independently in the community, then the ultimate outcome is that this is no longer a problem; rather, the child can function independently.

This symmetry also occurs with activities and intermediate outputs as each activity has a measure of service. In the partial hospitalization program, service activity was measured using a count or frequency of activity. If it was important, the evaluator might have used a measure of time such as the number of hours spent completing assessments each month. And remember, this count (or length of time) is how many times (or how much time) the staff person spent on the activity with all clients in that month, not how much time the client spent on each activity.

As you can see, a logic model succinctly summarizes a great deal of information about the program. After completing the logic model, the evaluator, and often the stakeholders, should have a better understanding about the logic underlying the program. It can be used to identify questions of interest to the stakeholders.

🔲 Questions for Evaluation Research

Evaluation projects can focus on different questions related to the operation of social programs and the impact they have:

- Is the program needed?
- How does the program operate?
- What is the program's impact?
- How efficient is the program?

You can see how a logic model is helpful because it provides details associated with these questions. If you want to measure program activities, the outputs column provides measures. If you are interested in the program's impact, then the initial and final outcomes can serve as a guide. The specific methods used in an evaluation research project depend in part on the particular question of interest.

Needs Assessment

Is a new program needed, or is an old one still required? Is there a need at all? A **needs assessment** attempts to answer this question with systematic, credible evidence. Need may be identified and enumerated by social indicators (secondary data) such as the poverty rate or school dropout rate, by interviews with local experts such as mental health providers, by surveys of populations in need or service providers, by structured groups such as focus groups with community residents, or by taking a resource inventory of available services and service capacity, as is often done by local planning groups (McKillip, 1987). The evaluation will enumerate need, whereas the assessment of need and subsequent priorities will depend ultimately on the final judgment of key stakeholders.

> **Needs assessment** A type of evaluation research that is used to determine the needs of some population.

It is not as easy as it sounds. Whose definitions or perceptions should be used to shape our description of the level of need? How will we deal with ignorance of need? How can we understand the level of need without understanding the social context from which that level of need emerges? (Short answer to that one: We can't!) What, after all, does "need" mean in the abstract? We will not really understand what the level of need is until we develop plans for implementing a program in response to identified needs.

Research In the News

For Further Thought **?**

WHAT MOTIVATES POLICY SHIFTS?

A report from the American Civil Liberties Union (ACLU) documented a national corrections overall that is fragile but growing. After decades of increased incarceration and skyrocketing prison populations, states from the South to the Midwest are starting to see decreases. Much of the motivation behind these policy shifts is financial: Housing prisoners is far more expensive than parole or drug treatment. Social science researchers have identified the value of alternative approaches to incarceration in many studies, but budget pressures are often more powerful than statistics.

1. What hypothesis would you propose to test the value of reducing rates of incarceration and what research design would you suggest using to test it?

2. Why do you think stakeholders tend to discount evaluation/research findings?

Source: Savage (2011, p. A12).

The results of a needs assessment survey conducted by Rosalyn Darling and colleagues (Darling, Hager, Stockdale, & Heckert, 2002) reveal the importance of taking a multidimensional approach to the investigation of need. This survey was conducted in Indiana County, a rural county in western Pennsylvania. The area had experienced an economic downturn with the loss of industrial jobs that were being replaced by lower wage, service sector jobs. At the time of the survey, the poverty rate was 19%. Darling and colleagues (2002) conducted a survey with clients of nine social service agencies and all professionals working at any of the 75 social service agencies in the area. They asked both groups to assess the frequency of need for 67 different specific items using a 3-point scale.

Did clients and professionals identify different needs? Darling and colleagues (2002) found that there were differences in need perception. Professionals and clients differed on every question; professionals consistently rated the need to be greater than did clients. For example, about 25% of clients reported that not having enough money to continue their education was a frequent concern in contrast to 43% of professionals believing that this was a frequent problem for clients. Clients were much more likely to offer "not a problem" as a response to the items than professionals; nearly 70% of client responses were "not a problem" in contrast to 28% of professional responses. When items were categorized into one of six broad concerns, there were some similarities as well as differences. For example, both groups believed that security and safety-related issues were not very important but professionals felt that formal support issues were very important while clients were less likely to identify the need for formal support (Darling et al., 2002).

What should we make of these differences? Did the professionals understand what was important to their clients? Do the discrepancies suggest the need for more collaboration among clients and professionals in establishing client service-related goals?

The methodological lesson here is that in a needs assessment, as in other forms of evaluation research, it is a good idea to use multiple indicators. You can also see that there is no absolute definition of need in this situation, nor is there likely to be in any but the most simplistic evaluation projects. Good evaluation researchers will do their best to capture different perspectives on need and help others make sense of the results.

A wonderful little tale, popular with evaluation researchers, reveals the importance of thinking creatively about what people need:

> The manager of a 20-story office building had received many complaints about the slowness of the elevators. He hired an engineering consultant to propose a solution. The consultant measured traffic flow and elevator features and proposed replacing the old elevators with new ones, which could shave 20 seconds off the average waiting time. The only problem: it cost $100,000. A second consultant proposed adding 2 additional elevators, for a total wait time reduction of 35 seconds and a cost of $150,000. Neither alternative was affordable. A third consultant was brought in. He looked around for a few days and announced that the problem was not really the waiting times, but boredom. For a cost of less than $1,000, the manager had large mirrors installed next to the elevators so people could primp and observe themselves while waiting for an elevator. The result: no more complaints. Problem solved. (B. Witkin & Altschuld, 1995, p. 38)

Process Evaluation

What actually happens in a social program? The purpose of a **process evaluation** is to investigate how the program is operating. Process evaluations are completed to answer a variety of questions related to the operation of a particular program. Two questions focus concerns program coverage: Is the program serving its target population? What proportion of the eligible population is being served by the program? Other questions focus on service delivery: Has the program been implemented as designed? What are the outputs of various program activities? In the past, process evaluations were the primary response to funders who wanted to know whether the agency had actually carried out its planned activities. Increasingly, process evaluations are conducted to identify specific activities that produced program outcomes as well as to determine client satisfaction with the program activities.

Process evaluation Type of program evaluation that investigates the process of service delivery.

Process evaluation can employ a wide range of indicators. Program coverage can be monitored through program records, participant surveys, and community surveys or by comparing program users with dropouts and ineligibles. Service delivery can be monitored through service records completed by program staff, a management information system maintained by program administrators, or reports by program recipients (Rossi & Freeman, 1989).

Qualitative methods are often a key component of process evaluation studies because they can be used to elucidate and understand internal program dynamics—even those that were not anticipated (Patton, 2002; Posavac & Carey, 2010). Qualitative researchers may develop detailed descriptions of how program participants engage with each other, how the program experience varies for different people, and how the program changes and evolves over time.

Process evaluation is particularly useful when complex programs are evaluated. Many social programs involve multiple elements and are delivered over an extended period of time, often by different providers in different areas. Due to this complexity, it is quite possible that the program as delivered is not the same for all program recipients or consistent with the formal program design.

The evaluation of D.A.R.E. by Research Triangle Institute researchers Christopher Ringwalt and colleagues (1994) included a process evaluation with three objectives:

1. Assess the organizational structure and operation of representative D.A.R.E. programs nationwide.

2. Review and assess factors that contribute to the effective implementation of D.A.R.E. programs nationwide.

3. Assess how D.A.R.E. and other school-based drug prevention programs are tailored to meet the needs of specific populations. (p. 7)

The process evaluation (they called it an *implementation assessment*) was an ambitious research project, with site visits, informal interviews, discussions, and surveys of D.A.R.E. program coordinators and advisers. These data indicated that D.A.R.E. was operating as designed and was running relatively smoothly. As shown in Exhibit 13.3, drug prevention coordinators in D.A.R.E. school districts rated the program components as more satisfactory than did coordinators in school districts with other types of alcohol and drug prevention programs.

Process evaluation can be used to identify the specific aspects of the service delivery process that have an impact. This, in turn, will help to explain why the program has an effect and which conditions are required for these effects. (In Chapter 6 we described this as identifying the causal mechanism.) In the case of early D.A.R.E process evaluations, implementation problems identified in site visits included insufficient numbers of officers to carry out the program as planned and a lack of Spanish-language D.A.R.E. books in a largely Hispanic school. There were as well positive findings; classroom observations indicated engaging presentations and active student participation (Ringwalt et al., 1994).

Exhibit 13.3	Components of D.A.R.E. and Other Alcohol and Drug (AOD) Prevention Programs Rated as Very Satisfactory (%)	
Components	D.A.R.E. Program (*N* = 202)	Other AOD Programs (N = 406)
Curriculum	67.5	34.2
Teaching	69.7	29.8
Administrative Requirements	55.7	23.1
Receptivity of Students	76.5	34.6
Effects on Students	63.2	22.8

Source: Ringwalt et al. (1994, p. 58).

The term **formative evaluation** may be used instead of process evaluation when the evaluation findings are used to help shape and refine the program (Rossi & Freeman, 1989). Formative evaluation procedures that are incorporated into the initial development of the service program can specify the treatment process and lead to changes in recruitment procedures, program delivery, or measurement tools (Patton, 2002).

> **Formative evaluation** Process evaluation that is used to shape and refine program operations.

Susan Franzen, Susan Morrell-Samuels, Thomas Reischl, and Marc Zimmerman's (2009) process evaluation of the Youth Empowerment Solutions for Peaceful Communities (YES) illustrates how such an assessment can improve program delivery. YES was designed to address youth violence. The program had three components: empowering youth, building adult capacity, and community development. The youth component involved meetings addressing personal issues such as self-esteem, citizenship, and ethnic pride as well as learning about resources, team building, and learning to develop community plans. The participants would be supervised and mentored by adult staff and neighborhood advocates prepared by the program to work with youth.

The process evaluation was conducted at the ends of the first and second years of the program. The process evaluation used both quantitative methods and qualitative methods and integrated different perspectives into the evaluation. The youth participants completed a 15-item quantitative questionnaire to rate both program activities and the quality of the adults engaged in the program. The youth were then split into several focus groups designed to elicit more depth about the program activities as well as their work with adults. The neighborhood advocates participated in a semi-structured telephone interview to learn their opinions about the program, their work with youth, and the program's impact on the community.

After the first-year evaluation, program staff met to review the data, identify areas in which there was a need for improvement, and the types of program changes that would be made going into Year Two (see Exhibit 13.4). The result of the program changes? At the end of Year Two, the youth quantitative assessments of staff and adult advocates

---

Exhibit 13.4 | **Indicated Need for Improvement and Improvement Implemented**

Indicated Need for Improvement	Improvements Implemented
Youth wanted greater control over selection of adults (S, F)	Interview process altered, greater choices of advocates for youth
Youth wanted greater control over community development projects (F)	Provided additional training for adults: discussing adultism and the concept of youth empowerment
Youth would like to work with younger adults (S, F)	Summer program staff all 25 or younger, mural project artist was under 30
Youth and adults desired increased listening skills of adults (S, F, I)	Increase number of adult trainings, modify training curriculum
Youth would like less strictness and controlling adults (S, F)	Increase number of adult trainings, modify training curriculum
Adults desired a greater understanding of the youth (I)	Provided additional training for adults: methods of getting to know youth
Youth and adults desired skills for intergenerational communication (F, I)	Provided additional training for youth and adults: how to be an intergenerational bridge

Source: Franzen, S., Morrel-Samuels, S., Reischl, T. M., Zimmerman, M. A. (2009). Using process evaluation to strengthen intergenerational partnerships in the Youth Empowerment Solutions Program. *Journal of Prevention & Intervention in the Community, 37*, 289–301

Note: S = Youth Evaluation Questionnaire, F = Youth Focus Groups, I = Adult Interview.

improved in every category except one, and there were more positive comments and fewer negative expressions in the focus groups (Franzen et al., 2009).

Service delivery can also be reviewed through the use of a flowchart to describe program activities. The flowchart typically includes program activities, decision points at which a client may receive a different set of activities, and points at which documentation is necessary (see Exhibit 13.5). Flowcharts are used to answer questions such as these: Are all necessary activities present in the program, or are there missing activities? Do the steps flow in a logical order? Is there duplication of service effort? How long does it take for a client to go through the entire process? How long does it take for a client to go from initial intake to assessment to intervention?

Increasingly, both program providers and those funding programs are interested in client satisfaction with program processes. A well-designed client satisfaction survey focused on the specific operation of the program can provide useful information about how to improve the program. Lawrence Martin and Peter Kettner (2010) suggest that rather than using global measures of satisfaction, providers should include questions that focus on particular dimensions of interest to the agency, such as the accessibility of services, courtesy of staff, timeliness of services, competency of practitioners, attitudes of the staff toward the client, or the appearance of the facilities, staff, and program materials.

Outcome evaluation A program evaluation designed to measure client or participant outcomes.

Outcome Evaluation

The core questions of evaluation research are: Did the program work? Did the intervention have the intended result? This part of the research is called **outcome evaluation**

Exhibit 13.5	Common Flowchart Symbols

Symbol	Description
☐	Process: Describes on activity or event
◇	A decision or alternative. A path will depend on the answer to the decision question. For example. Eligible: yes/no. Someone eligible (yes) will follow one path and someone ineligible (no) will follow another path.
→	Direction arrow connecting the flow from one activity to another or activity to a decision point.
▱	Document such as an application form.
⊠	Collate information
○	Exit from a process

or, in some cases, impact or summative evaluation. Formally speaking, outcome evaluation compares what happened after a program with what would have happened had there been no program.

Elizabeth D'Amico and Kim Fromme's (2002) study of a new Risk Skills Training Program (RSTP) is a good example of a more elaborate study. They compared the impact of RSTP on adolescents 14 to 19 years of age to that of an abbreviated version of D.A.R.E and to a control group. The impacts they examined included positive and negative "alcohol expectancies" (the anticipated effects of drinking) as well as perception of peer risk taking and actual alcohol consumption. They found that negative alcohol expectancies increased for the RSTP group in the posttest but not for the D.A.R.E. group or the control group, while weekly drinking and "positive expectancies" for drinking outcomes actually *increased* for the D.A.R.E. group and/or the control group by the 6-month follow-up, but not for the RSTP group.

Think of the program—a new strategy for combating domestic violence, an income supplement, whatever—as an independent variable and the result it seeks as a dependent variable. The D.A.R.E. program (independent variable), for instance, tries to reduce drug use (dependent variable). When the program is present, we expect less drug use. In a more elaborate study, we might have multiple values of the independent variable; for instance, we might look at no program, D.A.R.E. program, and other drug/alcohol education conditions and compare the results of each.

It is often impractical for agencies to utilize an experimental design and may not be necessary given the particular purpose of the evaluation. A large-scale randomized design can be expensive, particularly if it is for a large evaluation and one that is designed to follow participants over time. If the evaluation is designed to provide feedback about how the program is doing rather than focusing on causality, then there is no need to establish the conditions of a true experimental design. There are times when trying to establish a true experimental design is simply not feasible or ethically permissible. Therefore, program outcomes may be evaluated with quasi-experimental designs, particularly nonequivalent control group designs; nonexperimental designs such as the one group pretest–posttest design; and survey, single-subject, or field research methods.

Outcome evaluation is an important undertaking that fully deserves the attention it has been given in the program funding requirements of local United Ways, foundations, and the government. It is now common for grant applications to foundations and United Ways to include a requirement for the measurement of outcomes. In one geographic area, a large number of foundations are using a common grant application that requires a logic model and a plan to document program progress and program outcomes.

Efficiency Analysis

Whatever the program's benefits, are they sufficient to offset the program's costs? Are the funders getting their money's worth? These efficiency questions can be the primary reason that funders require evaluation of the programs they fund. As a result, efficiency analysis, which compares program effects to costs, is sometimes a component of an evaluation research project.

A **cost-benefit analysis** must identify the specific costs and benefits that will be studied, which requires in turn that the analyst identify whose perspective will be used to determine what can be considered a benefit rather than a cost. Program clients will have a different perspective on these issues than do taxpayers or program staff. Consider, for example, the costs and benefits you might list as a student versus the costs and benefits that the university might include. Tuition and fees, which are costs to you, are benefits for the university. Exhibit 13.6 lists factors that can be considered costs or benefits in an employment and training program from the standpoint of program participants, the rest of society, and society as a whole (the combination of program participants and the rest of society (Orr, 1999). Some anticipated impacts of the program, such as welfare benefits and wage subsidies, are considered a cost to one group and a benefit to the other, whereas some are not relevant to one of the groups.

Once potential costs and benefits have been identified, they must be measured. This is a need highlighted in recent government programs:

> **Cost-benefit analysis** A type of evaluation that compares program costs to the economic value of program benefits.

The Governmental Accounting Standards Board's (GASB) mission is to establish and improve standards of accounting and financial reporting for state and local governments in the United States. In June 1999, the GASB issued a major revision to current reporting requirements ("Statement 34"). The new reporting will provide information that citizens and other users can utilize to gain an understanding of the financial position and cost of programs for a government and a descriptive management's discussion and analysis to assist in understanding a government's financial results. (W. Campbell, 2002, p. 1)

In addition to measuring services and their associated costs, a cost-benefit analysis must be able to make some type of estimation of how clients benefit from the program. Normally, this will involve a comparison of some indicators of client status before and after clients received program services, or between clients who received program services and a comparable group that did not. In a cost-benefit analysis, these benefits are assigned a cash value.

A recent study of therapeutic communities provides a clear illustration. A therapeutic community (TC) is a method for treating substance abuse in which people participate in an intensive, structured living experience with other people who are attempting to stay sober. Because the treatment involves residential support as well as other types of services, it can be quite costly. Are those costs worth it?

Sacks, McKendrick, DeLeon, French, and McCollister (2002) conducted a cost-benefit analysis of a modified TC. Three hundred forty-two people who were homeless, mentally ill, and abusing substances were randomly assigned to either a TC or a treatment-as-usual comparison group. Employment status, criminal activity, and utilization of health care services were each measured for the 3 months prior to entering treatment and the 3 months after treatment. Earnings from employment in each period were adjusted for costs incurred by criminal activity and utilization of health care services.

Exhibit 13.6	Conceptual Framework for Cost-Benefit Analysis of an Employment and Training Program		
Costs/Benefits	**Perspective of Program Participants**	**Perspective of Rest of Society**	**Perspective of Entire Society**
Costs			
Operational costs of the program	O	—	—
Forgone leisure and home protection	—	O	—
Benefits			
Earnings gains	+	O	+
Reduced costs of nonexperimental services	O	+	+
Transfers			
Reduced welfare benefits	—	+	O
Wage subsidies	+	—	O
Net benefits	+/-	+/-	+/-

Source: Orr (1999, p. 224, Table 6.5).

Key: — = program costs; + = program benefits; +/- = program costs and benefits' O = no program costs or benefits.

Entire society = program participants + rest of society.

Was it worth it? The average cost of TC treatment for a client was $20,361. In comparison, the economic benefit (based on earnings) to the average TC client was $305,273, which declined to $273,698 after comparing post- and pre-program earnings, but it was still $253,337 even after adjustment for costs. The resulting benefit-cost ratio was 13:1, although this ratio declined to only 5.2:1 after further adjustments (for cases with extreme values). Nonetheless, the TC program studied seems to have had a substantial benefit relative to its costs.

It is often difficult to assign a dollar value to outcomes produced in social work programs. **Cost-effectiveness** is a common alternative to cost-benefit analysis; this analysis compares the costs of different programs (or interventions) to the actual program outcomes in lieu of assigning a dollar value to the outcomes. In

> **Cost effectiveness** A type of evaluation that compares program costs to program outcomes.

these comparisons, the program costs are calculated, whereas the benefits are listed and not assigned a cash value.

A study by Susan Essock, Linda Frisman, and Nina Kontos (1998) illustrates the use of cost-effectiveness analysis. They compared the costs and benefits of assertive community treatment (ACT) to standard case management (SCM) to help people with serious mental disorders function in the community. ACT used a multidisciplinary team and provided 24-hour coverage, whereas the SCM model offered only a case manager. The ACT team members offered and provided treatment services, whereas in SCM the case manager either provided the service or arranged for an independent provider to offer the service. The study included 262 participants with serious mental disorders who had difficulty functioning in the community. Participants were randomly assigned to ACT or SCM. Data were collected at baseline and 6, 12, and 18 months after baseline. Essock and colleagues examined the number of days hospitalized, quality of life, psychiatric symptoms, and family burden.

Over the 18-month period, ACT clients reported higher quality of life, including personal safety, leisure activities, living situation, and frequency of contact with friends, and they spent more days in the community. Although there were no overall differences in family burden as reported by family members, ACT client family members with high objective burden reported lower subjective burden than did SCM family members. The actual cost of the program to the state department of mental health, the state overall, or society did not differ significantly for ACT and SCM, although in each category the ACT program was slightly cheaper. Therefore, at about the same cost, the ACT program produced more desirable outcomes.

⊞ Design Decisions

Once we have decided on, or identified, the goal or focus for a program evaluation, important decisions must be made about how to design the specific evaluation project. The most important decisions are the following:

- *Black box or program theory:* Do we care how the program gets results?
- *Researcher or stakeholder orientation:* Whose goals matter most?
- *Quantitative or qualitative methods:* Which methods provide the best answers?
- *Simple or complex outcomes:* How complicated should the findings be?

Black Box or Program Theory?

The meat and potatoes of most evaluation research involves determining whether a program has the intended effect. If the effect occurred, the program "worked"; if the effect did not occur, then, some would say, the program should be abandoned or redesigned. In this approach, the process by which a program has an effect on outcomes is often treated as a **black box**—that is, the focus of the evaluation

> **Black box** Occurs when an evaluation of program outcomes ignores, and does not identify, the process by which the program produced the effect.

researcher is on whether cases seem to have changed as a result of their exposure to the program between the time they entered the program as inputs and when they exited the program as outputs (Chen, 1990). The assumption is that program evaluation requires only the test of a simple input–output model, like the one shown in Exhibit 13.1. There may be no attempt to open the black box of the program process.

But there is good reason to open the black box and investigate how the process works (or does not work), under what conditions it works and does not work, and for whom it works and does not work. Consider research on family preservation programs, which are child welfare interventions designed to reduce out-of-home placement and keep the family intact; the research findings about their effectiveness was mixed (Bagdasaryan, 2005). Sofya Bagdasaryan (2005) reframed the question from whether the program worked or not to the question, "Under what service conditions are family preservation services effective in preventing out-of-home placement and for which families?" (p. 619). So Bagdasaryan examined the interaction between family characteristics and service characteristics. For example, would out-of-home placement rates differ among parent status and mental health services (assuming mental health services were needed); that is, would single parents getting mental health services, single parents not getting mental health services, non-single parents getting mental health services, and non-single parents not getting mental health services have different out-of-home placement rates? By answering this question, services could be better matched to family characteristics with the intent of improving outcomes.

Delving further into program details can help researchers understand the context in which a program succeeds or fails. Wynne Korr and Antoine Joseph (1996) found that a demonstration case management program for homeless mentally ill people implemented at two different sites resulted in vastly different outcomes. At each site, clients were randomly assigned to a control group receiving the traditional case management program and an experimental group receiving assertive case management. The goals of the program were to identify and place clients in independent living situations and then help the clients maintain their independence. After 6 months, two thirds of clients in the experimental group at the first site were housed, compared with 34% of the control group, while at the second site, 53% of the experimental group and 66% of the control group were housed.

Why the contradictory findings? The investigators reviewed the client, organizational, and community context and found that there were differences that explained the contradictory outcomes. Most clients at the first site had been evicted from single resident occupancy rooms (SROs) and apartments, while most clients at the second site had lived with family or in board and care homes and were homeless because of family disputes. Although this was an interesting finding, it did not fully explain the differences. It turns out that the available housing also differed by location. The first site was located in a neighborhood with most of the city's single room occupancy housing, while the second site had few to no single room occupancy alternatives, but many board and care facilities. Because the ACT staff members at the second site were trying to stay faithful to the intervention's guidelines, their efforts to place clients in single room occupancy housing may have been contrary to the participants' wishes.

If an investigation of program process is conducted, a program theory may be developed. A program theory describes what has been learned about how the program has its effect. When a researcher has sufficient knowledge before the investigation begins, outlining a program theory can help to guide the investigation of program process in the most productive directions. This is termed a **theory-driven evaluation**.

Theory-driven evaluation A program evaluation that is guided by a theory that specifies the process by which the program has an effect.

A program theory specifies how the program is expected to operate and identifies which program elements are operational (Chen, 1990). In addition, a program theory specifies how a program is to produce its effects and so improves understanding of the relationship between the independent variable (the program) and the dependent variable (the outcome or outcomes). The logic model provides a simple depiction of the program theory (Savaya & Waysman, 2005).

Program theory can be either descriptive or prescriptive (Chen, 1990). Descriptive theory specifies what impacts are generated and how they occur. It suggests a causal mechanism, including intervening factors, and the necessary context for the effects. Descriptive theories are generally empirically based. In contrast, prescriptive theory specifies what should be done by the program and is not actually tested. Prescriptive theory specifies how to design or implement the treatment, what outcomes should be expected, and how performance should be judged. Comparison of the descriptive and prescriptive theories of the program can help to identify implementation difficulties and incorrect understandings that can be corrected (Patton, 2002).

Researcher of Stakeholder Orientation?

Whose prescriptions specify how the program should operate, what outcomes it should try to achieve, or who it should serve? Most social work research assumes that the researcher specifies the research questions, the applicable theory or theories, and the outcomes to be investigated. Social work research results are most often reported in a professional journal or at professional conferences, where scientific standards determine how the research is received. However, in program evaluation the question is often set by the program sponsors or a funding agency that is responsible for reviewing the program. It is to these authorities that research findings are reported. Sometimes, this authority specifies the outcomes to be investigated.

Should evaluation researchers insist on designing the evaluation project and specifying its goals, or should they accept the suggestions and adopt the goals of the funding agency? What role should the preferences of program staff or clients play? What responsibility do evaluation researchers have to politicians and taxpayers when evaluating government-funded programs? The different answers that various evaluation researchers have given to these questions are reflected in different approaches to evaluation (Chen, 1990).

Stakeholder approaches encourage researchers to be responsive to program stakeholders. Issues for study are to be based on the views of people involved with the program, and reports are to be made to program participants (Shadish, Cook, & Leviton, 1991). The program theory is developed by the researcher to clarify and develop the key stakeholders' theory of the program (Shadish et al., 1991). In one stakeholder approach, termed *utilization-focused evaluation*, the evaluator forms a task force of program stakeholders who help to shape the evaluation project so that they are most likely to use its results (Patton, 2002). In *participatory research*, or action research, program participants and stakeholders are engaged with the researchers as co-researchers and help to design, conduct, and report the research.

> **Stakeholder approaches** An orientation to evaluation research that expects researchers to be responsive primarily to the program stakeholders

Shantha Balaswamy and Holly Dabelko (2002) used the stakeholder participatory research approach to conduct a community-wide needs assessment of elderly residents. The agency initiating the project identified stakeholders, who were defined as "people with a vested interest in improving, protecting, and developing services for the community elders" (p. 60). An oversight committee was formed and included "aging service providers, funders, the city administrator, agency board members, research sponsors, administrators and faculty from local educational institutions, seniors, community residents, administrators from private corporations, private nonprofit funding organizations, and administrators from other social service agencies" (p. 60). This committee provided input and feedback on every phase of the needs assessment: establishing goals and objectives, developing the needs assessment tool, determining sampling issues and data collection methods, and implementing the actual data collection, data analysis, and dissemination. Because the stakeholders had been part of the entire evaluation, the findings were used even when they were unexpected and negative. The oversight committee even created subcommittees to follow up on the community's use of the information.

Social science approaches emphasize the importance of researcher expertise and maintenance of some autonomy to develop the most trustworthy, unbiased program evaluation. It is assumed that "evaluators cannot passively accept the values and views of the other stakeholders" (Chen, 1990, p. 78). Evaluators who adopt this approach derive a program theory from information they obtain on how the program operates and from extant social science theory and knowledge, not from the views of stakeholders. In one somewhat extreme form of this approach, *goal-free evaluation*, researchers do not even permit themselves to learn what goals the program

> **Social science approaches** An orientation to evaluation research that expects researchers to emphasize the importance of researcher expertise and maintenance of autonomy from program stakeholders.

stakeholders have for the program. Instead, researchers assess and then compare the needs of participants to a wide array of program outcomes (Scriven, 1972). Goal-free evaluators want to see the unanticipated outcomes and to remove any biases caused by knowing the program goals in advance.

Of course, there are disadvantages to both stakeholder and social science approaches to program evaluation. If stakeholders are ignored, researchers may find that participants are uncooperative, that their reports are unused, and that the next project remains unfunded. However, if social science procedures are neglected, standards of evidence will be compromised, conclusions about program effects will likely be invalid, and results are unlikely to be generalizable to other settings.

Integrative approaches Orientation to evaluation research that expects researchers to respond to the concerns of people involved with the program as well as to the standards and goals of the social science community.

These equally undesirable possibilities have led to several attempts to develop more integrated approaches to evaluation research. **Integrative approaches** attempt to cover issues of concern to both stakeholders and evaluators and to include stakeholders in the group from which guidance is routinely sought (Chen & Rossi, 1987). The emphasis given to either stakeholder or social science concerns is expected to vary with the specific project circumstances. Integrative approaches seek to balance the goal of carrying out a project that is responsive to stakeholder concerns with the goal of objective, scientifically trustworthy, and generalizable results. When the research is planned, evaluators are expected to communicate and negotiate regularly with key stakeholders and to take stakeholder concerns into account. Findings from preliminary inquiries are reported back to program decision makers so they can make improvements in the program before it is formally evaluated. When the actual evaluation is conducted, the evaluation research team is expected to operate more or less autonomously, minimizing intrusions from program stakeholders.

Many evaluation researchers now recognize that they must take account of multiple values in their research and be sensitive to the perspectives of different stakeholders, in addition to maintaining a commitment to the goals of measurement validity, internal validity, and generalizability (Chen, 1990).

Quantitative and/or Qualitative Methods?

Evaluation research that attempts to identify the effects of a social program typically is quantitative: Did housing retention improve? Did substance abuse decline? It's fair to say that when there is an interest in comparing outcomes between an experimental and a control group, or tracking change over time in a systematic manner, quantitative methods are favored.

But qualitative methods can add much to quantitative evaluation research studies, including more depth, detail, nuance, and exemplary case studies (Patton, 2002). Perhaps the greatest contribution qualitative methods can make in many evaluation studies is investigating program process—finding out what is "inside the black box." Although it is possible to track service delivery with quantitative measures like staff contact hours and frequency of referrals, finding out what is happening to clients and how clients experience the program can often best be accomplished by observing program activities and interviewing staff and clients intensively. For example, Patton (2002) describes a study in which process analysis in an evaluation of a prenatal clinic's outreach program led to program changes. The process analysis revealed that the outreach workers were spending too much time responding to immediate problems, such as needs for rat control, protection from violence, and access to English classes. As a result, the outreach workers were recruiting fewer community residents for the prenatal clinic. New training and recruitment strategies were adopted to lessen this deviation from program goals.

Another good reason for using qualitative methods in evaluation research is the importance of learning how different individuals react to the treatment. For example, a quantitative evaluation of student reactions to an adult basic skills program for new immigrants relied heavily on the students' initial statements of their goals. However, qualitative interviews revealed that most new immigrants lacked sufficient experience in America to set meaningful goals; their initial goal statements simply reflected their eagerness to agree with their counselors' suggestions (Patton, 2002).

Qualitative methods can also help in understanding how social programs actually operate. Complex social programs have many different features, and it is not always clear whether some particular feature or a combination of features is responsible for the program's effect—or for the absence of an effect.

The more complex the social program, the more value that qualitative methods can add to the evaluation process. Schorr and Yankelovich (2000) point to the Ten Point Coalition, an alliance of Black ministers that helped to reduce gang warfare in Boston through multiple initiatives "ranging from neighborhood probation patrols to safe havens for recreation" (p. A19). Qualitative methods would help to describe a complex, multifaceted program like this. A skilled qualitative or quantitative research will be flexible and creative in choosing methods for program evaluation and will often utilize mixed methods, so that the evaluation benefits from the advantages of both qualitative and quantitative techniques.

Simple or Complex Outcomes?

Does the program have only one outcome? That is unlikely. How many outcomes are anticipated? How many might be unintended? Which are the direct consequences of program action, and which are indirect effects that occur as a result of the direct effects (Mohr, 1992)? Do the longer term outcomes follow directly from the immediate program outcomes? Does the intermediate outcome (the increase in test scores at the end of the preparation course) result surely in the desired outcomes (increased rates of college admission)? Due to these and other possibilities, the selection of outcome measures is a critical step in evaluation research.

Most evaluation researchers attempt to measure multiple outcomes (Mohr, 1992). The result usually is a much more realistic, and richer, understanding of program impact. Some of the multiple outcomes measured in the evaluation of Project New Hope appear in Exhibit 13.7. Project New Hope was designed to answer the following critical policy question: If low-income adults are given a job at a sufficient wage, above the poverty level, with child care and health care assured, what will be the long-term impact on the adults and their children (Miller, Huston, Duncan, McLoyd, & Weisner, 2008)? Participants randomly assigned to the experimental group were offered a job involving work for 30 hours a week, earnings supplements, subsidized child care, and low-cost health care benefits for 3 years. What were the long-term outcomes 5 years after leaving the program? While there had been initial gains in employment and income and reductions in poverty, 5 years after the program had ended, these gains had disappeared. There were no differences between the experimental group and control group in any measure of parents' well-being. But there were some positive effects for their children: Children were more likely to participate in structured activities; had fewer reports of poor grades, being placed in special education, or repeating a grade; and were more engaged in school activities. In comparison to the control group, teachers and parents ranked the youth, especially boys, as better behaved, and the boys had higher reading scores. Finally, youth were more likely to have worked and were more optimistic about work in the future.

So did the New Hope Program "work"? Clearly, it did not live up to initial expectations, but it certainly showed that social interventions can have some benefits. Would the boys' gains continue through adolescence? Longer term outcomes would be needed. Why didn't girls (who were already performing better than the boys) benefit from their parents' enrollment in New Hope just as the boys did? A process analysis would add a great deal to the evaluation design. The long and short of it is that a collection of multiple outcomes gave a better picture of program impact.

Of course, there is a potential downside to the collection of multiple outcomes. Policy makers may choose to publicize those outcomes that support their own policy preferences and ignore the rest. Often evaluation researchers have little ability to publicize a more complete story.

In a sense, all of these choices (black box or program theory, researcher or stakeholder interests, etc.) hinge on (a) what your real goals are in doing the project and (b) how able you will be, in a "research for hire" setting, to achieve those goals. Not every agency really wants to know whether its programs work, especially if the answer is no. Dealing with such issues and the choices they require is part of what makes evaluation research both scientifically and politically fascinating.

Exhibit 13.7	Outcomes in Project New Hope: Year 8

Parents	New Hope	Control Group
Percent of quarters employed	56.3	54.2
Average annual earnings	11,319	11,031
Average income	13,595	13,285
Below poverty	63.1	67.1
Material hardship	.17	.17
Financial worry	2.52	2.45
Physical health	3.20	3.22
General stress	2.62	2.56
Depression	17.36	17.33
Hope	2.92	2.94
Children	New Hope	Control Group
Structure activities*	2.40	2.30
Reading score	93.31	91.86
Reading score boys*	93.35	90.98
Negative school progress	.22	.25
School engagement*	3.86	3.71
Social behavior*	3.84	3.77
Cynicism about work*	2.49	2.56
Pessimism about future employment	1.98	2.07
Employment and career preparation*	2.35	2.26

Source: Adapted from Miller, Huston, Duncan, McLoyd, and Weisner (2008).
* statistically significant difference.

⌨ Implications for Evidence-Based Practice

Evaluation research is connected to specific social work programs; as a result, you can learn lessons from the various evaluative questions that might apply to your own agency settings. Even more important, when an agency is engaged in ongoing evaluation to monitor program outcomes, the agency can adjust services or activities when the outcomes do not appear to be successful. Logic modeling and in-depth evaluations are two activities that enable agencies to integrate evidence-based practice (Whittaker et al., 2006).

When an agency completes a logic model of one or more of its programs, it is deconstructing its program. The logic model provides the basis for an agency asking a variety of evaluation questions. Is the program needed? Are the program assumptions correct? Is the treatment model appropriate? Are the activities implemented correctly with the right kinds of resources? Does the program produce the desired outcomes? The research literature may provide evidence about each of these questions, but this takes us back to our fundamental questions about the evidence—its validity and generalizability. To what extent are the findings from studies about client needs or program assumptions generalizable to the agency's target population? Are the interventions provided in one context generalizable to the agency's context? How valid are the findings about need or program outcome?

In-depth, ongoing program evaluation facilitates both the generation of evidence about a program's impacts as well as an understanding of what contributes to a program's success. Outcome evaluations provide some level of evidence about the effectiveness of the program for the target population; process evaluations can identify mechanisms of a program's implementation that contributes to the program's success (or lack of success). Including contextual factors in the evaluation process provides insight into the interaction of different systems with the program (Whittaker et al., 2006). In combination, such information is important for decision makers as they seek to ensure that they have the necessary inputs and activities to continue achieving desired client outcomes or as they reevaluate the inputs and activities of a less successful program. Therefore, ongoing monitoring of outcomes is a step toward ensuring that the program design is appropriate for the target population.

▣ Evaluation Research in a Diverse Society

Cultural competence has become a key requirement of ethical evaluation practice. Though not mentioned in early versions of the American Evaluation Association's (AEA) Guiding Principles, cultural competence is prominently discussed in the 2004 edition of these principles (Morris, 2011). Evaluation itself is not free of culture as evaluators bring their worldviews to the process; these views may shape the evaluation question, the design and methods used in the evaluation, and the analysis and interpretation of the findings (AEA, 2011).

Culturally competent evaluation practice is based on a respect for the people and groups represented in the evaluation, understanding how culture shapes perspectives and behaviors, and recognizing that there are power differentials (AEA, 2011). In addition to attitudes, culturally competent evaluation practice typically uses a participatory approach that engages the group or community at various stages of the evaluation starting with designing the question to disseminating the findings. Finally, evaluators must use research methods appropriate for the particular group (AEA, 2011).

Throughout this book, we have focused primarily on technical issues relative to our diverse society: Are the measures used reliable and valid for the target group? Is the sample representative? How do we recruit people of color to research studies? Is the question wording appropriate? These technical issues remain as concerns for evaluation research and are addressed elsewhere; in this section, we focus on both broader issues of categorization and ethical challenges with vulnerable participants.

Stanfield (1999) posed the question, "Even if the design and data meet the reliability and validity standards of Campbell and Stanley (1966) or of a particular social scientific or policy-making community, do the data fit the realities of the people it supposedly represents?" (p. 420). He refers to this idea as **relevance validity**. Although Stanfield was speaking about African Americans and people of color, the question is equally relevant for other population groups.

Relevance validity An aspect of validity regarding the usefulness of evaluation data to individuals or communities.

Researchers and agency administrators often define evaluation questions from a perspective that does not necessarily reflect the participants' perspectives. For example, we have argued that a logic model is a particularly useful tool for developing evaluation questions, but often this model is based on the agency's perspectives about a program: The assumptions are the agency's assumptions, the activities are the agency's activities, and the outcomes are those defined by the agency. You can probably begin to wonder whether clients or participants perceive things differently. I once evaluated a program whose intended outcomes were preventing substance abuse and building skills to resist peer pressure among a group of adolescents. Fortunately, I asked the parents of the participants what they saw as the benefits of the program. No parent mentioned anything related to substance abuse; rather, the parents spoke about better school attendance, improved grades, and improved behavior.

A second concern involves the process of categorizing clients by their characteristics. Categorizing clients (e.g., by race, gender, sexual orientation, or class) may reflect assumptions about the group's social and cultural characteristics and abilities. Such categorization ignores the heterogeneity within each classification and can result in an inaccurate assessment of a program's impact (AEA, 2011; Stanfield, 1999).

In research and evaluation, there is a tendency to compare other ethnic groups to Whites, suggesting that the White experience is the baseline to which other groups should aspire—that the majority's experience is what should be appropriate for other population groups (AEA, 2011; Stanfield, 1999). Similarly, differences between heterosexual participants and gay, lesbian, bisexual, or transgender participants should not be assumed to be deficits (Herek, Kimmel, Amaro, & Melton, 1991; J. Martin & Meezan, 2003).

This practice results in the application of a deficits model to evaluation; while in social work practice the focus on strengths is becoming more common, it is still emerging in evaluation. For example, needs assessments too often use a deficit model that identifies what are thought to be problems or gaps. A needs assessment that integrates questions to identify the strengths of individuals and the community may lead to different conclusions about "needs," as well as increase the number of options to deal with such needs.

▣ Ethics in Evaluation

Evaluation research can make a difference in people's lives while it is in progress, as well as after the results are reported. Job opportunities, welfare requirements, housing options, and treatment for substance abuse—each are a potentially important benefit, and an evaluation research project can change both their type and availability. This direct impact on research participants and, potentially, their families heightens the attention that evaluation researchers have to give to human subjects' concerns (Wolf, Turner, & Toms, 2009). Although the particular criteria that are at issue and the decisions that are most ethical vary with the type of evaluation research conducted and the specifics of a particular project, there are always serious ethical as well as political concerns for the evaluation researcher (Boruch, 1997; Dentler, 2002).

It is when program impact is the focus that human subjects' considerations multiply. What about assigning persons randomly to receive some social program or benefit? One justification given by evaluation researchers has to do with the scarcity of these resources. If not everyone in the population who is eligible for a program can receive it, due to resource limitations, what could be a fairer way to distribute the program benefits than through a lottery? Random assignment also seems like a reasonable way to allocate potential program benefits when a new program is being tested with only some members of the target recipient population. However, when an ongoing entitlement program is being evaluated and experimental subjects would normally be eligible for program participation, it may not be ethical simply to bar some potential participants from the program. Instead, evaluation researchers may test alternative treatments or provide some alternative benefit while the treatment is being denied.

There are many other ethical challenges in evaluation research:

- How can confidentiality be preserved when the data are owned by a government agency or subject to discovery in a legal proceeding?

- Who decides what level of burden an evaluation project may tolerably impose on participants?

- Is it legitimate for research decisions to be shaped by political considerations?

- Must evaluation findings be shared with stakeholders rather than only with policy makers?

- Is the effectiveness of the proposed program improvements really uncertain?

- Will a randomized experiment yield more defensible evidence that the alternatives?

- Will the results actually be used?

Evaluation researchers must consider whether it will be possible to meet each of these criteria long before they even design a study.

Ethical concerns must also be given special attention in human services as evaluations often involve vulnerable populations, some of whom are using agency programs by choice while others are legally mandated clients. Some of these participants may be marginalized and at risk of discrimination or violence (J. Martin & Meezan, 2003). This puts a particular onus on the agency to ensure that clients truly understand how the data are going to be used and participants' rights related to the use of such data.

English (1997) posed the question, "Does informed consent safeguard the interests of disadvantaged and minority target groups?" (p. 51). Gathering data is, first of all, intrusive, and the data-gathering process may impact negatively on the participants. In addition, the agency may produce information that could lead to some kind of sanction against the participants. English described an interview with a family that in the past had placed a disabled child in an institution, believing it was the right thing to do, but was now having that belief challenged by the interview process. The respondents were extremely distressed by the process. The ethical issue was whether the distress caused by the interview could have been anticipated and been alleviated in some fashion.

The problem of maintaining subject confidentiality is particularly thorny because researchers, in general, are not legally protected from the requirement that they provide evidence requested in legal proceedings, particularly through the process known as "discovery." However, it is important to be aware that several federal statutes have been passed specifically to protect research data about vulnerable populations from legal disclosure requirements.

The problem is that informed consent is linked to the use of the data by the sponsors and that sponsors may not use the data in a way that protects the interests of those providing the information. To protect participants, English (1997) recommends that participants be involved in all stages of the evaluation, including identifying the purposes and information requirements, how data should be obtained, data analysis, dissemination, and utilization. In this way, the evaluation will not distort the interests of the participants.

Finally, we know that participation must be voluntary. The challenges in agency-based evaluation are to reassure clients that there will be no ramifications for choosing not to participate and to emphasize that there no added benefits for clients who do participate. Think about how difficult this might be to a client, given the power differentials between clients and agency providers. You face a similar subtle pressure when a professor hands out a survey in class that the professor intends to use for a journal article; despite the guarantees offered about voluntary participation, it is normal to wonder if failing to complete the survey will somehow impact on your grade.

The American Evaluation Association has articulated five overarching principles to guide people involved in evaluation. These principles include the following (American Evaluation Association, 2004):

1. *Systematic inquiry: Evaluators conduct systematic, data-based inquiries.* This principle speaks directly to methodological decisions and their adequacy to answer particular questions (Morris, 2011).

2. *Competence: Evaluators provide competent performance to stakeholders.* Evaluators should have the skills necessary to carry out the evaluation including cultural competence.

3. *Integrity/Honesty: Evaluators should display honesty and integrity in their own behavior and attempt to ensure the honesty and integrity of the entire evaluation process.* This principle involves conflicts of interest, changes in design, reporting findings accurately, and the misuse of the findings by stakeholders (Morris, 2011; Chelimsky, 2008).

4. *Respect for People: Evaluators respect the security, dignity and self-worth of respondents, program participants, clients and other evaluation stakeholders.* Discussions about this principle include topics associated with informed consent, the idea of not causing harm, being proactive in reducing harm, and promoting the inclusion of vulnerable groups (Morris, 2011).

5. *Responsibilities for General and Public Welfare: Evaluators articulate and take into account the diversity of general and public interests and values that may be related to the evaluation.* This principle is fairly vague about the meaning of the general and public welfare and different views include pursuing social justice, advocating for recommendations emerging from an evaluation, and involving stakeholders in the evaluation process (Morris, 2011).

We conclude this discussion on ethics in evaluation by emphasizing one key point: It can be costly to society and potentially harmful to participants to maintain ineffective programs. In the long run, at least, it may be more ethical to conduct an evaluation study than to let the status quo remain in place.

回 Conclusion

Hopes for evaluation research are high: Society could benefit from the development of programs that work well, accomplish their goals, and serve people who genuinely need them. At least that is the hope. Unfortunately, there are many obstacles to realizing this hope (Posavac & Carey, 2010):

- Because social programs and the people who use them are complex, evaluation research designs can easily miss important outcomes or aspects of the program process.

- Because the many program stakeholders all have an interest in particular results from the evaluation, researchers can be subjected to an unusual level of cross-pressures and demands.

- Because the need to include program stakeholders in research decisions may undermine adherence to scientific standards, research designs can be weakened.

- Because some program administrators want to believe their programs really work well, researchers may be pressured to avoid null findings, or if they are not responsive, they may find their research report ignored. Plenty of well-done evaluation research studies wind up in a recycling bin or hidden away in a file cabinet.

- Because the primary audience for evaluation research reports is program administrators, politicians, or members of the public, evaluation findings may need to be overly simplified, distorting the findings.

The rewards of evaluation research are often worth the risks, however. Evaluation research can provide social scientists with rare opportunities to study complex social processes with real consequences and to contribute to the public good. Although evaluation researchers may face unusual constraints on their designs, most evaluation projects can result in high-quality analyses and publication in reputable social science journals. In many respects, evaluation research is an idea whose time has come. We may never achieve Donald Campbell's (Campbell & Russo, 1999) vision of an "experimenting society," in which research is consistently used to evaluate new programs and to suggest constructive changes, but we are close enough to continue trying.

Key Terms

Highlights

- Evaluation research is social work research that is conducted to investigate social problems.

- The evaluation process can be modeled as a feedback system with inputs entering the program, which generate outputs and then outcomes, which provide feedback to program stakeholders and effect program inputs.

- The evaluation process as a whole and the feedback process in particular can be understood only in relation to the interests and perspectives of program stakeholders.

- A logic model provides a schematic representation of the various components that make up a social service program.

- There are four primary types of program evaluation: needs assessment, process evaluation, outcome evaluation, and efficiency analysis.

- The process by which a program has an effect on outcomes is often treated as a "black box," but there is good reason to open the black box and investigate the process by which the program operates and produces, or fails to produce, an effect.

- A program theory may be developed before or after an investigation of program process is completed. It may be either descriptive or prescriptive.

- Qualitative methods are useful in describing the process of program delivery.

- Multiple outcomes are often necessary to understand program effects.

- Evaluation research raises complex ethical issues because it may involve withholding desired social benefits.

Discussion Questions

1. Evaluate the ethics of one of the studies discussed in this chapter. Which ethical guidelines seem most difficult to adhere to? Where do you think the line should be drawn between not taking any risks at all with research participants and developing valid scientific knowledge?

2. Select a social program with which you are familiar, and list its intended outcomes. What other outcomes might result from the program, both direct and indirect? Try to identify outcomes that would be deemed desirable as well as some that might not be desirable.

3. Describe a plan for an evaluation of a social program you have heard about. Identify a research question you would like to answer about this program, and select a method of investigation. Discuss the strengths and weaknesses of your proposed method.

Practice Exercises

1. Choose a social program with which you are familiar, and construct a logic model.

2. Find a recent article that evaluates a program or an intervention from a social work journal such as *Research Practice in Social Work*. Describe its strengths and weaknesses. Do the authors make claims about causality that are supported by their methodology?

3. Review a social work agency's description of one of its primary programs and the objectives it aims to meet. Create a flowchart illustrating the service delivery process. Do you believe that the program design reflects the stated goals? Are necessary activities absent or activities present that do not appear to contribute to the desired outcomes?

Web Exercise

1. Describe the resources available for evaluation researchers at one of the following websites: www.wmich.edu/evalctr, http://eevaluation.blogspot.com, http://ieg.worldbankgroup.org/ .

2. Check out the latest information regarding the D.A.R.E. program at www.dare.com. What is the current approach? Can you find information on the Web about current research on D.A.R.E.?

Developing a Research Proposal

1. Develop a logic model for a program that might influence the type of attitude or behavior in which you are interested. List the key components of this model.

2. Design a program evaluation to test the efficacy of your program model, using an impact analysis approach.

3. Add to your plan a discussion of a program theory for your model. In your methodological plan, indicate whether you will use qualitative or quantitative techniques and simple or complex outcomes.

4. Who are the potential stakeholders for your program? How will you relate to them before, during, and after your evaluation?

A Question of Ethics

1. Is it ethical to assign people to receive some social benefit on a random basis? Form two teams and debate the ethics of the New Hope randomized evaluation of employment described in this chapter.

2. Imagine that you are evaluating a group home for persons with serious mental illness and learn that a house resident has been talking about cutting himself. Would you immediately inform house staff about this? What if the resident asked you not to tell anyone? In what circumstances would you feel it is ethical to take action to prevent the likelihood of a subject harming himself or herself or others?

Quantitative Data Analysis

This chapter introduces several common statistics in social work research and evaluation and highlights the factors that must be considered in using and interpreting statistics. Think of it as a review of fundamental social statistics, if you have already studied them, or as an introductory overview, if you have not. Two preliminary sections lay the foundation for studying statistics. In the first, we discuss the role of statistics in the research process, returning to themes and techniques with which you are already familiar. In the second preliminary section, we outline the process of preparing data for statistical analysis. In the rest of the chapter, we explain how to describe the distribution of single variables and the relationship among variables. Along the way, we address ethical issues related to data analysis. This chapter will have been successful if it encourages you to use statistics responsibly, evaluate statistics critically, and seek opportunities for extending your statistical knowledge.

Although many colleges and universities offer social statistics in a separate course, and for good reason (there's a lot to learn), we do not want you to think of this chapter as somehow on a different topic than the rest of this book. Data analysis is an integral component of research methods, and it's important that any proposal for quantitative research or an evaluation plan include a section on data analysis that will follow data collection. You have to anticipate your data analysis needs if you expect your research or evaluation to secure the requisite data.

▣ Introducing Statistics

Statistics is often the word that social work students love to hate. We hope in this chapter to help you replace your fear of statistics with an appreciation of them as simply tools with which to summarize and analyze data. Statistics provide you with a means to report what you do as a social worker: to document what you do for agency administrators or funding agencies, to monitor your practice, to determine whether interventions are achieving the desired outcome, or to assess community needs. You need a sufficient understanding of basic statistical techniques to produce the kinds of reports that stakeholders and the general population demand. At the same time, a basic knowledge of statistics enables you to be informed consumers of research and helps you critically evaluate research findings reported in the professional literature.

Statistics play a key role in achieving valid research results in terms of measurement, causal validity, and generalizability. Some statistics are used to describe the results of measuring single variables. These statistics include graphs, frequency distributions, measures of central tendency, and variation. Other statistics are useful primarily to begin assessing causal validity by helping us describe the association among variables and to control for or otherwise take account of other variables. Cross-tabulation, the technique for measuring association and controlling other variables, is introduced in this chapter. All of these statistics are termed **descriptive statistics** because they are used to describe the distribution of and relationship among variables.

> **Descriptive statistics** Statistics used to describe the distribution of and relationship among variables.

You already learned in Chapter 5 that it is possible to estimate the degree of confidence that can be placed in generalizations from a sample to the population from which the sample was selected. The statistics used in making these estimates are termed inferential statistics. In this chapter, we refer briefly to inferential statistics, but on this book's website (www.sagepub.com/engelprsw4e) you will find a chapter describing some common statistical methods that are appropriate for hypothesis testing and program evaluation.

Social theory and the results of prior research should guide our statistical choices, as they guide the choice of other research methods. There are so many particular statistics and so many ways for them to be used in data analysis that even the best statisticians can become lost in a sea of numbers if they do not use prior research and theorizing to develop a coherent analysis plan. It is also important to choose statistics that are appropriate to the level of measurement of the variables to be analyzed. As you learned in Chapter 4, numbers used to represent the values of variables may not actually signify different quantities, meaning that many statistical techniques will not be applicable.

▣ Preparing Data for Analysis

If you have conducted your own survey or experiment, the information that you may have on assorted questionnaires, survey instruments, observational checklists, or tape transcripts needs to be prepared in a format suitable for analyzing data. Generally, this involves a process of assigning a number to a particular response to a question, observation, case record response, and the like. For the most part, this is a straightforward process. There are pitfalls and decisions you will have to make to ensure the consistency of how you transform these responses, and you will need to take steps to ensure the accuracy of the data you enter in the computer. If you are using an Internet survey tool such as Survey-Monkey or Qualtrics, you will not have many of these problems as they are designed to download data directly into a file; you are dependent on still setting up the survey and file structures correctly.

We suggest following these steps to prepare the data for analysis.

Assign a unique identifying number. A unique identifier such as a number should be assigned to each respondent, and this identifier should appear on the form, questionnaire, survey, or transcript. You should include the identifier as a variable in the data. Having an identifier enables you to go back to the original form if you find data entry errors or decide to enter additional information. If you are using data about the same people collected at different points in time, the unique identifier helps you link their responses.

Review the forms. As you review the instruments or questionnaires used to record responses, you may encounter mistakes or unanticipated problems. You need to establish rules that you will follow when you encounter such mistakes. Document the rules you establish so that corrections are made in a consistent fashion. Here are some of the problems you may encounter:

- *Responses that are not clearly indicated.* You may find mistakes such as a circle crossing more than one category or an X or a check mark falling between responses (see Exhibit 14.1). This presents a dilemma because the respondent has given a response, but because of the ambiguity of what was circled or checked, you may not be sure which response to consider correct. You have to make a decision about how you are going to treat such cases. One possibility is to simply take the first response or the second response. Although such decisions may ultimately lead you to overestimate certain responses while underestimating other responses, by being consistent you can identify the source of the bias. You may decide to treat the response as a missing response, accepting that you will lose information. The important point is that you establish a rule of thumb that you are going to follow and acknowledge the shortcomings of the decision you make.

- *Respondents misreading instructions.* Sometimes respondents do not follow instructions about how to respond to a question. We encountered this problem in a housing needs assessment survey. Respondents were asked to choose from a list of 25 different social services the 5 most important services by indicating with a 1 the most important, 2 the second most important, and so on. Instead, some respondents simply checked all (often more than five) that they thought were important (see Question 4 in Exhibit 14.1). When this happened, we decided to treat the responses as missing information. In a large sample, this decision might make little difference, but in a small sample, losing information might dramatically alter the findings.

- *Incomplete questionnaires.* Some respondents may not complete the entire instrument or may end the interview before it is completed. You have to decide whether to include the responses you have obtained and treat the rest as missing or consider the entire instrument as missing. There are no hard rules. Your decision is likely to be influenced by the sample size; when you have a large sample, there is less cost to treating the entire questionnaire as missing. In the case of the housing needs survey mentioned earlier, because there were only 20 respondents, the responses of the 2 people who completed only half the questionnaire were included. Your decision might be influenced by how many questions were answered or whether the questions crucial to your study were answered.

- *Unexpected responses.* You may get responses that you had not anticipated. For example, you might ask age and get responses like 30 1/2. Decide how you will treat such responses, and then be consistent throughout.

Exhibit 14.1   Unclear Responses

Thanks. This set of questions deals with different feelings and emotions. For each of these questions, please answer for how you felt over the past week by responding yes or no.
In the last week

Yes   No   1. Are you basically satisfied with your life?

Now I am going to ask you a couple of questions about your vision and health.

2. Overall, how would you rate your health? Would you say your health is excellent, very good, good, fair, or poor?

1   Excellent
2   Very good
3   Good
4   Fair
5   Poor

3. In which category does your annual earned income fall? (please check)

____   less than $10,000
____   10,000 - 14,999
____   15,000 - 19,999
✓/   20,000 - 24,999
____   25,000 - 29,999
____   30,000 or more

4. Please rank the top five housing options that are necessary for your agency to provide. Place a "1" by the most necessary option, a "2" by the second most necessary option, a "3" for the next third most necessary; a "4" for the fourth most necessary, and a "5" for the fifth most necessary.

X   Homeless shelter
___   Emergency rent & utilities financial help
___   Transitional/Bridge Housing

X   Shared with little/none support services
___   Subsidized Independent living no on site services

X   Long term rental/mortgage assistance
___   Shared with on-site support services
___   Housing and off-premise D&A use

X   Clean & Sober Housing program
___   Residential hospice
___   Skilled Nursing Facility

X   Personal care home/assisted living
___   Other, specify_____

Code open-ended questions. Two types of open-ended questions are common in structured surveys: (1) when the entire question is left open ended and (2) where you have *Other* (specify) _____ as a potential response in a list of responses. The process for developing categories is similar, although it is far easier to develop response categories for *Other* because the responses are likely to be far fewer in number, and the most common responses—or at least most anticipated responses—already appear in the questionnaire.

With open-ended questions, it is not unusual to get multiple responses to a question. For example, in a study assessing the potential roles of settlement houses in the community (Engel, 1994), respondents were asked to comment on a proposed definition. Many respondents gave lengthy responses that involved different ideas, such as this:

> I would revise activities to give stronger emphasis on the necessities of life. To feed the soul is an important task of course, but to feed the physical body and to keep people safe, warm, and dry is imperative. A neighborhood center, just as the neighborhood itself, should be open to all including those who may be attracted from without. It must also be a part of the larger community and not strive to protect itself or discourage its members from moving throughout this larger community. It must be democratic to a fault and find a meaningful role for all. (p. 6)

To identify possible response categories, you can rely on your own knowledge of the area and what might emerge as likely response categories. However, this list is still likely to be insufficient because if the options had been known, a closed-ended question probably would have been used. First, list the responses; if a respondent provides several answers, separate the responses and treat each as a unique response. One way to list the responses is to write the response on an index card (remember to include the respondent's identification number and question number on the card). In the previous example, you would identify different elements (i.e., different responses) and treat each as a different response. Next, review the separate responses to see whether patterns begin to emerge; these patterns represent potential response categories for the variable. This should be followed by additional reviews until you are convinced that you have interpreted the responses correctly and the categories are sufficient. Finally, a second opinion should be obtained with at least a subset of responses to establish consistency and accuracy for your conclusions. When you have a small number of respondents, all responses should be used to create the categories; with a large number of respondents, it is easier to use a sample of the responses to create the categories.

Create a codebook. A codebook contains the set of instructions used to link a number to a category for a particular variable. This is a record for you to know the values assigned to the response categories for each variable. You may define each variable as you build a data set in a statistical program, or you may create a paper version of your codebook. You should also use the codebook to keep track of any new variables you create as you analyze the data.

Enter the data. There are several common methods of data entry. Research studies using computer-assisted telephone interviews (CATI; described in Chapter 9) are designed so that as responses are given, the data are immediately entered into a computer program. Some Internet surveys are designed so that as participants complete the survey, their responses are entered immediately into a database. Another method is to use optical scan sheets. These are the familiar sheets many of us have used to take standardized tests or to do class evaluations. Data are coded on the sheets, and then the sheets are read by an optical scanner.

You may enter the data by hand into a spreadsheet such as Excel or Lotus or into a statistical package such as SPSS or SAS. If the data are entered directly into a statistics program, you have to define the data by identifying each variable and its characteristics. The procedures for doing so vary with the specific statistical or spreadsheet package. Exhibit 14.2 illustrates a variable definition file from SPSS. The information provided for each variable includes the variable name, variable label, labels for each of the variable values, values representing missing data, and the variable's level of measurement (note that in SPSS, *scale* combines interval and ratio).

Clean the data. After the data are entered, they must be checked carefully for errors—a process called *data cleaning.* If a data entry program has been used and programmed to flag invalid values, the cleaning process is

Exhibit 14.2 Data Definition File from SPSS

	Name	Type	Width	Decimals	Label	Values	Missing	Columns	Align	Measure
1	case	Numeric	8	0	Id Number	None	None	8	Right	Scale
2	gender	Numeric	8	0	Respondent's Gender	(1, female)...	9	8	Right	Nominal
3	ethnic	Numeric	8	0	Respondent's Ethnicity	(1, African American	9	8	Right	Nominal
4	q1t1	Numeric	8	0	Attitude 1 Time 1	(1, strongly agree)...	9	8	Right	Scale
5	q2t1	Numeric	8	0	Attitude 2 Time 1	(1, strongly agree)...	9	8	Right	Scale
6	q3t1	Numeric	8	0	Attitude 3 Time 1	(1, strongly agree)...	9	8	Right	Scale
7	q4t1	Numeric	8	2	Intensity Time 1	None	9.00	8	Right	Scale
8	q1t2	Numeric	8	0	Attitude 1 Time 2	(1, strongly agree)...	9	8	Right	Scale
9	q2t2	Numeric	8	0	Attitude 2 Time 2	(1, strongly agree)...	9	8	Right	Scale
10	q3t2	Numeric	8	0	Attitude 3 Time 2	(1, strongly agree)...	9	8	Right	Scale
11	q4t2	Numeric	8	2	Intensity Time 2	None	9.00	8	Right	Scale

Check coding A check of the accuracy of coding information; it is estimated by comparing the coding completed by one person with the coding completed by a second person.

much easier. If you do not have a programmed method to flag mistakes, there are other techniques that should be used.

When using **check coding**, a second person recodes a sample of the forms and then the percentage of agreement on all the items on the forms is computed. If the percentage falls below a pre-established criterion, then all forms should be recoded and reevaluated a second time.

You should also examine the frequency distribution for every variable to see if there are cases with values that fall outside the range of allowable values for a given variable. For example, if you were coding student status as 1 = full-time and 2 = part-time, finding 3 would mean that at least one or more cases had been miscoded or the data entered incorrectly. The cases for which this happened can be identified and corrections made.

At times, contingency questions may lead the interviewer or respondent to skip some questions. For example, a positive response to the question, "Are you currently employed?" might lead to additional questions about work, whereas a negative response would mean that those additional work-related questions should be skipped. To check that there were no errors in the coding, cross-tabulations are computed. A cross-tabulation (explained in far greater detail later) compares responses to two variables. Looking at the cross-tabulation, it is possible to identify instances where a person should have skipped a question but a response was actually coded.

When you find mistakes, you can easily correct them because you have established unique identifying numbers for each respondent. You can go back to the original questionnaire with the corresponding identification number, find the actual response, and make the correction in the computer file in which the data are stored. Unfortunately, what appears as a mistake may not always be a mistake nor be easily corrected. In a panel study conducted by the U.S. Census Bureau, several elderly women in their first interview reported that they were widowed, but 4 months later, they reported that they were divorced (Engel, 1988). In this case, it was impossible to determine what the correct marital status was.

囝 Displaying Univariate Distributions

The first step in data analysis is usually to display the variation in each variable of interest in what are called *univariate frequency distributions*. For many descriptive purposes, the analysis may go no further. Graphs and frequency distributions are the two most popular approaches for displaying variation; both allow the analyst to display the distribution of cases across the categories of a variable. Graphs have the advantage over numerically displayed frequency distributions because they provide a picture that is easier to comprehend. Frequency distributions are preferable when exact numbers of cases having particular values must be reported and when many distributions must be displayed in a compact form.

Whichever type of display is used, the primary concern of the data analyst is to accurately display the distribution's shape, that is, to show how cases are distributed across the values of the variable. The analyst may describe the shape in terms of the common or typical response, or **central tendency**; the spread or variability of the responses, or **variability**; and the shape of the responses, or **skewness**. These features of a distribution's shape can be interpreted in several ways, and they are not all appropriate for describing every variable. In fact, all three features of a distribution can be distorted if graphs, frequency distributions, or summary statistics are used inappropriately.

A variable's level of measurement is the most important determinant of the appropriateness of particular statistics. For example, we cannot talk about the skewness (lack of symmetry) of a variable measured at the nominal level (categorical or qualitative). If the values of a variable cannot be ordered from lowest to highest—if the ordering of the values is arbitrary—we cannot say whether the distribution is symmetric because we could just reorder the values to make the distribution more (or less) symmetric. Some measures of central tendency and variability are also inappropriate for nominal-level variables.

> **Central tendency** The most common value (for variables measured at the nominal level) or the value around which cases tend to center (for a quantitative variable).
>
> **Variability** The extent to which cases are spread out through the distribution or clustered in one location.
>
> **Skewness** The extent to which cases are clustered more at one or the other end of the distribution of a quantitative variable, rather than in a symmetric pattern around its center. Skew can be positive (a right skew) with the number of cases tapering off in the positive direction or negative (a left skew), with the number of cases tapering off in the negative direction.

The distinction between variables measured at the ordinal level and those measured at the interval or ratio level should also be considered when selecting statistics to use, but social work researchers differ in just how much importance they attach to this distinction. Many researchers think of ordinal variables as imperfectly measured interval-level variables and believe that, in most circumstances, statistics developed for interval-level variables also provide useful summaries for ordinal variables. Other researchers believe that variation in ordinal variables will be distorted by statistics that assume an interval level of measurement. We touch on some of the details in the following sections on particular statistical techniques.

We now examine graphs and frequency distributions that illustrate these three features of shape. Summary statistics used to measure specific aspects of central tendency and variability are presented in a separate section. There is a summary statistic for the measurement of skewness, but it is used only rarely in published research reports and is not presented here.

Graphs

A picture often is worth some immeasurable quantity of words. Even for the uninitiated, graphs can be easy to read, and they highlight a distribution's shape. They are useful particularly for exploring data because they show the full range of variation and identify data anomalies that might be in need of further study. Good professional-looking graphs can now be produced relatively easily with software available for personal computers. There are many types of graphs, but the most common and most useful are bar charts, histograms, frequency polygons, and, as you saw in Chapter 8, line graphs for displaying single-subject design data. Each has two axes, the vertical axis (the y-axis), which usually represents frequency counts or percentages, and the horizontal axis (the x-axis), which displays the values of the variable being graphed. Graphs should have labels to identify the variables and the values, with tick marks showing where each indicated value falls along the axis.

A **bar chart** contains solid bars separated by spaces. It is a good tool for displaying the distribution of variables measured at the nominal level and other discrete categorical variables because there is, in effect, a gap between each of

> **Bar chart** A graphic for categorical variables in which the variable's distribution is displayed with solid bars separated by spaces.

Histogram A graphic for quantitative variables in which the variable's distribution is displayed with adjacent bars.

Frequency polygon A graphic for quantitative variables in which a continuous line connects data points representing the variable's distribution.

the categories. The bar chart of marital status in Exhibit 14.3 indicates that less than half of adult Americans were married at the time of the survey. Smaller percentages were divorced, separated, widowed, or never married. The most common value in the distribution is married, so this would be the distribution's central tendency. There is a moderate amount of variability in the distribution because the half who are not married are spread across the categories of widowed, divorced, separated, and never married. Because marital status is not a quantitative variable, the order in which the categories are presented is arbitrary, and skewness is not defined.

Histograms are used to display the distribution of quantitative variables that vary along a continuum that has no necessary gaps. The bars in a histogram represent the number of cases falling in the intervals into which that continuum is divided, and so the bars are shown as adjacent to each other. Exhibit 14.4 shows a histogram of years of education. The distribution has a clump of cases centered at 12 years, with the most common value of 12. The distribution is negatively left-skewed as there are more cases just above the central point than below it.

In a **frequency polygon**, a continuous line connects the points representing the number or percentage of cases with each value. The frequency polygon is an alternative to the histogram when the distribution of a quantitative continuous variable must be displayed; this alternative is particularly useful when the variable has a wide range of values. It is easy to see in the frequency polygon of years of education in Exhibit 14.5 that the most common value is 12 years, high school completion, and that this value also seems to be the center of the distribution. There is moderate variability in the distribution, with many cases having more than 12 years of education and about one third having completed at least 4 years of college (16 years total). The distribution is highly skewed in the

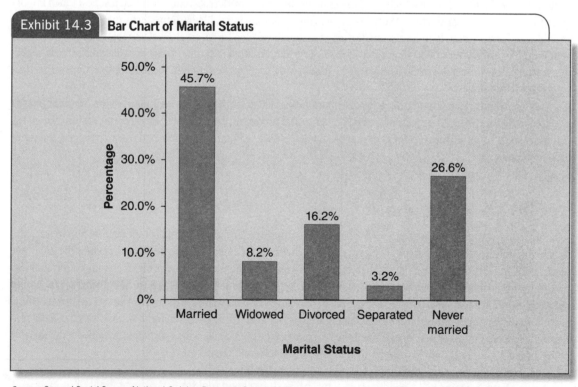

Exhibit 14.3 | **Bar Chart of Marital Status**

Source: General Social Survey, National Opinion Research Center, 2014.

Exhibit 14.4 **Histogram of Years of Education**

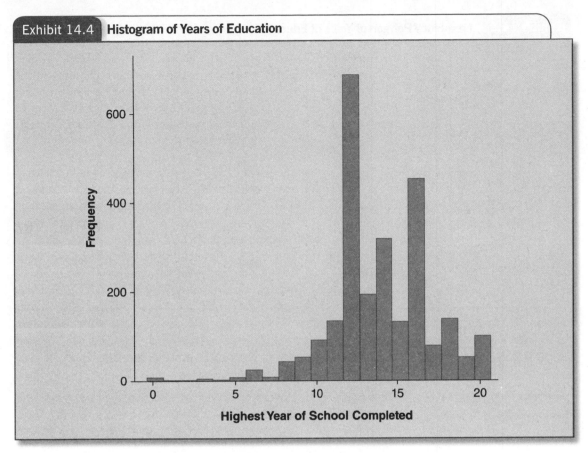

*Source:*General Social Survey, National Opinion Research Center, 2014.

negative direction, with few respondents reporting less than 10 years of education. This same type of graph can use percentages rather than frequencies.

If graphs are misused, they can distort, rather than display, the shape of a distribution. Adherence to several guidelines (Tufte, 1983; Wallgren, Wallgren, Persson, Jorner, & Haaland, 1996) will help you spot these problems and avoid them in your own work:

- The difference between bars can be exaggerated by cutting off the bottom of the vertical axis and displaying less than the full height of the bars. Instead, begin the graph of a quantitative variable at 0 on both axes. It may at times be reasonable to violate this guideline, as when an age distribution is presented for a sample of adults, but in this case, be sure to mark the break clearly on the axis.

- Bars of unequal width, including pictures instead of bars, can make particular values look as if they carry more weight than their frequency warrants. Always use bars of equal width.

- Either shortening or lengthening the vertical axis will obscure or accentuate the differences in the number of cases between values. The two axes usually should be of approximately equal length.

- Avoid chart junk that can confuse the reader and obscure the distribution's shape (a lot of verbiage or umpteen marks, lines, lots of cross-hatching, etc.).

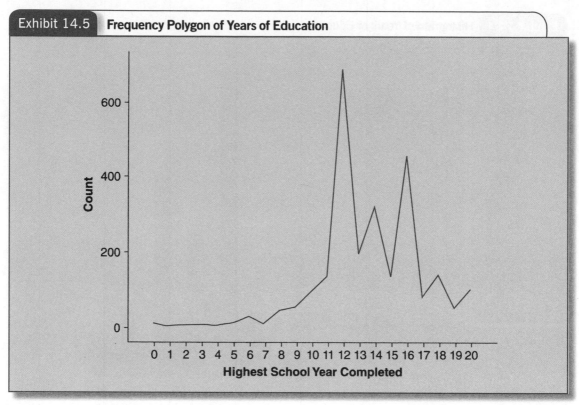

Exhibit 14.5 **Frequency Polygon of Years of Education**

Source: General Social Survey, National Opinion Research Center, 2014.

Frequency Distributions

A **frequency distribution** displays the number or percentage (the relative frequencies), or both, of cases corresponding to each of a variable's values or group of values. For continuous variables, a frequency distribution provides information about the spread of a variable, providing the lowest and highest categories with valid responses and some sense of the shape of the responses. The components of the frequency distribution should be clearly labeled, with a title; labels for the values of the variable; a caption identifying whether the distribution includes frequencies, percentages, or both; and perhaps the number of missing cases. If percentages rather than frequencies are presented (sometimes both are included), the total number of cases in the distribution (the base number *N*) should be indicated.

> **Frequency distribution** Numerical display showing the number of cases and usually the percentage of cases (the relative frequencies) corresponding to each value or group of values of a variable.

Ungrouped Data

Constructing and reading frequency distributions for variables with few values is not difficult. The frequency distribution of voting in Exhibit 14.6, for example, shows that 69.6% of the respondents eligible to vote said they voted and that 30.4% reported they did not vote. The total number of respondents to this question was 2,538, but voting behavior was reported by only 2,374 respondents. The rest were ineligible to vote, just refused to answer the question, said they did not know whether they had voted or not, or gave no answer.

Political ideology was measured with a question having seven response choices, resulting in a longer but still relatively simple frequency distribution (see Exhibit 14.7). The most common response was moderate, with 40.4% of the

Exhibit 14.6	Frequency Distribution of Voting in 2012 Election

Value	Frequency	Valid Percentage
Voted	1,652	69.6
Did not vote	722	30.4
Not eligible	135	-----
Don't know	23	-----
No answer	6	-----
Total	2,538	100.0
		(2,374)

Source: General Social Survey, National Opinion Research Center, 2014.

Exhibit 14.6	Frequency Distribution of Political Views

Value	Frequency	Valid Percentage	Cumulative Percentage
Extremely Liberal	94	3.8	3.8
Liberal	304	12.4	16.3
Slightly liberal	263	10.7	27.0
Moderate	989	40.4	67.6
Slightly conservative	334	13.6	81.0
Conservative	358	14.6	95.6
Extremely conservative	107	4.4	100.0
Total	2,449	100.0	

Source: General Social Survey, National Opinion Research Center, 2014.

sample choosing this label to represent their political ideology. The distribution has a symmetric shape, with about equal percentages of respondents identifying themselves as liberal and conservative. About 4% of the respondents identified themselves as extremely liberal and slightly more, 4.4%, as extremely conservative. This table also reports the *cumulative percentage*, which gives the total percentage below or above a category: 27.0% of the respondents lean to the liberal political identification, whereas 32.4% lean to the conservative political identification.

A frequency distribution can provide more precise information than a graph about the number and percentage of cases in a variable's categories. However, it is often easier to see the shape of a distribution when it is graphed. When the goal of a presentation is to convey a general sense of a variable's distribution, particularly when the presentation is to an audience that is not trained in statistics, the advantages of a graph outweigh those of a frequency distribution.

Grouped Data

Many frequency distributions (and graphs) require grouping of some values after the data are collected. Group data are used if there are too many values, say, 15 or more; if it is hard to display the data in an easily readable table; or if the distribution of the variable will be clearer or more meaningful if some of the values are combined. A frequency distribution of group data is made by combining scores into mutually exclusive and exhaustive categories. The categories should be logically defensible and preserve the distribution's shape.

Inspection of Exhibit 14.8 should clarify these reasons. In the first distribution, which is only a portion of the entire ungrouped age distribution, it is difficult to discern any shape, much less the central tendency. In the second distribution, age is grouped in the familiar 10-year intervals (except for the first, abbreviated category), and the distribution's shape is immediately clear.

| Exhibit 14.8 | **Ungrouped and Grouped Age Distributions** |

Ungrouped		Grouped		
Age	Percentage	Age	Percentage	Comulative Percentage
18	0.2	18–19	1.2	1.2
19	1.0	20–29	14.1	15.3
20	1.0	30–39	19.2	34.5
21	0.9	40–49	16.4	50.9
22	1.1	50–59	20.1	71.0
23	1.2	60–69	14.5	85.5
24	1.2	70–79	9.6	95.1
25	1.9	80–89	4.9	100.0
26	1.9		100.0	
27	1.6		(2,538)	
28	1.2			
29	2.0			
30	2.3			
31	1.9			
32	2.2			
33	1.9			
34	1.8			
35	1.6			
36	1.6			
37	2.1			
38	1.9			

Ungrouped		Grouped		
Age	Percentage	Age	Percentage	Comulative Percentage
39	2.1			
40	1.8			
41	2.1			
42	1.4			
43	2.1			
44	1.5			
45	1.6			
46	1.3			

Source: General Social Survey, National Opinion Research Center, 2014.

Combined and Compressed Distributions

Combined and compressed frequency displays facilitate the presentation of a large amount of data in a relatively small space. In a *combined frequency display*, the distributions for a set of conceptually similar variables having the same response categories are presented together. Exhibit 14.9 is a combined display reporting the frequency distributions in percentage form for 13 variables that indicate respondents' level of confidence in American institutions. The different variables are identified in the leftmost column, and their values are labeled along the top. By looking at the table, you can see that there is greatest confidence in the military and scientific community and low confidence in the U.S. Congress.

Compressed frequency displays also can be used to present cross-tabular data and summary statistics more efficiently by eliminating unnecessary percentages (such as those corresponding to the second value of a dichotomous variable) and reducing the need for repetitive labels. Exhibit 14.10 presents a compressed display of agreement that abortion should be allowed given particular situations. Note that this display presents the number of cases on which the percentages are based.

▣ Summarizing Univariate Distributions

Summary statistics focus attention on particular aspects of a distribution and facilitate comparison among distributions. For example, if your purpose is to report variation in income by state in a form that is easy for most audiences to understand, you would usually be better off presenting average incomes; many people would find it difficult to make sense of a display containing 50 frequency distributions, although they could readily comprehend a long list of average incomes. A display of average incomes would also be preferable to multiple frequency distributions if your only purpose was to provide a general idea of income differences among states.

Of course, representing a distribution in one number loses information about other aspects of the distribution's shape and so creates the possibility of obscuring important information. If you need to inform a discussion about differences in income inequality among states, for example, measures of central tendency and variability would miss the point entirely. You would either have to present the 50 frequency distributions or use some special

Exhibit 14.9	Confidence in Institutions				
Confidence in . . .	A Great Deal (%)	Only Some (%)	Hardly Any (%)	Total (%)	N
Congress	3.7	39.6	54.7	100	1,644
Press	8.2	47.0	44.8	100	1,663
Television	9.9	49.0	41.1	100	1,664
Executive branch of federal government	12.0	43.7	44.2	100	1,653
Organized labor	12.2	57.6	30.3	100	1,613
Banks and financial institutions	14.3	53.2	32.4	100	1,677
Major companies	18.9	62.2	18.9	100	1,655
Organized religion	20.7	54.8	24.6	100	1,636
Education	24.6	57.0	18.4	100	1,677
U. S. Supreme Court	24.1	55.6	20.4	100	1,641
Medicine	38.0	50.6	11.4	100	1,676
Scientific community	41.9	50.0	8.1	100	1,623
Military	50.5	40.1	9.4	100	1,670

Source: General Social Survey, National Opinion Research Center 2014.

Exhibit 14.10	Conditions When Abortion Should be Allowed	
Statement	% Agree	n
Women's health seriously endangered	88.2	1,647
Pregnant as a result of rape	78.3	1,629
Strong chance of serious defect	75.4	1,633
Married and wants no more children	47.5	1,642
Low income—can't afford more children	45.7	1,647
Abortion if woman wants for any reason	45.1	1,653
Not married	43.2	1,651

Source: General Social Survey, National Opinion Research Center, 2014.

statistics that represent the unevenness of a distribution. For this reason, analysts who report summary measures of central tendency usually also report a summary measure of variability, and sometimes several measures of central tendency, variability, or both.

Research In the News

For Further Thought **?**

GENERAL SOCIAL SURVEY SHOWS INFIDELITY ON THE RISE

Since 1972, about 12% of married men and 7% of married women have said each year that they have had sex outside their marriage. However, the lifetime rate of infidelity for men over age 60 increased from 20% in 1991 to 28% in 2006, whereas for women in this age group, it increased from 5% to 15%. Infidelity has also increased among those under age 35: from 15% to 20% among young married men and from 12% to 15% among young married women. However, couples appear to be spending slightly more time with each other.

1. Do you think that these changes reflect shifts in morals or other types of changes? What other variables would you want to include in an analysis to test alternative explanations for the change?

2. What would you want to measure about the characteristics of the interview situation itself so you could assess the likelihood of honest reporting about a behavior like infidelity?

Source: Parker-Pope, Tara. 2008. "Love, Sex, and the Changing Landscape of Infidelity." *The New York Times*, October 28, p. D1.

Measures of Central Tendency

Central tendency is usually summarized with one of three statistics: the mode, the median, or the mean. For any particular application, one of these statistics may be preferable, but each has a role to play in data analysis. To choose an appropriate measure of central tendency, you must consider a variable's level of measurement, the skewness of a quantitative variable's distribution, and the purpose for which the statistic is used.

Mode

The **mode** is the most frequent value in a distribution. It is also termed the probability average because, being the most frequent value, it is the most probable. For example, if you were to pick a case at random of views about confidence in the

> **Mode** The most frequent value in a distribution.

military (refer back to Exhibit 14.9), the probability of the case being a *great deal* would be 0.51 out of 1, or 51%—the most probable value in the distribution. When a variable distribution has one case or interval that occurs more often than others, it is called a *unimodal distribution.*

Sometimes the mode can give a misleading impression of a distribution's central tendency because there are two or more values with an equivalent number of cases. When this happens, the distribution is called *bimodal* (or trimodal, etc.). A bimodal distribution has two or more categories with an equal (or nearly equal) number of cases and with more cases than any of the other categories. There is no single mode. Imagine that a particular distribution has two categories, with each having just about the same number of cases, and these are the two most frequent categories. Strictly speaking, the mode would be the one with more cases, although the other frequent category had only slightly fewer cases. When the categories are close to each other, this is not really a problem; it becomes more of a problem when the categories are far apart. For example, the modal age of students at one school of social work is 24 (22%). The percentage at each age drops until 29 and then rises again until reaching the second most common age of 33 (20%). It is useful in this situation to report that the actual age distribution is bimodal.

Another potential problem with the mode is that it might happen to fall far from the main clustering of cases in a distribution. It would be misleading in most circumstances to say simply that the variable's central tendency was whatever the modal value was. In a study of caregivers, the modal response for monthly hours of respite care use was zero because a sizable proportion of caregivers did not use respite care (Cotrell & Engel, 1998). But to say the typical score was zero distorts the typical number of hours reported by those who did use respite care.

Nevertheless, on occasion, the mode is appropriate. Most important, the mode is the only measure of central tendency that can be used to characterize the central tendency of variables measured at the nominal level. The mode also is often referred to in descriptions of the shape of a distribution. The terms *unimodal* and *bimodal* appear frequently, as do descriptive statements such as "The typical [most probable] respondent was in her 30s." Of course, when you want to show the most probable value, the mode is the appropriate statistic. Which diagnostic category is most common in a community mental health center? The mode provides the answer.

Median

The **median** is the value that divides the distribution in half (the 50th percentile). The median is inappropriate for variables measured at the nominal level because their values cannot be put in order, so there is no meaningful middle position. To determine the median, we simply list the variable's values in numerical order and find the value of the case that has an equal number of cases above and below it. If the median point falls between two cases, which happens if the distribution has an even number of cases, the median is defined as the average of the two middle values and is computed by adding the values of the two middle cases and dividing by 2.

The median in a frequency distribution is determined by identifying the value corresponding to a cumulative percentage of 50. Starting at the top of the grouped age distribution in Exhibit 14.8, for example, and adding up the percentages, we find that we have reached 34.5% in the 30 to 39 years category and then 50.9% in the 40 to 49 years category. The median is therefore 40 to 49.

> **Median** The arithmetic or weighted average computed by adding up the value of all the cases and dividing by the number of cases.
>
> **Mean** The point that divides a distribution in half (the 50th percentile).

With most variables, it is preferable to compute the median from ungrouped data because that method results in an exact value for the median, rather than an interval. If we determine the median from the ungrouped data, we can state the exact value of the median as 49.

Mean

The **mean**, or arithmetic average, takes into account the values of each case in a distribution—it is a weighted average. The mean is computed by adding up the value of all the cases and dividing by the total number of cases, thereby taking into account the value of each case in the distribution:

$$\text{Mean} = \text{Sum of value of cases/number of cases}$$

In algebraic notation, the equation is $\bar{X} = \sum X_i / N$

For example, to calculate the mean value of eight cases, we add the value of all cases ($\sum X_i$) and divide by the number of cases (N):

$$(28 + 117 + 42 + 10 + 77 + 51 + 64 + 55) / 8 = 444 / 8 = 55.5$$

Because computing the mean requires adding up the values of the cases, it makes sense to compute a mean only if the values of the cases can be treated as actual quantities—that is, if they reflect an interval or ratio level of measurement, or if they are ordinal and we assume that ordinal measures can be treated as interval. It would make no sense to calculate the mean religion, for example. Imagine a group of four people in which there were two Protestants, one Catholic, and one Jew. To calculate the mean, you would need to solve the equation (Protestant + Protestant + Catholic + Jew)/ 4 = ?

Even if you decide that Protestant = 1, Catholic = 2, and Jewish = 3, for data entry purposes, it still doesn't make sense to add these numbers because they don't represent quantities of religion.

Median or Mean?

Both the median and the mean are used to summarize the central tendency of quantitative variables, but their suitability for a particular application must be carefully assessed. The key issues to be considered in this assessment are the variable's level of measurement, the shape of its distribution, and the purpose of the statistical summary. Consideration of these issues will sometimes result in a decision to use both the median and the mean, and sometimes neither measure is seen as preferable. But in many other situations, the choice between the mean and median will be clear-cut as soon as the researcher takes the time to consider these three issues.

Level of measurement is a key concern because, to calculate the mean, we must add up the values of all the cases—a procedure that assumes the variable is measured at the interval or ratio level. So although we know that coding *satisfied* with a 2 and *dissatisfied* with a 3 does not really mean that *dissatisfied* is 1 unit more satisfaction, the calculation of the mean assumes this difference to be true. Because calculation of the median requires only that we order the values of cases, we do not have to make this assumption. Technically speaking, then, the mean is an inappropriate statistic for variables measured at the ordinal level (and you already know that it is completely meaningless for nominal-level variables). In practice, however, many social work researchers use the mean to describe the central tendency of variables measured at the ordinal level for the reasons outlined earlier. So it is not unusual to see, for example, agencies report the mean (or average) satisfaction with services.

The shape of a variable's distribution should also be taken into account when deciding whether to use the median or mean. When a distribution is perfectly symmetric, so that the distribution of values below the median is a mirror image of the distribution of values above the median, the mean and median are the same. But the values of the mean and median are affected differently by skewness, or the presence of cases with extreme values on one side of the distribution but not on the other side. Because the median takes into account only the number of cases above and below the median point, not the value of these cases, it is not affected in any way by extreme values. Because the mean is based on adding the value of all the cases, it will be pulled in the direction of exceptionally high (or low) values. The average score on a test for a class of 10 can be easily distorted if one or two students did extremely well relative to everyone else; the median may be a more accurate reflection of the typical score. A small number of extreme cases can have a disproportionate effect on the mean.

This differential impact of skewness on the median and mean is illustrated in Exhibit 14.11. On the first balance beam, the cases (bags) are spread out equally, and the median and mean are in the same location. On the second and third balance beams, the median corresponds to the value of the middle case, but the mean is pulled toward the value of the one case with an extremely low value.

The single most important influence on the choice of the median or the mean should be the purpose of the statistical summary. If the purpose is to report the middle position in one or more distributions, then the median is the appropriate statistic regardless of whether the distribution is skewed. For example, with respect to the age distribution from the General Social Survey, you could report that half the American population is younger than 49 years old and that half the population is older than that. But if the purpose is to show how likely different groups are to have age-related health problems, the measure of central tendency for these groups should take into account people's ages, not just the number who are older and younger than a particular age. For this purpose, the median would be inappropriate because it would not distinguish the two distributions, as shown in Exhibit 14.12. In the top distribution, everyone is between the ages of 35 and 45 years, with a median of 41. In the bottom distribution, the median is still 41 years, but half of the cases have ages above 60. The higher mean in the second distribution reflects the fact that it has more older people.

Keep in mind that it is not appropriate to use either the median or the mean as a measure of central tendency for variables measured at the nominal level because at this level the different attributes of a variable cannot be ordered as higher or lower. Technically speaking, the mode should be used to measure the central tendency of variables measured

Exhibit 14.11   The Mean as a Balance Point

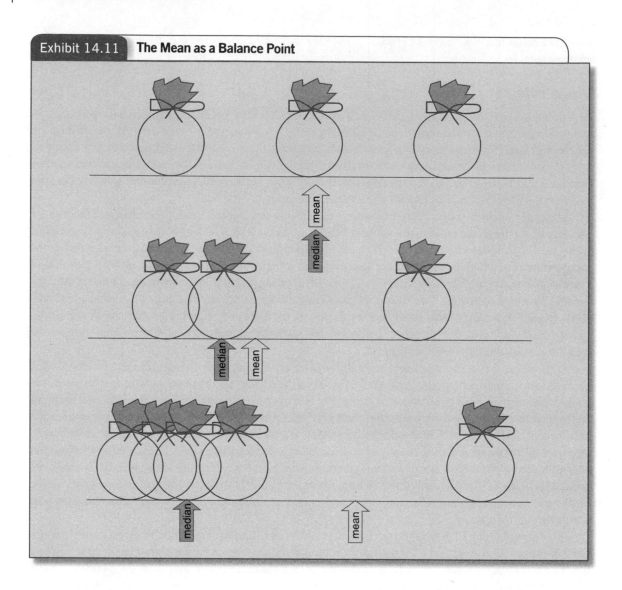

at the nominal level (and it can also be used to measure the central tendency of variables measured at the ordinal, interval, and ratio levels). The median is most suited to measure the central tendency of variables measured at the ordinal level (and it can also be used to measure the central tendency of variables measured at the interval and ratio levels). Finally, the mean is only suited to measure central tendency for variables measured at the interval and ratio levels.

It is not entirely legitimate to represent the central tendency of a variable measured at the ordinal level with the mean: Calculation of the mean requires summing the values of all cases, and at the ordinal level, these values indicate only order, not actual numbers. Nonetheless, as we have already said, many social work researchers use the mean with ordinal-level variables and find that this is potentially useful for comparison among variables and as a first step in more complex statistical analyses. The median and the mode can also be useful as measures of central tendency for variables measured at the interval and ratio levels, when the goal is to indicate middle position (the median) or the most frequent value (the mode).

Exhibit 14.13 summarizes the appropriate uses for each of the measures of central tendency. In general, the mean is the most commonly used measure of central tendency for quantitative variables because it takes into account the value of all cases in the distribution and because it is the foundation for many other more advanced statistics. However, the mean's popularity results in its use in situations for which it is inappropriate.

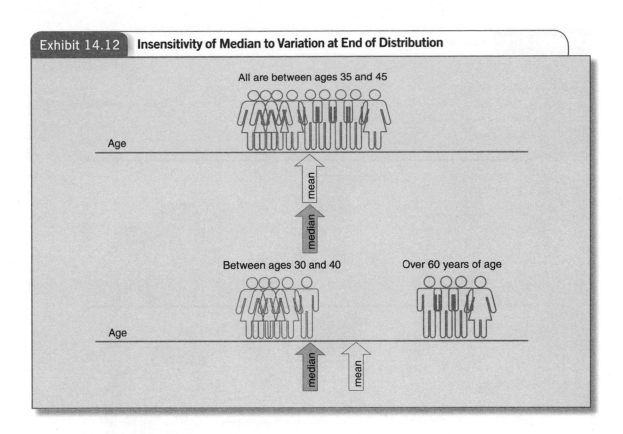

Exhibit 14.12 | Insensitivity of Median to Variation at End of Distribution

Exhibit 14.13 | Selection of Measures of Central Tendency (MCT)

Level of Measurement	Purpose of MCT	Most Appropriate MCT	Potentially Useful MCT	Definitely Inappropriate MCT
Nominal	Identify most frequent response	Mode	None	Median, Mean
Ordinal	Identify middle position	Median	Mean	None
Interval, Ratio	Identify arithmetic average	Mean	Median, Mode	None

Measures of Variation

You already have learned that central tendency is only one aspect of the shape of a distribution—the most important aspect for many purposes, but still just a piece of the total picture. A summary of distributions based only on their central tendency can be incomplete and even misleading. For example, three towns might have the same mean and median income but still be different in their social character due to the shape of their income distributions. As illustrated in Exhibit 14.14, Town A is a homogeneous middle-class community, Town B is very heterogeneous, and Town C has a polarized, bimodal income distribution, with mostly very poor and very rich people and few in between. However, all three towns have the same median income.

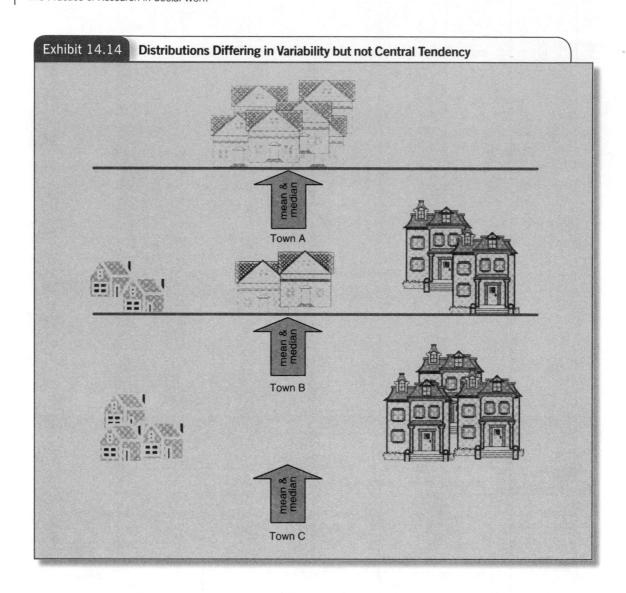

Exhibit 14.14 Distributions Differing in Variability but not Central Tendency

The way to capture these differences is with statistical measures of variation. Four popular measures of variation are the range, the interquartile range, the variance, and the standard deviation (which is the most popular measure of variability). To calculate each of these measures, the variable must be at the interval or ratio level. Statistical measures of variation are used infrequently with nominal-level variables, so these measures are not presented here.

Range

The **range** is a simple measure of variation, calculated as the highest value in a distribution minus the lowest value:

$$\text{Range} = \text{Highest value} - \text{Lowest value}$$

Range The true upper limit in a distribution minus the true lower limit (or the highest rounded value minus the lowest rounded value).

It often is important to report the whole range of actual values that might be encountered. However, because the range can be drastically altered by just one exceptionally high or low value, termed an *outlier*, it is not a good summary measure of a variable's distribution for most purposes.

Interquartile Range

The **interquartile range** avoids the problem created by outliers. **Quartiles** are the points in a distribution corresponding to the first 25% of the cases, the first 50% of the cases, and the first 75% of the cases. You already know how to determine the second quartile, corresponding to the point in the distribution covering half of the cases—it is another name for the median. The first and third quartiles are determined in the same way, but by finding the points corresponding to 25% and 75% of the cases, respectively. The interquartile range is the difference between the first and third quartiles.

Interquartile range The range in a distribution between the end of the first quartile and the beginning of the third quartile.

Quartile The point in a distribution corresponding to the first 25% of the cases, the first 50% of the cases, and the first 75% of the cases.

Variance A statistic that measures the variability of a distribution as the average squatted deviation of each case from the mean.

Variance

The **variance** provides a statistic that uses all the reported scores to determine the spread. The variance is the average squared deviation of each case from the mean. As you can see in Exhibit 14.15, you take each case, subtract it from the overall mean, and compute the square of the value. To get the *sample variance*, the result is summed across all cases and then divided by the number of cases minus 1. The formula for the *sample variance* is

$$s^2 = \frac{\Sigma\left(X_i - \overline{X}\right)^2}{n-1}$$

Exhibit 14.15 **Calculation of the Variance**

Case #	Score (X)	X_i-X	$(X_i$-X$)^2$
1	21	−3.27	10.69
2	30	5.73	32.83
3	15	−9.27	85.93
4	18	−6.27	39.31
5	25	0.73	0.53
6	32	7.73	59.75
7	19	−5.27	27.77
8	21	−3.27	10.69
9	23	−1.27	1.61
10	37	12.73	162.05
11	26	1.73	2.99
	267		434.15

Mean: X = 267/11 = 24.27.

Sum of squared deviations = 434.15.

Variance s^2_x = 434.15/(11 − 1) = 43.42.

where $\overline{X}$ is the sample mean, n is the sample size, Σ is the total for all cases and X_i is the value of each case i on variable X. The *population variance* only differs by dividing by the total number of cases. You also should note that the use of squared deviations in the formula accentuates the impact of relatively large deviations, since squaring a large number makes that number count much more.

The variance is used in many other statistics, although it is more conventional to measure variability with the closely related standard deviation than with the variance.

Standard Deviation

Because the variance provides a measure of the square of the deviations, it does not express the spread in the original units of the measure, and it is hard to interpret the variance. For example, what does a variance of 434.15 mean in relation to the actual reported scores in Exhibit 14.15? To correct this, variation is often expressed by the **standard deviation**, which is simply the square root of the variance. By taking the square root, the sample standard deviation is expressed in the original units of the measure. It is the square root of the average squared deviation of each case from the mean:

$$s = \sqrt{\frac{\Sigma\left(X_i - \overline{X}\right)^2}{n-1}}$$

Standard deviation The square root of the average squared deviation of each case from the mean.

Normal distribution A graph with a shape that looks like a bell, with one hump in the middle, centered around the population mean, and the number of cases tapering off on both sides of the mean. This shape is important for sampling and statistical analysis.

where $\sqrt{}$ is the square root. When the standard deviation is calculated from population data, the denominator is N, rather than $n - 1$, an adjustment that has no discernible effect when the number of cases is reasonably large.

The standard deviation has mathematical properties that make it the preferred measure of variability in many cases, particularly when a variable is normally distributed. A **normal distribution** results from chance variation around a mean. A graph of a normal distribution looks like a bell, with one hump in the middle, centered around the population mean, and the number of cases tapering off on both sides of the mean (see Exhibit 14.16). A normal distribution is symmetric: If you folded it in half at its center (at the population mean), the two halves would match perfectly. If a variable is normally distributed, 68% of the cases will lie

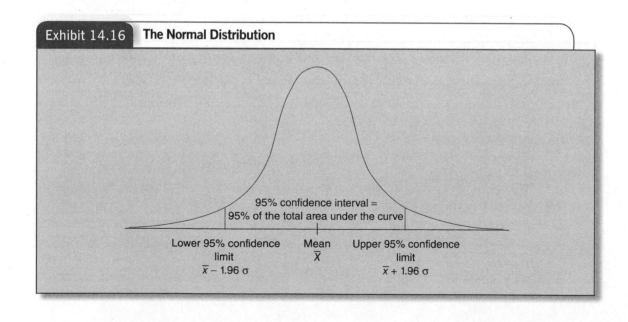

Exhibit 14.16 The Normal Distribution

95% confidence interval =
95% of the total area under the curve

Lower 95% confidence
limit
$\overline{x} - 1.96\ \sigma$

Mean
$\overline{X}$

Upper 95% confidence
limit
$\overline{x} + 1.96\ \sigma$

between plus and minus 1 standard deviation from the distribution's mean, and 95% of the cases will lie between 1.96 standard deviations above and below the mean.

The correspondence of the standard deviation to the normal distribution enables us to infer how confident we can be that the mean (or some other statistic) of a population sampled randomly is within a certain range of the sample mean. This is the logic behind calculating confidence intervals around the mean. Confidence intervals (see Chapter 5) indicate how confident we can be based on our particular random sample that the value of some statistic in the population falls within a particular range.

🔲 Describing Relationships Among Variables

Univariate distributions are useful, but they do not tell us how variables are related to each other. To establish a causal effect your first task is to determine whether there is an association between the independent and dependent variables (see Chapter 6). In this section, we describe how researchers start to examine these relationships.

Most data analyses focus on relationships among variables. The aim of many analyses is to test hypotheses about relationships among variables, while in some analyses the primary purpose is to describe or explore relationships. For each of these purposes, we must examine the association among two or more variables. **Cross-tabulation** is one of the simplest methods for doing so. A cross-tabulation displays the distribution of one variable for each category of another variable; it can also be termed a *bivariate distribution*. You can also display the association between two variables in a graph; we see an example in this section.

Exhibit 14.17 displays the cross-tabulation of self-reported health by education so that we can test the hypothesis that perceived health increases with education. The table is first presented with frequencies and then again with percentages. The cells of the table are defined by combinations of row and column values. Each

> **Cross-tabulation** In the simplest case, a bivariate (two-variable) distribution, showing the distribution of one variable for each category of another variable; can also be elaborated using three or more variables.
>
> **Marginal distributions** The summary distributions in the margins of a cross-tabulation that correspond to the frequency distribution of the row variable and the column variable.

cell represents cases with a unique combination of values of the two variables, corresponding to that particular row and column. The **marginal distributions** of the table are on the right (the row marginals) and underneath (the column marginals). These are just the frequency distributions for the two variables (in number of cases, percentages, or both), considered separately. In Exhibit 14.17, the column marginals are for the categories of education; the row marginals are for the distribution of health.

The first table in Exhibit 14.17 shows the number of cases with each combination of values of health and education. It is hard to look at the table in this form and determine whether there is a relationship between the two variables. We need to convert the cell frequencies into percentages, as in the second table in Exhibit 14.17. This table presents the data as percentages within the categories of the independent variable (the column variable, in this case). In other words, the cell frequencies have been converted into percentages of the column totals (the *n* in each column). For example, the number of people with less than a high school degree who felt in excellent health is 15 out of 108, or 13.9%. Because the cell frequencies have been converted to percentages of the column totals, the numbers add up to 100 in each column, but not across the rows. Note carefully: You must always calculate percentages within levels of the independent variable. In this example, we wanted to know if people with less education report poor health.

To read the percentage table, compare the percentage distribution of health across the columns, starting with the lowest educational category (in the left column). There is a strong association. As education increases, the percentage in excellent and very good health also rises, from about 29% of those with less than a high school degree (rounding added values 13.9 + 14.8 in the first two cells in the first column) up to 65% of those with a college degree (rounding added values 32 + 32.8 in the first two cells in the last column). This result is consistent with the hypothesis.

When the data in a table are percentages, usually just the percentages in each cell should be presented, not the number of cases in each cell. Include 100% at the bottom of each column (if the independent variable is the column variable)

Exhibit 14.17	Cross-Tabulation of Health by Education

Highest Grade Completed: Cell Counts				
Health	<High School	High School	College	Total
Excellent	15	121	168	304
Very Good	16	198	172	386
Good	46	214	134	394
Fair or Poor	31	79	51	161
Total (n)	108	612	525	1245
Highest Grade Completed: Percentages				
Health	<High School	High School	College	Total
Excellent	13.9	19.8	32.0	24.4
Very Good	14.8	32.4	32.8	31.0
Good	42.6	35.0	25.5	31.6
Fair or Poor	28.7	12.9	9.7	12.9
Total (n)[a]	100.0	100.1	100.0	99.9
	(108)	(612)	(525)	(1245)

Source: General Social Survey, National Opinion Research Center, 2014.

Gamma = .283 ($p < .001$).

[a] Due to rounding error, some percentages add up to 99.9% or 100.1%.

to indicate that the percentages add up to 100, as well as the base number (n) for each column (in parentheses). If the percentages add up to 99 or 101 due to rounding error, just indicate so in a footnote.

There is no requirement that the independent variable always be the column variable, although consistency within a report or paper is a must. If the independent variable is the row variable, we compute percentages based on the table's row totals (the n in each row), so the percentages add up to 100 across the rows.

Graphing Association

Graphs provide an efficient tool for summarizing relationships among variables. Exhibit 14.18 displays the relationship between age and poverty in graphic form. It shows that the percentage of the population whose income is below the official poverty line is highest among the youngest age cohorts (0 to 17 years old and 18 to 24 years).

A **scatterplot** is used to display the relationship between two continuous variables. Exhibit 14.19 displays the relationship between test scores and the number of hours studied. The dependent variable, test score, is placed on the y-axis while the independent variable, hours studied, is found on the x-axis. Visually, it appears that the distribution of responses confirms the expected relationship.

Scatterplot A graph of individual response to two continuous variables.

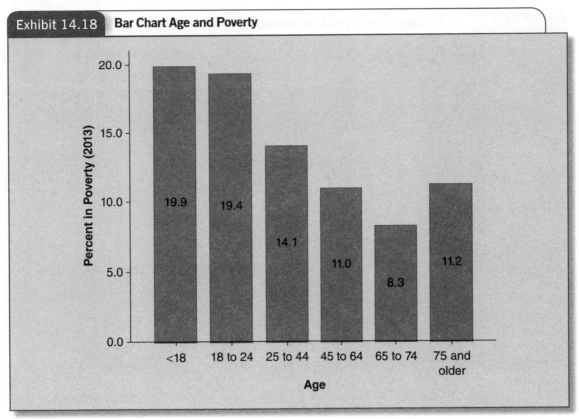

| Exhibit 14.18 | **Bar Chart Age and Poverty** |

Source: U.S. Census Bureau, Current Population Survey, Annual Social and Economic Supplement, CPS Table Creator, 2014.

Describing Association

A cross-tabulation table reveals four aspects of the association between two variables:

- *Existence.* Do the percentage distributions vary at all between categories of the independent variable?
- *Strength.* How much do the percentage distributions vary between categories of the independent variable?
- *Direction.* For quantitative variables, do values on the dependent variable tend to increase or decrease with an increase in value on the independent variable?
- *Pattern.* For quantitative variables, are changes in the percentage distribution of the dependent variable fairly regular (simply increasing or decreasing), or do they vary (perhaps increasing, then decreasing, or perhaps gradually increasing and then rapidly increasing)?

In Exhibit 14.17, an association exists; it is moderately strong (the difference in percentages between the first and last columns is about 15 percentage points), and the direction of association between perceived health and education is positive. The pattern in this table is close to what is termed monotonic. In a monotonic relationship, the value of cases consistently increases (or decreases) on one variable as the value of cases increases on the other variable. Monotonic is often defined a bit less strictly, with the idea being that as the value of cases on one variable increases (or decreases), the value of cases on the other variable tends to increase (or decrease) and at least does not change direction. This describes

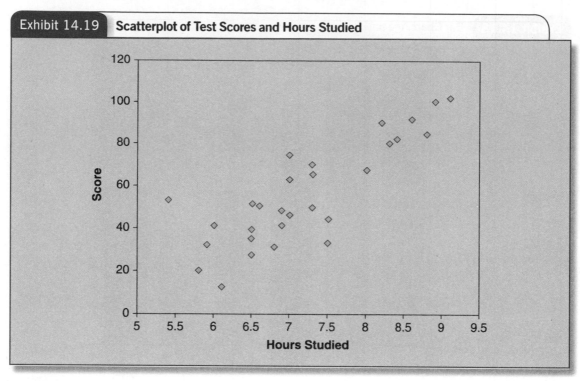

Exhibit 14.19 Scatterplot of Test Scores and Hours Studied

Correlation: .837.

the relationship between health and education: Self-reported health increases as education increases, with shifts in the direction of better health in the columns after the first.

Evaluating Association

When you read research reports and journal articles, you will find that social work researchers usually make decisions about the existence and strength of association on the basis of more statistics than just a single cross-tabulation. A **measure of association** is a type of descriptive statistic used to summarize the strength of an association. There are many measures of association, some of which are appropriate for variables measured at particular levels. One popular measure of association in cross-tabular analyses with variables measured at the ordinal level is gamma. As with many measures of association, the possible values of gamma vary from –1, meaning the variables are perfectly associated in an inverse direction; to 0, meaning there is no association of the type that gamma measures; to +1, meaning there is a perfect positive association of the type that gamma measures. In Exhibit 14.17, the gamma is .283, suggesting there is a moderate positive relationship between education and perceived health.

> **Measure of association** A type of descriptive statistic that summarizes the strength of an association. See also *association*.
>
> **Correlation coefficient** A statistic summarizing the strength of a relationship between two continuous variables.

The strength of a relationship for ratio variables can be determined using a **correlation coefficient** such as Pearson's *r*. The correlation coefficient can range from –1 to +1. Similar to gamma, the closer the correlation is to zero, the weaker the relationship; a correlation of +1 reflects a perfect positive relationship, while –1 reflects a perfect inverse relationship. In Exhibit 14.19, the correlation coefficient is .837, suggesting that there is a strong positive relationship between test scores and hours studied.

Note that the appropriate measure depends on the level of measurement of each of the variables. You may remember these measures of association from a statistics course.

Statistic	Minimum Level of Measurment
Phi	Nominal, both dichotomous
Cramer's *V*	Nominal, one dichotomous
Gamma	Ordinal
Spearman's Rho	Ordinal
Pearson's *r*	Both interval
Eta	One interval, one nominal with three or more categories
Point biserial	One interval, one dichotomous

🏛 Implications for Evidence-Based Practice

The effectiveness of a particular intervention is usually tested with statistical models beyond those we have described to this point. Even if it appears that there is a relationship between two variables that is consistent with the researcher's hypothesis, the association may have been due to chance—such are the vagaries of sampling on a random basis (of course, the problem is even worse if the sample is not random). Therefore, researchers perform tests of their hypotheses using *inferential statistics* to determine whether it is likely that an association exists in the larger population from which the sample was drawn. Inferential statistics include many different bivariate statistical tests (tests of the relationship of two variables) and multivariate statistical tests (tests of the relationship of three or more variables), which we do not describe here (see *Reviewing Inferential Statistics* on the text's study website, www.sagepub.com/engelprsw4e). It is these tests that enable practitioners to conclude that the effectiveness of an intervention is not just a function of chance.

Choosing a Statistical Test

There are many different statistical methods to test hypotheses. It is common for a researcher to start the analysis of an independent and a dependent variable with a **bivariate statistical test** (such as the chi-square test, paired *t* test, or independent samples *t* test). Bivariate statistics test the relationship between two variables. A **multivariate statistical test** is used when the analyst tests the relation of several independent variables with a dependent variable; these tests allow the analyst to test an independent

> **Bivariate statistical tests** Statistical tests of the relationship between two variables.
>
> **Multivariate statistical tests** Statistical tests involving two or more independent variables.

variable while controlling for the effects of other independent variables on the dependent variable. For example, we could test separately the relationship of education and health and marital status and health using bivariate tests. But we could test the relationship of education on health holding marital status constant and the relationship of marital status on health holding education constant using a multivariate test. It is not unusual to identify statistically significant relationships using bivariate statistic tests that are no longer statistically significant when the effects of other variables are controlled in a multivariate statistical test.

Different statistical tests depend on the level of measurement of the variables. For example

- The chi-square test requires the independent and dependent variable to be nominal measures.

- The independent student *t*-test requires that the independent variable be nominal and dichotomous and the dependent variable be at least an interval measure.

- The paired-samples *t*-test reports changes in a single group at two points in time; the dependent variable must be at least an interval measure.

- ANOVA (Analysis of Variance) is used when the independent variable is nominal and has at least three categories and the dependent variable is measured at the interval or ratio level.

- A bivariate regression analysis requires that both the independent and dependent variables must be at least interval measures.

The level of measurement of independent and dependent variables also influences the choice of multivariate tests.

Discussing each of these tests is beyond the focus of this book, and many of you have already taken a class in statistics. For those of you interested in a review, we have placed the chapter *Reviewing Inferential Statistics* on the text's study website, www.sagepub.com/engelprsw4e. To read most statistical reports and to conduct more sophisticated analyses of social data, you have to extend your statistical knowledge.

Hypothesis Testing and Statistical Significance

Quantitative findings that a practice method is effective rely on the analyst's ability to demonstrate that a relationship between two variables—an intervention and its effect or a comparison between two interventions and their effects on an outcome—is statistically significant. **Statistical significance** means that an association is not likely to be due to chance. Statistical significance answers the question: Does the treatment work? In other words, statistical significance is used to test the null hypothesis of no relationship versus the predicted relationship found in the alternative hypothesis.

> **Statistical significance** The mathematical likelihood that an association is due to chance, judged by a criterion set by the analyst (e.g., the probability of an association is due to chance is less than 5 out of 100 or $p < .05$)

> **Effect size:** A standardized measure of association; it may be the difference between the mean of the experimental group and the mean of the comparison group on the dependent variable, adjusted for the average variability in the two groups.

Researchers may also calculate **effect size**, which refers to the strength of the relationship between the independent and dependent variable. Effect size answers the practical questions: How much impact does the treatment have? and Is the effect small or large? There are a variety of different measures of effect size. Because effect size and statistical tests are answering two different questions, it is not uncommon in social work research for a finding to achieve statistical significance yet to involve a rather small effect size.

To assess statistical significance, researchers typically set a criterion often called the *alpha* level (α) or *p* value—the probability level that will be used to evaluate statistical significance. The *alpha* level is usually set by the researcher prior to the analysis, while the *p* value is the probability level often computed by statistical software packages. It is conventional in statistics to use an alpha level of .05, that is, to avoid concluding that an association exists in the population from which the sample was drawn unless the probability that the association was due to chance is less than 5%. In other words, a statistician normally will not conclude that an association exists between two variables unless he or she can be at least 95% confident that the association was not due to chance.

Note that we have emphasized that the analyst "feels reasonably confident" that the association is "not likely to be due to chance" when there is a statistically significant relationship. There is still a degree of doubt since statistical testing is based on probability, which means that whatever we conclude, it is possible we could be wrong. As we described in Chapter 5, when we draw a sample from a population, we have no guarantee that the sample is truly representative; rather, we are confident it is representative within some degree of error. Because the conclusion made from statistical testing is based on probability, it is possible to make the wrong conclusion. For example, we can test the relationship between the number of hours studied and student scores on examinations. The *null hypothesis* is that there is no relationship in the population, whereas the *alternative hypothesis* suggests that there is a relationship. With our sample of students, we find a statistically significant relationship and so we are 95% sure that a relationship exists in the population. Yet note: There still remains a 5% possibility that we have reached the wrong conclusion. We have to consider the possibility that we have concluded that there is a relationship based on our one sample, but in fact there is no relationship between the two variables in the population we sampled.

This type of error, called **Type I error**, threatens our ability to conclude that there is an association (see Exhibit 14.20). Type I error is easy to calculate as it is equal to the *alpha* level you chose as a criterion for statistical significance or the *p* value produced as part of an analysis computed by statistical software. A *p* value less than .03 means that there is less than a 3% chance of Type I error of wrongfully rejecting the null hypothesis.

> **Type I error** Error that occurs when there is evidence of a statistical relationship between two variables based on the sample, but in fact, there is no relationship between the two variables.

Type I error is influenced by the effect of the intervention or the strength of the relationship between an independent variable and a dependent variable. The greater the effect or impact of the intervention, the more likely the effect will be significant. Smaller effects or weaker relationships are less likely to provide statistically significant results.

Type I error is also influenced by sample size. A small sample is less likely to produce a statistically significant result for a relationship of any given strength. However, larger sample sizes are likely to find statistically significant relationships even when the strength of the relationship is weak. You may remember from Chapter 5 that sampling error decreases as sample size increases. For this same reason, an association is less likely to appear on the basis of chance in a larger sample than in a smaller sample. In a table with more than 1,000 cases, the odds of a chance association are often low indeed. For example, with our table based on 1,245 cases, the probability that the association between education and health (Exhibit 14.17) was due to chance was less than 1 in 1,000 ($p < .001$). The association in that table was only moderate, as indicated by a gamma of .283. Even rather weak associations can be statistically significant with such a large random sample, which means that the analyst must be careful not to assume that just because a statistically significant association exists, it is therefore important. In other words, in a large sample an association may be statistically significant, but still be too weak to be substantively significant (B. Thompson, 2002).

Type I error is not the only wrong conclusion that we can make. Let's return to the test of the relationship between the number of hours studied and examination scores. In our sample, we find that there is not a statistically significant relationship and conclude that the number of hours studied is unrelated to the examination scores. But we have to consider the possibility that we have concluded that there is no relationship based on our one sample, but in fact there is a relationship between the two variables in the population we sampled. This is referred to as **Type II error** and is summarized by *beta* (β; see Exhibit 14.20).

Type I and Type II errors are particularly important because finding an association between two variables is a necessary condition to establish causality. The problem that researchers encounter is that the risk of making Type I and Type II errors cannot be completely eliminated. When a researcher chooses an *alpha* level of .05, it means that the researcher is willing to accept a 5% chance of concluding

> **Type II error** Error that occurs when there is no evidence of a statistical relationship between two variables based on the sample, but in fact, the two variables are related.

Exhibit 14.20 **Type I and Type II Error**

In the Sample	In the Population	
	The groups differ	The groups do not differ
The groups differ by a statistically significant amount, so the researcher *Rejects the Null Hypothesis*	*The researcher's decision is* **CORRECT**	*The researcher has made a* **Type I Error** (α)
The groups do not differ by a statistically significant amount, so the researcher *Fails to Reject the Null Hypothesis*	*The researcher has made a* **Type II Error** (β)	*The researcher's decision is* **CORRECT**

that there is a relationship in a particular sample when there is no relationship in the population. The researcher could reduce Type I error by making it more difficult to find a statistically significant relationship: setting an *alpha* level of .01, which means that the researcher is willing to accept only a 1% chance of finding that there is a relationship when there is none in the population. By doing this, the likelihood of Type I error is reduced.

By minimizing Type I error, however, the researcher has increased the probability of Type II error. By making it less likely that we will falsely conclude that there is a relationship in the population, we have made it more likely that we will falsely conclude from sample data that there is no relationship when there is a relationship in the population.

Which type of error should be minimized? There is no easy answer to that question. It depends on the level of risk associated with concluding that there is a relationship when there is none (Type I error) or concluding that there is no relationship when there is a relationship (Type II error). For example, you might need to assess the risk or consequence of using an intervention shown to be effective in a research study that is really not effective (Type I error) versus the consequence of not using an intervention found to be ineffective in a research study (Type II error) when it really is effective. Statisticians normally focus on the risk of Type I error, to minimize the risk that they say that there is a relationship (that the favored hypothesis is supported) when there is not a relationship.

Statistical power analysis (see Chapter 5) is a tool used by researchers to determine the sample size necessary to detect an effect of specific size for a particular *alpha* level. Statistical power analysis is also used to determine Type II error for a sample of specific size, effect size, and the level of statistical significance.

Therefore, it is important to keep Type I error and Type II error in mind as you weigh the evidence about the effectiveness of a particular intervention from the research articles you read or the research that you conduct. What is the probability that these errors may explain the findings? Is the sample size so big that even trivial effects are statistically significant? It is through replication that researchers try to reduce doubts generated by the potential for Type I and Type II errors.

▣ Quantitative Data Analysis in a Diverse Society

One of the major concerns for intervention research is to have valid results that cut across population groups. Without such evidence, it is possible that we are offering interventions that will have limited impact on population subgroups.

Regardless of the group design used, ideally there should be sufficient numbers of specific ethnic groups or women to analyze their findings separately (Burlew, Feaster, Brecht, & Hubbard, 2009). Yet, as we noted in Chapter 7, there have been few mental health intervention studies with sufficient numbers of ethnic minorities and/or women included to do separate analyses (Mak et al., 2007; Miranda et al., 2003; Santiago & Miranda, 2014). Thus, the recruitment of diverse populations is crucial.

A second problem is that even when there is sufficient representation across groups, the study lacks separate analyses. José Szapocznik, Guillermo Prado, Ann Kathleen Burlew, Robert Williams, and Daniel Santisteban (2007) used the following criteria to identify substance abuse intervention research for Hispanic and African American youth published from 1985 to 2006: "(a) randomized controlled trials, (b) adolescents ages 12–17, and (c) primarily African American or Hispanic (i.e., 70% or greater) or reported separate results for either African Americans or Hispanics" (p. 83). They found only 12 studies; 10 focused on prevention and 2 on treatment. And none of the studies did a separate analysis for adolescent girls.

A third problem occurs when researchers do between-group comparisons. Many analyses involve comparing the means or average scores for each group; remember, the mean is just a summary of all the scores—it does not reflect the diversity of scores within each group. Ann Kathleen Burlew and her colleagues (2009, p. 37) note the following limitations with race-group comparisons:

1. It ignores within-group differences for each ethnic group. Such a strategy assumes that each group is homogeneous, yet this is not the case.

2. Both the presence and absence of mean score group differences may lead to wrong conclusions. The absence of group differences may lead to the premature combining of the groups; there may be relationships to other

variables that might be missed. The presence of mean score differences may lead the researcher to attribute too much meaning to the finding and may contribute to ethnic stereotyping.

3. The results may be misleading if the measures are not equivalent for each group. In Chapter 4, we discussed in detail the importance of having equivalent measures.

4. Intervention research samples tend to be convenience samples and therefore may not be representative of the broader population. Participants in treatment studies may differ from nonparticipants with the same presenting problem.

These comments apply to other diverse groups as well.

For between-group comparison studies to be useful, you need to go beyond just the statistical finding that one group does better than the other group. Is it something about the treatment? The treatment process? Other demographic differences? Cultural sensitivity? Understanding what causes group differences can improve practice.

Within-group analyses are useful as they offer researchers the opportunity to examine the diversity of scores within the group. For example, researchers can look at demographic differences within the group that might be related to the findings, or they can look at other factors (e.g., family-related variables) that might impact the findings (Burlew et al., 2009).

Therefore, a necessary step is to simply recognize the importance of doing within-group analyses. The other necessary step is to recruit and retain a sufficiently large sample to be able to do the analyses. Even with a small sample, researchers can compute an effect size (Burlew et al., 2009).

🖩 Ethical Issues: Avoiding Misleading Findings

Using statistics ethically means, first and foremost, being honest and open. Findings should be reported honestly, and researchers should be open about the thinking that guided their decision to use particular statistics. It is possible to distort social reality with statistics, and it is unethical to do so knowingly even when the error is due more to carelessness than deceptive intent.

When we summarize a distribution in a single number, even in two numbers, we are losing much information. Taken separately, neither central tendency nor variation alone tells us about the other characteristic of the distribution (central tendency or variation). So reports using measures of central tendency should normally also include measures of variation. Also, we should inspect the shape of any distribution for which we report summary statistics to ensure that the summary statistics do not mislead us (or anyone else) because of an unusual degree of skewness.

It is possible to mislead those who read statistical reports by choosing summary statistics that accentuate a particular feature of a distribution. Imagine an unscrupulous realtor trying to convince a prospective home buyer in Town B that it is a community with high property values when it actually has a positively skewed distribution of property values (see Exhibit 14.21). The realtor compares the mean price of homes in Town B to that for Town A (one with a homogeneous mid-priced set of homes) and therefore makes Town B look much better. In truth, the higher mean in Town B reflects a skewed, lopsided distribution of property values; most residents own small, cheap homes. A median would provide a better basis for comparison.

It is possible to distort the shape of a distribution by ignoring some of the guidelines for constructing graphs and frequency distributions. Whenever you need to group data in a frequency distribution or graph, you can reduce the potential for problems by inspecting the ungrouped distributions and then using a grouping procedure that does not distort the distribution's basic shape. When you create graphs, be sure to consider how the axes you choose may change the distribution's apparent shape.

Finally, when the data analyst begins to examine relationships among variables in some real data, social work research becomes most exciting. The moment of truth, it would seem, has arrived. Either the hypotheses are supported or they are not. But, in fact, this is also a time to proceed with caution and to evaluate the analyses of others with even more caution. Once large data sets are entered into a computer, it becomes easy to check out a great many relationships; when relationships are examined among three or more variables at a time, the possibilities become almost endless.

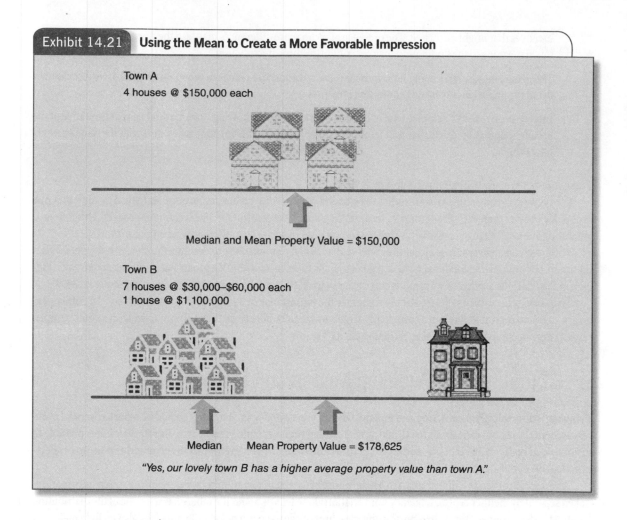

Exhibit 14.21   Using the Mean to Create a More Favorable Impression

Town A
4 houses @ $150,000 each

Median and Mean Property Value = $150,000

Town B
7 houses @ $30,000–$60,000 each
1 house @ $1,100,000

Median   Mean Property Value = $178,625

"Yes, our lovely town B has a higher average property value than town A."

However, this range of possibilities presents a great hazard for data analysis. It becomes tempting to search around in the data until something interesting emerges. Rejected hypotheses are forgotten in favor of highlighting what's going on in the data. It's not wrong to examine data for unanticipated relationships; the problem is that inevitably some relationships between variables will appear just on the basis of chance association alone. If you search hard and long enough, it will be possible to come up with something that really means nothing.

A reasonable balance must be struck between deductive data analysis to test hypotheses and inductive analysis to explore patterns in a data set. Hypotheses formulated in advance of data collection (*a priori*) must be tested as they were originally stated; any further analyses of these hypotheses (*post hoc*) that involve a more exploratory strategy must be so labeled in research reports. *Post hoc* analyses must use a more stringent level of significance to compensate for the increased possibility of finding results through chance, that is, making a Type I error. Unanticipated findings do not need to be ignored, but they must be reported as such. Subsequent researchers can try to test deductively the ideas generated by these explorations.

🏛 Conclusion

This chapter has demonstrated how a researcher can describe social phenomena, identify relationships among them, explore the reasons for these relationships, and test hypotheses about them. Statistics provide a remarkably useful tool for developing our understanding of the social world, a tool that we can use to both test our ideas and generate new ones.

Unfortunately, to the uninitiated, the use of statistics can seem to end debate right there—you can't argue with the numbers. You now know better than that. The numbers will be worthless if the methods used to generate the data are not valid, and the numbers will be misleading if they are not used appropriately, taking into account the type of data to which they are applied. Even assuming valid methods and proper use of statistics, there's one more critical step because the numbers do not speak for themselves. Ultimately, it is how we interpret and report the numbers that determines their usefulness.

Key Terms

Bar chart   376
Bivariate statistical test   395
Central tendency   375
Check coding   374
Correlation
   coefficient   394
Cross-tabulation   391
Descriptive statistics   370
Frequency distribution   378
Frequency polygon   376

Histograms   376
Interquartile range   389
Marginal distribution   391
Mean   384
Measure of association   394
Median   384
Mode   383
Multivariate statistical test   395
Normal distribution   390
Quartile   389

Range   388
Scatterplot   392
Skewness   375
Standard deviation   390
Statistical significance   396
Type I error   397
Type II error   397
Variance   389

Highlights

- Data must be prepared for analysis. This includes assigning unique identification numbers to each respondent, reviewing the forms for unclear responses, creating codes for open-ended questions, and developing a codebook.

- Data entry options include direct collection of data through a computer, use of scannable data entry forms, and use of data entry software. All data should be cleaned during the data entry process.

- Bar charts, histograms, and frequency polygons are useful for describing the shape of distributions. Care must be taken with graphic displays to avoid distorting a distribution's apparent shape.

- Frequency distributions display variation in a form that can be easily inspected and described. Values should be grouped in frequency distributions in a way that does not alter the shape of the distribution. Following several guidelines can reduce the risk of problems.

- Summary statistics are often used to describe the central tendency and variability of distributions. The appropriateness of the mode, the mean, and the median vary with a variable's level

of measurement, the distribution's shape, and the purpose of the summary.

- The variance and standard deviation summarize variability around the mean. The interquartile range is usually preferable to the range to indicate the interval spanned by cases, due to the effect of outliers on the range. The degree of skewness of a distribution is usually described in words rather than with a summary statistic.

- Some of the data in many reports can be displayed more efficiently by using combined and compressed statistical displays.

- Cross-tabulations should normally be percentaged within the categories of the independent variable. A cross-tabulation can be used to determine the existence, strength, direction, and pattern of an association.

- Inferential statistics are used to test hypotheses. There is the potential for Type I and Type II errors.

- Honesty and openness are the key ethical principles that should guide data summaries.

Discussion Questions

1. Consider the relationship between education and health that is presented in Exhibit 14.17. What third variables do you think should be controlled in the analysis to better understand the relationship? How might social policies be affected by finding out that this relationship was due to differences in eligibility to Medicaid rather than to educational differences?

2. Why does level of measurement matter in statistics?

3. What considerations come into play in choosing the mean versus the median?

4. Why should you be concerned with Type I and Type II errors?

Practice Exercises

1. Examine a quantitative study from a social work journal. Does the author provide summary statistics? Does the researcher provide information about the association among different variables? What statistics does the researcher use? Do these statistics support the researcher's hypotheses?

Web Exercise

1. Go to the Current Population Survey Table Creator (http://www.census.gov/cps/data/cpstablecreator.html). Use the CPS table creator to create frequency tables and cross-tabulations on variables of interest to you.

2. Do an online search for information on a social work subject that interests you. How much of the information you find relies on statistics as a tool for understanding the subject? How do statistics allow researchers to test their ideas about the subject and generate new ideas? Write your findings in a brief report, referring to the websites that you used.

Developing a Research Proposal

1. Develop a plan to prepare your data for analysis. How will you assure the quality of the data?

2. Describe how you would analyze and present your data. What descriptive or inferential procedures would you use?

A Question of Ethics

1. Review the frequency distributions and graphs in this chapter. Change one of these data displays so that you are "lying with statistics."

CHAPTER 15

Reporting Research

Y ou learned in Chapter 2 that research is a circular process, so it is appropriate that we end this book where we began. The stage of reporting research results is also the point at which the need for new research is identi- fied. It is the time when, so to speak, the rubber hits the road—when we have to make our research make sense to others. To whom will our research be addressed? How should we present our results to them? Will we seek to influence how our research report is used?

The primary goals of this chapter are to help you develop worthwhile reports for any research project you conduct and guide you in evaluating reports produced by others. We begin by discussing how to write research proposals as they also lay the groundwork for final research reports. We talk about the frustrations of writing and describe different approaches to writing for peer-reviewed journals and applied research reports. We conclude with the implications of each of these sections for our diverse society and the ethical issues you should consider.

回 Beginning With a Research Proposal

If you have been completing the Developing a Research Proposal exercises at the end of each chapter, you are already familiar with the process of proposal writing. Nonetheless, we suggest that you read through this section carefully as an overview of the entire process.

Most research proposals will have at least six sections (Locke, Spirduso, & Silverman, 2007):

1. *An introductory statement of the research problem.* Clarify what it is that you are interested in studying and the significance of the research problem.

2. *A literature review.* Explain your issue in greater detail and how you plan to build on what has already been reported in the literature on your topic.

3. *A methodological plan.* Detail the methods you will use, including the design, sample, measures and variables, and data collection procedures.

4. *An ethics statement.* Identify human subjects issues in the research and establish how you will respond to them in an ethical fashion.

5. *A statement of limitations.* Review weaknesses of the proposed research, and present plans for minimizing their consequences.

6. *A budget.* Present a careful listing of the anticipated costs.

If your research proposal will be reviewed competitively, it must present a compelling rationale for funding. It is not possible to overstate the importance of the research problem that you propose to study (see Chapter 2). If you pro- pose to test a hypothesis, be sure that it is one for which there are plausible alternatives.

When you develop a research proposal, it helps to ask yourself a series of questions like those posed in Exhibit 15.1. It is easy to omit important details and to avoid being self-critical while rushing to put a proposal together. However, it is even more painful to have a proposal rejected (or to receive a poor score). It is better to make sure the proposal covers what it should and confronts the tough issues that reviewers (or your professor) will be sure to spot.

The questions in Exhibit 15.1 can serve as a map to preceding chapters in this book and as a checklist of decisions that must be made throughout any research project. The questions are organized in five sections, each concluding with a *checkpoint* at which you should consider whether to proceed with the research as planned, modify the plans, or stop the project altogether. The sequential ordering of these questions obscures a bit the way in which they should be answered: not as single questions, one at a time, but as a unit—first as five separate stages, then as a whole. You may change your answers to earlier questions on the basis of your answers to later questions.

Exhibit 15.1 **Decisions in Research**

PROBLEM FORMULATION (Chapters 1–2)

1. Developing a research question
2. Assessing researchability of the problem
3. Consulting prior research
4. Relating to social theory
5. Choosing an approach: Deductive? Inductive? Descriptive?
6. Reviewing research guidelines

Checkpoint 1

Alternatives:

- Continue as planned.
- Modify the plan.
- STOP Abandon the plan.

RESEARCH VALIDITY (Chapters 4–6)

7. Establishing measurement validity:

   - How are concepts defined?
   - Choose a measurement strategy.
   - Assess available measures or develop new measures
   - What evidence of reliability and validity is available or can be collected?
   - Are the measures appropriate for use with the study population?

8. Establishing generalizability:

   $ Was a representative sample used?
   $ Are the findings applicable to particular subgroups?
   $ Does the population sampled correspond to the population of interest?

9. Establishing causality:

   $ What is the possibility of experimental or statistical controls?
   $ How to assess the causal mechanism?
   $ Consider the causal process

10. Data required: Longitudinal or cross-sectional?
11. Units of analysis: Individuals, families, groups, organizations, or communities?
12. What are the major possible sources of causal invalidity?

Checkpoint 2

Alternatives:

- Continue as planned.
- Modify the plan.
- STOP Abandon the plan.

RESEARCH DESIGN (Chapters 7–10, 12)

13. Choosing a research design and procedures:

    Experimental? Single-subject? Survey? Participant observation? Multiple methods?

(Continued)

Exhibit 15.1 (Continued)

14. Specifying the research plan: Type of surveys, observations, etc.
15. Secondary analysis? Availability of suitable data sets?
16. Causal approach: Idiographic or nomothetic?
17. Assessing ethical concerns

Checkpoint 3

Alternatives:

- Continue as planned.
- Modify the plan.
- STOP Abandon the plan.

DATA ANALYSIS (Chapters 10 and 14)

18. Choosing a statistical approach:

  - Statistics and graphs for describing data
  - Identifying relationships between variables
  - Deciding about statistical controls
  - Testing for interaction effects
  - Evaluating inferences from sample data to the population

Checkpoint 4

Alternatives:

- Continue as planned.
- Modify the plan.
- STOP Abandon the plan.

REVIEWING, PROPOSING, REPORTING RESEARCH (Chapters 2, 3, and 15)

19. Clarifying research goals
20. Identifying the intended audience
21. Searching the literature and the Web
22. Organizing the text
23. Reviewing ethical and practical constraints

Checkpoint 5

Alternatives:

- Continue as planned.
- Modify the plan.
- STOP Abandon the plan.

Case Study: Treating Substance Abuse

Particular academic departments, grant committees, and funding agencies will have more specific proposal requirements. As an example, Exhibit 15.2 lists the primary required sections of the Research Plan for proposals to the National Institutes of Health (NIH) together with excerpts from a proposal Russell Schutt submitted in this format to the National Institute of Mental Health (NIMH) with colleagues from the University of Massachusetts Medical School. The Research Plan is limited by NIH guidelines to 25 pages. It must be preceded by an abstract (which we have

| Exhibit 15.2 | A Grant Proposal to the National Institute of Mental Health |

Relapse Prevention for Homeless Dually Diagnosed

Abstract

This project will test the efficacy of shelter-based treatment that integrates Psychosocial Rehabilitation with Relapse Prevention techniques adapted for homeless mentally ill persons who abuse substances. Two hundred and fifty homeless persons, meeting . . . criteria for substance abuse and severe and persistent mental disorder, will be recruited from two shelters and then randomly assigned to either an experimental treatment condition . . . or to a control condition.

For one year, at the rate of three two-hour sessions per week, the treatment group (n=125) will participate for the first six months in "enhanced" Psychosocial Rehabilitation . . . , followed by six months of Relapse Prevention training. . . . The control group will participate in a Standard Treatment condition (currently comprised of a twelve-step peer-help program along with counseling offered at all shelters). . . .

Outcome measures include substance abuse, housing placement and residential stability, social support, service utilization, level of distress. . . . The integrity of the experimental design will be monitored through a process analysis. Tests for the hypothesized treatment effects . . . will be supplemented with analyses to evaluate the direct and indirect effects of subject characteristics and to identify interactions between subject characteristics and treatment condition . . . .

Research Plan

1. Specific Aims

The research demonstration project will determine whether an integrated clinical shelter-based treatment intervention can improve health and well-being among homeless persons who abuse alcohol and/or drugs and who are seriously and persistently ill—the so-called "dually diagnosed.". . . We aim to identify the specific attitudes and behaviors that are most affected by the integrated psychosocial rehabilitation/relapse prevention treatment, and thus to help guide future service interventions.

2. Background and Significance

Relapse is the most common outcome in treating the chronically mentally ill, including the homeless. . . . Reviews of the clinical and empirical literature published to date indicate that treatment interventions based on social learning experiences are associated with more favorable outcomes than treatment interventions based on more traditional forms of psychotherapy and/or chemotherapy. . . . However, few tests of the efficacy of such interventions have been reported for homeless samples.

3. Progress Report/Preliminary Studies

Four areas of Dr. Schutt's research help to lay the foundation for the research demonstration project here proposed. . . . The 1990 survey in Boston shelters measured substance abuse with selected ASI [Addiction Severity Index] questions. . . . About half of the respondents evidenced a substance abuse problem.

Just over one-quarter of respondents had ever been treated for a mental health problem. . . . At least three-quarters were interested in help with each of the problems mentioned other than substance abuse. Since help with benefits, housing, and AIDS prevention will each be provided to all study participants in the proposed research demonstration project, we project that this should increase the rate of participation and retention in the study. . . . Results [from co-investigator Dr. Walter Penk's research]. . . indicate that trainers were more successful in engaging the dually diagnosed in Relapse Prevention techniques. . . .

4. Research Design and Methods

Study Sample.

Recruitment. The study will recruit 350 clients beginning in month 4 of the study and running through month 28 for study entry. The span of treatment is 12 months and is followed by 12 months of follow-up. . . .

Study Criteria.

Those volunteering to participate will be screened and declared eligible for the study based upon the following characteristics:

(Continued)

Exhibit 15.2 (Continued)

1. Determination that subject is homeless using criteria operationally defined by one of the accepted definitions summarized by . . .

Attrition.

Subject enrollment, treatment engagement, and subject retention each represent potentially significant challenges to study integrity and have been given special attention in all phases of the project. Techniques have been developed to address engagement and retention and are described in detail. . . .

Research Procedures.

All clients referred to the participating shelters will be screened for basic study criteria. . . . Once assessment is completed, subjects who volunteer are then randomly assigned to one of two treatment conditions—RPST or Standard Treatment. . . .

Research Variables and Measures.

Measures for this study . . . are of three kinds: subject selection, measures, process measures, an outcome measures. . . .

5. Human Subjects

Potential risks to subjects are minor. . . . Acute problems identified . . . can be quickly referred to appropriate interventions. Participation in the project is voluntary, and all subjects retain the option to withdraw. . . at any time, without any impact on their access to shelter care or services regularly offered by the shelters. Confidentiality of subjects is guaranteed. . . . [They have] . . . an opportunity to learn new ways of dealing with symptoms of substance abuse and mental illness.

Source: Schutt et al. (1992).

---

excerpted), a proposed budget, biographical sketches of project personnel, and a discussion of the available resources for the project. Appendixes may include research instruments, prior publications by the authors, and findings from related work.

As you can see from the excerpt in Exhibit 15.2, the proposal was to study the efficacy of a particular treatment approach for homeless mentally ill people who abuse substances. The proposal included a procedure for recruiting subjects in two cities, randomly assigning half of the subjects to a recently developed treatment program, and measuring a range of outcomes. The NIMH review committee (composed of social scientists with expertise in substance abuse treatment and research methodology) approved the project for funding but did not rate it highly enough so that it actually was awarded funds. (It often takes several resubmissions before even a worthwhile proposal is funded.) The committee members recognized the proposal's strengths, but also identified several problems that they believed had to be overcome before the proposal could be funded. The problems were primarily methodological, stemming from the difficulties associated with providing services to, and conducting research on, this particular segment of the homeless population:

> The proposal has many strengths including the specially tailored intervention derived from psychiatric rehabilitation technology developed by Liberman and his associates and relapse prevention methods adapted from Marlatt. . . . [T]his fully documented treatment . . . greatly facilitates the generalizability and transportability of study findings. . . . The investigative team is excellent . . . also attuned to the difficulties entailed in studying this target group. . . . While these strengths recommend the proposal, . . . eligibility criteria for

inclusion of subjects in the study are somewhat ambiguous. . . . This volunteer procedure could substantially under-represent important components of the shelter population. . . . The projected time frame for recruiting subjects . . . also seems unrealistic for a three-year effort. . . . Several factors in the research design seem to mitigate against maximum participation and retention.

If you get the impression that researchers cannot afford to leave any stone unturned in working through procedures in an NIMH proposal, you are right. It is very difficult to convince a government agency that a research project is worth investing a lot of money in (the proposal requested about $2 million). That is as it should be: Your tax dollars should be used only for research that has a high likelihood of yielding findings that are valid and useful. But even when you are proposing a smaller project to a more generous funding source—or even presenting a proposal to your professor— you should scrutinize the proposal carefully before submission and ask others to comment on it. Other people will often think of issues you neglected to consider, and you should allow yourself time to think about these issues and to reread and redraft the proposal. Besides, you will get no credit for having thrown together a proposal as best you could in the face of an impossible submission deadline.

Let's review the issues identified in Exhibit 15.1 as they relate to the NIMH relapse prevention proposal (Schutt et al., 1992). The research question concerned the effectiveness of a particular type of substance abuse treatment in a shelter for homeless people—an evaluation research question [Question 1]. This problem certainly was suitable for social research, and it was one that could have been handled for the requested amount of money [2]. Prior research demonstrated clearly that the proposed treatment had potential and also that it had not previously been tried with homeless people [3]. The treatment approach was connected to psychosocial rehabilitation theory [4], and given prior work in this area, a deductive, hypothesis-testing stance was appropriate [5]. The review of research guidelines continued up to the point of submission and appeared to take each into account [6]. So it seemed reasonable to continue to develop the proposal [Checkpoint 1].

Measures were to include direct questions, observations by field researchers, and laboratory tests of substance abuse [7]. The proposal's primary weakness was in the area of generalizability [8]. Schutt and colleagues (1992) proposed to sample people in only two homeless shelters in two cities and could offer only weak incentives to encourage potential participants to start and stay in the study. The review committee believed that these procedures might result in an unrepresentative group of initial volunteers beginning the treatment and perhaps an even less representative group continuing through the entire program. The problem was well suited to a randomized experimental design [9] and was best addressed with longitudinal data [10] involving individuals [11]. The randomized design controlled for selection bias and endogenous change, but external events, treatment contamination, and treatment misidentification were potential sources of causal invalidity [12]. Clearly, the proposal should have been modified with some additional recruitment and retention strategies—although it may be that the research could not actually be carried out without some major modification of the research question [Checkpoint 2].

A randomized experimental design was preferable because this was to be a treatment-outcome study, but the researchers did include a field research component so that they could evaluate treatment implementation [13, 14]. Because the effectiveness of the proposed treatment strategy had not been studied before among homeless people, the researchers could not propose doing a secondary data analysis or meta-analysis [15]. They sought only to investigate causation from a nomothetic perspective, without attempting to show how the particular experiences of each participant may have led to the outcome [16]. Because participation in the study was to be voluntary and everyone received *something* for participation, the research design seemed ethical; it was also approved by the University of Massachusetts Medical School's Institutional Review Board and by the state mental health agency's human subjects committee [17]. Schutt and colleagues planned several statistical tests, but the review committee remarked that they should have been more specific [18]. The goal was to use the research as the basis for several academic articles, and the investigators expected that the funding agency would also require a report for general distribution [19, 20]. The research literature had been carefully reviewed [21], but as is typical in most research proposals, Schutt and colleagues did not develop research reporting plans any further [22, 23].

▣ Writing Can Be Frustrating!

Perfectionism is the voice of the oppressor; the enemy of the people. It will keep you cramped and insane your whole life and it is the main obstacle between you and a . . . first draft.

Lamott (1994, p. 28)

We often hear from students, "It is impossible to know where to begin," or "I have a hard time getting started." We have said it ourselves! To this we say, "Begin wherever you are most comfortable, but begin early." You do not have to start with the introduction; start in the methods section if you prefer. The main point is to begin somewhere and then keep typing, keep typing, and keep typing! It is easier to rewrite a paper than it is to write the first draft. The fine art of writing is really in the rewriting.

A successful report must be well organized and clearly written. Getting to such a product is a difficult but not impossible goal. Consider the following principles formulated by experienced writers:

- Respect the complexity of the task and do not expect to write a polished draft in a linear fashion. Your thinking will develop as you write, causing you to reorganize and rewrite.

- Leave enough time for dead ends, restarts, revisions, and accept the fact that you will discard much of what you write.

- Write as fast as you comfortably can. Do not worry about spelling, grammar, and so on until you are polishing things up.

- Ask anyone whom you trust for their reactions to what you have written.

- Write as you go along, so you have notes and report segments drafted even before you focus on writing the report. (Booth, Colomb, & Williams, 1995, pp. 150–151)

To start, create a timeline for the completion of the various tasks that you will need to accomplish. Such tasks may include making an outline and a title; finding, updating, and reviewing literature; writing the first draft; getting feedback and revising drafts; preparing tables and figures; writing an abstract; proofing the text; and checking references.

Once you have a timeline, you should start with an outline, but neither the report's organization nor the first written draft should be considered fixed. As you write, you will get new ideas about how to organize the report. Try them out. As you review the first draft, you will see many ways to improve your writing. Focus particularly on how to shorten and clarify your statements. Make sure each paragraph concerns only one topic. Remember the golden rule of good writing: Writing is revising!

Another useful tip is reverse outlining. After you have written a first complete draft, outline it on a paragraph-by-paragraph basis, ignoring the actual section headings you used. See if the paper you wrote actually fits the outline you planned.

If you began with a research proposal, you have a head start. Your proposal already has many of the components you will need for the final report. Reorganize and edit your proposal on your computer and ask the opinions of friends, teachers, and some of those to whom your report will be directed before turning in the final report. And most important, leave yourself enough time so that you *can* revise, several times if possible, before turning in the final draft.

So begin to write. Different types of reports typically pose different problems. Writing for your professor will be guided, in part, by the expectations of your professor. Thesis and dissertation writers have to meet the requirements of different committee members but can benefit greatly from the areas of expertise represented on a typical committee. Writing journal articles and applied reports tends to follow a common pattern of content.

▣ Reporting Results

The goal of research is not just to discover something, but to communicate that discovery to a larger audience: other social workers, consumer groups, government officials, your teachers, and the public—perhaps several of these

Research In the NEWS

For Further Thought **?**

HOW MUCH SHOULD SOCIAL SCIENTISTS REPORT

Marco Bertamini and Marcus Munafo discuss a trend emerging in research that puts a premium on shorter scholarly articles. Although "bite-size" science enables more work to be published and is supposedly easier to read, Bertamini and Munafo raise a number of concerns. They are also uneasy that articles are only written when the researchers are successful. Are scientific failures worth reporting?

1. Is shorter better? What are the advantages and disadvantages of compressing research reports into a few pages or even a paragraph or two? Do social scientists need to balance the type of audience and the complexity of the research in deciding how much to report?

2. "Scientific failures" in this sense mean research projects in which no association is found between variables that were hypothesized to be related, or more generally that do not lead to some interesting finding. It is hard to get a paper reporting such null results published because the tendency is to think that the researcher did not "find" anything. Do you see any hazards if social scientists do not publish such failures?

Source: Bertamini and Munafo (2012, p. SR12).

audiences. Whatever the study's particular outcome, if the intended audience for the research comprehends the results and learns from them, the research can be judged a success. If the intended audience does not learn about the study's results, the research should be judged a failure—no matter how expensive the research or how sophisticated its design.

Peer-Reviewed Journal Articles

Writing for academic journals is perhaps the toughest form of writing because articles are submitted to several other experts in your field for careful review—anonymously, with most journals—prior to acceptance for publication. This process is called *peer review*. Perhaps it would not be such an arduous process if so many academic journals did not have exceedingly high rejection rates as well as turnaround times for reviews that are, at best, several months. Even the articles that the reviewers judge initially to be the best are most often given a "revise and resubmit" after the first review and then are evaluated all over again after the revisions are concluded.

But there are some important benefits of journal article procedures. First and foremost is the identification of areas in need of improvement, as the author's eyes are replaced by those of previously uninvolved subject matter experts and methodologists. A good journal editor makes sure that he or she has a list of many different types of experts available for reviewing whatever types of articles the journal is likely to receive. There is a parallel benefit for the author: It is always beneficial to review criticisms of your own work by people who know the field well. It can be a painful and time-consuming process, but the entire field moves forward as researchers continually critique and suggest improvements in each other's research reports.

While there are slight variations in style across journals, there are typically seven standard sections in a journal article in addition to the title page:

1. *Abstract.* This concise summary of the research report describes the research problem, the sample, the method, and the findings. Though the abstract appears first, it is likely to be the last section that you write. Journals generally set limits on the number of words allowed in the abstract.

2. *Introduction.* The body of a paper should open with an introduction that presents the specific problem under study, highlights why such a study is important, and describes the research strategy. The first paragraph should identify the issue and should be written to engage the reader's attention (Kliewer, 2005). The next paragraph should convince the reader about the need for the research. The last paragraph should include the specific research question, and sometimes you might specify how the study was conducted. Therefore, a good intro-duction answers *what*, *why*, and *how* in a few paragraphs.

3. *Literature Review* (or Background). Discuss the literature relevant to the topic, including what is known about the particular topic and what has been left unanswered. At the end of this section, you are ready to conceptually define your variables and formally state your hypotheses.

4. *Method.* Describe in detail how the study was carried out. Although the headings used by journals may differ, the methods section generally includes information about the following:

   • *Research design.* The specific research design is described. The actual details differ by design. For example, a study about the effectiveness of an intervention might include the timing of when data were collected (e.g., measures were collected 1 week before the intervention and 1 week after the end of the intervention), the length of the intervention, whether there was a comparison group, and how participants were assigned to each of the groups. In contrast, a cross-sectional survey of community residents requires less information, and the researcher might just describe the length of time allocated to data collection.

   • *Setting.* The location of the study or where data are collected may be identified.

   • *Participants* or *sample.* This section describes the criteria used to include participants in the study. There may be information about the sampling frame, how the sample was recruited, and how the sample was selected based on the inclusion criteria. The overall sample size is described as well as the actual response rate or participation rate.

   • *Measures.* This section identifies the key independent and dependent variables and provides the variables' nominal and operational definitions. If scales are used, you should provide information about the reliability and validity of the measures and demonstrate that the measures are appropriate for the population with whom they are used. If relevant, variable categories should be specified, and for scales, the possible range of scores and the interpretation of the scores should be provided, including subscale scores. In intervention studies, there should be a clear description of the intervention.

   • *Data collection.* There should be a brief description of the data collection process, such as self-administered mail questionnaire, face-to-face interview, or observation. You will find that some studies will describe the arrangements made to collect data, particularly with interviews.

   • *Statistical methods* or *data analysis.* Description of how data are analyzed. This description enables the reader to evaluate the appropriateness of your methods and the reliability and validity of your results. It enables other researchers to replicate your study.

5. *Result* or *Findings.* Summarize the results of the statistical or qualitative analyses performed on the data. Generally, you start by describing the study participants, including their characteristics and the summary statistics for each of the variables. If the study requires several data collection points, you should report attrition rates as well as a brief description and analysis of comparing participants who remained in the study with participants who left the study. The remaining paragraphs focus on the study's results and tend to be organized around the study's specific objectives or hypotheses. Tables and figures should be used to display and summarize findings. They should be simple and clear, allowing the reader to easily grasp the contents (Kliewer, 2005).

6. *Discussion.* The discussion often begins with a one-paragraph summary of the key findings. The next several sections should focus on your evaluation and interpretation of the findings, taking into account the purpose of the study. This should include your interpretation, in light of the current state of knowledge as reflected in the literature review and the utility of the findings for social work practice and/or policy. Next, you should address the limitations of the study, the generalizability of the findings, and directions for future research. In the last paragraph you summarize the findings and their implications, unless the journal style includes a conclusion or summary section (Kliewer, 2005).

7. *References.* All citations in the manuscript must appear in the reference list, and all references must be cited in the text.

Exhibit 15.3 presents the outline of the sections in an academic journal article with some illustrative quotes.

Reporting Qualitative Research

The requirements for good research reports are similar in many respects for quantitative and qualitative research projects. Every research report should include good writing, a clear statement of the research question, an integrated literature review, and presentation of key findings with related discussion, conclusions, and limitations. However, the differences between qualitative and quantitative research approaches mean that it is often desirable for research reports based on qualitative research to diverge in some respects from those reflecting quantitative research.

Reports based on qualitative research should be enriched in each section with elements that reflect the more holistic and reflexive approach of qualitative projects. The introduction should include background about the development of the researcher's interest in the topic, while the literature review should include some attention to the types of particular qualitative methods used in prior research. The methodology section should describe how the researcher gained access to the setting or individuals studied and the approach used to manage relations with research participants. The presentation of findings may be organized into sections reflecting different themes identified in interviews or observational sessions. Quotes from participants or from observational notes should be selected to illustrate these themes, although qualitative research reports differ in the extent to which the researcher presents findings in summary form or uses direct quotes to identify key issues. The findings section may alternate between presentation of quotes or observations about the research participants, the researcher's interpretations of this material, and some commentary on how the researcher reacted in the setting, although some qualitative researchers will limit their discussion of their reactions to the discussion section.

Mixed Methods Research

Reports on mixed-methods projects should include subsections in the methods section that introduce each method, and then distinguish findings from qualitative and quantitative analyses in the findings section. Some mixed-methods research reports may present analyses that use both qualitative and quantitative data in yet another subsection, while others may just discuss implications of analyses of each type for the overall conclusions in the discussions and conclusions sections (Dahlberg, Wittink, & Gallo, 2010). However, findings based on each method are presented; it is important to consider explicitly both the ways in which the specific methods affected findings obtained with those methods and also to discuss the implications of findings obtained using both methods for the overall study conclusions.

Applied Research Reports

Applied research reports are written for a different audience than the professional social scientists and students who read academic journals. Typically, an applied report is written with a wide audience of potential users in mind and to

Exhibit 15.3 Sections in a Journal Article

Engel, R. J., Rosen, D., Weaver, A., & Soska, T. (2010). Raising the stakes: Assessing the human service response to the advent of a casino. *Journal of Gambling Studies, 26,* 611–622.

ABSTRACT

This article reports the findings of one county's human service network's readiness to treat gambling related problems in anticipation of the opening of a new casino. Using a cross-sectional survey design, questionnaires were mailed to executive directors of all mental health, family counseling, drug and alcohol, and faith-based, addiction-related organizations in the county (N = 248); 137 (55.2%) agency directors responded to the questionnaire . . .

INTRODUCTION

Over the last two decades, the worldwide proliferation of legalized gambling has led to remarkable growth in the number, visibility, and accessibility of gambling (Shaffer et al. 2006). Many state and local governments throughout the United States have legalized casino gambling as a strategy to increase revenue in lieu of raising taxes, and promote economic development. (p. 611).

Human Service Concerns

Organizational Readiness

METHODS

Setting and Background

Sample

Questionnaire

Procedures

RESULTS

Agency Activities

Staff Training

Screening

Treatment

Referral

Staff

Why Agencies Did Not Engage in These Activities

Staff Training

Screening

Treatment

Referral

Public Awareness/Education

DISCUSSION

. . . , agencies with a primary focus on mental health and/or substance abuse were more likely to be engaged in at least one problem gambling activity than agencies primarily providing other services. . . . Yet, because of the link between problem gambling and other social problems these other social service providers are likely to have clients . . . and can play a crucial service delivery role by identifying potential problem gamblers. . . (pp. 619–620).

LIMITATIONS

CONCLUSION

REFERENCES

serve multiple purposes. Often both the audience and purpose are established by the agency or other organization that funded the research project on which the report is based. Sometimes the researcher may use the report to provide a broad descriptive overview of study findings that will be presented more succinctly in a subsequent journal article. In either case, an applied report typically provides much more information about a research project than does a journal article and relies primarily on descriptive statistics, rather than only those statistics useful for the specific hypothesis tests that are likely to be the primary focus of a journal article.

Exhibit 15.4 outlines the sections in one applied research report. This particular report was funded by a foundation with a particular focus on mental health–related issues and was intended to inform a range of stakeholders and interested parties, including public officials, agency directors, and other foundations. The goals of the report were to provide description and recommendations. The body of the report presents findings on the extent to describe the capacity of social service providers to address gambling-related problems through assessment, referral, and treatment, and the barriers they faced in addressing such concerns. The recommendation section details specific recommendations for consideration with supporting summary evidence from the study. There was a single appendix locating Gamblers Anonymous sites on a county map.

You can see some of the differences in emphasis between a journal article and an applied research report by comparing Exhibits 15.3 and 15.4. The journal article came about as a result of the study done to do the applied research report. The journal article required an extensive background or literature review section and had a greater focus on methodological issues. The journal article's discussion focused on general lessons learned given the state of the literature that would have broad application. The discussion in the applied research report focused on

---

Exhibit 15.4   Sections in an Applied Report

Engel, R. J., Rosen, D., & Soska, T. January 2008. *Raising the stakes: Assessing Allegheny County's human service response capacity to the social impact of casino gambling.* Pittsburgh, PA: The University of Pittsburgh.

EXECUTIVE SUMMARY (p. 3)

The goal of the current project is to evaluate the capacity of human service providers in Allegheny County to engage in prevention and treatment efforts for gambling-related problems.

. . .

There is still time to take action before the casino's scheduled opening in May 2009 . . . to prepare for the anticipated increased demand for services related to gambling problems and to develop a coordinated and effective prevention, intervention, and treatment strategy.

OVERVIEW (pp. 4–5)

PROJECT DESIGN (pp. 5–6)

METHODOLOGY AND INTERPRETATION OF RESULTS (p. 6)

FINDINGS (pp. 7–14)

Overview of participating agencies

Activities to Prepare for Problem Gambling

Problem-Gambling Related Services

Public Awareness

RECOMMENDATIONS (pp. 15–16)

ACKNOWLEDGEMENTS (Frontend)

Advisory Committee

GAMBLERS ANONYMOUS MEETINGS (Backend)

recommendations specific to the county in which the study was conducted and were targeted to the needs of the stakeholders concerned about the topic.

▣ Poster Presentations

A poster is a very effective way to communicate the results of your research. You may find that you are required to develop a poster to report findings for a class or you have the opportunity to present a poster at a professional or scientific conference. In fact, many research studies that will be eventually published in peer-reviewed scientific journals are first presented in what are referred to as poster sessions at regional or national conferences.

A poster includes many of the same sections that are found in a published article: title, abstract (sometimes), introduction, methods, results, discussion, and references. However, a poster contains much less detail than an article. Text is often presented in bulleted lists of major points while findings may include bulleted texts but are often displayed in graphs and tables. It is common to find that a poster dimension ranges from 3 to 4 feet high and 5 to 6 feet wide.

While layouts may vary, you should think of your poster as comprising columns in which you are placing information. People tend to view information from left to right so the topics on a poster tend to move from left (e.g., introduction and methods) to the right (implications and literature review). People also tend to move their eyes from the top to bottom of the poster, so the most important information should be at the top and through the entire center of the poster ("Creating a Poster," n.d.). The least important information should be at the far right and bottom as this is generally the last area viewers will look, if they view it all.

Exhibit 15.5 displays a poster presented at a national gambling conference. The poster was split into three columns with the center column containing the most important information, including the research question (purpose) and the findings (with special boxes highlighting the most important findings). The far left column included the introduction and methods while the last column included implications and references. Notice that the least important information the presenters were trying to convey, the references, falls in the lower, far right corner.

▣ Implications for Evidence-Based Practice

One of the primary means by which social work practitioners learn about effective social work interventions is through the dissemination efforts of social work researchers and program evaluators. While journal articles and applied research reports differ in emphasis as well as the degree of review and scrutiny they each receive, both are vehicles to inform social work practice. It is likely that many of the readings used in your classes come from journal articles and applied research reports.

Just because a study is published does not mean that changes to practice come quickly. Therapeutic techniques for which there is a large body of evidence such as Cognitive-Behavioral Therapy took time to be widely utilized by practitioners in some fields of practice (Dattilio & Epstein, 2005; Probst, 2008). In health care, it takes an average of 17 years for clinical research findings to be used in practice (Balas & Boren, 2000; Institute of Medicine, 2001). Even when the findings are applied, interventions may be less effective when tried in real-word settings as the clients are more diverse with more diverse symptoms, less compliant than participants in research studies, and are seen by clinicians with a range of expertise (U.S. Department of Health and Human Services, 1999).

Such findings have led to the emergence of *translational research* or efforts to both speed the use of research findings into treatment settings and to make that research more relevant to these settings (Brekke, Ell, & Palinkas, 2009). The translational challenge is to figure out how to apply evidence-based findings to human service agencies with different community and organizational contexts than the setting for the research, with clients who may have different characteristics and motivations than the research participants and professionals whose incentive for following the intervention exactly is different than those testing the intervention (Probst, 2008). Therefore, there is a need for researchers to study how to best implement evidence-based findings in human service agencies (Brekke et al., 2009).

Exhibit 15.5   Example of a Poster

University of Pittsburgh

Older Adult Methadone Clients & Problem Gambling

Jody Bechtold, LCSW, NCGC, Rafael J. Engel, PhD, & Daniel Rosen, PhD

NIDA Grant #5 K08 DA021570-02

Purpose: This study examines the relationship of various demographic charateristics, mood, other substance use, health, and cognitive status to potential problem gambling.

Introduction. Addressing gambling-related problems for older adults in methadone treatment presents many challenges including gambling pathology, other substance abuse, comorbid mood disorders, and chronic medical conditions. Treatment engagement is impacted by age-related declines in health, social support, financial well-being, and neurocognitive ability. Previous research examining problem or pathological gambling and methadone recipients has not focused on older methadone users (Feigelman, Keinman, Lesieur, Millman, and Leeser, 1995; Ledgerwood and Downey, 2002

Sample and Methods. This availability sample included 129 Methadone clients of a methadone clinic, aged 50 and older. Th s sample is from a location located within 4 blocks of a casino in a region that experienced expanded legalized gambling in the past 5 years. Variables included:

- Demographics: age, race, gender, income, education, employment and living arrangement.
- problem Gambling: Based on responses to the Lie-Bet (Johnson et al., 1988), participants were divided into two groups, non-problem gambling (responded no to both questions) and potential problem gambling (responded yes to at least one question).
- Gambling Behaviour. Gambling activities dichotomized by "no or infrequently" and "frequently".
- Health measures. Cognitive status (Mental Status Exam), depress on (Patient Health Questionnaire-9), perceived health status, physical health, mental health, and overall health (all SF-12), current alcohol and marijuana use, and other substance use (urine screen).

Data were collected in a 1.5 hour face-to-face interview.

Findings

Lie-Bet Screen
1 in 5 endorsed at least one item (20.2%)

66% gamble "occasionally or frequently" and 1 in 4 endorsed at least one item (27.1%)

33% gamble "frequently" and 1 in 3 endorsed at least one item (32.6%)

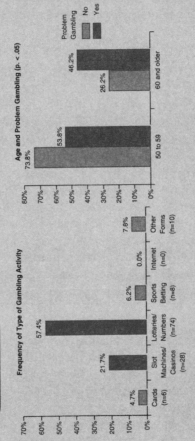

Frequency of Type of Gambling Activity

Age and Problem Gambling (p. < .05)

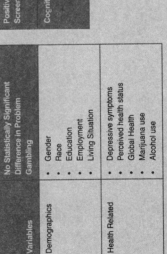

Implications for Future Research and Treatment:
Given that 20% of the sample respond positively to at least one Lie-Bet question, clinicians should be better trained to screen, assess, and treat problem gambling with older adult substances abusers. This research also calls to question whether there are more targeted interventions for specific age cohorts within the "older adult" category itself, given the differences reported between aged 50 and aged 60+. Developing and testing a problem gambling assessment (targeted to those responding positively on a Lie-Bet screen) that accounts for chronic substance misuse, specific forms of gambling and gambling behavior in older adults may yield more accurate information for developing tailored prevention and treatment interventions for older adults.

Future research should examine:

- Is problem gambling viewed as a "problem" by older adult methadone users; given the host of other issuess and addictions experienced by this group? What are the reasons older methadone users gamble and do they differ by age?
- Is there any significance to specific forms of gambling activities in older adult mathadone users?

Works Cited:

Feigelman, W. Keinman, P. H., Lesieur, H.R., Millman, R. B., Eistenstein, N., & Leesser, M. L. (1995). *Pathological gambling among methadone patients. Drug and Alcohol Dependence,* 39, 75–81.

Johnson, E. E., Hamer, R., Nora, R. M., Tan, B., Eistenstein, N., & Englehart, C. (1988). The lie/bet questionnaire for screening pathological gamblers. *Psychological Reports,* 80, 83–88.

Ledgerwood, D. M., & Downey, K.K. (2002). Relationship between problem gambling and substance use in a methadone maintenance population. *Addictive Behaviors,* 27, 483–491.

Spunt, B. (2002). Pathalogical Gambling and Substance misuse *Substance Use & Misuse,* 37, 1299–1304.

We do not mean to suggest that this challenge is so difficult that you should therefore ignore evidence-based findings. There are many examples of research findings applied to practice settings. The report summarized in Exhibit 15.4 led to a large-scale effort to train providers to address gambling-related issues. Carrilio (2001) described a process that one agency used to digest all the best evidence regarding early childhood and family intervention programs. She and her team adapted research findings regarding home visiting and center-based interventions to create a program integrating both approaches. And their experiences led them to conclude that prepackaged parenting curricula required time to process and practice the skills within a coordinated group setting.

Of course, one necessary requirement is for social work graduates to be prepared to understand, assess, and interpret research findings. Another necessary requirement is to assess how these findings might be applied to your clients and in your agency. We hope that much of what you have read in the previous chapters has prepared you to do these tasks.

▣ Social Work Research in a Diverse Society

We return to our admonition from Chapter 1—social work research is being conducted in an increasingly diverse society. It places a responsibility on researchers to develop proposals and report findings that recognize this diversity if we are to adequately address questions about the impact of interventions or to understand the nature of social problems. The findings we read about in journals or reports most often begin with formal research proposals, so writing the research proposal is part of the foundation for a successful research report. In turn, researchers are dependent on the quality of research reports when they synthesize studies to conduct meaningful meta-analyses in an attempt to clarify what works and for whom it works. So the decisions made in developing the proposal bear on reporting the findings in a single study and the synthesis of the findings of different studies.

We hope you have now learned the kinds of issues that you must consider in carrying out or evaluating research. The diversity of the populations that we study impacts all phases of the research process, whether it is the formulation of the research question, the meaning given to concepts and measurement of these concepts, the strategies used to recruit and retain participants, the kinds of categories used to classify participant characteristics, the analysis of the findings, or unique ethical concerns. These are all questions that must be addressed in the research proposal.

How the findings are reported is essential for reviewing individual studies and for conducting meta-analyses. It is not just enough to report the characteristics of the sample, such as the percentage who are female or the percentage who are African American, although this is certainly a good first step (Geller, Adams, & Carnes, 2006). To be meaningful, the analysis must account for group differences, whether by controlling for ethnicity or gender in a regression model or reporting group mean scores in intervention studies. Without these findings, it becomes more difficult for the meta-analyst to answer the "for whom" question.

You should be attentive to language and your choice of words. Some journal publication formats, such as those that use the American Psychological Association format, emphasize the use of written language that is sensitive to racial and ethnic identity, gender, age, sexual orientation, and disabilities. The goal is to eliminate sexism and ethnic bias in writing. For example, *gender* is the correct term to describe males and females as social groups. The term *sex* is the correct term to describe biological features of men and women. Nevertheless, gender pronouns can often be sexist; terms such as *he, his, man, men, mankind,* and so forth, display bias when representing both men and women.

In research reports of studies of persons with disabilities, be very mindful of the stigmatizing effects of diagnostic labels. For example, do not use the term *schizophrenic* as a noun, but rather use the phrase "a person with the diagnosis of schizophrenia." Similarly, when comparing a group of people with a diagnosis such as schizophrenia, with a control group, do not describe the control group as the "normal group." Instead, write, "We compared people with the disorder and without the disorder."

In describing people, a general rule is to refer to people in terms they prefer. Often the best policy is not to assume but rather to inquire politely and respectfully so that you will be sensitive to any terms or labels that might be offensive.

🔲 Ethical Considerations

At the time of reporting research results, the researcher's ethical duty to be honest becomes paramount. Here are some guidelines:

- *Provide an honest accounting of how the research was carried out and where the initial research design had to be changed.* Readers do not have to know about every change you made in your plans and each new idea you had, but they should be informed about major changes in hypotheses or research design. If important hypotheses were not supported, acknowledge this, rather than conveniently forgetting to mention them (Brown & Hedges, 2009)

- *Maintain a full record of the research project so that questions can be answered if they arise.* Many details will have to be omitted from all but the most comprehensive reports, but these omissions should not make it impossible to track down answers to specific questions about research procedures that may arise in the course of data analysis or presentation.

- *Avoid "lying with statistics" or using graphs to mislead.* There is a more subtle problem to be avoided, which is "cherry-picking" results to present. Many studies collect data that can be used to test many hypotheses, often with alternative measures. If many possible relationships have been examined with the data collected and only those found to yield a statistically significant result are reported, the odds of capitalizing on chance findings are multiplied. This is a major temptation in research practice that has the unfortunate result that published findings are often not replicated or do not stand up to tests over time (Lehrer, 2010).

- *Acknowledge the sponsors of the research.* This is important, in part, so that others can consider whether this sponsorship may have tempted you to bias your results in some way.

- *Thank staff who made major contributions.* This is an ethical as well as a political necessity. Let's maintain our social relations!

- *Be sure that the order of authorship for coauthored reports is discussed in advance and reflects agreed-upon principles.* Be sensitive to coauthors' needs and concerns.

Ethical research reporting should not mean ineffective reporting. You need to tell a coherent story in the report and avoid losing track of the story in a thicket of minuscule details. You do not need to report every twist and turn in the conceptualization of the research problem or the conduct of the research. But be suspicious of reports that do not seem to admit the possibility of any room for improvement. Social science is an ongoing enterprise in which one research report makes its most valuable contribution by laying the groundwork for another, more sophisticated research project. Highlight important findings in the research report, but use the research report also to point out what are likely to be the most productive directions for future researchers.

Communicating With the Public

Even following appropriate guidelines like these, however, will not prevent controversy and conflict over research on sensitive issues. Peter Rossi (1999) recounts the controversy that arose when he released a summary of findings conducted in his 1986 study of homeless people in Chicago, Illinois. In spite of important findings about the causes and effects of homelessness, media attention focused on Rossi's markedly smaller estimate of the numbers of homeless people in Chicago compared to the "guesstimates" that had been publicized by local advocacy groups. "Moral of the story: Controversy is news, to which careful empirical findings cannot be compared" (p. 2).

Does this mean that ethical researchers should avoid political controversy by sidestepping media outlets for their work? Many social scientists argue that the media offer some of the best ways to communicate the practical application of social work knowledge. Use the following principles for engaging the public through the media (Wilson, 1998, p. 438):

1. Focus on issues of national concern, issues that are high on the public agenda.

2. Develop creative and thoughtful arguments that are clearly presented and devoid of technical language.

3. Present the big picture whereby the arguments are organized and presented so that the readers can see how the various parts are interrelated.

Plagiarism

Since this is a chapter on writing reports, we would be remiss if we did not mention plagiarism. You likely have a course syllabus detailing instructor or university policies about plagiarism and specifying the penalties for violating that policy, so we know that you are aware of how serious its consequences are. It is an ongoing problem about taking work without attributing it to the author (Stephen, Young, & Calabrese, 2007) and purchasing papers (Broskoske, 2005).

You learned in Chapter 3 that maintaining professional integrity—honesty and openness in research procedures and results—is the foundation for ethical research practice. When it comes to research publications and reports, avoiding *plagiarism,* that is, presenting as one's own the ideas or words of another person or persons for academic evaluation without proper acknowledgment (Hard, Conway, & Moran, 2006). The National Association of Social Workers (2008) *Code of Ethics* states that "social workers should honestly acknowledge the work of and the contributions made by others" (Section 4.08b).

▣ Conclusion

A well-written research article or report requires (to be just a bit melodramatic) blood, sweat, and tears—and more time than you will at first anticipate. But the process of writing one will help you write the next. Also, the issues you consider, if you approach your writing critically, will be sure to improve your subsequent research projects and sharpen your evaluations of other investigators' research projects.

Good critical skills are essential when evaluating research reports, whether your own or those produced by others. There are *always* weak points in any research, even published research. It is an indication of strength, not weakness, to recognize areas where one's own research needs to be, or could have been, improved. It is really not just a question of sharpening your knives and going for the jugular. You need to be able to weigh the strengths and weaknesses of particular research results and to evaluate a study in terms of its contribution to understanding the social world—not in terms of whether it gives a definitive answer for all time.

But this is not to say that anything goes. Much research lacks one or more of the three legs of validity—measurement validity, causal validity, or generalizability—and contributes more confusion than understanding about the social world. Top journals generally maintain very high standards, partly because they have good critics in the review process and distinguished editors who make the final acceptance decisions. But some daily newspapers do a poor job of screening, and research reporting standards in many popular magazines, TV shows, and books are often abysmally poor. Keep your standards high and your view critical when reading research reports, but not so high or so critical that you turn away from studies that make tangible contributions to understanding the social world—even if they don't provide definitive answers. And don't be so intimidated by the need to maintain high standards that you shrink from taking advantage of opportunities to conduct research yourself.

The growth of social science methods from its infancy to adolescence, perhaps to young adulthood, ranks as a key intellectual accomplishment of the 20th century. Opinions about the causes and consequences of homelessness no longer need depend on the scattered impressions of individuals, criminal justice policies can be shaped by systematic evidence of their effectiveness, and changes in the distribution of poverty and wealth in populations can be identified and charted. Employee productivity, neighborhood cohesion, and societal conflict each may be linked to individual psychological processes and to international economic strains.

Of course, social work research methods are no more useful than the commitment of researchers to their proper application. Research methods, like all knowledge, can be used poorly or well, for good purposes or bad, when appropriate or not. A claim that a belief is based on research provides no extra credibility. As you have learned throughout this book, we must first learn which methods were used, how they were applied, and whether interpretations square with the evidence. Having done all that, we can enhance our efforts to improve the well-being of our clients and our communities.

Highlights

- Proposal writing should be a time for clarifying the research problem, reviewing the literature, considering the methods of implementation and data analysis, and thinking about the report that will be required. Trade-offs between different design elements should be considered and the potential for using multiple methods evaluated.

- Different types of reports typically pose different problems. Authors of student papers must be guided in part by the expectations of their professor. Thesis and dissertation writers have to meet the requirements of different committee members but can benefit greatly from the areas of expertise represented on a typical committee. Program evaluators and applied researchers are constrained by the expectations of the research sponsor. Journal articles must pass a peer review by other social scientists and often are much improved in the process.

- Research reports should include an introductory statement of the research problem; a literature review; a methodology section; a findings section with pertinent data displays; and a discussion/conclusions section that identifies the social work practice or policy implications of the findings, notes any weaknesses in the research methodology, and points out implications for future research. The report format should be modified according to the needs of a particular audience.

- All reports should be revised several times and critiqued by others before being presented in final form.

- To answer the "for whom" question, it is crucial to integrate diverse populations into research studies.

- The central ethical precept in research reporting is to be honest. This honesty should include providing a factual accounting of how the research was carried out, maintaining a full record about the project, using appropriate statistics and graphs, acknowledging the research sponsors, and being sensitive to the perspectives of coauthors.

Discussion Questions

1. List and describe the sections included in research proposals. How are the research proposal and the research report similar? How do they differ?

2. Describe the elements of successful research reporting. How does reverse outlining assist the writer? After the final draft of the article is written, how does the author find an appropriate audience?

3. Describe the similarities and differences between journal articles and applied research reports. Discuss the political and ethical considerations of research reporting in journals and in applied research.

Practice Exercises

1. Read a journal article about a social issue that interests you. Read an applied research report (these can easily be obtained online) on the same social issue focusing on the same population. Compare and contrast these two pieces.

2. Reread the journal article you chose for Practice Exercise 1. Was the research sponsored by any particular organization? If so, how might that sponsorship have influenced the reporting? How easy was the article to understand? Was the language simple

and clear, or did the author use technical jargon? Did the author include practice or policy recommendations?

3. Prepare an abstract of your research paper. Give the abstract to several students in your class, and have them edit and evaluate your work. Give the same abstract to several friends who are not students in social work. Have them also edit and evaluate your work. Compare the critiques.

Web Exercise

1. The National Academy of Sciences published a lengthy report on ethics issues in scientific research (http://www.nap.edu/openbook.php?record_id=4917). Read the report, and then summarize the information and guidelines in it.

2. Go online and find five examples of social science research projects that have been completed around the treatment of substance abuse and/or divorce and delinquency. Briefly describe each. How does each differ in its approach to reporting the research results? Who do you think the author of each is "reporting" to (i.e., who is the audience)? How do you think the predicted audience has helped to shape the author's approach to reporting the results? Be sure to note the websites where you located each of your five examples.

Developing a Research Proposal

1. Organize the proposal material you wrote for previous chapters in a logical order. Based on your research question, select the most appropriate research method as your primary method.

2. Select another research method that could add knowledge about your research question.

3. Rewrite the entire proposal, adding an introduction. Add sections that outline a budget and state the limitations of your study.

4. Think about how the study findings can be used to inform policies, service design, or practice activities. What future research might you suggest given the study findings?

5. How will the results of the study be disseminated? How will you make your findings known to the professional community?

A Question of Ethics

1. Would you recommend legal regulations about the release of research data? If so, what would those regulations be? Would they differ depending on the researcher's source of funding? Would you allow researchers exclusive access to their own data for some period of time after they have collected it?

2. Full disclosure of sources of research as well as of other medically related funding has become a major concern for medical journals. Should researchers publishing in social work journals also be required to fully disclose all sources of funding? Should full disclosure of all previous funds received by social work agencies be required in each published article? What about disclosure of any previous jobs or paid consultations with social work agencies? Write a short justification of the regulations you propose.

Appendix A

Questions to Ask About a Quantitative Research Article

1. What is the social concern under study? What is the basic research question, or problem? Try to state it in just one sentence. (Chapter 2)

2. Is the purpose of the study explanatory, evaluative, or descriptive? Did the study have more than one purpose? (Chapter 1)

3. How did the author(s) explain the importance of the research question? Is the research question relevant to social work practice and/or social welfare policy? (Chapter 2)

4. Was a theoretical framework presented? What was it? Did it seem appropriate for the research question addressed? Can you think of a different theoretical perspective that might have been used? (Chapters 1 and 2)

5. What prior literature was reviewed? Was it relevant to the research problem? To the theoretical framework? Does the literature review appear to be adequate? Are you aware of (or can you locate) any important omitted studies? Is the literature review up to date? (Chapter 2)

6. Were any hypotheses stated? Were these hypotheses justified adequately in terms of the theoretical framework? In terms of prior research? (Chapter 2)

7. What were the independent and dependent variables in the hypothesis or hypotheses? What direction of association was hypothesized? Were any other variables identified as potentially important? (Chapter 2)

8. What were the major concepts in the research? Did the author(s) provide clear and complete nominal definitions for each concept? What were the nominal definitions? Were some concepts treated as unidimensional that you think might best be thought of as multidimensional? (Chapter 4)

9. How were variables operationally defined by the author(s)? Are the operational definitions adequate? Did the instruments used and the measures of the variables seem valid and reliable? How did the author(s) attempt to establish measurement reliability and measurement validity? Could any more have been done in the study to establish measurement validity? Have the measures used in the study been evaluated in terms of reliability and validity with populations similar to the study sample? (Chapter 4)

10. Was a sample of the entire population of elements used in the study? Was a probability or nonprobability sampling method used? What specific type of sampling method was used? How was the sample recruited and selected? How large was the sample? Were women and people of color adequately represented in the sample? Did the authors think the sample was generally representative of the population from which it was drawn? Do you? How could you evaluate the likely generalizability of the findings to other populations? (Chapter 5)

11. Was the response rate or participation rate reported? Does it appear likely that those who did not respond or participate were markedly different from those who did participate? Why or why not? Did the author(s) adequately discuss this issue? (Chapters 5 and 9)

12. What were the units of analysis? Were they appropriate for the research question? If groups were the units of analysis, were any statements made at any point that are open to the ecological fallacy? If individuals were the units of analysis, were any statements made at any point suggesting reductionist reasoning? (Chapter 6)

13. Was the study design cross-sectional or longitudinal, or did it use both types of data? If the design was longitudinal, what type of longitudinal design was it? Could

the longitudinal design have been improved in any way, as by collecting panel data rather than trend data or by decreasing the dropout rate in a panel design? If cross-sectional data were used, could the research question have been addressed more effectively with longitudinal data? (Chapter 6)

14. Were any causal assertions made or implied in the hypotheses or in subsequent discussion? What approach was used to demonstrate the existence of causal effects? Were all five issues in establishing causal relationships addressed? What, if any, variables were controlled in the analysis to reduce the risk of spurious relationships? Should any other variables have been measured and controlled? (Chapter 6)

15. Was an experimental, single-subject, survey, or some other research design used? How does the author describe the design? How well was this design suited to the research question posed and the specific hypotheses tested, if any? Why do you suppose the author(s) chose this particular design? (Chapters 6–9, 12, and 13)

16. Did the design eliminate potential alternative explanations? Is so, how did the design do this? How satisfied (and why) are you with the internal validity of the conclusions? (Chapter 7)

17. What was the setting for the study? Does the setting limit the generalizability of the results to other similar settings or to the broader population? Is reactivity a problem? Are there other threats to external validity? (Chapters 1 and 7)

18. Was this an evaluation research project? If so, which type of evaluation was it? Which design alternatives did it use? (Chapter 13)

19. How were data collected? What are the advantages and disadvantages of the particular data-collection method? (Chapter 9)

20. What did the author(s) find? Are the statistical techniques used appropriate for the level of measurement of the variables? How clearly were statistical data presented and discussed? Were the results substantively important? (Chapter 14)

21. Did the author(s) adequately represent the findings in the discussion or conclusion sections? Were conclusions well grounded in the findings? Can you think of any other interpretations of the findings? (Chapter 15)

22. Compare the study to others addressing the same research question. Did the study yield additional insights? In what ways was the study design more or less adequate than the design of previous research? (Chapters 6–9, 12, and 13)

23. What additional research questions and hypotheses are suggested by the study's results? What light did the study shed on the theoretical framework used? On social work practice questions? On social policy questions? (Chapters 2 and 15)

24. How well did the study live up to the guidelines for science? Do you need additional information in any areas to evaluate the study? To replicate it? (Chapter 3)

25. Did the study seem consistent with current ethical standards? Were any trade-offs made between different ethical guidelines? Was an appropriate balance struck between adherence to ethical standards and use of the most rigorous scientific practices? (Chapter 3)

Appendix B

How to Read a Quantitative Research Article

The discussions of research articles throughout the text may provide all the guidance you need to read and critique research on your own. But reading an article in bits and pieces to learn about particular methodologies is not quite the same as reading an article in its entirety to learn what the researcher found out. The goal of this appendix is to walk you through an entire research article. Of course, this is only one article, and our walk will take different turns than a review of other articles might take, but after this review, you should feel more confident when reading other research articles on your own.

We use an article by Lani V. Jones and Lynn A. Warner (2011) on the use of a culturally appropriate group intervention designed to reduce depression and stress among African American women. This article is published in a leading journal, *Research on Social Work Practice* (volume 21, pp. 737–746). The article may be found on the study site, http://www.sagepub .com/pswr4e.

Our responses to the 25 questions listed in Appendix A follow. We indicate the chapter where the question was discussed, and after each answer, we cite the article page or pages to which we refer. You can also follow our review by reading through the article and noting our comments.

1. What is the social concern under study? What is the basic research question, or problem? Try to state it in just one sentence. (Chapter 2)

The specific concern in this study is depression and an intervention designed to treat depression among African American women. A clear statement of the research question is "This article details the efficacy of a culturally congruent group intervention aimed at enhancing psychosocial competence, while at the same time decreasing depressive symptoms and alleviating stress among Black women" (p. 737).

2. Is the purpose of the study explanatory, evaluative, or descriptive? Did the study have more than one purpose? (Chapter 1)

This is an explanatory study designed to assess the efficacy of "Claiming Your Connections" (CYC), a group intervention to treat depression.

3. How did the author(s) explain the importance of the research question? Is the research question relevant to social work practice and/or social welfare policy? (Chapter 2)

The authors noted the prevalence of health and mental health disparities. In particular, they reference the disproportionate prevalence of stress-related physical conditions. Further, they referred to research reporting that African American women are less likely to seek treatment, to be misdiagnosed, and to prematurely leave treatment. While these symptoms are due to chronic stress and lack of social support, there is evidence that "coping with structural barriers and racial bias may be a common underlying risk factor for stress-related illness" (p. 738). The authors concluded that to enhance mental health status among African American women, individual and societal stressors must be addressed in interventions and prevention. The study offers practitioners a model of a culturally appropriate intervention.

4. Was a theoretical framework presented? What was it? Did it seem appropriate for the research question addressed? Can you think of a different theoretical perspective that might have been used? (Chapters 1 and 2)

The authors provided a model, psychosocial competence, for the intervention. They noted that psychosocial competence is drawn from an ecological perspective.

Psychosocial competence is a way of "examining different patterns of human functioning that characterizes an individual's self-attitudes, world attributes and behavioral attributes" (p. 738). Next, they connected this model to practice with ethnic minority groups. They built the case that this is an appropriate perspective for social work practice.

5. What prior literature was reviewed? Was it relevant to the research problem? To the theoretical framework? Does the literature review appear to be adequate? Are you aware of (or can you locate) any important omitted studies? Is the literature review up to date? (Chapter 2)

The literature review constructs a coherent argument for the design of the particular intervention that is assessed in this study. The literature review began with reference to the nature of the problem and made a convincing argument that structural factors should be considered as risk factors to the mental and physical health of African American women (pp. 737–738). The next section provided the theoretical basis for psychosocial competence as an intervention model (p. 738). While research about psychosocial competence is referenced, no particulars are given about the studies. This section is followed by a discussion about the benefits of group interventions for African American women (pp. 738–739). Finally, the authors described the intervention, linking it to the previously described literature as well as other literature (p. 739). In general, the studies are up to date.

6. Were any hypotheses stated? Were these hypotheses justified adequately in terms of the theoretical framework? In terms of prior research? (Chapter 2)

Three hypotheses were stated with each addressing the impact of the group intervention (Claiming Your Connections) on different variables (p. 739). The authors based the hypotheses on one previous study and a solid framework of theoretical and practice literature.

7. What were the independent and dependent variables in the hypothesis or hypotheses? What direction of association was hypothesized? Were any other variables identified as potentially important? (Chapter 2)

The independent variable in each hypothesis was participation or nonparticipation in the CYC program. The dependent variables included: depressive symptoms, stress, external locus of control, and coping. The hypotheses were written with clear direction of association (p. 739).

8. What were the major concepts in the research? Did the author(s) provide clear and complete nominal definitions for each concept? What were the nominal definitions? Were some concepts treated as unidimensional that you think might best be thought of as multidimensional? (Chapter 4)

There are several key concepts in this study: culturally congruent, psychosocial competence, group intervention model, depressive symptoms, and stress. The authors provided nominal definitions for some terms. Culturally congruent means that a "treatment uses techniques and didactic content that addresses specific aspects of Black women's cultural experience" (p. 737). Psychosocial competence is "characterized by a person's active quest for 'personal effectiveness and mastery over his or her environment' (Tyler, 1991, cited in Jones & Warner, 2011, p.738)" and includes self-efficacy (locus of control), trust, social support, and behavioral attributes (p. 741). CYC was defined as a "manualized cognitive-based group treatment protocol . . . utilizing a psychosocial competence framework" and "treatment that teaches participants to recognize and examine their negative thoughts, beliefs, and feelings" (p. 739). Depressive symptoms included positive affect, depressive affect, somatic symptoms, and interpersonal relations (p. 740). Stress was defined as perceived stress or the degree to which life is seen as uncontrollable, unpredictable, and overwhelming (p. 741).

9. How were variables operationally defined by the author(s)? Are the operational definitions adequate? Did the instruments used and the measures of the variables seem valid and reliable? How did the author(s) attempt to establish measurement reliability and measurement validity? Could any more have been done in the study to establish measurement validity? Have the measures used in the study been evaluated in terms of reliability and validity with populations similar to the study sample? (Chapter 4)

The authors provided information about the CYC program intervention, including the number of sessions, length of sessions, session modules, session activities, and outcomes expected from the sessions (pp. 739–740). Depressive symptoms were measured with the Center for Epidemiologic Studies Depression Scale and a reliability coefficient is provided as well as a reference to known groups' validity (p. 740). Depressive symptoms were also measured using the Beck Depression Inventory-II; the authors reported internal consistency and criterion validity from other studies (p. 741).

Perceived stress was measured by the Perceived Stress Scale with reports of internal consistency, test-retest reliability, predictive validity, and discriminant validity. Locus of control was measured using the Internal-External Locus of Control Scale; the authors state the psychometric properties of the scale have been "well documented" (p. 741). Active coping was measured using the Behavioral Attributes of Psychosocial Competence Scale-Condensed Form; the authors note that reliability and validity have been assessed across ethnic groups.

The authors do report how each scale measures the concept. Based on the information in the methods section, it is not clear whether depression or depressive symptoms are measured as the authors refer to both total scores and cut-off scores; the problem is they do not specify what they are using. Another problem is the lack of clarity of some measures' psychometric properties as well as whether such assessments have been done with African American women.

10. Was a sample of the entire population of elements used in the study? Was a probability or nonprobability sampling method used? What specific type of sampling method was used? How was the sample recruited and selected? How large was the sample? Were women and people of color adequately represented in the sample? Did the authors think the sample was generally representative of the population from which it was drawn? Do you? How could you evaluate the likely generalizability of the findings to other populations? (Chapter 5)

The authors used a purposive sample. Potential participants had to self-identify as Black, female, and having difficulty coping with stresses of daily living; in addition, potential participants were not receiving mental health services at least from agency sites used for recruitment (p. 740). Flyers and mailings were used to recruit potential participants. From the attained pool, the first 20 women at each study site confirming their interest in the study became study subjects for that site. All participants were African American women. There is no generalizability to the target population.

11. Was the response rate or participation rate reported? Does it appear likely that those who did not respond or participate were markedly different from those who did participate? Why or why not? Did the author(s) adequately discuss this issue? (Chapters 5 and 9)

The participation rate was not reported. Although we know that the study was limited to 60 participants, 2 of whom withdrew, leaving 58. We do not know how many people were willing to participate in the study or refused to be considered as potential participants.

12. What were the units of analysis? Were they appropriate for the research question? If groups were the units of analysis, were any statements made at any point that are open to the ecological fallacy? If individuals were the units of analysis, were any statements made at any point suggesting reductionist reasoning? (Chapter 6)

The unit of analysis was the individual. There are no statements suggesting reductionist reasoning.

13. Was the study design cross-sectional or longitudinal, or did it use both types of data? If the design was longitudinal, what type of longitudinal design was it? Could the longitudinal design have been improved in any way, as by collecting panel data rather than trend data or by decreasing the dropout rate in a panel design? If cross-sectional data were used, could the research question have been addressed more effectively with longitudinal data? (Chapter 6)

Because of the experimental design used in this study, we are less concerned with this question.

14. Were any causal assertions made or implied in the hypotheses or in subsequent discussion? What approach was used to demonstrate the existence of causal effects? Were all five issues in establishing causal relationships addressed? What, if any, variables were controlled in the analysis to reduce the risk of spurious relationships? Should any other variables have been measured and controlled? (Chapter 6)

The causal assertion is that the CYC intervention will reduce depressive symptoms, stress, external locus of control will decrease, and active coping will increase. The experimental design used in this study is sufficient to establish an association, time order, and internal validity. Mechanism and context were not addressed.

15. Was an experimental, single-subject, survey, or some other research design used? How does the author describe the design? How well was this design suited to the research question posed and the specific hypotheses tested, if any? Why do you suppose the author(s) chose this particular design? (Chapters 6 – 9, 12, and 13)

The authors used a true experimental design, the Pretest-Posttest Control Group design. The design included random assignment, a control group, and pretests and posttests (p. 739). This design provides a plausible method to evaluate the effects of the intervention and answer the hypotheses identifying the proposed effects of the intervention.

16. Did the design eliminate potential alternative explanations? If so, how did the design do this? How satisfied (and why) are you with the internal validity of the conclusions? (Chapter 7)

To eliminate alternative explanations, the authors used random assignment into the two groups. To start, they created a list of participants. They randomly chose one participant to be in the treatment group. Starting with this participant, the authors next chose every other participant on the list to be in the treatment group. They described this process as a systematic random sample method to allocate participants (p. 740). They compared the demographic composition of the experimental and control groups and found only two differences; these characteristics were included in subsequent analyses and were found to have no impact on the study's findings (p. 741). Attrition was not a problem as of the 60 initial participants only two withdrew and that occurred prior to the start of the intervention.

17. What was the setting for the study? Does the setting limit the generalizability of the results to other similar settings or to the broader population? Is reactivity a problem? Are there other threats to external validity? (Chapters 1 and 7)

The study was conducted at three sites in a Northeastern United States metropolitan area: a women-only shelter, a residential drug treatment program, and a health center located in a Northeastern metropolitan area (p. 739). The settings might limit generalizability to a broader population, but having three distinctly different settings is an advantage of the study. The effect of site was considered in the analysis (p. 742). Because there was no subsequent follow-up it is not clear the extent to which the effects are due to reactivity to the experimental conditions. The primary investigator was a co-facilitator to ensure the proper use of the manualized intervention, suggesting that without proper training others might not be able to as adequately implement the treatment program; there may have been a social desirability effect (p. 740).

18. Was this an evaluation research project? If so, which type of evaluation was it? Which design alternatives did it use? (Chapter 13)

This is a research project.

19. How were data collected? What are the advantages and disadvantages of the particular data-collection method? (Chapter 9)

The research team administered the screening interviews and the standardized instruments (p. 740). The screenings were interviews, but it is not clear how the data for the pretest and posttest instruments were collected, that is, by an interview or completed by the participant.

20. What did the author(s) find? Are the statistical techniques used appropriate for the level of measurement of the variables? How clearly were statistical data presented and discussed? Were the results substantively important? (Chapter 14)

The authors found that the CYC group reported fewer depressive symptoms and perceived stress from pretest to posttest while there were no changes in depressive symptoms and perceived stress for the control group. There were no differences in locus of control or active coping. Site location had no impact on the findings as there was no interaction (p. 742). The authors used Multivariate Analysis of Variance (MANOVA), an appropriate analysis for this type of research. The article presents understandable tables and the authors use straightforward language to describe their findings.

21. Did the author(s) adequately represent the findings in the discussion or conclusion sections? Were conclusions well grounded in the findings? Can you think of any other interpretations of the findings? (Chapter 15)

The findings are briefly discussed in Discussion and Applications to Practice (p. 743) and are linked back to the literature review. The discussion is focused on the finding that the intervention is effective in treating depression and stress. The authors appropriately apply other literature to suggest why they did not find improvements in active coping or locus of control.

22. Compare the study to others addressing the same research question. Did the study yield additional

insights? In what ways was the study design more or less adequate than the design of previous research? (Chapters 6–9, 12, and 13)

This is a relatively new intervention. The findings in this study complement the findings of another study with higher income African American women.

23. What additional research questions and hypotheses are suggested by the study's results? What light did the study shed on the theoretical framework used? On social work practice questions? On social policy questions? (Chapters 2 and 15)

The authors note that future researchers might examine the need for ethnic matching of provider and client. Further, the process or content of the CYC intervention should be evaluated to determine what aspects of the program have the most impact on the outcomes. Researchers might try to disentangle the impact of the curriculum and therapeutic component of the intervention from the effect of social support available in a group process. There is a need to replicate the CYC intervention (p. 743).

24. How well did the study live up to the guidelines for science? Do you need additional information in any areas to evaluate the study? To replicate it? (Chapter 3)

The study clearly involves a test of ideas against empirical reality; in this case, a test of a clinical intervention and its impact on clients. The researchers carried out the investigation systematically and provided detail about the procedures used to carry out the study. The author specified the meaning of key terms, as required in scientific research. In general, the study seems to exemplify adherence to basic scientific guidelines and to be very replicable.

25. Did the study seem consistent with current ethical standards? Were any trade-offs made between different ethical guidelines? Was an appropriate balance struck between adherence to ethical standards and use of the most rigorous scientific practices? (Chapter 3)

The authors note that potential participants in the study were "provided with detailed information regarding the nature of the intervention and the randomization process" (p. 739). The authors did not note the receipt of Institutional Review Board approval. Because of the nature of the research design, at the end of the intervention, control group members were invited to participate in the intervention (p. 740). The authors responded to the journal requirement to declare potential conflicts of interest reporting that there were "no potential conflicts of interest with respect to the research, authorship, and/or publication of this article" (p. 744).

Appendix C

Questions to Ask About a Qualitative Research Article

1. What is the social condition under study? What is the basic research question or problem? Try to state it in just one sentence. (Chapter 2)

2. How does the author(s) explain the importance of the research question? Is the research question relevant to social work practice and/or social welfare policy? (Chapter 2)

3. What prior literature is reviewed? Is it relevant to the research question? Does the literature review appear to be adequate? Are you aware of (or can you locate) any important omitted studies? Is the literature review up to date? (Chapter 2)

4. Describe the orientation of the study. Is it described in general terms as a qualitative study, or is there a specific approach such as ethnography, grounded theory, or narrative analysis? (Chapters 10 and 11)

5. Do you think the methodological approach appears to be appropriate for the stated purpose or research question? Does the author offer a rationale for using the chosen method? Can you think of a different approach that might have been used? (Chapter 10)

6. Describe the setting or settings in which the study was conducted. Describe the life circumstances of the participants. Is the description sufficient to aid in judging the situations and people to which the study findings might be relevant? (Chapter 10)

7. What specific type of sampling method was used? How was the sample recruited and selected? How large was the sample? How do the authors justify the particular number of participants and the sampling method? (Chapters 5 and 10)

8. What methods were used to gather information (data)? What are the advantages and disadvantages of the particular data-collection method? (Chapter 10)

9. Who gathered the information? What kind of training was provided to prepare for data collection? (Chapter 10)

10. How do the researchers describe their theoretical orientations and biases? Do the authors describe how they minimize these biases? (Chapters 2 and 10)

11. Does the author(s) describe how data were analyzed? (Chapter 11)

12. What did the author(s) find? Are examples of the data provided? Do these examples illustrate the procedures used and the researcher's interpretations of the data? (Chapter 11)

13. How was consistency established? Are the codings and interpretations consistent? Was there an effort to triangulate findings? (Chapter 11)

14. Do the researchers use methods to check the credibility of their findings such as peer checking or checking their findings with participants or informants? (Chapter 11)

15. Was the methodological approach that was planned as stated in question 4 actually used? (Chapters 10 and 11)

16. Are the data, perspective, decisions, and situations documented? (Chapter 11)

17. Does the author(s) adequately represent the findings in the discussion or conclusion sections? Are conclusions grounded in the findings? (Chapters 10 and 11)

18. Are alternative explanations of findings offered? Do the authors describe and explain participants who may not fit the data? Can you think of any other interpretations of the findings? (Chapter 11)

19. Are the findings discussed in terms of their contribution to theory, content, method, or practical domains? (Chapter 11)

20. What study limitations are identified by the authors? What other limitations might the authors discuss? (Chapter 11)

21. What insights does the study offer for social work practice and social welfare policy? (Chapter 2)

22. Does the study seem consistent with current ethical standards? Are any trade-offs made between different ethical guidelines? Is an appropriate balance struck between adherence to ethical standards and use of the most rigorous scientific practices? (Chapters 3, 10, and 11)

Appendix D

How to Read a Qualitative Research Article

The goal of this appendix is to walk you through a qualitative research article, answering the review questions introduced in Appendix C. We use an article by Victoria Stanhope (2012) about engaging with people who have experienced long-term homelessness. This article, "The Ties That Bind: Using Ethnographic Methods to Understand Service Engagement," is published in a leading journal, *Qualitative Social Work* (Volume 11, pp. 412–430). The article has many strengths, yet, as you will see, there are gaps in the information reported by the author.

After each question, we indicate the chapter where the question was discussed, and after each answer, we cite the article page or pages to which we refer. You can also follow our review by reading through the article itself and noting our comments. The article is reproduced on the study site (http://www.sagepub.com/pswr4e).

1. What is the social condition under study? What is the basic research question or problem? Try to state it in just one sentence. (Chapter 2)

The purpose of this study is to understand how people with a history of social disengagement and program staff create a working partnership. As noted by the author, this is a study "based on a broad conceptualization of service engagement, which includes active collaboration and feeling valued . . . to explore the social interaction between case managers and service users" (p. 416).

2. How does the author(s) explain the importance of the research question? Is the research question relevant to social work practice and/or social welfare policy? (Chapter 2)

The housing first model has had success in providing stable housing for people experiencing long-term homelessness in contrast to the treatment first model. Having a better

understanding of why it is successful can assist other agencies in their adoption of this model (pp. 413 and 416).

3. What prior literature is reviewed? Is it relevant to the research question? Does the literature review appear to be adequate? Are you aware of (or can you locate) any important omitted studies? Is the literature review up to date? (Chapter 2)

The author reviewed literature focused on the housing first model, client-professional engagement, and the importance of engagement for successful social work practice. The housing first model and treatment first model were described followed by a summary of each model's success in providing stable housing. The engagement literature described the importance of engagement for successful case management. The literature review sections were brief but up to date (pp. 413–416).

4. Describe the orientation of the study. Is it described in general terms as a qualitative study or is there a specific approach such as ethnography, grounded theory, or narrative analysis? (Chapters 10 and 11)

The study is described as an ethnography using both participant observation and intensive interviews. The participation observation lasted for 10 months followed (with some overlap in time) by 2 months of interviews (p. 416).

5. Do you think the methodological approach appears to be appropriate for the stated purpose or research question? Does the author offer a rationale for using the chosen method? Can you think of a different approach that might have been used? (Chapters 10)

The author's approach seems appropriate for the research questions. The author explained that participant observation provided the research team the opportunity to observe and listen as the engagement process evolved in different settings and during different activities (p. 416). The interviews helped the research team to clarify observations and to learn what participants felt was relevant (p. 417).

6. Describe the setting or settings in which the study was conducted. Describe the life circumstances of the participants. Is the description sufficient to aid in judging the situations and people to which the study findings might be relevant? (Chapter 10)

The study was conducted in a midsized East Coast city; no other detail about the setting was provided. The participants included residents of a housing first program and members of two assertive community treatment (ACT) teams. We do not learn much about the background of the residents other than they had been homeless, had recently enrolled in the housing first program, and *may* have had co-occurring disorders. (p. 416). Background about ACT teams and case management was provided though not specific to the setting for the study. The author described in detail the philosophy of housing first programs (p. 415) and noted that "the structure of the Housing First program set the parameters within which the engagement process folded. In a concrete way, the program determined where and during which activities case managers and residents interacted and in a more abstract way, the program's values and expectations set the terms of these interaction. However, at the heart of the engagement process, there was a part of the interaction between the case managers and residents that was unscripted and spontaneous" (p. 419).

7. What specific type of sampling method was used? How was the sample recruited and selected? How large was the sample? How do the authors justify the particular number of participants and the sampling method? (Chapters 5 and 10)

The sample is a purposive sample. Resident participants had to have enrolled in the program within the preceding 12 months; all but one had enrolled within the preceding 2 months. The author justified this criterion noting that "this time period was chosen to include the most intense period of engagement for residents, including the beginning of their relationships with the case managers and being housed" (p. 416). All residents meeting the criterion were approached and nine agreed to participate. A 10th was added who had been recently rehoused to have enough women residents.

These ten residents were served by two different ACT teams, with 14 total members. All 14 agreed to participate though it was not stated how they were recruited.

8. What methods were used to gather information (data)? What are the advantages and disadvantages of the particular data-collection method? (Chapter 10).

Data were collected through both participant observation and intensive interviewing. The participant observation lasted for about 10 months and included 280 hours of observation. The researchers accompanied participant case managers on visits involving a variety of settings and for different activities. They collected data by observing and listening but also asked questions to "gain insight into what was taking place in real time" (p. 417). Field notes were written after each interaction, and descriptive notes were separated from memos relating to personal reactions and possible interpretations. The interviews were semistructured and were conducted starting near the end of the participation observation period. The interviews lasted between 20 minutes and 80 minutes and included all but one participant (p. 417).

The combination of data collection methods enabled the research team to observe behavior and ACT team member–resident interactions and then to clarify their observations as well as pursue other issues in greater depth. The downside was the 12-month period for data collection. That the interviews followed the behavioral observations allowed for triangulation.

9. Who gathered the information? What kind of training was provided to prepare for data collection? (Chapter 10)

The data were collected by two researchers who had no formal relationship with the agency prior to the start of the research. The author did not describe the training provided to the researchers but did note that both had previously been case managers, inferring that they had experience with other case managers and working with residents (p. 417).

10. How do the authors describe their theoretical orientations and biases? Do the authors describe how they minimize these biases? (Chapter 2 and Chapter 10)

The author noted that the "theoretical framework for the study was symbolic interactionism" (p. 418). This framework did focus the researchers' data collection and analysis as they focused on ways that respondents felt connected to providers and "how to identify commonalities across varied contexts and events" (p. 418). Because they were focused on understanding how program staff created positive relationships, the researchers tended to ignore negative interactions.

11. Does the author(s) describe how data were analyzed? (Chapter 11)

During data collection the researchers met to review the data. The author noted that data were organized and analyzed with a computer program. Open coding was used to categorize observations while focused coding was used to create subcategories and refine insights (p. 418). The researchers developed axial codes to connect and link the different coding families together.

12. What did the author(s) find? Are examples of the data provided? Do these examples illustrate the procedures used and the researcher's interpretations of the data? (Chapter 11)

The author reported two major themes: (1) creating a shared narrative and (2) creating ties that bind. The shared narrative refers to program-related experiences shared by residents and caseworkers including move-in, home meetings, life events, activities in the community, office meetings, and on-call requirements (pp. 419–423). Creating ties that bind came through the quality of the interactions and included paying attention and communication based on mutual regard. The quality of the interactions resulted in making a connection between caseworkers and residents (pp. 423–426). The author provides quotes to illustrate the meaning of the categories that helped clarify the researchers' interpretations.

13. How was consistency established? Are the codings and interpretations consistent? Was there an effort to triangulate findings? (Chapter 11)

As noted earlier, the themes emerged through ongoing discussion and use of memoing to describe how the themes evolved. Triangulation occurred as the result of the timing of the two data collection efforts. The behaviors and interactions learned through the participant observation period were verified (or disconfirmed) as part of the interview.

14. Do the researchers use methods to check the credibility of their findings such as peer checking or checking their findings with participants or informants? (Chapter 11)

The authors do not use any other method to check their findings.

15. Was the methodological approach that was planned as stated in question 4 actually used? (Chapters 10 and 11)

As reported in the article, the methodological approach was carried out as planned. The author did note that the research team spent more time with caseworkers and, therefore, collected more data from the caseworkers (p. 427).

16. Are the data, perspective, decisions, and situations documented? (Chapter 11)

The author provided detailed information about data collection and data analysis and how conclusions were reached but provided less information about her own perspective.

17. Does the author(s) adequately represent the findings in the discussion or conclusion sections? Are conclusions grounded in the findings? (Chapters 10 and 11)

The conclusions were grounded in the findings, and the author linked the findings to the discussion. The author provided a brief conclusion and summarized the findings associated with that conclusion (pp. 426–427).

18. Are alternative explanations of findings offered? Do the authors describe and explain participants who may not fit the data? Can you think of any other interpretations of the findings? (Chapter 11)

The author did address interactions and participants who failed to achieve engagement with their caseworkers. For example, some residents did not make close connections with the caseworkers. Caseworkers felt that gender and racial differences factored in the failure to make connections (p. 426). This was reported in the findings and not the discussion section.

19. Are the findings discussed in terms of their contribution to theory, content, method, or practical domains? (Chapter 11)

The findings briefly touch on theory but much more so on practice. For example, the nature of the social interactions was linked to case management and how case managers have situational power that extends beyond a program's structural requirements (p. 427). The author used the findings to recommend strategies for program implementation.

20. What study limitations are identified by the authors? What other limitations might the authors discuss? (Chapter 11)

The author identified several limitations including: (1) the sampling strategy led to few observations of negative interactions; (2) the presence of the researcher during the course of the participant observation may have influenced the interactions between residents and caseworkers; (3) the researchers traveled with case managers, therefore spending more time with them so more data were from the case manager perspective; and (4) the researchers were ex-case managers, and therefore they understood better the subjective experiences of case managers (p. 427). The author suggested that a future study design should include shadowing residents separately and interviewing outside the agency. The study findings might have been richer by forgoing the use of a particular theory as the theoretical framework bounded what the researchers observed. Given that these were new residents, the researchers may be overstating the link between connectedness resulting in permanent shelter.

21. What insights does the study offer for social work practice and social welfare policy? (Chapter 2)

The study offered some practical considerations for engaging people who are long-term homeless. While the program design created many opportunities for interaction, it was the skills in communication and trust building that contributed to program success. Developing these skills should be a crucial component of case manager training and evaluation.

22. Does the study seem consistent with current ethical standards? Are any trade-offs made between different ethical guidelines? Is an appropriate balance struck between adherence to ethical standards and use of the most rigorous scientific practices? (Chapters 3, 10, and 11)

The study seemed consistent with current ethical standards. The author noted that the study was submitted to both university and agency Institutional Review Boards, and all participants signed consent forms (p. 416). Before each interaction between caseworker and resident, the researchers asked participants for permission to observe (p. 416).

Glossary

Adherence to authority: Unquestioning acceptance of statements by authority figures such as parents, teachers, and professionals.

Aggregate matching: Two or more groups, such as classes, are matched and then randomly assigned to the experimental and control conditions.

Alternate-forms reliability: A procedure for testing the reliability of responses to survey questions in which subjects' answers are compared after the subjects have been asked slightly different versions of the questions or when randomly selected halves of the sample have been administered slightly different versions of the questions.

Anonymity: Provided by research in which no identifying information is recorded that could be used to link respondents to their responses.

Assent: Requirement that a child provide affirmative agreement to participate in a research study.

Association: A criterion for establishing a nomothetic causal relationship between two variables: variation in one variable is related to variation in another variable.

Authenticity: When the understanding of a social process or social setting is one that reflects fairly the various perspectives of participants in that setting.

Availability sampling: Sampling method in which elements are selected on the basis of convenience.

Bar chart: A graphic for categorical variables in which the variable's distribution is displayed with solid bars separated by spaces.

Baseline phase: The initial phase of a single-subject design, typically abbreviated by the letter A; it represents the period in which the intervention to be evaluated is not offered to the subject. During the baseline phase, repeated measurements of the dependent variable are taken or constructed.

Behavior coding: Observation in which the researcher categorizes according to strict rules the number of times certain behaviors occur.

Belmont Report: The 1979 report of the Commission for the Protection of Human Subjects of Biomedical and Behavioral Research.

Big Data: Massive data sets produced or accessible in computer-readable form that are produced by people, available to social scientists, and manageable with today's computers.

Bivariate statistical tests: Statistical tests of the relationship between two variables.

Black box: Occurs when an evaluation of program outcomes ignores, and does not identify, the process by which the program produced the effect.

Block matching: A form of matching that groups individuals by their characteristics. Within each group, members are randomly assigned to the experimental and control groups.

Carryover effect: The impact of an intervention persists after the end of the treatment process.

Case study: A setting or group that the analyst treats as an integrated social unit that must be studied holistically and in its particularity.

Causal effect (ideographic perspective): The finding that a series of events following an initial set of conditions leads in a progressive manner to a particular event or outcome.

Causal effect (nomothetic perspective): The finding that change in one variable leads to change in another variable, other things being equal.

Causal validity: Exists when a conclusion that A leads to or results in B is correct. Also called *internal validity.*

Central tendency: The most common value (for variables measured at the nominal level) or the value around which cases tend to center (for a quantitative variable).

Certificate of Confidentiality: The National Institutes of Health can issue this to protect researchers from having to disclose confidential information.

Check coding: A check of the accuracy of coding information; it is estimated by comparing the coding completed by one person with the coding completed by a second person.

Clinical replication: Used to enhance generalizability of single-subject designs; clinical replication involves combining different interventions into a clinical package to treat multiple problems.

Clinical significance: The intervention led to a change in the actual clinical status of the participant.

Closed-ended question: A survey question that provides preformatted response choices for the respondent to check or circle.

Cluster: A naturally occurring, mixed aggregate of elements of the population.

Cluster sampling: Sampling method in which elements are selected in two or more stages, with the first stage being the random selection of naturally occurring clusters and the last stage being the random selection of elements within clusters.

Cognitive interview: A technique for evaluating questions in which researchers ask people test questions, then probe with follow-up questions to learn how they understood the questions and what their answers mean.

Cohort study: A type of longitudinal study in which data are collected at two or more points in time from individuals or groups with a common stating point. For example, people who were born in the 1940s and the 1950s (the "baby boom generation").

Community-based participatory research: A type of research in which the researcher involves some community and/or organizational members as active participants throughout the study. Also termed *participatory action research*.

Comparison group: In an experiment, a group that has been exposed to a different treatment (or value of the independent variable) than the experimental group.

Compensatory equalization of treatment: A threat to internal validity. When staff providing a treatment to a comparison group feel that it is unfair that the group is not getting the experimental treatment, the staff may work harder or do more than if there were no experiment.

Compensatory rivalry: A type of contamination in true experimental and quasi-experimental designs that occurs when control group members are aware that they are being denied some advantage and so increase their efforts by way of compensation.

Complete (covert) participant: A role in participant observation in which the researcher does not participate in group activities and is publicly identified as a researcher.

Complex design: Qualitative and quantitative methods are combined in a research project that uses more than one of the four basic types of mixed-methods designs or that repeats at least one of those basic types.

Concept: A mental image that summarizes a set of similar observations, feelings, or ideas.

Conceptualization: The process of specifying what we mean by a term. In deductive research, conceptualization helps to translate portions of an abstract theory into specific variables that can be used to test hypotheses. In inductive research, conceptualization is part of the process to make sense of related observations.

Concurrent validity: The type of validity that exists when scores on a measure are closely related to scores on a criterion measured at the same time.

Confidentiality: Provided by research in which identifying information that could be used to link respondents to their responses is available only to designated research personnel for specific research needs.

Conflicts of interest: When researchers have a significant stake in the design or outcome of their own research.

Construct validity: The type of validity that is established by showing that a measure is related to other measures as specified in a theory.

Constructivism: A perspective that emphasizes how different stakeholders in social settings construct their beliefs.

Contamination: A source of causal invalidity that occurs when either the experimental or the compassion group is aware of the other group and is influenced in the posttest as a result.

Content analysis: A research method for systematically analyzing and making inferences from text.

Content validity: The type of validity that exists when the full range of a concept's meaning is covered by the measure.

Context: A focus of idiographic causal explanation; a particular outcome is understood as part of a larger set of interrelated circumstances.

Context effects: Occur in a survey when one or more questions influence how subsequent questions are interpreted.

Contingency questions: Questions asked of the more limited group of people.

Continuous variable: A variable for which the number represents a quantity that can be described in terms of order, spread between the numbers, and/or relative amounts.

Control group: In an experiment, a comparison group that receives no treatment.

Convergent validity: The type of validity achieved when one measure of a concept is associated with different types of measures of the same concept.

Conversation analysis: A qualitative method for analyzing the sequential organization and details of a conversation.

Correlation coefficient: A statistic summarizing the strength of a relationship between two continuous variables.

Cost-benefit analysis: A type of evaluation that compares program costs to the economic value of program benefits.

Cost-effectiveness: A type of evaluation that compares program costs to program outcomes.

Counterfactual: The situation as it would have been in the absence of variation in the independent variable.

Cover letter: The letter sent with a mail questionnaire. It explains the survey's purpose and auspices and encourages the respondent to participate.

Covert observer: A role in field research in which the researcher does not reveal his or her identity as a researcher to those who are observed.

Criterion validity: The type of validity established by comparing the scores obtained on the measure being validated to scores obtained with a more direct or already validated measure of the same phenomenon (the criterion).

Critical theory: A research focus on examining structures, patterns of behavior, and meanings but rests on the premise that power differences, often manifested by discrimination and oppression, have shaped these structures and patterns

Cronbach's alpha coefficient: A statistic commonly used to measure interitem reliability.

Cross-population generalizability: Exists when findings about one group, population, or setting hold true for other groups, populations, or settings. Also called *external validity*.

Cross-sectional research design: A study in which the data are collected at only one point in time.

Cross-tabulation: In the simplest case, a bivariate (two-variable) distribution, showing the distribution of one variable for each category of another variable; can also be elaborated using three or more variables.

Cut-off score: A score used in a scale to distinguish between respondents with a particular status and respondents who do not have that status.

Cycle: A baseline phase pattern reflecting ups and downs depending on the time of measurement.

Debriefing: A researcher's informing participants after an experiment about the experiment's purposes and methods and evaluating participants' personal reactions to the experiment.

Decentering: Method of making equivalent different language versions of an instrument; it involves modifying both the original instrument and the translated instrument to increase their equivalence.

Deductive research: The type of research in which a specific expectation is deduced from a general premise and is then tested.

Dependent variable: A variable that is hypothesized to vary depending on or under the influence of another variable.

Descriptive research: Research in which social phenomena are defined and described.

Descriptive statistics: Statistics used to describe the distribution of and relationship among variables.

Differential attrition: A problem that occurs in experiments when comparison groups become different because subjects are more likely to drop out of one of the groups for various reasons.

Diffusion of treatment: A type of contamination in experimental and quasi-experimental designs that occurs when treatment and comparison groups interact and the nature of the treatment becomes known to the comparison group.

Direct replication: Used to enhance the generalizability of a single-subject design; the single-subject design is repeated using the same procedures by the same researchers and the same providers, in the same setting, and in the same situation with different clients.

Direction of association: A pattern in a relationship between two variables; the values of one variable tend to change consistently in relation to change in the value of the second variable.

Discriminant validity: An approach to construct validity; the scores on the measure to be validated are compared to scores on another measure of the same variable and to scores on variables that measure different but related concepts. Discriminant validity is achieved if the measure to be validated is related most strongly to its comparison measure and less so to the measures of other concepts.

Disproportionate stratified sampling: Sampling in which elements are selected from strata in different proportions from those that appear in the population.

Double-barreled questions: A single survey question that actually asks two questions but allows only one answer.

Double-blind procedures: An experimental method in which neither the subjects nor the staff delivering the experimental treatments know which subjects are getting the treatment and which are receiving a placebo.

Duration: The length of time an event of some symptom lasts and usually is measured for each occurrence of the event or symptom.

Ecological fallacy: An error in reasoning in which the incorrect conclusions about individual-level processes are drawn from group-level data.

Effect size: A standardized measure of association; it may be the difference between the mean of the experimental group and the mean of the comparison group on the dependent variable, adjusted for the average variability in the two groups.

Elements: The individual members of the population whose characteristics are to be measured.

Embedded design: Qualitative and quantitative methods are used concurrently in the research but one is given priority.

Empirical generalization: A statement that describes patterns found in data.

Enumeration units: Units that contain one or more elements and that are listed in a sampling frame.

Ethnography: The study of a culture shared by some group of people, using participant observation over an extended period.

Ethnomethodology: A qualitative research method focused on the way that participants in a social setting create and sustain a sense of reality.

Evaluation research: Research that describes or identifies the impact of social programs and policies.

Exempt status: IRB review for research studies that involve minimal human subject involvement.

Exhaustive: Every case can be classified as having at least one attribute (or one value) for the variable.

Expedited review: IRB reviews that are done for new or continuing studies that present minimal risk of harm to the participant.

Experimental group: In an experiment, the group of subjects that receives the treatment or experimental manipulation.

Explanatory research: Seeks to identify causes and effects of social phenomena and to predict how one phenomenon will change or vary in response to variation in some other phenomenon.

Exploratory research: Seeks to find out how people get along in the setting under question, what meanings they give to their actions, and what issues concern them.

External validity: See cross-population generalizability.

Face validity: The type of validity that exists when an inspection of items used to measure a concept suggests that they are appropriate "on their face."

Factorial validity: A form of construct validity used to determine if the scale items relate correctly to different dimensions of the concept.

False negative: The participant does not have a particular problem according to a screening instrument, but the participant really does have the problem based on a clinical evaluation.

False positive: A respondent has a particular problem according to a screening instrument but in reality does not have the problem based on a clinical evaluation.

Feminist research: Research with a focus on women's lives and often including an orientation to personal experience, subjective orientations, and the researcher's standpoint.

Fence-sitters: Survey respondents who see themselves as being neutral on an issue and choose a middle (neutral) response.

Field notes: Notes that describe what has been observed, heard, or otherwise experienced in a participant observation study. These notes usually are written after the observation session.

Filter question: A survey question used to identify a subset of respondents who are then asked other questions.

Floaters: Survey respondents who provide an opinion on a topic in response to a closed-ended question that does not include a *don't know* option, but who will choose *don't know* if it is available.

Focus groups: A qualitative method that involves unstructured group interviews in which the focus group leader encourages discussion among participants on the topics of interest.

Formative evaluation: Process evaluation that is used to shape and refine program operations.

Frequency: In a single-subject design, counting the number of times a behavior occurs or the number of times people experience different feelings within a particular time period.

Frequency distribution: Numerical display showing the number of cases, and usually the percentage of cases (the relative frequencies) corresponding to each value or group of values of a variable.

Frequency polygon: A graphic for quantitative variables in which a continuous line connects data points representing the variable's distribution.

Full review: IRB reviews that are completed for research studies with vulnerable populations or when there is the potential for harm. These extensive reviews are conducted, vetted, and voted on by the full IRB committee.

Grand tour question: A broad question at the start of an interview that seeks to engage the respondent in the topic of interest.

Grounded theory: Systematic theory developed inductively, based on observations that are summarized into conceptual categories, reevaluated in the research setting, and gradually refined and linked to other conceptual categories.

Group-administered survey: A survey that is completed by individual respondents who are assembled in a group.

Histograms: A graphic for quantitative variables in which the variable's distribution is displayed with adjacent bars.

History: A source of causal invalidity that occurs when something other than the treatment influences outcome scores; also called an effect of *external events*.

Hypothesis: A tentative statement about empirical reality involving a relationship between two or more variables.

Idiographic causal explanation: An explanation that identifies the concrete, individual sequence of events, thoughts, or actions that resulted in a particular outcome for a particular individual or that led to a particular event.

Illogical reasoning: Occurs when we prematurely jump to conclusions or argue on the basis of invalid assumptions.

Inaccurate observation: Observations based on faulty perceptions of empirical reality.

Independent variable: A variable that is hypothesized to cause, or lead to, variation in another variable.

Inductive research: The type of research in which general conclusions are drawn from specific data; compare with *deductive research*.

Inferential statistics: Mathematical tools for estimating how likely it is that a statistical result based on data from a random sample is representative of the population from which the sample is assumed to have been selected.

Informed consent: Potential research study participants have sufficient information about the costs and benefits of participating in the study, what their participation involves, and their rights as participants in the study to make an "informed" decision to participate.

In-person interview: A survey in which an interviewer questions respondents face-to-face and records their answers.

Inputs: The resources, raw materials, and staff that go into a program.

Institutional review board (IRB): A group of organizational and community representatives required by federal law to review the ethical issues in all proposed research that is federally funded, involves human subjects, or has any potential harm to subjects.

Instrumentation: A problem that occurs in experimental designs when the measurement methods are not stable or equivalent.

Integrated design: Qualitative and quantitative methods are used concurrently and both are given equal importance.

Integrative approaches: Orientation to evaluation research that expects researchers to respond to the concerns of people involved with the program as well as to the standards and goals of the social science community.

Intensive interviewing: A qualitative method that involves open-ended, relatively unstructured questioning in which the interviewer seeks in-depth information on the respondent's feelings, experiences, and perceptions.

Internal consistency: An approach to reliability based on the correlation among multiple items used to measure a single concept.

Internal validity: A criterion necessary to demonstrate causality; it is the ability to rule out all other explanations for the findings.

Interpretivism: Methodology based on the belief that reality is socially constructed and that the goal of social scientists is to understand the meanings people give to reality.

Interquartile range: The difference in a distribution between the end of the first quartile and the beginning of the third quartile.

Interrater reliability: The degree of agreement when similar measurements are obtained by different observers rating the same people, events, or places.

Intersubjective agreement: Agreement between scientists about the nature of reality.

Interval: Used in single-subject design, a measure of the length of time between events, behaviors, or symptoms.

Interval level of measurement: A measurement of a variable in which the numbers indicating a variable's values represent fixed measurement units but have no absolute, or fixed, zero point.

Intervening variables: Variables that are influenced by independent variables and in turn influence variation in a dependent variable, thus helping to explain the relationship between the independent and dependent variables.

Interview schedule: The survey instrument containing the questions asked by the interviewer in an in-person or phone survey.

Intrarater reliability: Consistency of ratings by an observer of an unchanging phenomenon at two or more points in time.

Jottings: Brief notes written in the field about highlights of an observation period.

Justice: Ethical principle that benefits and risks of research should be fairly distributed.

Known-groups validity: Demonstrating the validity of a measure using two groups with already-identified characteristics.

Leading questions: Question phrasing meant to bias the response.

Level: Flat lines reflecting the amount or magnitude of the target variable; used in a single-subject design.

Level of measurement: The mathematical precision with which the values of a variable can be expressed.

Likert-type responses: Response categories that generally ask respondents to indicate the extent to which they agree or disagree with statements.

Logic model: A schematic representation of the various components that make up a social service program, including the assumptions underlying the program, inputs, activities, outputs, and outcomes.

Longitudinal research design: A study in which data are collected that can be ordered in time; research in which data are collected at two or more points in time.

Magnitude: Measuring the intensity of a particular behavior or psychological state.

Mailed survey: A survey involving a mailed questionnaire to be completed by the respondent.

Marginal distributions: The summary distributions in the margins of a cross-tabulation that correspond to the frequency distribution of the row variable and the column variable.

Matrix: A form on which to systematically record particular features of multiple cases or instances that a qualitative data analyst needs to examine.

Matrix questions: A series of questions that concern a common theme and have the same response choices.

Maturation: A threat to internal validity; changes that naturally occur with the passage of time.

Mean: The arithmetic or weighted average computed by adding up the value of all the cases and dividing by the number of cases.

Measure of association: A type of descriptive statistic that summarizes the strength of an association. See also *association*.

Measurement validity: Exists when a measure measures what we think it measures.

Mechanism: A discernible process that creates a causal connection between two variables.

Median: The point that divides a distribution in half (the 50th percentile).

Mediating variable: The independent variable impacts the mediating variable, and the mediating variable affects the dependent variable. The effect of the independent variable on the dependent variable becomes zero.

Member checking: When a qualitative researcher seeks input from participants about the interviews, findings, and interpretations.

Meta-analysis: The quantitative analysis of findings from multiple studies.

Meta-synthesis: The qualitative analysis of findings from multiple studies.

Mixed methods: The use of both qualitative and quantitative methods in a research study.

Mode: The most frequent value in a distribution.

Moderator variable: A third variable that interacts with the independent variable.

Multidimensional scale: A scale containing subsets of questions that measure different aspects of the same concept.

Multivariate statistical tests: Statistical tests involving two or more independent variables.

Mutually exclusive: A variable's attributes or values are mutually exclusive when every case can be classified as having only one attribute or value.

Narrative analysis: A form of qualitative analysis in which the analyst focuses on how respondents impose order on their experiences and make sense of events and actions in which they have participated.

Needs assessment: A type of evaluation research that is used to determine the needs of some population.

Netnography: The use of ethnographic methods to study online communities.

Nominal definition: Defining a concept using other concepts.

Nominal level of measurement: Variables whose values have no mathematical interpretation; they vary in kind or quality, but not in amount.

Nomothetic causal explanation: An explanation that identifies common influences on a number of cases or events.

Nonexperimental designs: Weakest form of group research designs in attributing causality. Often used for program evaluation.

Nonprobability sampling methods: Sampling methods in which the probability of selection of population elements is unknown.

Nonspuriousness: A criterion for establishing a causal relation between two variables; when a relationship between two variables is not due to variation in a third variable.

Normal distribution: A graph with a shape that looks like a bell, with one hump in the middle, centered around the population mean, and the number of cases tapering off on both sides of the mean. This shape is important for sampling and statistical analysis.

Open-ended question: A survey question to which the respondent replies in his or her own words, by either writing or talking.

Operational definition: The set of rules and operations used to find the value of cases on a variable.

Operationalization: The process of specifying the operations that will indicate the value of cases on a variable.

Ordinal level of measurement: A measurement of a variable in which the numbers indicating a variable's values specify only the order of the cases, permitting *greater than* and *less than* distinctions.

Outcome evaluation: A program evaluation designed to measure client or participant outcomes.

Outcomes: The impact of the program process on participants.

Output: Measures of the services delivered by the program process.

Overgeneralization: Occurs when we unjustifiably conclude that what is true for some cases is true for *all* cases.

Panel study: A longitudinal study of the same individuals.

Participant observer: A qualitative method for gathering data that involves developing a sustained relationship with people while they go about their normal activities.

Peer debriefing: A qualitative researcher receives feedback from a second party like a colleague.

Permission: Parent or guardian agreement to a child's participation in a research study.

Phone survey: A survey in which interviewers question respondents over the phone and then record their answers.

Photovoice: A qualitative method in which participants both photograph meaningful scenes and interpret the photographs.

Pilot study: A small initial study to determine the quality of the data collection procedures that will be used in a larger study.

Placebo effect: A source of treatment misidentification that can occur when subjects who receive a treatment that they consider likely to be beneficial improve because of that expectation rather than because of the treatment itself.

Population: The entire set of individuals or other entities to which study findings are to be generalized.

Population parameter: The value of a statistic, such as a mean, computed using the data for the entire population; a sample statistic is an estimate of a population parameter.

Positivism: The philosophical view that an external objective reality exists apart from human perceptions of it.

Postpositivism: A philosophical view that modifies the positivist premise of an external reality by recognizing its complexity, the limitations of human observers, and, therefore, the impossibility of developing more than a partial understanding of reality.

Posttest: In experimental research, the measurement of an outcome (dependent variable) after an experimental intervention or after a presumed independent variable has changed for some other reason.

Pragmatism: A philosophy that emphasizes the importance of taking action and learning from the outcomes to generate knowledge.

Predictive validity: The type of validity that exists when a measure predicts scores on a criterion measured in the future.

Pretest: In experimental research, the measurement of an outcome (dependent variable) prior to an experimental intervention or change in a presumed independent variable.

Probability of selection: The likelihood that an element will be selected from the population for inclusion in the sample.

Probability sampling methods: Sampling methods that rely on a random or chance selection method so that the probability of selection of population elements is known.

Process consent: An interpretation of the ethical standard of voluntary consent that allows participants to change their decision about participating at any point by requiring that the researcher check with participants at each stage of the project about their willingness to continue in the project.

Process evaluation: Type of program evaluation that investigates the process of service delivery.

Program process: The complete treatment or service delivered by the program.

Progressive focusing: The process by which a qualitative analyst interacts with the data and gradually refines his or her focus.

Proportionate stratified sampling: Sampling method in which elements are selected from strata in exact proportion to their representation in the population.

Purposive sampling: A nonprobability sampling method in which elements are selected for a purpose, usually because of their unique position.

Qualitative comparative analysis: A systematic type of qualitative analysis that identifies the combination of factors that had to be present across multiple cases to produce a particular outcome.

Qualitative methods: Methods such as participant observation, intensive interviewing, and focus groups that are designed to capture social life as participants experience it, rather than in categories predetermined by the researcher. These methods typically involve exploratory research questions, inductive reasoning, an orientation to social context, human objectivity, and the meanings attached by participants to events.

Quantitative methods: Methods such as surveys and experiments that record variation in social life in terms of categories that vary in amount. Data that are treated as quantitative are either numbers or attributes that can be ordered in terms of magnitude.

Quartile: The point in a distribution corresponding to the first 25% of the cases, the first 50% of the cases, and the first 75% of the cases.

Quasi-experimental design: A research design in which there is a comparison group that is comparable with the experimental group in critical ways, but participants are not randomly assigned to the comparison and experimental groups.

Questionnaire: The survey instrument containing the questions in a self-administered survey.

Quota sampling: A nonprobability sampling method in which elements are selected to ensure that the sample represents certain characteristics in proportion to their prevalence in the population.

Random assignment: A procedure using chance to assign each research participant to an experimental or comparison group.

Random digit dialing: The random dialing by a machine of numbers within designated phone prefixes, which creates a random sample for phone surveys.

Random error: Errors in measurement that are due to chance and are not systematic in any way.

Random numbers table: A table containing lists of numbers that are ordered solely on the basis of chance; it is used for drawing a random sample.

Random sampling: A method of sampling that relies on a random or chance selection method so that every element of the sampling frame has a known probability of being selected.

Randomization: Placing participants into an experimental or control group using some chance method such as by the toss of a coin.

Range: The true upper limit in a distribution minus the true lower limit (or the highest rounded value minus the lowest rounded value).

Ratio level of measurement: A measurement of a variable in which the numbers indicate a variable's values represent fixed measuring unit and an absolute zero point.

Reactive effects: The changes in an individual or group behavior due to being observed or otherwise studied.

Reactivity: Changes in an individual or group behavior due to the nature of the experimental conditions or process of measurement.

Recall loss: Problems of remembering events or details about events.

Reductionist fallacy: An error in reasoning that occurs when an incorrect conclusion about group-level processes is based on individual-level data.

Relevance validity: An aspect of validity regarding the usefulness of evaluation data to individuals or communities.

Reliability: A criterion to assess the quality of scales based on whether the procedure yields consistent scores when the phenomenon being measured is not changing.

Representative sample: A sample that "looks like" the population from which it was selected in all respects potentially relevant to the study. The distribution of characteristics among the elements of a representative sample is the same as the distribution of those characteristics among the total population. In an unrepresentative sample, some characteristics are overrepresented or underrepresented.

Resentful demoralization: This problem for experimental designs occurs when comparison group members perform worse than they otherwise might have because they feel that they have been left out of a valuable treatment.

Resistance to change: The reluctance to change our ideas in light of new information.

Response set: When a series of questions have the same set of response categories, there is the possibility that the respondent provides the same response for each question.

Sample: A subset of a population that is used to study the population as a whole.

Sample generalizability: Exists when a conclusion based on a sample, or subset, of a larger population holds true for that population.

Sample statistic: The value of a statistic, such as a mean, computed from sample data.

Sampling distribution: The hypothetical distribution of a statistic across all the random samples that could be drawn from a population.

Sampling error: Any difference between the characteristics of a sample and the characteristics of a population. The larger the sampling error, the less representative the sample.

Sampling frame: A list of all elements or other units containing the elements in a population.

Sampling interval: The number of cases from one sampled case to another in a systematic random sample.

Sampling units: Units listed at each stage of a multistage sampling design.

Saturation point: The point at which subject selection is ended in intensive interviewing, when new interviews seem to yield little additional information.

Scale: A composite measure based on combining the responses to multiple questions pertaining to a common concept.

Scatterplot: A graph of individual response to two continuous variables.

Secondary data: Previously collected data that are used in a new analysis.

Secondary data analysis: The method of using preexisting data in a different way or to answer a different research question than intended by those who collected the data.

Secular drift: A type of contamination in true experimental and quasi-experimental designs that occurs when broader social or economic trends impact the findings of a study.

Selection bias: The lack of similarity between groups may offer an alternative explanation for an experiment's findings as opposed to the effect of the independent variable on the dependent variable.

Selective observation: Choosing to look only at things that are in line with our preferences or beliefs.

Sensitivity: The proportion of true positives that is based on the number of people assessed as having a diagnosis by a screening instrument to the number of people who actually have the condition.

Serendipitous findings: Unexpected patterns in data that stimulate new ideas or theoretical approaches.

Simple random sampling: A method of sampling in which every sample element is selected only on the basis of chance through a random process.

Skewness: The extent to which cases are clustered more at one or the other end of the distribution of a quantitative variable, rather than in a symmetric pattern around its center. Skew can be positive (a right skew), with the number of cases tapering off in the positive direction, or negative (a left skew), with the number of cases tapering off in the negative direction.

Skip patterns: The unique combination of questions created in a survey by filter questions and contingency questions.

Snowball sampling: A method of sampling in which sample elements are selected as they are identified by successive informants or interviewees.

Social desirability: The tendency for individuals to respond in ways that make them appear in the best light to the interviewer.

Social science: The use of scientific methods to investigate individuals, groups, communities, organizations, societies, and social processes; the knowledge produced by these investigations.

Social science approach: An orientation to evaluation research that expects researchers to emphasize the importance of researcher expertise and maintenance of autonomy from program stakeholders.

Specificity: The proportion of true negatives based on the number of people assessed as not having a diagnosis by a screening instrument relative to the number who really do not have the diagnosis.

Split-half reliability: Reliability achieved when responses to the same questions by two randomly selected halves of a sample are about the same.

Spurious relationship: When the relationship between two variables is actually caused by a third variable.

Stable line: A line in the baseline phase that is relatively flat, with little variability in the scores so that the scores fall in a narrow band.

Staged design: Qualitative and quantitative methods are used in sequence in the research.

Stakeholder approaches: An orientation to evaluation research that expects researchers to be responsive primarily to the people involved with the program.

Stakeholders: Individuals and groups that have some basis of concern with the program.

Standard deviation: The square root of the average squared deviation of each case from the mean.

Statistical control: A method in which one variable is held constant so that the relationship between two (or more) variables can be assessed without the influence of variation in the control variable.

Statistical regression: People experience cyclical or episodic changes that result in different scores with repeated measurement.

Statistical significance: The mathematical likelihood that an association is due to chance, judged by a criterion set by the analyst (e.g., the probability of an association is due to chance is less than 5 out of 100 or $p < .05$)

Stratified random sampling: A method of sampling in which sample elements are selected separately from population strata that are identified in advance by the researcher.

Survey research: Research in which information is obtained from a sample of individuals through their responses to questions about themselves or others.

Systematic bias: Overrepresentation or underrepresentation of some population characteristics due to the method used to select the sample.

Systematic error: Error due to a specific process that biases the results.

Systematic observation: A strategy that increases the reliability of observational data using explicit rules that standardize coding practices across observers.

Systematic random sampling: A method of sampling in which sample elements are selected from a list or from sequential files, with every nth element being selected after the first element is selected randomly within the first interval.

Systematic replication: Repeating a single-subject design in different settings, using different providers and other related behaviors to increase generalizability.

Systematic reviews: Summary review about the impact of an intervention in which the analyst tries to account for differences in design and participant characteristics, often using statistical techniques such as meta-analysis.

Tacit knowledge: In field research, a credible sense of understanding of social processes that reflects the researcher's awareness of participants' actions as well as their words, and of what they fail to state, feel deeply, and take for granted.

Target population: A set of elements larger than or different from the population sampled and to which the researcher would like to generalize study findings.

Telescoping effect: Remembering an event as happening more recently than when it really occurred.

Test–retest reliability: A type of reliability that is demonstrated by showing that the same measure of a phenomenon at two points in time is highly correlated, assuming that the phenomenon has not changed.

Testing effect: Measurement error related to how a test is given; the conditions of the testing, including environmental conditions; and acclimation to the test itself.

Theoretical sampling: A sampling method recommended for field research; the sample is drawn in a sequential fashion, with settings or individuals selected for study as earlier observations or interviews indicate that these settings or individuals are influential.

Theory: A logically interrelated set of propositions about reality.

Theory-driven evaluation: A program evaluation that is guided by a theory that specifies the process by which the program has an effect.

Thick description: A rich description that conveys a sense of what a phenomenon or situation is like from the standpoint of the actors in that setting.

Time order: A criterion for establishing a causal relation between two variables. The variation in the presumed cause (the independent variable) must occur before the variation in the presumed effect (dependent variable).

Treatment as usual: When the comparison group in an experiment receives the intervention that is normally given.

Treatment fidelity: Delivering an intervention as it was designed to be provided.

Treatment phase: The intervention phase of a single-subject design.

Trend: Repeated measurement scores that are ascending or descending in magnitude; used in single-subject design.

Trend studies: A longitudinal study in which data are collected at two or more points in time from different samples of the same population.

Triangulation: The use of multiple methods to study one research question.

True experiments: Group designs that are used to test the causal relationship between the independent and dependent variables. These designs enable the researcher to show that the independent variable occurs prior to the change in the dependent variable, that there is a statistical association, and that other explanations (internal validity) can be ruled out.

True negative: When it is determined from a screening instrument score that the participant does not have a particular status and the participant really does not have the status based on a clinical evaluation.

True positive: When it is determined from a screening instrument score that the participant has a particular status and the participant really does have the status based on a clinical evaluation.

Type I error: Error that occurs when there is evidence of a statistical relationship between two variables based on the sample, but in fact, there is no relationship between the two variables.

Type II error: Error that occurs when there is no evidence of a statistical relationship between two variables based on the sample, but in fact, the two variables are related.

Units of analysis: The level of social life on which a research question is focused.

Units of observation: The cases about which measures actually are obtained in a sample.

Validity: The state that exists when statements or conclusions about empirical reality are correct.

Variability: The extent to which cases are spread out through the distribution or clustered in just one location.

Variables: Characteristics or properties that can take on different values or attributes.

Variance: A statistic that measures the variability of a distribution as the average squared deviation of each case from the mean.

References

Abbott, A. (1992). From causes to events: Notes on narrative positivism. *Sociological Methods and Research, 20*, 428–455.

Abel, D. (2008, February 24). For the homeless, keys to a home. *The Boston Globe*, pp. A1, A14.

Abildso, C., Zizzi, S., Gilleland, D., Thomas, J., & Bonner, D. (2010). A mixed methods evaluation of a 12-week insurance-sponsored weight management program incorporating cognitive-behavioral counseling. *Journal of Mixed Methods Research, 4*, 278–294.

Aiden, E., & Michel, J.-B. (2013). *Unchartered: Big Data as a lens on human culture*. New York, NY: Riverhead Books.

Altheide, D. L., & Johnson, J. M. (1994). Criteria for assessing interpretive validity in qualitative research. In N. K. Denzin & Y. S. Lincoln (Eds.), *Handbook of qualitative research* (pp. 485–499). Thousand Oaks, CA: Sage.

American Association of Public Opinion Research (AAPOR). (2014). *Nonresponse in RDD cell phone surveys*. Retrieved from http://www.aapor.org/AAPORKentico/Education-Resources/Reports/Cell-Phone-Task-Force-Report/Coverage-and-Sampling-(1).aspx

American Evaluation Association. (2004). *Guiding principles for evaluators*. Retrieved from http://www.eval.org

American Evaluation Association. (2011). *Public statement on cultural competence in evaluation*. Fairhaven, MA: Author. Retrieved from http://www.eval.org

American Medical Association. (2011). *AMA code of medical ethics*. Retrieved from http://www.ama-assn.org/ama/pub/physician-resources/medical-ethics/code-medical-ethics.page

American Psychological Association. (2006). Evidence-based practice in psychology. *American Psychologist, 61*, 271–285.

American Psychiatric Association. (2013). *Diagnostic and statistical manual of mental disorders (DSM-5)* (5th ed.). Arlington, VA: American Psychiatric Publishing.

Anderson, E. (1990). *Streetwise: Race, class, and change in an urban community*. Chicago, IL: University of Chicago Press.

Anderson, E. (1999). *Code of the street: Decency, violence, and the moral life of the inner city*. New York, NY: W. W. Norton.

Anderson, E. (2005). Jelly's Place: An ethnographic memoir. *International Journal of Politics, Culture and Society, 19*, 35–52.

Anderson-Butcher, D., Khairallah, A. O., & Race-Bigelow, J. (2004). Mutual support groups for long-term recipients on TANF. *Social Work, 49*, 131–140.

Angell, B., Mahoney, C. A., & Martinez, N. I. (2006). Promoting treatment adherence in assertive community treatment. *Social Service Review, 80*, 485–526.

Arbin, A. O., & Cormier, E. (2005). Racial disparity in nursing research: Is single subject experimental design a solution? *Journal of Theory Construction and Testing, 9*, 11–13.

Armstrong, K., (2008). Ethnography and audience. In P. Alasuutari, L. Bickman., & J. Brannen (Eds.), *The SAGE handbook of social research methods* (pp. 54–63). Thousand Oaks, CA: Sage.

Arumi, A. M., Yarrow, A. L., Ott, A., & Rochkind, J. (2007). *Compassion, concern, and conflicted feelings: New Yorkers on homelessness and housing*. New York, NY: Public Agenda. Retrieved from http://www.publicagenda.org/files/pdf/homeless_nyc.pdf

Arwood, T., & Panicker, S. (2007). Assessing risk in social and behavioral sciences. *Collaborative Institutional Training Initiative*. Retrieved from https://www.citiprogram.org/members/learners

Auerbach, C., & Schudrich, W. Z. (2013). SSD for R: A comprehensive statistical package to analyze single-system data. *Research on Social Work Practice, 23*, 346–353.

Axinn, W., Pearce, L., & Ghimire, D. (1999). Innovations in life history calendar applications. *Social Science Research, 28*, 243–264.

Ayalon, L., & Young, M. A. (2003). A comparison of depressive symptoms in African Americans and Caucasian Americans. *Journal of Cross-Cultural Psychology, 34*, 111–124.

Ayón, C., & Aisenberg, E. (2010). Negotiating cultural values and expectations within the public child welfare system: A look at familismo and personalismo. *Child & Family Social Work, 15*, 335–344.

Bachman, R. (1992). *Death and violence on the reservation*. Westport, CT: Auburn House.

Bae, S.-W., & Brekke, J. S. (2003). The measurement of self-esteem among Korean Americans: A cross-ethnic study. *Cultural Diversity and Ethnic Minority Psychology, 9*, 16–33.

Baffour, T. D. (2011). Addressing health and social disparities through community-based participatory research in rural communities: Challenges and opportunities for social work. *Contemporary Rural Social Work, 3*, 4–16.

Bagdasaryan, S. (2005). Evaluating family preservation services: Reframing the question of effectiveness. *Children and Youth Services Review, 27*, 615–635.

Bainbridge, W. S. (1989). *Survey research: A computer-assisted introduction*. Belmont, CA: Wadsworth.

Baker, T. A., & Wang, C. C. (2006). Photovoice: Use of a participatory action research method to explore the chronic pain experience in older adults. *Qualitative Health Research, 16*, 1405–1413.

Balas, E. A., & Boren, S. A. (2000). Managing clinical knowledge for health care improvement. In *Yearbook of medical informatics*. Bethesda, MD: National Library of Medicine. Available at http://www.ihi.org/resources/Pages/Publications/Managingclinicalknowledgeforhealthcareimprovement.aspx

Balaswamy, S., & Dabelko, H. I. (2002). Using a stakeholder participatory model in a community-wide service needs assessment of elderly residents: A case study. *Journal of Community Practice, 10*, 55–70.

Barresi, P., Husnick, M., Camacho, M., Powell, B., Gage, R., LeBlanc, D., . . . Koblin, B. (2010). Recruitment of men who have sex with men for large HIV intervention trials: Analysis of the EXPLORE study recruitment effort. *AIDS Education and Prevention, 22*, 28–36.

Barlow, D., Nock, M. K., & Hersen, M. (2009). *Single case experimental designs: Strategies for studying behavior change* (3rd ed.). Boston, MA: Pearson.

Baron, R. M., & Kenny, D. A. (1986). The moderator-mediator variable distinction in social psychological research: Conceptual, strategic, and statistical considerations. *Journal of Personality and Social Psychology, 51*, 1173–1182.

Barusch, A., Gringeri, C., & George, M. (2011). Rigor in qualitative social work research: A review of strategies used in published articles. *Social Work, 35, 1,* 11–19.

Bates, B. R., & Harris, T. M. (2004). The Tuskegee study of untreated syphilis and public perceptions of biomedical research: A focus group study. *Journal of the National Medical Association, 96,* 1051–1064.

Baumrind, D. (1964). Some thoughts on ethics of research: After reading Milgram's "Behavioral Study of Obedience." *American Psychologist, 19,* 421–423.

Baumrind, D. (1985). Research using intentional deception: Ethical issues revisited. *American Psychologist, 40,* 165–174.

Beals, J., Manson, S. M., Mitchell, C. M., Spicer, P., & the AI-SUPERPFP Team. (2003). Cultural specificity and comparison in psychiatric epidemiology: Walking the tightrope in American Indian research. *Culture, Medicine, and Psychiatry, 27,* 259–289.

Bechtold, J., Engel, R. J., & Rosen, D. (2012, September). *Older adult methadone clients and problem gambling.* Paper presented at the National Center for Responsible Gambling Conference on Gambling and Addiction, Las Vegas, Nevada.

Becker, H. S. (1958). Problems of inference and proof in participant observation. *American Sociological Review, 23,* 652–660.

Bellah, R. N., Madsen, W. M., Sullivan, A. S., Swidler, A., & Tipton, S. M. (1985). *Habits of the heart: Individualism and commitment in American life.* New York, NY: Harper & Row.

Belle, S., & REACH II Investigators. (2006). Enhancing the quality of life of dementia caregivers from different ethnic or racial groups. *Annals of Internal Medicine, 145,* 727–738.

Bennett, L. W., Stoops, C., Call, C., & Flett, H. (2007). Program completion and re-arrest in a batterer intervention system. *Research on Social Work Practice, 17,* 42–54.

Berk, R. A., Campbell, A., Klap, R., & Western, B. (1992). The deterrent effect of arrest: A Bayesian analysis of four field experiments. *American Sociological Review, 57,* 698–708.

Berman, G., & Fox, A. (2009). *Lessons from the battle over D.A.R.E.: The complicated relationship between research and practice.* Washington, DC: Center for Court Innovation and Bureau of Justice Assistance, U.S. Department of Justice.

Bertamini, M., & Munafo, M. R. (2012, January 29). The perils of "bite size" science. *New York Times,* SR 12.

Beyer, W. H. (Ed.). (1979). *CRC handbook of tables for probability and statistics* (2nd ed.). Boca Raton, FL: CRC Press.

Biesta, G. (2010). Pragmatism and the philosophical foundations of mixed methods research. In A. Tashakkori & C. Teddlie (Eds.), *SAGE handbook of mixed methods in social and behavioral research* (2nd ed., pp. 95–118). Thousand Oaks, CA: Sage.

Birkeland, A., Murphy-Graham, E., & Weiss, C. (2005). Good reasons for ignoring good evaluation: The case of the Drug Abuse Resistance Education (D.A.R.E.) Program. *Evaluation and Program Planning, 28,* 247–256.

Black, M. C., Basile, K. C., Breiding, M. J., Smith, S. G., Walters, M. L., Merrick, M. T., . . . Stevens, M. R. (2011). *The National Intimate Partner and Sexual Violence Survey (NISVS): 2010 summary report.* Atlanta, GA: National Center for Injury Prevention and Control, Centers for Disease Control and Prevention.

Blank, R. M. (2008). Presidential address: How to improve poverty measurement in the United States. *Journal of Policy Analysis and Management, 27,* 233–254.

Bledsoe, K. L., & Hopson, R. K. (2009). Conducting ethical research and evaluation in underserved communities. In D. M. Mertens & P. E. Ginsberg (Eds.), *The handbook of social research ethics* (pp. 391–496). Thousand Oaks, CA: Sage.

Bloom, M., Fischer, J., & Orme, J. (2009). *Evaluating practice: Guidelines for the accountable professional* (6th ed.). Boston, MA: Allyn & Bacon.

Blumberg, S. J., & Luke, J. V. (2014). *Wireless substitution: Early release of estimates from the National Health Interview Survey, January–June 2014.* Washington, DC: Centers for Disease Control. Retrieved from http://www.cdc.gov/nchs/data/nhis/earlyrelease/wireless201412.pdf

Bogdewic, S. P. (1999). Participant observation. In B. F. Crabtree & W. L. Miller (Eds.), *Doing qualitative research* (2nd ed., pp. 33–45). Thousand Oaks, CA: Sage.

Bohn, A., Buchta, C., Hornik, K., & Mair, P. (2014). Making friends and communicating on Facebook: Implications for access to social capital. *Social Networks, 37,* 29–41.

Bond, G. R., Drake, R. E., McHugo, G. J., Rapp, C. A., & Whitley, R. (2009). Strategies for improving fidelity in the National Evidence-Based Practices Project. *Research on Social Work Practice, 19,* 569–581.

Booth, W. C., Colomb, G. G., & Williams, J. M. (1995). *The craft of research.* Chicago, IL: University of Chicago Press.

Borckardt, J. J., Murphy, M. D., Nash, M. R., & Shaw, D. (2004). An empirical examination of visual analysis procedures for clinical practice evaluation. *Journal of Social Service Research, 30,* 55–73.

Borckardt, J. J., Nash, M. R., Murphy, M. D., Moore, M., Shaw, D., & O'Neil, P. (2008). Clinical practice as natural laboratory for psychotherapy research: A guide to case-based time-series analysis. *American Psychologist, 63,* 77–95.

Boruch, R. F. (1997). *Randomized experiments for planning and evaluation: A practical guide.* Thousand Oaks, CA: Sage.

Bradshaw, W. (1997). Evaluating cognitive-behavioral treatment of schizophrenia: Four single-case studies. *Research on Social Work Practice, 7,* 419–445.

Bradshaw, W. (2003). Use of single-system research to evaluate the effectiveness of cognitive-behavioural treatment of schizophrenia. *British Journal of Social Work, 33,* 885–899.

Bradshaw, W., & Roseborough, D. (2004). Evaluating the effectiveness of cognitive-behavioral treatment of residual symptoms and impairment in schizophrenia. *Research on Social Work Practice, 14,* 112–120.

Breiding, M. J., Smith, S. G., Basile, K. C., Walters, M. L., Chen, J., & Merrick, M. T. (2014). Prevalence and characteristics of sexual violence, stalking, and intimate partner violence victimization—National Intimate Partner and Sexual Violence Survey, United States, 2011. *Morbidity and Mortality Weekly Report (MMWR), Centers for Disease Control and Prevention.* Retrieved from http://www.cdc.gov/mmwr/preview/mmwrhtml/ss6308a1.htm?s_cid=ss6308a1_e

Brekke, J. S., Ell, K., & Palinkas, L. A. (2009). Translational science at the National Institute of Mental Health: Can social work takes its rightful place? *Research on Social Work Practice, 17,* 123–133.

Brennan, N., Oelschlaeger, A., Cox, C., & Tavenner, M. (2014). Leveraging the Big-Data revolution: CMS is expanding capabilities to spur health system transformation. *Health Affairs, 33,* 1195–1202.

Brewer, J., & Hunter, A. (2005). *Foundations of multimethod research: Synthesizing styles.* Thousand Oaks, CA: Sage.

Bridges, G. S., & Weis, J. G. (1989). Measuring violent behavior: Effects of study design on reported correlates of violence. In N. A. Weinar & M. E. Wolfgang (Eds.), *Violent crime, violent criminals* (pp. 14–34). Newbury Park, CA: Sage.

Broad, W. J. (1990, January 23). After 400 years, a challenge to Kepler: He fabricated his data, scholar says. *New York Times,* Retrieved from http://www.nytimes.com/1990/01/23/science/after-400-years-a-challenge-to-kepler-he-fabricated-his-data-scholar-says.html

Brock, T., & Harknett, K. (1998). A comparison of two welfare-to-work case management models. *Social Service Review, 72*, 493–520.

Broskoske, S. (2005). How to prevent paper recycling. *The Teaching Professor, 19*, 1–4.

Brown, A., & Patten, E. (2014, April 29). Statistical portrait of the foreign-born population in the United States, 2012. Pew Research Center. Retrieved from http://www.pewhispanic.org/2014/04/29/statistical-portrait-of-the-foreign-born-population-in-the-united-states-2012/

Brown, B. L., & Hedges, D. (2009). Use and misuse of quantitative methods: Data collection, calculation, and presentation. In D. M. Mertens & P. E. Ginsberg (Eds.), *The handbook of social research ethics* (pp. 373–386). Thousand Oaks, CA: Sage.

Brown, J. B. (1999). The use of focus groups in clinical research. In B. F. Crabtree & W. L. Miller (Eds.), *Doing qualitative research* (2nd ed., pp. 109–124). Thousand Oaks, CA: Sage.

Brown, R. A., Kennedy, D. P., Tucker, J. S., Golinelli, D., & Wenzel, S. L. (2013). Monogamy on the street: A mixed methods study of homeless men. *Journal of Mixed Methods Research, 7*, 328–346.

Burlew, A. K., Feaster, D., Brecht, M., & Hubbard, R. (2009). Measurement and data analysis in research addressing health disparities in substance abuse. *Journal of Substance Abuse Treatment, 36*, 25–43.

Burt, M. R. (1996). Homelessness: Definitions and counts. In J. Baumohl (Ed.), *Homelessness in America* (pp. 15–23). Phoenix, AZ: Oryx Press.

Byrne, T., Munley, E. A., Fargo, J. D., Montgomery, A. E., & Culhane, D. P. (2012). New perspectives on community-level determinants of homelessness. *Journal of Urban Affairs, 35*, 607–625.

Cambron, C., Gringeri, C., & Vogel-Ferguson, M. B. (2014). Physical and mental health correlates of adverse childhood experiences among low-income women. *Health and Social Work, 39*, 221–229.

Campbell, D. T., & Russo, M. J. (1999). *Social experimentation*. Thousand Oaks, CA: Sage.

Campbell, D. T., & Stanley, J. C. (1966). *Experimental and quasi-experimental designs for research*. Boston, MA: Houghton Mifflin.

Campbell, R. T. (1992). Longitudinal research. In E. F. Borgatta & M. L. Borgatta (Eds.), *Encyclopedia of sociology* (pp. 1146–1158). New York, NY: Macmillan.

Campbell, W. (2002). *A statement from the Government Accounting Standards Board and Performance Measurement staff* (American Society for Public Administration). Retrieved from http://64.91.242.87/cap/forum_statement.html

Carrilio, T. (2001). Family support program development: Integrating research, practice and policy. *Journal of Family Social Work, 6*, 53–78.

Cava, A., Cushman, R., & Goodman, K. (2007). HIPAA and human subjects research. *Collaborative Institutional Training Initiative*. Retrieved from https://www.citiprogram.org/members/learners

Cave, E., & Holm, S. (2003). Milgram and Tuskegee—Paradigm research projects in bioethics. *Health Care Analysis, 11*, 27–40.

Centers for Disease Control and Prevention. (1997). *Remarks by the President in apology for study done in Tuskegee*. Retrieved from http://www.cdc.gov/tuskegee/clintonp.htm

Centers for Disease Control and Prevention. (2010). *Distinguishing public health research and public health non-research*. Retrieved from http://www.cdc.gov/od/science/integrity/docs/cdc-policy-distinguishing-public-health-research-nonresearch.pdf

Chambliss, D. E., & Schutt, R. K. (2013). *Making sense of the social world: Methods of investigation* (4th ed.). Thousand Oaks, CA: Sage.

Chavez, L., Matías-Carrelo, L., Barrio, C., & Canino, G. (2007). The cultural adaptation of the Youth Quality of Life Instrument-Research Version for Latino children and adolescents. *Journal of Child and Family Studies, 16*, 75–89.

Chelimsky, E. (2008). A clash of cultures: Improving the "fit" between evaluative independence and the political requirements of a democratic society. *American Journal of Evaluation, 29*, 400–415.

Chen, H.-T. (1990). *Theory-driven evaluations*. Newbury Park, CA: Sage.

Chen, H.-T., & Rossi, P. (1987). The theory-driven approach to validity. *Evaluation and Program Planning, 10*, 95–103.

Cheung, K. M. (1999). Effectiveness of social work treatment and massage therapy for nursing home clients. *Research on Social Work Practice, 9*, 229–247.

Cho, H., & Wilke, D. J. (2005). How has the Violence Against Women Act affected the response of the criminal justice system to domestic violence. *Journal of Sociology and Social Welfare, 32*, 125–140.

Christian, L., Keeter, S., Purcell, K., & Smith, A. (2010). *Assessing the cell phone challenge to survey research in 2010*. Washington, DC: Pew Research Center for the People & the Press and Pew Internet & American Life Project.

Chung, P., Grogan, C. M., & Mosley, J. E. (2012). Residents' perceptions of effective community representation in local health decision-making. *Social Science & Medicine, 74*, 1652–1659.

Clark, H. W., Power, A. K., Le Fauve, C. E., & Lopez, E. I. (2008). Policy and practice implications of epidemiological surveys on co-occurring mental and substance use disorders. *Journal of Substance Abuse Treatment, 34*, 3–13.

Cocks, A. (2008). Researching the lives of disabled children. *Qualitative Social Work, 7*, 163–180.

Coffey, A., & Atkinson, P. (1996). *Making sense of qualitative data: Complementary research strategies*. Thousand Oaks, CA: Sage.

Cohen, J. (1988). *Statistical power analysis for the behavioral sciences*. Hillsdale, NJ: Lawrence Erlbaum.

Cole, D., Panchanadeswaran, S., & Daining, C. (2004). Predictors of job satisfaction of licensed social workers: Perceived efficacy as a mediator of the relationship between workload and job satisfaction. *Journal of Social Service Research, 31*, 1–12.

Cole, S. R., Kawachi, I., Maller, S. J., & Berkman, L. F. (2000). Test of item-response bias in the CES-D scale: Experience from the New Haven EPESE study. *Journal of Clinical Epidemiology, 53*, 285–289.

Collins, P. H. (2008). Learning from the outsider within: The sociological significance of Black feminist thought. In A. M. Jagger (Ed.), *Just methods: An interdisciplinary feminist reader* (pp. 280–310). Boulder, CO: Paradigm.

Colon, I., &, Marston, B. (1999). Resistance to a residential AIDS home: An empirical test of NIMBY. *Journal of Homosexuality, 37*, 135–145.

Converse, J. M. (1984). Attitude measurement in psychology and sociology: The early years. In C. F. Turner & E. Martin (Eds.), *Surveying subjective phenomena* (Vol. 2, pp. 3–40). New York, NY: Russell Sage.

Convery, I., & Cox, D. (2012). A review of research ethics in Internet-based research. *Practitioner Research in Higher Education, 6*, 50–57.

Cook, T. D., & Campbell, D. T. (1979). *Quasi-experimentation: Design and analysis issues for field settings*. Chicago, IL: Rand McNally.

Cooper, H., & Hedges, L. V. (1994). Research synthesis as a scientific enterprise. In H. Cooper & L. V. Hedges (Eds.), *The handbook of research synthesis* (pp. 3–14). New York, NY: Russell Sage.

Costner, H. L. (1989). The validity of conclusions in evaluation research: A further development of Chen and Rossi's theory-driven approach. *Evaluation and Program Planning, 12*, 345–353.

Cotrell, V., & Engel, R. J. (1998). Predictors of respite service utilization. *Journal of Gerontological Social Work, 30*, 117–132.

Council on Social Work Education. (2015). *2015 Educational Policy and Accreditation Standards*. Washington, DC: Council on Social Work Education. Retrieved from http://www.cswe.org/File.aspx?id=13780

Counts, D. A., & Counts, D. R. (1996). *Over the next hill: Ethnography of RVing seniors in North America*. Orchard Park, NY: Broadview Press.

Couper, M. P., Baker, R. P., Bethlehem, J., Clark, C. Z. F., Martin, J., Nicholls II, W. L., & O'Reilly, J. M. (Eds.). (1998). *Computer assisted survey information collection*. New York, NY: John Wiley.

Couper, M. P., & Miller, P. V. (2008). Web survey methods: Introduction. *Public Opinion Quarterly, 72*, 831–835.

Creating a poster. Undergraduate symposium 2015. (n.d.). Retrieved from http://www.learning.wisc.edu/ugsymposium/poster.html

Cress, D. M., & Snow, D. A. (2000). The outcomes of homeless mobilization: The influence of modernity and proto-modernity on political and civil rights, 1965 to 1980. *American Sociological Review, 60*, 702–718.

Creswell, J. W. (2010). Mapping the developing landscape of mixed methods research. In A. Tashakkori & C. Teddlie (Eds.), *SAGE handbook of mixed methods in social and behavioral research* (2nd ed., pp. 45–68). Thousand Oaks, CA: Sage.

D'Amico, E. J., & Fromme, K. (2002). Brief prevention for adolescent risk-taking behavior. *Addiction, 97*, 563–574.

Dahlberg, B., Wittink, M. N., & Gallo, J. J. (2010). Funding and publishing integrated studies: Writing effective mixed methods manuscripts and grant proposals. In A. Tashakkori & C. Teddlie (Eds.), *SAGE handbook of mixed methods in social & behavioral research* (2nd ed., pp. 775–802). Thousand Oaks, CA: Sage.

Darling, R. B., Hager, M. A., Stockdale, J. M., & Heckert, D. A. (2002). Divergent views of clients and professionals: A comparison of responses to a needs assessment instrument. *Journal of Social Service Research, 28*, 41–63.

Dattalo, P. (1998). Time series analysis: Concepts and techniques for community practitioners. *Journal of Community Practice, 5*, 67–85.

Dattilio, F., & Epstein, N. B. (2005). Introduction to the special section: The role of cognitive-behavioral interventions in couple and family therapy. *Journal of Marital and Family Therapy, 31*, 7–13.

Davis, R. E., Couper, M. P., Janz, N. K., Caldwell, C. H., & Resnicow, K. (2010). Interviewer effects in public health surveys. *Health Education Research, 25*, 14–26.

Deegan, A., (2012). Stranger in a strange land: The challenges and benefits of online interviews in the social networking space. In J. Salmons (Ed.), *Cases in online interview research* (pp. 69–99). Thousand Oaks, CA: Sage.

Dentler, R. A. (2002). *Practicing sociology: Selected fields*. Westport, CT: Praeger.

Denzin, N. K. (2002). The interpretive process. In A. M. Huberman & M. B. Miles (Eds.), *The qualitative researcher's companion* (pp. 349–368). Thousand Oaks, CA: Sage.

Denzin, N. K. (2005). The First International Congress of Qualitative Inquiry. *Qualitative Social Work, 4*, 105–111.

Denzin, N. K., & Lincoln, Y. S. (1994). Introduction: Entering the field of qualitative research. In N. K. Denzin & Y. S. Lincoln (Eds.), *Handbook of qualitative research* (pp. 1–17). Thousand Oaks, CA: Sage.

Denzin, N. K., & Lincoln, Y. S. (Eds.). (2000). *Handbook of qualitative research* (2nd ed.). Thousand Oaks, CA: Sage.

Denzin, N. K., & Lincoln, Y. S. (2008). *Strategies of qualitative inquiry* (3rd ed.). Thousand Oaks, CA: Sage.

Deochand, N., Costello, M. S., & Fuqua, R. W. (2015). Phase-changing lines, scale breaks, and trend lines using Excel 2013. *Journal of Applied Behavior Analysis, 48*, 1–16.

DeWard, S. L., & Moe, A. M. (2010). "Like a prison!": Homeless women's narratives of surviving shelter. *Journal of Sociology and Social Welfare, 37*, 115–135.

Diamond, T. (1992). *Making gray gold: Narratives of nursing home care*. Chicago, IL: University of Chicago Press.

Dillman, D. A. (2000). *Mail and Internet surveys: The tailored design method*. New York, NY: John Wiley.

Dillman, D. A. (2007). *Mail and Internet surveys: The tailored design method* (2nd ed.). Hoboken, NJ: John Wiley.

Dillman, D. A., & Christian, L. M. (2005). Survey mode as a source of instability in response across surveys. *Field Methods, 17*, 30–52.

Dilworth-Anderson, P., & Williams, S. W. (2004). Recruitment and retention strategies for longitudinal African American caregiving research: The Family Caregiving Project. *Journal of Aging and Health, 165*, 137S–156S.

Dohrenwend, B. P., & Dohrenwend, B. S. (1982). Perspectives on the past and future of psychiatric epidemiology. *American Journal of Public Health, 72*, 1271–1279.

Donahue, W. H. (1988). Kepler's fabricated figures—Covering up the mess in the new astronomy. *Journal of the History of Astronomy, 19*, 217–237.

Drake, R. E., McHugo, G. J., & Biesanz, J. C. (1995). The test-retest reliability of standardized instruments among homeless persons with substance use disorders. *Journal of Studies on Alcohol, 56*, 161–167.

Drew, P. (2005). Conversation analysis. In K. L. Fitch & R. E. Sanders (Eds.), *Handbook of language and social interactions* (pp. 71–102). Mahwah, NJ: Lawrence Erlbaum.

Drisko, J. W., & Grady, M. D. (2012). *Evidence-based practice in clinical social work*. New York. NY: Springer.

Dulmus, C. N., & Cristalli, M. E. (2012). A university-community partnership to advance research in practice settings: The HUB research model. *Research on Social Work Practice, 22*, 195–202.

Eckholm, E. (2014, February 23). Opponents of same-sex marriage take bad-for-children argument to court. *New York Times*, A16.

Economic Policy Institute. (2015). Economic Policy Institute, family budget calculator. Retrieved from http://www.epi.org/resources/budget

Edin, K., & Lein, L. (1997). *Making ends meet: How single mothers survive welfare and low-wage work*. New York, NY: Russell Sage.

Elliott, J., Holland, J., & Thompson, R. (2008). Longitudinal and panel studies. In P. Alasuutari, L. Bickman, & J. Brannen (Eds.), *The SAGE handbook of social research methods* (pp. 228–248). Thousand Oaks, CA: Sage.

Emerson, R. M., Fretz, R. I., & Shaw, L. L. (1995). *Writing ethnographic fieldnotes*. Chicago, IL: University of Chicago Press.

Engel, R. J. (1988). *The dynamics of poverty for the elderly* (Unpublished doctoral dissertation). University of Wisconsin, Madison.

Engel, R. J. (1994). *Settlement house survey final report*. Pittsburgh, PA: United Way of Allegheny County and University of Pittsburgh Institute of Politics.

Engel, R. J., Rosen, D., & Soska, T. (2008, January). *Raising the stakes: Assessing Allegheny County's human service response to the social impact of casino gambling*. Pittsburgh, PA: School of Social Work, University of Pittsburgh.

Engel, R. J., Rosen, D., Weaver, A., & Soska, T. (2010). Raising the stakes: Assessing the human service response to the advent of a casino. *Journal of Gambling Studies, 26*, 611–622.

English, B. (1997). Conducting ethical evaluations with disadvantaged and minority target groups. *Evaluation Practice, 18*, 49–55.

Erikson, K. T. (1967). A comment on disguised observation in sociology. *Social Problems, 12*, 366–373.

Essock, S. M., Frisman, L. K., & Kontos, N. J. (1998). Cost-effectiveness of Assertive

Community Treatment teams. *American Journal of Orthopsychiatry, 68*, 179–190.

Eurostat. (2003). *ECHP UDP manual: European Community Household Panel Longitudinal users' database*. Brussels, Belgium: European Commission.

Eynon, R., Fry, J., & Schroeder, R. (2008). The ethics of Internet research. In N. Fielding, R. M. Lee, & G. Blank (Eds.), *The SAGE handbook of online research methods* (pp. 23–41). Thousand Oaks, CA: Sage.

Federal Bureau of Investigation, U.S. Department of Justice. (2013). Table 29: Estimated number of arrests, in *Crime in the United States: 2012*. Retrieved from http://www.fbi.gov/about-us/cjis/ucr/crime-in-the-u.s/2012/crime-in-the-u.s.-2012/tables/29tabledatadecpdf

Fenno, R. F., Jr. (1978). *Home style: House members in their districts*. Boston, MA: Little, Brown.

Ferguson, K. M., Bender, K., Thompson, S. J., Maccio, E. M., & Pollio, D. (2012). Employment status and income generation among homeless young adults: Results from a five-city, mixed methods study. *Youth & Society, 44*, 385–404.

File, T. (2013). The diversifying electorate—Voting rates by race and Hispanic origin in 2012 (and other recent elections). *Population Characteristics: Current Population Survey*. Washington, DC: U.S. Census Bureau.

Fink, A. (2005). *Conducting research literature reviews: From Internet to paper* (2nd ed.). Thousand Oaks, CA: Sage.

Fischer, J., & Corcoran, K. (2013). *Measures for clinical practice and research* (5th ed.). Oxford, UK: Oxford University Press.

Fisher, C. B., & Anushko, A. E. (2008). Research ethics in social science. In P. Alasuutari, L. Bickman, & J. Brannen (Eds.), *SAGE handbook of social research methods* (pp. 94–109). Thousand Oaks, CA: Sage.

Flaherty, J. A., Gaviria, M., Pathak, D., Mitchell, T., Wintrob, R., Richman, J., & Birz, S. (1988). Developing instruments for cross-cultural psychiatric research. *The Journal of Nervous and Mental Disease, 176*, 257–263.

Forte, J. (2010). Transformation through interaction: A meta-ethnographic synthesis of research reports on mutual aid groups. *Qualitative Social Work, 9*, 151–168.

Fowler, F. J. (1988). *Survey research methods* (Rev. ed.). Newbury Park, CA: Sage.

Fowler, F, J. (1995). *Improving survey questions: Design and evaluation*. Thousand Oaks, CA: Sage.

Fram, A., & Tompson, T. (2008, March 19). Many college students stressed out, poll finds. *Boston Globe*. Retrieved from http://www.boston.com/news/nation/articles/2008/03/19/many_college_students_stressed_out_poll_finds/

Franzen, S., Morrel-Samuels, S., Reischl, T. M., & Zimmerman, M. A. (2009). Using process evaluation to strengthen inter-generational partnerships in the Youth Empowerment Solutions Program. *Journal of Prevention & Intervention in the Community, 37*, 289–301.

Gaiser, T. J., & Schreiner, A. E.'(2009). *A guide to conducting online research*. Thousand Oaks, CA: Sage

Gallup Poll. (2013). *Election polls—Accuracy record in Presidential elections*. Retrieved from http://www.Gallup.com/poll/9442/Election-Polls-Accuracy-Record-Presidential-Elections.aspx

Galvan, J. L. (2013). *Writing literature reviews: A guide for students of the social and behavioral sciences* (5th ed.). Glendale, CA: Pyrczak Publishing.

Gambrill, E. (1999). Evidence-based practice: An alternative to authority-based practice. *Journal of Contemporary Human Services, 80*, 341–350.

Gambrill, E. (2001). Social work: An authority-based profession. *Research on Social Work Practice, 11*, 166–175.

Gambrill, E. (2006). Evidence-based practice and policy: Choices ahead. *Research on Social Work Practice, 16*, 338–357.

Garbarski, D., Schaeffer, N. C., & Dykema, J. (2015). The effects of response option order and question order on self-rated health. *Quality of Life Research, 24*, 1443–1453.

Garland, D., Rogers, R., Singletary, J., & Yancey, G. (2005). *The faith factor in effective models of multi-sector collaboration: A final report to the Pew Charitable Trusts*. Waco, TX: Baylor University. Retrieved from http://www.baylor.edu/content/services/document.php/22985.pdf

Garner, T. I. (2010). Supplemental poverty measure thresholds: Laying the foundation. Retrieved from http://www.census.gov/hhes/povmeas/methodology/supplemental/research/ASSAGarner%20Poverty%20Thresholds%20paper%2012-29-10.pdf

Geertz, C. (1973). Thick description: Toward an interpretive theory of culture. In C. Geertz (Ed.), *The interpretation of cultures* (pp. 3–30). New York, NY: Basic Books.

Geller, S. E., Adams, M. G., & Carnes, M. (2006). Adherence to federal guidelines for reporting of sex and race/ethnicity in clinical trials. *Journal of Women's Health, 15*, 1123–1131.

Gellis, Z. D., McGinty, J., Tierney, L., Jordan, C., Burton, J., & Misener, E. (2008). Randomized controlled trial of problem-solving therapy for minor depression in home care. *Research on Social Work Practice, 18*, 596–606.

Gelman, C. R. (2002). The elderly Latino population in Holyoke, MA: A qualitative study of unmet needs and community strengths. *Journal of Gerontological Social Work, 39*, 89–114.

George, S., Duran, N., & Norris, K. (2014). A systematic review of barriers and facilitators to minority research participation among African Americans, Latinos, Asian Americans, and Pacific Islanders. *American Journal of Public Health, 104*, e16–e31.

Gjesfjeld, C. D., Greeno, C. G., Kim, K. H., & Anderson, C. M. (2010). Economic stress, social support, and maternal depression: Is social support deterioration occurring? *Social Work Research, 34*, 135–143.

Glaser, B. G., & Strauss, A. L. (1967). *The discovery of grounded theory: Strategies for qualitative research*. London, UK: Weidenfeld and Nicholson.

Gobo, G. (2008). Reconceptualizing generalization: Old issues in a new frame. In P. Alasuutari, L. Bickman, & J. Brannen (Eds.), *The SAGE handbook of social research methods* (pp. 193–213). Thousand Oaks, CA: Sage.

Goleman, D. (1993, August 17). Placebo effect is shown to be twice as powerful as expected. *New York Times*, C3.

Gordon, R. (1992). *Basic interviewing skills*. Itasca, IL: Peacock.

Grady, J. (1996). The scope of visual sociology. *Visual Sociology, 11*, 10–24.

Gray, M., Joy, E., Plath, D., & Webb, S. A. (2012). Implementing evidence-based practice: A review of the empirical research literature. *Research on Social Work Practice, 23*, 157–166.

Green, B. L., Chung, J. Y., Daroowalla, A., Kaltman, S., & DeBenedictis, C. (2006). Evaluating the cultural validity of the Stressful Life Events Screening Questionnaire. *Violence Against Women, 12*, 191–213.

Griffin, C., & Phoenix, A. (1994). The relationship between qualitative and quantitative research: Lessons from feminist psychology. *Journal of Community and Applied Social Psychology, 4*, 287–298.

Grinnell, F. (1992). *The scientific attitude* (2nd ed.). New York, NY: Guilford Press.

Groves, R. M. (1989). *Survey errors and survey costs*. New York, NY: John Wiley.

Groves, R. M., & Couper, M. P. (1998). *Nonresponse in household interview surveys*. New York, NY: John Wiley.

Guba, E. G., & Lincoln, Y. S. (1989). *Fourth generation evaluation*. Newbury Park, CA: Sage.

Gubrium, J. F., & Holstein, J. A. (1997). *The new language of qualitative method*. New York, NY: Oxford University Press.

Gubrium, J. F., & Holstein, J. A. (2000). Analyzing interpretive practice. In N. Denzin & Y. S. Lincoln (Eds.), *The handbook of qualitative research* (2nd ed., pp. 487–508). Thousand Oaks, CA: Sage.

Guterbock, T. M. (2008, May 9). *Strategies and standards for reaching respondents in an age of new technology*. Presentation to the Harvard Program on Survey Research Spring Conference, New Technologies and Survey Research, Harvard University, Cambridge, MA.

Hacker, K., Collins, J., Gross-Young, L., Almeida, S., & Burke, N. (2008). Coping with youth suicide and overdose: One community's efforts to investigate, intervene, and prevent suicide contagion. *Crisis, 29*, 86–95.

Hafner, K. (2008, May 3). Exercise your brain, or else you'll . . . Uh . . . . *New York Times*. Retrieved from http://www.nytimes.com/2008/05/03/technology/03brain.html?_r=0

Hage, J., & Meeker, B. F. (1988). *Social causality*. Boston, MA: Unwin Hyman.

Hakimzadeh, S., & Cohn, D. (2007). *English usage among Hispanics in the United States*. Washington, DC: Pew Hispanic Center. Retrieved from http://pewhispanic.org/files/reports/82.pdf

Halcón, L. L., & Lifson, A. R. (2004). Prevalence and predictors of sexual risks among homeless youth. *Journal of Youth & Adolescence, 33*, 71–80.

Haley, L., & Bangs, R. (2000). *Impact of welfare reform on nonprofit organizations in Pennsylvania* (Proposal to Aspen Institute, Nonprofit Sector Research Fund). Pittsburgh, PA: University of Pittsburgh.

Hall, J. A., Dineen, J. P., Schlesinger, D. J., & Stanton, R. (2000). Advanced group treatment for developmentally disabled adults with social skill deficits. *Research on Social Work Practice, 10*, 301–326.

Hamilton, R. J., & Bowers, B. J. (2006). Internet recruitment and e-mail interviews in qualitative studies. *Qualitative Health Research, 16*, 821–835.

Hammersley, M. (2008). Assessing validity in social research. In P. Alasuutari, L. Bickman, & J. Brannen (Eds.), *The SAGE handbook of social research methods* (pp. 42–53). Thousand Oaks, CA: Sage.

Hann, D., Winter, K., & Jacobsen, P. (1999). Measurement of depressive symptoms in cancer patients: Evaluation of the Center for Epidemiological Studies Depression Scale (CES-D). *Journal of Psychosomatic Research, 46*, 438–443.

Hard, S. F., Conway, J. M., & Moran, A. C. (2006). Faculty and college student beliefs about the frequency of student academic misconduct. *Sociological Review, 72*, 341–364.

Haynes, R. B, Devereaux, P. J., & Guyatt, G. H. (2002). Clinical expertise in the era of evidence-based medicine and patient choice. *Evidence Based Medicine, 7*, 36–38.

Heaton, J. (2008). Secondary analysis of qualitative data. In P. Alasuutari, L. Bickman, & J. Brannen (Eds.), *The SAGE handbook of social research methods* (pp. 506–535). Thousand Oaks, CA: Sage.

Henderson, J. N. (1994). Ethnic and racial issues. In J. F. Gubrium & A. Sankar (Eds.), *Qualitative methods in aging research* (pp. 33–50). Thousand Oaks, CA: Sage.

Hendryx, M., Onizuk, R., Wilson, V., & Ahern, M. (2012). Effects of a cost-sharing policy on disenrollment from a state health insurance program. *Social Work in Public Health, 27*, 671–686.

Herek, G., Kimmel, D. C., Amaro, H., & Melton, G. B. (1991). Avoiding heterosexist bias in psychological research. *American Psychologist, 46*, 957–963.

Hergenrather, K. C., Rhodes, S. D., & Clark, G. (2006). Windows to work: Exploring employment-seeking behaviors of persons with HIV/AIDS through Photovoice. *AIDS Education and Prevention, 18*, 243–258.

Herrera, C. D. (2003). A clash of methodology and ethics in "undercover" social science. *Philosophy of the Social Sciences, 33*, 351–362.

Hesse-Biber, S, & Leavy, P. L. (2007). *Feminist research practice: A primer*. Thousand Oaks, CA: Sage.

Heyman, J. C., & Gutheil, I. A. (2010). Older Latinos' attitudes toward and comfort with end-of-life planning. *Social Work, 35*, 17–26.

Hirsch, K. (1989). *Songs from the alley*. New York, NY: Doubleday.

Holbrook, A. L., Green, M. C., & Krosnick, J. A. (2003). Telephone versus face-to-face interviewing of national probability samples with long questionnaires: Comparisons of respondent satisficing and social desirability response bias. *Public Opinion Quarterly, 60*, 58–88.

Holden, G., Barker, K., Kuppens, S., Rosenberg, G., & LeBreton, J. (2015). A replication of failure, not a failure to replicate. *Research on Social Work Practice, 25*, 313–321.

Holmes, S. (2009). Methodological and ethical considerations in designing an Internet study of quality of life: A discussion paper. *International Journal of Nursing Studies, 46*, 394–405.

Horney, J. D., Osgood, W., & Marshall, I. H. (1995). Criminal careers in the short-term: Intra-individual variability in crime and its relation to local life circumstances. *American Sociological Review, 60*, 655–673.

Horowitz, C. R., Robinson, M., & Seifer, S. (2009). Community-based participatory research from the margin to the mainstream: Are researchers prepared? *Circulation, 119*, 2633–2642.

Huberman, A. M., & Miles, M. B. (1994). Data management and analysis methods. In N. K. Denzin & Y. S. Lincoln (Eds.), *Handbook of qualitative research* (pp. 428–444). Thousand Oaks, CA: Sage.

Hui, C. H., & Triandis, H. C. (1985). Measurement in cross-cultural psychology: A review and comparison of strategies. *Journal of Cross-Cultural Psychology, 16*, 131–152.

Humphries, C. (2011, May 15). Deeply conflicted: How can we insulate ourselves from conflicts of interest? The most popular solution—disclosing them turns out not to help. *Boston Globe*, K1, K3.

Humphrey, N. (1992). *A history of the mind: Evolution and the birth of consciousness*. New York, NY: Simon & Schuster.

Huston, P., & Naylor, C. D. (1886). Health services research: Reporting on studies using secondary data sources. *Canadian Medical Association Journal, 155*, 1697–1702.

Ingersoll-Dayton, B., Neal, M. B., Ha, J.-H., & Hammer, L. B. (2003). Collaboration among siblings providing care for older parents. *Journal of Gerontological Social Work, 40*, 51–66.

Ingraham, C. (2014, October 29). Child poverty in the U.S. is among the worst in the developed world. *Washington Post*. Retrieved from http://www.washingtonpost.com/news/wonkblog/wp/2014/10/29/child-poverty-in-the-u-s-is-among-the-worst-in-the-developed-world/

Institute of Medicine. (2001). *Crossing the quality chasm: A new health system for the 21st century—brief report*. Retrieved from http://www.nap.edu/html/quality_chasm/reportbrief.pdf

Irvine, L. (1998). Organizational ethics and fieldwork realities: Negotiating ethical boundaries in Codependents Anonymous. In S. Grills (Ed.), *Doing ethnographic research: Fieldwork settings* (pp. 167–183). Thousand Oaks, CA: Sage.

Israel, B. A., Eng, E., Schulz, A. J., & Parker, E. A. (2005). Introduction to methods in community-based participatory research for health. In B. A. Israel, E. Eng, A. J. Schulz, & E. A. Parker (Eds.), *Methods in community-based participatory research for health* (pp. 3–26). San Francisco, CA: Jossey-Bass.

James, N., & Busher, H. (2009). *Online interviewing.* Thousand Oaks, CA: Sage.

Jang, D.-H. (2009). Significance of variations between income transfers and social care services development. *Journal of Comparative Social Welfare, 25,* 37–48.

Jarrett, M. A., & Ollendick, T. H. (2012). Treatment of comorbid attention-deficit/hyperactivity disorder and anxiety in children: A multiple baseline design analysis. *Journal of Consulting and Clinical Psychology, 80,* 239–244.

Jenson, W., Clark, E., Kircher, J. C., & Kristjansson, S. D. (2007). Statistical reform: Evidence-based practice, meta-analyses, and single subject designs. *Psychology in the Schools, 44,* 483–493.

Johnson, C., & Golden, J. (1997). Generalization of social skills to peer interactions in a child with language delays. *Behavioral-Interventions, 12,* 133–147.

Johnson, R. B., Onwuegbuzie, A., & Turner, L. A. (2007). Toward a definition of mixed methods research. *Journal of Mixed Methods Research, 1,* 112–133.

Johnston, M., Sherer, M., & Whyte, J. (2006). Applying evidence standards to rehabilitation research. *American Journal of Physical Medicine and Rehabilitation, 85,* 292–309.

Jones, K., & Benda, B. (2004). Alcohol use among adolescents with non-residential fathers: A study of assets and deficits. *Alcoholism Treatment Quarterly, 22,* 3–25.

Jones, L. V., & Warner, L. A. (2011). Evaluating culturally responsive group work with Black women. *Research on Social Work Practice, 21,* 737–746.

Kagawa-Singer, M. (2000). Improving the validity and generalizability of studies with underserved U.S. populations expanding the research paradigm. *Annals of Epidemiology, 10,* S92–S103.

Kahana, B., & Kahana, E. (1970). Changes in mental status of elderly patients in age integrated and age segregated hospital milieus. *Journal of Advanced Psychology, 75,* 177–181.

Kahana, E., Kahana, B., & Riley, K. P. (1988). Contextual issues in quantitative studies of institutional settings for the aged. In S. Reinharz & G. D. Rowles (Eds.), *Qualitative gerontology* (pp. 197–216). New York, NY: Springer.

Kang, S.-Y., Domanski, M. D., & Moon, S. S. (2009). Ethnic enclave resources and predictors of depression among Arizona's Korean immigrant elders. *Journal of Gerontological Social Work, 52,* 489–502.

Kaufman, S. R. (1986). *The ageless self: Sources of meaning in late life.* Madison: University of Wisconsin Press.

Kaufman, S. R. (1994). In-depth interviewing. In J. F. Gubrium & A. Sankar (Eds.), *Qualitative methods in aging research* (pp. 123–136). Thousand Oaks, CA: Sage.

Kayser-Jones, J., & Koenig, B. A. (1994). Ethical issues. In J. F. Gubrium & A. Sankar (Eds.), *Qualitative methods in aging research* (pp. 15–32). Thousand Oaks, CA: Sage.

Keenan, E. K. (2004). From sociocultural categories to socially located relations using critical theory in social work practice. *Families in Society, 85,* 539–548.

Kenney, C. (1987, August 30). They've got your number. *Boston Globe Magazine,* pp. 12, 46–56, 60.

Kincaid, H. (1996). *Philosophical foundations of the social sciences: Analyzing controversies in social research.* Cambridge, UK: Cambridge University Press.

King, G., Keohane, R. O., & Verba, S. (1994). *Scientific inference in qualitative research.* Princeton, NJ: Princeton University Press.

King, N., & Horrocks, C. (2010). *Interviews in qualitative research.* Thousand Oaks, CA: Sage.

Kinnevy, S. C., Healey, B. P., Pollio, D. E., & North, C. S. (1999). BicycleWORKS: Task-centered group work with high-risk youth. *Social Work With Groups, 22,* 33–47.

Kirkpatrick, S. I., & Tarasuk, V. (2011). Housing circumstances are associated with household food access among low-income families. *Journal of Urban Health, 88,* 284–296.

Kitchner, K. S., & Kitchner, R. E. (2009). Social science research ethics: Historical and philosophical issues. In D. M. Mertens & P. E. Ginsberg (Eds.), *The handbook of social research ethics* (pp. 5–22). Thousand Oaks, CA: Sage.

Kliewer, M. A. (2005). Writing it up: A step-by-step guide to publication for beginning investigators. *American Journal of Roentgenology, 185,* 591–596.

Klinenberg, E. (2012, February 5). One's a crowd. *New York Times,* SR4.

Koegel, P. (1987). *Ethnographic perspectives on homeless and homeless mentally ill women.* Washington, DC: U.S. Department of Health and Human Services, Public Health Service, Alcohol, Drug Abuse, and Mental Health Administration.

Koeske, G. (1994). Some recommendations for improving measurement validation in social work research. *Journal of Social Service Research, 18,* 43–72.

Kohut, A., Keeter, S., Doherty, C., Dimock, M., & Christian, L. (2012, May 15). *Assessing the representativeness of public opinion surveys.* Washington DC: Pew Research Center. Retrieved from http://www.people-press.org/files/legacy-pdf/Assessing%20the%20Representativeness%20of%20Public%20Opinion%20Surveys.pdf

Kolata, G. (2013, October 18). Decades later, condemnation for a skid row cancer study. *New York Times,* A1.

Korr, W. S., & Joseph, A. (1996). Effects of local conditions on program outcomes: Analysis of contradictory findings from two programs for homeless mentally ill. *Journal of Health and Social Policy, 8,* 41–53.

Kotsopoulos, S., Walker, S., Beggs, K., & Jones, B. (1996). A clinical and academic outcome study of children attending a day treatment program. *Canadian Journal of Psychiatry, 41,* 371–378.

Kozinets, R. V. (2010). *Netnography: Doing ethnographic research online.* Thousand Oaks, CA: Sage.

Kreuger, R. A., & Casey, M. A. (2009). *Focus groups: A practical guide for applied research* (4th ed.). Thousand Oaks, CA: Sage.

Kreuter, F., Presser, S., & Tourangeau, R. (2008). Social desirability bias in CATI, IVR, and web surveys: The effects of mode and question sensitivity. *Public Opinion Quarterly, 72,* 847–865.

Kroenke, K., & Spitzer, R. L. (2002). The PHQ-9: A new depression diagnostic and severity measure. *Psychiatric Annals, 32,* 509–515.

Krosnick, J. A. (1999). Survey research. *Annual Review of Psychology, 50,* 537–567.

Krout, J. A. (1985). Service awareness among the elderly. *Journal of Gerontological Social Work, 9,* 7–19.

Kuzel, A. J. (1999). Sampling in qualitative inquiry. In B. F. Crabtree & W. L. Miller (Eds.), *Doing qualitative research* (2nd ed., pp. 33–45). Thousand Oaks, CA: Sage.

Kvale, S. (1996). *Interviews: An introduction to qualitative research interviewing.* Thousand Oaks, CA: Sage.

Kvale, S. (2002). The social construction of validity. In N. k. Denzin & Y. S. Lincoln (Eds.), *The qualitative inquiry reader* (pp. 299–325). Thousand Oaks, CA: Sage.

Labaw, P. J. (1980). *Advanced questionnaire design.* Cambridge, MA: ABT Books.

Lamott, A. (1994). *Bird by bird: Some instructions on writing and life.* New York, NY: Anchor Books.

Larsen, D. L., Attkisson, C. C., Hargreaves, W. A., & Nguyen, T. D. (1979). Assessment of client/patient satisfaction: Development of a general scale. *Evaluation and Program Planning, 2,* 197–207.

Layte, R., & Whelan, C. T. (2003). Moving in and out of poverty: The impact of welfare regimes on poverty dynamics in the EU. *European Societies, 5,* 167–191.

Lee, B. A., Farrell, C. R., & Link, B. G. (2004). Revisiting the contact hypothesis: The case of public exposure to homelessness. *American Sociological Review, 69,* 40–63.

Lehrer, J. (2010, December 12). The truth wears off: Is there something wrong with the scientific method? *The New Yorker,* 52–57.

Leiter, J. (2007). School performance trajectories after the advent of reported maltreatment. *Children and Youth Services Review, 29,* 363–382.

Levy, P. S., & Lemeshow, S. (2008). *Sampling of populations: Methods and applications* (4th ed.). New York, NY: John Wiley.

Lewis-Fernandez, R., Raggio, G. A., Gorritz, M., Duan, N., Marcus, S., Cabassa, L. J., . . . Hinton, D. E. (2013). GAP-REACH: A checklist to assess comprehensive reporting of race, ethnicity, and culture in psychiatric publications. *The Journal of Nervous and Mental Disease, 201,* 860–871.

Li, Y., Mills, B., Davis, G. C., & Mykerezi, E. (2014). Child food insecurity and the Food Stamp program: What a difference monthly data make. *Social Service Review, 88,* 322–348.

Lietz, C. (2006). Uncovering stories of family resilience: A mixed methods study of resilient families, Part 1. *Families in Society: Journal of Contemporary Social Services, 87,* 575–581.

Lietz, C. (2007). Uncovering stories of family resilience: A mixed methods study of resilient families, Part 2. *Families in Society: Journal of Contemporary Social Services, 88,* 147–155.

Lin, J., & Bernstein, J. (2008). *What we need to get by* (EPI Briefing Paper #224). Washington, DC: Economic Policy Institute. Retrieved from http://epi.3cdn.net/0136f3b9a1aa8e2a34_f0m6bnry2.pdf

Lincoln, Y. S. (2009). Ethical practices in qualitative research. In D. M. Mertens & P. E. Ginsberg (Eds.), *The handbook of social research ethics* (pp. 150–169). Thousand Oaks, CA: Sage.

Lindsey, M. A., Korr, W. S., Broitman, M., Bone, L., Green, A., & Leaf, P. J. (2006). Help-seeking behaviors and depression among African American adolescent boys. *Social Work, 51,* 49–58.

Lipp, A. (2007). Using systematic reviews. *Nursing Management, 14,* 30–32.

Lipsey, M. W., & Wilson, D. B. (2001). *Practical meta-analysis.* Thousand Oaks, CA: Sage.

Littell, J. H. (2005). Lessons from a systematic review of effects of multisystemic therapy. *Children and Youth Services Review, 27,* 445–463.

Litwin, M. S. (1995). *How to measure survey reliability and validity.* Thousand Oaks, CA: Sage.

Locke, L. F., Spirduso, W. W., & Silverman, S. J. (2007). *Proposals that work: A guide for planning dissertations and grant proposals* (5th ed.). Thousand Oaks, CA: Sage.

Lofland, J., & Lofland, L. H. (1984). *Analyzing social settings: A guide to qualitative observations and analysis* (2nd ed.). Belmont, CA: Wadsworth.

Luna, I., de Ardon, E. T., Lim, Y. M., Cromwell, S., Phillips, L., & Russell, C. (1996). The relevance of familism in cross-cultural studies of family caregiving. *Journal of Nursing Research, 18,* 267–283.

Lundahl, B. W., Nimer, J., & Parsons, B. (2006). Preventing child abuse: A meta-analysis of parent training programs. *Research on Social Work Practice, 16,* 251–262.

Lyman, K. A. (1994). Fieldwork in groups and institutions. In J. F. Gubrium & A. Sankar (Eds.), *Qualitative methods in aging research* (pp. 155–170). Thousand Oaks, CA: Sage.

Lynch, M., & Bogen, D. (1997). Sociology's asociological "core": An examination of textbook sociology in light of the sociology of scientific knowledge. *American Sociological Review, 62,* 481–493.

Mabry, L. (2008). Case study in social research. P. Alasuutari, L. Bickman, & J. Brannen (Eds.), *The SAGE handbook of social research methods* (pp. 214–227). Thousand Oaks, CA: Sage.

Macgowan, M. J., & Wong, S. E. (2014). Single-case designs in group work: Past applications, future directions. *Group Dynamics: Theory, Research and Practice, 18,* 138–158.

Madden, R. (2010). *Being ethnographic: A guide to the theory and practice of ethnography.* Thousand Oaks, CA: Sage.

Magnuson, K. A., Meyers, M. K., & Waldfogel, J. (2007). Public funding and enrollment in formal child care in the 1990s. *Social Service Review, 81,* 47–83.

Mak, W. W. S., Law, R. W., Alvidrez, J., & Perez-Stable, E. J. (2007). Gender and ethnic diversity in NIMH-funded clinical trials: Review of a decade of published research. *Administration & Policy in Mental Health & Mental Health Services Research, 34,* 497–503.

Mangione, T. W. (1995). *Mail surveys: Improving the quality.* Thousand Oaks, CA: Sage.

Marin, G., & Marin, B. V. (1991). *Research with Hispanic populations.* Newbury Park, CA: Sage.

Marini, M. M., & Singer, B. (1988). Causality in the social sciences. In C. C. Clogg (Ed.), *Sociological methodology* (Vol. 18, pp. 347–409). Washington, DC: American Sociological Association.

Markham, A., & Buchanan, E. (2012). Ethical decision-making and Internet research: Recommendations from the AoIR Ethics Working Committee. Retrieved from http://aoir.org/reports/ethics2.pdf

Marshall, C., & Rossman, G. B. (1999). *Designing qualitative research* (3rd ed.). Thousand Oaks, CA: Sage.

Martin, J. I., & Knox, J. (2000). Methodological and ethical issues in research on lesbians and gay men. *Social Work Research, 24,* 51–59.

Martin, J. I., & Meezan, W. (2003). Applying ethical standards to research and evaluations involving lesbian, gay, bisexual, and transgender populations. *Journal of Gay and Lesbian Social Services, 15,* 181–201.

Martin, L., & Kettner, P. (2010). *Measuring the performance of human service programs* (2nd ed.). Thousand Oaks, CA: Sage.

Martin, S. S., Trask, J., Peterson, T., Martin, B. C., Baldwin, J., & Knapp, M. (2010). Influence of culture and discrimination on care-seeking behavior of elderly African Americans: A qualitative study. *Social Work in Public Health, 25,* 311–326.

Matt, G. E., & Cook, T. D. (1994). Threats to the validity of research syntheses. In H. Cooper & L. V. Hedges (Eds.), *The handbook of research synthesis* (pp. 503–520). New York, NY: Russell Sage.

Max, W., Rice, D. P., Finkelstein, E., Bardwell, R. A., & Leadbetter, S. (2004). The economic toll of intimate partner violence against women in the United States. *Violence and Victims, 19,* 259–272.

Maxwell, J. A. (2005). *Qualitative research design: An interactive approach* (2nd ed.). Thousand Oaks, CA: Sage.

Mayer-Schönberger, V., & Cukier, K. (2013). *Big Data: A revolution that will transform how we live, work, and think.* Boston, MA: Houghton Mifflin Harcourt.

Maynard, D. W., Freese, J., & Schaeffer, N. C. (2010). Calling for participation: Requests, blocking moves, and rational (inter) action in survey introductions. *American Sociological Review, 75,* 791–814.

McCarter, S. A. (2009). Legal and extralegal factors affecting minority overrepresentation in Virginia's juvenile justice system: A mixed-methods study. *Child and Adolescent Social Work Journal, 26,* 533–544.

McCoyd, J. L. M., & Kerson, T. S. (2006). Conducting intensive interviews using email: A serendipitous comparative opportunity. *Qualitative Social Work, 5,* 389–406.

McGeeney, K., & Keeter, S. (2014, January 15). Pew Research increases share of interviews conducted by cellphone. Pew Research Center. Retrieved from http://www.pewresearch.org/fact-tank/2014/01/15/pew-research-increases-share-of-interviews-conducted-by-cellphone

McGinn, T., Taylor, B., McColgan, M, & McQuilkan, J. (2014). Social work literature searching: Current issues with databases and online search engines. *Research on Social Work Practice*. doi: 10.1177/1049731514549423 2.

McKee, M. B., Picciano, J. F., Roffman, R. A., Swanson, F., & Kalichman, S. C. (2006). Marketing the "Sex Check": Evaluating recruitment strategies for a telephone-based HIV prevention project for gay and bisexual men. *AIDS Education and Prevention, 18*, 116–131.

McKillip, J. (1987). *Need analysis: Tools for the human services and education.* Newbury Park, CA: Sage.

McMillen, J. C., Fedoravicius, N., Rowe, J., Zima, B. T., & Ware, N. (2007). A crisis of credibility: Professionals' concerns about the psychiatric care provided to clients of the child welfare system. *Administration and Policy in Mental Health and Mental Health Services Research, 34*, 203–212.

McNamara, J. R., Tamanini, K., & Pelletier-Walker, S. (2008). The impact of short-term counseling at a domestic violence shelter. *Research on Social Work Practice, 18*, 132–136.

McNeill, T. (2006). Evidence-based practice in an age of relativism: Toward a model for practice. *Social Work, 51*, 147–156.

Mertens, D. M. (2012). Transformative mixed methods: Addressing inequities. *American Behavioral Scientist, 56*, 802–813.

Mertens, D. M., Bledsoe, K. L., Sullivan, M., & Wilson, A. (2010). Utilization of mixed methods for transformative purposes. In A. Tashakkori & C. Teddlie (Eds.), *SAGE handbook of mixed methods in social and behavioral research* (2nd ed.). Thousand Oaks, CA: Sage.

Miles, M. B., & Huberman, A. M. (1994). *Qualitative data analysis* (2nd ed.). Thousand Oaks, CA: Sage.

Miles, M. B., Huberman, A. M., & Saldaña, J. (2014). *Qualitative data analysis: A methods sourcebook* (3rd ed.). Thousand Oaks, CA: Sage.

Milgram, S. (1963). Behavioral study of obedience. *Journal of Abnormal and Social Psychology, 67*, 371–378.

Milgram, S. (1964). Issues in the study of obedience: A reply to Baumrind. *American Psychologist, 19*, 848–852.

Milgram, S. (1965). Some conditions of obedience and disobedience to authority. *Human Relations, 18*, 57–76.

Milgram, S. (1974). *Obedience to authority: An experimental view.* New York, NY: Harper & Row.

Milgram, S. (1977, October). Subject reaction: The neglected factor in the ethics of experimentation. *Hastings Law Review,* pp. 19–23.

Milgram, S. (1992). *The individual in a social world: Essays and experiments* (2nd ed.). New York, NY: McGraw-Hill.

Miller, A. G. (1986). *The obedience experiments: A case study of controversy in social science.* New York, NY: Praeger.

Miller, C., Huston, A. C., Duncan, G. J., McLoyd, V. C., & Weisner, T. S. (2008). *New Hope for the working poor: Effects after eight years for families and children.* New York, NY: MDRC. Retrieved from http://www.mdrc .org/sites/default/files/full_458.pdf

Miller, D. C., & Salkind, J. N. (2002). *Handbook of research design and social measurement* (6th ed.). Thousand Oaks, CA: Sage.

Miller, S. (1999). *Gender and community policing: Walking the talk.* Boston, MA: Northeastern University Press.

Miller, W. L., & Crabtree, B. F. (1999). Clinical research: A multimethod typology and qualitative roadmap. In B. F. Crabtree & W. L. Miller (Eds.), *Doing qualitative research* (2nd ed., pp. 127–140). Thousand Oaks, CA: Sage.

Minkler, M. (2005). Community-based research partnerships: Challenges and opportunities. *Journal of Urban Health: Bulletin of the New York Academy of Medicine, 82*(Suppl. 2), ii3–ii12.

Miranda, J., Azocar, F., Organista, K. C., Munoz, R. F., & Lieberman, A. (1996). Recruiting and retaining low-income Latinos in psychotherapy research. *Journal of Consulting and Clinical Psychology, 64*, 868–874.

Miranda, J., Nakamura, R., & Bernal, G. (2003). Including ethnic minorities in mental health intervention research: A practical approach to a long-standing problem. *Culture, Medicine, and Psychiatry, 27*, 467–486.

Mirowsky, J., & Ross, C. E. (2003). *Education, social status, and health.* New York, NY: Aldine de Gruyter.

Mitchell, C. G. (1999). Treating anxiety in a managed care setting: A controlled comparison of medication alone versus medication plus. *Research on Social Work Practice, 9*, 188–200.

Mitchell, R. G. (1993). *Secrecy and fieldwork.* Newbury Park, CA: Sage.

Moe, A. (2007). Silenced voices and structural survival—battered women's help seeking. *Violence Against Women, 13*, 676–699.

Moher, D., Liberati, A., Tetzlaff, J., & Altman, D. G. (2009). Preferred reporting items for systematic reviews and meta-analyses: The PRISMA statement. *Open Medicine, 3*, 123–130.

Mohr, L. B. (1992). *Impact analysis for program evaluation.* Newbury Park, CA: Sage.

Molloy, J. K. (2007). Photovoice as a tool for social justice workers. *Journal of Progressive Human Services, 18*, 39–55.

Mongan-Rallis, H. (2014, November 21). *Guidelines for writing a literature review.* Retrieved from http://www.duluth.umn.edu/~hrallis/ guides/researching/litreview.html

Moran, J. R., & Bussey, M. (2007). Results of an alcohol prevention program with urban American Indian youth. *Child and Adolescent Social Work Journal, 24*, 1–21.

Morano, C. L. (2003). The role of appraisal and expressive support in mediating strain and gain in Hispanic Alzheimer's disease caregivers. *Journal of Ethnic & Cultural Diversity in Social Work, 12*, 1–18.

Moreno-John, G., Gachie, A., Fleming, C. M., Napoles-Springer, A., Mutran, E., Manson, S., & Peréz-Stable, E. J. (2004). Ethnic minority older adults participating in clinical research: Developing trust. *Journal of Aging and Health, 16*, 93S–123S.

Morgan, D. L. (2014). *Integrating qualitative & quantitative methods: A pragmatic approach.* Thousand Oaks, CA: Sage.

Morrill, C., Yalda, C., Adelman, M., Musheno, M., & Bejarano, C. (2000). Telling tales in school: Youth culture and conflict narratives. *Law and Society Review, 34*, 521–565.

Morris, M. (2011). The good, the bad, and the evaluator: 25 years of AJE ethics. *American Journal of Evaluation, 32*, 134–151.

Mosley, J. E. (2010). Organizational resources and environmental incentives: Understanding the policy advocacy involvement of human service nonprofits. *Social Service Review, 84*, 57–76.

Motel, S., & Patten, E. (2013, January 29). Statistical portrait of the foreign-born population in the United States, 2011. Retrieved from http://www.pewhispanic. org/2013/01/29/statistical-portrait-of-the-foreign-born-population-in-the-united-states-2011/

Muhr, T., & Friese, S. (2004). *User's manual for ATLAS.ti 5.0* (2nd ed.). Berlin, Germany: Scientific Software Development.

Mullen, E. J., Bledsoe, S. E., & Bellamy, J. L. (2008). Implementing evidence-based social work practice. *Research on Social Work Practice, 18*, 325–338.

Nápoles-Springer, A. M., Santoyo-Olsson, J., O'Brien, H., & Stewart, A. L. (2006). Using cognitive interviews to develop surveys in diverse populations. *Medical Care, 44*, S21–S30.

Nápoles-Springer, A. M., & Stewart, A. L. (2006). Overview of qualitative methods in research with diverse populations: Making research reflect the population. *Medical Care, 44*, S5–S9.

Nassar-McMillan, S. C., & Borders, L. D. (2002). Use of focus groups in survey item development. *Qualitative Report 7*:1. Retrieved from http://nsuworks.nova.edu/tqr/vol7/iss1/3/

National Association of Social Workers. (2001). *NASW standards for cultural competence in the practice of social work*. Washington, DC: Author. Retrieved from http://www.socialworkers.org/practice/standards/NASWCulturalStandards.pdf

National Association of Social Workers. (2008). *Code of ethics of the National Association of Social Workers*. Retrieved from http://www.naswdc.org/pubs/code/code.asp

National Highway Traffic Safety Administration. (2013). *Traffic safety facts 2012 data: Alcohol-impaired driving*. Washington, DC: NHTSA Center for Statistical Analysis. Retrieved from http://www-nrd.nhtsa.dot.gov/Pubs/811870.pdf

National Institute on Alcohol Abuse and Alcoholism. (n.d.). *Five year strategic plan*. Retrieved from http://www.niaaa.nih.gov/about-niaaa/our-work/strategic-plan

National Institutes of Health. (1994). *NIH guidelines on the inclusion of women and minorities as subjects in clinical research*. Retrieved from http://grants.nih.gov/grants/guide/notice-files/not94-100.html

National Opinion Research Center. (2014). *General Social Survey*. Chicago, IL: Author.

Navarro, M. (2013, November 22). Homeless tally taken in January found 13% rise in New York. *New York Times*, A24.

Nelson, J. C. (1994). Ethics, gender, and ethnicity in single-case research and evaluation. *Journal of Social Service Research, 18*, 139–152.

Neuendorf, K. A. (2002). *The content analysis guidebook*. Thousand Oaks, CA: Sage.

Newcomer, R., Kang, T., & Graham, C. (2006). Outcomes in a nursing home transition case-management program targeting new admissions. *The Gerontologist, 46*, 385–390.

Newmann, J. P. (1987). Gender differences in vulnerability to depression. *Social Service Review, 61*, 447–468.

Newmann, J. P. (1989). Aging and depression. *Psychology and Aging, 4*, 150–165.

Norton, I. M., & Manson, S. P. (1996). Research in American Indian and Alaska Native communities: Navigating the cultural universe of values and process. *Journal of Consulting and Clinical Psychology, 64*, 856–860.

Noss, A. (2014, September). Household income: 2013. *American Community Survey Briefs*. Washington, DC: U.S. Census Bureau. Retrieved from https://www.census.gov/content/dam/Census/library/publications/2014/acs/acsbr13-02.pdf

Nugent, W. (2000). Single case design visual analysis procedures for use in practice evaluation. *Journal of Social Service Research, 27*, 39–75.

O'Connell, H., Chin, A.-V., Hamilton, F., Cunningham, C., Walsh, J. B., Coakley, D., & Lawlor, B. A. (2004). A systematic review of the utility of self-report alcohol screening instruments in the elderly. *International Journal of Geriatric Psychiatry, 19*, 1074–1086.

O'Connor, C. M., Smith, R., Nott, M. T., Lorang, C., & Mathews, R. M. (2011). Using video simulated presence to reduce resistance to care and increase participation of adults with dementia. *American Journal of Alzheimer's Disease & Other Dementias, 26*, 312–325.

Ofstedal, M. B., & Weir, D. R. (2011). Recruitment and retention of minority participants in the Health and Retirement Study. *The Gerontologist, 51*(Suppl.), S8–S20.

Onoye, J. M., Goebert, D. A., & Nishimura, S. T. (2012). Use of incentives and web-based administration for surveying student alcohol and substance use in an ethnically diverse sample. *Journal of Substance Use, 17*, 61–71.

Onwuegbuzie, A. J., & Combs, J. P. (2010). Emergent data analysis techniques in mixed methods research: A synthesis. In A. Tashakkori & C. Teddlie (Eds.), *SAGE handbook of mixed methods in social and behavioral research* (pp. 397–430). Thousand Oaks, CA: Sage.

Orr, L. (1999). *Social experiments: Evaluating public programs with experimental methods*. Thousand Oaks, CA: Sage.

Orshansky, M. (1977). Memorandum for Daniel P. Moynihan. Subject: History of the poverty line. In M. Orshansky (Ed.), *The measure of poverty: Technical paper I: Documentation of background information and rationale for current poverty matrix* (pp. 232–237). Washington, DC: U.S. Department of Health, Education, and Welfare.

Ortega, D. M., & Richey, C. A. (1998). Methodological issues in social work research with depressed women of color. *Journal of Social Service Research, 23*, 47–68.

O'Toole, T. P., Aaron, K. F., Chin, M. H., Horowitz, C., & Tyson, F. (2003). Community-based participatory research: Opportunities, challenges, and the need for a common language. *Journal of General Internal Medicine, 18*, 592–594.

Padgett, D. K. (2008). *Qualitative methods in social work research* (2nd ed.). Thousand Oaks, CA: Sage.

Padgett, D. K., Gulcur, L., & Tsemberis, S. (2006). Housing first services for people who are homeless with co-occurring serious mental illness and substance abuse. *Research on Social Work Practice, 16*, 74–83.

Papineau, D. (1978). *For science in the social sciences*. London, UK: Macmillan.

Parker-Pope, T. (2010, February 16). As girls become women, sports pay dividends. *New York Times*, D5.

Parks, K. A., Pardi, A. P., & Bradizza, C. M. (2006). Collecting data on alcohol use and alcohol-related victimization: A comparison of telephone and web-based survey methods. *Journal of Studies on Alcohol, 67*, 318–323.

Parlett, M., & Hamilton, D. (1976). Evaluation as illumination: A new approach to the study of innovative programmes. In G. Glass (Ed.), *Evaluation studies review annual: Vol. 1* (pp. 140–157). Beverly Hills, CA: Sage.

Pasick, R. J., Stewart, S. L., Bird, J. A., & D'Onofrio, C. N. (2001). Quality of data in multiethnic health surveys. *Public Health Reports, 116*, 223–244.

Pate, A. M., & Hamilton, E. E. (1992). Formal and informal deterrents to domestic violence: The Dade County spouse assault experiment. *American Sociological Review, 57*, 691–697.

Patton, M. Q. (2002). *Qualitative research and evaluation methods* (3rd ed.). Thousand Oaks, CA: Sage.

Payne, M. (1997). *Modern social work theory: A critical introduction* (2nd ed.). Chicago, IL: Lyceum.

Perry, G. (2013). *Behind the shock machine: The untold story of the notorious Milgram psychology experiments*. New York, NY: New Press.

Peterson, R. A. (2000). *Constructing effective questionnaires*. Thousand Oaks, CA: Sage.

Pew Research Center. (2013). *Social networking use*. Retrieved from http://www.pewresearch.org/data-trend/media-and-technology/social-networking-use/

Pew Research Center. (2014). *Pew Research Internet project: Internet user demographics*. Retrieved from http://www.pewinternet.org/data-trend/internet-use/latest-stats/

Phillips, J. C., Ingram, K. M., Smith, N. G., & Mindes, E. J. (2003). Methodological and content review of lesbian-, gay-, and bisexual-related articles in counseling journals: 1990–1999. *The Counseling Psychologist, 31*, 25–62.

Plath, D. (2006). Evidence-based practice: Current issues and future directions. *Australian Social Work, 59*, 56–72.

Polizzi, K. G., & Millikin, R. J. (2002). Attitudes toward the elderly: Identifying problematic usage of ageist and overextended terminology in research instructions. *Educational Gerontology, 28*, 367–377.

Pollio, D. (2006). The art of evidence-based practice. *Research on Social Work Practice, 16*, 224–232.

Posavac, E. J., & Carey, R. G. (1997). *Program evaluation: Methods and case studies* (5th ed.). Upper Saddle River, NJ: Prentice Hall.

Posavac, E. J., & Carey, R. G. (2010). *Program evaluation: Methods and case studies* (8th ed.). Upper Saddle River, NJ: Prentice Hall.

Presser, S., & Blair, J. (1994). Survey pretesting: Do different methods produce different results? *Sociological Methodology, 24*, 74–104.

Presser, S., Coupter, M. J., Lessler, J. T., Martin, E., Martin, J., Rothgeb, J. M., & Singer, E. (2004). Methods for testing and evaluating survey questions. *Public Opinion Quarterly, 68*, 109–130.

Probst, B. (2008). Issues in portability of evidence-based treatment for adolescent depression. *Child and Adolescent Social Work Journal, 25*, 111–123.

Proctor, E. K., & Rosen, A. (2008). From knowledge production to implementation: Research challenges and imperatives. *Research on Social Work Practice, 18*, 285–291.

Prohaska, T. R., & Etkin, C. D. (2010). External validity and translation from research to implementation. *Generations, 34*, 59–65.

Punch, M. (1994). Politics and ethics in qualitative research. In N. K. Denzin & Y. S. Lincoln (Eds.), *The handbook of qualitative research* (pp. 83–97). Thousand Oaks, CA: Sage.

Quenqua, D. (2015, May 25). Public defender beats partner on happiness scale for lawyers, study finds. *New York Times*, A19.

Radloff, L. (1977). The CES-D scale: A self-report depression scale for research in the general population. *Applied Psychological Measurement, 1*, 385–401.

Ragin, C. C. (1987). *The comparative method: Moving beyond qualitative and quantitative strategies*. Berkeley: University of California Press.

Ragin, C. C. (1994). *Constructing social research*. Thousand Oaks, CA: Pine Forge Press.

Ramsay, J., Carter, Y., Davidson, L., Dunn, D., Eldridge, S., Feder, G., . . . Warburton, A. (2009). *Advocacy interventions to reduce or eliminate violence and promote the physical and psychosocial well-being of women who experience intimate partner abuse*. Available at http://www.campbellcollaboration.org/reviews_social_welfare/index.php

Reed, P. S., Foley, K. L., Hatch, J., & Mutran, E. J. (2003). Recruitment of older African Americans for survey research: A process evaluation of the community and church-based strategy in the Durham Elders Project. *The Gerontologist, 43*, 52–61.

Reich, C. M., & Berman, J. S. (2015). Do financial literacy classes help? An experimental assessment in a low-income population. *Journal of Social Service Research, 41*, 193–203.

Reinharz, S. (1992). *Feminist methods in social research*. New York, NY: Oxford University Press.

Rew, L., Koniak-Griffin, D., Lewis, M. A., Miles, M., & O'Sullivan, A. (2000). Secondary data analysis: New perspective for adolescent research. *Nursing Outlook, 48*, 223–229.

Richards, T. J., & Richards, L. (1994). Using computers in qualitative research. In N. K. Denzin & Y. S. Lincoln (Eds.), *Handbook of qualitative research* (pp. 445–462). Thousand Oaks, CA: Sage.

Richards, T. N., Garland, T. S., Bumphus, V. W., & Thompson, R. (2010). Personal and political? Exploring the feminization of the American homeless population. *Journal of Poverty, 14*, 97–115.

Richardson, L. (1995). Narrative and sociology. In J. V. Maanen (Ed.), *Representation in ethnography* (pp. 198–221). Thousand Oaks, CA: Sage.

Riedel, M. (2000). *Research strategies for secondary data: A perspective for criminology and criminal justice*. Thousand Oaks, CA: Sage.

Riessman, C. K. (2002). Narrative analysis. In A. M. Huberman & M. B. Miles (Eds.), *The qualitative researcher's companion* (pp. 217–270). Thousand Oaks, CA: Sage.

Riessman, C. K. (2008). *Narrative methods for the human sciences*. Thousand Oaks, CA: Sage.

Ringwalt, C. L., Greene, J. M., Ennett, S. T., Iachan, R., Clayton, R. R., & Leukefeld, C. G. (1994). *Past and future directions of the D.A.R.E. program: An evaluation review*. Research Triangle, NC: Research Triangle Institute.

Roffman, R., Downey, L., Beadnell, B., Gordon, J., Craver, J., & Stephens, R. (1997). Cognitive-behavioral group counseling to prevent HIV transmission in gay and bisexual men: Factors contributing to successful risk reduction. *Research on Social Work Practice, 7*, 165–186.

Roffman, R., Picciano, J., Wickizer, L., Bolan, M., & Ryan, R. (1998). Anonymous enrollment in AIDS prevention telephone group counseling: Facilitating the participation of gay and bisexual men in intervention and research. *Journal of Social Service Research, 23*, 5–22.

Rogers, R. K., Yancey, G., & Singletary, J. (2005). Methodological challenges in identifying promising and exemplary practices in urban faith-based social service programs. *Social Work & Christianity, 32*, 189–208.

Romans, S. E., Tyas, J., Cohen, M. M., & Silverstone, T. (2007). Gender differences in the symptoms of major depressive disorder. *The Journal of Nervous and Mental Disease, 195*, 905–911.

Rosal, M. C., Carbone, E. T., & Goins, K. V. (2003). Use of cognitive interviewing to adapt measurement instruments for low-literate Hispanics. *The Diabetes Educator, 29*, 1006–1017.

Rosen, A. (2003). Evidence-based social work practice: Challenges and promises. *Social Work, 27*, 197–208.

Rosen, D., Goodkind, S., & Smith, M. L. (2011). Using Photovoice to identify service needs of older African American methadone clients. *Journal of Social Service Research, 37*, 526–538.

Rosenbaum, D. P. (2007). Just say no to D.A.R.E. *Criminology & Public Policy, 6*, 815–824.

Rosenbaum, D. P., & Hanson, G. S. (1998). Assessing the effects of school-based drug education: A six-year multi-level analysis of Project D.A.R.E. *Journal of Research in Crime and Delinquency, 35*, 381–412.

Ross, C. E. (1990). Work, family, and the sense of control: Implications for the psychological well-being of women and men (Proposal submitted to the National Science Foundation). Urbana: University of Illinois.

Rossi, P. H. (1999). Half-truths with real consequences: Journalism, research, and public policy. Three encounters. *Contemporary Sociology, 28*, 1–5.

Rossi, P. H., & Freeman, H. F. (1989). *Evaluation: A systematic approach* (4th ed.). Newbury Park, CA: Sage.

Rossman, G. B., & Rallis, S. F. (1998). *Learning in the field: An introduction to qualitative research*. Thousand Oaks, CA: Sage.

Rowles, G. D. (1978). *Prisoners of space? Exploring the geographical experience of older people*. Boulder, CO: Westview Press.

Royse, D., Thyer, B. A., Padgett, D. K., & Logan, T. K. (2006). *Program evaluation: An introduction* (4th ed.). Belmont, CA: Thomson Brooks/Cole.

Rubin, H. J., & Rubin, I. S. (1995). *Qualitative interviewing: The art of hearing data*. Thousand Oaks, CA: Sage.

Ruderman, W. (2012, June 29). Crime report manipulation is common among New York police, study finds. *New York Times*, A17.

Sacks, S., McKendrick, K., DeLeon, G., French, M. T., & McCollister, K. E. (2002). Benefit-cost analysis of a modified therapeutic community for mentally ill chemical abusers. *Evaluation and Program Planning, 25,* 137–148.

Salmons, J. (2012). Designing and conducting research with online interviews. In J. Salmons (Ed.), *Cases in online interview research* (pp. 1–35). Thousand Oaks, CA: Sage.

Sampson, R. J. (1987). Urban Black violence: The effect of male joblessness and family disruption. *American Journal of Sociology, 93,* 348–382.

Sands, R. G., & Goldberg-Glen, R. S. (2000). Factors associated with stress among grandparents raising their grandchildren. *Family Relations: Interdisciplinary Journal of Applied Family Studies, 49,* 97–105.

Sanger-Katz, M. (2014, November 21). Oregon Health Study: The surprises in a randomized trial. *New York Times.* Retrieved from http://www.nytimes.com/2014/11/22/upshot/oregon-health-study-the-surprises-in-a-randomized-trial.html?_r=0&abt=0002&abg=1

Santiago, C. D., & Miranda, J. (2014). Progress in improving mental health services for racial-ethnic minority groups: A ten-year perspective. *Psychiatric Services, 65,* 180–185. Retrieved from http://dx.doi.org/10.1176/appi.ps.201200517

Sarri, R., & Sarri, C. M. (1992). Organizational and community change through participatory action research. *Administration in Social Work, 16,* 99–122.

Savage, C. (2011, August 13). Trend to lighten harsh sentences catches on in conservative states. *New York Times,* A12.

Savaya, R., & Waysman, M. (2005). The logic model: A tool for incorporating theory in development and evaluation of programs. *Administration in Social Work, 29,* 85–103.

Schaeffer, N. C., & Presser, S. (2003). The science of asking questions. *Annual Review of Sociology, 29,* 65–88.

Schaie, K. W. (1993). Ageist language in psychological research. *American Psychologist, 48,* 49–51.

Schegloff, E. (1996). Issues of relevance for discourse analysis: Contingency in action, interaction, and coparticipant context. In E. H. Hovy & D. R. Scott (Eds.), *Computational and conversational discourse: Burning issues—An interdisciplinary account* (pp. 3–35). New York, NY: Springer.

Schein, R. L., & Koenig. H. G. (1997). The Center for Epidemiological Studies-Depression scale: Assessment of depression in the medically ill elderly. *International Journal of Geriatric Psychiatry, 12,* 436–446.

Schober, M. F. (1999). Making sense of survey questions. In M. G. Sirken, D. J. Herrmann, S. Schechter, N. Schwartz, J. M. Tanner, & R. Tourangeau (Eds.), *Cognition and survey research* (pp. 77–94). New York, NY: John Wiley.

Schofield, J. W. (2002). Increasing the generalizability of qualitative research. In A. M. Huberman & M. B. Miles (Eds.), *The qualitative researcher's companion* (pp. 171–203). Thousand Oaks, CA: Sage.

Schorr, L. B., & Yankelovich, D. (2000, February 18). In search of a gold standard for social programs. *Boston Globe,* p. A19.

Schuman, H., & Presser, S. (1981). *Questions and answers in attitude surveys: Experiments on question form, wording, and context.* New York, NY: Academic Press.

Schutt, R. K. (2011). *Homelessness, housing, and mental illness.* Cambridge, MA: Harvard University Press.

Schutt, R. K., Penk, W. E., Barreira, P. J., Lew, R., Fisher, W. H., Browne, A., & Irvine, E. (1992). Relapse prevention for dually diagnosed homeless (Proposal to National Institute of Mental Health, for Mental Health Research on Homeless Persons, PA-91-60). Worcester: University of Massachusetts Medical School.

Schwandt, T. A. (1994). Constructivist, interpretivist approaches to human inquiry. In N. K. Denzin & Y. S. Lincoln (Eds.). *Handbook of qualitative research* (pp. 118–137). Thousand Oaks, CA: Sage.

Scriven, M. (1972). The methodology of evaluation. In C. H. Weiss (Ed.), *Evaluating action programs: Readings in social action and education* (pp. 123–136). Boston, MA: Allyn & Bacon.

Seefeldt, K. S., & Orzol, S. M. (2005). Watching the clock tick: Factors associated with TANF accumulation. *Social Work Research, 29,* 215–229.

Shadish, W. R., Cook, T. D., & Leviton, L. C. (Eds.). (1991). *Foundations of program evaluation: Theories of practice.* Newbury Park, CA: Sage.

Shapiro, J. R., & Mangelsdorf, S. C. (1994). The determinants of parenting competence in adolescent mothers. *Journal of Youth and Adolescence, 23,* 621–641.

Sharp, L. K., & Lipsky, M. S. (2002). Screening for depression across the lifespan: A review of measures for use in primary care settings. *American Family Physician, 66,* 1001–1008.

Shepherd, J., Hill, D., Bristor, J., & Montalvan, P. (1996). Converting an ongoing health study to CAPI: Findings from the National Health and Nutrition Study. In R. B. Warnecke (Ed.), *Health survey research methods conference proceedings* (pp. 159–164). Hyattsville, MD: U.S. Department of Health and Human Services.

Sherman, L. W. (1992). *Policing domestic violence: Experiments and dilemmas.* New York, NY: Free Press.

Sherman, L. W., & Berk, R. A. (1984). The specific deterrent effects of arrest for domestic assault. *American Sociological Review, 49,* 261–272.

Sherman, L. W., Smith, D. A., Schmidt, J. D., & Rogan, D. P. (1992). Crime, punishment, and stake in conformity. *American Sociological Review, 57,* 680–690.

Shrout, P. E. (2011). Integrating causal analysis into psychopathology research. In P. E. Shrout, K. M. Keyes, & K. Ornstein (Eds.), *Causality and psychopathology: Finding the determinants of disorders and their cures* (pp. 3–24). New York, NY: Oxford University Press.

Sieber, J. E. (1992). *Planning ethically responsible research: A guide for students and internal review boards.* Newbury Park, CA: Sage.

Sieber, J. E., & Tolic, M. B. (2013). *Planning ethnically responsible research* (2nd ed.). Thousand Oaks, CA: Sage

Sigmon, S. T., Pells, J. J., Boulard, N. E., Whitcomb-Smith, S., Edenfield, T. M., Hermann, B. A., . . . Kubik, E. (2005). Gender differences in self-reports of depression: The response bias hypothesis revisited. *Sex Roles, 53,* 401–411.

Silvestre, A. J. (1994). Brokering: A process for establishing long-term and stable links with gay male communities for research and public health education. *AIDS Education and Prevention, 6,* 65–73.

Silvestre, A. J,, Hylton, J. B., Johnson, L. M., Houston, C., Witt, M., Jacobson, L., & Ostrow, D. (2006). Recruiting minority men who have sex with men for HIV research: Results from a 4-city campaign. *American Journal of Public Health, 96,* 1020–1027.

Simpson, G. M., & Cornelius, L J. (2007). Overlooking African American males. *Journal of Human Behavior in the Social Environment, 15,* 147–170.

Sin, C. H. (2005). Seeking informed consent: Reflections on research practice. *Sociology, 39,* 277–294.

Singer, E. (2006). Introduction: Nonresponse bias in household surveys. *Public Opinion Quarterly, 70,* 637–645.

Singer, M. (2005). A twice-told tale: A phenomenological inquiry into clients' perceptions of therapy. *Journal of Marital and Family Therapy, 31,* 269–281.

Skinner, H. A., & Sheu, W.-J. (1982). Reliability of alcohol use indices: The lifetime drinking history and the MAST. *Journal of Studies on Alcohol, 43,* 1157–1170.

Sloboda, Z., Stephens, R. C., Stephens, P. C., Grey, S. E., Teasdale, B., Hawthorne, R. D.,

... Marquette, J. F. (2009). The Adolescent Substance Abuse Prevention Study: A randomized field trial of a universal substance abuse prevention program. *Drug and Alcohol Dependence, 102*, 1–10.

Slutske, W. S. (2005). Alcohol use disorders among US college students and their non-college-attending peers. *Archives of General Psychiatry, 62*, 321–327.

Smedslund, G., Clench-Aas, J., Dalsbo, T. K., Steiro, A., & Winsvold, A. (2011). *Cognitive behavioural therapy for men who physically abuse their female partner.* Available at http://www.campbellcollaboration.org/reviews_social_welfare/index.php

Smith, J. (1991). A methodology for twenty-first century sociology. *Social Forces, 70*, 1–17.

Smith, T. W. (1984). Nonattitudes: A review and evaluation. In C. F. Turner & E. Martin (Eds.), *Surveying subjective phenomena: Vol. 22* (pp. 215–255). New York. NY: Russell Sage.

Smith, T. W. (1987). That which we call welfare by any other name would smell sweeter: An analysis of the impact of question wording on response patterns. *Public Opinion Quarterly, 51*, 75–83.

Smith, T. W., & Kim, S. (2003). *A review of CAPI-effects on the 2002 General Social Survey* (GSS Methodology Report No. 98). Chicago, IL: NORC/University of Chicago.

Smithson, J. (2008). Focus groups. In P. Alasuutari, L. Bickman, & J. Brannen (Eds.), *The SAGE handbook of social research methods* (pp. 357–370). Thousand Oaks, CA: Sage.

Smyth, J. D., Dillman, D. A., Christian, L. M., & Stern, M. J. (2004, May 13). *How visual grouping influences answers to Internet surveys.* Extended version of paper presented at the annual meeting of the American Association for Public Opinion Research, Phoenix, AZ. Retrieved from http://www.amstat.org/sections/srms/Proceedings/y2004/files/Jsm2004-000194.pdf

Sobeck, J. L., Chapleski, E. E., & Fisher, C. (2003). Conducting research with American Indians: A case study of motives, methods, and results. *Journal of Ethnic and Cultural Diversity, 12*, 69–84.

Solari, C. D., Cortes, A., Henry, M., Matthews, N., & Morris, S. (2014). The 2013 Annual Homeless Assessment Report (AHAR) to Congress: Part 2: Estimates of homelessness in the United States. Retrieved from https://www.hudexchange.info/onecpd/assets/File/2013-AHAR-Part-2.pdf

Solberg, J. (2011). Activation encounters: Dilemmas of accountability in constructing clients as "knowledgeable." *Qualitative Social Work, 10*, 381–398.

Sood, J. R., & Stahl, S. M. (2011). Community engagement and Centers for Minority Aging Research. *The Gerontologist, 51*(Suppl.), S5–S8.

Stake, R. E. (1995). *The art of case study research.* Thousand Oaks, CA: Sage.

Stanfield, J. H. (1999). Slipping through the front door: Relevant social scientific evaluation in the People of Color century. *American Journal of Evaluation, 20*, 415–431.

Stanhope, V. (2012). The ties that bind: Using ethnographic methods to understand service engagement. *Qualitative Social Work, 11*, 412–430.

Starin, A. (2006). Clients role choices: Unexplored factors in intervention decisions. *Clinical Social Work Journal, 34*, 101–119.

Staudt, M. (1997). Pseudoissues in practice evaluation: Impediments to responsible practice. *Social Work, 42*, 99–106.

Stein, G. L., Beckerman, N. L., & Sherman, P. A. (2010). Lesbian and gay elders and long-term care: Identifying the unique psychosocial perspectives and challenges. *Journal of Gerontological Social Work, 53*, 421–435.

Steng, J. M., Rhodes, S. D., Rhodes, G. X., Eng, E., Arceo, R., & Phipps, S. (2004). Realidad Latina: Latino adolescents, their school, and a university use Photovoice to examine and address the influence of immigration. *Journal of Interprofessional Care, 18*, 403–415.

Stephen, J. M., Young, M. F., & Calabrese, T. (2007). Does moral judgment go offline when students are online? A comparative analysis of undergraduates' beliefs and behaviors related to conventional and digital cheating. *Ethics and Behavior, 17*, 233–254.

Stevens, C. A. (2006). Being healthy: Voices of adolescent women who are parenting. *Journal for Specialists in Pediatric Nursing, 11*, 28–40.

Stewart, A. L., & Nápoles-Springer, A. (2000). Health-related quality of life assessments in diverse population groups in the United States. *Medical Care, 38*(Suppl. II), 102–124.

Stewart, D. W., & Kamins, M. A. (1993). *Secondary research: Information sources and methods* (2nd ed.). Newbury Park, CA: Sage.

Stewart, D. W., Shamdasani, P. N., & Rook, D. W. (2007). *Focus groups: Theory and practice* (2nd ed.). Thousand Oaks, CA: Sage.

Stewart, M., Makwarimba, E., Barnfather, A., Letourneau, N., & Neufeld, A. (2008). Researching reducing health disparities: Mixed-methods approaches. *Social Science & Medicine, 66*, 1406–1417.

Straus, S., Richardson, W. S., Glasziou, P. S., & Haynes, R. B. (2005). *Evidence-based medicine: How to practice and teach EBM* (3rd ed.). Edinburgh; New York, NY: Elsener/Churchill Livingstone.

Straus, S., Richardson, W. S., Glasziou, P. S., & Haynes, R. B. (2011). *Evidence-based medicine: How to practice and teach it* (4th ed.). Edinburgh; New York, NY: Elsener/Churchill Livingstone.

Strauss, A. L., & Corbin, J. (1990). *The basics of qualitative research: Grounded theory procedures and techniques.* Newbury Park, CA: Sage.

Substance Abuse and Mental Health Services Administration, Office of Applied Studies. (2013). *Results from the 2012 National Survey on Drug Use and Health: Summary of national findings* (NSDUH Series H-34. HHS Publication No. SMA 13-4795). Rockville, MD. Retrieved from http://www.samhsa.gov/data/NSDUH/2012SummNatFindDetTables/NationalFindings/NSDUHresults2012.htm

Sudman, S. (1976). *Applied sampling.* New York, NY: Academic Press.

Sue, V. M., & Ritter, L. A. (2012). *Conducting online surveys* (2nd ed.). Thousand Oaks, CA: Sage.

Sulkunen, P. (2008). Social research social practice in post-positivist society. In P. Alasuutari, L. Bickman, & J. Brennan (Eds.), *The SAGE handbook of social research methods.* Thousand Oaks, CA: Sage.

Sullivan, M. K., Larrison, C. R., Nackerud, L., Risler, E., & Bodenschatz, L. (2004). Examining the relationship between psychological well-being and the need for continued public assistance benefits. *Journal of Contemporary Social Services, 85*, 425–429.

Szapocznik, J., Prado, G., Burlew, A. K., Williams, R. A., & Santisteban, D. (2007). Drug abuse in African American and Hispanic adolescents: Culture, development, and behavior. *Annual Review of Clinical Psychology, 3*, 77–105.

Tavernise, S. (2002, October 10). How many Russians? Let us weigh the count, cooperation or no. *New York Times*, A13.

Tavernise, S. (2011, April 21). Youth, mobility, and poverty help drive cellphone-only status. *New York Times*, p. A13.

Teddlie, C., & Tashakkori, A. (2010). Overview of contemporary issues in mixed methods research. In A. Tashakkori & C. Teddlie (Eds.), *SAGE handbook of mixed methods in social and behavioral research* (2nd ed., pp. 1–41). Thousand Oaks, CA: Sage.

Testa, M., Livingston, J. A., & VanZile-Tamsen, C. (2011). Advancing the study of violence against women using mixed methods:

Integrating qualitative methods into a quantitative research program. *Violence Against Women, 17*, 236–250.

Thompson, B. (2002). "Statistical," "practical," and "clinical": How many kinds of significance do counselors need to consider? *Journal of Counseling Development, 80*, 64–71.

Thompson, E. E., Neighbors, H. W., Munday, C., & Jackson, J. S. (1996). Recruitment and retention of African American patients for clinical research: An exploration of response rates in an urban psychiatric hospital. *Journal of Consulting and Clinical Psychology, 64*, 861–867.

Thompson, N. C., Hunter, E. E., Murray, L., Ninci, L., Rolfs, E. M., & Pallikkathayil, L. (2008). The experience of living with chronic mental illness: A Photovoice study. *Perspectives in Psychiatric Care, 44*, 14–24.

Thorne, B. (1993). *Gender play: Girls and boys in school.* New Brunswick, NJ: Rutgers University Press.

Thorne, S., Jensen, L., Kearney, M. H., Noblit, G., & Sandelowski, M. (2004). Qualitative metasynthesis: Reflections on methodological orientation and ideological agenda. *Qualitative Health Research, 14*, 1342–1365.

Thyer, B. A. (2001). What is the role of theory in research on social work practice? *Journal of Social Work Education, 37*, 9–21.

Thyer, B. A. (2006). What is evidence-based practice? In A. R. Roberts & K. R. Yeager (Eds.), *Foundation of evidence-based practice* (pp. 35–46). Cary, NC: Oxford University Press.

Tichon, J. G., & Shapiro, M. (2003). The process of sharing social support in cyberspace. *Cyber Psychology and Behavior, 6*, 161–170.

Tinkler, P. (2013). *Using photographs in social and historical research.* Thousand Oaks, CA: Sage.

Toby, J. (1957). Social disorganization and stake in conformity: Complementary factors in the predatory behavior of hoodlums. *Journal of Criminal Law, Criminology and Police Science, 48*, 12–17.

Toppo, G. (2002, October 29). Antidrug program backed by study. *Boston Globe*, p. A10.

Tourangeau, R. (2004). Survey research and social change. *Annual Review of Psychology, 55*, 775–801.

Tourangeau, R., Conrad, F. G., & Couper, M. J. (2012). *The science of web surveys.* Oxford. UK: Oxford University Press.

Townsend, L., Floersch, J., & Findling, R. L. (2010). The conceptual adequacy of the Drug Attitude Inventory for measuring youth attitudes toward psychotropic medications: A mixed methods evaluation. *Journal of Mixed Methods Research, 4*, 32–55.

Tran, T. V., Khatutsky, G., Aroian, K., Balsam, A., & Conway, K. (2000). Living arrangements, depression, and health status among elderly Russian-speaking immigrants. *Journal of Gerontological Social Work, 33*, 63–77.

Tripodi, T. (1994). *A primer on single-subject design for clinical social workers.* Washington, DC: National Association of Social Workers.

Tufte, E. R. (1983). *The visual display of quantitative information.* Cheshire, CT: Graphics Press.

Turkle, S. (2011). *Alone together: Why we expect more from technology and less from each other.* New York, NY: Basic Books.

Turner, C. F., & Martin, E. (Eds.). (1984). *Surveying subjective phenomena* (Vols. 1 & 2). New York, NY: Russell Sage.

UK Data Service. (2014). *Key data.* Retrieved from http://ukdataservice.ac.uk/get-data/key-data.aspx

U.S. Census Bureau. (2015). *Surveys & programs.* Retrieved from http://www.census.gov/programs-surveys/surveys-programs.html

U.S. Census Bureau, Current Population Survey, Annual Social and Economic Supplement, CPS Table Creator, 2014. Retrieved from http://www.census.gov/cps/data/cpstablecreator.html

U.S. Conference of Mayors. (2015, December). *Hunger and homelessness survey: A status report on hunger and homelessness in America's cities: A 25-city survey.* Washington, DC. Retrieved from http://www.usmayors.org/pressreleases/uploads/2013/1210-report-HH.pdf

U.S. Department of Health, Education, and Welfare. (1979). *Belmont report: Ethical principles and guidelines for the protection of human subjects of research.* Washington, DC: Author.

U.S. Department of Health and Human Services. (1999). *Mental health: A report of the Surgeon General—Executive summary.* Rockville, MD: U.S. Department of Health and Human Services, Substance Abuse and Mental Health Services Administration, Center for Mental Health Services, National Institutes of Health, and National Institute of Mental Health.

U.S. Department of Health and Human Services. (2001). *Mental health: Culture, race, and ethnicity—A supplement to mental health: A report of the Surgeon General.* Rockville, MD: U.S. Department of Health and Human Services, Office of the Surgeon General. Retrieved from http://www.ncbi.nlm.nih.gov/books/NBK44243/pdf/Bookshelf_NBK44243.pdf

U.S. Department of Health and Human Services. (2009). *Code of Federal Regulations Title 45 Public Welfare Department of Health and Human Services Part 46: Protection of Human Subjects.* Retrieved from http://www.hhs.gov/ohrp/policy/ohrpregulations.pdf

U. S. Department of Housing and Urban Development. (2011). *The 2010 Annual Homeless Assessment Report to Congress.* Washington, DC: Author.

Van den Berg, N., & Crisp, C. (2004). Defining culturally competent practice with sexual minorities: Implications for social work education and practice. *Journal of Social Work Education, 40*, 221–238.

Van Maanen, J. (1995). An end to innocence: The ethnography of ethnography. In J. Van Maanen (Ed.), *Representation in ethnography* (pp. 1–35). Thousand Oaks, CA: Sage.

Van Selm, M., & Jankowski, N. W. (2006). Conducting online surveys. *Quality and Quantity, 40*, 435–456.

Vega, W. A., Kolody, B., Aguilar-Gaxiola, S., Alderete, E., Catalano, R., & Caraveo-Anduaga, J. (1998). Lifetime prevalence of DSM-III-R psychiatric disorders among urban and rural Mexican Americans in California. *Archives of General Psychiatry, 55*, 771–778.

Vincus, A. A., Ringwalt, C., Harris, M. S., & Shamblen, S. R. (2010). A short-term, quasi-experimental evaluation of D.A.R.E.'s revised elementary school curriculum. *Journal of Drug Education, 40*, 37–49.

Violence Policy Center. (2014, September). *When men murder women: An analysis of 2012 homicide data.* Retrieved from http://www.vpc.org/studies/wmmw2014.pdf

W. K. Kellogg Foundation. (2004). *Using logic models to bring together planning, evaluation, and action: Logic model development guide.* Battle Creek, MI: Author. Retrieved from http://www.smartgivers.org/uploads/logicmodelguidepdf.pdf

Wallace, J. B. (1994). Life stories. In J. F. Gubrium & A. Sankar (Eds.), *Qualitative methods in aging research* (pp. 137–154). Thousand Oaks, CA: Sage.

Wallace, W. L. (1983). *Principles of scientific sociology.* New York, NY: Aldine.

Wallgren, A., Wallgren, B., Persson, R., Jorner, U., & Haaland, J. (1996). *Graphing statistics and data: Creating better charts.* Thousand Oaks, CA: Sage.

Walsh, J. (1994). Social support resource outcomes for the clients of two assertive community treatment teams. *Research on Social Work Practice, 4*, 448–463.

Walton, E. (2001). Combining abuse and neglect investigations with intensive family preservation services: An innovative approach to protecting children. *Research on Social Work Practice, 11,* 627–644.

Walton, E., Fraser, M. W., Lewis, R. E., Pecora, P. J., & Walton, W. K. (1993). In-home family-focused reunification: An experimental study. *Child Welfare, 72,* 473–487

Wang, C., & Burris, M. A. (1997). Photovoice: Concept, methodology, and use for participatory needs assessment. *Health Education and Behavior, 24,* 369–387.

Warnick, E. M., Weersing, V. R., Scahill, L., & Woolston, J. L. (2009). Selecting measures for use in child mental health services: A scorecard approach. *Administration and Policy in Mental Health, 36,* 112–122.

Weaver-Hightower, M. (2013). A mixed methods approach for identifying influences on public policy. *Journal of Mixed Methods Research, 20,* 1–24.

Webb, E. J., Campbell, D. T., Schwartz, R. D., & Sechrest, L. (2000). *Unobtrusive measures* (Rev. ed.). Thousand Oaks, CA: Sage.

Weber, M. (1949). *The methodology of the social sciences.* (E. A. Shils, Trans., & H. A. Finch, Ed.). New York, NY: Free Press.

Weber, R. P. (1985). *Basic content analysis.* Beverly Hills, CA: Sage.

Wechsler, H., Lee, J. E., Kuo, M., Seibring, M., Nelson, T. F., & Lee, H. (2002). Trends in college binge drinking during a period of increased prevention efforts. *Journal of American College Health, 50,* 203–217.

Weeks, L. E., & LeBlanc, K. (2011). An ecological synthesis of research on older women's experiences of intimate partner violence. *Journal of Women & Aging, 23,* 283–304.

Weinberg, D. (2000). "Out there": The ecology of addiction in drug abuse treatment discourse. *Social Problems, 47,* 606–621.

Weintraub, K. (2013, July 22). Monitoring social media to cut the military suicide rate. *New York Times,* B5.

Weiss, C. H. (1998). *Evaluation* (2nd ed.). Upper Saddle River, NJ: Prentice Hall.

Wengraf, T. (2001). *Qualitative research interviewing: Biographic narrative and semi-structured methods.* Thousand Oaks, CA: Sage.

West, S. L., & O'Neal, K. K. (2004). Project D.A.R.E. outcome effectiveness revisited. *American Journal of Public Health, 94,* 1027–1029.

Whittaker, J. K., Greene, K., Schubert, D., Blum, R., Cheng, K., Blum, K., . . . Roy, R. (2006). Integrating evidence-based practice in the child mental health agency: A template for clinical and organizational change. *American Journal of Orthopsychiatry, 76,* 94–201.

Whyte, W. F. (1955). *Street corner society.* Chicago, IL: University of Chicago Press.

Wikoff, N., Linhorst, D. M., & Morani, N. (2012). Recidivism among participants of a reentry program for prisoners released without supervision. *Social Work Research, 36,* 289–299.

Wilson, W. J. (1987). *The truly disadvantaged: The inner city, the underclass, and public policy.* Chicago, IL: University of Chicago Press.

Wilson, W. J. (1998). Engaging publics in sociological dialogue through the media. *Contemporary Sociology, 27,* 435–438.

Witkin, B. R., & Altschuld, J. W. (1995). *Planning and conducting needs assessments: A practical guide.* Thousand Oaks, CA: Sage.

Witkin, S. L. (2001). The measure of things. *Social Work, 46,* 101–104.

Witkin, S. L., & Harrison, W. D. (2001). Whose evidence and for what purpose? *Social Work, 46,* 293–296.

Wolcott, H. F. (1995). *The art of fieldwork.* Walnut Creek, CA: AltaMira Press.

Wolf, A., Turner, D., & Toms, K. (2009). Ethical perspectives in program evaluation. In D. M. Mertens & P. E. Ginsberg (Eds.), *The handbook of social research ethics* (pp. 170–184). Thousand Oaks, CA: Sage.

Wolff, E. N. (2009). *Poverty and income distribution* (2nd ed.). Chichester, UK: Wiley-Blackwell.

Wooffitt, R. (2005). *Conversation analysis and discourse analysis: A comparative and critical introduction.* Thousand Oaks, CA: Sage.

World Medical Association. (2011). *WMA international code of medical ethics.* Retrieved from http://www.wma.net/en/30publications/10policies/c8/index.html

Xiang, X. (2013). A review of interventions for substance use among homeless youth. *Research on Social Work Practice, 23,* 34–45.

Yamatani, H., Mann, A., & Wright, P. (2000). *Garfield community needs assessment.* Pittsburgh, PA: University of Pittsburgh.

Yancey, A. K., Ortega, A. N., & Kumanyika, S. K. (2006). Effective recruitment and retention of minority research participants. *Annual Review of Public Health, 27,* 1–28.

Yin, R. K. (2003). *Case study research: Design and methods* (3rd ed.). Thousand Oaks, CA: Sage.

Yoon, I. (2009). A mixed-method study of Princeville's rebuilding from the flood of 1999: Lessons on the importance of invisible community assets. *Social Work, 54,* 19–28.

Yoshihama, M., Gillespie, B., Hammack, A. C., Belli, R. F., & Tolman, R. (2005). Does the life history calendar method facilitate the recall of intimate partner violence? Comparison of two methods of data collection. *Social Work Research, 29,* 151–163.

Zauszniewski, J. A., Fulton Picot, S. J. Debanne, S. M., Roberts, B. L., & Wykle, M. L. (2002). Psychometric characteristics of the depressive cognition scale in African American women. *Journal of Nursing Measurement, 10,* 83–95.

Zayas, L. H., Cabassa, L., & Perez, M. C. (2005). Capacity to consent in psychiatric research: Development and preliminary testing of a screening tool. *Research on Social Work Practice, 15,* 545–556.

Zimet, G. D., Dahlem, N. W., Zimet, S. G., & Farley, G. K. (1988). The multidimensional scale of perceived social support. *Journal of Personality Assessment, 52,* 30–41.

Index

NOTE: Page references to exhibits are identified as (exhibit).

About the Authors

Rafael J. Engel, PhD, is associate professor at the University of Pittsburgh. He received his PhD (1988) from the University of Wisconsin, his MSW (1979) from the University of Michigan, and his BA (1978) from the University of Pennsylvania. He coordinates the graduate certificate program in aging and is the principal investigator for the Hartford Partnership Program for Aging Education. He has written *Fundamentals of Social Work Research* (with Russell Schutt) and *Measuring Race and Ethnicity* (with Larry E. Davis). He is coeditor in chief of the journal *Intergenerational Relationships* and is a member of the editorial board of *Race and Social Problems.* He has authored journal articles on such topics as poverty in later life, welfare benefits, and depressive symptomatology, and he has written a variety of monographs reporting agency-based evaluations. His research experience includes funded research studies on gambling, faith-based organizations, and employment in later life as well as funded evaluation research studies on welfare-to-work programs and drug and alcohol prevention programs. His most recent research involves older adults and gambling prevention.

Russell K. Schutt, PhD, is professor and chair of sociology at the University of Massachusetts, Boston, and lecturer on sociology in the Department of Psychiatry (Beth Israel-Deaconess Medical Center) at the Harvard Medical School. He completed his BA, MA, and PhD (1977) at the University of Illinois at Chicago and a postdoctoral fellowship at Yale University (1977–1979). His other books include *Investigating the Social World: The Process and Practice of Research*, and *Fundamentals of Social Work Research* (with Ray Engel), *Making Sense of the Social World* (with Dan Chambliss), and *Research Methods in Psychology* (with Paul G. Nestor)—all with SAGE Publications, as well as *Homelessness, Housing, and Mental Illness* (Harvard University Press) and *Social Neuroscience: Brain, Mind, and Society* (coedited with Larry J. Seidman and Matcheri S. Keshavan, also Harvard University Press). Most of his peer-reviewed journal articles and book chapters focus on the effect of social context on cognition, satisfaction, and functioning, the service preferences of homeless persons and service personnel, and the organization of health and social services. He is currently a co-investigator for a randomized trial of peer support for homeless dually diagnosed veterans, funded by the Veterans Administration.